T0178172

FROM DISCOURSE TO LOGIC

The titles published in this series are listed at the end of this volume.

FROM DISCOURSE TO LOGIC

Introduction to Modeltheoretic Semantics of Natural Language, Formal Logic and Discourse Representation Theory

by

HANS KAMP
and
UWE REYLE

Institute for Computational Linguistics,
University of Stuttgart

KLUWER ACADEMIC PUBLISHERS

DORDRECHT / BOSTON / LONDON

Library of Congress Cataloging-in-Publication Data

ISBN: 0-7923-1028-4

Published by Kluwer Academic Publishers,
P.O. Box 17, 3300 AA Dordrecht, The Netherlands.

Kluwer Academic Publishers incorporates
the publishing programmes of
D. Reidel, Martinus Nijhoff, Dr W. Junk and MTP Press.

Sold and distributed in the U.S.A. and Canada
by Kluwer Academic Publishers,
101 Philip Drive, Norwell, MA 02061, U.S.A.

In all other countries, sold and distributed
by Kluwer Academic Publishers Group,
P.O. Box 322, 3300 AH Dordrecht, The Netherlands.

Printed on acid-free paper

Printed in the Netherlands

Contents

PART 1

PART 2

Preface

This book is about semantics and logic. More specifically, it is about the semantics and logic of natural language; and, even more specifically than that, it is about a particular way of dealing with those subjects, known as Discourse Representation Theory, or DRT. DRT is an approach towards natural language semantics which, some thirteen years ago, arose out of attempts to deal with two distinct problems. The first of those was the semantic puzzle that had been brought to contemporary attention by Geach's notorious "donkey sentences" - sentences like **If Pedro owns some donkey, he beats it**, in which the anaphoric connection we perceive between the indefinite noun phrase **some donkey** and the pronoun **it** may seem to conflict with the existential meaning of the word **some**. The second problem had to do with tense and aspect. Some languages, for instance French and the other Romance languages, have two morphologically distinct past tenses, a simple past (the French Passé Simple) and a continuous past (the French Imparfait). To articulate precisely what the difference between these tenses is has turned out to be surprisingly difficult.

One feature the two problems seemed to have in common was that neither allowed for a natural solution within the framework of modeltheoretic semantics, the dominant formal approach towards semantics in the seventies; and the ultimate reason appeared to be the same in each case: the static perspective behind modeltheoretic semantics, which tries to give an exhaustive characterization of the meaning of a linguistic expression in terms of the referential relations that it bears to the subject matter that it is used to speak about, ignores a dimension of linguistic meaning that is crucial both to the analysis of aspectual matters and to questions of anaphora. This is the dimension of *interpretation*: the meanings of linguistic expressions are - or so we would want to claim - inextricably linked with the interpretive canons that must be brought into play by anyone who wants to grasp their sense. DRT tries to remedy the one-sidedness of the model-theoretic paradigm by combining its referential perspective with this second interpretation-oriented viewpoint. It is this more complex view of linguistic meaning - as subject-related on the one hand, and as bound up with the interpretation of language on the other - which is the central conception that informs the theory presented in this book.

The intention to write a book of this sort goes back to the early eighties, when the first work on DRT (see [Kamp 1981]) and the independent, but closely related investigations of Heim (most extensively reported in [Heim 1982]) had just become available. In fact, writing such a book had got off to a false start more than once. In the fall of 1987, the authors jointly taught a seminar on DRT at the University of Stuttgart and it was this seminar which provided the two of us with the impetus to produce the text that has now at last appeared in print. The particular circumstances of the book's origin have been responsible for two salient properties. First, since the book started out in the form of teaching material, it was set up as a textbook from the outset. Having decided that this wasn't necessarily a bad thing, we carried on in the same vein. The result is a manuscript which we hope can serve as a textbook on DRT.

It would not be right, however, to simply describe the book as a textbook and say no more. Only the first part, consisting of Chapters 0, 1 and 2, clearly deserves this description. This part of the book has been tested repeatedly in seminars at Stuttgart University and elsewhere, and the feedback received from those who have used it has led to a certain consolidation of both content and form. The matter is different for the remaining chapters. These contain material that has for the most part not yet been published, even if it has figured in oral presentations or been circulated in unpublished manuscripts. It is possible that these chapters will need substantial modification in the light of criticisms that the publication of this book will provoke, and thus that they have not yet reached the degree of maturity that may be expected of classroom material.

The substance of the book is to be found in Chapters 1, 2, 4 and 5. Chapters 1 and 2 give a systematic presentation of the theory as it is outlined in [Kamp 1981]. In addition, Chapter 1 offers a treatment of negation and Chapter 2 treatments of both disjunction and conjunction; the analysis we propose for conjunctions is, to our knowledge, new. Chapters 4 and 5 extend the theory of the preceding chapters into new territory. Chapter 4 deals with plural constructions, Chapter 5 with questions of tense and aspect. The proposals discussed in Chapter 4 are largely based on unpublished work by Frey and Kamp from 1985/1986. (Some of the ideas that are central to the DR-theoretical aproach to questions of plurals have been used by others. See in particular the work of Roberts ([Roberts 1987b]) and of Kadmon ([Kadmon 1987a], [Kadmon 1987b], [Kadmon 1990]).) The material of Chapter 5 is in part quite old, going back to the origins of DRT hinted at in the opening paragraph. Those original ideas, buried almost beyond recognition in [Kamp 1979], have undergone many refinements in the course of the past 15 years. Perhaps their most explicit elaboration to date is to be found in a nearly finished book manuscript by Kamp and Rohrer on the system of tense and aspect of French. Preliminary sketches of that work can be found in [Kamp 1981b], [Kamp & Rohrer 1983] and [Rohrer 1986]. The method outlined in these papers has also been used in other studies of tense and aspect – see for instance [Partee 1984], [Abusch 1988], [Ogihara 1989], [Smith 1991].

Chapter 0 deals with preliminaries. The chapter consists of two quite different parts. The first part gives an informal discussion of some of the fundamental issues – conceptual as well as methodological – relating to the book's principal concerns, semantics and logic. Introductions of this sort are notorious for being to the liking of nobody. The cognoscenti, if not actually infuriated by what they read, are inevitably bored, while the novice, for whom the introduction is primarily intended, finds himself unable to make sense of an exposé for which he lacks the necessary presuppositions. Although we are aware of these pitfalls, we have thought it nevertheless necessary to try and say something about semantics and logic as we understand these fields and their mutual relationship, as well as about the place of the particular approach we pursue within a wider linguistic, logical and philosophical perspective.

The second part of Chapter 0 serves an entirely different purpose. As we said, this is a book about logic and semantics. It is not a book about syntax. But even so, we cannot make do without syntax altogether for one of our central objectives is to describe how syntactic form determines linguistic meaning. So we must avail ourselves of some means for representing syntactic form, even if these means fall short of satisfying those who expect syntactic descriptions to reveal the deeper principles of grammar. We fully acknowledge the central importance of syntactic theory as the systematic study of those principles, and we should have much preferred to use a syntax that has a better claim to capturing them than the one we have chosen. But to present such a better motivated syntax would have involved us in syntactic discussions far more extensive than seems compatible with the true purpose of this book. So we have decided to stick with the policy followed in the first explicit description of DRT ([Kamp 1981]) which makes use of a simple phrase structure grammar. The second part of Chapter 0 defines a phrase structure grammar that is slightly more complicated in that it has been enriched with various syntactic features. Later on, this feature system is significantly expanded. However, the basic architecture of our syntax remains the same throughout.

The one chapter that we have not yet mentioned is Chapter 3. This chapter is a kind of interlude between Chapters 1 and 2 on the one hand, and Chapters 4 and 5 on the other. Some parts of it deal with issues, such as for instance reflexives or scope ambiguity, which pertain directly to the theory developed in Chapters 1 and 2, but which we have chosen ignore for reasons of presentation. The other parts of Chapter 3 contain fairly brief discussions of linguistic constructions that the book does not treat in depth, but which, we found, kept turning up in sentences that illustrate the phenomena focussed on in Chapters 4 and 5. To demonstrate the viability of the theoretical proposals we make in those chapters it is important that they can be applied to such sentences, i.e. that they can be used in the conversion of those sentences into DRSs which represent them. But in order to convert a sentence into a DRS we must have principles to deal with every linguistic construction that it contains, including those that may have no direct bearing on the issues at hand.

So it is important that we have some understanding – even if it be lacking in theoretical depth – of those other constructions as well. Some of the constructions touched upon in Chapter 3 will be discussed in greater detail in Volume 2.

The second feature which this book owes to the particular circumstances of its origin is connected with the students who took the seminar that made us write it. To our considerable consternation, almost none of those students had had any previous training in either semantics or logic. At first, teaching a course in DRT to students whose preparation was so truly minimal seemed an enterprise that was bound to end in disaster. However, things turned out a lot better than we expected. No doubt this was due in large part to the exceptional ability of those who attended the course (for the most part computer scientists taking linguistics as a secondary subject). But we'd like to think that the manuscript which we were producing as we went along did its bit too; and that it helped as much as it did, because of the conscientious effort we were making to explain everything that someone without previous exposure to either formal semantics or logic would need to be told. In this way we ended up writing a book without prerequisite. This is not to say that some antecedent knowledge of logic or semantics would not be useful. For instance, we think the reader should have an easier time if he has had at least some exposure to formal logic, so that he is familiar with the syntax, and preferably also with the basics of the model theory, of the predicate calculus. But while such knowledge will undoubtedly make it easier to assimilate many of the book's details, it is not a prerequisite in a strict sense. In fact, the book contains, as part of the general development, an account of the syntax and semantics of predicate logic that presupposes no antecedent knowledge whatsoever.

The table of contents we planned originally included much that is not to be found within the present volume. As time went on, we discovered that things always take longer, not only longer in the sense of time but also in terms of the number of pages that are needed to say anything properly. Thus it became inevitable, lest we produce a book that would be as impossible to carry as to read, that certain parts of the original project be shelved. These parts will be published in a second volume. The main topics of this second book are: 1. Implications of DRT for certain issues in the philosophy of language and logic (relating to reference, truth, propositions, presupposition, ambiguity and the relation between semantics and pragmatics). 2. The proof theory of so-called "DRS-languages" (DRSs, or Discourse Representation Structures are the formal representations postulated by the theory developed in this book; these structures can be treated as formulas of certain symbolic languages, called 'DRS-languages'). 3. The theory of propositional attitudes (like belief, desire etc) and the semantics of attitude reports, i.e. sentences which ascribe attitudes to those who have them, like 'John believes that Mary is drunk'.) 4. The theory of verbal communication, of common knowledge and of common reference.

To make the book more useful as a textbook we have included a smattering of exercises. Some of these are routine, and only serve to give the student a chance to test his understanding of the preceding section. But there are also some exercises which touch upon matters of independent theoretical interest, and by illustrating substantive points which we decided to keep out of the main body of the text for reasons of exposition. The exercises constitute perhaps the most obvious point on which the book is open to improvement. It would be an exaggeration to claim that no textbook could ever have too many exercises. But it is not much of an exaggeration, and in practice there are few textbooks that could not have done with more exercises than they in fact contain. Certainly the present book doesn't have enough of them, not at any rate by our own lights. However, producing good exercises is not easy, and it takes time. The stock of exercises that we have collected up to this point (and which for the most part has found its way into the book) has been the fruit of an ongoing effort, closely connected with the series of DRT seminars that we ourselves and others at Stuttgart University have been teaching, and which, each time, have yielded a few new additions. We hope that the stock will continue to grow, and that now that the book is out, its growth rate will even accelerate. If, a few years from now, we find ourselves with a substantially richer collection than the one contained in the book, we may decide to make that collection publicly available.

A considerable number of people have influenced the content and/or form of the text that has now appeared in print. We are much indebted to Bernd Langner, who has been almost singlehandedly responsible for the visual appearance of what lies before you. (The manuscript was delivered camera-ready to the publishers, so everything looks just the way Bernd made it look.) Also, he and Bianca Dorn displayed a growing and eventually uncanny virtuosity turning what most people would perceive as random distributions of ink into digitalized script. Those who have had an effect on content as well as form include not only the ones who have given us their comments on earlier versions of the present manuscript, but also the many others with whom we interacted in relevant ways before the manuscript was started, and specifically those who read and criticised its abortive precursors. Without serious hope that we will succeed in mentioning everyone who should be, we want to express our explicit thanks to: Dorit Abusch, Joseph Almog, Nicholas Asher, Rainer Bäuerle, Johan van Benthem, Steve Berman, Daniel Bonevac, Gennaro Chierchia, Robin Cooper, Jan van Eijck, Werner Frey, Franz Guenthner, Irene Heim, Nirit Kadmon, Ewan Klein, Fred Landman, Hubert Lehmann, Arthur Merin, Michael Morreau, Toshi Ogihara, Stanley Peters, Manfred Pinkal, Craige Roberts, Christian Rohrer, Mats Rooth, Antje Rossdeutscher, Hans Rott, Görel Sandstrom, Andy Schwartz, Peter Sells, Bonnie Webber, Jürgen Wedekind and Ede Zimmermann.

A special tribute is owed to Victoria Rosen, who proof-read the first part of the book with exceptional care, and to whom we owe a large number of substantive as well as stylistic improvements. If the first three chapters read better and seem more coherent than those that follow, her scrutiny must surely be a major reason. Perhaps an even greater tribute must go to Barbara Partee. Among other things it was her penetrating criticisms of an unpublished manuscript by Frey & Kamp on plurals that led us to correct a good many mistakes that might otherwise have slipped into Chapter 4.

The list of those we mentioned in the last two paragraphs is long and diverse enough to suggest that the sentence you are reading right now may well be the only one in this book to which everyone on that list would happily agree. So, prudence would seem to command that we disclaim responsibility for all the remaining sentences. However, as we are the ones who wrote them all, the blame should be all ours too.

Hans Kamp
Uwe Reyle
Stuttgart, April 1993

Chapter 0

Preliminaries

0.1 Theories of Meaning

Languages are for communication. To know a language is to know how to communicate with it, and this involves two separate, albeit related, capacities. As speakers we must be able to put words to our thoughts, and as hearers we must be able to recognize the thoughts expressed from the words we perceive. Similarly when we express ourselves in writing, or read the writings of others.

These two capacities, that of finding words to fit the content we want to convey, and that of recognizing content from the words that reach us, presuppose a third one. This is the capacity to recognize the systematic connections between meaning and linguistic form. If the connection were not systematic – were not, in some sense or other, *rule-based* – language could not function in the way it does. For there would then be no guarantee that the recipient of an utterance could recover from it the thought which the speaker meant to express by it.

Formal semantics, which tries to come up with rigorous and detailed descriptions of the meaning-form relation, has taken the view that this is *all* that semantics can be asked to do. The question of how the relation is known and how that knowledge is exploited in the practice of language use are, according to this view, the concerns of pragmatics, of psycholinguistics, or perhaps of cognitive psychology generally. A theorist of this persuasion perceives language as an abstract symbolic system, governed by a form-meaning relation which in particular assigns *propositional content* to each symbol combination that has the form of a grammatically correct sentence.

A very different view of the tasks of semantics is entertained by those who see human language as the crystallization of human thought and regard linguistic meaning as an essentially psychological phenomenon. For them a theory of meaning must explain what it is for a linguistic expression to have a certain meaning *for the language user*, who grasps that meaning when he reads or hears the expression or chooses the expression as a carrier for the meaning he wants to convey. For him an abstract characterization of the relation between meaning and linguistic form could only be a part of the larger story semantics has to tell.

Theories which view their task this way have as a rule not gone very far. The principal reason for this is that they have not applied themselves enough to the description of the form-meaning relation itself. Evidently a precise semantical theory cannot afford to ignore this relation even if its central purpose is to explain how meaning is associated with form in actual language use. For surely, if we have no account of what the relation between meaning and form *is* we cannot hope to say anything precise about the user's capacity to *recognize* particular meanings and forms as related.

Although the approach we have adopted in this book is inspired by the second view, we will in fact be almost exclusively concerned with describing the form-meaning relation itself. But – and this is something that sets the present method apart from all existent semantic theories that have been inspired by either of the two mentioned views – this description is conceived as an (idealized) analysis of the process whereby the recipient of an utterance comes to grasp the thoughts that the utterance contains. We have been led towards our description of the relation between meaning and form by a firm conviction that it is only in this way that a comprehensive range of semantic facts can be explained.

We have been speaking of the relation between meaning and linguistic form. But we have said nothing so far about what meaning and form are. In fact it is anything but clear how these terms should be understood; and the different ways in which they have been understood have led to a further ramification of semantic theories.

The notion of linguistic form appears to be the less controversial of the two. Linguistic form, or *grammatical* or *syntactic* form, has been a central topic in the study of language virtually from the moment language was made into a subject of scientific reflection at all. It is *the* topic of what we usually refer to as *grammar*. However, what traditional grammars – which are typically concerned with spelling out which expressions are grammatically correct – have to say about syntactic form was often only implicit, and it was not until this century that linguists came to see the central goal of grammar, or *syntax* as it is now normally called, to be that of discovering the pattern of syntactic structures which the expressions of a given language realize. (Once the system of possible syntactic structures realized in the given language has been identified and the theory has made explicit how these structures are realized as actual – i.e. written or spoken – expressions of the language, the problem of defining the set of grammatical expressions of the language has been solved too: the grammatical expressions are precisely those which realize one of the possible syntactic structures.) Syntactic theory as it exists today owes its impetus and general form primarily to Noam Chomsky (*1928), whose

Syntactic Structures (1957) marks the beginning of *generative syntax*. Generative syntax is so called because its central component consists of rules by means of which syntactic structures (or at any rate a core set of syntactic structures) can be generated.[1] In the years following 1957 Chomsky's ideas have been elaborated in various directions, partly by himself and partly by other linguists. The syntax we have adopted here is a version of the so-called Generalized Phrase Structure Grammar (GPSG) first developed by Gerald Gazdar (*1949).

The notions of meaning and content are much more problematic than the notion of linguistic form. Talking of "putting" content "into" linguistic form, or of "extracting" a content "from" such a form, as we did above, has a tendency to make us think of contents as some kinds of "objects", and of the putting into and the extracting as going from one kind of object (a content or a linguistic form) to another (a linguistic form or a content). And from here it is only an apparently small and natural step to look upon these processes as some sort of translations – from linguistic expressions (or their grammatical structures) to expressions of some "language of thought" and vice versa. This view of uttering and understanding language as involving translations from and into a certain language of the mind has, over the past 20 years or so, been defended with particular force by the psychologist Jerry Fodor (*1935)[2]. Fodor's strongest argument for this view (or, at any rate, what seems to be his strongest argument to us) is that mental states which have propositional content, such as, say, beliefs and intentions, must be, as he puts it, *computational*. What he means is this. One of the central features of cognitively complex beings like ourselves is that they reason. They move, with greater or lesser confidence, from beliefs they hold, hypotheses they entertain, desires they harbour, and intentions they have, to new beliefs and new intentions, and in this way they arrive at new ways of seeing the world and are propelled into new ways of acting upon it.

However, the processes of reasoning *cannot* be understood, Fodor argues, unless we assume that both the beliefs, desires etc. which act as the premises of mental inferences and the conclusions that are drawn from them have some kind of formal, language-like, representational structure within which the particular inference drawn instantiates a general formal inferential pattern, defined in terms of the structural relations between premises and conclusion as they appear within that mode of representation. The mind must be able to "compute" the conclusion from the premises on the basis of their structural characteristics, or at least it should be able to verify by some sort of computation on the representational structures involved that the inference instantiates a valid formal inference pattern. Thus beliefs etc. must have a representational structure; and when somebody aquires a new belief by receiving, understanding and accepting as true something that someone else

[1] How this works is explained in Section 0.4.

[2] See [Fodor 1975], [Fodor 1983].

has said or written, this process of acquisition must be seen as his going from the linguistic form he receives as input to the mental representation whose structural features are essential to its subsequent exploitation as premise.

We find this position persuasive. Indeed, it is nothing other than the old view that deduction and inference are based on formal relations, the view that has informed the discipline of logic from the time it was born, presumably in the mind of Aristotle (384–322 BC). But as a basis for semantic theory the view faces two serious difficulties, one circumstantial and one fundamental. The circumstantial problem is that the only access which the theorist seems to have to the language of thought is *via* the languages we speak. Looking into people's heads, subjecting them to all sorts of experiments that might reveal details of cognitive processes and their correlation with physiological processes in the brain, is an option that is simply not available.[3] Consequently, the semantic programme of explaining linguistic meaning in terms of the language of thought looks like it is condemned to be circular at least in practice: it won't do to base whatever one has to say about mental representation of content solely on what can be learned from studying the linguistic expressions through which these contents are publicly expressed, and then to offer mental representations as explaining the content of the corresponding expressions of the public language.

The second difficulty goes deeper, and would remain even if it were possible to ground an account of the language of thought on evidence other than how people express their thoughts in natural language. Even if the grammars of both natural language and the language of thought could be established independently, and if it would also be possible to state how expressions of natural language translate into mental representations and conversely, this, it has been argued, would still fall fundamentally short of an account of what either language *means.* Indeed, explaining natural language solely by referring to mental representations would only shift the problem of meaning to another language. For what could we reply if, having proposed such an account of the meaning of expressions of natural language, we were then asked what endows the expressions of the language of thought with the meaning they are supposed to have? The whole enterprise, so the argument goes, is really no different from trying to account for the meaning of English by articulating how English expressions are translated into French, and equating the meaning of each English expression with that of the expression or expressions of French into which it translates. What are we to say to the skeptic who then asks for an account of the meaning of French? Refer back to the corresponding expressions

[3]Note that this is, presumably, not simply a matter of ethics: it is not only immoral to subject fellow human beings to experiments that would endanger their physical or spiritual health; it is not even remotely clear what such experiments *could* possibly teach us about the structure of the language of thought. In any case, even if relevant experiments could be designed, the ethical issues involved would rule out most or all of them.

of English? Obviously that would not do.

What is missing from a theory of meaning along these lines, the objection continues, is something that is fundamental to the phenomenon of linguistic meaning, viz. that when we speak or think we typically speak or think *about* something. And in the cases that matter most to us, creatures which must get on in a world that is as full of dangers as it is of opportunities, what we speak or think about are things in, or, more generally, parts of, that actual world.

For thoughts and utterances that concern the actual world there arises the question whether they are *true* or *false*. A thought or utterance about the actual world is true if it correctly reflects the way the actual world *is*, false otherwise. Moreover, truth and falsity are not just any concepts that apply to world-directed utterances and thoughts. Evidently, truth is of the utmost importance to us. This is especially so in the context of *practical reasoning*. When I reason my way towards a plan of action, and then act according to that plan, my action will be prone to fail, or even to lead to disaster, if the factual beliefs underlying my deliberation are false – even if my deliberation cannot be faulted in any other way.

Since truth and falsity are of such paramount importance, and since it is in virtue of their meaning that thoughts and utterances can be distinguished into those that are true and those that are false, it is natural to see the world-directed, truth value-determining aspect of meaning as central; and, consequently, to see it as one of the central obligations of a theory of meaning to explain how meaning manifests itself in the determination of truth and falsity. But how should such an explanation proceed? To address this question let us concentrate on meaning in natural language, ignoring for now any questions concerning the language of thought.

Evidently the truth or falsity of a natural language utterance is the product of two independent factors, on the one hand the meaning of the expression uttered and on the other the factual constitution of its subject matter. A theory explaining the part which meaning plays in the determination of truth must succeed in separating these factors. For only then will it enable us to perceive clearly what is being contributed by either. The method which has thus far proved to be the most effective in achieving this separation is that of *model-theoretic semantics*. This method was introduced to the study of natural language in the late 60s by the logician Richard Montague (1932–1971). In model-theoretic semantics – including the specific form of it which is exemplified by Montague's own work and which is now generally referred to as *Montague Grammar* ([Partee 1973a], [Thomason 1974], [Dowty et. al. 1981]) – the subject matter is represented by way of a *model*, an abstract structure that can be seen as encoding, in some natural and direct way, the kind of factual information that is pertinent to the truth values of the sentences of the language or language fragment that is being studied. The object, then, becomes that of articulating, for each sentence S of this language or language fragment, in which of the possible models S is true and in which it is false.

The interest of such an articulation resides in its details. These details depend on two kinds of structure, on the one hand the structure of the models the theory adopts, and on the other that of the sentences with which it is concerned. Sentence structure, in the sense of syntactic structure, we have already discussed. This subject is comparatively uncontroversial, even if the structure of certain sentences is still being explored and debated. On the other hand, what structure should be assumed for the models is a much more difficult problem which raises a number of deep and fundamental philosophical questions. This is a matter that we cannot go into here, but which will be taken up in Sections 1.2, 4.3 and 5.6.

The interest, we have said, of a model-theoretic semantics lies in the details of how it exploits both model structure and sentence structure. What renders such accounts especially valuable as accounts of meaning is that they make precise how each structural component of a sentence contributes to the determination of the truth values which the sentence assumes in each of the models considered. For such an account will not only, by making explicit what truth values a sentence assumes in the various models, tell us a good deal about the meaning of the sentence itself. By specifying what contribution each sentence constituent makes to the truth of the many different sentences in which it occurs as constituent, it tells us also something about the meanings of these constituents. In particular, it will show how the meaning of a complete sentence is connected with the meanings of its constituent parts. (How all this might work is, we realize, hard to comprehend for one who is unfamiliar with the inner workings of model-theoretic semantics; the matter will become clear when, in the course of this book, we will develop such a semantics in detail.)

The central ideas which motivate the model-theoretic analysis of linguistic meaning go back to the German mathematician and philosopher Gottlob Frege (1848–1925). Frege came to see the problem of giving an account of linguistic meaning as first and foremost that of describing the meanings of complete sentences. To explain the meanings of other linguistic units – e.g., descriptions, such as **the man on the moon**, or **the largest proper divisor of 145**, or **the woman with a Martini in her hand**, or predicates, such as **owns a dog**, or **is divisible by 37**, or **doesn't like meals prepared without garlic** – it would be enough, he held, to explain how those constituents contribute to the meaning of the sentences in which they occur. It was also Frege's insight that to explain the meaning of a sentence one must explain under what conditions the sentence is or would be true. Together these two views lead naturally to the kind of analysis of meaning that model-theoretic semantics offers.

More recently such a view has been defended by the philosopher Donald Davidson (*1915) who, in the late 60s, proposed that a definition of truth for a language which reveals how the truth values of sentences are determined by their syntactic structure and the meanings of their component words is about all that a theory of meaning for that language could be asked to deliver (cf. [Davidson 1967c]). Our own view of the matter is less extreme. On the one hand we are, with Frege, Davidson and many others, convinced that the links between language and the world – those links in virtue of which, as it is often put, words and larger linguistic units are able to *refer* to things in the world – are essential to what constitutes linguistic meaning, and therefore that no theory of the meaning of language is complete unless it accounts for the connection between meaning and truth. On the other hand, we have become persuaded that a theory of meaning must also have things to say about *interpretation*. A speaker's grasp of the meaning of his language manifests itself partly in his ability to interpret the sentences that reach him, i.e. to assign a meaning to the strings of signs or sounds which he reads or hears, and which he recognizes as conforming to the grammar of his language. The theory of meaning which we will develop in this book attempts to do justice to both convictions. In fact, the treatment it offers of either aspect of meaning – the one which links it to truth, and that which links it to interpretation – is inseparable from what it has to say about the other. Its implicit message is that truth and interpretation are connected in a way which earlier treatments appear to have overlooked.

0.2 Logic

Systematic semantics is one of the younger sciences; it has been with us for little more than half a century. Logic, in contrast, dates back to the time of Aristotle, whose work contains most of the substantial and methodological insights which characterize the subject as it is understood today. This vast chronological discrepancy between semantics and logic suggests that the two disciplines would be very different, or at least that, whether or not semantics presupposes logic, logic does not presuppose semantics. However, according to our understanding of the two subjects today they are intimately connected, and neither can be effectively pursued without the other. This interconnectedness of semantics and logic is particularly important in the approach taken in this book, where it gains an extra dimension that is absent from other contemporary approaches, such as, for instance, the strictly model-theoretic approach of Montague Grammar.

Logic is the science of inference. It is based on two central assumptions which are fully present in Aristotle's work. The first of these is:

(i) in order that an inference be *sound*, two separate conditions must be fulfilled

(a.) the premises from which the inference proceeds must be trustworthy;

and

(b.) the inferred conclusion must stand to these premises in a certain "logical" relation which guarantees that the trustworthiness of the premises transfers to the conclusion.

Before we state the second assumption we must say a little more about (i), in particular about the term "trustworthy". "Trustworthy" is vague. A proposition may be said to be trustworthy simply because it is true, i.e. because it has that property which trust ascribes to it. But we might also regard it as worthy of our trust because it is plausible or probable, even though that does not exclude the possibility of its being false. Whether or not this possibility is admitted makes a crucial difference to the meaning of soundness, and in fact to the entire enterprise of logic that builds upon that concept. If we permit the possibility, then it may happen that the conclusion of an argument, though no less probable than the premises, is nevertheless in fact false while the premises are true. So no matter how firm the guarantee that trustworthiness, in the sense of probability, is preserved, the inference may still lead from true assumptions to a false conclusion. With transfer of trustworthiness in the first sense - i.e. transfer of truth - this is by definition not so. Transfer of truth simply *means* that the conclusion must be true unless one or more of the premises are false. So only a guarantee that there is transfer of trustworthiness in this sense will be a foolproof protection against erring, by mere inference, from the path of truth.

Thus the two conceptions of soundness - the one based on probability and the one based on truth - yield two distinct conceptions of logic, a narrower conception, according to which logic is concerned exclusively with relations which preserve truth, and a broader one which concerns itself with the preservation of probability, of which the preservation of truth appears as a special, limiting case. Logic in the first, narrower sense is called *deductive logic*, as distinct from *inductive logic*, which is concerned with soundness in the sense of probability. In this book we will be interested only in deductive logic, and we will refer to it simply as *logic*.

The second of the two central assumptions is one which has application to inductive as well as to deductive logic, but it is in the context of deductive logic that it has had the greatest impact - indeed, deductive logic as it has been understood from Aristotle to this day is inseparable from this assumption. This is the assumption that:

(ii) The relation between premises and conclusion which guarantees transfer of truth is a *formal* relation, one that can be analysed as a relation between sentence *forms*. It can be seen as a relation between sentence forms inasmuch as its holding between given premises $A_1,\ldots,A_n$ and conclusion B implies that it will hold equally between any other combination of premises $A_1,\ldots,A_n$ and conclusion B which instantiates the same formal pattern - any other combination of the same n+1 forms related to each other by the same formal connections.

The forms of premises and conclusion that are implied in this assumption are often referred to as *logical forms.* The relation between $A_1,...,A_n$ and B spoken of in (ii) is often referred to as the relation of *logical consequence* or *logical entailment* – we say 'B *is a logical consequence of* $A_1,...,A_n$', or $A_1,...,A_n$ *entail* B. One also says in this situation that the inference from $A_1,...,A_n$ to B is *logically valid.*

The research programme that assumptions (i) and (ii) suggest is two-fold. First there is the task of explaining how the logical consequence relation can be recognized. Evidently this is something that people are able to do (though, admittedly, some of them are better at it than others), for how else would they distinguish good modes of reasoning from bad ones? In the light of assumption (ii) this task entails another. If the relation in question is a relation between the logical forms of premises and conclusion, then an explanation of that relation must include an account of logical form. The second task is that of developing such an account. It is one of the many tributes to Aristotle's genius that he recognized the accomplishment of this second task as indispensible to the theory of logic, and that he developed an account of logic and logical form – his doctrine of the *syllogism* – which, for all its limitations, survived largely unchallenged until well into the 19th century.

Aristotle's syllogistic logic can be described as a comparatively simple and limited logic of classes. Typical examples of the argument patterns with which it is concerned are:

(0.1)

	All Ps are Qs
	All Qs are Rs
therefore:	All Ps are Rs

(0.2)

	All Ps are Qs
	Some Qs are Rs
therefore:	Some Ps are Rs

(0.3)

	Some Ps are Qs
	All Qs are Rs
therefore:	Some Ps are Rs

(0.4)

	No Ps are Qs
	All Qs are Rs
therefore:	No Ps are Rs

(0.5)

	All Ps are Qs
	No Qs are Rs
therefore:	No Ps are Rs

Of these (0.1), (0.3) and (0.5) are valid patterns, while (0.2) and (0.4) are not. In general the patterns consist of a conclusion and a couple of premises; each of these states a simple relation between two classes - either one class is included in the other, or they have something in common, or the two have nothing in common; the classes themselves are usually designated by schematic letters, such as the P, Q, R of the examples above.

By combining valid patterns of this kind into chains we can account for a substantially larger set of "extended" inference patterns, e.g. the pattern:

(0.6)

	All Ps are Qs
	All Qs are Rs
	No Rs are Ss
therefore:	No Ps are Ss

can be justified by noting that the first two premises yield 'All Ps are Rs' by (0.1), and this together with the third premise yields the conclusion 'No Ps are Ss' by pattern (0.5). Even by chaining valid Aristotelean patterns together, however, we cover, as it turns out, only a minor part of the variety of valid inference forms that figure prominently in daily reasoning and, more significantly perhaps, in the typically more rigorous and complex reasoning that is found in mathematics and science. The problem is not just detecting which are the valid patterns expressible in the formal notation of syllogistic logic; more fundamentally, it concerns its logical forms. These forms are unable to display enough of the logical structure of many of the propositions with which we operate in much of our ordinary and scientific thought.

As a consequence, no real advance in logical theory was possible until Aristotle's conception of logical form made way for one more adequate to the true complexities of propositional structure. It is one of the more remarkable facts of the history of science that this did not happen until the late 19th century. Only in 1879 Frege, in his famous *Begriffsschrift* ([Frege 1964]), introduced a new notion of logical form, and an elaborate, rigorously defined notation for representing it. (A similar discovery was made at about the same time, by the American philosopher Charles Sanders Peirce (1839–1914), whose work ([Roberts 1973]), however, has had, partly for contingent reasons, a much more modest influence on the dramatic logical developments of the early parts of this century.) The formal system Frege developed is still with us today, in a form that differs only superficially from the original. It is commonly known as *predicate logic*, or as the *predicate calculus*.

As a matter of fact, not all of the drawbacks of Aristotelean logic, as it was taught and practiced during the long centuries when it reigned supreme, related to the limitations of its concept of logical form. Another deficiency was the lack of any sufficiently general method for determining which of the inference patterns expressible in syllogistic notation are valid and which are not. Consequently, a good part of syllogistic theorizing consisted in discovering particular valid patterns, and arguing why these were in fact valid - an activity not unlike that of collecting biological specimens (which even today some people seem to consider the true mission of "natural history").

This second deficiency was overcome not long before the advent of predicate logic, when, in the second part of the 19th century, the logician John Venn (1834–1923) developed a method, usually referred to as the *method of Venn-diagrams*, for "modelling" the premises and conclusions of syllogistic inferences in a systematic way. To determine the validity of a given pattern it suffices to construct the relevant Venn-diagram or diagrams for it. The answer can then be read off these diagrams mechanically. In a Venn-diagram the classes that are given in our syllogistic notation by the letters P, Q, R, ... are represented by circles (or other closed curves) whose relations of inclusion and intersection conform to the premises of the pattern under consideration. If *every* such diagram also verifies the conclusion of the pattern, then the pattern will be valid, and otherwise not. Thus, for instance, the following diagram verifies the two premises of pattern (0.1):

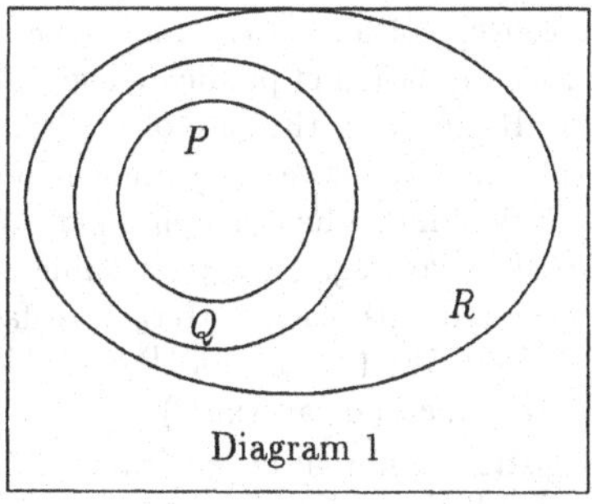

Diagram 1

P is included in Q, i.e. 'all Ps are Q', and Q is included in R, i.e. 'all Qs are Rs'. As the diagram shows, we also have then, inevitably, that P is included in R, i.e. that 'all Ps are Rs', and it is evident that any other diagram which verifies the premises will verify the conclusion as well. Thus the pattern is valid. In contrast, a diagram reflecting the two premises of (0.2) might look like this:

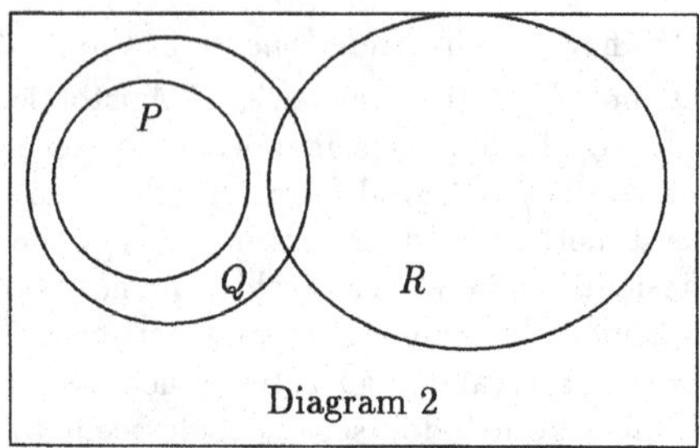

Diagram 2

Here the overlap of Q and R verifies the premise that some Qs are Rs, while, as in Diagram 1, the inclusion of P within Q captures the content of the first premise. According to this diagram the conclusion is not true and consequently pattern (0.2) is not valid. As these examples show, Venn's method of checking the validity of syllogistic inference patterns is quite straightforward. Moreover, it has the desirable property of being a *decidable* method: for any fixed number of classes (and in particular for the type of case with which we have been dealing, where there are just three classes P, Q, R), there exists only a finite number of diagrams that differ from each other in some relevant way (i.e. by making different claims about inclusion or intersection). Therefore it is always possible to determine, by checking each of the diagrams in this finite list, whether the given pattern is indeed valid or not; proceeding in this manner we can be sure to reach, after a finite number of checks, a definite answer, yes or no.

Venn's method may be called a "semantic" method inasmuch as it involves, through its diagrams, the concept of an *interpreting structure.* The method has an analogue for the much richer notation of predicate logic, which we will study in detail later on in this book. However, in the case of predicate logic the variety of interpreting structures is infinite. Therefore one cannot hope for a simple finitary way of determining the validity of individual inference patterns such as that which we have in the case of Aristotelian logic, where it suffices to run through the finitely many diagrams associated with each pattern. (In fact, we know through the work of Kurt Gödel (1906–1978) ([Gödel 1931]) and Alonso Church (*1903) ([Church 1936]) that no finitary method can exist.)

Both in the case of syllogistic and in that of predicate logic the semantic method for analysing validity must be distinguished from another, in which a small number of inference patterns are selected as basic and the validity of other patterns is established by chaining two or more applications of the basic patterns together. This second method, which we already mentioned briefly in connection with syllogistic logic, is known as the *proof-theoretic* or *deductive* method. It captures an aspect of deduction which the semantic definition of validity does not touch: in many cases where we reason from given premises to a certain conclusion it is only by moving in small steps that we succeed in arriving at the final conclusion; in others, where we may see the inference more or less directly, it may nevertheless be necessary to break it up into a chain of simple inferences to persuade others that our conclusion really follows. The more sophisticated the inferences, the more important this breaking up into intermediate steps becomes. This is especially true in the mathematical sciences; the point of a mathematical proof is that it moves from premises to conclusion by inferences simple enough to be readily verified. It is this feature – that by combining inference steps which are all of them individually simple and transparent one can arrive at chains of reasoning that lead from accepted assumptions to conclusions that are anything but obvious – which appears as central to the phenomenon of deduction to anyone familiar with its more impressive manifestations. It is not surprising therefore that the great logicians of the late 19th and early 20th century (Giuseppe Peano (1858–1932), David Hilbert (1862–1943), Bertrand Russell (1872–1970), Alfred North Whitehead (1861–1947) and Gerhard Gentzen (1909–1945)) whose background was largely mathematical and whose interest in logic arose out of a desire to place mathematics on a more solid logical foundation, should have put great emphasis upon this feature, and that they were thus led to tackle the problems of logic primarily by the deductive method.

They and others showed that even the most complicated mathematical proofs can be rephrased as sequences of inferences each of which instantiates one of a very small number of basic patterns. The validity of these patterns can be seen by direct inspection, and they may be regarded as "purely logical" in that their validity has to do only with general logical concepts such as those expressed by the words **and**, **not** or **every**, and not with any notions privy to some particular domain, such as, e.g., the concepts **plus**, **perpendicular**, **gravity** or **molecule**, from arithmetic, geometry, physics and chemistry. In this way the logicians of the late 19th and early 20th centuries were able to unify the methods of scientific deduction, and so vindicated formal logic as the general foundation of scientific methodology.

Important as the proof-theoretic approach towards inference is, it has two crucial drawbacks, and these are drawbacks that affect the deductive method generally. First, how are we to know, after we have tried but failed to vindicate a given pattern in this way, that there might not be some other combination of rule applications we have overlooked and which shows that the pattern does follow from the basic patterns after all? Second and more importantly, how do we know that the given basic patterns suffice even in principle for the validation of all inferences that should be acknowledged as valid, i.e. of all those patterns that preserve truth? It is true that after a good deal of successful experimentation with a given system of basic inference principles one may become convinced that these principles provide all that could ever be needed. As a matter of fact, by showing that a representative sample of mathematical proofs could be transformed into deductions exploiting only the few patterns they had postulated as basic, the logicians we have mentioned succeeded in building up an impressive amount of evidence that these patterns do cover all patterns of valid reasoning that would ever be needed. But such evidence, no matter how much of it there may be, can never add up to conclusive proof. If proof is what we want - and the issue at stake, the relation between logic and knowledge, is important enough for us to insist upon proof - it is necessary to proceed in some other way.

Before we can even contemplate how such a proof might go, we must settle what precisely it is that should be proved. In other words, we need an independent, intuitively correct and mathematically rigorous definition of logical validity. Only then does the statement that all logically valid inferences can be reduced to chains of applications of the basic patterns of some given system have the degree of precision that makes it possible to show it by an argument that meets the standards of mathematical demonstration.

The definition of validity that is needed here, however, must not only be mathematically rigorous, it must also be intuitively correct - i.e. we must be able to see, on the strength of our informal understanding of what validity amounts to, that the definition captures the notion. It is here that we need to come back to our earlier characterization of an inference as logically valid iff it necessarily preserves truth, i.e. if it is such that its conclusion cannot be false if all its premises are true. To cast this principle in the form of an exact definition we must reflect on the meaning of "necessarily" (or "cannot", which plays the same role in our second formulation). The established way of interpreting "necessarily" in the present context is that the truth of the premises must entail that of the conclusion, irrespective of how the world or subject matter about which premises and conclusions speak turns out to be. In other words, for our argument with premises $A_1,...,A_n$ and conclusion B to be valid it should be necessary and sufficient that in every possible circumstance in which $A_1,...,A_n$ are true B is true as well.

This is the blueprint for the definition of validity on which modern formal logic is based. But as it stands it isn't quite the mathematically rigorous definition which we were looking for; for the notion of a possible circumstance has not yet been made precise, nor have we said anything about the question (how could we have, so long as we haven't studied what circumstances are!) of what accounts for a statement being true with respect to a given circumstance rather than false. Clarifying these issues is the task of semantics.

The first and most important part of this task is to develop an exact notion of possible circumstance. It has become customary in semantics to identify circumstances with so-called *models.* A *model* for an inference I, with premises A_1, ..., A_n and conclusion B, is a structure which supplies an exact interpretation for each of the expressions occurring in either premises or conclusion except those which are treated as purely logical notions (expressions such as **not**, **and** or **all**). These interpretations determine unequivocally for any sentence that can be constructed from the vocabulary occurring in I, whether it is true or false in the model. Thus for any well-defined class **K** of models for I the question whether B is true in every member of **K** in which A_1, ..., A_n are true is well-defined as well. And if we can persuade ourselves that the models in **K** are representative of all possible circumstances, we can accept the well-defined property of being truth-preserving in all members of **K** as an explication of our intuitive concept of validity.

It should be clear that the role which models play in relation to the language of modern logic resembles that played by Venn-diagrams in the theory of the syllogism. In both cases the interpreting structure (model or Venn-diagram) assigns truth values to each sentence of the language for which it is designed. But *how* precisely are these truth values determined? This is a question that we have not so far addressed. We didn't explicitly discuss it when we talked about Venn-diagrams because there the answer seemed straightforward enough. But for the languages of modern logic, with their much more comprehensive notational capabilities, the matter is not that simple. In fact, the definition of the *truth relation* – the relation which holds between a formula and a model if the formula is true in the model – has been one of the milestones in the development of 20th century logic. (Strictly speaking the discovery was made in two steps. The decisive break-through occurred when in 1935 Alfred Tarski (1901–1983) produced his famous essay *The Concept of Truth in Formalized Languages* ([Tarski 1935/36]). An explicit model-theoretic truth definition became available – through the continued research of Tarski and his students – only in the late forties.) It is precisely because the definition of validity requires the concept of truth-in-a-model, and because that is a concept which cannot be taken for granted but needs to be carefully and explicitly defined, that semantics has become an integral part of modern logic.

0.3 Logic and Semantics

From what we have said so far it appears that while the initial goals of logic and semantics are quite different, their pursuits have a good deal in common. In particular, we have seen that something like the model-theoretic approach we described in Section 0.1 is also needed in a satisfactory account of logic. Yet, how much overlap we may expect between logic and the semantics of natural language is far from clear for that will depend in part on how closely the notational systems of formal logic resemble, in syntactic and/or semantic structure, natural languages such as English, Greek or Eskimo. There would seem to be good reason for doubting that their similarity will go very far; for it was precisely with the aim of overcoming the perceived inadequacies of natural language as a tractable vehicle for expressing scientific propositions with the required precision that the symbolisms of modern logic – that of the predicate calculus foremost among them – were developed. It is not surprising therefore that superficially at least the languages of symbolic logic do not seem to be at all like natural languages. In fact, from the time the predicate calculus was invented until the mid-sixties there was a general belief that natural languages were too unsystematic to allow analysis by the rigorous methods of formal logic including those of model theory. This conviction held for several decades after the model theory for predicate logic had been developed. It was thought not just that a model theory for, say, English would have to be quite unlike that for predicate logic; people believed that such a model theory could not be developed at all.

It was against the background of this scepticism that Montague's papers on natural language semantics, which were mentioned in the first part of this chapter, made their dramatic impact. These papers showed once and for all that the model-theoretic approach towards natural language was viable. They also demonstrated that the model theories for natural and those for symbolic languages have a great deal in common.

Montague himself made a point of stressing the similarities and playing down the differences. On the one hand this brought criticism from linguistic quarters. Natural languages, it was argued, were importantly different from constructed symbolic languages such as the predicate calculus; and Montague's treatment of, in particular, the syntactic structure of natural language showed not enough sensitivity to the distinctive features of natural language syntax. There is some truth in this criticism, but nevertheless Montague was right in emphasizing the similarities. For from a fundamental standpoint the tasks of explicating the meaning of a formal language such as predicate logic and of accounting for meaning of a natural language such as English are not really different.

Indeed, in retrospect it seems obvious that some such approach as Montague's should have been possible. To see this we must return to what we said earlier about logic and reasoning. Inference and deduction are activities in which human beings engaged long before logical theory began and which they engage in irrespective of whether the theory of logic is known to them or not. Logical theory must explain the nature of this activity (and, where possible, but only *via* this explanation, provide canons which might help us to improve it). However, the deductive practices and capacities that motivate the theory of logic, and to which it must be ultimately accountable, are practices and capacities which manifest themselves typically in the context of *natural* language. Inasmuch as we have a (pretheoretical) ability to tell good arguments from bad ones, it is *natural* language arguments which we can divide into those that are good and those that are bad. This implies that we have some way of recognizing whether premises and conclusions *phrased in natural language* are related in such a way that the premises could not be true without the conclusion being true as well. Thus our ability to reason in natural language entails that we are able to recognize how the truth conditions of different sentences are systematically related to each other. But what would permit us to recognize the truth conditions of a sentence if it weren't its overtly recognizable form – as a string of words which follow each other in a particular, semantically significant order? Montague's model-theoretic semantics for natural language constitutes one way of explicating the human ability to recognize truth conditions from perceptible sentence form.

It should be noted in this connection that Montague's professed aim was to clarify, through his model-theoretic treatment of English, what inferential relations exist between its different sentences. His work is as much a contribution to the theory of the *logic* of English as it is a contribution to the theory of its semantics. Until recently this deductive aspect of model-theoretic semantics of natural language seemed to be only of abstract interest. For there seemed little point in trying to design, on the basis of a semantic analysis such as Montague's, a particular system of deductive rules that would capture all, or at any rate a significant part, of the inferences which that analysis satisfies. Anyone who is really serious about deduction or proof, so the general attitude was, had better stick to the formal languages that have been specifically designed for proof and deduction and which are so eminently suited to it.

In recent years, however, the perspective has changed. In large part the change has come about through the advent of cognitive science, the science of how the mind works. Reasoning is one of the most significant mental functions, which enters, in one form or another, into almost all types of intellectual performance. In many instances – if not, presumably, in all – the reasoning which constitutes all or part of the performance is closely tied with the ways in which we normally express ideas, that is in the forms which natural language makes available. The understanding of these reasoning processes which cognitive science should eventually produce must include an understanding of how human beings reason with thoughts as natural language enables them to express these.

In the theory developed in this book semantics and logic are connected in yet another way. As we mentioned in the first part of this chapter, the approach we will pursue is not, in the way of model-theoretic semantics, just concerned with articulating the truth conditions of the natural language sentences under study, but also with the phenomenon of natural language *interpretation*. We will assume that interpretations of sentences and texts are constructed in the form of abstract structures, so-called *Discourse Representation Structures* or DRSs. These DRSs are obtained through the application of certain rules to the input sentences, the so-called *DRS Construction Rules*. In general these rules do not look just at the sentence or sentence component that is being interpreted, but also at the DRS that has already been built and into which the results of the present interpretation step are to be incorporated. How the form of the already constructed DRS influences the application of a construction rule varies from rule to rule. In some cases – discussed for the most part in Volume 2 – this influence can be determined only by performing certain logical deductions on the already constructed DRS. Thus logical deduction reveals itself as an integral part of interpretation, i.e. of the process by which we determine what the sentences we hear or read mean.

Within the perspective of this theory the interconnection between semantics and logic is complete. Not only does it seem impossible to give a satisfactory account of logical deduction without accounting also for meaning; conversely, if a theory of meaning is to include – as we think it should – a theory of interpretation, an account of meaning includes in its turn an account of deduction – at least, it will have to include all those forms of deduction that enter into the process or processes of interpretation; but those forms cover, as we will see in Volume 2, a very substantial part of deduction in general – and for all that is known at present, they may well cover all.

0.4 Syntax

As we explained in the introduction, a systematic account of semantics presupposes a theory of syntactic form. So we will have to begin by presenting such a theory. This is what we will do in the present section.

It must be emphasized again that syntactic form is not, in and of itself, a topic of this book. Therefore, our presentation of syntax will proceed briskly and fairly perfunctorily. Also, our choice of syntactic theory has been guided by opportunism. We have opted for a syntax that assigns to each of the sentences of the English fragment with which we will deal a syntactic structure that suits the needs of the interpretation procedure which we will describe in the following chapters (and which *is* of central importance to what we intend to accomplish in this book). But in choosing a particular set of syntactic rules which define these syntactic structures we have been largely oblivious to the more profound questions which motivate much of contemporary syntactic theorizing.

In particular, we have stayed aloof from the question whether our rules capture the deeper syntactic regularities which a self-respecting syntactician would see it as his primary duty to discover. We believe, however, that such expedience is fairly harmless. For all existing experience with the semantic theory we will present here suggests that it can easily be adapted to fit a theory of syntactic form which does justice to the issues that make syntax an important and fascinating subject in its own right.

Our syntax follows in outline the *Generalized Phrase Structure Grammar* (GPSG) of Gazdar and his associates (1985). To explain how such a grammar is set up it is best to look, right from the start, at some examples. Consider the sentence:

(0.7) Jones likes Anna Karenina.

It is a piece of age-old wisdom that such a sentence can be analysed as consisting of a *subject*, **Jones** and a *predicate*, which is made up of the remainder of the sentence, i.e. of the words **likes Anna Karenina** and that this predicate can, in its turn, be analysed into the transitive verb **likes** and the direct object **Anna Karenina**. Thus we can decompose the sentence into three grammatical *constituents*, as in the following diagram:

(0.8)

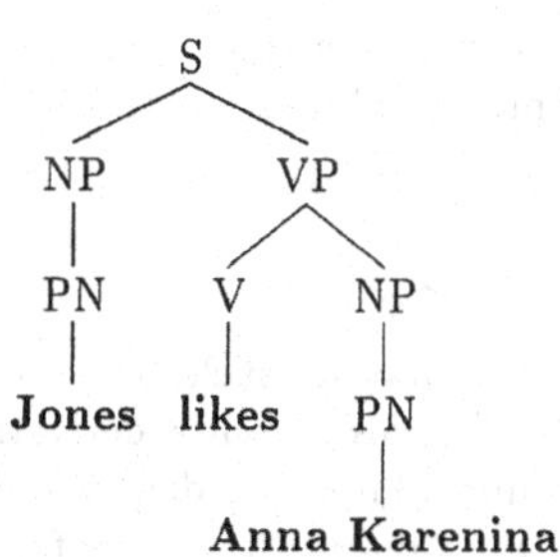

Here the top node, marked S (which denotes the syntactic category of *sentence*) is the node representing the entire sentence (0.7). As the diagram shows, this sentence can be decomposed into a subject – the node, marked NP, denoting the category of *Noun Phrase* – on the left and a predicate, or, as we will call it, *verb phrase*, the node on the right bearing the category label VP. So the subject NP **Jones** and the VP **likes Anna Karenina** are the principal constituents of (0.7). The VP can be further decomposed into a verb constituent, the node marked V and another noun phrase constituent, **Anna Karenina**, represented by the second node marked NP, the one underneath the VP-node. Note that a syntactic constituent may itself be composed of smaller constituents, as here the VP-constituent is a compound consisting of the V constituent **likes** and its direct object, the NP constituent **Anna Karenina**. Immediately below each of the two NP nodes there is a node marked PN, for *Proper Name*. This is to distinguish the type of noun phrases that are found in (0.7), i.e. the proper names **Jones** and **Anna Karenina**, from other types such as for instance *personal pronouns* (**he**, **she**, **it**) or *indefinite descriptions* (**a book, a man whom Mary abhors, a magazine that fascinates Jones**).

It was first realized by the linguist Noam Chomsky (*1928) that constituent analyses like that in (0.8) can be described by means of so-called *phrase structure rules* ([Chomsky 1957]). Thus the fact that English has the sentence pattern exemplified by (0.7), which is analysable as the concatenation of a subject NP and a VP, is captured by a rule of the form:

(0.9) S $\rightarrow$ NP VP

Similarly, that there are VPs which, like the one of (0.7), consist of a V-constituent and an object NP is captured by the rule

(0.10) VP $\rightarrow$ V NP

and that among the English NPs there are those which have the form of proper names can be codified in the form of a rule

(0.11) NP $\rightarrow$ PN

These rules enable us to derive the syntactic "skeleton" of (0.8), i.e. all of it except for the words that occupy the end nodes. Such a derivation can be carried out as follows. We start with a rudimentary tree diagram, consisting of only one node labeled 'S'. We then apply the rules in the sense of inserting, with each rule application, underneath an end node of the tree so far obtained which bears the left-hand symbol of the applied rule as its label, successor nodes whose labels are the category symbols mentioned in the rule on the right-hand side of the arrow. Thus we obtain successively:

(0.12)

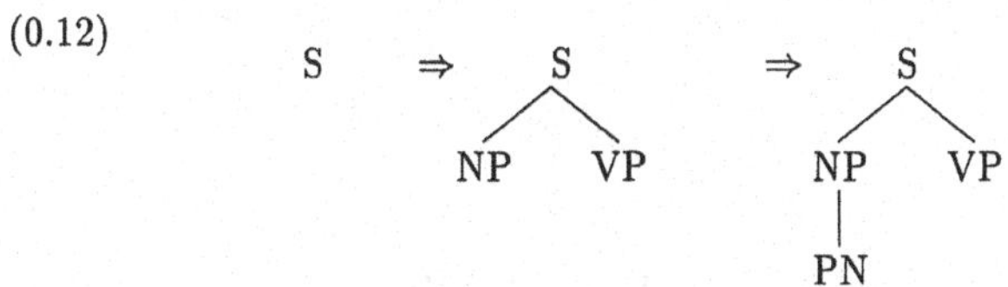

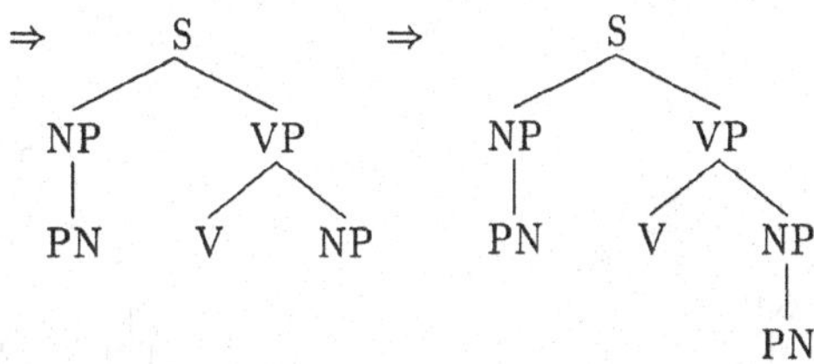

To complete the derivation of (0.8) we need rules that enable us to insert the lexical items – **Jones, likes** and **Anna Karenina** – underneath the end nodes of the last tree of(0.12). The rules which will permit us to do this are called *lexical insertion rules.* A lexical insertion rule tells us for some particular syntactic category which words fall under that category. For instance, the lexical insertion rule for proper names will have the form

(0.13) PN → **Jones, Smith, Mary, ..., Anna Karenina, Middlemarch, Buddenbrooks, ...**

with on the right-hand side a list of all the proper names our fragment of English is to take into account. And the lexical insertion rule for verbs will specify all the verbs we include, and this will be something like:

(0.14) V → **likes, loves, abhors, arises, rotates, ...**

When a lexical rule is applied one of the words on the right-hand side is inserted under a node bearing the category label occurring on the left-hand side of the rule. So three applications to the last tree of (0.12) give the structure (0.8), e.g.:

(0.15)

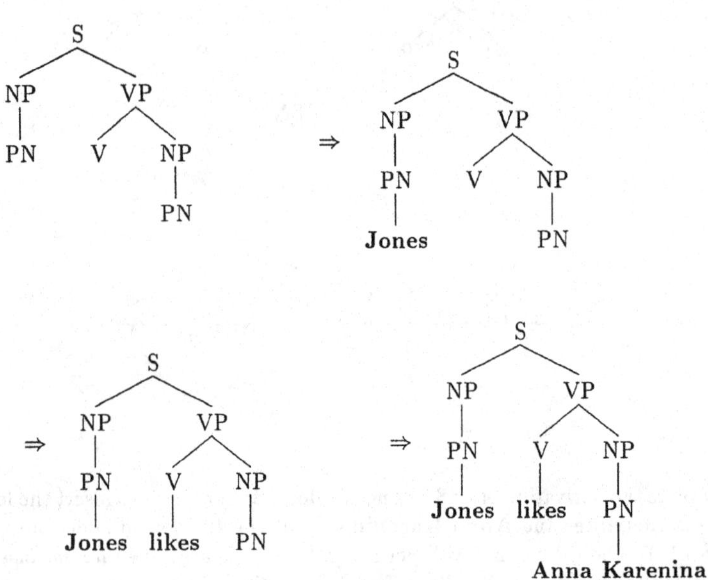

The idea behind systems of rules such as the one consisting of (0.9), (0.10), (0.11), (0.13) and (0.14) is that they *define* classes of sentences (and expressions belonging to other grammatical categories, such as the category of NPs and that of VPs). A sentence, i.e. an expression of category S, is *generated* by the given rules if the rules enable us to derive a tree structure all end nodes of which are English words and which yields the sentence if we string these words together in the left-right order in which they appear in the tree. Of course, the few rules so far given allow us to derive only a handful of sentences. Besides (0.7) we get for instance

(0.16) Jones loves Anna Karenina

(0.17) John likes Mary

and the, somewhat dubious,

(0.18) Anna Karenina likes Jones

(dubious in that one may wonder if a book can be the grammatical subject of the verb **likes**). But that is about it. More substantial fragments of English require more rules, and all of English requires a whole lot more rules. Here we do not aim for a grammar that covers all, or even a substantial percentage, of English; but, still, we want to cover a non-trivial English fragment, and so we will have to adopt quite a few more rules than have been given so far. For instance, we will want to generate not only sentences with proper names but also sentences with pronouns and with indefinite descriptions. Specifically we will adopt one new rule which says that an NP can be developed into a pronoun:

(0.19) NP → PRO

and a rule which says that an NP can be complex, consisting of a so-called *determiner* (the determiners of English include on the one hand the articles '**a**' and '**the**', and on the other particles such as **some**, **every**, **all**, **most** and others) and a *Noun*:

(0.20) NP → DET N

In addition, we need lexical insertion rules for the categories PRO, DET and N. For PRO, the category of personal pronouns, the list of words is finite and includes in particular the third singular pronouns, to which we will confine our attention for the time being. So we may approximate the rule as:

(0.21) PRO → **he, him, she, her, it, they**

The insertion rule for DET will be something like this:

(0.22) DET → **a, every, the, some, all, most**, ...

And the rule for the category N will typically be quite a long one, listing on the right all the common nouns that are to be included in the fragment. Mentioning just some of the nouns we will use later in examples we get something like:

(0.23) N → **book, stockbroker, man, woman, widow, donkey,**
horse, Porsche, bicycle, ...

However, if we enlarge our fragment by simply adding new rules in this fashion we soon run into trouble. For instance, in Chapter 3, we will be looking at the semantics of certain plural sentences, such as, e.g. **Jones and Smith like Anna**

Karenina. To generate such a sentence we need a rule which tells us that there are NPs which result from combining two NPs with the word **and**. The simplest rule to do this is

(0.24) NP $\rightarrow$ NP **and** NP.

We also need a rule to tell us that the verb **to like** occurs not only in the form **likes**, but also in a form without final '**s**', viz. as **like**. But it won't do to add the form **like** without further qualification to the list of words which can be inserted underneath nodes of the category V. In fact, keeping the form **likes** as one of the items on the right-hand side of the lexical insertion rule for V gets us into trouble as soon as we add rule (0.24). For with (0.24) we can derive the ungrammatical string

(0.25) Jones and Smith likes Anna Karenina.

The source of this trouble is obvious. Like most languages English is subject to certain *agreement* rules. For instance, English singular subjects combine with singular verb forms and English plural subjects with plural verb forms, but not vice versa. This is something that a grammar must account for, but for which one cannot account by means of the simple rule systems we have so far considered. In a sense we will cope with the problem of agreement in the most simple-minded way possible: to distinguish, say, between singular and plural sentences we duplicate all the relevant rules, keeping one for the singular case while adding a new one for the plural case. Thus we will have a rule which asserts that an expression of the category S can be a compound of a singular NP and a singular VP.

(0.26) $S_{sing} \rightarrow NP_{sing}\ VP_{sing}$

and another rule which asserts that a sentence can be composed of a plural NP and a plural VP:

(0.27) $S_{plur} \rightarrow NP_{plur}\ VP_{plur}$.

In addition to these we need separate rules to tell us what expressions of each of the categories NP_{sing}, NP_{plur}, VP_{sing}, VP_{plur} can be like. Thus we will have for NP_{sing} the rules

(0.28) $NP_{sing} \rightarrow PN_{sing}$

(0.29) $NP_{sing} \rightarrow PRO_{sing}$

and

(0.30) $NP_{sing} \rightarrow DET_{sing}\ N_{sing}$

with the lexical insertion rules

(0.31) $DET_{sing} \rightarrow$ **a, every, the, some**

(0.32) $PRO_{sing} \rightarrow$ **he, him, she, her, it**

and

(0.33) $N_{sing} \rightarrow$ **book, stockbroker, woman, ...**

On the other hand we will have a set of rules for plural NPs, among which there will be in particular:

(0.34) $NP_{plur} \rightarrow NP_{sing}$ and NP_{sing}

as well as

(0.35) $NP_{plur} \rightarrow PRO_{plur}$

and

(0.36) $NP_{plur} \rightarrow DET_{plur}\ N_{plur}$

In addition we have:

(0.37) $DET_{plur} \rightarrow$ **all, most, the, some, ...**

(0.38) $PRO_{plur} \rightarrow$ **they, them**

and

(0.39) $N_{plur} \rightarrow$ **books, stockbrokers, women, ...**

Similarly we will now have separate rules for VP_{sing} and VP_{plur}:

(0.40) $VP_{sing} \rightarrow V_{sing}\ NP_{sing}$

(0.41) $VP_{sing} \rightarrow V_{sing}\ NP_{plur}$

(0.42) $\mathrm{VP}_{plur} \rightarrow \mathrm{V}_{plur}\ \mathrm{NP}_{sing}$

(0.43) $\mathrm{VP}_{plur} \rightarrow \mathrm{V}_{plur}\ \mathrm{NP}_{plur}$

and for V_{sing} and V_{plur} we have the separate lexical insertion rules:

(0.44) $\mathrm{V}_{sing} \rightarrow$ **likes, loves, abhors, owns, rotates, ...**

(0.45) $\mathrm{V}_{plur} \rightarrow$ **like, love, abhor, own, rotate, ...**

But English does not only have a principle of *number agreement* (i.e. that singular subjects go with singular verbs and plural subjects with plural verbs). It is subject to a considerable number of other agreement constraints as well. To name but two: subject and verb must agree also as to person; and, when the verb is reflexive, the subject must also agree with the object in person and gender. Thus we can say **the man likes himself** and **the woman likes herself** but not **the man likes herself** or **the woman likes himself.** If these and other agreement phenomena are to be dealt with by the kind of rule duplication just proposed for coping with number agreement, the result will be a huge system of rules with an apparently high degree of redundancy. To keep the proliferation of rules within bounds we will make use of a device known in linguistics as *subcategorization through features.* Strictly speaking features do not reduce the number of rules. But they permit us to keep down the number of rules that actually need to be written down in any presentation of the rule system. In other words, they permit us to keep the full abundance of rules off the page on which the grammar is displayed, and thus mercifully conceal it from the eye which confronts that page.

To explain how this works we will continue to focus on number agreement. Like any other feature the number feature has a *feature name.* We will use for this the syllable *Num.* Secondly a feature always has two or more values. In particular, the number feature has two values, which we will refer to as *sing* and *plur.* Thirdly, each feature applies to a certain set of syntactic categories. Thus the feature *Num* applies, among the categories we have already encountered, to: S, NP, PN, DET, N, VP, and V. This means that each rule in which one of these categories occurs on the left-hand side must be interpreted as in fact splitting into a pair of rules – one for each of the two feature values. But we will set things up in such a way that we will in general still have to write down only one rule, viz.:

(0.46) $\mathrm{S}_{Num=\alpha} \rightarrow \mathrm{NP}_{Num=\alpha}\ \mathrm{VP}_{Num=\alpha}$

The interpretation of (0.46) is subject to the following conventions:

(i) α acts as a variable ranging over the values of *Num*, and so (0.46) represents two rules, one in which α takes the value *sing* and one in which it takes the value *plur*.

(ii) the fact that α occurs in several places in (0.46) means that it must take the *same* value in all these places. In other words, (0.46) can be turned into just two explicit rules, viz.

(0.47) $\quad S_{Num=sing} \rightarrow NP_{Num=sing}\ VP_{Num=sing}$

and

(0.48) $\quad S_{Num=plur} \rightarrow NP_{Num=plur}\ VP_{Num=plur}$

In contrast the rule for VP, which we can now state as

(0.49) $\quad VP_{Num=\alpha} \rightarrow V_{Num=\alpha}\ NP_{Num=\beta}$

expands into four rules:

(0.50) $\quad VP_{Num=sing} \rightarrow V_{Num=sing}\ NP_{Num=sing}$

(0.51) $\quad VP_{Num=sing} \rightarrow V_{Num=sing}\ NP_{Num=plur}$

(0.52) $\quad VP_{Num=plur} \rightarrow V_{Num=plur}\ NP_{Num=sing}$

(0.53) $\quad VP_{Num=plur} \rightarrow V_{Num=plur}\ NP_{Num=plur}$

We will refer to rules such as (0.46) and (0.49), which have variables for feature values in one or more places, as *covering rules*, and to their expansions (such as (0.47–0.48) or (0.50–0.53)) as *explicit rules.*

Besides covering rules which have variables in all places where a feature value must be specified in a fully explicit way, we must also acknowledge rules in which one or more feature values are fixed from the start. For instance, an NP of the form 'NP **and** NP' is always plural. So the rule which says that there are such NPs must make this explicit. So it must have the form

(0.54) $\quad NP_{Num=plur} \rightarrow NP_{Num=\alpha}$ **and** $NP_{Num=\beta}$

Here the value of the category at the left is fixed as *plur*. On the other hand the variables α and β on the right imply that the rule is a covering rule. In fact, since α and β are distinct, it covers four explicit rules, for each of the two variables can be turned into either *sing* or *plur*. This reflects the grammatical fact that, for instance, **Jones and Smith**, **Jones and all women**, **all women and Jones** and **all women and all men**, which are conjunctions of two singular NPs, of a singular and a plural NP, of a plural and a singular NP and of two plural NPs, respectively are all grammatically well formed plural NPs.

There are two ways in which covering rules may be used in the derivation of tree structures. First, we can turn the covering rules, whenever we apply them, into explicit rules by fixing the values of the feature variables. This will produce the same type of derivation of the same type of tree structure that was discussed earlier. For instance, paralleling the derivation of (0.8), we now have the derivation:

(0.55)

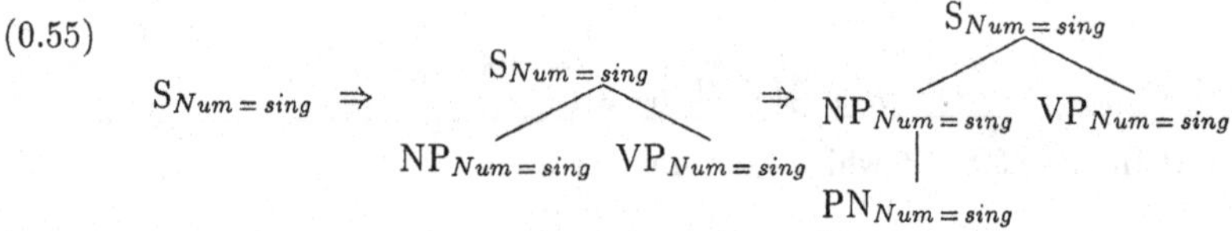

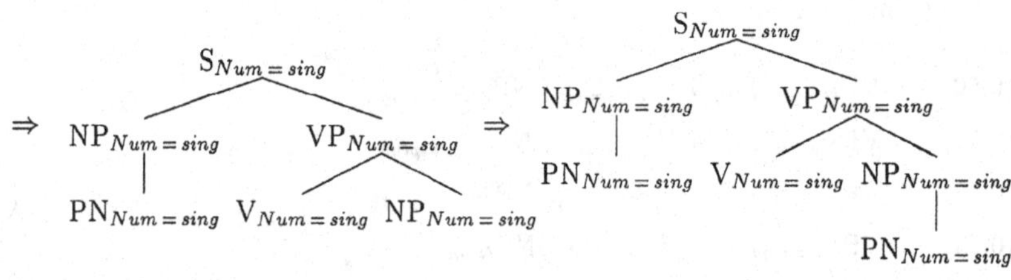

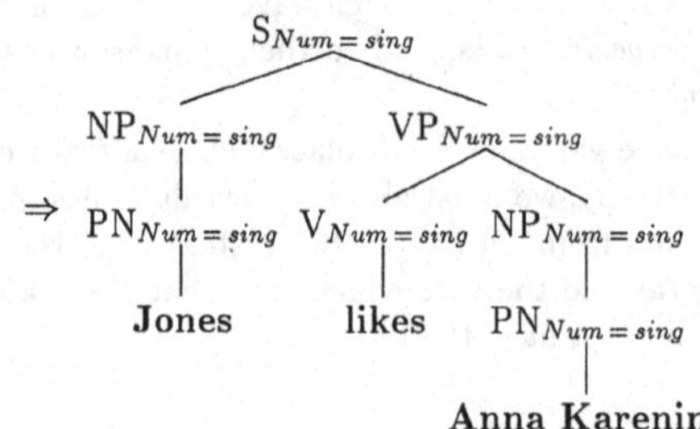

(In the last step we carried out all three lexical insertions at once. Things had been going on long enough already!)

But there is also a way of using covering rules in tree derivations which retains the feature variables. The result here is what we earlier called a tree "skeleton", a structure which must still be subjected to lexical insertion before it becomes the derivation of an actual expression of English. Thus we can perform the following derivation:

(0.56)

$S_{Num=\alpha}$ $\Rightarrow$

$S_{Num=\alpha}$
$NP_{Num=\alpha}\ VP_{Num=\alpha}$

$\Rightarrow$

$S_{Num=\alpha}$
$NP_{Num=\alpha}\ VP_{Num=\alpha}$
$PN_{Num=\alpha}$

$\Rightarrow$

$S_{Num=\alpha}$
$NP_{Num=\alpha}\quad VP_{Num=\alpha}$
$PN_{Num=\alpha}\ V_{Num=\alpha}\ NP_{Num=\beta}$

$\Rightarrow$

$S_{Num=\alpha}$
$NP_{Num=\alpha}\quad VP_{Num=\alpha}$
$PN_{Num=\alpha}\ V_{Num=\alpha}\ NP_{Num=\beta}$
$PN_{Num=\beta}$

Lexical insertion can turn this structure into a complete syntactic structure of an English sentence. But here the use of lexical insertion will include making certain choices for the feature values α and β. Thus for instance, if we insert underneath the first PN-node the singular proper name **Jones** we thereby fix the value of α as *sing.* This means that we can no longer insert underneath the V-node a plural verb form such as **like**. Thus, lexical insertion into skeletons of this sort must be carried out in such a way that the values assigned to the variables are *consistent.*

Pronouns will play an important part in the semantic theory that we will develop starting in the next chapter. So we really do need them. However, for our syntax they are troublemakers for they make it necessary to introduce two features which otherwise we would have managed to do without. The first of these is *Case.* In English case distinctions have almost completely disappeared from morphology. (The personal pronouns are the only items in which case distinctions are overtly marked.)

The distinction between **he** and **she** on the one hand and **him** and **her** on the other is that between *nominative* case, which is borne by subject NPs and *non-nominative* cases, which one finds with direct, indirect and prepositional objects (as in **Jones likes her**, **Jones gave her a book**, or **Jones dotes on her**). Since the pronominal forms **him** and **her** are used whenever the case is other than nominative and since our little grammar will make no other use of case distinctions, we need not consider whether English should be regarded as having one or several non-nominative cases. So we will assume that the feature *Case* has just two values, which we will denote as $+nom$ and $-nom$. The categories to which case applies will be NP and PRO.[4]

The introduction of case affects the phrase structure rules as follows. First, the rule (0.46) now becomes:

$$(0.57) \qquad S_{Num=\alpha} \rightarrow NP_{\left[\begin{array}{l} Num = \alpha \\ Case = +nom \end{array}\right]} VP_{Num=\alpha}$$

and the rule (0.55) becomes:

$$(0.58) \qquad VP_{Num=\alpha} \rightarrow V_{Num=\alpha}\ NP_{\left[\begin{array}{l} Num = \beta \\ Case = -nom \end{array}\right]}$$

Secondly, rules (0.29) and (0.35) become:

$$(0.59) \qquad NP_{\left[\begin{array}{l} Num = \alpha \\ Case = \beta \end{array}\right]} \rightarrow PRO_{\left[\begin{array}{l} Num = \alpha \\ Case = \beta \end{array}\right]}$$

The other rules which have NP on the left-hand side involve no specification of *Case* on the right-hand side of the arrow since the feature applies to none of the categories occurring there. So the new version of (0.30) and (0.36) would be expected to look like this:

$$(0.60) \qquad NP_{\left[\begin{array}{l} Num = \alpha \\ Case = \beta \end{array}\right]} \rightarrow DET_{Num=\alpha}\ N_{Num=\alpha}$$

However, here we will adopt a further convention: when a feature applies only to the category mentioned on the left-hand side of a rule, but not to any of the categories mentioned on its right-hand side, then we simply don't mention the feature on the left-hand side either. This allows us to simplify (0.60) to:

$$(0.61) \qquad NP_{Num=\alpha} \rightarrow DET_{Num=\alpha}\ N_{Num=\alpha}$$

The intended meaning is that the left-hand side can have either of the case values $+nom$ and $-nom$. So when we apply the rule in tree derivations it permits us to insert a pair of nodes labeled $DET_{Num=\alpha}$ and $N_{Num=\alpha}$ underneath a node labeled either as

[4] In a language such as German, where case marking is much more extensive, the case feature would also have to apply to the other categories subordinate to NP, i.e. DET, N, PN and, in a more comprehensive system, also the category of Adjectives.

$$\text{'NP}\begin{bmatrix} Num = \alpha \\ Case = +nom \end{bmatrix}\text{' or as 'NP}\begin{bmatrix} Num = \alpha \\ Case = -nom \end{bmatrix}\text{'}$$

The only lexical insertion rules affected by *Case* are those for PRO. We now have four such rules, viz.

(0.62) $\text{PRO}\begin{bmatrix} Num = sing \\ Case = +nom \end{bmatrix} \rightarrow$ **he, she, it**

(0.63) $\text{PRO}\begin{bmatrix} Num = sing \\ Case = -nom \end{bmatrix} \rightarrow$ **him, her, it**

(0.64) $\text{PRO}\begin{bmatrix} Num = plur \\ Case = +nom \end{bmatrix} \rightarrow$ **they**

(0.65) $\text{PRO}\begin{bmatrix} Num = plur \\ Case = -nom \end{bmatrix} \rightarrow$ **them**

The second feature made necessary by the presence of pronouns is one we already briefly encountered. It is the agreement feature of gender, to which we will henceforth refer as *Gen*. We noted that this feature is needed in connection with reflexives (**himself, herself, itself**). We will discuss reflexive pronouns in Section 3.1. But the personal pronouns we have already included require the feature as well. The need for it becomes apparent in connection with a phenomenon about which we shall have a good deal to say in the following chapters, that of *pronominal anaphora*. An example of pronominal anaphora is the sentence pair:

(0.66) Jones owns Ulysses. It fascinates him.

which will be discussed at length in Section 1.1. The natural way to interpret the pronouns **it** and **him** is to take them as referring back (hence the term "anaphora") to the book "Ulysses" and the man "Jones", which were mentioned in the first sentence.[5] Our intuition that **it** refers to the book and **him** to the man is partly guided by consideration of gender: **him** must refer to a human male and **it** to something non-human. In other words, the anaphoric link between a pronoun and its *antecedent* (i.e. the noun phrase which introduced the individual which the anaphoric pronoun picks up) must respect the constraint of gender agreement. It should be evident from what we have so far said that *Gen* must distinguish between three distinct values, which we will refer to as *male*, *fem* and *−hum*. The categories affected by *Gen* are: NP, N, PN and PRO. The changes which

[5] There is also an interpretation of **it** according to which it refers to the fact of Jones's owning Ulysses, but let us ignore that possibility for now.

the introduction of *Gen* occasions in the rules that involve these categories ought, after all that has been said about rules and features already, to be fully predictable. (0.57) becomes

(0.67) $$S_{Num=\alpha} \rightarrow NP_{\begin{bmatrix} Num = \alpha \\ Gen = \beta \\ Case = +nom \end{bmatrix}} VP_{Num=\alpha}$$

whereas (0.60), (0.28) and (0.59) become

(0.68) $$NP_{\begin{bmatrix} Num = \alpha \\ Gen = \beta \\ Case = \gamma \end{bmatrix}} \rightarrow DET_{Num=\alpha}\ N_{\begin{bmatrix} Num = \alpha \\ Gen = \beta \end{bmatrix}}$$

(0.69) $$NP_{\begin{bmatrix} Num = \alpha \\ Gen = \beta \\ Case = \gamma \end{bmatrix}} \rightarrow PN_{\begin{bmatrix} Num = \alpha \\ Gen = \beta \end{bmatrix}}$$

and

(0.70) $$NP_{\begin{bmatrix} Num = \alpha \\ Gen = \beta \\ Case = \gamma \end{bmatrix}} \rightarrow PRO_{\begin{bmatrix} Num = \alpha \\ Gen = \beta \\ Case = \gamma \end{bmatrix}}$$

The lexical insertion rules for N, PRO and PN are also affected. The rules for N must now distinguish between the different gender values associated with names. Thus the rule for N_{sing} splits up into three rules, which will look something like:

(0.71) $N_{\begin{bmatrix} Num = sing \\ Gen = male \end{bmatrix}}$ → **stockbroker, man, ...**

(0.72) $N_{\begin{bmatrix} Num = sing \\ Gen = fem \end{bmatrix}}$ → **stockbroker, woman, widow, ...**

(0.73) $N_{\begin{bmatrix} Num = sing \\ Gen = -hum \end{bmatrix}}$ → **book, donkey, horse, Porsche, bicycle, ...**

The lexical rules for personal pronouns, which are responsible for all this fuss, become

(0.74) $PRO_{\begin{bmatrix} Num = sing \\ Gen = male \\ Case = +nom \end{bmatrix}}$ → **he**

(0.75) PRO $\begin{bmatrix} Num = sing \\ Gen = male \\ Case = -nom \end{bmatrix}$ → **him**

(0.76) PRO $\begin{bmatrix} Num = sing \\ Gen = fem \\ Case = +nom \end{bmatrix}$ → **she**

(0.77) PRO $\begin{bmatrix} Num = sing \\ Gen = fem \\ Case = -nom \end{bmatrix}$ → **her**

(0.78) PRO $\begin{bmatrix} Num = sing \\ Gen = -hum \\ Case = -nom/+nom \end{bmatrix}$ → **it**

(0.79) PRO $\begin{bmatrix} Num = plur \\ Gen = male/fem/-hum \\ Case = +nom \end{bmatrix}$ → **they**

(0.80) PRO $\begin{bmatrix} Num = plur \\ gen = male/fem/-hum \\ Case = -nom \end{bmatrix}$ → **them**

In the last three rules we have made use of a natural device that is probably self-explanatory: The slash is used to seperate two possible feature values each of which is meant to be included. Again this is just a matter of notational convenience which could be dispensed with through multiplication of rules. Thus (0.78) could be replaced by the pair of rules

(0.78.a) PRO $\begin{bmatrix} Num = sing \\ Gen = -hum \\ Case = +nom \end{bmatrix}$ → **it**

and

(0.78.b) PRO $\begin{bmatrix} Num = sing \\ Gen = -hum \\ Case = -nom \end{bmatrix}$ → **it**

When a feature specification mentions all the values in the range of the given feature as it does in (0.78–0.80), its effect is, in view of our cenvention regarding unmentioned features, equivalent to not mentioning the feature at all. So for instance (0.78) could also have been written as

(0.78)′ $\text{PRO}_{\left[\begin{array}{l} Num = sing \\ Gen = -hum \end{array}\right]} \rightarrow$ **it**

However, we will also have occasion to use the slash notation to specify non-exhaustive disjunctions of feature values.

What about the lexical insertion rule for proper names? Here we enter one of those grey areas between what belongs, by anyone's standards, to linguistics proper, and what lies beyond and is part, rather, of general "world" knowledge. A reasonably educated person may know that **Anna Karenina, Buddenbrooks** and **Madame Bovary** are names of books, and thus that they should occur among the list of names headed by the label $\text{PN}_{Gen=-hum}$. But is this knowledge of language or knowledge of literary history? Or take the name **Mary**. As a rule we would take it to be the name of a human female, and this suggests that it should appear in the lexical insertion rule for $\text{PN}_{Gen=fem}$. But again, is this linguistic knowledge or knowledge of social conventions, relating to what names parents in our culture are likely to give to their daughters and sons? Besides, **Mary** can be used, and sometimes is used, as a name for non-humans, e.g. as a name for a racehorse, a ship or a cow. Where such knowledge belongs is one of the issues that do not concern us here. The policy we have adopted is to allow the names we introduce into our fragment to occur only in lexical rules with feature values that reflect the name's most common use. That the name does not occur with other feature values does not mean that it could not be used to name an individual characterized by those values, but only that our fragment ignores that possibility. The open-ended format in which we state lexical rules supports this interpretation. For now (0.81–0.83) gives us enough to go on:

(0.81) $\text{PN}_{\left[\begin{array}{l} Num = sing \\ Gen = male \end{array}\right]} \rightarrow$ **Jones, Smith, Bill, ...**

(0.82) $\text{PN}_{\left[\begin{array}{l} Num = sing \\ Gen = fem \end{array}\right]} \rightarrow$ **Jones, Smith, Mary, Anna Karenina, Madame Bovary, ...**

(0.83) $\text{PN}_{\left[\begin{array}{l} Num = sing \\ Gen = -hum \end{array}\right]} \rightarrow$ **Anna Karenina, Buddenbrooks, Middlemarch, Ulysses, Madame Bovary, ...**

Another use of features has to do with the distinction between transitive and intransitive verbs. So far we have only considered simple transitive verbs such as **like** and **love**. But besides these there are also *intransitive* verbs, verbs which do not take a direct object.[6] If we add intransitive verbs to our fragment we also need

[6] In English stative intransitive verbs are comparatively hard to come by. Stative verbs are

a new phrase structure rule, which enables us to expand a VP into a simple verb, rather than a verb followed by a direct object. In other words, we need some such rule as

(0.84) $\mathrm{VP}_{Num=\alpha} \rightarrow \mathrm{V}_{Num=\alpha}$

However, this by itself won't do, for now we can form both the ungrammatical **Jones likes** and the ungrammatical **Jones stinks Anna Karenina.** To prevent these ungrammatical strings from being generated we introduce a feature, *Trans*, with two values '+' and '–', which distinguishes between the two types of verbs. With this feature we can rewrite the two relevant phrase structure rules as

(0.85) $\mathrm{VP}_{Num=\alpha} \rightarrow \mathrm{V}_{\begin{bmatrix} Num = \alpha \\ Trans = - \end{bmatrix}}$

and

(0.86) $\mathrm{VP}_{Num=\alpha} \rightarrow \mathrm{V}_{\begin{bmatrix} Num = \alpha \\ Trans = + \end{bmatrix}} \mathrm{NP}_{\begin{bmatrix} Num = \beta \\ Gen = \gamma \\ Case = -nom \end{bmatrix}}$

At the same time the lexical insertion rules for Vs are modified so as to make explicit which verbs are transitive and which are intransitive. So we get for instance for singular verbs the pair of insertion rules:

(0.87) $\mathrm{V}_{\begin{bmatrix} Num = sing \\ Trans = + \end{bmatrix}}$ → **likes, loves, abhors, rotates, ...**

(0.88) $\mathrm{V}_{\begin{bmatrix} Num = sing \\ Trans = - \end{bmatrix}}$ → **stinks, rotates, ...**

It should be noted that the distinction between transitive and intransitive verbs is only the tip of an iceberg. A language like English has besides the simple transitive verbs also so-called *ditransitive* verbs, such as **give**, which can take two objects, as we get in the sentence **Jones gave Mary the book.** Moreover, there are verbs that take *prepositional* objects, as for instance the verb **rely**, which occurs in a

verbs which occur freely in the simple present tense and do not require the progressive; for reasons that it would carry us too far to properly explain at this point we have decided to restrict our attention in Chapters 1 and 2 of this book to present tense stative verbs. One of the comparatively few stative intransitive verbs which can be applied to both persons and books is the verb **stink**. Although this is not our favorite English verb we will occasionally use it in illustrations.

sentence such as **he relied on his wife**, or as **put** in **he put the book in the drawer**. Sometimes as with the verbs **put** or **rely**, such prepositional phrases are obligatory – **he put the book** or **she relies** are not well-formed English sentences. But in other cases, and in fact more commonly, prepositional phrases are optional. Thus we can say: **He located the book on the shelf**, as well as **He located the book**. These, however, are complications with which we will not be concerned in this text, and so we leave the topic without making an attempt to treat it adequately.

Even for the limited purposes of the present book the syntax we have outlined here is very far from complete. But as we go along and add new syntactic constructions to the fragment with which our semantics will deal, we will introduce additional grammatical categories, features, phrase structure rules and lexical insertion rules. However, features can serve a variety of purposes which we have not yet discussed. Two of these, in particular, are important enough for what will be done in later chapters, and also different enough from the features we have so far considered, to merit a separate discussion before we move on.

The first feature relates to negation. Modern English has the peculiarity that verb negation requires, in all cases except when the main verb is the verb **to be**, an auxiliary verb. This will often be an auxiliary that would have been required in any case for reasons of tense or modality (we have **has not liked, will not like, must not like** besides **has liked, will like, must like**). But also in contexts where the unnegated verb occurs without an auxiliary – that is to say, when it occurs in the simple present or the simple past tense – negation will force the introduction of the auxiliary **do**. We have **he likes her**; but **he likes her not** is ungrammatical or at best archaic, the proper form being **he does not like her**.[7]

Since we will for the time being be interested only in the present tense and only in negations formed with the help of the particle **not**, we are in a position to keep things comparatively simple. To distinguish between negated and unnegated verb phrases we introduce two new categories. The first is the category AUX which can be expanded into an auxiliary verb form. (In the present fragment these forms will be only **does** and **do**, but we will include also **has, have, will, can, must, may**, etc. in the fragment of Chapter 5). Secondly we split the original category VP into two. One of these carries the old label 'VP' while the other is called 'VP''. The split is required for the following reason. A verb phrase can either be negated, in which case it will be of the form

(0.89) AUX **not** VP

[7]In fact the auxiliary **do** can also combine with an infinitival verb in the absence of negation, in which case it has the effect of placing special emphasis on the fact that the verb is being used without negation. But this is a construction we will ignore.

or it will be unnegated, in which case it is like the VPs generated by the rule system we have given above. However, we do not want to expand the VP in (0.89) once again into a negated structure – we do not want, that is, strings of the form

(0.90) AUX **not** AUX **not** VP

(which could be lexicalized into such ungrammatical strings as **does not do not like**). We prevent this by allowing only VP′s to expand into negated structures. That is, we replace the old rule (0.67) by

(0.91) $$S_{Num=\alpha} \rightarrow NP_{\begin{bmatrix} Num = \alpha \\ Gen = \beta \\ Case = +nom \end{bmatrix}} VP'_{Num=\alpha}$$

retain the old rules

(0.85) $$VP_{Num=\alpha} \rightarrow V_{\begin{bmatrix} Num = \alpha \\ Trans = - \end{bmatrix}}$$

(0.86) $$VP_{Num=\alpha} \rightarrow V_{\begin{bmatrix} Num = \alpha \\ Trans = + \end{bmatrix}} NP_{\begin{bmatrix} Num = \beta \\ Gen = \gamma \\ Case = -nom \end{bmatrix}}$$

and add the rules

(0.92) $VP'_{Num=\alpha} \rightarrow AUX_{Num=\alpha}$ **not** VP

and

(0.93) $VP'_{Num=\alpha} \rightarrow VP_{Num=\alpha}$

together with the lexical insertion rules:

(0.94) $AUX_{Num=sing} \rightarrow$ **does**

and

(0.95) $AUX_{Num=plur} \rightarrow$ **do**

This is almost right. But there remains one complication. The VP in the string 'AUX **not** VP' must be expanded into an infinitival verb form, whereas an unnegated VP, obtained via the rule (0.93), must be expanded into a finite form. To make these constraints explicit we introduce a further feature, called *Fin*, with two values which we will simply refer to as '+' and '–'. This feature applies to VP′s, VPs and Vs. With the help of the feature *Fin* we can restate the rules involving VP′, VP and V in the desired way:

(0.96) $$S_{Num=\alpha} \rightarrow NP_{\begin{bmatrix} Num = \alpha \\ Gen = \beta \\ Case = +nom \end{bmatrix}} \; VP'_{\begin{bmatrix} Num = \alpha \\ Fin = + \end{bmatrix}}$$

(0.97) $$VP'_{\begin{bmatrix} Num = \alpha \\ Fin = \beta \end{bmatrix}} \rightarrow AUX_{\begin{bmatrix} Num = \alpha \\ Fin = \beta \end{bmatrix}} \; \textbf{not} \; VP_{Fin=-}$$

(0.98) $$VP'_{\begin{bmatrix} Num = \alpha \\ Fin = + \end{bmatrix}} \rightarrow VP_{\begin{bmatrix} Num = \alpha \\ Fin = + \end{bmatrix}}$$

(0.99) $$VP_{\begin{bmatrix} Num = \alpha \\ Fin = \beta \end{bmatrix}} \rightarrow V_{\begin{bmatrix} Num = \alpha \\ Fin = \beta \\ Trans = + \end{bmatrix}} \; NP_{\begin{bmatrix} Num = \gamma \\ Gen = \delta \\ Case = -nom \end{bmatrix}}$$

(0.100) $$VP_{\begin{bmatrix} Num = \alpha \\ Fin = \beta \end{bmatrix}} \rightarrow V_{\begin{bmatrix} Num = \alpha \\ Fin = \beta \\ Trans = - \end{bmatrix}}$$

Infinitival verbs now get their separate insertion rule – one for the transitive and one for the intransitive verbs.

(0.101) $$V_{\begin{bmatrix} Trans = + \\ Fin = - \end{bmatrix}} \rightarrow$$ **like, love, abhor, own, fascinate, rotate, ...**

(0.102) $$V_{\begin{bmatrix} Trans = - \\ Fin = - \end{bmatrix}} \rightarrow$$ **stink, rotate, ...**

On the other hand we must have new versions of the old lexical rules for verbs, in all of which the feature equation $Fin = +$ will now appear on the left-hand side – as for instance in the following revision of rule (0.87):

(0.103) $$V_{\begin{bmatrix} Num = sing \\ Fin = + \\ Trans = + \end{bmatrix}} \rightarrow$$ **likes, loves, abhors, owns, fascinates, rotates, ...**

To list all forms of English verb morphology separately under different categories is clearly inelegant. A more sophisticated grammar will make the regularities explicit that connect different forms. We will avoid a naïve duplication of lexical insertion rules by the following procedure:

English verb morphology is more complex than the morphology of nouns, as it involves, first, the distinction between finite forms, on the one hand, and, on the other, further forms: infinitive, gerund and past participle. Second the finite-forms differ from each other depending on person, number and tense. In toto this gives us morphological verb transformations: 'Inf', 'Ger', 'PPart', together with functions which we will label with the particular values they represent of the relevant features – 'Person', 'Number', 'Tense'. Of these features 'Person' has the values $\{1, 2, 3\}$, 'Number' the values $\{sing, plur\}$ and 'Tense' the values *past* and *present*. This gives $3 \times 2 \times 2 = 12$ different functions; these, however, can be reduced to a mere five, in view of the fact that for all English verbs (i) the simple past tense has the same form for all combinations of 'Person' and 'Number', and (ii) the plural present tense forms are the same for 1st, 2nd and 3rd person. We will label these five functions Past, ⟨Pres, plur⟩, ⟨Pres, sing1^{st}⟩, ⟨Pres, sing2^{nd}⟩ and ⟨Pres, sing3^{rd}⟩. Following again standard dictionary practice we use for the underlying verb form the infinitive, so that Inf becomes the identity function. The explicit definition of the morphological transformations of nouns and verbs belongs to the province of morphology. Morphology is of no direct interest to the topics of this book, and we will dispense with the tedious and detracting enterprise of giving the definitions.

Applying this procedure to the formulation of (0.103) results in (0.103′):

(0.103′) $$V_{\begin{bmatrix} Num = sing \\ Fin = + \\ Trans = + \end{bmatrix}} \rightarrow \langle \text{Pres}, \text{sing}3^{\text{rd}} \rangle(\alpha), \text{ where } \alpha \in V_{Trans=+}$$

The last use of the features which we discuss in this section concerns the formation of relative clauses. A relative clause is a sentence-like construction that typically begins with a relative pronoun (**who(m)**, **which**, **that**) and which is appended to a noun. Examples are the strings beginning with **who** and **which** in the sentences:

(0.104) Jones likes a stockbroker who loves Mary.

and

(0.105) Mary loves a book which Smith abhors.

We adopt the syntactic analysis of sentences with relative clauses according to which the noun with the relative clause appended to it form a simple constituent, which is of the category N. (In other words, expressions such as **book which Smith abhors** and **stockbroker who loves Mary** are treated as "complex nouns".) The main difference between relative clauses and the English sentences we have been considering up to this point is that the former have a *gap*. This is most clearly perceived with a relative clause like

(0.106) **which Smith abhors**

In an ordinary sentence the transitive verb **abhor** would be followed by a direct object NP, but in the relative clause (0.106) the role of direct object is played by the relative pronoun **which**, and the position behind the verb is left unoccupied. With relative clauses in which the relative pronoun plays the role of subject such as it does in

(0.107) **who loves Mary**

this is less obvious, but the received view among linguists is that here too the relative pronoun is followed by a gap in the place which would be occupied by the grammatical subject in an ordinary, non-relativized sentence.

We want to exploit the grammatical similarity of relative clauses and ordinary sentences, and analyse relative clauses in the way we have informally described them, i.e. as sentences, but distinguished from the sentences which our rules already generate precisely in that they have gaps. More exactly, we will analyse relative clauses as resulting from combining a relative pronoun with an expression which is marked as one with a gap.

To do this we need two new syntactic categories, the category of relative clauses, called 'RC', and the category of relative pronouns, called 'RPRO'; and a new feature, which we call *Gap* and which serves to distinguish the "gappy" from the "gap free" instances of the category S. In our grammar *Gap* may be assumed to have just two values, which we will refer to as '–' (meaning there is no gap; this will be the value marking the ordinary sentences which our rules generate already), and as 'NP' (meaning intuitively "the expression has a gap because it is missing an NP"). In the present limited fragment an expression of category S which has a gap has it in either one of two places – that of the grammatical subject or that of the direct object. Thus an expression of this category can be expanded in two different ways, depending on where the gap is to be. Correspondingly, we get two phrase structure rules expanding gapped Ss. (The old S-rule (0.96) now should have the form:

$$(0.108)\quad S\begin{bmatrix} Num = \alpha \\ Gap = - \end{bmatrix} \rightarrow NP\begin{bmatrix} Num = \alpha \\ Gen = \beta \\ Case = +nom \\ Gap = - \end{bmatrix} \; VP'\begin{bmatrix} Num = \alpha \\ Fin = + \\ Gap = - \end{bmatrix}$$

We will return to the old rules presently.)

$$(0.109)\quad S\begin{bmatrix} Num = \alpha \\ Gap = NP \end{bmatrix} \rightarrow NP\begin{bmatrix} Num = \alpha \\ Gen = \beta \\ Case = +nom \\ Gap = NP \end{bmatrix} \; VP'\begin{bmatrix} Num = \alpha \\ Fin = + \\ Gap = - \end{bmatrix}$$

$$(0.110)\quad S\begin{bmatrix} Num = \alpha \\ Gap = NP \end{bmatrix} \rightarrow NP\begin{bmatrix} Num = \alpha \\ Gen = \beta \\ Case = +nom \\ Gap = - \end{bmatrix} \; VP'\begin{bmatrix} Num = \alpha \\ Fin = + \\ Gap = NP \end{bmatrix}$$

Moreover, a VP′ can be expanded into either a negated or an unnegated VP with the same *Gap* value:

$$(0.111)\quad VP'\begin{bmatrix} Num = \alpha \\ Fin = \beta \\ Gap = \gamma \end{bmatrix} \rightarrow AUX\begin{bmatrix} Num = \alpha \\ Fin = \beta \end{bmatrix} \; \textbf{not} \; VP\begin{bmatrix} Fin = - \\ Gap = \gamma \end{bmatrix}$$

$$(0.112)\quad VP'\begin{bmatrix} Num = \alpha \\ Fin = + \\ Gap = \gamma \end{bmatrix} \rightarrow VP\begin{bmatrix} Num = \alpha \\ Fin = + \\ Gap = \gamma \end{bmatrix}$$

VPs with the *Gap* value NP must be expanded into a transitive verb followed by a gap. So we have the rule:

$$(0.113)\quad VP\begin{bmatrix} Num = \alpha \\ Fin = \beta \\ Gap = NP \end{bmatrix} \rightarrow V\begin{bmatrix} Num = \alpha \\ Fin = \beta \\ Trans = + \end{bmatrix} \; NP\begin{bmatrix} Num = \gamma \\ Gen = \delta \\ Case = -nom \\ Gap = NP \end{bmatrix}$$

but *no* rule of the form

$$(*)\quad VP\begin{bmatrix} Num = \alpha \\ Fin = \beta \\ Gap = NP \end{bmatrix} \rightarrow V\begin{bmatrix} Num = \alpha \\ Fin = \beta \\ Trans = - \end{bmatrix}$$

We need a further rule to tell us what to do with NPs that carry the *Gap* value NP. As we have been saying, such NP nodes should be "lexicalized" as gaps. So we need a kind of "lexical insertion" rule to capture this. We give it as

$$(0.114) \qquad \mathrm{NP}\begin{bmatrix} Num = \alpha \\ Gen = \beta \\ Case = \gamma \\ Gap = NP \end{bmatrix} \rightarrow \phi$$

using ϕ to denote the empty string.

Now that we have introduced the feature *Gap*, and have used it in application to a considerable number of categories, viz. S, VP′, VP, and NP, we are under an obligation to restate all our earlier rules involving these categories as rules involving categories that are marked as having the *Gap* value '–'. We will escape this obligation, however, by adopting a new convention, of which feature based rule systems make frequent use. This convention involves selecting one of the values of some given feature as a so-called *default value*, and to understand this value as attached to any node of a category to which the feature applies, and for which no specification of the feature is given. (This convention is especially useful when the default value occurs substantially more often than any of the other values of the feature.) Choosing '–' as default value for the feature *Gap* we can retain all our old rules in precisely the form in which they have already been given. Thus for instance the S-rule

$$(0.96) \qquad \mathrm{S}_{Num=\alpha} \rightarrow \mathrm{NP}\begin{bmatrix} Num = \alpha \\ Gen = \beta \\ Case = +nom \end{bmatrix} \mathrm{VP'}\begin{bmatrix} Num = \alpha \\ Fin = + \end{bmatrix}$$

of which we noted above that it should now be restated as

$$(0.108) \qquad \mathrm{S}\begin{bmatrix} Num = \alpha \\ Gap = - \end{bmatrix} \rightarrow \mathrm{NP}\begin{bmatrix} Num = \alpha \\ Gen = \beta \\ Case = +nom \\ Gap = - \end{bmatrix} \mathrm{VP'}\begin{bmatrix} Num = \alpha \\ Fin = + \\ Gap = - \end{bmatrix}$$

can in fact be retained in its original form (0.96); but the choice of '–' as default value for gap means that (0.96) now has in effect the same meaning as (0.108).

There is one more rule we need. This is the lexical insertion rule for relative pronouns. Limiting ourselves, as we said we would, to the words **who** and **which**, we would be naturally led to state the rule as

(0.115) RPRO → **who, which**

However, a little reflection shows that this cannot be right. For the choice between **who** and **which** is not arbitrary. Which of the two is to be used depends on whether the noun to which the relative clause is appended is or is not human: We say

(0.116) a man who Mary likes

and

(0.117) a book which Mary likes

but not

(0.118) a man which Mary likes

or

(0.119) a book who Mary likes

Here, for the first time, we find ourselves in a position where the feature distinction we need has already been introduced. For the feature *Gen* gives us precisely what we need or almost precisely. Ideally we should have a feature with two values, one that selects for **which** and one that selects for **who**. As it is, *Gen* has three values, *-hum*, which selects for **which** and *male* and *fem* which both select for **who**. However, making once again use of the "slash" notation to indicate that either one of the two indicated values applies, we can restate the lexical insertion rule for RPRO in a way that insures that the selection restrictions on **who** and **which** are observed. It should be noted in this connection that the selection of relative pronouns is insensitive to number and, if we adopt the dialect of many contemporary speakers of English who do not have the non-nominative form **whom** as a lexical item distinct from **who**, also to case. For this dialect the insertion rules for RPRO can be given as follows:

(0.120) $\mathrm{RPRO}_{Gen=male/fem} \rightarrow$ **who**

(0.121) $\mathrm{RPRO}_{Gen=-hum} \rightarrow$ **which**

We still need two further rules. The first of these says that a node of category N can be expanded into a "complex noun" consisting of a noun and a relative clause:

(0.122) $N_{\begin{bmatrix} Num = \alpha \\ Gen = \beta \end{bmatrix}} \rightarrow N_{\begin{bmatrix} Num = \alpha \\ Gen = \beta \end{bmatrix}} \; RC_{\begin{bmatrix} Num = \alpha \\ Gen = \beta \end{bmatrix}}$

The second rule is needed to express that a relative clause consists of a relative pronoun and a gapped sentence. It might be thought that the appropriate form for this rule should be as follows:

(0.123) $RC_{\begin{bmatrix} Num = \alpha \\ Gen = \beta \end{bmatrix}} \rightarrow RPRO_{\begin{bmatrix} Num = \alpha \\ Gen = \beta \end{bmatrix}} \; S_{\begin{bmatrix} Num = \alpha \\ Gap = NP \end{bmatrix}}$

However, there is one last complication here. Some but not all relative clauses are subject to a constraint of number agreement with the nouns to which the clause is appended. More precisely, whenever the relative pronoun of a relative clause plays the role of subject, the VP′ of the relative clause must agree in number with the noun. But when the relative pronoun stands proxy for the direct object, no such agreement is required. Thus

(0.124) Stockbroker who loves Mary

and

(0.125) Stockbrokers who love Mary

are both good, while

(0.126) Stockbroker who love Mary

and

(0.127) Stockbrokers who loves Mary

are both ill-formed. On the other hand, when the relative pronoun acts as direct object, all possible combinations of number values for the governing noun and the embedded VP′ are possible, as witnessed by

(0.128) Stockbroker who Mary loves

(0.129) Stockbrokers who Mary loves

(0.130) Stockbroker who Jones and Smith love

(0.131) Stockbrokers who Jones and Smith love

The simplest and most natural way to make sure that this agreement constraint is satisfied is to insist upon agreement both between the noun and the relative pronoun and between the relative pronoun and the gap. This, however, makes it necessary to distinguish between two different types of gaps, viz. between "singular NP gaps" and "plural NP gaps". Thus *Gap* will now have *three*, rather than *two* values: besides the default value '–' there is one value which we will denote as '$\mathrm{NP}_{Num=sing}$', and one which we denote as '$\mathrm{NP}_{Num=plur}$'. The choice of this particular way of denoting the new values is motivated by how we want to exploit this notation. In some of the rules we will formulate below we will allow a variable to occur in the subscripted equation of the label; in other words, we will use expressions such as '$Gap = \mathrm{NP}_{Num=\alpha}$', in which the expression on the right-hand side denotes either the *Gap* value $\mathrm{NP}_{Num=sing}$ or the *Gap* value $\mathrm{NP}_{Num=plur}$, depending on whether the variable α takes the value *sing* or *plur*.

Using this new set of values of *Gap* and the notational convention just described for designating these values, we can restate the rules involving categories which carry the *Gap* values $\mathrm{NP}_{Num=sing}$ and $\mathrm{NP}_{Num=plur}$ in such a way that the number agreement between noun and embedded verb is satisfied whenever it has to be:

(0.132) $$\mathrm{RC}\begin{bmatrix} Num = \alpha \\ Gen = \beta \end{bmatrix} \rightarrow \mathrm{RPRO}\begin{bmatrix} Num = \alpha \\ Gen = \beta \end{bmatrix} \mathrm{S}\begin{bmatrix} Num = \gamma \\ Gap = \mathrm{NP}_{Num=\alpha} \end{bmatrix}$$

(0.133) $$\mathrm{S}\begin{bmatrix} Num = \alpha \\ Gap = \mathrm{NP}_{Num=\gamma} \end{bmatrix} \rightarrow \mathrm{NP}\begin{bmatrix} Num = \{\alpha, \gamma\} \\ Gen = \beta \\ Case = +nom \\ Gap = \mathrm{NP}_{Num=\gamma} \end{bmatrix} \mathrm{VP}'\begin{bmatrix} Num = \alpha \\ Fin = + \\ Gap = - \end{bmatrix}$$

(0.134) $$\mathrm{S}\begin{bmatrix} Num = \alpha \\ Gap = \mathrm{NP}_{Num=\gamma} \end{bmatrix} \rightarrow \mathrm{NP}\begin{bmatrix} Num = \alpha \\ Gen = \beta \\ Case = +nom \\ Gap = - \end{bmatrix} \mathrm{VP}'\begin{bmatrix} Num = \alpha \\ Fin = + \\ Gap = \mathrm{NP}_{Num=\gamma} \end{bmatrix}$$

(0.111) $$\mathrm{VP}'\begin{bmatrix} Num = \alpha \\ Fin = \beta \\ Gap = \gamma \end{bmatrix} \rightarrow \mathrm{AUX}\begin{bmatrix} Num = \alpha \\ Fin = \beta \end{bmatrix} \textbf{not } \mathrm{VP}\begin{bmatrix} Fin = - \\ Gap = \gamma \end{bmatrix}$$

(0.112) $$\mathrm{VP}'\begin{bmatrix} Num = \alpha \\ Fin = + \\ Gap = \gamma \end{bmatrix} \rightarrow \mathrm{VP}\begin{bmatrix} Num = \alpha \\ Fin = + \\ Gap = \gamma \end{bmatrix}$$

$$(0.135)\ \mathrm{VP}\begin{bmatrix} Num = \alpha \\ Fin = \beta \\ Gap = \mathrm{NP}_{Num=\gamma} \end{bmatrix} \rightarrow \mathrm{V}\begin{bmatrix} Num = \alpha \\ Fin = \beta \\ Trans = + \end{bmatrix} \mathrm{NP}\begin{bmatrix} Num = \gamma \\ Gen = \delta \\ Case = -nom \\ Gap = \mathrm{NP}_{Num=\gamma} \end{bmatrix}$$

$$(0.136)\ \mathrm{NP}\begin{bmatrix} Num = \alpha \\ Gen = \beta \\ Case = \gamma \\ Gap = \mathrm{NP}_{Num=\alpha} \end{bmatrix} \rightarrow \phi$$

The one rule in this list that requires explanation is (0.133). Here we have something which we have not encountered earlier, viz. the pair of variables $\{\alpha,\gamma\}$ which is used to specify the number value of the NP-constituent. The intention of this is that whether the *Num* value of this constituent is going to be *sing* or *plur*, it must be the value of *both* α and γ. In other words, the only correct applications of (0.133) are those in which α and γ are given the *same* value, and thus are in fact identified. We could have achieved this same effect by identifying the variables throughout, and thus stating the rule in the form:

$$(0.133')\ \mathrm{S}\begin{bmatrix} Num = \alpha \\ Gap = \mathrm{NP}_{Num=\alpha} \end{bmatrix} \rightarrow \mathrm{NP}\begin{bmatrix} Num = \alpha \\ Gen = \beta \\ Case = +nom \\ Gap = \mathrm{NP}_{Num=\alpha} \end{bmatrix} \mathrm{VP}'\begin{bmatrix} Num = \alpha \\ Fin = + \\ Gap = - \end{bmatrix}$$

We have chosen to present the rule in the form (0.133) because that form seems to bring out more transparently how placing the *Gap* in subject position of the relative clause *forces* the number of the clause to be the same as that of the noun to which it is appended. It shows, to use some popular contemporary jargon, how the number values of N and the verb of the appended relative clause must *unify*.

We conclude with a complete list of all the rules introduced so far, presented in the feature notation we have reached at this point. We emphasize once more that in the chapters that follow (and these are the ones that really matter!) we will not be interested in *how* precisely sentences are derived, but only in the final forms – the tree structures – which the derivations produce. We will as a rule simply use those syntactic structures as inputs for the interpreting algorithm that we will be discussing, without bothering to verify in any detail that our rules actually generate these structures.

Complete set of rules[8]

Phrase structure rules:

(PS 1) (= 0.96)

$$S_{Num=\alpha} \rightarrow NP_{\begin{bmatrix} Num=\alpha \\ Gen=\beta \\ Case=+nom \end{bmatrix}} VP'_{\begin{bmatrix} Num=\alpha \\ Fin=+ \end{bmatrix}}$$

(PS 2) (= 0.133)

$$S_{\begin{bmatrix} Num=\alpha \\ Gap=NP_{Num=\gamma} \end{bmatrix}} \rightarrow NP_{\begin{bmatrix} Num=\{\alpha,\gamma\} \\ Gen=\beta \\ Case=+nom \\ Gap=NP_{Num=\gamma} \end{bmatrix}} VP'_{\begin{bmatrix} Num=\alpha \\ Fin=+ \\ Gap=- \end{bmatrix}}$$

(PS 3) (= 0.134)

$$S_{\begin{bmatrix} Num=\alpha \\ Gap=NP_{Num=\gamma} \end{bmatrix}} \rightarrow NP_{\begin{bmatrix} Num=\alpha \\ Gen=\beta \\ Case=+nom \\ Gap=- \end{bmatrix}} VP'_{\begin{bmatrix} Num=\alpha \\ Fin=+ \\ Gap=NP_{Num=\gamma} \end{bmatrix}}$$

(PS 4) (= 0.111)

$$VP'_{\begin{bmatrix} Num=\alpha \\ Fin=+ \\ Gap=\gamma \end{bmatrix}} \rightarrow AUX_{\begin{bmatrix} Num=\alpha \\ Fin=+ \end{bmatrix}} \text{ not } VP_{\begin{bmatrix} Num=\delta \\ Fin=- \\ Gap=\gamma \end{bmatrix}}$$

(PS 5) (= 0.112)

$$VP'_{\begin{bmatrix} Num=\alpha \\ Fin=+ \\ Gap=\gamma \end{bmatrix}} \rightarrow VP_{\begin{bmatrix} Num=\alpha \\ Fin=+ \\ Gap=\gamma \end{bmatrix}}$$

(PS 6) (= 0.135)

$$VP_{\begin{bmatrix} Num=\alpha \\ Fin=\beta \\ Gap=\gamma \end{bmatrix}} \rightarrow V_{\begin{bmatrix} Num=\alpha \\ Fin=\beta \\ Trans=+ \end{bmatrix}} NP_{\begin{bmatrix} Num=\gamma \\ Gen=\delta \\ Case=-nom \\ Gap=\gamma \end{bmatrix}}$$

(PS 7) (= 0.100)

$$VP_{\begin{bmatrix} Num=\alpha \\ Fin=\beta \end{bmatrix}} \rightarrow V_{\begin{bmatrix} Num=\alpha \\ Fin=\beta \\ Trans=- \end{bmatrix}}$$

(PS 8) (= 0.136)

$$NP_{\begin{bmatrix} Num=\alpha \\ Gen=\beta \\ Case=\gamma \\ Gap=NP_{Num=\alpha} \end{bmatrix}} \rightarrow \phi$$

[8]We list the rules with new labels (PS 1 – PS 2 – ...). The numbers with which they appeared earlier in this section are given in parentheses.

(PS 9) (= 0.68)

$$NP_{\begin{bmatrix} Num = \alpha \\ Gen = \beta \\ Case = \gamma \end{bmatrix}} \rightarrow DET_{Num=\alpha}\ N_{\begin{bmatrix} Num = \alpha \\ Gen = \beta \end{bmatrix}}$$

(PS 10) (= 0.69)

$$NP_{\begin{bmatrix} Num = \alpha \\ Gen = \beta \end{bmatrix}} \rightarrow PN_{\begin{bmatrix} Num = \alpha \\ Gen = \beta \end{bmatrix}}$$

(PS 11) (= 0.70)

$$NP_{\begin{bmatrix} Num = \alpha \\ Gen = \beta \\ Case = \gamma \end{bmatrix}} \rightarrow PRO_{\begin{bmatrix} Num = \alpha \\ Gen = \beta \\ Case = \gamma \end{bmatrix}}$$

(PS 12) (= 0.54′)

$$NP_{\begin{bmatrix} Num = plur \\ Gen = \beta \\ Case = \gamma \end{bmatrix}} \rightarrow NP_{\begin{bmatrix} Num = \delta \\ Gen = \epsilon \\ Case = \gamma \end{bmatrix}}\ \textbf{and}\ NP_{\begin{bmatrix} Num = \eta \\ Gen = \theta \\ Case = \gamma \end{bmatrix}}$$

(PS 13) (= 0.136)

$$N_{\begin{bmatrix} Num = \alpha \\ Gen = \beta \end{bmatrix}} \rightarrow N_{\begin{bmatrix} Num = \alpha \\ Gen = \beta \end{bmatrix}}\ RC_{\begin{bmatrix} Num = \alpha \\ Gen = \beta \end{bmatrix}}$$

(PS 14) (= 0.132)

$$RC_{\begin{bmatrix} Num = \alpha \\ Gen = \beta \end{bmatrix}} \rightarrow RPRO_{\begin{bmatrix} Num = \alpha \\ Gen = \beta \end{bmatrix}}\ S_{\begin{bmatrix} Num = \gamma \\ Gap = NP_{Num=\alpha} \end{bmatrix}}$$

Lexical insertion rules:

(LI 1) (= 0.31)

$$DET_{Num=sing} \rightarrow \textbf{a, every, the, some}$$

(LI 2) (= 0.74)

$$PRO_{\begin{bmatrix} Num = sing \\ Gen = male \\ Case = +nom \end{bmatrix}} \rightarrow \textbf{he}$$

(LI 3) (= 0.75)

$$PRO_{\begin{bmatrix} Num = sing \\ Gen = male \\ Case = -nom \end{bmatrix}} \rightarrow \textbf{him}$$

(LI 4) (= 0.76)

$$PRO_{\begin{bmatrix} Num = sing \\ Gen = fem \\ Case = +nom \end{bmatrix}} \rightarrow \textbf{she}$$

(LI 5) (= 0.77)

$$\mathrm{PRO}_{\left[\begin{smallmatrix} Num = sing \\ Gen = fem \\ Case = -nom \end{smallmatrix}\right]} \rightarrow \textbf{her}$$

(LI 6) (= 0.78)

$$\mathrm{PRO}_{\left[\begin{smallmatrix} Num = sing \\ Gen = -hum \\ Case = -nom/+nom \end{smallmatrix}\right]} \rightarrow \textbf{it}$$

(LI 7) (= 0.79)

$$\mathrm{PRO}_{\left[\begin{smallmatrix} Num = plur \\ Gen = male/fem/-hum \\ Case = +nom \end{smallmatrix}\right]} \rightarrow \textbf{they}$$

(LI 8) (= 0.80)

$$\mathrm{PRO}_{\left[\begin{smallmatrix} Num = plur \\ Gen = male/fem/-hum \\ Case = -nom \end{smallmatrix}\right]} \rightarrow \textbf{them}$$

(LI 9) (= 0.81)

$$\mathrm{PN}_{\left[\begin{smallmatrix} Num = sing \\ Gen = male \end{smallmatrix}\right]} \rightarrow \textbf{Jones, Smith, Bill, ...}$$

(LI 10) (= 0.82)

$$\mathrm{PN}_{\left[\begin{smallmatrix} Num = sing \\ Gen = fem \end{smallmatrix}\right]} \rightarrow \textbf{Jones, Smith, Mary, Anna Karenina, Madame Bovary, ...}$$

(LI 11) (= 0.83)

$$\mathrm{PN}_{\left[\begin{smallmatrix} Num = sing \\ Gen = -hum \end{smallmatrix}\right]} \rightarrow \textbf{Anna Karenina, Buddenbrooks, Middlemarch, Ulysses, Madame Bovary, ...}$$

(LI 12) (= 0.71)

$$\mathrm{N}_{\left[\begin{smallmatrix} Num = sing \\ Gen = male \end{smallmatrix}\right]} \rightarrow \textbf{stockbroker, man, ...}$$

(LI 13) (= 0.72)

$$\mathrm{N}_{\left[\begin{smallmatrix} Num = sing \\ Gen = fem \end{smallmatrix}\right]} \rightarrow \textbf{stockbroker, woman, widow, ...}$$

(LI 14) (= 0.73)

$$\mathrm{N}_{\left[\begin{smallmatrix} Num = sing \\ Gen = -hum \end{smallmatrix}\right]} \rightarrow \textbf{book, donkey, horse, Porsche, bicycle, ...}$$

(LI 15) (= 0.94)

$$\mathrm{AUX}_{\left[\begin{smallmatrix} Num\, =\, sing \\ Fin\, =\, + \end{smallmatrix}\right]} \rightarrow \textbf{does}$$

(LI 16) (= 0.95)

$$\mathrm{AUX}_{\left[\begin{smallmatrix} Num\, =\, plur \\ Fin\, =\, + \end{smallmatrix}\right]} \rightarrow \textbf{do}$$

(LI 17) (= 0.101)

$$\mathrm{V}_{\left[\begin{smallmatrix} Num\, =\, sing/plur \\ Trans\, =\, + \\ Fin\, =\, - \end{smallmatrix}\right]} \rightarrow \textbf{like, love, abhor, own, fascinate, rotate, ...}$$

(LI 18) (= 0.102)

$$\mathrm{V}_{\left[\begin{smallmatrix} Num\, =\, sing/plur \\ Trans\, =\, - \\ Fin\, =\, - \end{smallmatrix}\right]} \rightarrow \textbf{stink, rotate, ...}$$

(LI 19) (= 0.103′)

$$\mathrm{V}_{\left[\begin{smallmatrix} Num\, =\, sing \\ Trans\, =\, \beta \\ Fin\, =\, + \end{smallmatrix}\right]} \rightarrow \langle \mathrm{Pres}, \mathrm{sing3^{rd}}\rangle(\alpha), \text{ where } \alpha \in \mathrm{V}_{\left[\begin{smallmatrix} Num\, =\, sing/plur \\ Trans\, =\, \beta \\ Fin\, =\, - \end{smallmatrix}\right]}$$

(LI 20)

$$\mathrm{V}_{\left[\begin{smallmatrix} Num\, =\, plur \\ Trans\, =\, \beta \\ Fin\, =\, + \end{smallmatrix}\right]} \rightarrow \langle \mathrm{Pres}, \mathrm{plur}\rangle(\alpha), \text{ where } \alpha \in \mathrm{V}_{\left[\begin{smallmatrix} Num\, =\, sing/plur \\ Trans\, =\, \beta \\ Fin\, =\, - \end{smallmatrix}\right]}$$

(LI 21) (= 0.120)

$$\mathrm{RPRO}_{\left[\begin{smallmatrix} Num\, =\, sing/plur \\ Gen\, =\, male/fem \end{smallmatrix}\right]} \rightarrow \textbf{who}$$

(LI 22) (= 0.121)

$$\mathrm{RPRO}_{\left[\begin{smallmatrix} Num\, =\, sing/plur \\ Gen\, =\, -hum \end{smallmatrix}\right]} \rightarrow \textbf{which}$$

Exercises

1. In the syntax trees that appear later in the book only those feature value specifications will be displayed which will be important in connection with the construction of the semantic representation. Give syntactic analyses of the following sentences in order to make sure that these displays result from syntactic trees that correspond to the grammar of this section simply by erasing the features that are irrelevant for the interpretation process.

(a) Jones owns Ulysses.

(b) It fascinates him.

(c) Jones owns a Porsche.

(d) He does not like it.

(e) Jones does not own a Porsche.

(f) Jones owns a book which Smith adores.

2. Give a sequence of five sentences of increasing length (i.e. number of words) that are all generated by the grammar of this section. Show that our fragment generates sentences of arbitrary length.

3. Add the following rules to our fragment.

$$\text{VP}\begin{bmatrix} Num = \alpha \\ Fin = \beta \end{bmatrix} \rightarrow \text{BE}\begin{bmatrix} Num = \alpha \\ Fin = \beta \end{bmatrix} \quad \text{ADJ}$$

$$\text{VP}\begin{bmatrix} Num = \alpha \\ Fin = \beta \end{bmatrix} \rightarrow \text{BE}\begin{bmatrix} Num = \alpha \\ Fin = \beta \end{bmatrix} \quad \textbf{not} \quad \text{ADJ}$$

ADJ → **happy, unhappy, foolish, fat, dum, ...**

$$\text{BE}\begin{bmatrix} Num = sing \\ Fin = \beta \end{bmatrix} \rightarrow \textbf{is}$$

Give analyses of the following sentences.

(a) Bill admires a woman who is not unhappy.

(b) He is happy.

4. The sentence

'Jones knows a woman who knows a man who is happy.'

is – according to our syntax – ambiguous in constituent-structure.

(a) Show this by giving two syntactic analyses of the sentence that differ in constituent-structure.

(b) Are there other sources of constituent-structure ambiguity in our grammar than the one exemplified under (a)?

(c) Give examples of ambiguities arising from different feature annotations.

5. Write lexical insertion rules for all finite verb forms of English, as well as for infinitives, gerunds and past participles.

Chapter 1

DRT and Predicate Logic

1.1 Simple Sentences

The central task of this book is to show how English sentences give rise to semantic representations. We will refer to the semantic representations we will be constructing as *Discourse Representation Structures*, or, more succinctly, *DRSs*.

In general, DRSs will not be representations of single sentences. Rather, they often represent larger linguistic units, multisentential passages, paragraphs, discourses or texts. Nevertheless the construction of DRSs for such larger units proceeds sentence by sentence. As each next sentence S gets processed, it contributes its information to the DRS that has already been constructed from the preceding sentences, thereby transforming that DRS into a new one which represents the discourse segment which ends with, but includes S.

The incremental nature of interpretation is closely connected with a ubiquitous feature of discourse, its *semantic cohesiveness*. Typically the sentences that make up a coherent piece of discourse are connected by various kinds of cross-reference. As a consequence it is often impossible to analyse the meaning of cohesive discourse as a simple conjunction of the separate meanings of the individual sentences that make it up. The meaning of the whole is more, one might say, than the conjunction of its parts. The connection between cohesiveness and incremental discourse processing is, in rough outline, this: to understand what information is added by the next sentence of a discourse to what he has learned already from the sentences preceding it, the interpreter must *relate* that sentence to the information structure he has already obtained from those preceding sentences. Thus his interpretation of the new sentence must rely on two kinds of structures, the syntactic structure of the sentence itself and the structure representing the context of the earlier sentences.

One linguistic phenomenon which exemplifies discourse cohesion and illustrates the connection between cohesion and incremental interpretation is *pronominal anaphora.* We have already said a few words about this in Chapter 0. But there is a good deal more that will have to be said in this chapter.

Consider the following pair of sentences.

(1.1) Jones owns Ulysses. It fascinates him.

As we naturally interpret this two-sentence passage - indeed, in the absence of further contextual information, there seems to be no other way of interpreting it - the pronouns **it** and **him** of the second sentence refer back to the entities introduced by the NPs **Ulysses** and **Jones** of the first sentence. Thus the sentence pair gets understood as claiming that *one* pair of entities stands in each of *two* relations, one expressed by the verb **owns** of the first sentence and the other by the verb **fascinates** of the second. In order to describe how the interpreter succeeds in connecting the pronouns **it** and **him** with their antecedents, we must first describe how a semantic representation is constructed from the first sentence of (1.1).

In a case like this, where the sentence that must be interpreted is the *initial* sentence of a passage, we assume that there is no information structure into which the new information is to be integrated, but only the syntactic structure of the sentence itself.[1]

(1.2)

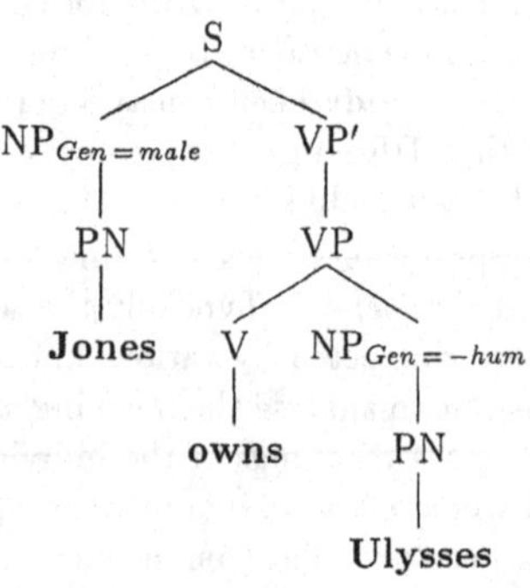

(Note that we have omitted almost all feature value specifications from (1.2). Only those values have been displayed which will be important in connection with the

[1]In reality this is rarely if ever true. Almost always interpretation relies on antecedent information, deriving from general knowledge and from earlier communications between the speaker and the recipient. We will have more to say about this in Volume 2. Until then, however, our theory will always assume that initial sentences are always interpreted against the background of a 'tabula rasa'.

interpretation of (1.1). This is a policy we will follow from now on; only feature values that matter to the interpretation process will be shown in the display of the syntactic structures that serve as inputs to that process.)

The first construction step which (1.2) invites exploits the fact that the represented sentence is analysable as a combination of subject and predicate. This structural aspect of the sentence is made explicit by the top-part of (1.2), consisting of the S-node and its daughters NP and VP′. In fact, the various operations which the step involves are determined by a small part of (1.2), which subsumes these three nodes but includes one more, and which reveals also that the NP is a proper name:

(1.3)

S

$NP_{Gen=male}$ VP′

PN

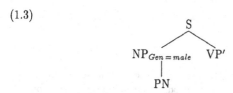

Semantically the combination of subject NP and VP′ signifies that the individual indicated by the NP satisfies the *predicate* expressed by the VP′. We represent this information by introducing a formal representative (a so-called *discourse referent*) for the indicated individual and encode the claim that the individual satisfies the predicate in the form of a *DRS-condition*, a formula in which the predicate is combined with the chosen discourse referent. This formula is obtained by substituting the discourse referent - let us assume it to be the symbol **x** - for the subject NP in the syntactic structure of (1.2); the result of this substitution is

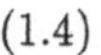

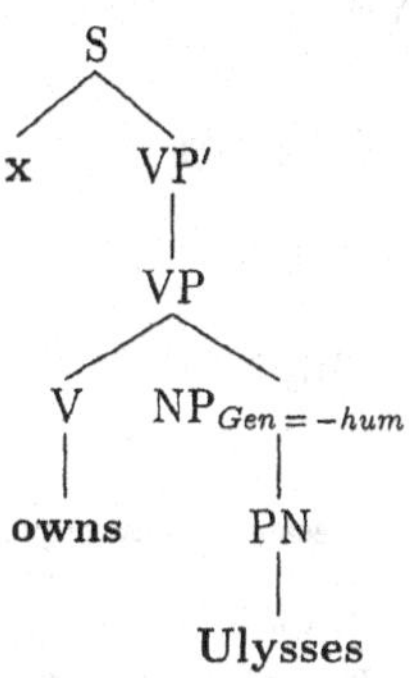

Often, we will give such DRS-conditions in simplified, linearized form. (1.4), for instance, will also be presented as

(1.5) **[x owns Ulysses]**

Here the brackets indicate that expressions such as (1.5) are shorthand for the more elaborate structures exemplified by (1.4).

In addition to (1.4), we also need a DRS-condition which captures the information that the discourse referent **x** represents the individual indicated by the NP **Jones**. We will use for this purpose the expression

(1.6) **Jones(x)**

(1.6) is to be interpreted as saying that **x** stands for the individual denoted by the proper name **Jones** (as that name is being used in the sentence in question).[2] Thus the first construction step transforms (1.2) into the representation given in (1.7), or alternatively, using the shorthand (1.5), in (1.8).

(1.7) 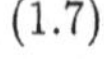

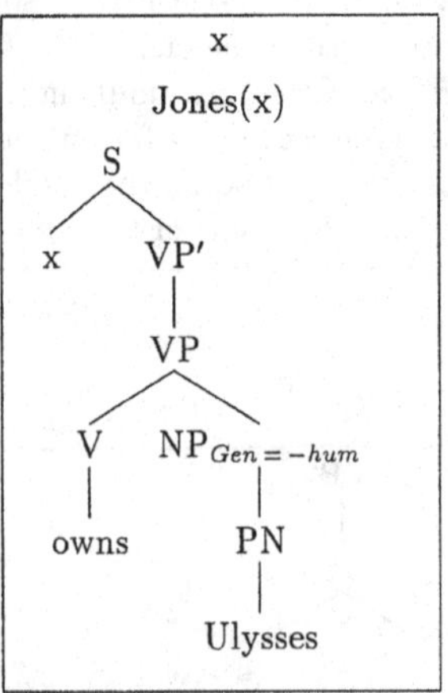

[2]The parenthetical qualification is needed because many proper names, and especially such highly common names as **Jones**, have many bearers. Who is meant by **Jones** depends on the context (including the speaker's intentions), in which the sentence is being used. Besides this ambiguity problem the correct analysis of proper names encounters several others. We cannot go into any of these issues here, but some of them will be taken up in Chapter 3.

(1.8)

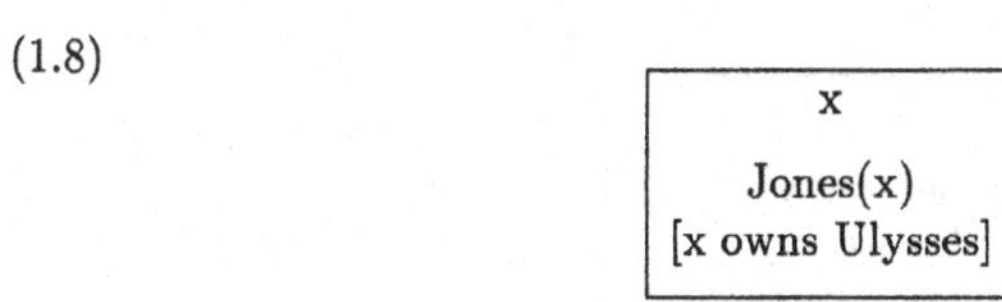

(1.7) is our first example of a DRS. Like all DRSs it consists of two components:

(i) a set of discourse referents, called the *universe* of the DRS, which will always be displayed at the top of the diagram; and

(ii) a set of DRS-conditions, typically displayed below the universe.

In (1.7), evidently, the universe consists of the single discourse referent **x** and the condition set of **Jones(x)** and the tree structure (1.4).

The second of the two conditions of (1.7), (1.4), is still of a complexity that invites further semantic analysis. For note that this condition involves the complex predicate **owns Ulysses**, which is a compound of the verb **owns** and the direct object NP **Ulysses**. Such conditions, which are of a complexity that needs to be further reduced, will be called *reducible* conditions.

Note that we can look at (1.4) in two different ways. We can either see it as a predication of the individual represented by **x**, the claim that that individual has the property of owning Ulysses. This is how we have looked at it so far. But we can also look at it as a predication of the other individual mentioned, the one indicated by the NP **Ulysses**, as the claim that that individual has the property of being owned by the one represented by **x**. This second analysis of (1.4) can be made explicit in the same way in which we represented the first, viz. by introducing a new discourse referent, say **y**, for the NP **Ulysses** and replacing (1.4) in (1.7) by two new conditions, one obtained by substituting **y** for the NP in (1.4) and the other, **Ulysses(y)**, expressing that **y** represents the bearer of **Ulysses**. The part of (1.4) which triggers this set of operations is the tree

(1.9)

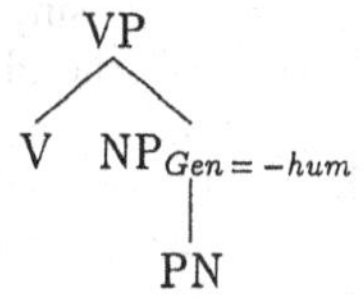

and the result of applying them to (1.7) is the DRS

(1.10)

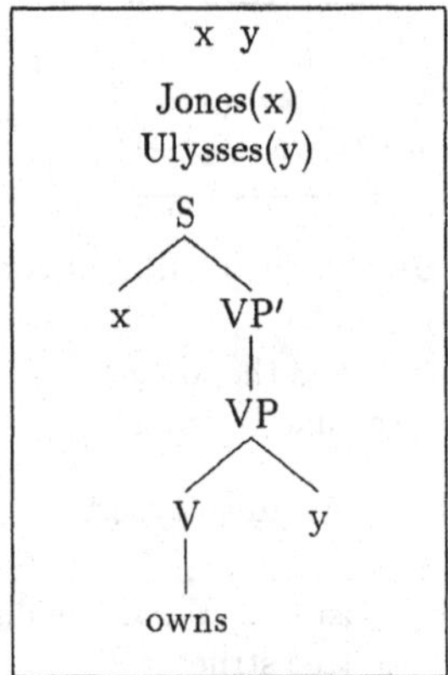

The condition [**x owns y**]cannot be decomposed any further. Such conditions are called *irreducible.* We write (1.10) in abridged form

(1.11)

x y
Jones(x) Ulysses(y) x owns y

The two construction steps triggered by (1.3) and (1.9) are, in the account presented here, the only ones required to obtain a semantic representation of the first sentence of (1.1).[3]

As we have argued, the two steps are meant to capture one and the same semantic relation – that between an individual and the predicate which it is claimed to satisfy. Moreover, in each of the two cases the individual is indicated by a proper name. The representation of this relation involves the introduction of a new discourse referent and two conditions, one expressing the predication and the other the information given by the NP concerning the identity of the individual. We will refer to the rule which involves these three operations as the *Construction Rule for Proper Names*, or CR.PN, for short. In the English fragment we study in this book this rule will be triggered by two syntactic configurations

[3]We will say more about the general processing *rule* which both these steps instantiate at the end of this section.

(1.12)

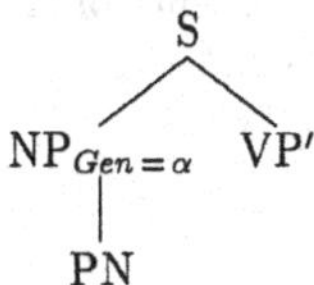

and

(1.13)

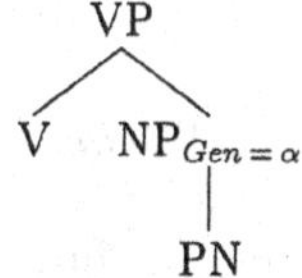

(in which the *Gen*-values *male* and $-hum$ of (1.3) and (1.9) have been replaced by the variable α.) It may be summarized as follows:

CR.PN

1. Introduce a new discourse referent into the universe.
2. Introduce into the condition set a condition formed by placing the discourse referent in parentheses behind the proper name which, in the syntactic structure (of the sentence or DRS-condition) from which the triggering configuration (i.e. (1.12) or (1.13)) is drawn, is inserted below the PN-node of the configuration.
3. Introduce into the condition set a condition obtained by replacing, in the syntactic structure referred to (under 2), the NP-constituent by the new discourse referent.
4. Delete the syntactic structure containing the triggering configuration from the DRS.

The form of the first of the two conditions that this rule asks us to introduce has to do with the type of NP in question, viz. that it is a proper name. Other types of NPs, such as pronouns or indefinite descriptions, call for different conditions, reflecting the kind of information they contribute. However, in two other respects the rules triggered by the configurations with such NPs are like CR.PN. All such rules involve the introduction of a new discourse referent and of a condition obtained through substituting that referent for the NP. We will see this presently for the case of pronouns when we process the second sentence of (1.1).

The syntactic structure of that sentence is:

(1.14)

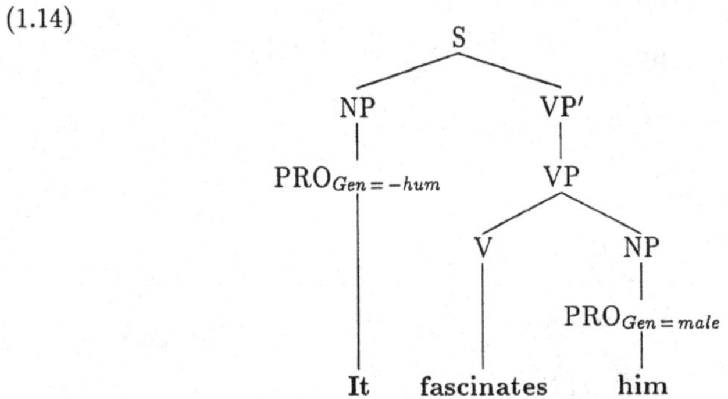

The only difference between (1.14) and the syntactic tree (1.2) is that the NPs of (1.14) are not proper names but pronouns. To see what difference this makes to the process of interpreting (1.14) it will be necessary to go into some preliminary observations about the role which pronouns play in discourse. This will be our first concern in the next section.

1.1.1 Pronouns

Personal pronouns have two distinct (albeit related) functions. They can be used either *deictically* or *anaphorically.* A pronoun is used deictically when its utterance is accompanied by a *deictic act*, i.e. by the pointing of the finger, a nod of the head or some other demonstrating gesture towards that object to which the speaker intends the pronoun to refer. A pronoun is anaphoric when it refers to some item mentioned elsewhere in the discourse in which the pronoun occurs. As we will be concerned only with the interpretation of written language, to which demonstrating gestures are irrelevant, deictic pronouns fall outside the scope of our theory. Thus we will need to confront only the anaphoric uses of pronouns.

The central problem for a theory of pronominal anaphora is often seen as that of defining and explaining the relation which holds between the anaphoric pronoun and its *anaphoric antecedent*, i.e. that noun phrase which introduced the entity or entities into the discourse to which the pronoun is understood to refer. This view regards pronominal anaphora as a grammatical relationship between certain kinds of NPs. The relationship is subject to a variety of syntactic and other constraints that it is the task of linguistic theory to identify.

The perspective adopted here is somewhat different. We will analyse anaphora not as a relation between pronouns and other NPs, but as one between pronouns and discourse referents that are already present in the semantic representation under construction. Thus, for instance, the problem of interpreting the pronouns **it** and **him** of (1.14) we treat as the problem of finding for each of them that discourse referent in the universe of (1.10) which represents the individual to which the pronoun is understood to refer.

In the present case the selection problem is comparatively simple. In the first place the DRS universe from which a discourse referent for each pronoun must be selected contains only two members, **x** and **y**. Secondly, the choice between these referents is determined, for each of the two pronouns, by constraints of gender agreement: if it is assumed that **Jones** is the name of a person and **Ulysses** the name of a book, it follows that **it** must refer to the latter and **him** to the former. In general, however, matters are not that simple. Consider, for instance, the following, often discussed example:

(1.15) Billy hit Johnny with his baseball bat. He burst into tears.

Who is bursting into tears here? There may be a tendency to interpret **he** as referring back to Johnny. For Johnny was the one that got hit. But then Billy might have burst into tears out of frustration, rage or remorse. So, if we knew more about the situation, we would take **he** to refer to Billy after all.

(1.15) illustrates two points. First, it shows that pronouns may be genuinely ambiguous – the recipient may simply not know what he should take the pronoun's antecedent to be. Secondly, (1.15) indicates that often when the interpreter is able to reach a decision as to what the intended antecedent is, he does so on the strength of what he knows about the kind of situation that is being described and not exclusively on the basis of his knowledge of grammar or linguistic meaning. Such extraneous clues, which involve world knowledge rather than knowledge about language, are extremely difficult to analyse in any detail, and would require a much more elaborate theoretical framework than we could develop here. The best we will be able to do, therefore, when formulating the construction rule for anaphoric pronouns, is to state it in a manner which finesses these complications.

Before trying to state the rule let us consider what should be involved in processing the particular pronouns of (1.1). The first construction step prompted by (1.14) is triggered by the configuration:

(1.16)

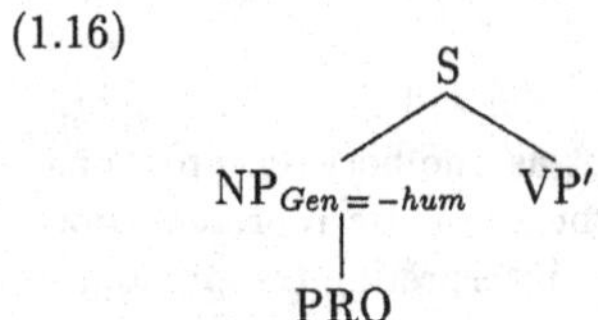

As we already mentioned at the end of the last section, two of the operations which this step requires are also involved in the construction step which led to the DRS (1.10). First, the NP-node requires the introduction of the condition obtained by substituting the referent for the NP-node in (1.14). The only difference between the present step and the two we have already described concerns the remaining condition. This time, when the NP is an anaphoric pronoun, this condition must identify the pronoun's antecedent. We will represent this information in the form of an equation, with the new marker (here **u**) on the left and the marker that is chosen as antecedent on the right of the equality sign '='. Thus we get:

(1.17) **u = y**

Incorporating the three new elements into (1.11) we obtain

(1.18)

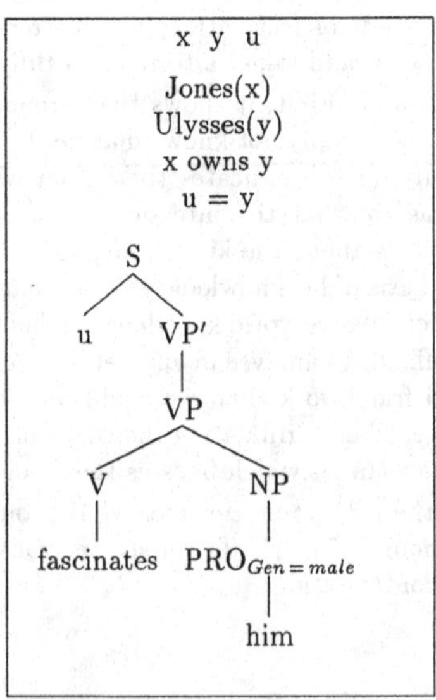

or, in abridged form:

(1.19)

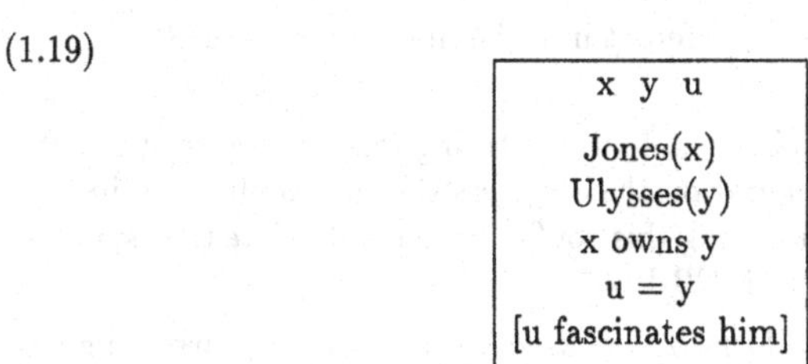

The second step, triggered by the local configuration

(1.20)

```
        S
      /   \
     V    NP_{Gen = -hum}
             |
            PRO
```

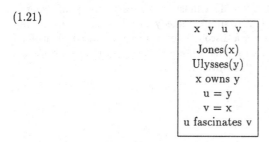

is much like the one just described. The NP-node occasions the introduction of a new discourse referent. Let this be **v**. Furthermore, the last condition of (1.18) is replaced by one in which **v** has been substituted for the remaining NP-constituent, and finally a new condition is added which equates **v** with its 'antecedent' **x**. So the final result is the DRS (1.21), which we present only in the space-saving abridged form:

(1.21)

x y u v
Jones(x)
Ulysses(y)
x owns y
u = y
v = x
u fascinates v

As noted on page 67, we lack the tools to give a statement of the construction rule triggered by (1.16) and (1.20) which takes all relevant factors into account on which the choice of the antecedent might depend. But we can give the promised "minimal" formulation. which acknowledges the existence of such factors implicitly, without actually saying what they are, as follows:

CR.PRO

1. Introduce a new discourse referent into the universe of the DRS (= CR.PN.1).
2. Introduce a condition obtained by substituting this referent for the NP-node of the local configuration that triggers the rule application in the syntactic structure containing this configuration and delete that syntactic structure (= CR.PN.3, CR.PN.4).
3. Add a condition of the form $\alpha = \beta$ where α is a new discourse referent and β is a *suitable* discourse referent chosen from the universe of the DRS.

This formulation of CR.PRO.3 has the unexplained qualification 'suitable'. What makes a particular choice of β *suitable* may depend, as our discussion of (1.15) suggested, on all sorts of considerations, non-linguistic as well as linguistic. Thus, the present statement is capable of an indefinite variety of improvements, which would spell out, in ever greater detail, what "suitability" comes to.[4] By way of example let us see how the statement of CR.PRO could be improved so that it incorporates the constraints of gender agreement, which suffice, we noted, to render the reference of the pronouns **it** and **him** in (1.1) determinate. It is fairly easy to incorporate this criterion into the rule for pronominal anaphora, since the information needed to apply it is contained in the syntactic structures that are generated by the grammar we adopted in Section 0.4.

There is nevertheless a slight complication which arises from the circumstance that, as we have described the DRS-construction procedure so far, no gender information is explicitly associated with the discourse referents which are already in the DRS, and from which the antecedent must be chosen at the point where the pronoun gets to be interpreted. A simple remedy to this problem would be to encode such information whenever a discourse referent is introduced. Thus for instance we might, when processing the first sentence of (1.1), introduce, together with the discourse referents x and y, conditions

(1.22) $\quad Gen(\mathbf{x}) = male$

and

(1.23) $\quad Gen(\mathbf{y}) = -hum$

[4]Most of the research on anaphora within computational linguistics and Artificial Intelligence has been concerned with such refinements of the rule. See [Bullwinkle 1977], [Grosz 1977], [Grosz et.al. 1983], [Sidner 1979], [Webber 1978].

expressing that **x** comes from an NP carrying the value *male* and **y** from an NP carrying the value *-hum*. Similarly, the pronouns **it** and **him** could give rise to conditions

(1.24) $Gen(\mathbf{u}) = -hum$

and

(1.25) $Gen(\mathbf{v}) = male$

and the anaphoric pronoun rule CR.PRO can now be expanded to include the stipulation that in the condition '$\alpha = \beta$' α and β must have the same gender values. Formally this would entail that both CR.PRO and the rule CR.PN which was applied in the construction of (1.10) should be extended with an additional clause stipulating the introduction of a condition such as (1.22–1.25). The additions to CR.PN and CR.PRO would be identical.

CR.PN.5 (= CR.PRO.4)

Add a condition of the form $Gen(\alpha) = \beta$ where α is the new discourse referent and β is the gender value of the NP-node in the local configuration which triggers the rule application.

The third clause of the pronoun rule should then be modified to read:

CR.PRO.3

Add a condition of the form $\alpha = \beta$, where α is the new discourse referent and β is a discourse referent already in the DRS, such that:

1. $Gen(\alpha) = Gen(\beta)$

and

1. β must be a *suitable* antecedent also in other respects.

There is an alternative strategy for dealing with the gender agreement constraint which does not involve introducing with each discourse referent a condition that encodes the gender information associated with it, but instead *recovers* that information at the point where an anaphoric pronoun needs to be interpreted from DRSs such as (1.10), in which that information is not explicitely encoded. Typically the information can be recovered. For instance, in (1.10), the information we need is contained in the conditions **Jones(x)** and **Ulysses(y)**.

But how is the information to be recovered from these names? Evidently this is possible only if the interpreter has access to the lexical insertion rules for proper names from which the gender values for the NP-nodes in (1.2) were got in the first place. As long as these rules can be consulted for "looking up" the *Gen*-values of the names in question the recovery problem will be solved in principle.

From an intuitive point of view it is of course natural enough to assume that the lexical insertion rules remain available for consultation throughout the interpretation process. For after all such information is part of the interpreter's knowledge of language (including certain social conditions about the use of proper names), and thus will be at his disposal at any point in which he might use his linguistic knowledge. Given this assumption, it is reasonably straightforward to formulate a precise procedure for recovering the relevant *Gen*-values. We will not spell this out here. But we have mentioned this second strategy nevertheless because it is representative of a class of methods for "unpacking" information contained in a DRS by relating that DRS to other kinds of information (such as the lexical rules from which the needed *Gen*-values must be called).

Methods for "unpacking" information could equally well be described as *methods of inference*, for the "unpacking" of implicit information is really just drawing conclusions from premises one already has. As we said in the introduction, inference is the topic of Volume 2; and we will not pursue this topic here. They are equally important as tools for obtaining that information from the linguistic input in the first place. We think that it is important to stress this point, as it implies that there is, besides the connection between semantics and logic to which we drew attention in the introduction, also another link. To give a theory of linguistic meaning, we claimed, it is necessary to articulate the procedures by which information is extracted from incoming strings of phonemes or words. As inference is an indispensible ingredient of these procedures, this indicates that our grasp of meaning is dependent on our understanding of inference, just as our grasp of valid inference is (according to what was argued in the introduction) dependent upon a grasp of meaning.

To sum up, we have described two different methods for incorporating the *Gender Agreement Constraint* into the processing rule for anaphoric pronouns. The first involves transfer, with the introduction of each discourse referent, of additional information from the syntactic input to the resulting DRS. The second involves a process of inference from the DRS, together with other information that is also at the interpreter's disposal. Although neither of these two methods will be incorporated into the theory presented in this volume, we have taken time out to discuss them; for they are paradigmatic of the devices of which a more comprehensive account of natural language interpretation must avail itself.

As new aspects of the processes and results of interpretation are brought into the theory, more of the information that is carried by syntactic structures is likely to become relevant. Such information must be either explicitly encoded in the structures which the interpretation process produces; or else, the theory must rely on inferential mechanisms which succeed in recovering the information from those results in some other, typically indirect way.

1.1.2 Truth Conditions (informally)

DRSs have well-defined truth conditions. We will give a precise statement of these in Section 1.4. However, for a proper appreciation of the DRSs that have been constructed in this and the preceding sections a preliminary informal statement of the truth definition for DRSs should be helpful.

The central idea on which the definition is based is simple and intuitive:

(1.26) A DRS is true provided we can find individuals for each of the discourse referents in its universe in such a way that the conditions which the DRS contains for particular discourse referents are satisfied by the corresponding individuals.

Thus the DRS (1.11) is true if we can find real individuals a and b such that a satisfies the condition **Jones(x)**, b satisfies **Ulysses(y)** and a and b together satisfy the condition **x owns y**. In other words, a must be the bearer of the name **Jones**, b the book entitled **Ulysses** and a must own b. Similarly, for (1.21) to be true there must be, corresponding to **x**, **y**, **u** and **v**, individuals a, b, c and d that satisfy all of (1.21)'s DRS-conditions. In particular, c and b must satisfy the condition **u = y**, which means that they must be identical; for the same reason d must be identical with a. So we can restate the truth conditions of (1.21) as:

(1.27) There are individuals a and b such that
- (i) a is the bearer of the name **Jones**,
- (ii) b is the book entitled **Ulysses**,
- (iii) a owns b
- (iv) b fascinates a.

The truth conditions of (1.21) reveal an aspect of natural language discourse which we stressed in the introduction. Meaningful discourse is invariably *cohesive*, and its cohesion often shows itself in the impossibility of analysing it as a simple propositional conjunction where each conjunct is the proposition expressed by one of the sentences of which the discourse consists. Our first sample discourse (1.1) shows nothing quite so dramatic. Its cohesion is manifest in the identification of the individuals mentioned in the second sentence with those that the first sentence talks about. The DRS (1.21) makes this identification explicit by means of its equational conditions **u** = **y** and **v** = **x**. The effect of these conditions on the truth conditions of (1.21) is that the predication made by the first sentence of (1.1) and that made by the second sentence must be understood as pertaining to *the same* individuals a and b.

As a result, (1.21) assigns to (1.1) truth conditions to the effect that (i) the individual named Jones stands in the relation of ownership to the object known as Ulysses and (ii) that the object known as Ulysses stands to the individual Jones in the relationship expressed by the verb **fascinate**. These truth conditions bear witness to the cohesiveness of (1.1) in that (i) and (ii) are about the same individuals Jones and Ulysses. Nevertheless, they do amount to a conjunction of two independent propositions, each corresponding to one of the sentences of (1.1). But in general such a propositional "factorization" of the content of a multi-sentence discourse is not possible. It is important in this connection to stress the *existential* character of the truth conditions defined in (1.26): A DRS is true if (and only if) *there are* individuals in its universe corresponding to the discourse referents which satisfy the conditions. This existential aspect of the definition will become visible in a more dramatic way in the next section, where we look at discourses that contain indefinite desriptions.

1.1.3 Indefinite Descriptions

It is instructive to compare (1.1) with a discourse like

(1.28) Jones owns a Porsche. It fascinates him.

The main difference between (1.28) and (1.1) is that the direct object of the first sentence of (1.28) is not a proper name, but an indefinite description.

The first construction step to be performed on the syntactic tree of (1.28) is the same as the first step triggered by (1.2) and yields the DRS (1.29). The next step, however, is different, as it must deal with an indefinite description, and not a proper name. We will refer to the rule that is applied in this step as CR.ID. In the present instance it is triggered by the configuration (1.30).

(1.29)

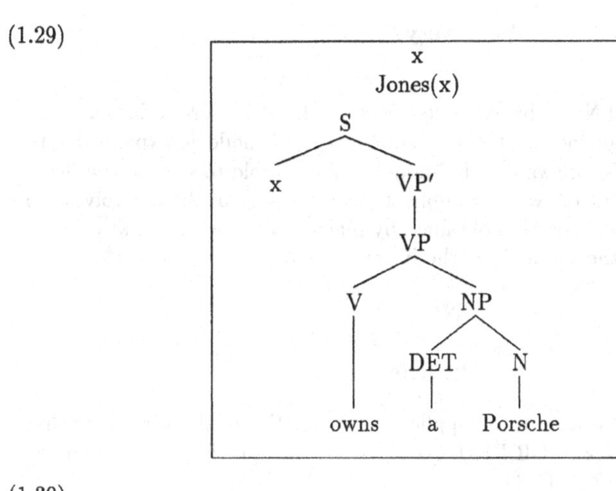

(1.30)

```
        VP
       /  \
      V    NP
          /  \
        DET   N
         |
        a(n)
```

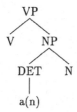

Like the pronoun rule CR.ID differs from the rule for proper names only in regard of the condition which reflects the contribution of the NP. The condition we need here must capture the contribution made by the indefinite description **a Porsche**. Intuitively it is fairly clear what this contribution is. The information which the phrase **a Porsche** contains is that the individual must be of the kind indicated by the noun, in other words that it must satisfy the predicate **Porsche**. We represent this information by means of a DRS-condition in which the noun **Porsche** is followed by the new discourse referent in parentheses. Thus, if the new referent is **y**, we get[5]

[5]A condition such as (1.31), in which a discourse referent occurs in combination with a common noun, should not be confused with conditions like **Jones(x)** or **Ulysses(y)**, which contain proper names. Whereas **Jones(x)** signifies that **x** stands for the (intended) bearer of the name **Jones**, (1.31) signifies that the individual represented by **y** *has the property* of being a Porsche. Thus, whereas the former condition determines the represented individual *uniquely*, conditions like (1.31) do as a rule not do this.

(1.31) **Porsche(y)**

Because a node labelled N can be expanded either by lexical insertion into a single noun (this is what happens in (1.29) where the only N-node is expanded into **Porsche**) or into an N-node and an RC-node, it is desirable to see the condition **Porsche(y)** as the result of two rule applications. The first of these involves the rule CR.ID, and yields a condition obtained by placing the new discourse referent in parentheses behind the top node of the N-constituent.

(1.32)

N(y)
|
Porsche

The other operations involved in the application of CR.ID are the very same that are required by CR.PN and CR.PRO. So the result of applying the rule to the second condition of (1.29) is (1.33).

(1.33)

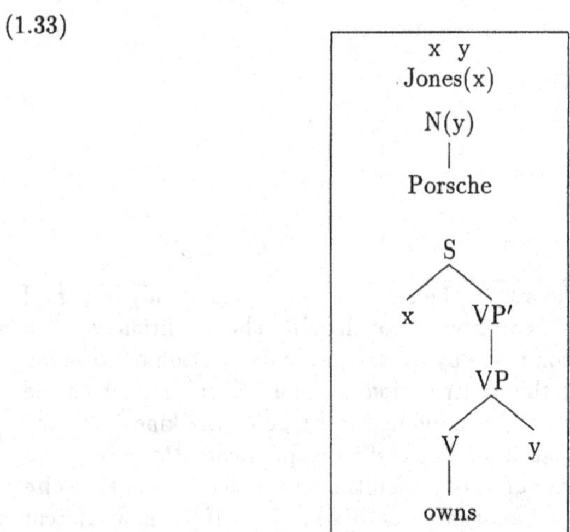

The second rule, which we will refer to as CR.LIN (for 'lexical insertion into N'), transfers the discourse referent from the N-node to the realizing noun, and thus gives us condition (1.31): **Porsche(y)**. CR.LIN is triggered by a configuration that includes the entire DRS-condition to which the rule is being applied. In particular, in the case under consideration, (1.32) is the triggering configuration as well as the condition to which the rule applies, and that gets replaced by (1.31) in the course of this application. Applying CR.LIN to (1.33) we obtain the desired DRS, which in abridged notation looks like this (1.34). To incorporate the second sentence of (1.28) into (1.34) one proceeds in the same way in which we dealt with the second sentence of (1.1). The result is – again in abridged notation – (1.35).

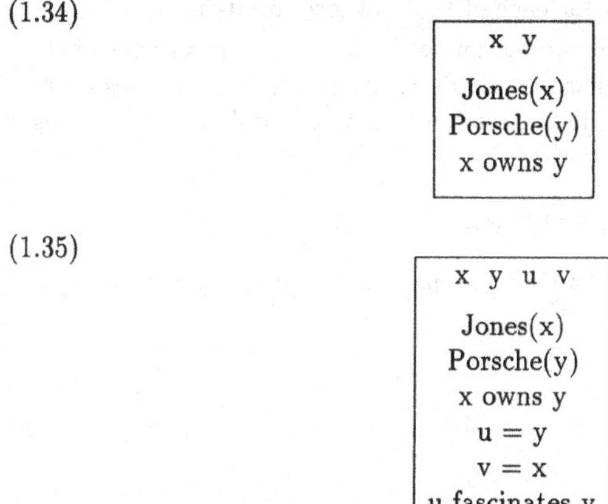

Let us consider the truth conditions of (1.34) and (1.35), as specified by (1.26). According to (1.26), (1.34) is true iff there are individuals a and b such that a is the bearer of the name **Jones**, b is an individual satisfying the predicate **Porsche** and a owns b. In other words, (1.34) is true iff there is a Porsche such that Jones owns it; which is just what the first sentence of (1.28) says. Similarly, (1.35) is true iff there are individuals a, b, c, d such that a is the bearer of the name **Jones**, b is a Porsche, c is identical with a, d is identical with b, a owns b and d (that is, b) fascinates c (that is, a); or, more succinctly,

(1.36) there are individuals a and b such that a is Jones, b is a Porsche, a owns b, and b fascinates a.

The truth conditions of (1.34) and (1.35) demonstrate how the existential character of (1.26) turns into an existential interpretation of the indefinite description **a Porsche**. According to our informal gloss of (1.34) this DRS is true iff

there is a Porsche such that the bearer of the name Jones owns it.[6]

[6]Many sentences with indefinite descriptions permit such paraphrases. But not all: in Chapter 2 we will encounter sentences for which this is not so.

The existential element in the truth condition (1.36) for (1.35) highlights the cohesiveness of the represented discourse (1.28). For as (1.36) has it, *there is* some Porsche to which both the predication of the first sentence and the predication of the second sentence of (1.28) apply – these predications must apply to *one and the same* Porsche. Such an interpretation can only be captured by a single representation that captures the joint content of the two sentences together, not by a pair of unconnected representations, one for each of the sentences on its own.

Our syntax allows not only for indefinites consisting of the article a and a single noun, but also for more complex indefinites in which the constituent of category N contains a relative clause. We conclude this section with an example which contains such a complex indefinite. Consider

(1.37) Jones owns a book which Smith adores.

According to the syntax of Section 0.4 this sentence has the structure:

(1.38)

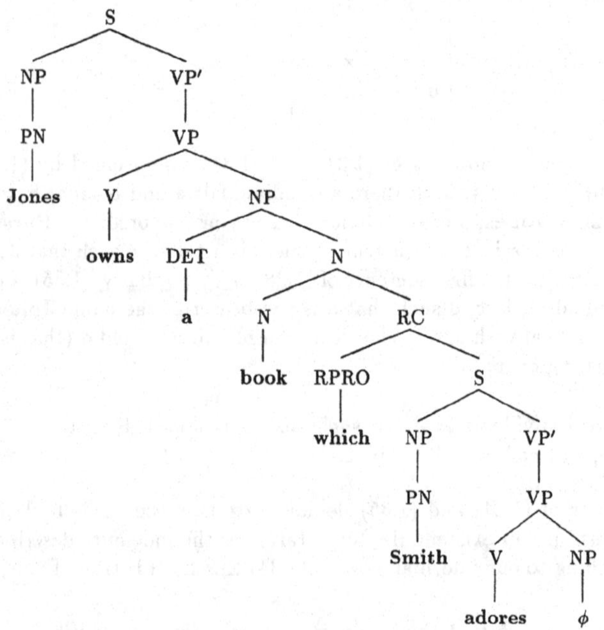

The first step in the construction of a DRS for (1.38) gives

(1.39)

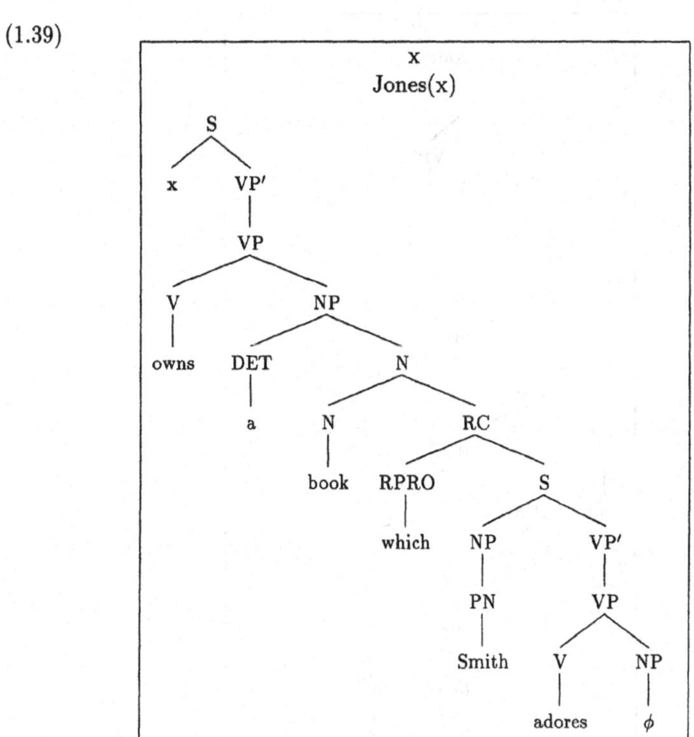

The next step is an application of CR.ID, which yields the DRS

(1.40)

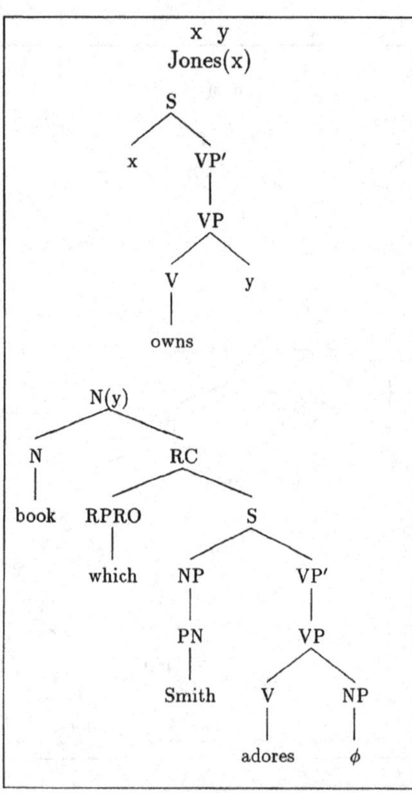

The last condition of (1.40) calls for further reduction. Intuitively it is clear how the predication this condition expresses may be broken down into its constituent predications. Satisfying the complex noun **book which Smith adores** is equivalent to satisfying the head noun **book** and satisfying the predicate expressed by the relative clause. For the first of these predications we already have a form of DRS-condition, viz.

(1.41) **book(y)**

Again, this condition will be reached in two steps via an intermediate condition of the form

(1.42)

which an application of CR.LIN will then transform into (1.41) itself. What about the second predicate? A little reflection should suffice to see that the predication which a relative clause imposes on the individual indicated by the NP of which the clause is part is the same as would be expressed by a sentence got by putting an NP indicating the individual in the gap corresponding to the relative pronoun. For instance, the relative clause **which Smith adores** predicates of the individual, call it b, indicated by the NP **a book which Smith adores** what would also be predicated of b by the sentence **Smith adores** b. A natural way to represent this predication is to insert the new discourse referent for the empty NP-node of the S-constituent. Thus we get, in the present instance, the condition

(1.43)

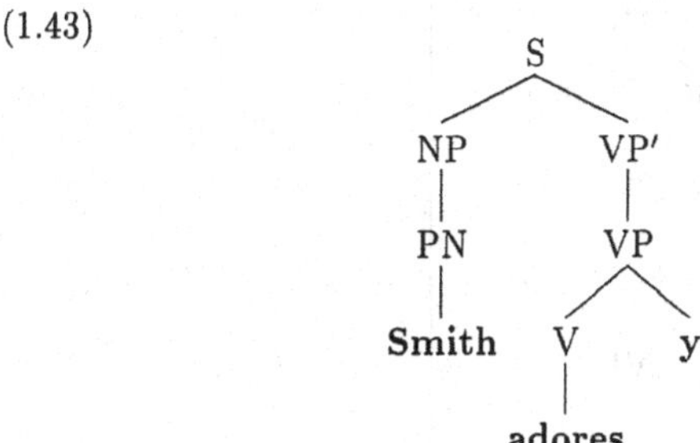

The new rule then, which we will call CR.NRC and which is triggered by the configuration

(1.44)

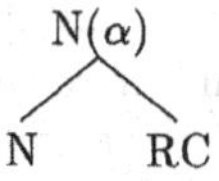

N(α)

N RC

involves the following operations:

CR.NRC

1. Introduce a condition obtained by taking the subtree whose top node is the daughter N-node of the triggering configuration and place α in parentheses behind the top node of this subtree.

2. Introduce a condition obtained by taking the S-part of that constituent of the DRS-condition whose top node is the RC-node of (1.44) and replace the empty NP-node in that S-part by α.

Application of this rule to (1.40) produces

(1.45)

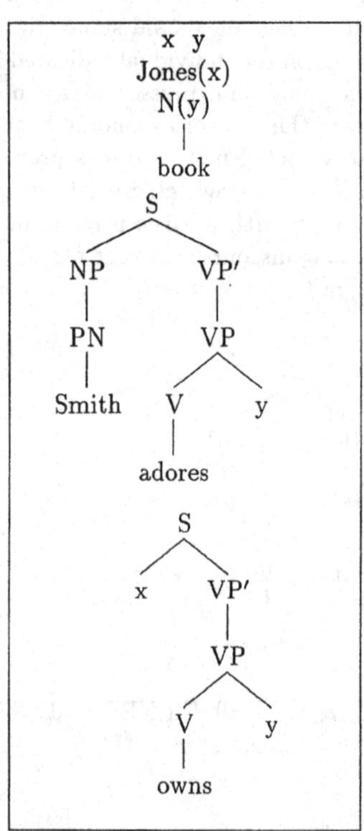

(1.45) contains two conditions which invite further reduction. The first is (1.42) which, as we already noted, is turned into (1.41) by an application of CR.LIN. The second is the S-structure which occurs as the penultimate DRS-condition of (1.45). The top configuration of that structure,

S
NP VP′
PN

asks for an application of CR.PN. Applying both rules at once we get (1.46) or, in abridged notation, (1.47).

(1.46)

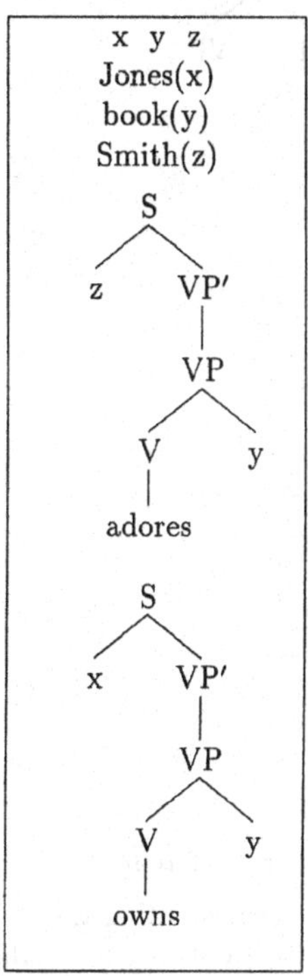

(1.47)

x y z
Jones(x)
book(y)
Smith(z)
z adores y
x owns y

We conclude this section with a brief summary of what our exploration of indefinite noun phrases has taught us.

We have been led to adopt three new construction rules. The first of these, CR.ID, is triggered by either of the configurations (1.48) and (1.49).

(1.48)

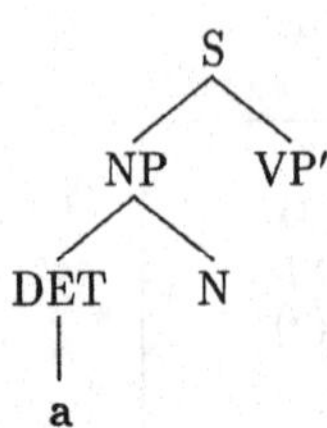

(1.49)

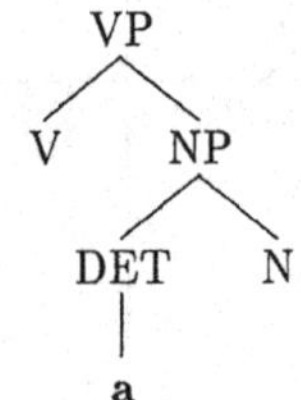

It involves the operations:

CR.ID

1. Introduce a new discourse referent.
2. Introduce the result of substituting this discourse referent for the NP-constituent in the syntactic structure to which the rule is being applied.
3. Introduce a condition obtained by placing the discourse referent in parentheses behind the top node of the N-constituent.

Secondly, we found the need for a rule CR.LIN triggered by the configuration:

(1.50) $N(\alpha)$
|
β

which converts the condition to which it applies (and which is always identical with (1.50)) into $\beta(\alpha)$.

Thirdly, a rule is needed to deal with the configuration (1.44) which replaces the condition to which it is applied by two conditions. The first of these is obtained by taking the constituent whose top node is the N-daughter of (1.44) and placing α in parentheses behind that node. The second is obtained by taking the S-constituent α for the empty NP-node.

1.1.4 The Construction Algorithm

So far we have only given a fairly informal sketch of the construction algorithm which converts English sentences and texts into DRSs. In this section we want to show how the algorithm can be rigorously defined, although even now we do not intend to spell out the formal definition in full detail.

The DRS-construction algorithm involves two *recursions*. The first recursion operates at the level of the complete sentence that the discourse consists of: when the algorithm is applied to a sequence of sentences S_1, ..., S_n it deals with these sentences in order of appearence. It first incorporates S_1 into the starting DRS K_0, then it incorporates S_2 into the DRS K_1 resulting from the first incorporation, etc. The first step of the process by which S_i gets incorporated into K_{i-1} consists in adding the syntactic analysis $[S_i]$ of S_i to the set of conditions of K_{i-1}: As we have explained at length, K_{i-1} acts as a *context of interpretation* for S_i.

The construction algorithm describes how the interpretation of S_i makes use of this context and how, as a result, the context gets transformed into a new context K_i. What it does not specify is the context for the very first sentence. This omission has been intentional. The initial context K_0 for a given discourse should be a DRS incorporating that (relevant) information which is available to the recipient of that discourse at the point when he starts processing it. However, what contextual information is available to the recipient at that point will depend on the circumstances under which the discourse is being received, among them on what the recipient happens to know already about its subject matter; so a general definition of the initial context of a discourse should say very little, lest it misrepresents what happens in actual communication for all but a tiny fraction of all cases. Nothing of importance is lost, however, if we make the simplifying assumption that the initial context contains no information at all. (This is the assumption we made tacitly in all the examples of DRS-constructions we have given so far.) Formally the assumption comes to this: The initial DRS, K_0, is always taken to be what we call the *empty* DRS, the DRS which consists of an empty set of discourse referents and an empty set of conditions.

DRS-Construction Algorithm
Input: a discourse D = S_1, ..., S_i, S_{i+1}, ..., S_n the empty DRS K_0 **Keep repeating for** i = 1, ..., n: (i) add the syntactic analysis [S_i] of (the next) sentence S_i to the conditions of K_{i-1}; call this DRS K_i*. Go to (ii). (ii) Input: a set of reducible conditions of K_i* Keep on applying construction principles to each reducible condition of K_i* until a DRS K_i is obtained that only contains irreducible conditions. Go to (i).

We have nothing more to say here about the global aspect of DRS-construction described under (i), and so we will now focus on the second aspect described under (ii). This second recursion enters into the construction at the level of the processing of individual sentences, of *sentence-incorporation*, as we will call it. To make the process of sentence incorporation fully explicit, we need to articulate three things:

(i) The operations that are to be carried out in the applications of each of the different DRS-construction rules.

(ii) The syntactic configurations that trigger applications of the different rules.

(iii) The order in which the rules are to be applied in the processing of a given syntactic structure.

We begin with (ii) and (iii). The first step in the processing of a sentence always deals, we have seen, with the decomposition of its highest node (which is always an S-node). Thus in processing (1.1), whose syntactic structure, we saw, is the tree (1.2), the S-node triggers the application of a certain rule, viz. the rule for proper names CR.PN. That it is this rule which should be applied and not some other rule can be read off from the syntactic tree. In fact, it is only a small part of the tree consisting of the S-node, its immediate daughter nodes – the subject NP-node and the VP-node – and finally the PN-node which is immediately below the subject NP-node, which represents all the information needed to determine that it is CR.PN which should be applied here.

We call the subtree (1.3) of (1.2) which consists of these nodes a *triggering configuration*. More specifically, it is a *triggering configuration for* the rule CR.PN. An important part of specifying the construction algorithm is to describe for each of the construction principles that constitute it that principle's triggering configuration or configurations.

We have seen that each of the "NP-rules" (in other words of each of the construction principles that deal with the syntactic combination of an NP and a VP′ or transitive verb) introduces a new discourse referent and replaces the NP by that discourse referent in the condition to which the rule is being applied. The result of such an application will either be an irreducible condition or else it will contain in its turn one or more triggering configurations (for that same rule and/or some other(s)). Note, however, that when construction rules are applied to syntactic trees, the resulting DRS-conditions will, strictly speaking, not be syntactic trees; they are not generated by the grammar of Chapter 0, for some of their nodes will have discourse referents attached to them. Even so, the results of rule applications are very much like syntactic trees. (They are syntactic trees, but for the presence of discourse referents that have come to supplant the corresponding noun phrases.) So there is, in particular, a perfectly good sense in which they can be said to contain certain triggering configurations as parts. A telling example is (1.4), which resulted through application of the rule CR.PN to the first sentence of (1.1). In a strict sense (1.4) is not a syntactic tree according to our grammar; but the sense in which it contains the triggering configuration (1.9) is nevertheless transparent.

Given this obvious extension of the notion of "containing a triggering configuration" to arbitrary DRS-conditions we can formally characterize what it is for a DRS-condition to be reducible: A *reducible* DRS-condition is one containing at least one triggering configuration for some construction rule.

Now that reducible DRS-conditions have been identified as tree structures with triggering configurations as subtrees, what can we say about the order of rule application? There are two distinct questions which we must adress in this connection. The first is: When a DRS contains several reducible conditions, which of these should be reduced first? The second: When a condition contains more than one triggering configuration, which of these should trigger the rule application by which this condition is to be reduced?

We begin with the second question. It is not hard to verify that the ordering principle by which thus far we have been led comes to this: A reducible condition γ must be reduced by applying the appropriate rule to its *highest* triggering configuration, i.e. that triggering configuration τ such that the highest node of τ dominates the highest node of any other triggering configuration that γ contains. A particularly simple and special case of this principle is provided by (1.2). This condition has two triggering configurations, viz. (1.3) and (1.9). Of these (1.3) is obviously the highest, as its highest node, the S-node, is the highest node of the entire condition and thus dominates every other node of the tree, including the highest node of the other triggering configuration (1.9). It is interesting to compare the case of (1.2) with that of (1.4). The relevant configuration in (1.4) is not (1.3), but (1.9). In fact, (1.9) is the only triggering configuration of (1.4), for the subtree (1.51) fails to be a triggering configuration for CR.PN. The reason is that in order to qualify as a triggering configuration for CR.PN – or, for that matter, for any other rule we formulated up to now – the configuration ought to contain a daughter of the S-node which is a NP-node, and not just a simple discourse referent, such as **x**.[7]

(1.51)

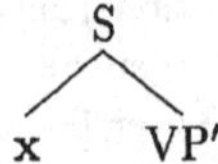

In the last paragraph we have spoken of "the highest triggering configuration" as the one which triggers the reducing rule application. But what guarantees that there always is a highest triggering configuration in any condition that contains triggering configurations at all? The answer to this question is two-fold. On the one hand there is no fundamental reason we can see why a DRS-condition could not in principle contain two triggering configurations neither of which is higher than the other. But on the other hand this is a situation that, as a matter of fact, does not arise in the English fragment we have so far defined. Nor does it arise in any of the extensions of the present fragment that will be studied later on in this book. We hypothesize that, were further extensions ever to give rise to DRS-conditions containing incomparable triggering configurations, the correct stipulation concerning the processing of such a condition should be: the condition may be reduced either via the one of these configurations or via the other.

This element of order indeterminacy would parallel another one which is directly relevant for our present fragment, and which has to do with the occurrence of two reducible conditions within the same DRS. Where a DRS contains two or more such conditions – and this brings us to the first of the two questions about order of rule application we have stated – it is indeterminate which of these is to be reduced first. Note well, this indeterminacy is intentional. It is needed because which of the two reducible conditions is to be processed first may vary from case to case. Compare, for instance, the two sentences (1.52) and (1.53).

(1.52) A stockbroker who knows him likes Bill.

(1.53) A stockbroker who knows Bill likes him.

[7]From this observation it is clear that an explicit description of the construction algorithm must provide an exhaustive enumeration of the possible triggering configurations. Such an enumeration would make explicit among other things that (1.51) is not one of them.

The DRS-construction starts in each case with the same steps, those of applying CR.ID, CR.NRC and CR.LIN.

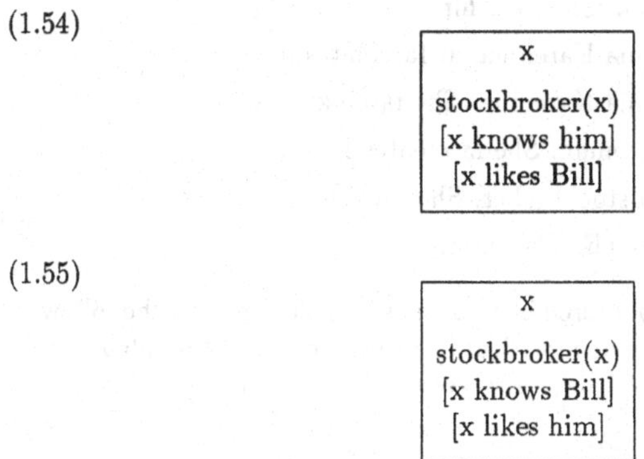

At this point both DRSs (1.54) and (1.55) contain two reducible conditions. But now, to complete the two constructions so that the resulting DRSs represent the natural readings of (1.52) and (1.53) in which **him** is anaphoric to **Bill**, it is necessary to proceed differently in the two cases. In the case of (1.52) we must first reduce the condition representing the content of the main clause, so that we have a discourse referent for **Bill** when we reduce the (condition representing the content of the) relative clause, which requires that we deal with the pronoun **him**. In the case of (1.53) the order of reduction that produces the right DRS is the opposite: first reduce the relative clause and then the main clause.

As often as not it is immaterial which of the two reducible conditions is processed first. In such cases the construction algorithm does not specify a precise order of processing, but irrespective of the order of which one proceeds, the final result, i.e. the completed DRS, will be the same. Here the indeterminacy serves no purpose, but neither does it any harm.

In essence, this completes our specification of the construction algorithm. In the next chapters we will gradually extend the fragment of English to which our theory applies; as a crucial part of this we will formulate further construction principles to deal with the new syntactic constructions that will be added to our fragment.

Exercises

1. Describe the DRS-constructions for (a)–(f) below. The discourses (b)–(d) are intuitively not acceptable. They are, however, analysable by our construction algorithm, which assigns each of them a well-formed, completed DRS. How

might the algorithm be modified, so that the construction of these DRSs be blocked?

(a) A man admires a woman. She likes him.
(b) Buddenbrooks loves Anna Karenina. It fascinates it.
(c) Buddenbrooks loves Anna Karenina. She fascinates it.
(d) Buddenbrooks loves a woman. She fascinates him.
(e) A stockbroker abhors a stockbroker. She loves him.
(f) Jones admires a woman who likes him.

2. Similar problems as are encountered in 1. arise in connection with the following sentences and text. Do your modifications to the construction algorithm to deal with the problems of 1.b–d, also cope with these new problems? If not, modify further.

   (a) Jones admires him.
   (b) Jones admires a woman who likes her.
   (c) Jones admires a woman. She likes her.
   (d) Jones admires a woman who she likes.

3. Formulate DRS-construction rules that cover the fragment extension given in Exercise 3 of Section 0.4. Construct the DRSs for the sentences (a) and (b) of that exercise.

4. Give the set of possible DRSs for the following discourses.

   (a) Jones knows a woman. He admires her. She fascinates him.
   (b) Jones knows a woman. Jones admires her. She fascinates him.
   (c) Jones knows a woman. He admires a woman. She fascinates him.

5. Do the following sequences describe correct DRS-constructions for the discourses (5a), (5b) and (5c) they are supposed to analyse?

   (a) Jones admires a woman.

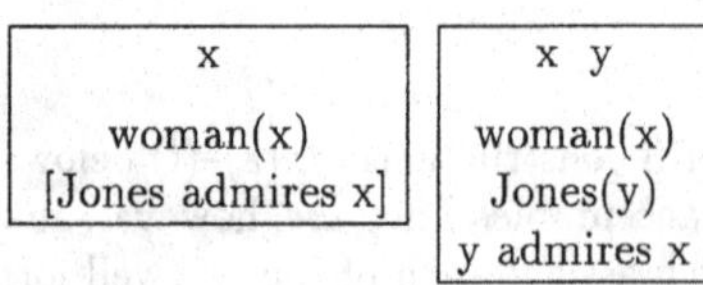

(b) Jones admires a woman. She loves him.

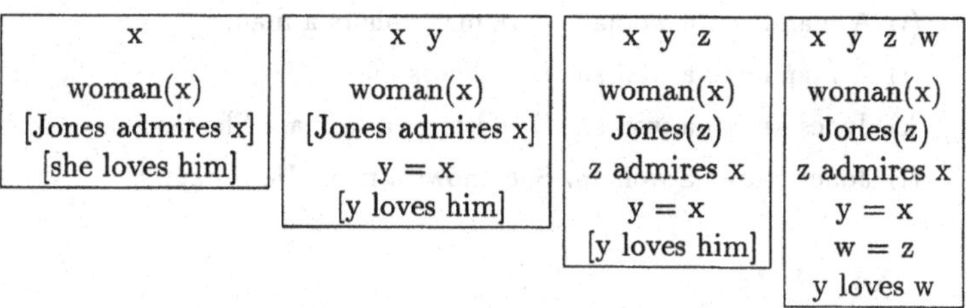

(c) Jones admires a woman who loves him.

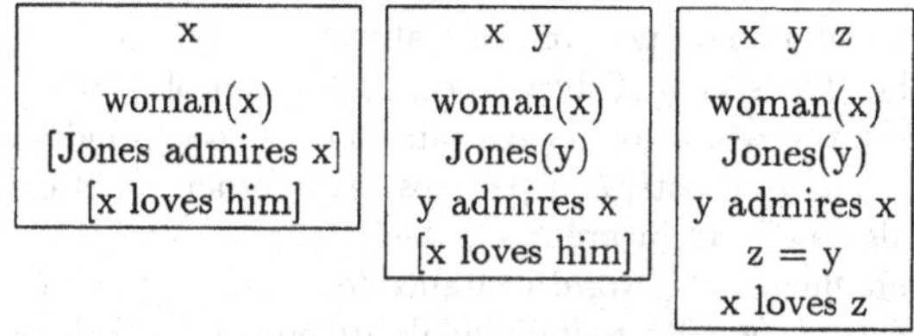

6. Instead of adding a condition of the form **u** = **v** we could have formulated CR.PRO in such a way that no new referent **u** is introduced and identified with **v** but that the referent **v** is inserted into the relevant place in the syntax tree. Formulate this alternative rule CR.PRO′.

   Extend this CR.PRO′ according to the two alternative strategies for dealing with the gender agreement constraint.

7. For each of the discourses below answer the following questions: Does a DRS-derivation exist for the given discourse – and if yes, which? Does the resulting DRS match the intuitive meaning of the discourse? Is the discourse ambiguous?

   (a) Anna loves Carl. Betty abhors Carl.
   (b) Anna loves Carl. Betty abhors him.
   (c) Anna loves him. Betty abhors Carl.
   (d) Anna loves Carl. Carl abhors Carl.
   (e) Anna loves Carl. Carl abhors him.
   (f) Anna loves Carl. He abhors him.

(g) Anna loves a man. Betty abhors a man.

(h) Anna loves a man. Betty abhors him.

(i) A man loves a woman. A woman abhors a man.

(j) A man loves a woman. She abhors him.

(k) Jones knows a woman. He admires a woman. She fascinates him.

(l) Jones knows a woman. She knows a man. He is happy.

1.2 Models

We have so far stated the truth conditions of the DRSs we have constructed by relating each DRS to the "world" of which it – or, rather, the discourse from which it was derived – is taken to be speaking about. But what is a "world"? When a discourse is about some aspect of the real world – e.g. the adventures of Oliver Cromwell in the 1650's or of Oliver North in the fall of 1986 – the notion may be clear enough: the world, or its relevant part, contains individuals of various kinds – people, places, events, and perhaps many other varieties of things – and these individuals have certain properties and stand to each other in certain relations. What individuals the world contains determines what mappings from the discourse referents of the DRS to individuals are possible and the properties of and relations between those individuals determine which of those mappings verify the conditions of the DRS. When a discourse is not about the real world but rather about some world of fiction or fantasy, the notion of a world seems more problematic. A particular difficulty seems to arise for what we might call *original fiction*, fiction which tells a story for the first time (rather than making it the subject of further, secondary reflection, as happens, for instance, in literary criticism). What is a world of primary fiction if it is not the world created by the very piece of fiction itself? But if that is all there is to such a world, how could a truth definition which proposes to evaluate the fictional discourse, or its derived DRS, with respect to this "world" be anything other than circular?

As a matter of fact a related difficulty arises for factual discourse, which aims to talk directly of the real world in which we live. For, as we said in the introduction, the point of a truth conditional account of *meaning* is not simply that it tells us whether a given sentence or discourse is true (in relation to its purported subject!) but also that it shows what the truth value of the sentence or discourse would have been, had its subject matter been different (in any one of the innumerable ways in which things could have turned out otherwise than they actually do). To repeat the words we already used there, the truth conditional account should define not only what the *actual* truth values are of the sentences or discourses to which it applies, but also what their truth values are in each of the *possible* (but non-actual) worlds.

But – and this is a question echoing the one just asked about fictional worlds – what is a non-actual possible world?

These questions, and especially the last one, have been the subject of ceaseless (and, it seems, literally interminable) debate among philosophers. The issue is important, but it is also very difficult, and for reasons that go well beyond what could be meaningfully discussed here.[8] We have judged it wise therefore not to become too deeply involved in these problems.

In order to sidestep them, we will adopt the more abstract point of view of *model-theoretic semantics.* In model-theoretic semantics the place of possible worlds is taken by models. A *model* is a certain information structure, relative to which it is possible to evaluate the expressions of some given language, and in particular to evaluate the sentences of that language in respect of truth and falsity.[9] The structure of a *model* will depend in general on the expressions whose evaluation is at stake. In the present chapter, where the DRSs considered will be comparatively simple, we will be able to make do with correspondingly simple kinds of models.[10] The structure these models have can be read off from the few DRSs we have so far considered. The truth or falsity of those DRSs depended, we saw, on what *individuals* there are, on what *properties* these individuals have and in what *relations* they stand to each other, and finally on which individuals are denoted by which *names.*

There are many different ways in which this kind of information could be represented. We will use the way (standard nowadays in formal logic and semantics) according to which a model M is a structure consisting of

i) a set U_M (which we will assume to be non-empty) of individuals, called the *universe* of M;

ii) for each name A of the language an individual i_A of U_M, the *individual named by* A *in* M; and

iii) for each predicate P_i of the language (i.e. for each one of its primitive expressions of category N or V) an *extension* $P_{i,M}$ for that predicate, *relative to* the universe U_M.

To explain the notion of *extension*, it is best to begin by concentrating on the case of predicates which express properties (or *unary* predicates, as they are also

[8] For an excellent defence of one position on possible worlds see [Lewis 1986].

[9] In our case the "expressions" we are concerned to evaluate are DRSs; but in fact DRSs can be regarded as expressions of a certain formal language – the DRS-language, as we will call it – which we will define in detail later on; see Def. 1.4.1.

[10] Models of essentially the same structure will continue to serve us through Chapter 4. Only in Chapter 5 we will have a need for models of a significantly greater complexity.

called). We already observed that the information what the model needs to tell us about such a predicate is which individuals satisfy it and which do not. This information is evidently fully determined by the set of precisely those individuals which do satisfy the predicate: an individual satisfies the predicate if and only if it belongs to the set. This set is called the predicate's *extension.*

In the case of *relational* predicates, a set of individuals would not suffice to provide the information we require. Suppose for instance that P is a binary predicate (i.e. one that expresses a two-place relation). What we need to know concerning P is whether, with regard to any two of the relevant individuals a and b, a stands in the expressed relation to b. Evidently this information is completely determined by the set consisting of just those pairs ⟨a,b⟩ where a stands in the given relation to b. This set of pairs is called the extension of the predicate. Similarly for predicates expressing relations between three things, the extensions are sets whose members are tuples each consisting of three elements, for predicates expressing relations between four things the extensions are sets whose members are tuples each consisting of four elements, etc.

We already said that what information is encoded in a model will in general depend on the purpose to which the model is put. More specifically, for which names the model specifies bearers, and for which predicates it provides extensions, will depend on what names and predicates occur in the expressions that are to be evaluated in it. Since in general we are concerned about the evaluation of all expressions of a given language, we will be interested in models which provide bearers and extensions for all the names and predicates of that language. This leads naturally to the notion of a model for a given vocabulary. By a *vocabulary* we will here understand any collection of names and predicates. M is a *model for a vocabulary* V iff it provides bearers for all and only the names in V and appropriate extensions (i.e. subsets of its universe for the unary predicates, sets of pairs for the binary predicates, etc.) for all and only the predicates of V.

Definition 1.2.1

We define a *model* M *for a vocabulary* V to be a triple $\langle U_M, Name_M, Pred_M \rangle$, consisting of

i) M's universe U_M,

ii) a function $Name_M$ from the set of individual constants of V into U_M. For each constant c of V $Name_M(c)$ is called the *bearer of* c *(according to* M)

iii) a function $Pred_M$ from the set of predicate constants of V into suitable objects associated with U_M: if P is a 1-place predicate of V, then $Pred_M(P)$ is a subset of U_M; and if P is an n-place predicate with $n \geq 2$

then $\mathsf{Pred}_{\mathsf{M}}(\mathsf{P})$ is a set of n-tuples of numbers of U_{M}. $\mathsf{Pred}_{\mathsf{M}}(\mathsf{P})$ is called the *extension of* P *in* M.

Let us look at a couple of toy examples to get a better feel of what models are like and how DRSs are evaluated in them.

First consider $\mathsf{M}_1 = \langle \mathsf{U}_{\mathsf{M}_1}, \mathsf{Name}_{\mathsf{M}_1}, \mathsf{Pred}_{\mathsf{M}_1} \rangle$, where

$\mathsf{U}_{\mathsf{M}_1}$ is the set of individuals {a,b,c,d,e,f};

$\mathsf{Name}_{\mathsf{M}_1}$ is the set of pairs {⟨**Jones**,a⟩, ⟨**Smith**,b⟩, ⟨**Ulysses**,d⟩, ⟨**Candide**,e⟩}

$\mathsf{Pred}_{\mathsf{M}_1}$ is the set consisting of

i) the pair ⟨**owns**, $\mathsf{owns}_{\mathsf{M}_1}$⟩ where $\mathsf{owns}_{\mathsf{M}_1}$ is the set of pairs {⟨a,d⟩, ⟨a,e⟩, ⟨b,e⟩, ⟨b,f⟩, ⟨c,f⟩};

ii) the pair ⟨**fascinates**, $\mathsf{fascinates}_{\mathsf{M}_1}$⟩, where $\mathsf{fascinates}_{\mathsf{M}_1}$ is the set of pairs {⟨e,a⟩, ⟨f,a⟩, ⟨d,b⟩, ⟨a,b⟩, ⟨c,a⟩, ⟨d,a⟩, ⟨c,b⟩}; and

iii) the pair ⟨**Porsche**, $\mathsf{Porsche}_{\mathsf{M}_1}$⟩, where $\mathsf{Porsche}_{\mathsf{M}_1}$ is the set {f} (i.e. the set whose only member is the individual f).

It is easy to see that the function f which maps the discourse referents **x** and **v** onto the individual a and the discourse referents **y** and **u** onto the individual d verifies all conditions of the DRS (1.21). Thus (1.21), and therewith the discourse (1.1) from which it was derived, is true in the model M_1. On the other hand, it is also easily seen that there is no function mapping the discourse referents of the DRS (1.35) onto individuals of M_1 which verifies all the conditions of (1.35). So (1.35), and the discourse (1.28) which it represents, are false in M_1.

Next, let M_2 be the model $\langle \mathsf{U}_{\mathsf{M}_2}, \mathsf{Name}_{\mathsf{M}_2}, \mathsf{Pred}_{\mathsf{M}_2} \rangle$ for which $\mathsf{U}_{\mathsf{M}_2}$ is the set {a,b,c,d,e,f,g,h,k}, and $\mathsf{Name}_{\mathsf{M}_2}$ and $\mathsf{Pred}_{\mathsf{M}_2}$ are the same as $\mathsf{Name}_{\mathsf{M}_1}$ and $\mathsf{Pred}_{\mathsf{M}_1}$, except that $\mathsf{Porsche}_{\mathsf{M}_2}$ is the set {f,g,h,k}. Again it is easy to see that (1.21) is true in M_2 – in fact, it will be verified by the same function f that verified (1.21) in M_1. (1.35) is false in M_2, intuitively because none of the members of the set $\mathsf{Porsche}_{\mathsf{M}_2}$ stand in the right relation to a. (For f the situation is the same here as it was in M_1, and the new elements g,h,k do not stand to a in either of the required relations.)

The third model we consider, M_3, has the same universe and naming relation as M_2, but it assigns different extensions to the predicates **owns** and **fascinates**. In particular, $\mathsf{owns}_{\mathsf{M}_3}$ is the set {⟨a,d⟩, ⟨a,e⟩, ⟨b,e⟩, ⟨b,f⟩, ⟨a,g⟩, ⟨a,k⟩} and $\mathsf{fascinates}_{\mathsf{M}_3}$ the set {⟨d,a⟩, ⟨e,a⟩, ⟨f,a⟩, ⟨d,b⟩, ⟨a,b⟩, ⟨c,a⟩, ⟨c,b⟩, ⟨h,a⟩, ⟨k,a⟩}. The extension of **Porsche** in M_3 is the same as it was in M_2.

In this model (1.21) is once again true. But now (1.35) is true also; it is verified by the function which maps x and v onto a and y and u onto k (and, as can be readily checked, this is the only function which will verify all the conditions of (1.35) in M_3).

As a last example, let M_4 be the model which is like M_3 except that its universe is the larger set {a,b,c,d,e,f,g,h,k,l,m,n}. As in M_3, both (1.21) and (1.35) are true.

The reader may have noted that whenever a DRS was true in any one of the models M_1–M_4, it was also true in the subsequent models we looked at, and in fact the very same function that verified the DRS in the first model also verified it in the later ones. This is no accident. It is a consequence of two facts, one about the models M_1–M_4 we have considered, and one concerning the DRSs we have constructed up to this point (including in particular the two, (1.21) and (1.35), which we have been evaluating in M_1–M_4). The first fact is that each next model *extended*, in some sense, the preceding one. Thus M_2 extends M_1 in that its universe is larger while it has the same naming relation and the same predicate extensions. M_4 extends M_3 in the same way. M_3 also extends M_2, but in a slightly different sense. Here the two universes are the same, and so is the naming relation; but the extensions of some of the predicates are larger in M_3 than they are in M_2.

The second fact is that the DRSs we have so far encountered only contain what might be called *positive* information. Thus all the information carried by (1.21) is that there exist certain individuals bearing certain names, and standing in certain relations. The information conveyed by (1.35) is of the same sort. It should be clear that when a function verifies a DRS of this kind in a given model M it will do so also in any model that extends M in either of the two senses just considered. For the positive information that M contains – which suffices for the truth of the DRS, and which is all that matters to its truth – is preserved in all of M's extensions.

We can make this more exact as follows.

Definition 1.2.2

i) For any two models M and M′ for V we say that M′ *extends* M (in symbols: $M \subseteq M'$) iff $U_M \subseteq U_{M'}$; $Name_M = Name_{M'}$; and for each predicate Q, $Pred_M(Q) = Pred_{M'}(Q) \cap U_M$.

ii) We call a DRS K *persistent* iff whenever M is a model in which K is true, and M′ extends M, then K is true in M′.

The persistent DRSs are those which, in the more intuitive terminology used above, contain only positive information.

All three DRSs we have so far seen are persistent. In fact, they are, from a logical point of view, extremely simple. And so is their relation to the models in which they are evaluated. In fact, it is not all that easy to see any very clear difference between models and DRSs at this point: both provide sets of "individuals", to which they assign names, properties and relations. Presently we will encounter other DRSs with a more complicated structure, and which no longer have the persistence property. These DRSs will look increasingly different from the models in which they are evaluated, and the illusion that DRSs are just small models will quickly evaporate.

However, even the persistent DRSs to which our experience has been limited so far differ from models in at least one crucial respect. DRSs are partial information structures, not only in that they will typically assert the existence of only a small portion of the totality of individuals that are supposed to exist in the worlds of which they intend to speak, but also in that they will specify only some of the properties and relations of those individuals they mention. Thus a DRS may, for given discourse referents x and y belonging to its universe, simply leave it open whether or not they stand in a certain relation. Models, in contrast, leave no relevant information out. Thus if a and b are individuals in the universe of the model M and the pair ⟨a,b⟩ does not belong to the extension in M of, say, the predicate **owns**, then this means that a does not own b, not that the question whether a owns b is, as far as M is concerned, undecided.

We should point out that the notion of a model for a vocabulary V is a strictly mathematical one. That is, every mathematically possible combination of choices of extensions for the predicates of V and bearers for the names in V qualifies as a model. In other words, the class of all models for the vocabulary V is the class consisting of all structures $\langle U_M, Name_M, Pred_M \rangle$ such that U_M is a non-empty set, $Name_M$ associates with each name of V some element of U_M and $Pred_M$ assigns to each predicate of V a subset of U_M (in case the predicate is unary) or a set of tuples of the appropriate number of places (in case the predicate is n-place with n greater or equal than 2) the members of which all belong to U_M. The question whether these assignments are plausible in the light of the intuitive meaning of the names of predicates is one which simply does not arise in this connection.

We turned to models in order to avoid inopportune questions about possible worlds. Indeed, we will not speak of possible worlds again, except occasionally in informal comments. Yet, before we abandon worlds altogether, a few words ought to be said about the relation between them and the models that we use as their substitutes. Very roughly, the relation is this. Let us restrict attention to the models for some fixed vocabulary V in which there are no names. For each possible world w there is a unique corresponding model M(w) (for V), whose universe consists of the individuals existing in w and which assigns to each of the predicates in V the extension it has in w. In particular, there will be a unique model $M(w_0)$ corresponding to the actual world w_0.

Is there conversely for each model M for V a corresponding possible world w such that M = M(w)? This is less obvious. In fact, the answer should probably be in the negative. Suppose, for instance, that V contains the predicate **owns** and the predicate **Porsche**. Are there possible worlds in which Porsches own things? It would seem that our concept of ownership doesn't provide for this possibility: with Porsches the preconditions for owning simply are not met given our cultural conditions and conventions; and it is difficult to imagine what cultural conditions and conventions should have to be like so that Porsches being owners becomes a genuine possibility.

This point can be made in countless different ways. For instance, suppose that V contains also the predicate **person**. Can Porsches be persons? Wouldn't something just cease to qualify as a Porsche – in the literal sense of the word – if it turned out to be a person? Or suppose that V contains the predicates **alive** and **dead**. Could there be things – i.e. are there possible worlds in which there are things – which are both dead and alive (at the same time)? Or could there be persons who were neither alive nor dead? There isn't any straightforward answer to these questions. Indeed, their difficulty is of a piece with the deepest problems that beset the notion of a possible world itself. Still, to some of the questions we would be inclined to answer: no. Thus, that nothing can be at the same time both dead and alive would seem to be simply a consequence of the fact that these predicates are mutually exclusive because of what they *mean*; their incompatibility is part of their "logic".

If this is indeed so, then not every model would correspond to a possible world. Besides those models that do there are also those which violate some aspect of the logic or meaning of the predicates for which they provide extensions, and thus represent what are in fact impossibilities. It might perhaps be felt that such models should be excluded from consideration – that evaluation in such a model won't tell us anything of importance about the evaluated expression, and could only distort the truth-conditional account of meaning in the context of which such evaluations would primarily arise. However, if we were to try to exclude such models, we would find ourselves once again in the midst of the very difficulties that the switch from possible worlds to models was intended to circumvent.

We will therefore stick with the notion of a model for a given vocabulary V as we defined it above, and make no attempt to eliminate any of the models that fall under Definition 1.2.2 as it stands. In adopting this definition we follow the lead of standard ("classical") logic.

Exercises

1. Consider the model M_1 defined on page 95 and the extension V′ of the vocabulary V of that model which we get by adding the 1-place predicates **unicorn** and **stinks** and the 2-place predicate **likes**. Let M be the model for V′ which

we get by extending $\mathsf{Pred}_{\mathsf{M}_1}$ to include the following extensions for these new predicates:

- the pair ⟨**unicorn**, $\mathsf{unicorn}_\mathsf{M}$⟩, where $\mathsf{unicorn}_\mathsf{M}$ is the empty set $\emptyset$;
- the pair ⟨**stinks**, $\mathsf{stinks}_\mathsf{M}$⟩, where $\mathsf{stink}_\mathsf{M}$ is the set {c,f};
- the pair ⟨**likes**, $\mathsf{likes}_\mathsf{M}$⟩, where $\mathsf{likes}_\mathsf{M}$ is the set of pairs {⟨a,c⟩, ⟨a,d⟩, ⟨a,e⟩, ⟨d,e⟩, ⟨f,g⟩}

For each of the following texts construct a DRS for it and check whether that DRS is verified in M_1.

(a) Jones likes a unicorn which stinks.

(b) Jones owns a Porsche. It stinks.

(c) Smith owns a Porsche which Jones likes. It fascinates Smith.

2. As under 1. obtain a model M′ for the vocabulary V′ by expanding the model M_3 of page 95 by adding to $\mathsf{Pred}_{\mathsf{M}_3}$ the extensions:

- the pair ⟨**unicorn**, $\mathsf{unicorn}_{\mathsf{M}'}$⟩, where $\mathsf{unicorn}_{\mathsf{M}'}$ is the set {c};
- the pair ⟨**stinks**, $\mathsf{stinks}_{\mathsf{M}'}$⟩, where $\mathsf{stink}_{\mathsf{M}'}$ is the set {c,f,h,k};
- the pair ⟨**likes**, $\mathsf{likes}_{\mathsf{M}'}$⟩, where $\mathsf{likes}_{\mathsf{M}'}$ is the set of pairs {⟨a,c⟩, ⟨a,d⟩, ⟨a,e⟩, ⟨d,e⟩, ⟨f,g⟩, ⟨a,f⟩, ⟨a,k⟩, ⟨b,d⟩, ⟨g,h⟩}

Check the verifiablity of the DRSs for (a)–(c) in M′.

1.3 Negation

Our near-exclusive concern so far has been with construction principles corresponding to the rules S → NP VP′ and VP → V NP. But even for these rules we haven't given a complete statement of the corresponding construction principles. For there are two types of NPs in our fragment which we haven't yet considered: definite descriptions and phrases beginning with **every**. Before we consider these, however, it will be helpful to look at some simple instances of *negation*. So far we have concentrated on sentences and types of discourse which typically serve to communicate information. The correctness criterion we stated for the DRSs which these sentences or discourses produce was inspired by the intuition that the DRS derived from such a sentence or discourse gives some kind of schematic 'picture' of the world, a picture which is right if its discourse referents can be taken as representations of real objects with the 'depicted' properties and relations. It is part and parcel of this idea that to assert one or more sentences is to claim that the world accords with the 'picture' which the utterance induces; in other words, that there exists some correct map from the set of discourse referents of that picture to objects in the world.

Assertion is only one of the many different purposes to which linguistic expressions can be put. It is, as contemporary terminology has it, only one of a number of different types of *speech acts.*[11] Among the various other speech act types there is one which is not always distinguished from assertion, and which evidently has close affiliations with it. This is *denial.* The paradigmatic situation in which denial occurs is that where the recipient understands what is said to him, rejects it, and lets that be known to the speaker. Denial is also a common reaction to claims that are made tentatively, e.g. by tagging a question to the relevant sentence (as in **Bill has returned the book, hasn't he**?); or it may occur in response to actual questions (**Hasn't Bill repaid you the money**?). In all these cases the effect of the denial is to repudiate something that has been put forward tentatively or confidently by someone else; it is to reject, as the present theory suggests, the 'picture' which the previous speaker has presented as certainly or possibly correct. The force of denial is thus that a certain picture is *not* correct; i.e. that there is *no* map from its referents to objects such that these objects satisfy the depicted conditions.

There are various forms in which denial can be expressed. Often, when it is clear from context what it is that is being denied, it is enough simply to say **no**, or shake one's head. But on other occasions a simple **no** might leave doubt as to *what* it is meant to repudiate. The speaker may have made several claims before the addressee has a chance to respond, and the addressee may wish to reject only one of them. In these cases the act of denial must identify the rebutted content, as well as make clear that this content is being rebutted (rather than, say for instance, affirmed). There is no a priori limit to the variety of linguistic conventions that could serve this double purpose. But those that English, and probably all other natural languages, employ seem to be particularly natural: use a construction from which the sentence expressing the rejected content can easily be recovered and which at the same time makes it explicit that this content is being rejected. We shall call such a linguistic construction, which is typically used to deny the content of the sentence that is recoverable from it, a *negation of* that sentence.

English has several such constructions. Of these, the one we have included in our fragment appears to be the most basic – where it can be used at all it tends to be preferred over the other constructions that express negation. In this construction the word **not** is added to the VP of the sentence, often accompanied by an obligatory tensed occurrence of the verb **do**.[12]

[11]See e.g. [Austin 1962], [Gazdar 1979], [Searle 1969], [Cole/Morgan 1975].

[12]Such "verb phrase" negations, in which **not** is added, with or without a supporting form of

Once a language has one or more constructions for expressing negation from which the embedded – i.e. negated – sentence can be effortlessly recovered, there are two ways in which we can look upon what is done by a speaker who utters such a construction. We have just been describing such utterances as denials of the embedded sentence. But they can equally well be regarded as assertions – not of the sentence which the uttered expression negates, but of the uttered expression as a whole. (Thus, on this second view, the asserted content is not the proposition expressed by the embedded sentence, but rather the complement of that proposition, which is true if and only if the first proposition is false.) In fact, this second view is clearly to be preferred, as it is continuous with what we will have to say in any case about utterances in which negations are themselves embedded – e.g. under disjunction, as in the sentence **Either Jones does not like Mary or she does not invite him**. The natural perspective on utterances of such sentences is that they are assertions whose content relates to that of their "minimal propositional constituents" (in the example: **Jones does not like Mary** and **she does not invite him**) via operations such as disjunction and negation. (The alternative view would force us to devise, for each sentence form in which negation somewhere occurs, a corresponding utterance type, which would relate to that form in the same way as denial stands to unembedded negation. It is not hard to see that this enterprise quickly leads to absurdity.) Thus we shall treat sentences which contain negations as sentences that are typically used in assertions, just as we have been treating the negation-free sentences discussed in the first three sections of this chapter.

How do we semantically represent the content of a sentence φ which is the negation of some other sentence ψ? The main principle to guide us here is that the representation of φ should involve, in some way or other, the representation of the sentence ψ which φ negates. For the content of φ is evidently a function of that of ψ. The most natural way to achieve this is by combining the representation of ψ with something which represents the function itself – that which turns the content of ψ into that of its negation φ. We represent the function by one of the symbols which have been traditionally used for this purpose within formal logic, viz. the

---

do, to the verb phrase of the sentence that is being negated, are not applicable to all English sentences. For instance it can not be applied to a sentence whose verb phrase is already negated. In this regard English differs from certain other languages such as e.g. German and Dutch. An English verb phrase can be negated once more by embedding it into a construction that applies to a very much more comprehensive class of declarative sentences than does verb phrase negation itself, viz. that where one prefixes to the sentence some such phrase as **it is not true that** or **it is not the case that**. But these constructions are not part of our fragment and we will ignore them here. However, for our purposes the variety of the sentences to which it applies is large enough. In particular, the English fragment that we built up in Section 0.4, in which the verb phrase negation described is the only form of negation, has the same expressive power as first order predicate logic.

symbol '¬'. It will act as a kind of operator on the representation of the negated sentence, in other words, on its DRS. Thus the DRS of (1.56) will look like (1.57).

(1.56) Jones does not own a Porsche.

(1.57)

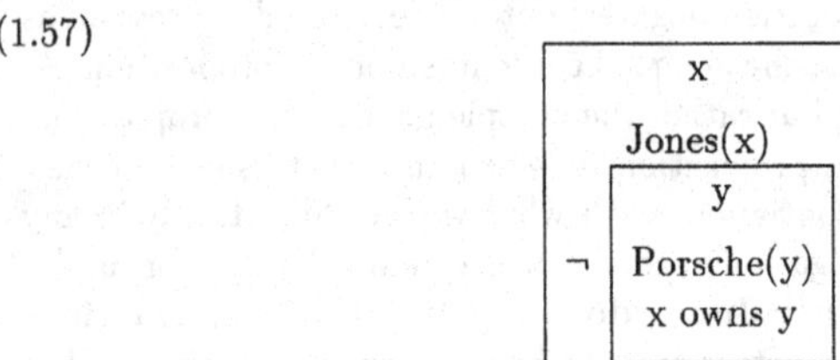

We should see (1.57) as a DRS with one discourse referent **x** and two conditions. The first of these, **Jones(x)**, we have encountered several times already. The second, however, consisting of the internal box with its contents and its affixed '¬', is quite different from what we have seen so far. One feature which distinguishes it from earlier conditions is that it contains a DRS as a component. The satisfaction criteria for conditions of this new sort naturally depend on the satisfaction conditions of their component DRSs. For the particular case of (1.57) we have already informally agreed on what that dependency should be: the condition will be verified by an embedding function f (which associates an individual **a** with the single discourse referent **x**) iff there is no way of associating an individual **b** with the discourse referent **y** of the component DRS which, in combination with f, gives us a correct embedding of that DRS. In other words, f satisfies the condition if, for no **b**, **b** is a Porsche such that f(**x**) owns **b**.

Evidently this imposes the right truth conditions on (1.57); and it generalizes naturally to all conditions that negated sentences give rise to. Each such condition consists of a DRS K marked with '¬'; it is satisfied by a given map f if there is no way of combining f with a map g which associates objects with the discourse referents of K, so that the combination of f and g constitutes a correct embedding of K.

How is (1.57) obtained? To answer this we must make a decision for which we are not in a position to give an adequate justification. It concerns the *scope* of negation. Does verb phrase negation embrace the subject or doesn't it? We will assume that it does not. Our principal reason for this relates to such sentences as (1.58).

(1.58) Somebody does not own a Porsche.

(1.58) cannot be understood as denying the assertion that somebody owns a Porsche. Therefore, **not**, the negative element, cannot be understood as having wide scope over **somebody**.[13]

With this assumption the DRS-construction for (1.56) starts off in just the same fashion as we began those for (1.1), (1.28) and (1.37). Such a beginning accords, by the way, with our earlier commitment to let the order in which the construction steps are to be carried out be determined by syntactic structure. For as our syntax has it, the first syntactic rule to be applied in analysing (1.56) should indeed be the rule S → NP VP′. Applying the relevant construction principle (the one suited to proper names) we get:

(1.59)

x
Jones(x) [x does not own a Porsche]

What next? Let us look at the syntactic tree for (1.56):

(1.60)

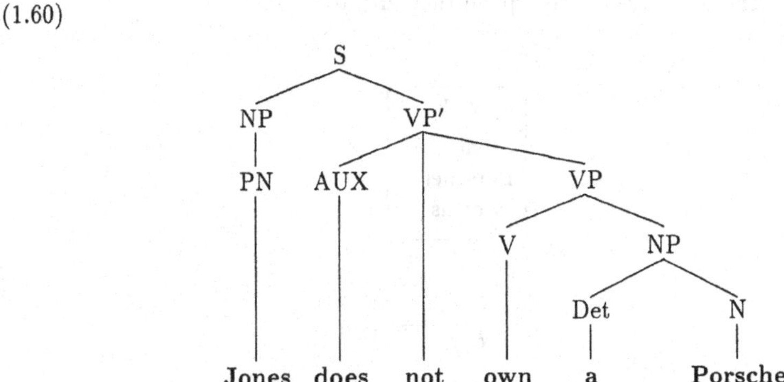

According to this tree the node we must deal with next is the VP′ node. We assume that it is a rule associated with the syntactic rule in question (the rule VP′ → AUX **not** VP) which introduces the sub-DRS of (1.57). Applying this rule, we obtain

[13]This matter is really much more involved than our cavalier treatment of it reveals. It is one of several problems which are intimately connected with deeper issues in syntax, and thus lie outside the reach of the theory developed here.

(1.61)

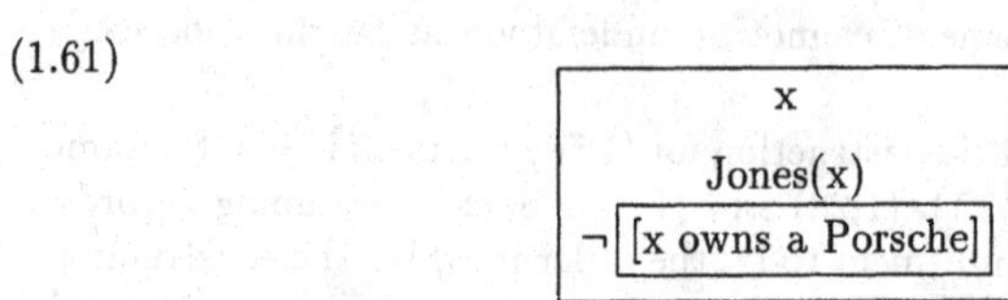

The next step must deal with the condition **x owns a Porsche**. Following the principle that sentences in the scope of negation should be treated as they would be if the negation were absent, we arrive at (1.57).

In expanding a subordinate DRS introduced by negation we may draw on discourse referents introduced earlier, just as we did when we had to deal with anaphoric pronouns. Thus, consider

(1.62) Jones owns a Porsche. He does not like it.

Processing of the first sentence gives us (1.63). The first two construction steps triggered by the second sentence expand this DRS to (1.64).

(1.63)

(1.64)

x y z
Jones(x)
Porsche(y)
x owns y
z = x
¬ [z likes it]

The last step must deal with the pronoun **it** in the subordinate DRS. It can link the pronoun to the NP **a Porsche** in the by now familiar fashion:

(1.65)

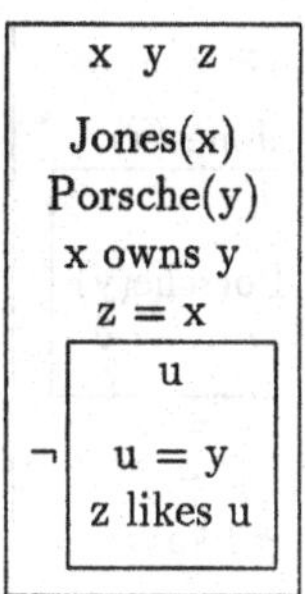

In contrast, a discourse referent introduced into a subordinate box is not accessible to anaphoric pronouns in subsequent discourse. For instance,

(1.66) Jones does not own a Porsche. He likes it.

does not seem to admit a reading which interprets **it** as anaphorically linked to **a Porsche**. Thus, having arrived at the DRS (1.67), we cannot proceed to obtain (1.68) because the referent **y** is in a position which is "inaccessible" from the position of **it**.

(1.67)

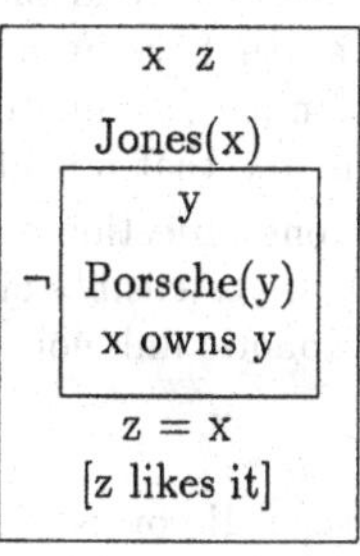

(1.68)

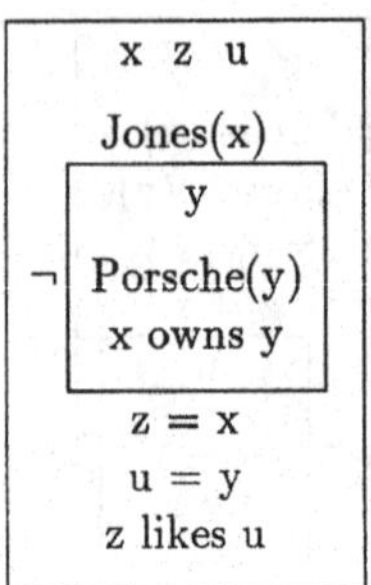

We will encounter this phenomenon in a variety of contexts. As we have set things up, inaccessibility arises whenever the referent introduced for the putative (but impossible) antecedent occurs in a subordinate DRS; or, more accurately, the referent x is *accessible* to the pronoun α (if and) only if the condition γ from which α is to be eliminated belongs to the DRS containing x, or to one which is subordinate to that DRS. The *subordination* relation to which we have referred here is an important, empirically significant component of DRT. It is, as we shall see, one of the two primary factors which determine what anaphoric links are possible. Subordination holds not only between a main DRS and the DRSs that it includes, but also between certain subordinate DRSs of a given DRS; and to make sure that things come out right we will have to be careful that the relation be defined just right. For the moment, however, all that we need to remember about it is that any DRS K′ introduced by a negation is subordinate to the DRS K containing the condition to which the construction step that introduces K′ is applied.

We hasten to forestall at least one objection that may have occurred to the reader. There are discourses, which are ostensibly of the form of (1.66), but which nevertheless seem to permit the anaphoric link not allowed in (1.66). Thus it is at least arguable that

(1.69) Jones doesn't like a Porsche. He owns it.

can be interpreted as saying, roughly, that there is some Porsche which Jones both dislikes and owns. The principles we have formulated thus far do not enable us to construct a DRS which assigns this reading to (1.69).

There are two routes towards a solution of this problem: (i) defer the treatment of negation until after a discourse referent has been introduced for the object NP and (ii) introduce an alternative processing principle for the indefinite description, by which the new discourse referent gets introduced into the universe of the main

DRS (and not into that of the subordinate DRS containing the condition to which the principle is being applied). Without further comment both adjustments may seem ad hoc. About the first we will say no more just now. But the second invites an observation which should be made in any case. Whereas (1.66) does not allow us to interpret **it** as anaphorically related to the direct object of its first sentence, such an anaphoric link is perfectly possible for

(1.70) Jones doesn't own Ulysses. He likes it (however).

The reason for this is a difference between the construction principle for indefinite descriptions and that for proper names which we were not in a position to formulate when we first stated them: whereas the discourse referent introduced for an indefinite description is to become part of the DRS which contains the relevant condition γ, the referent introduced for a proper name (as well as the condition containing the proper name) must be added to the universe of the main DRS (i.e. that DRS that is not a sub-DRS of any other DRS), whether γ be one of the conditions of that DRS itself or of some DRS subordinate to it. Thus, subjecting (1.70) to all but the very last processing step, we obtain the DRS

(1.71)

x y z
Jones(x)
Ulysses(y)
¬ [x owns y]
z = x
[z likes it]

Since **y** belongs to the same DRS as the condition **z likes it**, we may link the discourse referent **u** we introduce for **it** with **y** (by means of the condition **u** = **y**).

The intuitive motivation for the requirement that a referent introduced for a proper name be put into the universe of the main DRS is this: proper names serve – or so we believe, following philosophers like Kripke, Kaplan and others – to refer 'directly' to their bearers. It is the bearer of a proper name that any assertion containing that name is 'about'. In our terminology this means that the DRS for the assertion is correct only if we can suitably correlate its discourse referents with real objects in such a way that, in particular, the bearer of the name is associated with the discourse referent which the name introduced.

It should be pointed out that the rule according to which the discourse referent for a proper name is always placed in the universe of the main DRS is by itself not sufficient to capture all implications of the view that names refer directly. This is a matter that will be discussed at length in Volume 2; a brief preview of that discussion can be found in Section 3.3. At present, our main concern is to account for the different capacities that names and indefinite descriptions in contexts such as (1.62) and (1.69) act as antecedents for anaphoric pronouns. This we accomplish by insisting that the discourse referents for proper names do always go into the universe of the main DRS but those for indefinite descriptions do not. (1.69) shows that under certain circumstances the discourse referent for an indefinite description which is situated (at the point where the discourse referent is introduced) in some subordinate DRS may also end up in the universe of the main DRS. Precisely when this should happen turns out to be a quite complicated issue. We will take up this issue in Chapter 3, where we will also touch upon the related question whether there are besides the universe of the sub-DRS of the indefinite NP and that of the main DRS also additional intermediate "landing sites" for the discourse referent. (This last question can of course only arise when the indefinite NP ends up in a multiply embedded position.)

Exercises

1. Consider the following discourses:

   (a) Bill admires a woman who doesn't admire him. He is unhappy. She is not unhappy. She is happy. She doesn't admire a man.

   (b) Bill admires Anna. Anna admires a man who admires a woman who owns a dog. Anna doesn't own a dog. Anna is unhappy. Bill is foolish.

   Construct all possible DRSs for these two texts.

2. Give DRS-analyses of the following sentences:

   (a) Jones does not like a unicorn.

   (b) A Porsche does not stink.

   (c) Jones does not own a Porsche which does not fascinate him.

   (d) Jones does not like a Porsche which he does not own.

   Do these DRSs correctly reflect the meaning of these sentences as you understand them?

1.4 Verification, Truth and Accessibility

When we introduced the notion of a model we gave an informal definition of what it is for a DRS to be true in a model: The DRS K is true in the model M iff there is a way of associating members of U_M with the discourse referents of K so that each of the conditions in K is verified in M. When we gave this definition, its content was clear enough since the DRS-conditions were all of particularly simple forms. But this situation has now changed, for the DRSs we have been constructing in the last section contain besides the "atomic" conditions we encountered in earlier sections also complex conditions beginning with '¬'. We should remind ourselves in this connection that conditions of this latter kind may themselves contain conditions beginning with '¬', and so on, so that there is in principle no limit to their complexity. This complicates the general statement of the verification conditions for such conditions and requires us to proceed more carefully, and more formally, than has been necessary so far.

First, we have to be more explicit about what we understand in general by an *embedding*. This is important because it will be necessary to refer, in the formal statement of the verification conditions for DRSs we will give below, to arbitrary embeddings satisfying certain conditons. The notion of embedding we will use is basically that of a *function*, as it occurs in modern set theory. According to set theory the identity of a function is completely determined by what values it associates with each of the arguments for which it is defined. The precise form in which the association is conceived or defined is immaterial. Thus if two algorithms or computer programmes compute exactly the same numbers when given the same numbers as inputs, then they will, according to the set-theoretic conception, specify the same function even if the computation strategies they follow are very different (perhaps so different that no one would be able to prove that the algorithms will always produce the same outputs for the same inputs). It follows that a function in the sense of set theory is fully characterized by the set of all pairs consisting of an argument for which the function is defined and the value which it assigns to that argument. In other words, we may think of functions as sets of argument-value pairs. By the Domain of a function or embedding f (Dom(f)), we understand the set consisting of all arguments for which f is defined, i.e. the set of all a such that for some b the pair ⟨a,b⟩ belongs to f. Similarly the Range of f, Ran(f), is the set of all possible values under f, i.e. the set of all b such that for some a the pair ⟨a,b⟩ belongs to f.

When f is a function and a is in Dom(f) we will use the familiar notation 'f(a)' to denote the value which f associates with a. (Thus the statements 'f(a) = b' and '⟨a,b⟩ belongs to f' are interchangeable.) We say that two functions f and g are *compatible* if they assign the same values to those arguments for which they are both defined – i.e., if for any a which belongs to both Dom(f) and Dom(g) f(a) = g(a). g is called an *extension of* f if g is compatible with f and the Domain of g includes the Domain of f – thus, if g is an extension of f then f and g assign the same values to all arguments for which f is defined, while g may (though it need not) be defined for some additional arguments as well.

It should be obvious from these definitions that f and g are compatible functions iff f ∪ g (i.e. the set of all pairs that belong either to f or to g) is a function. Note that by the definition of function we have just adopted the second and third component of a model M, i.e., Name_M and Pred_M, are in fact functions. So it is legitimate to write, as we have in fact already done, say, Name_M(**Jones**) to denote the individual which acts as the bearer of the name **Jones** in M (thus the individual a such that ⟨**Jones**, a⟩ belongs to Name_M) or writing Pred_M(**stockbrocker**) to denote the extension of the predicate **stockbroker** in M; etc.

Second, we need to define precisely what the conditions are which can occur in DRSs. Since the conditions beginning with '¬' do themselves contain DRSs, this requires a precise definition of what a DRS can be like. In fact, the two definitions, of a *DRS* and of a *DRS-condition*, must be dovetailed, and thus given simultaneously, for each will have to rely on the other. (Such definitions, where two notions are defined in such a way that the more complex instances of the first notion are characterized with the help of simpler instances of the second notion and the more complex instances of the second with the help of simpler instances of the first, are called *definitions by simultaneous recursion.*) Here is the combined definition, relativized to a given vocabulary V and a set R of discourse referents:

Definition 1.4.1

(i) A *DRS* K *confined to* V *and* R is a pair, consisting of a subset U_K (possibly empty) of R and a set Con_K of DRS-conditions confined to V and R;

(ii) A *DRS-condition confined to* V *and* R is an expression of one of the following forms:

(a) **x** = **y**, where **x**, **y** belong to R

(b) π(**x**), where **x** belongs to R and π is a name from V

(c) η(**x**), where **x** belongs to R and η is a unary predicate (corresponding to a common noun) from V

(d) **x**ζ, where **x** belongs to R and ζ is a unary predicate (corresponding to an intransitive verb) from V

(e) **x**ξ**y**, where **x**, **y** belong to R and ξ is a binary predicate from V

(f) ¬K, where K is a DRS confined to V and R

Of the different kinds of conditions Def. 1.4.1 specifies, only those given under (f) have DRSs for constituents. Later we will encounter more conditions with this same property. Such conditions are called *complex conditions.* Conditions of the forms given under (a)–(e) are called *simple* or *atomic conditions.*

When we discuss a given DRS K – say the DRS constructed from a given discourse or sentence – it will often be convenient to distinguish K from its various subordinate DRSs. We will do this by referring to K itself (as in fact we already started doing on the last section) as the *main* or *principal* DRS.

Each of the DRSs which we constructed before we came to deal with negation had the property that every discourse referent occurring in one of its conditions also occurred in its universe. The DRSs we want to consider in the present section are meant to have a similar property, but it is one that is a little more difficult to state correctly. Roughly, when a discourse referent occurs in a condition, either of the principal DRS or in one of the "sub-DRSs" which enter into the principal DRS as part of conditions beginning with '$\neg$', then this discourse referent belongs to the universe of either the principal DRS or to that of some sub-DRS so that the universe in which it occurs "dominates" the condition of which the discourse referent is a constituent. To make this precise, we must define the notion of a discourse referent being *free* in a DRS or DRS-condition. The definition is as follows:

Definition 1.4.2

(i) A discourse referent z is *free in* a DRS K iff it is free in some condition in Con_K and does not belong to U_K.

(ii) If γ is a DRS-condition and z a discourse referent then z is *free in* γ iff

(a) γ is of the form x = y and z is x or z is y

(b) γ is of the form π(x) and z is x

(c) γ is of the form η(x) and z is x

(d) γ is of the form xζ and z is x

(e) γ is of the form xξy and z is x or z is y

(f) γ is of the form $\neg$K and z is free in K

It is easy to verify that none of the DRSs constructed so far has any free discourse referents. (Although sometimes a discourse referent was free in a sub-DRS in which it occurred.) For a DRS which is to represent a definite proposition, which has a truth value in each model (for the given V and R), this is how things ought to be. For a free discourse referent would have no "proper home". It would, as will be seen from the definitions below, have no determinate semantic role and thus prevent the DRS as a whole from having a determinate propositional content. These considerations motivate the following definition.

Definition 1.4.3

A DRS is *proper* iff no discourse referent is free in it.

We can now proceed to state the verification conditions for DRSs and DRS-conditions. We consider DRSs and DRS-conditions that are confined to V and R.

Let M be a model for V. We want to define both what it means for an embedding f to *verify* a DRS *in* M and what it means for f to *verify a DRS-condition in* M. Again these are two notions which dovetail, just as the concepts of a DRS and of a DRS-condition which occur in it are dovetailed. And so we are once again led to a definition by simultaneous recursion:

Definition 1.4.4

Let K be a DRS confined to V and R, let γ be a DRS-condition, and let f be a (possibly partial) *embedding from* R *into* M, i.e. a function whose Domain is included in R and whose Range is included in U_M

(i) f *verifies* the DRS K in M iff f verifies each of the conditions belonging to Con_K in M

(ii) f *verifies* the condition γ in M iff

(a) γ is of the form $x = y$ and f maps x and y onto the same element of U_M

(b) γ is of the form $\pi(x)$ and f maps x onto the element a of U_M such that $\langle \pi, a \rangle$ belongs to $Name_M$

(c) γ is of the form $\eta(x)$ and f maps x onto an element a of U_M such that a belongs to $Pred_M(\eta)$

(d) γ is of the form $x\zeta$ and f maps x onto an element a of U_M such that a belongs to $Pred_M(\zeta)$

(e) γ is of the form $x\xi y$ and f maps x and y onto elements a and b of U_M such that $\langle a,b \rangle$ belongs to $Pred_M(\xi)$

(f) γ is of the form $\neg K'$ and there is no embedding g from R into M which extends f, such that $Dom(g) = Dom(f) \cup U_{K'}$ and g verifies K′ in M

In Section 1.3 we already used the notion of verification when we talked about the evaluation of the DRSs (1.11) and (1.35) in the models M_1 to M_4. There the DRSs did not yet contain the recursive element that came into play when we introduced negation. Take, for example, the DRS (1.73) representing the first sentence of (1.72):

(1.72) Jones likes Ulysses. He doesn't own a Porsche.

(1.73)

x y
Jones(x) Ulysses(y) x likes y

Let us show that there is an embedding of (1.73) into the following model $\mathsf{M}_1 = \langle \mathsf{U}_{\mathsf{M}_1}$, $\mathsf{Name}_{\mathsf{M}_1}$, $\mathsf{Pred}_{\mathsf{M}_1} \rangle$, where

- $\mathsf{U}_{\mathsf{M}_1}$ is the set of individuals {a,b,c,d,e};
- $\mathsf{Name}_{\mathsf{M}_1}$ is the set of pairs {⟨**Jones**,a⟩, ⟨**Smith**,b⟩, ⟨**Ulysses**,d⟩, ⟨**Candide**,e⟩}
- $\mathsf{Pred}_{\mathsf{M}_1}$ is the set consisting of

  i) the pair ⟨**likes**, $\mathsf{likes}_{\mathsf{M}_1}$⟩ where $\mathsf{likes}_{\mathsf{M}_1}$ is the set of pairs {⟨a,d⟩, ⟨a,e⟩, ⟨b,e⟩};

  ii) the pair ⟨**owns**, $\mathsf{owns}_{\mathsf{M}_1}$⟩, where $\mathsf{owns}_{\mathsf{M}_1}$ is the set of pairs {⟨e,a⟩, ⟨b,d⟩, ⟨a,b⟩, ⟨d,a⟩, ⟨b,c⟩};
  and

  iii) the pair ⟨**Porsche**, $\mathsf{Porsche}_{\mathsf{M}_1}$⟩, where $\mathsf{Porsche}_{\mathsf{M}_1}$ is the set {c} (i.e. the set whose only member is the individual c).

It is easy to see that the function f which maps the discourse referent **x** onto the individual a and the discourse referent **y** onto the individual d is an embedding of $\mathsf{U}_{(1.73)}$ into M_1 that verifies all conditions in $\mathrm{Con}_{(1.73)}$: ⟨**Jones**, f(**x**)⟩ and ⟨**Ulysses**, f(**y**)⟩ belong to $\mathsf{Name}_{\mathsf{M}_1}$, and ⟨f(**x**), f(**y**)⟩ belongs to $\mathsf{likes}_{\mathsf{M}_1}$. If we add the second sentence of (1.72), we have to deal with the complex condition ¬K when we try to find an embedding of (1.74).

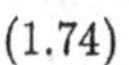
(1.74)

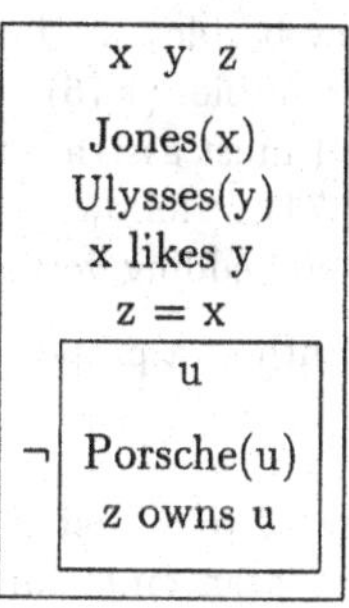

(1.74) is verified by an embedding f which maps the discourse referents **x** and **z** onto the individual a and the discourse referent **y** onto the individual d. It is straightforward to check the first four conditions: ⟨**Jones**, f(**x**)⟩ and ⟨**Ulysses**, f(**y**)⟩ belong to $\mathsf{Name}_{\mathsf{M}_1}$, ⟨f(**x**), f(**y**)⟩ belongs to $\mathsf{likes}_{\mathsf{M}_1}$, and **x** and **z** are mapped to the same element. In order to show that f verifies the last condition in (1.74), namely

(1.75) ¬

u
Porsche(u) z owns u

we have to show that there is no embedding g from {**x**,**y**,**z**,**u**} into $\mathsf{U_M}$ which extends f such that Dom(g) = Dom(f) ∪ $\mathrm{U_K}$, and which verifies the DRS (1.75) in M which appears inside the scope of '¬'. To show this let us first look if there is an embedding h of this DRS, which we give once more in (1.76);

(1.76)

u
Porsche(u) z owns u

The extension of **Porsche** in M_1 is the singleton set {c}. So if h is to fulfill the first condition of (1.76), it must map **u** to c. Furthermore, h must also verify the second condition, **z owns u**. Since h(**z**) = f(**z**) = f(**u**) = a this is impossible. So no such h exists and f verifies (1.75). Thus f verifies verifies all the conditions of (1.74) and, by Def. 1.4.4.(a), f verifies the DRS (1.74) itself.

Next, let M_2 be the model $\langle \mathsf{U}_{\mathsf{M}_2}, \mathsf{Name}_{\mathsf{M}_2}, \mathsf{Pred}_{\mathsf{M}_2}\rangle$ for which $\mathsf{U}_{\mathsf{M}_2} = \{\mathsf{a,b,c,d,e,p}\}$, $\mathsf{Name}_{\mathsf{M}_2}$ is the same as $\mathsf{Name}_{\mathsf{M}_1}$, and $\mathsf{Pred}_{\mathsf{M}_2}$ extends $\mathsf{Pred}_{\mathsf{M}_1}$ in such a way that $\mathsf{Pred}_{\mathsf{M}_2}$(**likes**) = $\mathsf{Pred}_{\mathsf{M}_1}$(**likes**), $\mathsf{Pred}_{\mathsf{M}_2}$(**owns**) is the set {⟨e,a⟩, ⟨b,d⟩, ⟨a,b⟩, ⟨d,a⟩, ⟨b,c⟩, ⟨a,p⟩} and $\mathsf{Pred}_{\mathsf{M}_2}$(**Porsche**) = {⟨c,p⟩}. It is easy to see that (1.74) fails to be true in M_2, because there is now besides the function h considered in the last paragraph another function j which verifies (1.76), viz. the one which maps **u** to p. So, f does not verifiy (1.75). Since f must assign a to **x** and **z** and d to **y** in order to verify the other conditions of (1.74), it follows that no embedding can verify all conditions of (1.74). Therefore no embedding verifies (1.74).

We now give the definition of truth of a proper DRS in a model M.

Definition 1.4.5

Let K be a proper DRS confined to V and R and M a model for V. We say that K is *true in* M iff there is an embedding f from R into M such that Dom(f) = $\mathrm{U_K}$ and f verifies K in M.

The notion of truth in a model enables us to define two other concepts which are of primary importance in semantics and logic, *logical consequence* and *logical truth*:

An expression is a *logical truth* (or is *logically true*) if it is true in all models; and one expression is a *logical consequence* of some other expression (or of a set of such) if it is true in every model in which the latter is true (or in which all of the latter are true). The intuitions behind these definitions ought to be fairly obvious. A logical truth is an expression which is true no matter how the subject matter of which it could be used to speak might turn out; and a logical consequence of one or more expressions is one whose truth is guaranteed, no matter how the subject matter might turn out, by the truth of the expression or expressions of which it is a consequence.

As it stands, Def. 1.4.5 puts us in a position to define these notions only for DRSs – for the expressions, in other words, of our formal DRS-languages. Even for those there is a tiny wrinkle to the definitions as we have just given them. Def. 1.4.5 involves, like the earlier definitions of DRSs and models, a parameter for the vocabulary V. So the definitions of logical consequence and truth, which build on the concept that 1.4.5 defines, should be relativized to this parameter as well. So once more we confine our attention to DRSs relative to some vocabulary V and set of discourse referents R. For these we define:

Definition 1.4.6

(i) a DRS is *logically true* iff it is true in all models for V;

and

(ii) a DRS K is a *logical consequence* of DRSs $K_1,\ldots,K_n$ iff for every model M for V if $K_1,\ldots,K_n$ are all true in M then so is K.

Our primary aim is to define logical truth and consequence, not for the DRSs, to which Defs. 1.4.5 and 1.4.6 apply directly but for the sentences and discourses from which these DRSs derive. However, the transfer of these notions from DRSs to the natural language inputs from which they can be constructed runs into a slight complication. Natural language is often ambiguous, and this is true also for the English fragments studied in this book, including the one for which the semantics has been given in the present chapter. As far as this last fragment is concerned, ambiguity is quite limited, however, since in choosing it we have made sure that it is free both from syntactic ambiguity (of the kind exemplified by **They are flying planes**, **Visiting relatives can be boring** or **I saw a man with a telescope**) and from lexical ambiguity (as in, say, **My pen is empty**). But even in this fragment discourses, and even individual sentences, can still be ambiguous because of the anaphoric ambiguities of pronouns. When a discourse is ambiguous in this way, the construction rules permit the derivation of two or more non-equivalent DRSs from the discourse, even though each sentence of the discourse has a unique syntactic analysis. (We call two DRSs *non-equivalent* if they determine distinct truth conditions, so that there are models in which one DRS is true and the other false.) Evidently we cannot talk about the truth conditions of an ambiguous discourse without qualification, but only relative to some particular DRS that can be derived from it. Thus we come to the following definition.

Definition 1.4.7

Let D be a discourse whose names and predicates all belong to the vocabulary V. Let K be a DRS derived from D. And let M be a model for V. Then D is *true in* M *according to the interpretation* K iff K is true in M.

Only when all DRSs that can be constructed from D are equivalent can we speak of the truth or falsity of D in M simpliciter. A special case of this would be that where the number of DRSs that can be derived from D equals one. But strictly speaking, this is a situation which never arises. For as the construction algorithm has been stated, there are no constraints on the choice of new discourse referents, other than that they do not yet occur in the DRS into which they are to be introduced. Of course, there is a good sense in which DRSs that differ from each other only in the choice of certain discourse referents do not differ from each other in any essential way, and there ought to be a way of identifying them whenever we want to. To this end we define two DRSs K_1 and K_2 to be *essentially the same* if one can be obtained from the other by replacing some or all of its discourse referents by others: K_1 and K_2 are essentially the same if there is a one-to-one map g from the discourse referents of K_1 to the discourse referents of K_2, so that K_2 is obtained by replacing in K_1 each discourse referent u by the corresponding referent g(u).[14]

DRSs K_1 and K_2 which are essentially the same according to the definition just given are also called *alphabetic variants* (K_1 is an alphabetic variant of K_2 and vice versa). It is a straightforward exercise to show that if K_1 and K_2 are alphabetical variants, then for any model M K_1 is true in M iff K_2 is. So, if D is a discourse such that any two DRSs derivable from D are alphabetical variants, then we can talk about the truth or falsity of D without reference to DRSs. Let us call such discourses *unambiguous.*

Definition 1.4.8

A discourse D is *unambiguous* iff any two DRSs derived from it are alphabetic variants.

[14]By a one-to-one correspondence between two sets A and B we understand a function f with Dom(f) = A and Ran(f) = B, such that for any distinct elements a_1, a_2 from A $f(a_1) \neq f(a_2)$.

Definition 1.4.9

Suppose that D is an unambiguous discourse and that M is a model for a vocabulary V which contains all the names and predicates that occur in D. Then D is *true* in M iff any DRS derivable from D is true in M. Otherwise D is false in M.

From Def. 1.4.5 it follows that the DRS (1.74) is true in M_1, but false in M_2. Since M_2 extends M_1 this shows that (1.74) is not persistent, in the sense of persistence defined in Def. 1.2.2. Evidently it is the last condition of (1.74), viz. (1.75), which is responsible for this failure of persistence. In general, DRSs cease to be persistent as soon as they contain conditions of the form $\neg$K.

From Def. 1.4.7 it follows that the discourse (1.72) from which (1.74) was derived is true in M_1 according to (1.74) and false in M_2 according to (1.74). These results would seem to agree with our intuitive understanding of (1.72) - and indeed one would think that it should be possible to show that (1.72) is true in M_1 and false in M_2 simpliciter. To draw this conclusion on the basis of our formal definitions, however, it is necessary to show that (1.72) is unambiguous. But whether (1.72) is unambiguous depends on how the processing rule for anaphoric pronouns is stated. To wit, it depends on whether the rule does or does not exclude the intuitively inacceptable link between the pronoun **he** and the noun phrase **Ulysses**. This is a matter about which we have not so far been entirely explicit. If we build into the rule a sensitivity to the feature *Gen* and specify (i) that **he** can only be linked with (the discourse referent introduced by) an NP which assigns *Gen* the value *male*, and (ii) that **Ulysses** assigns *Gen* the value *-hum*; then (1.72) emerges as unambiguous. But relative to a processing rule for pronouns which ignores such feature information (1.72) would not be unambiguous, as it would permit, besides the interpretation that we recognize as correct, also the one according to which it is Ulysses which doesn't own a Porsche.

We found that in the context of negation, proper names and indefinite noun phrases have distinct anaphoric properties: in some cases where a pronoun can refer back to a proper name such anaphoric reference becomes impossible when the proper name is replaced by an indefinite description (recall the examples (1.66) and (1.70)!).

We accounted for this difference by arguing

(i) that when they occur in conditions which belong to subordinate DRSs (i.e. DRSs that are themselves part of a condition $\neg$K) proper names and indefinite descriptions yield discourse referents in distinct DRS universes, and

(ii) that the possibility of interpreting a pronoun π as anaphorically linked to some other noun phrase η depends on the configurational relation between the position of π at the stage when an antecedent must be found for it, and that of the discourse referent that has already been introduced for η.

When this configurational relation is such that it permits the anaphoric link between η and π, we will say that the discourse referent is *accessible* from the position of the pronoun (at the processing stage in question); otherwise the discourse referent is said to be *inaccessible.*

Accessibility is a central concept for the present treatment of anaphora, and it is therefore important that we define it exactly. As we have described it, it is a relation between constituents of DRS-conditions and discourse referents. But from our description of it, it is clear that whether the relation holds between, say, a pronoun π and a discourse referent $\mathbf{x}$ depends on the one hand on the DRS which contains the syntactic tree in which π is a constituent as one of its conditions, and on the other hand on the DRS whose universe contains $\mathbf{x}$. Whether $\mathbf{x}$ is accessible to π is fully determined by the configurational relationship between these two DRSs. We will exploit this fact by first defining the relevant relation between DRSs, a relation which we will call *subordination*, and then define accessibility in terms of subordination.

Before stating the definition of subordination we should note that the DRSs of which we are speaking here are not in general those that were defined in Def. 1.4.1. The DRSs of Def. 1.4.1 are all *completed* DRSs, DRSs to which no further construction rules can be applied. Compare the description of the DRS-Construction Algorithm on page 85. But in connection with subordination, and the notion of accessibility which we will define in terms of it, it is precisely the uncompleted DRSs, those that still contain reducible DRS-conditions, that are of importance.

If we were to proceed in perfect compliance with the canons of proper methodology we would at this point have to define, in the formally precise manner of Def. 1.4.1, the class consisting of all completed and uncompleted DRSs. This would require in turn that we give a precise definition of all the conditions which are found in uncompleted DRSs, that is, of all possible reducible conditions. Since there is no real obstacle to such a definition and since it involves a number of tedious details, we have decided to leave this matter to the reader, trusting that he has already developed a sufficiently clear sense of what reducible conditions look like.

In the remainder of this section we will use the term 'DRS' to refer to both completed and uncompleted DRSs. And after that we will, whenever there is a danger of confusion, make explicit whether we are talking about completed DRSs only or about the uncompleted ones as well.

The definition of *subordination* is very simple. First, if $\neg K'$ is a condition of a DRS K, then K′ is subordinate to K. Second, if K′ contains in its turn a condition $\neg K''$, then K″ is subordinate to K′, and also to the DRS K to which K′ is subordinate; and so on. As this informal description indicates, the concept of subordination has a recursive element. A correct formal definition of the notion must capture this. We proceed in a way that is standard in mathematics. We first provide a non-recursive definition of an auxiliary concept, that of *immediate subordination*, and then give a recursive definition of subordination in which immediate subordination constitutes the base case.

Definition 1.4.10

(i) K_1 is *immediately subordinate* to K_2 iff Con_{K_2} contains the condition $\neg K_1$

(ii) K_1 is *subordinate* to K_2 iff either

(a) K_1 is immediately subordinate to K_2, or

(b) there is a DRS K_3 such that K_3 is subordinate to K_2 and K_1 is immediately subordinate to K_3.

Graphically the subordination relation has a very simple interpretation. If a DRS K is represented, in the manner of this book, as a structure of nested boxes, then K′ is a DRS subordinate to K if it occurs somewhere inside the box that identifies K. Similarly K_2 is subordinate to K_1 if and only if K_2 is inside the box that identifies K_1. Thus the relation of subordination can be directly read off the way in which the boxes are nested. For instance, in the DRS K_0 K_1, K_2 and K_3 are all subordinate to K_0, and K_2 is subordinate to K_1. But neither K_1 nor K_2 is subordinate to K_3, nor is K_3 subordinate to either K_1 or K_2.

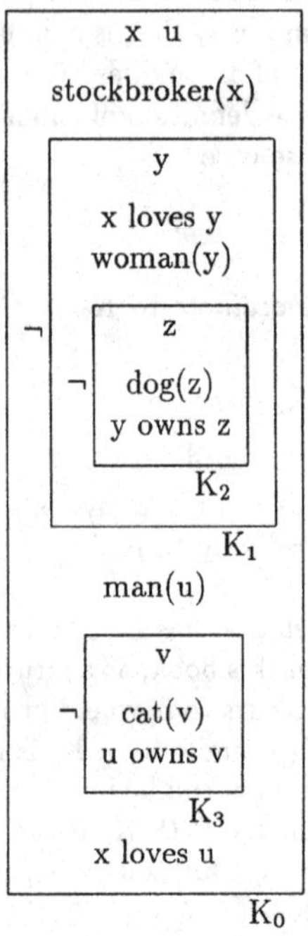

It will be convenient to have a compact notation for what we will call *weak subordination*, the relation which holds between K_1 and K_2 if either K_1 is identical to K_2 or K_1 is subordinate to K_2 (in the sense of Def. 1.4.10). We write '$K_1 \leq K_2$' for weak subordination.

Accessibility is now readily defined in terms of '$\leq$'. We define it as a relation between discourse referents and DRS-conditions.

Definition 1.4.11

> Let K be a DRS, **x** a discourse referent and γ a DRS-condition. We say that **x** is *accessible from* γ *in* K iff there are $K_1 \leq K$ and $K_2 \leq K_1$ such that **x** belongs to U_{K_1} and γ belongs to Con_{K_2}.

The accessibility relation between discourse referents and pronouns reduces to this relation between discourse referents and conditions: **x** is accessible to π in K, at a given stage of processing, iff at that stage π is a constituent of a condition γ from which **x** is accessible in K.

Construction Rules

We conclude the section with a complete list of the construction principles we have so far formulated. For each principle the specification involves (i) its triggering configuration or configurations, and (ii) its 'modus operandi'. Our specifications of the latter will presuppose throughout that the condition to which the rule is being applied belongs to Con_K where K is part of some DRS K′. K may be either a proper part, i.e. a sub-DRS, of K′ or an improper part, that is, coincide with K′. In general the triggering configuration will only be a proper subtree of the condition to which the rule is being applied. When this is the case, we write **Triggering Configuration** $\gamma \subseteq \overline{\gamma} \in$ **Con**$_{\mathbf{K}}$, to indicate that γ is the configuration that triggers the application of the rule and that $\overline{\gamma}$ is the treated condition that contains it as a subtree. Two of the rules, CR.PRO and CR.LIN, can be stated here only in a preliminary version. We have indicated this by framing them within a single (as opposed to a double) line. The definitive versions of CR.PRO and CR.LIN will be given in Sections 3.1 and 4.2.2, respectively.

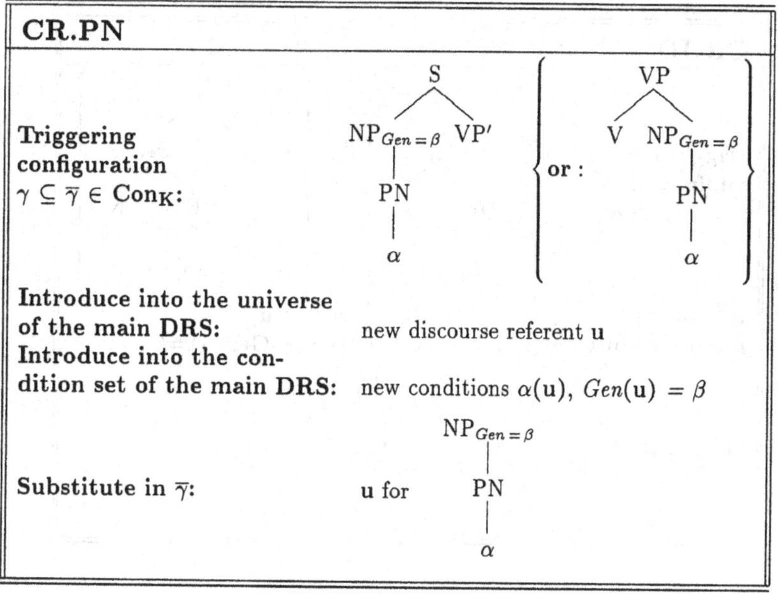
CR.PN
Triggering
configuration
$\gamma \subseteq \overline{\gamma} \in$ Con$_K$:
S
NP$_{Gen=\beta}$ VP′
PN
α
or :
VP
V NP$_{Gen=\beta}$
PN
α
Introduce into the universe
of the main DRS: new discourse referent u
Introduce into the con-
dition set of the main DRS: new conditions α(u), Gen(u) $= \beta$
Substitute in $\overline{\gamma}$: u for
NP$_{Gen=\beta}$
PN
α

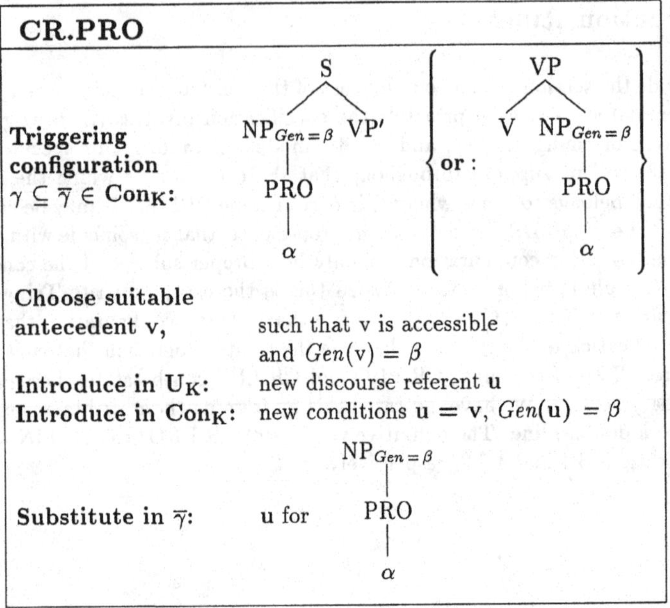
CR.PRO
Triggering configuration
$\gamma \subseteq \overline{\gamma} \in Con_K$:
S
$NP_{Gen=\beta}$ VP′
PRO
α
or :
VP
V $NP_{Gen=\beta}$
PRO
α
Choose suitable antecedent v,
such that v is accessible and $Gen(v) = \beta$
Introduce in U_K:
new discourse referent u
Introduce in Con_K:
new conditions $u = v$, $Gen(u) = \beta$
Substitute in $\overline{\gamma}$:
u for
$NP_{Gen=\beta}$
PRO
α

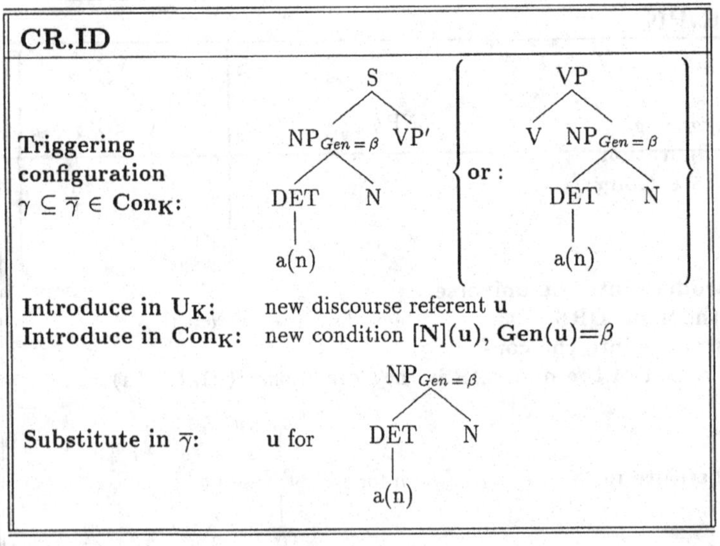
CR.ID
Triggering configuration
$\gamma \subseteq \overline{\gamma} \in Con_K$:
S
$NP_{Gen=\beta}$ VP′
DET N
a(n)
or :
VP
V $NP_{Gen=\beta}$
DET N
a(n)
Introduce in U_K:
new discourse referent u
Introduce in Con_K:
new condition [N](u), Gen(u)=β
Substitute in $\overline{\gamma}$:
u for
$NP_{Gen=\beta}$
DET N
a(n)

CR.NEG

Triggering configuration
$\gamma \subseteq \overline{\gamma} \in$ **Con**$_K$:

S
u VP′
AUX **not** VP

Replace $\overline{\gamma}$ **by:** $\neg$

S
u VP′
VP

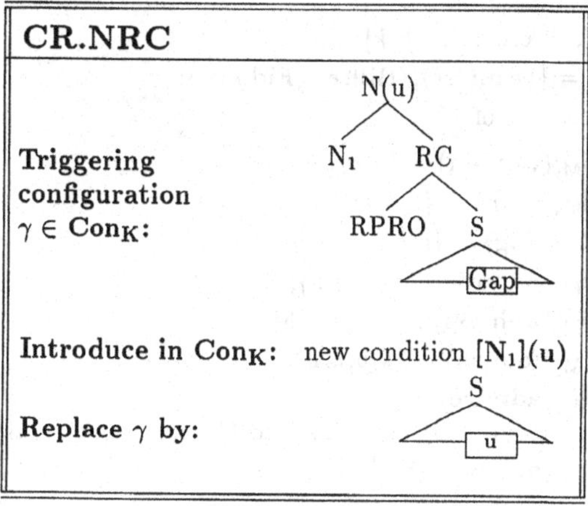

CR.LIN	
Triggering configuration $\gamma \in$ **Con**$_K$:	N(v) — α
Replace γ **by:**	α(v)

Exercises

1. Given the following models M_1 – M_3:

   (M_1) $U_{M_1} = \{a, b, c, d, e, f\}$
   $Name_{M_1} = \{\langle \textbf{Anna}, c\rangle, \langle \textbf{Bill}, e\rangle\}$
   $Pred_{M_1}$ consists of
   - $Pred_{M_1}(\textbf{woman}) = \{a, b, c\}$
   - $Pred_{M_1}(\textbf{man}) = \{d, e, f\}$
   - $Pred_{M_1}(\textbf{dog}) = \{\ \}$
   - $Pred_{M_1}(\textbf{happy}) = \{a, b, c\}$
   - $Pred_{M_1}(\textbf{unhappy}) = \{d, e, f\}$
   - $Pred_{M_1}(\textbf{foolish}) = \{a, b, c, d, e, f\}$
   - $Pred_{M_1}(\textbf{admire}) =$
     $\{\langle a, b\rangle, \langle b, c\rangle, \langle c, d\rangle, \langle c, f\rangle, \langle d, e\rangle, \langle d, b\rangle, \langle e, c\rangle, \langle e, b\rangle, \langle e, a\rangle\}$
   - $Pred_{M_1}(\textbf{own}) = \{\ \}$

   (M_2) $U_{M_2} = \{a, b, c, d, e, f, g, h, k\}$;
   $Name_{M_2} = \{\langle \textbf{Anna}, c\rangle, \langle \textbf{Bill}, e\rangle, \langle \textbf{Fido}, h\rangle\}$;
   $Pred_{M_2}$ consists of
   - $Pred_{M_2}(\textbf{woman}) = \{a, b, c\}$;
   - $Pred_{M_2}(\textbf{man}) = \{d, e, f\}$;
   - $Pred_{M_2}(\textbf{dog}) = \{g, h\}$;
   - $Pred_{M_2}(\textbf{happy}) = \{a, b, d, h\}$;
   - $Pred_{M_2}(\textbf{unhappy}) = \{c, e, f, h\}$;
   - $Pred_{M_2}(\textbf{foolish}) = \{a, b, c, d, e, f\}$;
   - $Pred_{M_2}(\textbf{admire}) =$
     $\{\langle a, b\rangle, \langle b, c\rangle, \langle c, d\rangle, \langle c, f\rangle, \langle d, e\rangle, \langle d, b\rangle, \langle e, c\rangle, \langle e, b\rangle, \langle e, a\rangle\}$;
   - $Pred_{M_2}(\textbf{own}) = \{\langle b, h\rangle, \langle e, g\rangle\}$.

(M_3) As M_2, with the only difference that $Pred_{M_2}$(**admire**) is extended with the pairs $\langle a, e\rangle$, $\langle b, e\rangle$ and $\langle c, e\rangle$; i.e.
$Pred_{M_3}$(**admire**) =
$\{\langle a,b\rangle, \langle b,c\rangle, \langle c,d\rangle, \langle c,f\rangle, \langle d,e\rangle, \langle d,b\rangle, \langle e,c\rangle, \langle e,b\rangle, \langle e,a\rangle, \langle a,e\rangle, \langle b,e\rangle, \langle c,e\rangle\}$

Decide for the DRSs K_1 and K_2 of Exercise 1 in Section 1.3 and each of the models M_1–M_3 if the DRS is true in the model. In case the DRS is true in a model give an embedding function that verifies it.

2. (a) Show that the DRS (1.34) is a logical consequence both of the DRS (1.35) and (1.65).
   (b) Show that that the converse does not hold.

3. Show that the following DRSs are logically true:

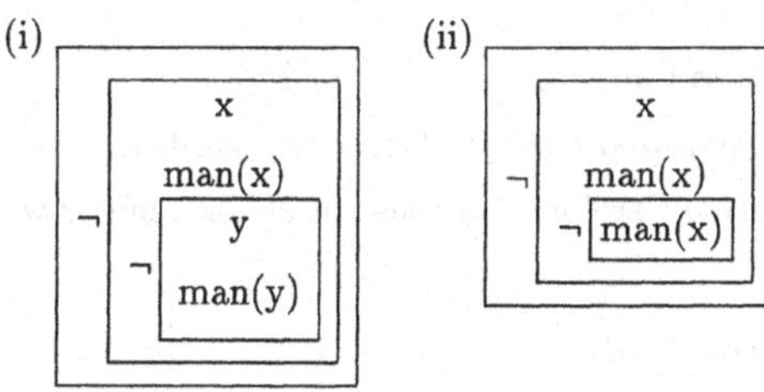

4. Think of sentences of our fragment of English the DRSs of which are logically true.

5. For each of the following sentences construct a maximal (possibly empty) set of DRSs, which are not essentially equivalent to each other.

   (a) A man who knows a stockbroker who Fred likes doesn't own a dog which hates her.
   (b) A man who knows a stockbroker who Fred likes doesn't own a dog which hates him.
   (c) A man who doesn't know a stockbroker who Fred likes owns a dog which hates him.
   (d) A man who doesn't know a stockbroker who Fred likes owns a dog which hates her.

6. Which truth values do the sentences (a)–(d) of Exercise 2 in Section 1.3 have with respect to the models M and M′ of Exercise 1 in Section 1.2?

7. Consider the model $M = \langle U_M, Name_M, Pred_M\rangle$ with

U_M = {a,b,c,d,e,f,g,h}
$Name_M$ = {⟨**Princess Caroline**,a⟩, ⟨**James** ,d⟩, ⟨**Madame Bovary**,h⟩}
$Pred_M$(**woman**) = {a,b,c,}
$Pred_M$(**man**) = {d,e,f,g,h}
$Pred_M$(**gardener**) = {b,d,e}
$Pred_M$(**butler**) = {c,f,g}
$Pred_M$(**book**) = {h}
$Pred_M$(**loves**) = {⟨a,d⟩, ⟨b,c⟩, ⟨d,a⟩, ⟨d,b⟩, ⟨d,c⟩, ⟨e,c⟩, ⟨g,c⟩}
$Pred_M$(**likes**) = {⟨a,d⟩, ⟨d,a⟩, ⟨d,c⟩, ⟨e,b⟩, ⟨f,a⟩, ⟨f,c⟩, ⟨g,c⟩}
$Pred_M$(**fascinates**) = {⟨a,d⟩, ⟨a,f⟩, ⟨b,e⟩, ⟨c,d⟩, ⟨c,g⟩}
$Pred_M$(**abhors**) = {⟨a,h⟩, ⟨b,a⟩, ⟨c,a⟩, ⟨d,d⟩, ⟨e,a⟩, ⟨g,a⟩}
$Pred_M$(**reads**) = {⟨a,h⟩, ⟨b,h⟩, ⟨d,h⟩}

Construct the DRSs of the following sentences:

(i) James does not like Princess Caroline.

(ii) James does not like a woman who does not fascinate a gardener.

(iii) A man does not like Princess Caroline. He does not abhor a butler who fascinates her.

Determine, whether they are true in M.

1.5 From DRT to Predicate Logic

We have remarked already that the DRSs we have defined in Def. 1.4.1 can be seen as the expressions of a formally defined language, expressions which may be regarded as meaningful sentences on two separate grounds – on the one hand because they arise as "translations" of meaningful sentences and discourses of English, and thus must be seen as carrying the same meaning as those sentences and discourses from which they derive – on the other hand because of the independent account we have provided, through definitions Def. 1.4.3 to Def. 1.4.5, of the conditions under which DRSs are true.

In fact, in these as well as in certain other respects, the DRSs of Def. 1.4.1 have a close affinity with certain formulas of symbolic logic, more specifically of the so-called *lower* (also *first-order*) *predicate calculus*, the logical language which has formed the backbone of the disciplines of mathematical and philosophical logic ever since Frege first formulated it in the late 19th century.[15] The affinity is very close indeed, for as we will explain in this section, the DRS-language we have defined

[15] Compare the reference to Frege in Section 0.2.

is in truth nothing but a notational variant of standard predicate logic. In other words, each DRS can be regarded as a formula of predicate logic in disguise – a disguise, moreover, that neither is nor is intended to be a particularly effective one.

The most striking difference (but one that on closer analysis shows itself to be quite superficial) is that the formulas of predicate logic are, like the sentences of English, *linear*, i.e. are strings of symbols – something that DRSs, as we have defined them, are not. Here, when we say that DRSs are not linear, we do not think so much of the fact that the diagrams we have used to display them are two-dimensional structures enclosed in boxes, rather than lines of symbolism or prose. We ourselves find these diagrams comparatively easy to read and work with, but their two-dimensional character is no more relevant to the real structure of the DRSs than the font used in the published version of this manuscript is to the linguistic structure and identity of the English sentences it contains.

There is, however, also a more important sense in which DRSs are non-linear. For they are pairs of *sets*, a set of discourse referents and a set of conditions; and sets are unordered, i.e. they do not impose any order on the elements they contain. In fact, in this regard the diagrams we have been using display *more* linearity than there really is, in-so-far as they present both discourse referents and conditions in a certain order (from left to right in the first, and from top to bottom in the second case).

Since the formulas of predicate logic are linear, we must, when going from a DRS ⟨U,Con⟩ to a corresponding formula, impose a certain order on the sets U and Con – which particular order is not important. For, although the particular predicate logic formula which we get will depend on the chosen order, the different formulas which result from different orders of the given sets U and Con will always be equivalent in meaning.

There is one further point that needs to be made here before we start describing how the translation from DRSs to predicate logic is to go. It is this: as we have characterized DRSs in Def. 1.4.1 nothing prevents them from being infinite. In fact, for all Def. 1.4.1 says, the universe of a DRS and/or the set of its conditions might be infinite. Of course, all examples we have seen of DRSs were finite; and indeed, any DRS constructed from a given bit of discourse or text will be finite – unless the text or discourse itself were infinitely long, but that is an abstract possibility with which we need not be seriously concerned.

We might have excluded the possibility of infinite DRSs directly in Def. 1.4.1, by allowing in clause (a) only finite sets of discourse referents and conditions. But there is nevertheless a good logical reason for not imposing such a restriction once and for all. As Def. 1.4.1 stands, it characterizes what is in fact a very powerful formal language, much more powerful than the language of predicate logic we will define below. Nevertheless, it corresponds to a kind of logic that has been closely studied and has interesting properties. This is the system of *infinitary logic* usually denoted as $L_{\infty\infty}$. $L_{\infty\infty}$ has many interesting and well studied subsystems, whose expressive power lie somewhere between $L_{\infty\infty}$ itself and the much weaker system of (finite) first order logic. The equivalents of such systems can be obtained by imposing certain restrictions on U and Con, without insisting that both be finite. (A particularly important and well-understood system is the language which we obtain by requiring that U be always finite and that Con be at most denumerable.) There is no question of studying infinitary languages in this introductory text. However, as it appears to be the simpler definition of DRSs that yields the more powerful DRS-language, it seemed natural to us to give the definition of DRSs first in that form.

For the remainder of this volume we will restrict our attention to finite DRSs.[16] The concept of a *finite* DRS and the corrected notion of a *finite* DRS-condition must, strictly speaking, be defined *ab initio*, and by the same kind of simultaneous recursion that is found in Def. 1.4.1. In fact the new definition is just like Def. 1.4.1 except that, as indicated, we require the sets U and Con to be finite.

Definition 1.5.1

(i) If U is a finite set of discourse referents belonging to the set R and Con a finite set of finite DRS-conditions confined to V *and* R, then ⟨U,Con⟩ is a *finite DRS confined to* V and R.

(ii) A *finite DRS-condition confined to* V *and* R is an expression of one of the following forms:

(a) $\mathbf{x} = \mathbf{y}$, where $\mathbf{x}$, $\mathbf{y}$ belong to R

(b) $\pi(\mathbf{x})$, where $\mathbf{x}$ belongs to R and π is a name from V

(c) $\eta(\mathbf{x})$, where $\mathbf{x}$ belongs to R and η is a unary predicate from V

(d) $\mathbf{x}\zeta$, where $\mathbf{x}$ belongs to R and ζ is a unary predicate from V

(e) $\mathbf{x}\xi\mathbf{y}$, where $\mathbf{x}$, $\mathbf{y}$ belong to R and ξ is a binary predicate from V

(f) $\neg$K, where K is a finite DRS confined to V and R

Since only finite conditions and DRSs will be considered, we may drop the qualification 'finite' again. But it will always be implicitly understood.

Let us indicate the result of imposing a certain order on a given set X by placing an arrow above it: $\vec{\mathrm{X}}$. Thus $\vec{\mathrm{U}}$ is the result of imposing a certain order on the discourse referents in U, and similarly for $\overrightarrow{\mathrm{Con}}$.

The next step we must perform in turning a DRS into a corresponding formula is to form what we will call its *matrix*. The matrix of a DRS $\langle\vec{\mathrm{U}},\overrightarrow{\mathrm{Con}}\rangle$ (in which discourse referents and conditions have already been ordered) is a single expression

[16]We will make use of the possibility of having infinite sets U and Con, however, when we give the completeness proof for a DRS-calculus in Volume 2.

in which the conditions in $\vec{\text{Con}}$ follow each other in the chosen order. In principle we could do this by simply stringing the conditions together. But it is established and good logical practice to separate them by tokens of a so-called *conjunction* sign. Symbolic logic has used various symbols for this purpose, among them '∧', '&' and also the dot, '.'. We will use the ampersand, '&'. Moreover, we will, for reasons that will become clear presently, enclose the entire string of ampersands and conditions that represent a given ordered set $\vec{\text{Con}}$ within parentheses. Thus the matrix of the DRS (1.77) is (1.78).

(1.77)

(1.78) **(Mary(x) & dog(y) & x owns y)**

Similarly, in

(1.79)

x y
Mary(x) dog(y) x owns y ¬ [u z | u = x, cat(z), u owns z] K_1

the matrix of the embedded DRS K_1 is the formula

(1.80) **(u = x & cat(z) & u owns z)**

The next step is to combine the matrix m of a simple DRS with its (ordered) universe $\vec{U}$. Let us assume that $\vec{U}$ consists of the discourse referents $\mathbf{u}_1, \mathbf{u}_2, \ldots, \mathbf{u}_n$ in this order. The way in which this is done should convey the semantic role that is played by the discourse referents in the universe of a simple DRS. This role is revealed by the *existential* character of the truth definition. A DRS K is true in a model M, we have stipulated, if *there exists* a function f which maps the discourse referents in U_K to elements of U_M and verifies the conditions in Con_K. Given that U_K consists of the referents $u_1, ..., u_n$ this can be roughly rephrased as

(1.81) K is true in M iff there are corresponding to the members of $u_1, ..., u_n$ of U_K objects $a_1, ..., a_n$ in M such that the conditions in K are satisfied in M by the objects which correspond to the referents that these conditions contain as arguments.

We make the existential role of the discourse referents $u_1, ..., u_n$ explicit by means of the symbol '∃'. '∃' is just what it looks, i.e. an inverted 'E', and is called the *existential quantifier.* To get the predicate logic formula for the DRS K as a whole we place the quantifier '∃' in front of the sequence $u_1, ..., u_n$ of discourse referents of K and prefix the entire sequence to the matrix of K. (A string consisting of '∃' and a finite string of variables will be called a *quantifier prefix.*) Then the formula corresponding to (1.77) is

(1.82) $\exists xy(\mathbf{Mary(x)}\ \&\ \mathbf{dog(y)}\ \&\ \mathbf{x\ owns\ y})$

and that corresponding to the embedded DRS K_1 of (1.79) is

(1.83) $\exists uz(\mathbf{u = x}\ \&\ \mathbf{cat(z)}\ \&\ \mathbf{u\ owns\ z})$

(1.82) may be read informally as: "there are individuals x and y such that x is Mary, and y is a dog, and x owns y" – thus just as one might paraphrase the content of the DRS (1.77). Similarly, (1.83) may be read as "there are individuals u and z such that u is equal to x and z is a cat and u owns z". Note that this last sentence cannot be determined as true or false as long as it is not known what **x** stands for. Only when we integrate (1.83) into the predicate logic formulation of the entire DRS (1.79) – which we will show how to do below – will this question be settled. The indeterminate status of **x** in the formula (1.83) is a reflection of the fact that the subordinate DRS of (1.79) is not a proper DRS, in the sense of Def. 1.4.3.

We have now fully explained how simple DRSs should be translated into predicate logic, but not how we are to deal with complex DRSs. To obtain the translation of a complex DRS we work "from the inside out", first translating the smallest subordinate DRSs, e.g. those which are themselves simple, then those which only contain simple DRSs as subordinate DRSs and so forth. To carry this procedure through, however, we need a way of making explicit the role of negation. More precisely, we must decide how to obtain a translation for a condition of the form

$\neg$K from a translation for K. All that is needed here is a notational device which indicates the role that the translation of K plays within the formula translating the DRS which contains $\neg$K as a condition. What symbol we use for this purpose is, once more, strictly a matter of convention. Symbolic logic uses among others '$\neg$', '$\sim$' and a bar over the entire negated formula. We will use the hook '$\neg$', the same symbol we have already been using in connection with DRSs.

The translation, then, of a condition $\neg$K is the formula which is obtained by putting '$\neg$' in front of the translation of K. We can now get the translation of (1.79) as follows.

First, we must first obtain its matrix. There is a slight difference between the situation we must deal with here and the one we encountered when dealing with simple DRSs, such as (1.77) and the subordinate DRS of (1.79). For now we have besides simple conditions also a complex one. This one cannot be taken over simply as it is, but rather contributes to the matrix its translation. In other words, to form the matrix we must now string together the simple conditions of (1.79) and the translation

(1.84) $\neg\exists$uz(u = x & cat(z) & u owns z)

of the complex condition $\neg K_1$. We already got, in (1.83), the translation of the subordinate DRS K_1. So, combining this translation with the simple conditions of (1.79), we get the matrix:

(1.85) **(Mary(x) & dog(y) & x owns y &**
$\neg\exists$uz(u = x & cat(z) & u owns z))

To complete the translation of (1.79) we prefix the string '$\exists$xy' to (1.85), thus obtaining

(1.86) **$\exists$xy(Mary(x) & dog(y) & x owns y &**
$\neg\exists$uz(u = x & cat(z) & u owns z))

This completes the description of the procedure for translating DRSs into formulas of predicate logic. The predicate logic formulas that are produced by this translation procedure still deviate in some respects from what is nowadays considered standard. The differences are strictly cosmetic, but since they might obscure how DRS-notation relates to those forms of predicate logic used in most writings on logic, we may as well point them out here and now.

First, it is common in predicate logic to write the arguments of a predicate always behind the predicate; in some versions the arguments are enclosed in parentheses, as in, say, **cat(z)**, while in other versions the parentheses are left out, i.e.

one simply writes **cat z**. We choose here the first option, which means that we will write not only, as we have been doing already, **cat(z)**, but also, say, **rotates(u)** and **likes(x,y)**.

Secondly, proper names are normally treated in predicate logic as *terms* (or, in the terminology common within symbolic logic, *individual constants*). This means that they play roughly the same syntactic role within the formalism of predicate logic that noun phrases play in natural language. In particular, they can occur in the argument positions of predicates, but cannot themselves combine, in the way of predicates, with other expressions that can fill argument positions. Thus the proper name **Mary** becomes within predicate logic a symbol which can occur in such formulas as **stockbroker(Mary)**, **loves(y, Mary)** and **x = Mary**; but there won't be any such formulas as **Mary(x)**. The DRS-condition **Mary(x)**, which is now no longer admissible as a formula itself, must be translated as **x = Mary**. (Intuitively this latter formula says that **x** stands for the individual that is identical with the bearer of the name **Mary**, which is precisely what the DRS-condition **Mary(x)** means.)

Adopting these minor changes we get as translation of (1.79), not (1.86) but the slightly different:

(1.87) $\exists$**xy(x = Mary & dog(y) & owns(x,y) &**
$\neg\exists$**uz(u = x & cat(z) & owns(u,z)))**

The translation procedure we have given implicitly defines a class of predicate logic formulas – the class of all those formulas which can be obtained by applying the procedure to some DRS or other. It will be useful, however, to have an independent definition of the formulas of predicate logic, just as we have found it useful to have, in Def. 1.4.1, an independent definition of DRSs. Actually, the phrase 'the formulas of predicate logic' from the last sentence could be misleading. For there are many versions of first order predicate logic, even if these differ from each other only in inessential ways. The version we present now differs from another which we will present in Chapter 2. We will refer to the present version as PL_0.

As we did when defining the class of DRSs, we will give an inventory of the symbols from which these formulas are to be built before we define the class of formulas of PL_0. First, we must take over all the symbols that occur in simple DRS-conditons. For, as we saw, these conditions either remain unchanged, or they translate into formulas in which their symbols reoccur. In addition, we have the special symbols '$\exists$', '&' and '$\neg$'.

Definition 1.5.2

The *logical vocabulary* of PL_0 consists of the following symbols:

(i) *Variables*: **x, y, z, u, v, ..., x_1, x_2, x_3, ...**
(These are the same symbols that we have been calling *discourse referents* in the context of DRSs. They fulfill a roughly similar function within the formulas of predicate logic, but the name by which they go there is that of *variables.*[17])

(ii) *Logical constants*:

(a) the negation sign: $\neg$

(b) the conjunction sign: &

(c) the existential quantifier sign: $\exists$

(d) the identity sign: $=$

(iii) Parentheses: (,)

Besides the logical symbols, every non-degenerate language of predicate logic involves a collection of non-logical symbols. As before, these non-logical symbols come in a number of distinct categories. The following definition makes this explicit.

Definition 1.5.3

A *non-logical vocabulary* V of PL_0 consists of symbols of the following types:

(i) *Individual constants*: e.g. **Jones, Smith, Fred, Mary, Ulysses, Candide, ...**

(ii) *Predicates*:

(a) one-place predicates: e.g. **stockbroker, dog, eat, rotates, stinks, ...**

(b) two-place predicates: e.g. **loves, hates, uses, owns, ...**

We will refer to any set V consisting of such symbols as a *non-logical vocabulary* for PL_0. Each non-logical vocabulary V for PL_0 determines a *total* vocabulary V′ for PL_0, consisting of the symbols in V together with the logical vocabulary of PL_0, and this vocabulary V′ determines in its turn a particular class of formulas

[17] The roles played by discourse referents in DRT and by variables in predicate logic are not exactly the same, and it was to stress the differences that the new term discourse referent was introduced when DRT was first developed. In relation to the presentation of DRT given in this book, however, these differences are not particularly important; and if we have nonetheless stuck with the two-pronged terminology – 'variables' for predicate logic and 'discourse referents' for DRT – this has been only because each term has become firmly established in its own domain.

to which we will refer as the (formulas of the) language $PL_0(V)$. As with DRSs we will, for the time being, restrict our attention to non-logical vocabularies in which all predicates are either one-place or two-place.

The definition of the class of formulas of $PL_0(V)$ is, once again, a definition by recursion – though it is simpler than the corresponding definition for DRSs, as now we do not have to define two notions by simultaneous recursion (recall that the definition of the notion of a DRS required the simultaneous definition of that of a DRS-condition), but only one, viz. the notion of formula itself. The definition holds no surprises:

Definition 1.5.4

(a) If π is a one-place predicate and τ is either a variable or an individual constant, then $\pi(\tau)$ is a *formula of* PL_0.

(b) If π is a two-place predicate and each of σ and τ is either a variable or an individual constant, then $\pi(\sigma,\tau)$ is a *formula of* PL_0.

(c) If each of σ and τ is either a variable or an individual constant, then $\sigma = \tau$ is a *formula of* PL_0.

(d) If φ is a formula of PL_0, then $\neg\varphi$ is a *formula of* PL_0.

(e) If $\varphi_1, ..., \varphi_n$ is any finite collection of formulas of PL_0, then $(\varphi_1 \,\&\, \varphi_2 \,\&\, ... \,\&\, \varphi_n)$ is a *formula of* PL_0.

(f) If $\alpha_1, ..., \alpha_n$ is any finite collection of variables, and φ is a formula of PL_0, then $\exists\alpha_1\alpha_2...\alpha_n\varphi$ is a *formula of* PL_0.

We have already described the procedure for translating DRSs into PL_0-formulas, but it won't hurt to restate what we have said about this in the form of an exact definition. Again we must proceed by simultaneous recursion, defining at the same time what it is for a PL_0 formula to translate a DRS and what it is for a PL_0 formula to translate a DRS-condition.

Definition 1.5.5

(i) Let K be a DRS $\langle U, Con\rangle$ confined to V and R

(a) Suppose $U = \{\ \}$.
Then φ is *a translation of* the DRS K *into* PL_0 iff φ is of the form $(\varphi_1 \,\&\, \varphi_2 \,\&\, ... \,\&\, \varphi_n)$, where for $i = 1, ..., n$ φ_i is a translation of γ_i and $\langle\gamma_1, \gamma_2, ..., \gamma_n\rangle$ is some ordering of Con.

(b) Suppose $U = \{\alpha_1, ..., \alpha_n\}$
Then φ is *translation of* the DRS K *into* PL_0 iff φ is of the form $\exists\alpha_1 ... \alpha_n (\varphi_1 \,\&\, \varphi_2 \,\&\, ... \,\&\, \varphi_n)$, where $\varphi_1, ..., \varphi_n$ are as under (a) and $\langle\alpha_1, ..., \alpha_n\rangle$ is some ordering of U.

(ii) Suppose γ is a DRS-condition confined to V and R.

(a) Suppose γ has the form $\nu(\alpha)$, where α is a discourse referent in R and ν is a proper name in V, then φ is a *translation of γ into* PL_0 iff φ is the formula $\alpha = \nu$.

(b) Suppose γ has the form $\nu(\alpha)$, where α is a discourse referent in R and ν is a common noun in V, then φ is a *translation of γ into* PL_0 iff φ is the formula $\nu(\alpha)$.

(c) Suppose γ has the form $\nu\alpha$, where α is a discourse referent in R and ν is an intransitive verb in V, then φ is a *translation of γ into* PL_0 iff φ is the formula $\nu(\alpha)$.

(d) Suppose γ has the form $\alpha\nu\beta$, where α and β are discourse referents in R and ν is a transitive verb in V, then φ is a *translation of γ into* PL_0 iff φ is the formula $\nu(\alpha,\beta)$.

(e) Suppose γ has the form $\alpha = \beta$, where α and β are discourse referents in R, then φ is a *translation of γ into* PL_0 iff φ is the formula $\alpha = \beta$.

(f) Suppose γ has the form $\neg$K, where K is a DRS confined to V and R, then φ is a *translation of γ into* PL_0 iff φ is the formula $\neg\psi$, where ψ is a translation of K.

Using the translation relation between DRSs and formulas of PL_0 we can transfer the truth definition we have already given for DRSs (Def. 1.4.4, Def. 1.4.5, and Def. 1.4.7) to formulas: A PL_0-formula is true in a model M iff it is a translation of some DRS K which is true in M. As a truth definition for PL_0, however, this is not satisfactory, if only because many of its formulas do not qualify as translations of any DRS. It is therefore desirable to define the concept of truth for PL_0 separately.

We can proceed in much the same way as we did before. Here too, however, the terminology that has become standard in the course of the history of predicate logic is somewhat different from the one we have been using in relation to DRSs; and here too we will do well to adopt the standard terminology when speaking of predicate logic, while retaining the terms we introduced earlier when we dealt with DRT. The main terminological differences concern the functions which connect linguistic structures with models and the three-place relation between such functions, linguistic items and models which was the subject of Def. 1.4.4. In the context of predicate logic the functions are usually called *assignments* and the relation *satisfaction*. First we give an explicit definition of assignments.

Definition 1.5.6

Let M be a model for a vocabulary V. An *assignment in* M is a function f such that Dom(f) is a set of variables of PL_0 and Ran(f) $\subseteq U_M$.

Next, we define, preparatory to the definition of satisfaction, an auxiliary notion, that of a term (i.e. a variable or individual constant) τ *denoting, according to* an assignment f, an object *in* M.

Definition 1.5.7

Let M be a model for V. Let τ be either an individual constant in V or a variable, f an assignment in M, and a an element of U_M, then τ *denotes* a *in* M *according to* f iff either

(i) τ is an individual constant and $Name_M(\tau) = a$; or

(ii) τ is a variable, τ belongs to Dom(f) and $f(\tau) = a$.

The definition of satisfaction can now be stated as follows.

Definition 1.5.8

Let M be a model for V, φ a formula of $PL_0(V)$ and f an assignment.

(a) If φ is of the form $\pi(\tau)$, then f *satisfies* φ *in* M iff there is an element a in U_M such that τ denotes a in M according to f and a belongs to $Pred_M(\pi)$.

(b) If φ is of the form $\pi(\sigma,\tau)$, then f *satisfies* φ *in* M iff there are elements a and b in U_M such that σ denotes a and τ denotes b in M according to f and $\langle a,b \rangle$ belongs to $Pred_M(\pi)$.

(c) If φ is of the form $\sigma = \tau$, then f *satisfies* φ *in* M iff there is an element a in U_M such that σ and τ both denote a in M according to f.

(d) If φ is of the form $\neg\psi$, then f *satisfies* φ *in* M iff f does not satisfy ψ in M.

(e) If φ is of the form $(\varphi_1 \;\&\; \varphi_2 \;\&\; ... \;\&\; \varphi_n)$, then f *satisfies* φ *in* M iff f satisfies φ_i in M for $i = 1, ..., n$.

(f) If φ is of the form $\exists \alpha_1 \, \alpha_2 \, ... \, \alpha_n \, \psi$, then f *satisfies* φ *in* M iff there is an extension g of f such that $Dom(g) = Dom(f) \cup \{\alpha_1, \alpha_2, ..., \alpha_n\}$ and g satisfies ψ in M.

Again we want to define truth in terms of satisfaction. And we want to do this in much the same way as before (Def. 1.4.5), viz. by stipulating that a formula φ is true in M iff there is some assignment *with the right domain* which satisfies φ in M. But what is the right domain here? Note that there is one important difference between DRSs and the predicate logic formulas into which they translate. A DRS K has a universe, which more often than not is non-empty – this has been the case in particular for all the DRSs we have constructed so far. This universe determines the domain of the verifying embeddings which have to be considered in determining its truth. In contrast, a formula φ which translates K does not strictly speaking have anything that could qualify as a "universe". As is illustrated by (1.82) and (1.86), – and this can easily be shown to hold in general for the translations of proper DRSs – every variable which occurs anywhere in such a formula occurs somewehere in it as part of a quantifier prefix – i.e. of a sequence of variables following the symbol '$\exists$'. Whenever we encounter, in the process of evaluating whether an assignment f satisfies a formula, a subformula of φ beginning with a string $\exists\alpha_1, ..., \alpha_n$ we must consider extensions of f which include $\alpha_1, ..., \alpha_n$ in their domains. In this way each quantifier string extends the domain of the assignment functions at some stage along the path the evaluation takes. The assignment function with which we should start the evaluation should be one which doesn't contain anything in its domain at all – that function, in other words, which doesn't assign anything to anything. This is a kind of "dummy" function; but in the set-theoretic sense of 'function' we have adopted, according to which a function is a set of ordered pairs, it really *is* a function nonetheless, viz. the empty set (of ordered pairs). We will denote this function by 'Λ'.

For PL_0 formulas which are translations of proper DRSs, then, we may define truth in a model M by:

φ is true in M iff Λ satisfies φ in M

However, not all formulas of PL_0 have the property that the variables they contain invariably occur also in quantifier strings. This is not so, for instance, of the translations of improper DRSs. For if α is a discourse referent which occurs in the DRS K but is a member neither of U_K nor of the universe of any DRS subordinate to K, then α will occur as a variable in any translation φ of K but won't occur in any of its quantifier prefixes. Such variable occurrences which are not accompanied by any occurrence of α in strings of the form $\exists\alpha_1, ..., \alpha_n$, are called *free*. Evidently, this is essentially the same notion as that of a free discourse referent defined in Def. 1.4.2, and it should be clear how that definition can be recast to give us the notion of a variable of PL_0 being free in a PL_0 formula. But let us, to guard against all possible misunderstanding, state the new definition explicitly:

Definition 1.5.9

Let φ be a formula and γ a variable. Then γ *is free in* φ iff

(a) φ is of the form $\pi(\alpha)$ and α is the variable γ.

(b) φ is of the form $\pi(\alpha,\beta)$ and either α or β is the variable γ.

(c) φ is of the form $\alpha = \beta$ and either α or β is the variable γ.

(d) φ is of the form $\neg\psi$ and γ is free in ψ.

(e) φ is of the form $(\varphi_1$ & ... & $\varphi_n)$ and γ is free in at least one of $\varphi_1, ..., \varphi_n$.

(f) φ is of the form $\exists\alpha_1...\alpha_n\ \psi$, γ is free in ψ and γ does not occur among $\alpha_1, ..., \alpha_n$.

Variable occurrences that are not free are called *bound.* Moreover, we will speak of the particular quantifier prefix which puts an end to the freedom of a variable occurrence α as *binding* that occurrence. Thus if α is one of the variables occurring in the particular quantifier prefix $\exists\alpha_1...\alpha_n$ of the formula $\exists\alpha_1...\alpha_n\ \psi$, then this prefix $\exists\alpha_1...\alpha_n$ is said to *bind in* $\exists\alpha_1...\alpha_n\ \psi$ all the occurrences of α in ψ which are free in ψ; and, by the same token, the prefix is also said to bind those occurrences of ψ in any larger formula which contains $\exists\alpha_1...\alpha_n\ \psi$ as a subformula.

Now that we have defined the notion of α occurring free in φ we can restate our earlier observation about the translations of proper DRSs: in such formulas no variable is free. Such formulas are usually called *closed formulas*, or *sentences.*

Definition 1.5.10

A formula φ of PL_0 is *closed* (or is a *sentence*) if no variable is free in φ. Otherwise φ is called *open.*

The view that symbolic logic has traditionally taken of open formulas is that they are not the kinds of expressions that can be used to make statements. Consider for instance the formula

(1.88) $\quad \exists \mathbf{y}(\mathbf{y} = \mathbf{Mary}\ \&\ \mathbf{loves}(\mathbf{x},\mathbf{y}))$

As it stands, the argument goes, (1.88) doesn't express a proposition. For in order to determine what proposition is expressed, one would have to know what individual the variable **x** stands for. Only when this question has been settled can we regard (1.88) as making a definite claim, and only then does the issue of truth or falsity arise. A truth definition that accords with this perspective should not determine whether an open formula is true or false absolutely but only whether it is true or false *relative* to particular ways of fixing values for its free variables. This is precisely what is accomplished by an assignment whose domain consists of just those variables that are free. We are thus led to the following

Definition 1.5.11

Let φ be a formula of $PL_0(V)$ and let M be a model for V. Let U be the set of variables that are free in φ and let f be an assignment in M such that Dom(f) = U. Then φ is *true in* M *relative to* f iff f satisfies φ in M.

This definition implies that if φ is a closed formula, then φ is true iff it is satisfied by the empty function. So in this case the relativity of truth to particular assignments is only apparent: φ is true in M, *simpliciter*, iff φ is satisfied in M by the empty function 'Λ'.

Chapter 2

Quantification and Connectives

2.1 Conditionals

The discourses we have considered so far were all cumulative: each next sentence added new constraints to those imposed by its predecessors. This was reflected by the DRSs we have constructed for these discourses: The DRS for a discourse $\langle S_1, ..., S_n\rangle$ was constructed in stages, each stage K_i corresponding to the processing of one of the sentences S_i. At each of these stages the new DRS K_i represented more information than its predecessor K_{i-1}, and, consequently, was true in a smaller class of models. As yet another illustration of this, consider (2.1). The first sentence of (2.1) yields the DRS (2.2).

(2.1) Jones owns a book on semantics. He uses it.

(2.2)

x y
Jones(x)
book on semantics(y)
x owns y

Processing of the second sentence then transforms this into the DRS

(2.3)

x y u v
Jones(x)
x owns y
book on semantics(y)
u = x
v = y
u uses v

Evidently (2.3) is stronger than (2.2), as it adds a number of further constraints to those (2.2) already imposes. As a consequence, whenever f is an embedding verifying (2.3) in some model M, f will also verify (2.2) in M; while on the other hand there are f and M such that f verifies (2.2) in M but not (2.3).

The transition from (2.2) to (2.3) reflects what we might call the 'rhetorical structure' of the mini-discourse (2.1): the first sentence posits a certain quantity of information and the second sentence simply adds further information to this first quantity. This kind of rhetorical structure is common enough. But it is by no means the only one there is. A distinctly different structure is found in

(2.4) Suppose Jones owns a book on semantics. Then he uses it.

Here the first sentence does not assert a certain amount of information to which the second sentence then adds a little more. Rather, as the word **suppose** makes explicit, the first sentence conveys a certain *supposition* under which the information supplied by the next sentence is claimed to be correct. In fact, in contrast to the first sentence of (2.1), the first sentence of (2.4) does not by itself make any assertion. It is only the sentence pair (2.4) as a whole which makes a claim, a claim to the effect that if the information carried by the first sentence is correct then so is the additional information carried by the second.

This is an obvious difference between (2.1) and (2.4). But there are also striking similarities. In particular, the pronouns of the second sentences of (2.1) and (2.4) are in each of the two discourses interpreted with reference to the information that has already been extracted from the first sentence, and in fact each time the pronouns exploit that information in exactly the same way. These similarities are not surprising if we look upon what the discourse (2.4) accomplishes as follows: the first sentence of (2.4), we could say, is to describes a hypothetical situation; the second sentence *extends* the description of that situation; and the sentence *pair* asserts that if a situation is of the first kind it is also of the more fully specified second kind. If we put things this way we see that what (2.4) does with the two situation descriptions is different from what is done with them by (2.1). But the process of obtaining the fuller description from the sparser one is the same.

Although (2.4) consists of two separate sentences, it must be considered as making a single claim. How are we to represent this claim? First, it is clear that the representation must show that the two situation descriptions of which we have been speaking, i.e. (2.2) and (2.3), stand in the hypothetical relation which holds between them according to (2.4). We will indicate this by connecting them through an arrow, as in (2.5).

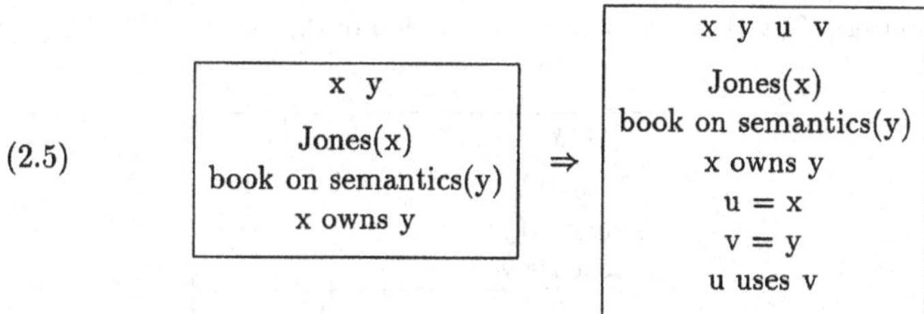

As it stands, however, (2.5) does not appear to be a DRS. DRSs, we said, are pairs consisting of a set of discourse referents and a set of conditions. But (2.5) does not seem to be of that form. Is there any natural way in which we can turn it into a DRS?

To see more clearly what is involved we must look at a larger discourse which contains (2.4) as a proper part. Consider (2.6).

(2.6) Jones teaches linguistics. Suppose he owns a book on semantics. Then he uses it.

The first sentence of (2.6) gives rise to a DRS in the familiar way. (We treat **linguistics** as the proper name of a certain scientific field, and treat scientific fields, like books and people, as individuals of our ontology.) This DRS is given in

(2.7)

x y

Jones(x)
linguistics(y)
x teaches y

The next two sentences add to the information captured in (2.7) the conditional claim we have represented as (2.5). The DRS which results from incorporating into (2.7) the information these two sentences add must combine our representation of that information, i.e. the structure (2.5), with what is already present in (2.7).

But how could the two be combined? Here we can rely upon what we learned in our study of negation. A negated sentence that is part of a larger discourse, we saw, contributes to the DRS of that discourse a complex condition of the form $\neg$K. It is in this same sense that we may understand the pair consisting of the second and the third sentence of (2.6) contributing a single complex condition of the form of (2.5) to the DRS of (2.6). More generally, hypothetically connected sentence pairs like (2.4) contribute to the DRSs of the discourses in which they occur conditions of the form $K_1 \Rightarrow K_2$, where K_1 is the DRS of the first sentence and K_2 the result of incorporating the second sentence into K_1. So in particular, the result of processing the last two sentences of (2.6) is the following extension of (2.7).

(2.8)

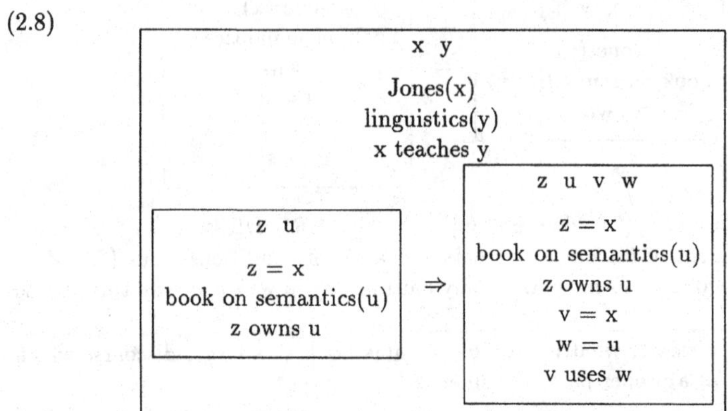

We will refer to complex conditions like the final one of (2.8) – thus to conditions of the form $K_1 \Rightarrow K_2$, where K_1 and K_2 are DRSs – as *implicative* conditions.

In those cases where the entire discourse involves a single conditional claim – as for instance in that of (2.4) – the resulting DRS consists of just the corresponding complex condition. Thus the DRS to which (2.4) gives rise is not the structure given in (2.5) but rather (2.9).[1]

(2.9)

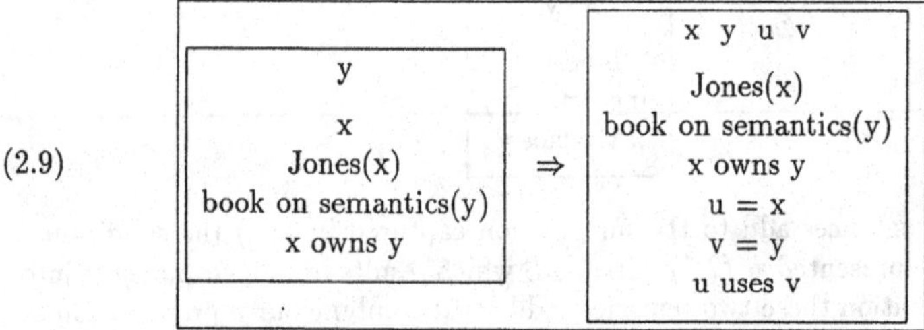

Conditional claims can be made by means of pairs of sentences the first of which begins with some such phrase as **suppose** or **assume**. But this is not the only possibility. In the first place – but this is only a minor variant of the form of hypothetical discourse we have just been discussing – the suppositional part and/or the hypothetically asserted one need not consist of a single sentence. For instance in

[1]In fact, we will find below that (2.9) isn't quite the right DRS for (2.4) either, since the discourse referent **x** that is introduced by the name **Jones** must be introduced into the universe of the outer DRS; but this need not worry us just yet.

(2.10) Suppose Jones owns a book on semantics. And suppose he likes it. Then he will use it. Moreover, he will recommend it to his friends.

the suppositional part and the hypothetically asserted part comprise two sentences each. In fact, since both the suppositional and the hypothetically asserted part may consist of one or of more sentences, it is often not easy to know exactly where these parts begin or end. With the suppositional part this tends to be less of a problem, for as a rule each of the sentences belonging to it is marked as such by a word like **suppose** or **assume**. But for the sentences which make up the hypothetically asserted part this is normally not so. Consequently no simple algorithm exists for deciding where the hypothetically asserted part ends and the text continues with assertions that are made categorically (i.e. not conditionally upon the assumption expressed be the suppositional part). For instance, consider the following text.

(2.11) Suppose Jones owns Formal Philosophy. Then he uses it. But he doesn't like it.

Is the last sentence part of the hypothetical assertion, or does it function as a separate, unconditional assertion? Probably the latter, for it would be odd if Jones's not liking the book were conditional on his owning it. But this is a consideration which among other things depends on the meanings of the individual verbs involved. A general mechanism for deciding where a hypothetically asserted part ends would have to be sensitive to such considerations. How such a mechanism should be formulated, and what range of factors it ought to take into account, are questions to which no satisfactory answers yet exist. (The general problem to which these questions are subordinate – that of how the language user perceives the logical and rhetorical structure of a discourse or text – is still poorly understood, and very far from being solved!) Since we cannot answer these questions in this book, we do better to side-step them. We will therefore ignore all hypothetical assertions of the **suppose ... . Then ...** variety, those which involve just two sentences as well as those which involve more.

This does not entail, however, that we disallow hypothetical claims altogether. For such claims can also be made by single sentences. For instance the information expressed in (2.4) can also be conveyed by the single sentence

(2.12) If Jones owns a book on semantics then he uses it.

Such sentences, in which a subordinate clause beginning with **if** combines with a main clause, (which, when it follows the **if**-clause may, though it need not, begin with the word **then**), are usually referred to as *conditional* sentences, or simply as *conditionals.* The suppositional part of a conditional sentence, i.e. its **if**-clause, is called the *antecedent* of the conditional and the hypothetically asserted part, i.e. the main clause, its *consequent.*

If ... then-sentences are not the only sentence forms that serve the purpose of making hypothetical claims. In English for instance we can also use sentences beginning with **provided, in case**, or **supposing** for this purpose and there are other possibilities besides. But we will confine ourselves to conditional sentences whose subordinate clauses begin with **if**, and, moreover, to those sentences in which the **if**-clause precedes the main clause. (Thus we include (2.12) but exclude **Jones will use a book on semantics if he owns it.**)

There is at present no complete agreement among syntacticians as to what the constituent structure of a sentence such as (2.12) should be. We adopt here an analysis according to which conditional sentences are formed by combining the distinctive particles **if** and **then** with two expressions which are in turn of the category S. Specifically, we adopt the phrase structure rule:

(PS 15) S $\rightarrow$ **if** S **then** S

which permits the derivation of (2.12) from the S-expressions **Jones owns a book on semantics** and **he uses it**. The rule (PS 15) triggers a construction rule which sets up the kind of complex condition exemplified by (2.5). More specifically, when applied to a conditional sentence of the form '**if** A **then** B' the rule introduces a DRS-condition of the form $K_1 \Rightarrow K_2$, where K_1 is a DRS corresponding to A and K_2 is the DRS resulting from extending K_1 through incorporation of B. This is still too loose a formulation to allow us to see how a sentence like (2.12) is to yield a completed DRS, however, and something more will have to be said. As we have indicated in our informal discussion of (2.4), the completed DRS for a hypothetical statement should involve the same processing rules (for proper names, indefinite descriptions, pronouns and so forth) which we have introduced to deal with non-hypothetical discourse. The conditional rule we have just described should as it were "prepare the ground" for these other rules. It should set up the implicative condition which will capture the hypothetical character of the represented statement, but in such a way that the components of that condition can be developed into completed DRSs using the construction rules we already have. Thus the new rule should, in the case of (2.12), leave behind a structure of some such form as (2.13).

(2.13)

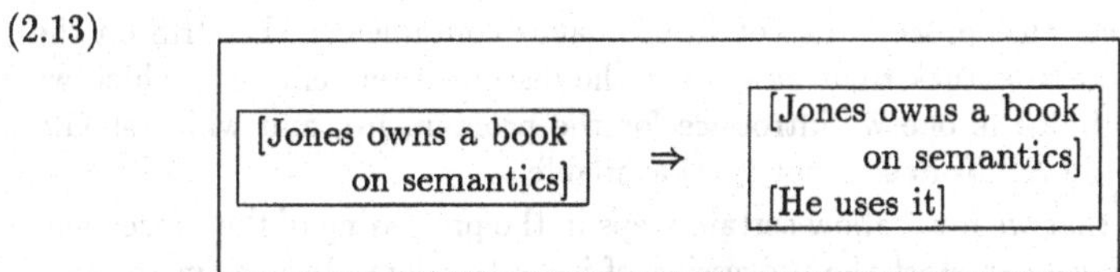

But how should the construction be completed? From the motivation we gave when we first introduced representations of this form[2] it would seem clear how the remainder of the construction is meant to proceed: it must first deal with [**Jones owns a book on semantics**] and then with [**he uses it**]. From this point of view the fact that [**Jones owns a book on semantics**] occurs twice, i.e. once on the left and once on the right, is misleading. Clearly (2.12) involves *one* antecedent, which needs to be interpreted only once. (We return to thus point below – see the discussion starting at page 149.) If the completion of (2.13) is to reflect this intuition it ought to proceed along the following lines: first the antecedent is processed as it occurs on the left, then the results of this process are copied on the right, and after that the right-hand DRS is completed by processing the consequent. In general, however, the construction procedure cannot proceed in a manner quite as simple as this. Consider for instance the following two sentences:

(2.14) If he likes it, then Jones owns Buddenbrooks.

(2.15) If he likes Buddenbrooks, then Jones owns it.

These sentences are perhaps not quite as natural as

(2.16) If Jones likes Buddenbrooks, then he owns it.

but they seem perfectly grammatical (on the interpretation which links **he** to **Jones** and **it** to **Buddenbrooks**). However, if we were to proceed according to the strategy sketched, we would not arrive at the right DRS. Consider for instance (2.14). Application of the rule for conditional sentences gives

(2.17)

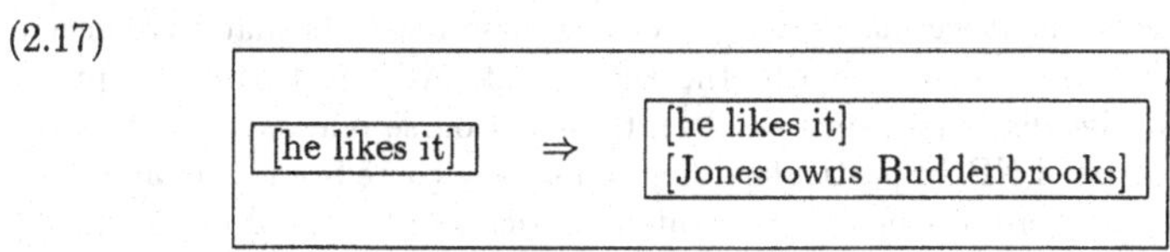

[2]Compare our comments on (2.5)!

At this point we must process the condition that is contained in the DRS on the left. But here we are stuck right away. For the discourse referent with which we would want to link the one we introduce for the pronoun **he**, and which should originate with the NP **Jones**, is not (yet) available.

This shows that we must allow certain steps in the processing of the consequent of (2.14) before we can start the processing of its antecedent. In fact, in the case of (2.14) the consequent must be processed *completely* before the processing of the antecedent can be brought to a conclusion, for we also need a discourse referent for the proper name **Buddenbrooks** before we can deal with the pronoun **it**. For (2.15) the situation is a little different. Here too we must start the processing of the consequent before we can do anything to the antecedent; but then we must carry on with the antecedent until we can deal with the pronoun **it** in the consequent to complete the DRS on the right-hand side.

From these observations it might appear that the interpretation of the antecedent may depend on that of the consequent in the same way as that of the consequent may depend on that of the antecedent. But that isn't really so. For, as we saw,

(2.12) If Jones owns a book on semantics, he uses it.

can be interpreted in a way which links **it** with **a book on semantics**. In contrast,

(2.18) If Jones owns it, he likes a book on semantics.

has no such interpretation. The data revealed by (2.12), (2.14), (2.15) and (2.18) fall into place, however, if we remind ourselves of the difference between proper names and indefinite descriptions which we noticed when dealing with negation.[3] Remember that we were led to the conclusion that the discourse referents introduced by proper names always go into the universe of the main DRS while those introduced by indefinite descriptions end up normally in the universe of the DRS which contains the condition to which the processing rule for indefinite descriptions is being applied. Remember also that our first gloss of hypothetical assertion was that the antecedent describes a hypothetical situation and the consequent can be interpreted as extending that description. This means in particular that in interpreting the consequent we may make use of discourse referents that have been introduced in the course of interpreting the antecedent. And, just as in the processing of cumulative discourses such as (2.1), these discourse referents could have arisen from any type of NP. In particular, they could have come from indefinite descriptions as well as from proper names. Sentences such as (2.14) and (2.15) show

[3]See Section 1.3, p. 104.

that the interpretation of the antecedent may depend to some extent on that of the consequent. But the phrase 'to some extent' is crucial here. For the difference between (2.14) and (2.15) on the one hand and (2.18) on the other indicates that when a discourse referent comes from an NP occurring in the consequent, then it is available for pronouns in the antecedent when the NP is a proper name, but not when it is an indefinite description.

Thus it appears that, just as we saw in our discussion of negation, it is the *relation* between the position of the pronoun which is in search of an anaphoric antecedent and that of the discourse referent which it selects that is the factor which decides whether the anaphoric link is possible or not, and not the question whether the discourse referent which is identified as anaphoric antecedent comes from an NP occurring in the antecedent of the conditional or from an NP occurring in its consequent. More precisely, the pronouns that occur in conditions of the left-hand DRS K_1 can be linked with discourse referents that belong either to the universe of K_1 or to that of the DRS K_0 which contains $K_1 \Rightarrow K_2$ as a condition; (or, in the general case, belong to the universe of any DRS to which K_0 is subordinate). They do *not* have access, however, to the discourse referents occurring in the universe of the right-hand DRS K_2 (unless, of course those discourse referents are part of the universe of K_1 as well). In contrast, the pronouns occurring in conditions of K_2 have access not only to discourse referents occurring in the universe of K_2, but also to those occurring in the universe of K_1 (as well as, of course, to all those belonging to the universe of K_0 and to those of any DRSs which contain K_0 as a subordinate part). As long as we observe these accessibility constraints we may allow the interpretation processes for antecedent and consequent to take place in either order, and even concurrently – something which we saw to be indispensible if the discourse referents that are needed as anaphoric antecedents are always to be available at the point where the pronouns for which they are needed must be processed.

There is a further problem with the construction procedure for hypothetical conditional sentences as we outlined it on page 147. As we put it there, the antecedent appears twice, once in the left-hand side subordinate DRS and once in the subordinate DRS on the right; since these two entries correspond to the same *occurrence* of the antecedent phrase in the processed sentence or text, they should be processed only once; otherwise we might end up with interpretations that are not available. Consider for instance

(2.19) Smith teaches linguistics. Jones teaches philosophy. If he owns a book on semantics, he uses it.

The first two sentences of (2.19) give rise to a DRS of the form (2.20).

(2.20)

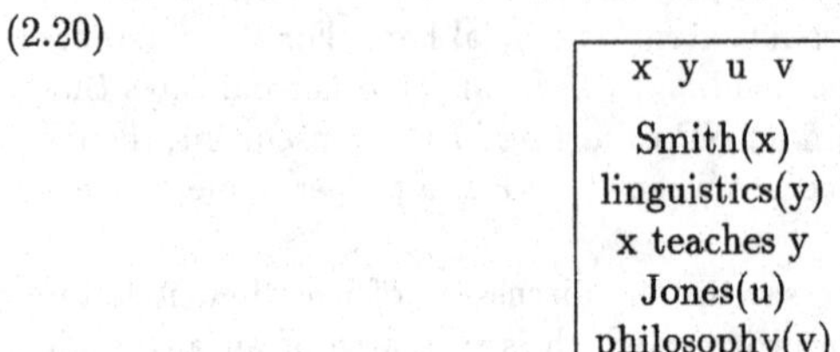

The first step in the interpretation of the third sentence transforms (2.20) into (2.21).

(2.21)

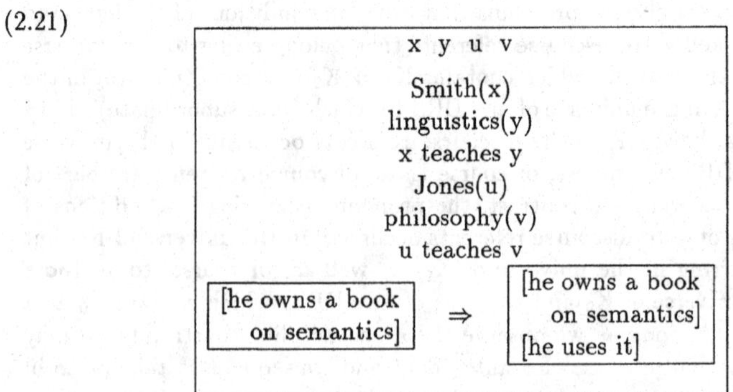

If we were to separately process the occurrences of [**he owns a book on semantics**] on the left and on the right, then nothing – at any rate nothing that has so far been said – would prevent us from deriving the following DRS:

(2.22)

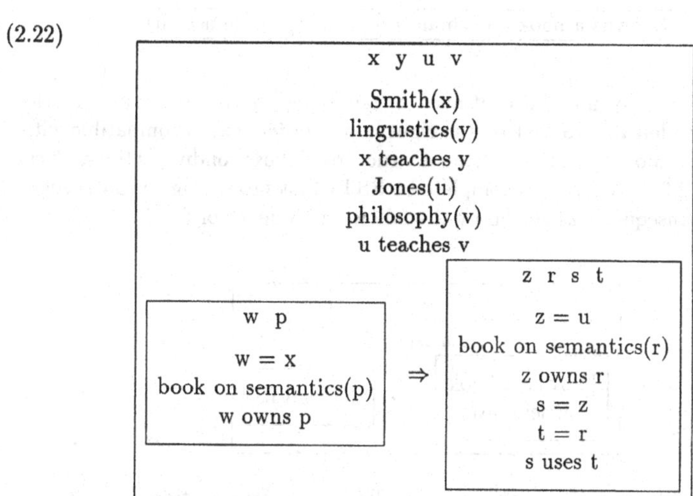

There are two things wrong with this interpretation. The most obvious error is that the pronoun **he** of the condition [**he owns a book on semantics**] is linked to **Smith** in the left-hand DRS and to **Jones** in the right-hand DRS. As a consequence the implicative condition of (2.22) entails that if Smith owns a book on semantics then so does Jones. It is clear that whatever reading (2.19) may have, it has no reading which carries this implication. The second error is that for the indefinite description **a book on semantics** two different discourse referents have been introduced, **p** on the left and **r** on the right. Why this is wrong is perhaps not so obvious in connection with (2.22) as it stands. But suppose we had not made the first error and had interpreted both the **he** of **he owns a book on semantics** on the left and the **he** of that same condition on the right as linked to **Smith**. Then the implicative condition, with **p** and **r**, would have said that if Smith owns a book on semantics then there also is a book on semantics (but possibly another) which he owns and, moreover, uses. This too is not right.

These problems demonstrate what has been intuitively clear all along – that interpreting a conditional sentence involves interpreting its antecedent one time only. The simplest way to ensure that the processing mechanism we are defining conforms to this is to enter the antecedent into the complex DRS-condition which represents the conditional claim in only one place. This is what we will do. We will enter the antecedent only into the left-hand DRS of the two of which this condition consists. Proceeding this way we obtain in particular, after performing the first step in the DRS-construction for (2.12)

(2.23)

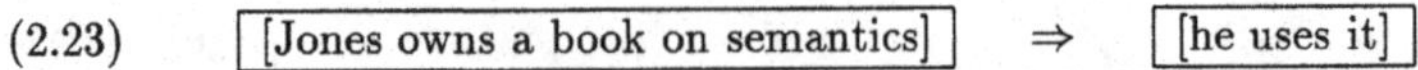

The construction may now be continued by applying construction rules to the condition on the left and to that on the right in any order that is compatible with the constraints imposed by the constituent structure of those conditions themselves. In the case of (2.23) we obtain a completed DRS by first processing the antecedent and then the consequent, as shown by the following sequence of DRSs:

(2.24)

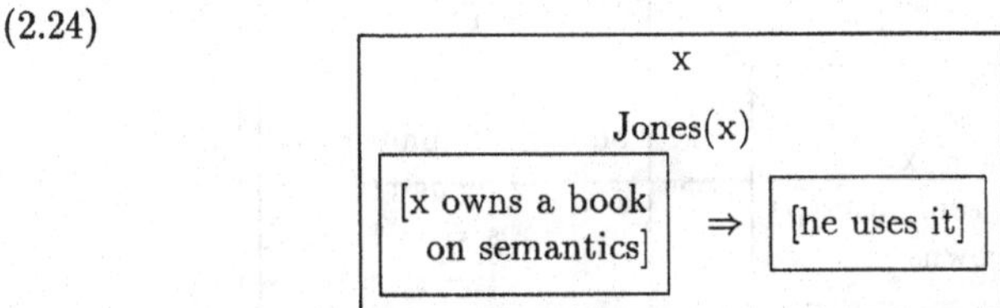

Note that contrary to what is shown in the preliminary representation (2.9) we gave earlier as for the hypothetical discourse (2.4), the discourse referent **x** for the proper name **Jones** and the accompanying condition **Jones(x)** have been entered into the universe and condition set of the main DRS, not in the universe and condition set of the left-hand DRS of the implicative condition.

(2.25)

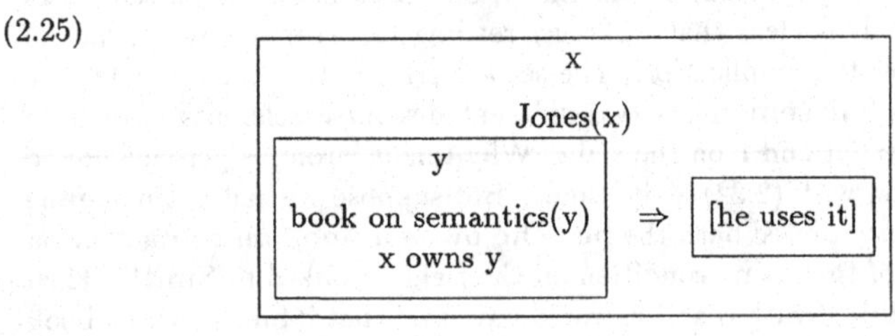

(2.26)

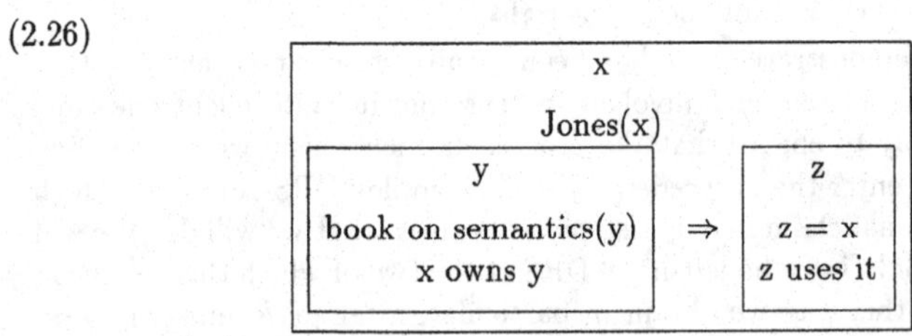

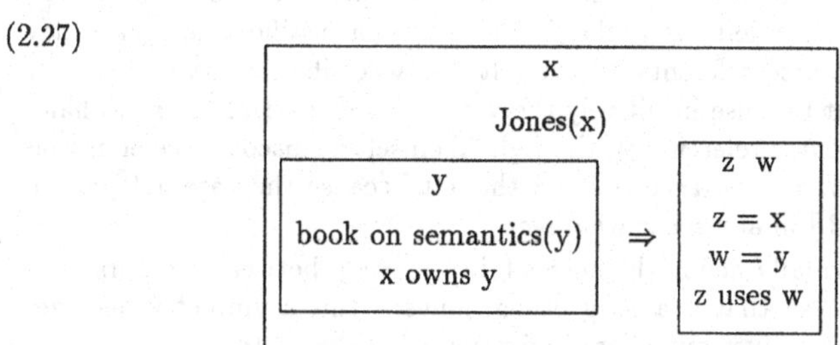

As we have already seen, in other cases a different order may be required. Thus to obtain the intuitively right DRS for (2.14), we have to deal first with the consequent. That is, from (2.28) we first move in two steps to (2.29) and then in two further steps to (2.30).

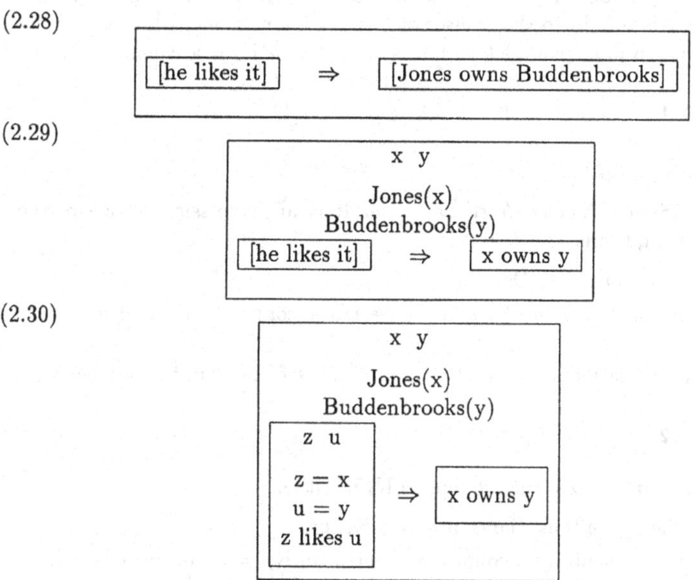

We must emphasize that representing conditionals by DRSs such as (2.27) and (2.30), in which the antecedent only occurs on the left, rather than by DRSs such as (2.5) where the antecedent occurs twice over, is a matter of convenience, not of substance. And it should be kept in mind that even though we adopt the mode of representation in which the antecedent occurs only on the left, the *intuition behind* this representional form is the one from which we started, according to which the right-hand side DRS provides a situational description which *extends* that given by the DRS on the left. It is this intuition which justifies the asymmetry in accessibility: discourse referents on the left are accessible as antecedents for pronouns on the right because intuitively they are as much part of the right-hand side DRS as the discourse referents on the right themselves; discourse referents on the right, in contrast, are not accessible on the left because they are not part of the left-hand side DRS in any sense whatever.

Before we can formally define the accessibility relation between discourse referents and pronouns, so that – among other things – this asymmetry becomes explicit, we must first adjust our characterization of DRSs to the demands that conditional sentences place upon them. The DRSs we have been constructing in this section contain conditions of the form $K_1 \Rightarrow K_2$, and we need a new definition of DRSs which takes this into account. Strictly speaking our task is twofold, for we have to adjust both the notion of a completed and that of a possibly uncompleted DRS. The first adjustment can be carried out formally. It is very simple. All that needs to be done is to add to the clauses of Def. 1.4.1 a new one, which stipulates that when K_1 and K_2 are (completed) DRSs, then $K_1 \Rightarrow K_2$ is a *condition*. Thus:

Definition 2.1.1

(i) as in Def. 1.4.1

(ii) a DRS-*condition confined to* V *and* R is an expression of one of the following forms

  (a) ... (f) are as in Def. 1.4.1

  (g) $K_1 \Rightarrow K_2$, where K_1 and K_2 are DRSs confined to V and R.[4]

The subordination relation is adjusted by extending Def. 1.4.10 in the obvious way.

Definition 2.1.2

(i) K_1 is *immediately subordinate* to K_2 iff either

  (a) Con_{K_2} contains the condition $\neg K_1$; or

  (b) Con_{K_2} contains a condition of the form $K_1 \Rightarrow K_3$ or one of the form $K_3 \Rightarrow K_1$ for some DRS K_3

(ii) K_1 is *subordinate* to K_2 iff either

  (a) K_1 is immediately subordinate to K_2; or

[4]The corresponding adjustment to the notion of a (possibly) uncompleted DRSs, should be obvious. A possibly uncompleted DRS may now contain conditions of the form $K_1 \Rightarrow K_2$ where K_1 and K_2 are again possibly uncompleted DRSs of the new kind.

(b) there is a K_3 such that K_3 is subordinate to K_2 and K_1 is immediately subordinate to K_3.[5]

(iii) K_1 is weakly subordinate to K_2 iff either $K_1 = K_2$ or K_1 is subordinate to K_2. As before, we write $K_1 \leq K_2$ for weak subordination.

The new notion of accessibility we need can now be defined in terms of the new subordination relation as follows:

Definition 2.1.3

Let (as in Def. 1.4.11) K be a DRS, x a discourse referent and γ a DRS-condition. We say that x is *accessible from* γ *in* K if x belongs to U_{K_1} where

(i) $K_1 \leq K$, and

(ii) for some K_2, γ occurs in Con_{K_2}, and either

(a) $K_2 \leq K_1$; or

(b) there is a DRS K_3 and a DRS $K_4 \leq K$ such that $K_1 \Rightarrow K_3$ is in Con_{K_4} and $K_2 \leq K_3$.

By way of illustration consider the DRS:

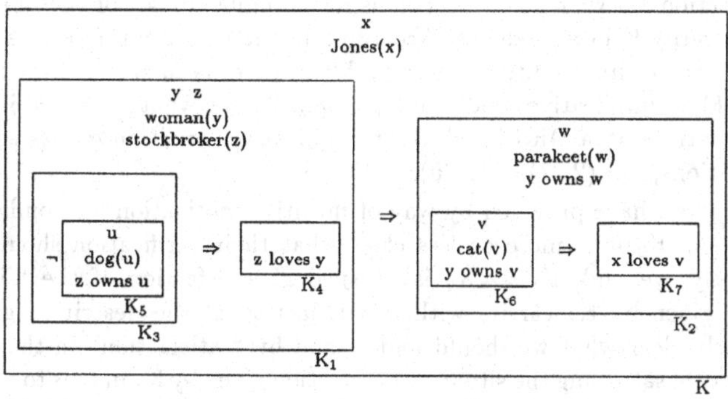

Here we have the immediate subordination relations:

$K_5 < K_3 < K_1 < K$, $K_4 < K_1 < K$, $K_6 < K_2 < K$, $K_7 < K_2 < K$

(where we have used '<' to indicate immediate subordination)

[5]Note that part (ii) is identical with the second part of Def. 1.4.10!

Furthermore, the discourse referents **z**, **y** and **x** are accessible to the condition **z loves y** in Con_{K_4}, but not the referents **u**, **w** and **v**. Similarly, **x**, **y**, **w**, **z** and **v** are accessible to the condition **x loves v** in Con_{K_7}, but **u** isn't.

As we have seen, DRS construction for conditionals requires only one new construction rule, which sets up the implicative condition. We call this rule CR.COND and state it as follows.

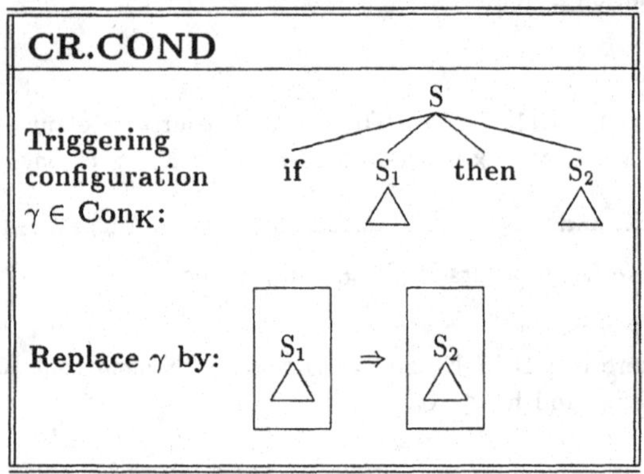

Next, we must define the verification and truth definitions for the new (completed) DRSs. In Section 1.5 we defined what it is for an embedding f of the universe of a DRS K to verify K in a model M. According to the definition, f verifies K in M iff it verifies each of its conditions. Our problem, then, is to state what it is for f to verifiy in M an implicative condition $K_1 \Rightarrow K_2$. To see what is needed it will be best to concentrate on a DRS in which an implicative condition occurs as one of several conditions, e.g. (2.27) or (2.30).

From what we have provided by way of intuitive motivation for conditions of the form $K_1 \Rightarrow K_2$ it is more or less clear what their verification should come to. Intuitively, we said, $K_1 \Rightarrow K_2$ is satisfied iff satisfaction of the "situation description" given by K_1 carries with it satisfaction of the descrition given by K_2. It is fairly clear what we should understand by "satisfaction" in the present context: a way of satisfying the situation description given by K_1 in M is to associate elements of M with the discourse referents of the DRS K_1 so that the conditions of K_1 are satisfied in M; and similarly of course for K_2. Thus the natural way of understanding satisfaction of the implicative condition $K_1 \Rightarrow K_2$ as a whole is that any assignment g of elements to the discourse referents of K_1 which verifies the conditions of K_1 yields satisfaction in M of K_2.

A complication here is that K_2 may contain new discourse referents, so that satisfaction of K_2 must involve, besides the assignments already made to the discourse referents of K_1, also assignments to these additional referents. Thus, in the general case we must interpret the phrase "the assignment g yields satisfaction of the DRS K_2" as "g can be extended to an assignment h which also takes into account the new discourse referents of K_2 such that h verifies (the conditions of) K_2".

There is still a further point which we must take into account. Our problem is to define what it is for the given assignment f (of elements of M to the discourse referents of the DRS containing $K_1 \Rightarrow K_2$ among its conditions) to verify $K_1 \Rightarrow K_2$. So, inasmuch as it makes sense to talk about "satisfaction" of $K_1 \Rightarrow K_2$ in M in this context, we must keep in mind that we are talking about "satisfaction *relative* to the given assignment f". What this relativity amounts to should be clear after what we went through in dealing with negation: some of the discourse referents which may occur in the conditions of K_1 and K_2 have already been assigned elements of M by f; and these assignments should remain fixed when we consider the possible "satisfactions" of K_2. In other words, the extension g of which we were speaking must be an extension of f, one which associates elements with those discourse referents of K_1 which are not in the larger DRS, but which retains the assignments already established by f.

Combining these various considerations we arrive at the following condition:

(2.31) f *verifies* $K_1 \Rightarrow K_2$ *in* M iff for every extension g of f such that $\text{Dom}(g) = \text{Dom}(f) \cup U_{K_1}$ which verifies K_1 in M there is an extension h of g such that $\text{Dom}(h) = \text{Dom}(g) \cup U_{K_2}$ and h verifies K_2 in M.

To get our revised definitions of DRS verification and truth, (2.31) must be integrated into Def. 1.4.4. This is straightforward. Relying on Def. 1.4.4 we can state the new definition as follows:

Definition 2.1.4

Let K, γ, and M be as in Def. 1.4.4 and f an embedding from K into M

(i) as in Def. 1.4.4

(ii) f *verifies* the condition γ *in* M iff

(a) ... (f) are as in Def. 1.4.4

(g) γ is of the form $K_1 \Rightarrow K_2$ and for every extension g of f such that $\text{Dom}(g) = \text{Dom}(f) \cup U_{K_1}$ which verifies K_1 in M there is an extension h of g such that $\text{Dom}(h) = \text{Dom}(g) \cup U_{K_2}$ and h verifies K_2 in M.

Having adopted this definition of what it is for a function to verify a DRS, we can now take over the truth definition, Def. 1.4.5, exactly as it stands: the proper DRS K is true in the model M iff there is an embedding f of U_K in M which verifies K in M. The same goes for the definitions of logical consequence and logical truth.

2.1.0.1 Material Interpretation of Conditionals

These are the definitions of verification and truth which we will adopt. It is however not quite as clear as the preceding discussion may have suggested that they capture the meaning of conditional statements correctly. The problem is most easily seen in connection with conditionals in which there is no anaphoric connection between antecedent and consequent. Consider for instance the sentence

(2.32) If Jones owns a Porsche then Smith owns a Ferrari.

Constructing the DRS for (2.32) in the now familiar way we get

(2.33)

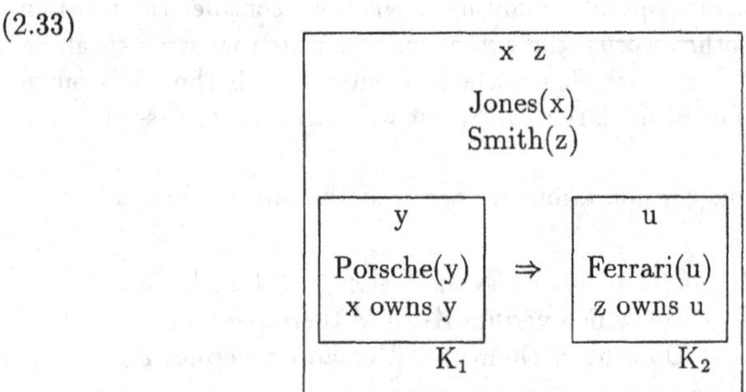

The problem is this. According to (2.31), a function f which maps **x** onto the bearer of the name **Jones** in M and **z** onto the bearer of the name **Smith** verifies the implicative condition of (2.32) iff

(2.34) every extension g of f such that $Dom(g) = Dom(f) \cup U_{K_1}$ and g verifies K_1 has an extension h such that $Dom(h) = Dom(g) \cup U_{K_2}$ and h verifies K_2.

Let us see what this amounts to in the case of (2.33). We have that $U_{K_1} = \{y\}$ and $U_{K_2} = \{u\}$. Furthermore, the discourse referent **y** *only* occurs in K_1 – just as **u** occurs only in K_2. Thus for the question whether a function h, which assigns elements of M to **x**, **y**, **z** and **u**, verifies K_2 it is immaterial what it assigns to **y** (it is also immaterial what it assigns to **x**, but this is irrelevant to the argument). In fact, h will verify K_2 iff K_2 is verified by the more restrictive assignment h′, which assigns the same elements as h to **x**, **z** and **u** but leaves **y** out. Thus, in relation to (2.33), (2.34) is equivalent to the statement that

(2.35) for every extension g of f which assigns an element of M to **y** and verifies K_1 there is an extension h′ of f which assigns an element of M to **u** and verifies K_2.

It is easy to see that because h′ does not in any way depend on g, this last condition is equivalent to the statement

(2.36) either there is no extension g of f which (assigns an element to **y** and) verifies K_1 in M or there is an extension h′ of f which (assigns an element to **u** and) verifies K_2 in M.

Recalling the connection between verification and truth we can rephrase (2.36) in less technical terms as

(2.37) either the antecedent of (2.32), **Jones owns a Porsche**, is false (in M) or the consequent, **Smith owns a Ferrari**, is true (in M).

It follows that, still according to (2.31), (2.33) and the sentence (2.32) from which it derives, are true (in a model M) if either the antecedent of (2.32) is false or else its consequent is true. Evidently this conclusion follows whenever there are no anaphoric ties between the consequent of the conditional and its antecedent, i.e. when the discourse referents of U_{K_1} do not occur in the conditions of U_{K_2}.

A conditional which obeys such truth conditions, according to which it is equivalent to the *disjunction* of its consequent and the negation of its antecedent is known as a *material conditional.* But, it has often been claimed, the conditionals one finds in natural language, among them in particular those which get expressed with the help of **if** and **then**, are in general not material conditionals. (2.32), for instance, would not normally be understood as synonymous with

(2.38) Either Jones does not own a Porsche or Smith owns a Ferrari.

Rather, it would be thought to convey that Smith's owning a Ferrari *depends* in some way on Jones's owning a Porsche. This dependence would not be captured by the factual claim (2.38), for it would also have implications for various situations other than the one which actually obtains: it would imply that in each of those possible situations in which Jones owns a Porsche it is also the case that Smith owns a Ferrari.

The dispute whether material conditionals can be used to represent the conditionals of natural language is almost as old as formal logic itself and goes back to antiquity.[6] Many of the traditional arguments against the material conditional do not stand up to scrutiny. In fact, part of what leads to the feeling that the conditionals of natural language are in general not material conditionals seems to derive from a one-sided perspective on truth and information generally, a perspective which does not clearly distinguish between the *information* which a sentence or discourse provides and the question whether what it says is *true* or *false*. In the theory of truth and interpretation we are adopting in this book these two aspects of the concept of meaning are more clearly separated, and the temptation to accept the faulty argument we will present below is correspondingly smaller.

As should have become clear by now, the DRSs which the present theory associates with sentences, discourses or texts play a double role. On the one hand they serve to identify the truth conditions of the bits of language from which they derive. On the other they capture, in an appropriately idealized way, the information which the recipient obtains when he processes the words that reach him, and thereby grasps the content they carry. There is an important sense in which this information that the recipient grasps is nothing but the truth conditions of the sentence or sentences he has processed. For having that information is tantamount to expecting the world to be in accordance with it, i.e. to expect it to be one of those possible worlds for which the obtained information is correct. And the class of these possible worlds is, as we noted above, the natural reflection of the truth conditions of the sentence or discourse from which the information has been extracted. When the words from which the given information derives take the form of a conditional sentence (which is moreover free of anaphoric links between the two parts), this class consists of all possible worlds in which either the antecedent of the conditional fails or the consequent holds. It is natural enough to think of this information as telling the recipient something not only about the world as it actually is (and may reveal itself in more detail to him subsequently), but also about any of the other worlds that are compatible with what further information he possesses. In *each* of these worlds the truth of the antecedent carries with it that of the consequent.

It is only a small step from this correct observation to the unwarranted conclusion that the information which a conditional sentence conveys is about worlds other than the actual one. In particular, it is tempting, but cannot be right to conclude just from this that a statement of the verification conditions of (the DRSs representing) conditional sentences must refer to worlds or models other than the one in which the conditional is being evaluated. For, as we just saw, in the very

[6]The issue was extensively and at times emotionally disputed in particular by the 'Megarian School', a school of logicians from the Greek city of Megara in the late 5th to the early 3rd century BC. ([Kneale/Kneale 1962])

same sense in which conditional sentences appear to tell us something about more worlds than the one which is in fact real, the sentence **Mary owns a dog** might be said to tell us something about more than one world too – for it might be said to tell us that among all the worlds compatible with what other information we possess only those could be actual in which Mary owns a dog. Yet no-one has ever claimed this as a reason why the truth or falsity of **Mary owns a dog** in a world w should be seen as depending on what is the case in worlds other than w. If this is right – as it surely must be – it cannot be equally right to conclude from the very same consideration that conditional sentences depend for their truth at w on what is the case at other worlds.

While these reasons for thinking conditional sentences do not have the meaning of material conditionals are clearly inadequate, there are others which carry more weight. The most persuasive arguments of which we are aware involve complex sentences which contain conditional sentences as proper parts. Consider for instance the case of an engine which, for reasons of safety, will run if both the main switch and the auxiliary switch are up, but not if only one of them is. In such a situation it seems correct to say:

(2.39) If the main switch is up and the auxiliary switch is up then the engine is running.

But the statement

(2.40) Either the engine is running if the main switch is up or the engine is running if the auxiliary switch is up.

seems quite absurd in these circumstances. Yet it can be shown without too much difficulty that if each of the conditionals is true if either its antecedent is false or its conclusion true, then the truth of (2.40) is entailed by that of (2.39). Since the inference is untenable, the material interpretation of the conditionals involved, which appears to licence that inference, cannot be correct.[7]

Examples such as these indicate that the "material" interpretation of conditional statements to which our analysis reduces in the absence of anaphoric links between antecedent and consequent, cannot be the final word about the meaning of such sentences. And they provide part of the justification for the voluminous amount of literature – much of it from the past two decades – which develops various alternative accounts of the meaning of conditional sentences. Nevertheless, the material interpretation of the conditional, on which these proposals try to improve, is, for the reasons we have touched upon, much less inadequate than the authors of many of these studies seem to think. Moreover, the material conditional is an

[7] See [Veltman 1985].

ingredient of the standard system of symbolic logic, viz the classical predicate calculus, which it is one of the aims of this book to present and develop. Also it is much simpler than any of those alternative proposals. For all these reasons we will stick with it here.[8]

Exercises

1. Construct DRSs for the following discourses.

   (a) Fred likes Mary. If she likes a book then he likes it.

   (b) Fred doesn't like Mary. If she likes a book then he doesn't like it.

   (c) If Mary likes a man then he likes Fred.

2. Decide for each of the DRSs of excercise (1) if they are true in the following models M_1, M_2 and M_3.

   M_1 is defined by:
   $U_{M_1} = \{a, b, c, d, e, f\}$;
   $Name_{M_1} = \{\langle \text{Mary}, a\rangle, \langle \text{Fred}, f\rangle\}$;
   $Pred_{M_1}(\text{man}) = \{d, e, f\}$;
   $Pred_{M_1}(\text{book}) = \{b\}$;
   $Pred_{M_1}(\text{likes}) = \{\langle a,a\rangle, \langle a,b\rangle, \langle b,b\rangle, \langle a,d\rangle, \langle d,b\rangle, \langle a,e\rangle, \langle e,f\rangle\}$.

   M_2 is defined by:
   $U_{M_2} = \{a, b, c, d, e, f\}$;
   $Name_{M_2} = \{\langle \text{Mary}, a\rangle, \langle \text{Fred}, f\rangle\}$;
   $Pred_{M_2}(\text{man}) = \{d, e, f\}$;
   $Pred_{M_2}(\text{book}) = \{b, c\}$;
   $Pred_{M_2}(\text{likes}) =$
   $\{\langle a,a\rangle, \langle a,b\rangle, \langle a,c\rangle, \langle a,e\rangle, \langle b,b\rangle, \langle d,b\rangle, \langle e,f\rangle, \langle f,a\rangle, \langle f,b\rangle, \langle f,d\rangle, \langle f,e\rangle, \langle f,f\rangle\}$.

   M_3 is defined by:
   $U_{M_3} = \{a, b, c, d, e, f\}$;
   $Name_{M_3} = \{\langle \text{Mary}, a\rangle, \langle \text{Fred}, f\rangle\}$;
   $Pred_{M_3}(\text{man}) = \{d, e, f\}$;
   $Pred_{M_3}(\text{book}) = \{b, c\}$;
   $Pred_{M_3}(\text{likes}) = \{\langle a,a\rangle, \langle a,b\rangle, \langle a,c\rangle, \langle b,b\rangle, \langle d,b\rangle, \langle a,e\rangle, \langle a,f\rangle, \langle e,f\rangle, \langle f,a\rangle,$
   $\langle f,b\rangle, \langle f,c\rangle, \langle f,d\rangle, \langle f,f\rangle\}$.

[8]The reader who wants to learn about alternative treatments may consult the works of [Lewis/Langford 1932], [Stalnaker 1968], [Adams 1970], [Lewis 1973], [Pollock 1976], [Veltman 1985].

3. The following examples seem to be possible under the interpretations indicated by the coindexations. According to our theory the anaphoric links are excluded, however. Show that this is indeed the case. (Treat **has bought**, **has read**, and **need to park** as transitive verbs.)

   (a) If Fred owns a dog which Susan owns, then he feeds it. If Fred doesn't own $[$a dog which Susan owns$]_1$, then he doesn't feed it$_1$.

   (b) Fred doesn't like $[$a book which Susan has bought$]_1$. He has read it$_1$.

   (c) If Fred doesn't own $[$a car$]_1$, then he doesn't need to park it$_1$.

   How could we possibly explain these phenomena and integrate the explanations into our theory?

4. (a) According to most speakers

   (1) If she supports Bill, he admires Suzie.

   can be understood so that **she** is anaphoric to **Suzie** and **him** to **Bill**. (Though not everybody accepts the sentence with this reading and nobody seems to like it very much.) As it stands, our construction algorithm is not able to assign this reading to (1). Why?

   (b) One way in which the algorithm may be altered so that it can represent (1) as having the reading in question is to allow object NPs to be treated before subject NPs.

   Question: Why does this help? Construct a DRS for (1) using this altered mechanism!

Allowing object NPs to be processed before subject NPs, however, would be allowing far too much, unless we impose some restrictions. At this point we can only hint at the problems which an unrestricted version of the object-before-subject option would create. (We return to this issue at some length in 3.7, where we will in fact argue towards a restricted form of this option, although we will still be lacking the means for developing it fully.) Here we can only give a hint of what is wrong with the unrestricted version. One of the undesirable effects it would have is that a sentence such as

(2) He courts a girl who loathes a stockbroker.

could, if the option were freely available, be converted into a DRS which would assign it the meaning of

(3) A stockbroker courts a girl who loathes him.

(**Task:** Show this!)

Evidently (2) does not have this meaning. So if the object-before-subject option is adopted, some constraint must be introduced which blocks the derivation of the DRS.

One possible restriction on the liberalization we first proposed would be to allow early processing of object NPs in those cases where they are proper names (or other NP types that are used to designate particular objects, like e.g. *definite descriptions* i.e. complex noun phrases beginning with **the** such as **the King of Denmark, the church in the town square of Waiblingen, the smallest perfect number**, etc. For a brief discussion of these see Section 3.4).

Lest such a move seems very much ad hoc, we should point out that it corresponds to the following intuition. The recipient of an utterance has in general knowledge of a great many individuals, and of many more than those that have been mentioned within the particular discourse D of which the utterance is part. In our terms: his background knowledge will contain many more discourse referents than those which were introduced in the course of processing D. In general, however, these discourse referents are not readily available as antecedents: in order for them to become available they must be rendered *salient*; they must, in some suitable sense, be brought into the recipient's field of attention.

One way to do this is to explicitely refer to the individual that such a discourse referent represents. However, since the discourse referent is already present in some non-salient way, it should be possible for such a reference to mediate the identification of the intended antecedent even if it becomes available to the recipient shortly after the pronoun which is meant as anaphoric to it.

If this is indeed correct, then we should expect that those NPs which are typically used to refer to things that are presumed to be already in some way familiar, can serve as antecedents also to pronouns which precede them. Thus proper names and all definite descriptions, which are typically used to remind of entities that are already familiar, can serve as antecedents in cases of *kataphora*, (i.e. cases where the pronoun precedes its antecedent) while NPs beginning with **every** or **a** cannot.

If this is the intuitively correct explanation of kataphora involving proper names, our proposal for early processing of proper names would not appear to be quite right, even if it produces the desired results for the examples we have looked at here. A more truthful account would, rather, allow for certain delays in the determination of a pronoun's antecedent, provided the antecedent can, once it is identified, be seen to have been available in principle already at the point where the pronoun came up for interpretation. Formally such an account would involve, at the very least, a distinction between two categories of discourse referents, those that are "currently active" from the point of anaphora and those that are not. Processing of a pronoun could then take the following form just as in our earlier formulation of the rule: a new discourse referent **x** is introduced for the pronoun, and the processed condition is replaced by the result γ' of substituting **x** for the pronoun in γ. Moreover, either a condition of the form $\mathbf{x} = \mathbf{y}$ is added, where **y** is an (accessible) active discourse referent, or else a "promissary note" for such a condition is given, which must then be reduced subsequently by an actual equation $\mathbf{x} = \mathbf{y}$ where **y** is a discourse referent that (i) is active at that point, and (ii) already belonged to the set of inactive discourse referents at the point where the pronoun was processed. However, to make a construction algorithm which incorporates this "promissory note" device formally explicit requires a considerable machinery, which we will not develop here.

Moreover, the proposal raises a number of further questions. For instance, when we study kataphora more closely we find that the 'reminding' NP must follow the pronoun fairly shortly. But how shortly? Another, more general problem with a sentence such as (1) is that it is (on its intended reading) neither perfect nor wholly bad. For such in-between cases there is, in a theory like the one of this book, which is set up to make only bivalent distinctions between what is possible and what is impossible, no proper place.[9]

Task: Restate the construction algorithm so that it permits processing of object before subject when the object is a proper name, and use the revised algorithm to construct a DRS for (1).

5. The following sentences seem to have the indicated interpretations. According to our theory the anaphoric links are excluded, however. Show that this is so.

   (a) If [a student]$_2$ owns [a book by Goethe]$_1$, then he$_2$ likes it$_1$.

   (b) If Jones$_1$ owns it$_2$, then he$_1$ likes Faust$_2$.

   (c) If Jones$_1$ owns it$_2$, then he$_1$ likes [a book by Goethe]$_2$.

   (d) If he$_1$ knows him$_2$, then John reads Goethe$_2$.

   (e) If he$_1$ knows Faust$_2$, then it$_2$ fascinates Jones$_1$.

6. Does our fragment of English generate a sentence that gets transformed into the DRS K on page 155?

[9]See on this point a similar, and slightly more extensive remark at the end of Section 2.4, p. 226, as well as remarks scuttered throughout Section 4.4.

2.2 Universal Quantification

There exists an intimate connection between conditionals and the words **every**, **all** and **each**. We get a glimpse of this connection when we compare, say

(2.41) If a farmer owns a Mercedes he thrives.

and

(2.42) Every farmer who owns a Mercedes thrives.

Although these sentences may not have exactly the same meaning, their meanings are certainly very close. In particular, each provides the information on the basis of which we can, whenever we encounter an individual whom we recognize to be a farmer and in a possession of a Mercedes, infer that that individual thrives.

This is as correct an assessment of (2.42) as it is of (2.41), and it is an assessment that can be generalized to all instances of the word **every**: the contribution which is made by a noun phrase of the form **every** α to the clause in which it occurs is that whatever satisfies the condition expressed by α also satisfies the predicate expressed by that of the clause which remains after we extract the noun phrase. This informal description of what **every**-phrases contribute to the clauses of which they are part contains a clear suggestion of the rule by means of which such NPs should be handled in the process of DRS-construction. The rule ought to yield the introduction of a conditional structure in which the suppositional part contains the condition of satisfying α and the conditionally asserted part that of satisfying the predicate identified by the remainder of the clause. More precisely, the first part should contain the information that some arbitrary individual **x** satisfies α and the second part the information that **x** satisfies the other predicate. In the case of (2.42) this leads to a DRS with a single implicative condition:

(2.43)

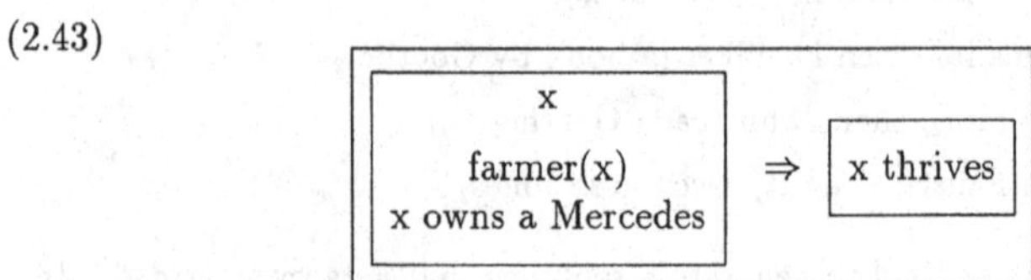

To complete (2.43) we need to perform another construction step on the condition **x owns a Mercedes**, after which we get

(2.44)

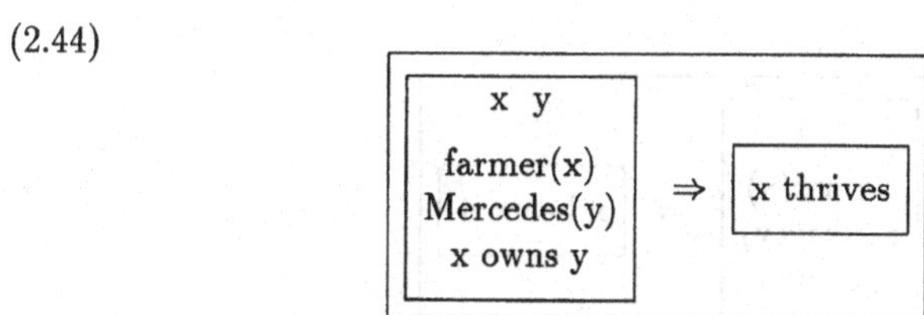

Note that if we construct, according to the rules we already had, the DRS for (2.41) we obtain virtually the same DRS, viz.

(2.45)

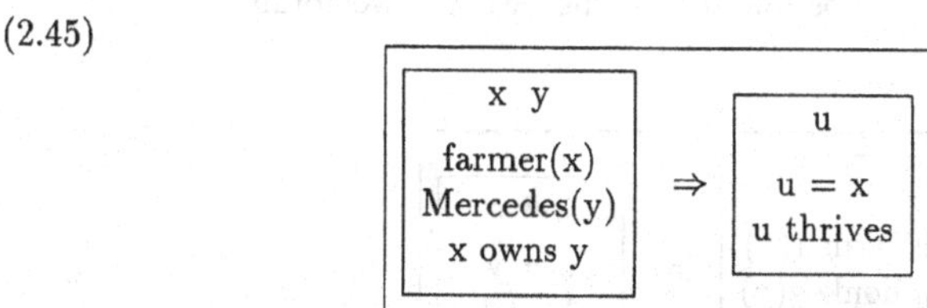

Since any verifying embedding of the right-hand DRS must map **u** and **x** to the same individual, (2.45) evidently has the same truth conditions as (2.44).

That it is right to use implicative conditions to represent the semantic contributions of **every**-phrases is further confirmed by the anaphoric similarities between clauses with such noun phrases and conditional sentences. Compare for instance

(2.46) Every farmer who owns a donkey beats it.

and

(2.47) If a farmer owns a donkey he beats it.

In both (2.46) and (2.47) the pronoun **it** can be interpreted as anaphorically connected with the indefinite noun phrase **a donkey**. What we have said in the preceding section about the treatment of conditionals entails that this possibility exists in the case of (2.47). But the rule we have just proposed for dealing with **every**-phrases makes the same prediction. In fact, the two sentences lead, like (2.41) and (2.42), to virtually identical DRSs, with clearly identical truth conditions.

(2.49) gives the completed DRS for (2.46); it is preceded by (2.48), which represents that intermediate construction stage where the processing mechanism must turn to the pronoun **it**.

(2.48)

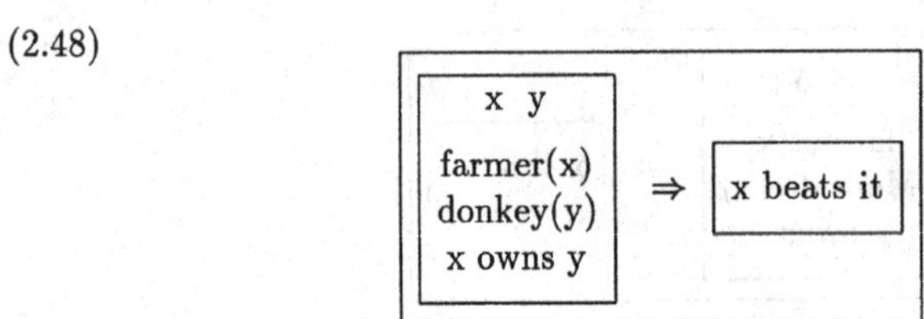

Since, according to Def. 2.1.4, the discourse referent **y** is accessible to the position occupied by **it** in (2.48), it is possible to link the two; and we obtain

(2.49)

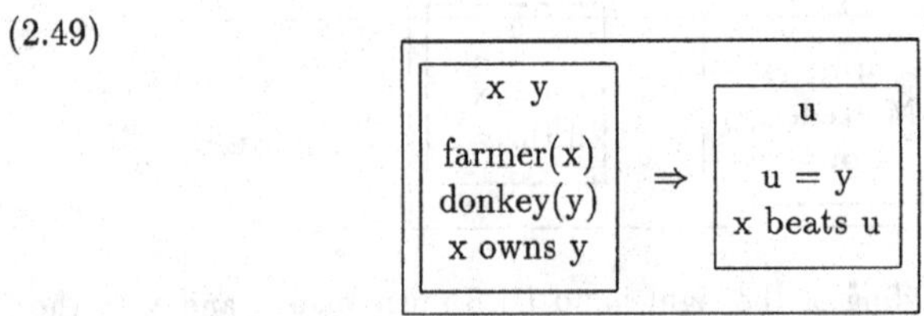

As our illustrations (2.43) and (2.48) have shown, the application of the new rule for **every**-phrases involves the introduction of a discourse referent.[10] In this regard the new rule **CR.EVERY** is like the rules we have adopted for other types of NPs. All these rules introduce a discourse referent for the NP to which they are applied, as well as a couple of conditions, one obtained by substituting the referent for the NP in the condition to which the rule is being applied and one which captures the descriptive content of the NP itself.

There is, however, one important difference between the rule for **every**-phrases and the NP rules we have encountered in earlier sections. All the other rules introduce discourse referents either into the universe of the very DRS to which they are applied or into the universe of a superordinate DRS. The new rule, in contrast, places its discourse referent into the universe of a newly created *sub*ordinate DRS, one which, according to the accessibility definition we have already adopted, is inaccessible to pronouns occurring at the level of the condition to which the rule is applied.

[10]In both cases the referent happened to be **x** but of course what particular referent is chosen is of no more significance here than it is in connection with the processing of any other type of NP. The only requirement is, as before, that the chosen referent be new to the DRS into which it is introduced.

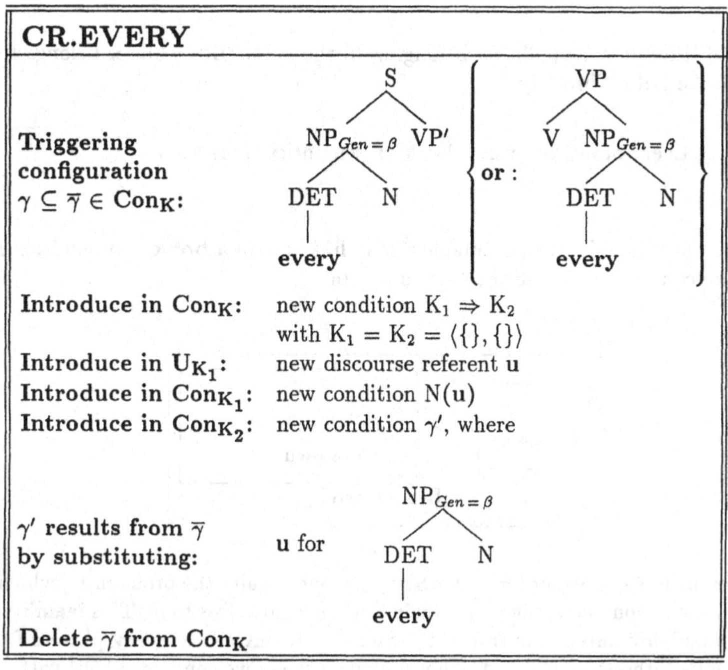

We would expect this to have implications for the possibilities of anaphora, and indeed, the facts bear out what our theoretical assumptions suggest. Consider, for instance,

(2.50) Every professor owns Buddenbrooks. He likes it.

In (2.50) **he** cannot be interpreted as anaphorically related to **every professor**. The reason, we maintain, is that the relevant referent is in subordinate position: at the crucial point we have the DRS

(2.51)

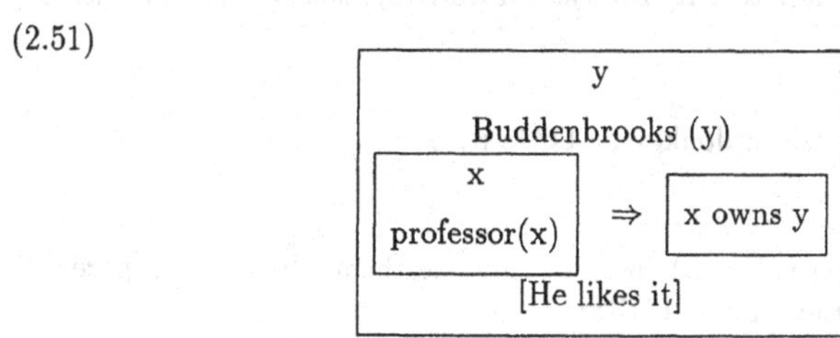

Here **He likes it** is a condition belonging to the main DRS while **x** belongs to a subordinate DRS. Similarly,

(2.52) Every professor owns a book on semantics. It is bizarre.

does not allow **it** to be read as anaphorically linked with **a book**, a prohibition for which we can account along the same lines: In

(2.53)

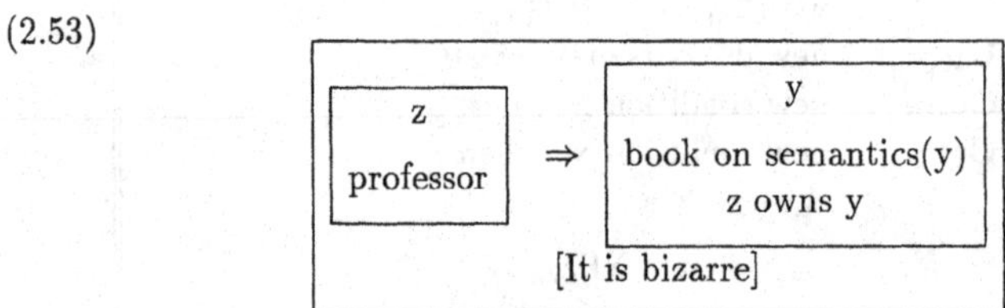

the referent **y** is in a subordinate DRS and so, once again, the pronoun **it**, which is part of a condition belonging to the main DRS, has no access to it. This inability to act as anaphoric antecedent in certain contexts distinguishes **every**-phrases from all the NPs hitherto considered. This is evident when we compare (2.50) with

(2.54) Bill owns a book on semantics. He likes it.

Processing the first sentence of (2.54) produces, in contrast with what happened in the case of (2.50), discourse referents for both **Bill** and **a book on semantics** in the main DRS, and these are thus accessible to **he** and **it**.

The difference between **every**-phrases and indefinite descriptions shows itself also at the level of subordinate DRSs. For instance, while the **he** and **it** of (2.47) can be interpreted as anaphoric to **a farmer** and **a donkey**, no such interpretation is possible for the sentence

(2.55) If every farmer owns a donkey he beats it.

That such an interpretation is indeed ruled out by the theory becomes apparent when we try to construct the intended DRS:

(2.56)

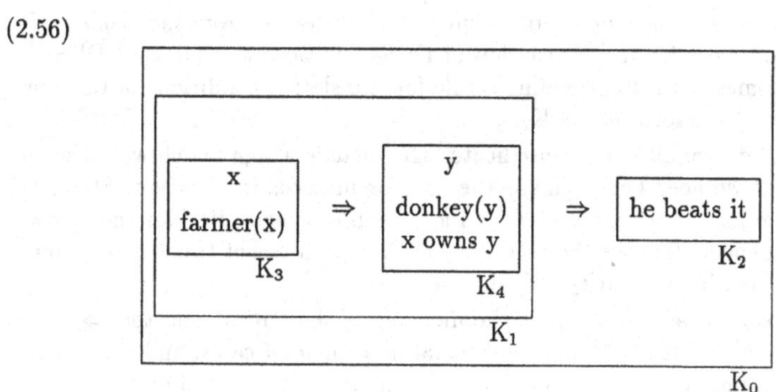

In view of the positions they occupy – viz. as constituents of a condition of K_2 – **he** and **it** would have access to the universes of K_2, of K_1 and of K_0. But these are all empty. On the other hand, the universes of K_3 and K_4, which contain **x** and **y** respectively, are inaccessible.

We noted in passing that the same semantic role that is played by the word **every** is also played by **all** and **each**. Of these **all** is a word that requires the plural. Thus to include it in our fragment we have to deal with plurals more generally. We will do this in Chapter 4.

This is not a reason for excluding **each**, which, just like **every**, forms singular noun phrases from our present fragment. There are however, as it turns out, subtle differences between **every** and **each**, which can, if we are right, only be explained within a much more elaborate theoretical framework than we offer in this book. Since we cannot do justice here to the distinctive characteristics of **each**, we have decided to exclude it too.[11]

2.2.0.2 Translation into Predicate Logic

How should DRSs with implicative conditions be translated into predicate logic? There is more than one way in which this question might be understood. One way to understand it is: How should DRSs from the more comprehensive class characterized in Def. 2.1.1 be translated into formulas of the language of predicate logic PL_0? This is a question we will address below (see (2.75)). But there is also another interpretation, viz.: How should we extend our language PL_0 so that the new DRSs can be translated into the extended language in a comparatively natural and direct manner? It is this last question which we will address now.

[11]For a discussion of some of the uses of **each** see Sections 4.4.3 and 4.4.4.

In view of the way in which we have set up the translation procedure for DRSs without implicative conditions – a procedure which operates "from the inside out" and is based on rules for the translation of DRS-conditions as well as of DRSs – the problem comes down to providing a rule for translating conditions of the new kind, i.e. those of the form $K_1 \Rightarrow K_2$.

The standard formulations of predicate logic include a sign which would seem to be just what we need here. This is the sign for material implication. Material implication too has been represented by more than one sign. Besides the arrow, '$\rightarrow$', one often encounters the 'horseshoe', '$\supset$', though in recent times this symbol seems to have lost its popularity. We shall use '$\rightarrow$'.

We have seen in Section 2.1 that the meaning of the DRS connector '$\Rightarrow$' also boils down to that of the material conditional in a range of cases, and this might suggest that an implicative condition $K_1 \Rightarrow K_2$ should be translated into $\varphi_1 \rightarrow \varphi_2$, where φ_1 is the predicate logic translation of K_1 and φ_2 of K_2. In general, however, this won't do. To see why we must make explicit how the arrow of predicate logic works.

The syntactic role of '$\rightarrow$' is readily explained. '$\rightarrow$' acts as a formula connector which combines two predicate logic formulas, φ_1 and φ_2, say, into a new one, $(\varphi_1 \rightarrow \varphi_2)$. Thus if we add '$\rightarrow$' to the language PL_0 we should adjust the stipulations of Section 1.5, p. 133 as follows:

i) We add '$\rightarrow$' to the list of logical constants of predicate logic;

and

ii) we add to Def. 1.5.4 an extra clause of the form:

(2.57) if φ_1 and φ_2 are formulas then $(\varphi_1 \rightarrow \varphi_2)$ is a *formula*. (We refrain from introducing a separate name to the version of predicate logic which arises through these additions.)

The semantic role of the arrow is easily explicated also. All that we need to do is add to the definition of satisfaction, Def. 1.5.8, a further clause which says what it is for f to satisfy $(\varphi_1 \rightarrow \varphi_2)$ in M. The clause, which reflects the fact that '$\rightarrow$' represents material implication is

(2.58) f *satisfies* $(\varphi_1 \rightarrow \varphi_2)$ *in* M if f does not satisfy φ_1 in M or f satisfies φ_2 in M.

Since $\Rightarrow$ becomes equivalent to a material conditional when the DRSs K_1 and K_2 it connects are not linked in the way referred to earlier (i.e. when no discourse referent of U_{K_1} occurs in U_{K_2}) one would expect the translation of $K_1 \Rightarrow K_2$ as $\varphi_1 \rightarrow \varphi_2$ to be adequate as long as such links are absent. Indeed this is so. By way of an example, compare once more (2.59) with (2.60).

(2.59) If Bill owns a Porsche then Fred owns a Ferrari.

(2.60)

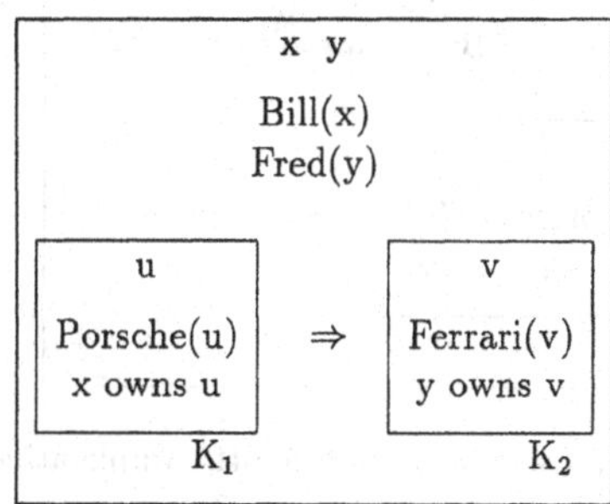

According to Def. 1.5.5 the translations of K_1 and K_2 are the formulas (2.61) and (2.62).

(2.61) $\exists$u(**Porsche(u)** & **owns(x,u)**)

(2.62) $\exists$v(**Ferrari(v)** & **owns(y,v)**)

So, if we translate $K_1 \Rightarrow K_2$ as suggested and then complete the translation, relying once more on Def. 1.5.5, we obtain

(2.63) $\exists$xy(x = **Bill** & y = **Fred** &
($\exists$u(**Porsche(u)** & **owns(x,u)**) $\rightarrow$ $\exists$v(**Ferrari(v)** & **owns(y,v)**)))

It is not hard to verify that (2.63) has the same truth conditions as (2.60).

The reason, however, why the suggested translation scheme works in the case of (2.60) is that the component DRSs of the implicative condition $K_1 \Rightarrow K_2$ happen to be free of the certain kind of connection that discourse referents often establish between the left-hand and the right-hand sides of such conditions. More precisely, if one or more discourse referents from U_{K_1} occur in conditions of K_2 then the given scheme no longer works. For instance consider

(2.64) Every professor who knows German owns Buddenbrooks.

which gives rise to the DRS[12]

(2.65)

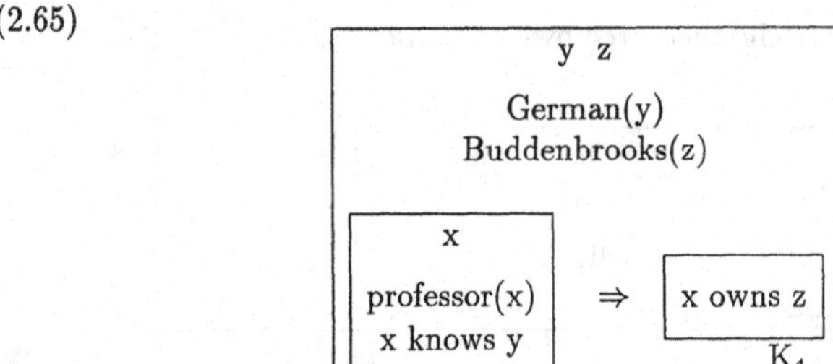

Proceeding as before we get as translation for the implicative condition $K_3 \Rightarrow K_4$ the formula

(2.66) $\exists$x(**professor**(x) & **knows**(x,y)) $\rightarrow$ **owns**(x,z)

and from this, as translation for (2.65)

(2.67) $\exists$yz(y = **German** & z = **Buddenbrooks** &
($\exists$x(**professor**(x) & **knows**(x,y)) $\rightarrow$ **owns**(x,z)))

This result cannot be right, for the occurrence of **x** as argument of the predicate **owns** is free in (2.67) (the quantifier string '$\exists$x' binds its occurrences following **professor** and **knows**, but not the one following **owns**!). Thus (2.67) isn't even a sentence in the sense of Def. 1.5.10, and fails, in the absence of an assignment which correlates the free occurrence of **x** with a particular individual, to determine any definite truth conditions. *A fortiori* it can't have the same truth conditions as (2.65).

The first remedy that comes to mind is to recall what we said when we first introduced implicative conditions as ways of representing suppositional discourse: the DRS on the right is strictly speaking an extension of that on the left, containing

[12]We have made use of the fact that in a sentence like (2.64) **German** is a proper name, the name of a particular language.

besides the discourse referents and conditions we overtly display also those that occur on the left. Thus (2.65) can be rewritten as

(2.68)

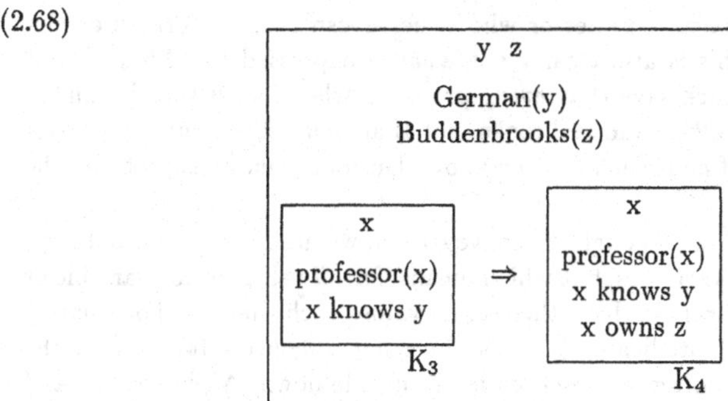

If we apply the present translation recipe to (2.68) we do indeed get a sentence of predicate logic rather than an open formula:

(2.69) $\exists$yz(y = **German** & z = **Buddenbrooks** &
($\exists$x(**professor**(x) & **knows**(x,y)) $\rightarrow$
$\exists$x(**professor**(x) & **knows**(x,y) & **owns**(x,z))))

However the formula does not give a correct rendition of what (2.68), or, equivalently, (2.65), means. (2.69) says that if there is a professor who knows German there also is a professor who knows German and owns Buddenbrooks. But this is a much weaker claim than the one made in (2.64), and represented by (2.65) and (2.68). What has gone wrong in the transition from (2.68) to (2.69) is that the connection which the discourse referent x establishes between the left and the right-hand side of the implicative condition in (2.69) has been broken. It has been broken because the occurrence of x on the right of the implicative condition is, in the part of (2.69) which translates the right-hand DRS, bound by a different quantifier string '$\exists$x' than the occurrence of x on the left-hand side. In order to get a correct translation of such implicative conditions, all occurrences of the variable x should be bound by the same quantifier string, which should come at the beginning of the (sub)formula that represents the implicative condition as a whole. But this quantifier string cannot be of the form '$\exists$x'. For suppose we were to translate (2.65) as

(2.70) $\exists$yz(y = **German** & z = **Buddenbrooks** &
$\exists$x((**professor**(x) & **knows**(x,y)) $\rightarrow$ **owns**(x,z)))

This formula says that there exists some professor such that if he knows German then he owns Buddenbrooks; or alternatively, since '$\rightarrow$' functions as the material conditional, that there exists a professor who either doesn't know German or else owns Buddenbrooks. This is also clearly not what is expressed by (2.64). What we want is a formula which says that *every* professor who is such that he knows German is such that he owns Buddenbrooks, not that *there exists some* professor of whom it is true that if he is such that he knows German then he is such that he owns Buddenbooks.

To convey what the formula ought to convey, then, we need a device which, like '$\exists$', is capable of binding variables, but which means 'for *all* values of the variable or variables such that ...' – rather than 'there exist values such that ...'. Fortunately the standard versions of predicate logic contain such a device. It is called the *universal quantifier*. It is often represented by an upside down 'A', i.e. as '$\forall$', and this is the symbol we will use also. The universal quantifier functions syntactically just like the existential quantifier. In other words, it is a logical constant that allows us to form formulas according to the principle

(2.71) If α_1, ..., α_n are variables and φ is a formula then $\forall\alpha_1...\alpha_n\ \varphi$ is a *formula*.

The semantics of '$\forall$' is captured by a clause that is to be added to Def. 1.5.8 and which forms the intuitively obvious counterpart to the clause for '$\exists$'.

(2.72) f *satisfies* $\forall\alpha_1...\alpha_n\varphi$ *in* M iff for every extension g of f such that Dom(g) = Dom(f) $\cup$ $\{\alpha_1, ...,\alpha_n\}$ g satisfies φ in M.

With the help of '$\forall$' we can translate (2.64) adequately, viz. as

(2.73) $\exists$**yz(y = German & z = Buddenbrooks &**
$\forall$x((professor(x) & knows(x,y)) $\rightarrow$ owns(x,z)))

But how do we get this formula from the DRS (2.65) for which it is proposed as translation? Or, more specifically, what is the rule which yields

(2.74) **$\forall$x((professor(x) & knows(x,y)) $\rightarrow$ owns(x,z)))**

as the translation of the implicative condition of (2.65)? In formulating this rule we must be a little careful. We cannot, in stipulating what should be the translation of the implicative condition $K_1 \Rightarrow K_2$, refer to the translations of K_1 and K_2. For the discourse referents of U_{K_1} have to be taken 'out of' the formula representing K_1, so that the quantifier string $\forall\alpha_1...\alpha_n$ can be on the outside of the formula ($\varphi_1 \rightarrow \varphi_2$) (where φ_2 translates the right-hand side of the implicative condition).

After all that has been said it should not be too difficult to persuade oneself that the following stipulation will do full justice to the meaning which implicative conditions carry.

(2.75) Let $K_1 \Rightarrow K_2$ be an implicative condition, where $K_1 = \langle U_1, Con_1 \rangle$, U_1 consists of the discourse referents $\alpha_1,...,\alpha_n$ and Con_1 consists of the conditions $\gamma_1,...,\gamma_m$. Then φ is a *translation* of $K_1 \Rightarrow K_2$ iff φ is a formula of the form $\forall\alpha_1...\alpha_n((\psi_1 \; \& \; \psi_2 \; ... \; \psi_m) \rightarrow \psi)$ where for $i = 1, ..., m$ ψ_i is a translation of γ_i and ψ is a translation of K_2.

It should be evident that applying (2.75) in the translation of (2.65) we do indeed obtain (2.73). For another illustration consider once more

(2.47) If a farmer owns a donkey then he beats it.

with its DRS

(2.76)

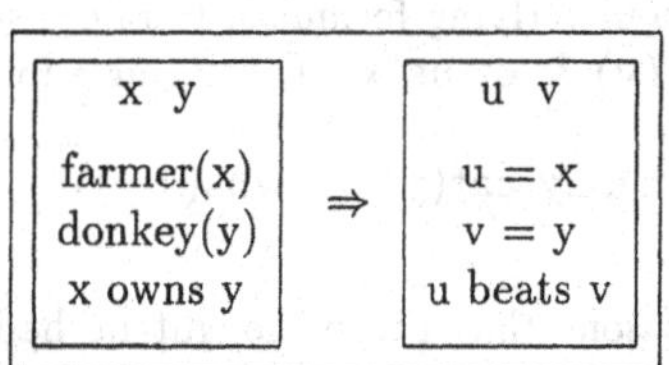

Applying (2.75) to the implicative condition of (2.76) we obtain

(2.77) $\forall$**xy((farmer(x) & donkey(y) & owns(x,y)) →**
∃uv(u = x & v = y & beats(u,v)))

The route we have followed towards our final statement (2.75) of how implicative conditions should be translated may well have seemed exceedingly circuitous. Indeed, we could have proceeded more directly by simply pointing out that standard predicate logic countenances the logical constants '→' and '∀', giving the conditions (2.71) and (2.72) which articulate their syntactic and semantic roles, and then presenting the translation stipulation (2.75), with a couple of illustrations, to show that this stipulation does what it is supposed to. The reason why we have walked the rather tortuous path we have chosen here, is that we wanted to make clear that it is through their implicative conditions that DRSs differ most importantly from the formulas of the predicate calculus. In fact, the implicative conditions of DRT seem to offer much more natural representations of the semantic contributions made by the words **if ... then** and **every** than are available in a formalism like predicate logic where these contributions have to be simulated by appropriate combinations of '$\forall$' and '$\rightarrow$'.

A historical remark on the origin of predicate logic is in order here. As we remarked in the introduction, predicate logic was first formulated by Frege. Crucial to Frege's achievement was his appreciation of the function of the particles **every** and **all**, and his recognition that a noun phrase like **every professor** makes a contribution to the statements in which it occurs that is fundamentally different from the contributions made by 'referring' NPs such as **the professor** or **Jones**. In particular, Frege was fully aware that **every** functions in the manner which implicative conditions make directly visible, viz. that it establishes a "universal-conditional" link between two predicates, one provided by the descriptive content of the simple or complex noun to which **every** is prefixed and the other by the remaining parts of the clause. In fact, it would have been straightforward to include within a system that in other respects would be like predicate logic as we have it today a device for representing **every** in a similarly direct way. For instance, one could have introduced a quantifier sign '$\forall'$' which is used to form new formulas not out of one, but out of two underlying formulas, forming, say, out of the formulas **professor(x)** and $\exists$**y(cat(y) & owns(x,y))** the single formula

(2.78) $\forall'$**x(professor(x),** $\exists$**y(cat(y) & owns(x,y)))**

We cannot go into the reasons that Frege thought he had for not choosing this way of formulating the meaning of **every**, but preferred to analyse it in terms of '$\forall$' and '$\rightarrow$'. With the benefit of hindsight, we can say that his reasons were not absolutely compelling. But compelling or not, the system of predicate logic that we have inherited from Frege has become so firmly and deeply entrenched that it would be quixotic to try and impose a switch from '$\forall$' to '$\forall'$', especially as the translation between the notation with '$\forall$' and that with '$\forall'$' is so straightforward.

Given the professed aims of predicate logic, which was intended as a kind of 'characteristica universalis', in which the propositions of mathematics, natural science and various other domains could be given logically transparent formalizations, the difference between $\forall$ and $\forall'$ is relatively immaterial, since going back and forth between the two notations is so straightforward. For DRT, however, the issues are somewhat different. Here we are not only concerned with developing a system in which the content of natural language sentences can be correctly and transparently expressed, but also with uncovering the systematic correlation between meaning and syntactic form of those sentences. Hence devising some formal representation system that is able to capture the truth conditions of the represented sentences and discourses isn't necessarily good enough.

The additional constraint that DRT's methodological foundations impose upon it become visible with particular clarity when we look at the account it gives of anaphora. It is easily seen that the treatment of anaphoric pronouns we have presented in this and the preceding chapters depends crucially on the structural organization of the DRSs into which each newly processed sentence of the discourse gets incorporated. In particular, a crucial role is being played by the notion of accessibility; but accessibility, as we have seen is a configurational relation between discourse referents, one which can be what it is only because of the structural organization that is specific to a DRS. Thus – and here we stress once more a point which we have made more than once before – it is in large part because of the *contextual* role that DRSs are made to play, as contexts for what is to be processed next, and not *only* as representations of what has been processed already, that they must display those structural properties which set them apart from the usual predicate logical formulas.

As a matter of fact the version of predicate logic we have so far presented is still a little closer to DRS structure than the versions one finds in most places. The remaining differences between the present version and those more familiar versions are minor, but should nonetheless be pointed out. We will do this in the next section.

Exercises

1. Show that the sentence

   'Every man who admires Casablanca owns a trenchcoat.'

   is true in the model $\mathsf{M} = \langle\{c,x,y\}, \mathsf{Pred_M}, \mathsf{Name_M}\rangle$,

   where $\mathsf{Pred_M} = \{\langle \mathbf{man}, \{x\}\rangle, \langle \mathbf{trenchcoat}, \{y\}\rangle, \langle \mathbf{admires}, \{\langle x, c\rangle\}\rangle, \langle \mathbf{owns}, \{\langle x, y\rangle\}\rangle\}$,

   and $\mathsf{Name_M}(\mathbf{Casablanca}) = c$

2. Construct all possible DRSs for the following discourses.

   (a) Fred owns a dog which doesn't wear a collar. It doesn't love him.

   (b) Fred doesn't own a dog which wears a collar. It loves him.

   (c) Fred likes Mary. If she likes a book then he likes it.

   (d) Fred doesn't like Mary. If she likes a book then he doesn't like it.

(e) Fred likes every man. If every man likes him then every man is happy.

(f) Fred likes every man who likes him. Fred doesn't like every man who Mary likes.

(g) If Mary likes a man then he likes Fred.

3. Decide for each of the DRSs of excercise (2c), (2d), (2f) and (2g) if they are true in the following models M_1, M_2 and M_3.

M_1 is defined by:
$U_{M_1} = \{a, b, c, d, e, f\}$;
$Name_{M_1} = \{\langle \text{Mary}, a\rangle, \langle \text{Fred}, f\rangle\}$;
$Pred_{M_1}(\text{man}) = \{d, e, f\}$;
$Pred_{M_1}(\text{book}) = \{b\}$;
$Pred_{M_1}(\text{likes}) =$
$\{\langle a,a\rangle, \langle a,b\rangle, \langle b,b\rangle, \langle a,d\rangle, \langle d,b\rangle, \langle a,e\rangle, \langle e,f\rangle, \langle f,a\rangle, \langle f,b\rangle\}$.

M_2 is defined by:
$U_{M_2} = \{a, b, c, d, e, f\}$;
$Name_{M_2} = \{\langle \text{Mary}, a\rangle, \langle \text{Fred}, f\rangle\}$;
$Pred_{M_2}(\text{man}) = \{d, e, f\}$;
$Pred_{M_2}(\text{book}) = \{b, c\}$;
$Pred_{M_2}(\text{likes}) =$
$\{\langle a,a\rangle, \langle a,b\rangle, \langle a,c\rangle, \langle b,b\rangle, \langle d,b\rangle, \langle a,e\rangle, \langle e,f\rangle, \langle f,a\rangle, \langle f,b\rangle, \langle f,d\rangle, \langle f,e\rangle, \langle f,f\rangle\}$.

M_3 is defined by:
$U_{M_3} = \{a, b, c, d, e, f\}$;
$Name_{M_3} = \{\langle \text{Mary}, a\rangle, \langle \text{Fred}, f\rangle\}$;
$Pred_{M_3}(\text{man}) = \{d, e, f\}$;
$Pred_{M_3}(\text{book}) = \{b, c\}$;
$Pred_{M_3}(\text{likes}) =$
$\{\langle a,a\rangle, \langle a,b\rangle, \langle b,b\rangle, \langle d,b\rangle, \langle a,e\rangle, \langle e,f\rangle, \langle f,a\rangle, \langle f,b\rangle, \langle f,c\rangle, \langle f,d\rangle, \langle f,f\rangle\}$.

4. Construct DRSs for each of the following sentences and discourses.

(a) Fred likes Susan. If she likes a man who he knows then Fred hates him.

(b) Every woman who loves every cat hates every dog who hates every cat.

(c) If a man likes a woman who loves every cat then, if she likes him then he hates every dog.

(d) If a stockbroker thrives, then he owns a palace. Mary knows a stockbroker who doesn't own a palace. Every stockbroker who Susan knows owns a palace.

(e) Susan knows every stockbroker who Mary knows.

5. The anaphoric relations indicated by indices in the following examples are all impossible. Show that our theory predicts this by constructing the DRSs up to the point where the indexed pronoun is to be processed.

   (a) If Fred doesn't own a car_1, then Susan uses it_1.
   (b) Fred loves [every dog which Susan owns]$_1$. He feeds it_1.
   (c) Fred loves every dog which she_1 owns. Susan_1 feeds it.
   (d) If Fred likes every woman who owns [a dachshund]$_1$, then it_1 bites him.

6. Show that for no model in which the discourse (4d) is true the discourse (4e) can be true also.

7. Construct a DRS for the following discourse.

   (a) Mary is a stockbroker. Every woman who is rich owns a Porsche. If a stockbroker does not own a Porsche then she is not rich. She is rich.

   (Analyse the copula **is** of the first sentence as transitive verb, and the phrase **be rich** as intransitive verb.[13]) Give a model in which this discourse is true.

8. Translate the DRSs for Exercise 2.(a–g) into formulas of predicate logic. Using the satisfaction definition for predicate logic evaluate your translations of the DRSs for 2.(c), (d), (f) and (g) in the models M_1–M_3 of Exercise 3.

2.3 Disjunction

This section will be concerned with the word **or**. In fact, our theme will be even more restricted than that, for we will look at only some of the uses which **or** has in English. We begin with an analysis of the particle **or** as connector of *sentences*. An example is the sentence

(2.79) The butler loves the baroness or the gardener loves her.

where **or** connects the complete sentences **the butler loves the baroness** and **the gardener loves her**. **Or** also occurs between expressions of other syntactic categories, as in (2.80)–(2.82).

[13] For more on the verb **to be** see Sections 3.5 and 3.6.

(2.80) The butler or the gardener loves the baroness.

(2.81) The butler loves or admires the baroness.

(2.82) The butler loathes the gardener or loves the baroness.

Here the particle connects two NPs, two transitive verbs and two VPs, respectively. We will consider uses of **or** where it connects constituents of some category other than S at the end of this section.

For the present we will concentrate on the sentential use of **or**. But even here our treatment will be far from exhaustive, excluding in particular certain contexts in which **or** seems to have roughly the force of **and**.[14]

The function of **or** is to allow for *alternatives.* The need for alternatives arises in cases where the speaker knows that what he wishes to speak of satisfies one of two or more alternative descriptions but does not know *which* of those descriptions it satisfies. A typical sort of case is that where we are concerned to identify the agent of a crime and have narrowed the field down to a couple of suspects. For instance, we may want to assert, at a fairly advanced stage of the investigation, that

(2.84) Either the butler assaulted the baroness or the gardener assaulted her.

Any representation of such a statement must make explicit what the alternative descriptions are, without making a choice between them. The natural way to achieve this within the DRS format is to represent the sets of alternatives as complex conditions which contain a DRS for each of the alternative descriptions the statement mentions. To see how this works let us begin by looking at the following sentence.

(2.85) Jones loves Lady Hermione or Smith loves her.

(2.85) – a variant of (2.79) in which we have replaced the definite descriptions **the butler, the baroness** and **the gardener** by proper names – will give rise to a representation which initially will look something like this:

[14]An example of the kind of context we will ignore is

(2.83) You may take an apple or you may take a pear.

which is often, perhaps typically, understood to imply that both the taking of an apple and the taking of a pear are permitted. Whether such uses of or are really different from the use on which we will concentrate here is a difficult and, to our knowledge, still unresolved question. See for instance [Lewis 1979] and [Kamp 1973].

(2.86)

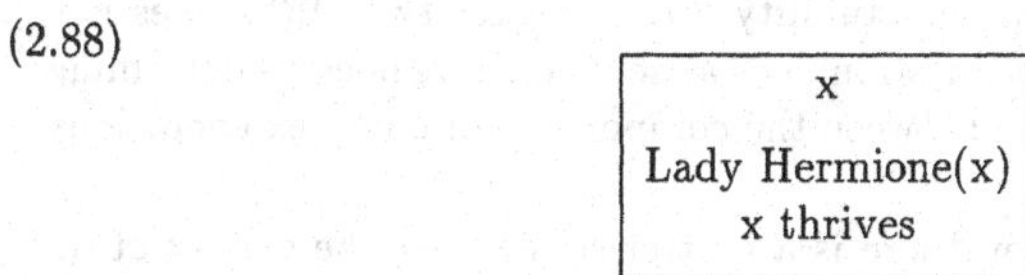

Here the sign '∨' indicates that the situation the represented statement (2.85) is about either fits the description given by K_1 or that given by K_2.

In (2.86), the complex consisting of K_1, '∨' and K_2 functions as a DRS-condition. To persuade ourselves that this is indeed how disjunctive sentences ought to be represented. We must, as we did in connection with complex conditions of the forms $\neg K$ and $K_1 \Rightarrow K_2$, look at cases where such sentences are part of larger discourses. For instance, the first sentence of (2.87) yields the DRS (2.88).

(2.87) Lady Hermione thrives. Either Jones loves her or Smith loves her.

(2.88)

x
Lady Hermione(x) x thrives

Incorporation of the second sentence of (2.87) into (2.88) should provide a pair of alternatives one of which must be true *in addition to* what is specified by (2.88) if (2.87) is to count as true. Thus the representation of the pair of alternatives should take the form of a new condition that is to be conjoined with the two conditions which (2.88) already contains. Thus we are led to a structure of the following form.

(2.89)

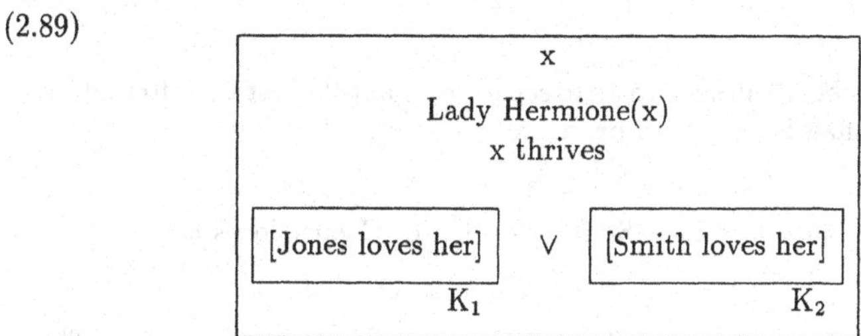

To complete this representation we must process the conditions **Jones loves her** and **Smith loves her** in their respective subordinate DRSs. This can be done by applying the by now familiar rules for proper names and pronouns. (It should be kept in mind that the discourse referents introduced by proper names are to be added to the universe of the main DRS!) We end up with the completed DRS

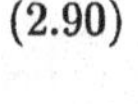
(2.90)

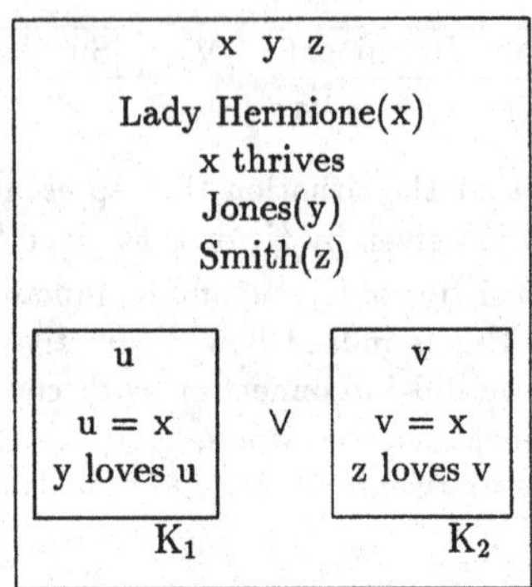

The completion of the subordinate DRSs K_1 and K_2 is unproblematic because in this particular case the question of accessibility *between* these two DRSs does not arise. In other cases, however, this question does arise, and so we need to determine what the accessibility relations are between the components of complex conditions involving '$\vee$'.

Before we address this question there is a matter concerning the syntax of **or** and the form of the DRS-conditions by which **or**-sentences are to be represented which we must settle first. The examples of **or**-sentences we have so far given each involve two alternatives. But this is not always so; it is possible to form sentences involving three alternatives or more, as in

(2.91) Jones loves Lady Hermione or Smith loves her or Cooper loves her.

Sometimes it sounds better in such cases to separate all but the last two alternatives by commas rather than by the word **or**, as in

(2.92) Jones loves Lady Hermione, Smith loves her or Cooper loves her.

It is this latter type of **or**-sentence that we will incorporate into our fragment. This means that we must add to our phrase structure grammar one or more rules that allow us to form out of any set consisting of n expressions σ_1, ..., σ_n of the category S (where $n \geq 2$) a sentence of the form

(2.93) σ_1, ..., σ_{n-1} **or** σ_n

What rule or rules will do this job has been left as an exercise[15]. Sentences of the general form shown in (2.93) are called *disjunctive* sentences or *disjunctions*, and their components, σ_1, ..., σ_n, are called the *disjuncts* of the larger disjunctive sentence.

Any disjunctive sentence will have to yield, when it is incorporated into a DRS, a condition which displays each of the n alternatives as a separate DRS. The form of this condition is essentially the one we have already encountered in (2.89) and (2.90), with the additional proviso that the DRSs representing *any* two adjacent disjuncts are separated by the symbol '∨'. Thus the first step in the processing of (2.92) is the DRS

(2.94)

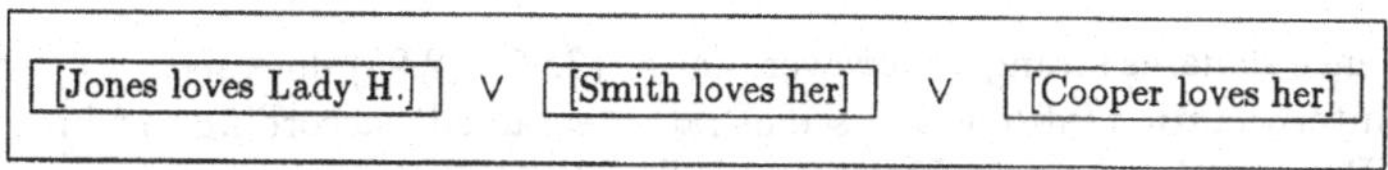

We will call the DRS-conditions that arise through the processing of disjunctive sentences *disjunctive conditions* and will also speak of the component DRSs as the *disjuncts* of these conditions.

2.3.1 Accessibility

We return to the issue of accessibility. In connection with disjunction this appears to be a more complicated matter than with the logical operators we have looked at so far – negation, conditionals and universal quantification.[16] We will follow the same policy as before, however, and present a comparatively simple definition of accessibility, after which we will list some cases that do not seem to fit the anaphoric patterns this definition predicts. Again, the proper solution of some of these cases involves theoretical tools which we do not develop, so the reader will have to be content with hints of solutions in lieu of solutions that are fully worked out. (In some of the exercises at the end of the section the questions raised by the examples we will discuss below will be pursued a little further, but these exercises will not add up to exhaustive treatments either.)

Our basic assumption about accessibility in disjunctive DRS-conditions is that no disjunct of a disjunctive condition is accessible from any other. In other words, if K_1 and K_2 are two such disjuncts then no discourse referent in U_{K_1} is accessible from (pronouns occurring in conditions of) K_2 and no discourse referent in U_{K_2} is

[15]See Exercise 2.

[16]Although, with those other constructions too the issues are not as simple as our initial presentation of them suggested – see Section 3.7.

accessible from K_1. In other words, in a disjunctive condition no one of the components is subordinate to any of the others. That a later disjunct of a disjunction is not accessible from an earlier one will probably not be surprising. Consider e.g. (2.95), which clearly supports the assumption.

(2.95) Bill owns it or Fred owns a Porsche.

It seems quite impossible to interpret the **it** of the first disjunct as anaphoric to the indefinite description **a Porsche** occurring in the second disjunct.

But even when we switch the indefinite and the pronoun around, as in

(2.96) Bill owns a Porsche or Fred owns it.

the sentence remains strange. However, unlike (2.95), (2.96) does seem to permit a certain interpretation (although it seems rather strained), according to which there is some Porsche that is owned by either Bill or Fred.

Inasmuch as such an interpretation is available for (2.96), it might seem to contradict the basic assumption just made. But this is only a matter of appearance. It is important to distinguish between two issues: (i) whether a discourse referent in the universe U_{K_1} of the first disjunct K_1 of a disjunctive condition $K_1 \vee K_2$ is accessible from K_2, and (ii) whether the discourse referent introduced by an indefinite belonging to a reducible condition in K_1 introduces its discourse referent into U_{K_1} or some other universe. The possibility of interpreting **it** as anaphoric to **a Porsche** in (2.96) arises because it is possible to interpret **a Porsche** as introducing its discourse referent not into U_{K_1} but into that of the main DRS. This view is supported not only by the apparent truth conditions which (2.96) has on the interpretation we are discussing – these truth conditions are correctly captured by a DRS in which the discourse referent for **a Porsche** belongs to the main universe – but also by the fact that sentences of the general form (2.96) improve as the indefinite NP is made longer – or 'heavier' to use the linguistic jargon. For instance, when **a Porsche** is replaced by **a Porsche which I have seen race past our house several times this morning** the resulting sentence is entirely felicitous. The natural explanation is that indefinite NPs with a more specific descriptive content are more readily interpreted as referring to some particular object – as "specific indefinites" – and thus as introducing their discourse referents at the highest level. (For specific indefinites see Section 3.7.3.)

There are however sentences which have the same form as (2.96) and in which the anaphoric link seems fairly good even though the indefinite description is short and comparatively uninformative. The sort of case we have in mind is exemplified by

(2.97) Jones has borrowed a bicycle or he has rented it.

Again, it seems to us that (2.97) falls short of being perfect; but it nevertheless has a high degree of acceptability and what renders it (more or less) acceptable is something that does not seem to enter into our understanding of (2.96). It is possible to get the anaphoric link in (2.97), we think, because one takes the second disjunct as providing an alternative description of the same event that is described by the first disjunct, an event which might also be described, in a manner that is neutral between what either of the two disjuncts has to say about it, as Jones's *acquiring* of a bicycle. Indicative of this being a crucial factor is that, in our judgement, (2.97) is much improved when rephrased as:

(2.98) Jones has borrowed a bicycle, or perhaps he has rented it.

where the comma before **or** and the added **perhaps** manage to convey that the second disjunct acts as a qualification of what has been claimed in the first disjunct. A proper analysis of such sentences must make explicit that disjunctive sentences can often be interpreted as providing alternative descriptions of one and the same event.

A very different sort of apparent counterexample to our characterization of accessibility within disjunctions is the following:

(2.99) Either Jones does not own a car or he hides it.

Note that as we have defined accessibility the intended anaphoric antecedent **a car** is as it were inaccessible "twice over" to the pronoun **it**. For if we start constructing the DRS for (2.99) we reach at the relevant point

(2.100)

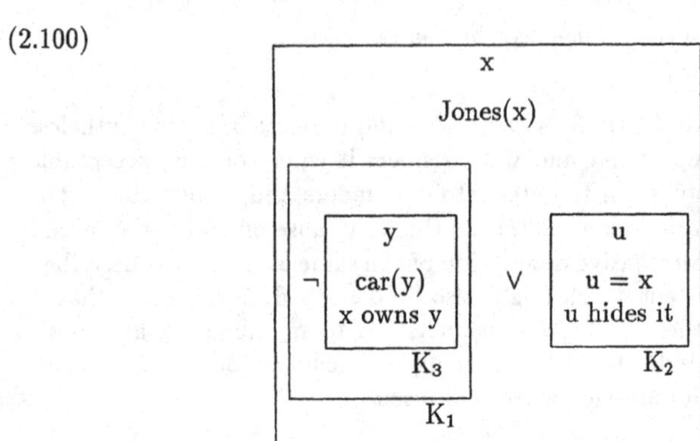

By our stipulations the discourse referent y would already be inaccessible from the position of **it** were it to belong to U_{K_1}. But in fact it occurs even more deeply embedded, viz. as an element of U_{K_3}. Interestingly enough, sentences where there is such an apparent "double" relation of inaccessibility are often much better than those we get from them by removing the negation, an operation which would seem – to continue the same metaphor – to reduce the inaccessibility of the intended antecedent by half. For instance,

(2.101) Jones owns a car or he hides it.

seems very odd indeed; and even if the oddity of (2.101) may be blamed in part on the particular choice of verbs, there is also a structural problem which (2.101) shares with (2.96) above. So it looks as if it is in fact the *presence* of negation which saves (2.99). The reason why the presence of negation saves (2.99) becomes visible when we note that the sentence can be felicitously rephrased as in:

(2.102) Either Jones doesn't own a car or $\left\{\begin{array}{c}\text{else}\\ \text{otherwise}\end{array}\right\}$ he hides it.

(2.102) is as good as, perhaps even better than (2.99). That adding either **else** or **otherwise** should improve the sentence invites the following explanation. **Otherwise** refers to "the other case"; in the present context it refers to the case other than the one described by the first disjunct (**else** seems to have a similar meaning – compare **someone else, elsewhere**). So, it is consistent with much that we have said earlier, about conditional sentences and hypothetical discourse, to suppose that the interpretation of **otherwise he hides it** involves postulating a representation for what is referred to by **otherwise** and then extending that representation by incorporating **he hides it** into it. This strategy is, we hypothesize, generally available for the interpretation of disjunctive sentences – especially when a word like **else** or **otherwise** is present, but also when these particles are absent; for after all, almost any disjunction of the form 'A **or** B' can be paraphrased as 'A **or else** B'. When the first disjunct is an unnegated sentence then the only straightforward way of characterizing the other case is by negating the description this sentence provides. So if we apply the processing principle we have just hypothesized to a sentence of this kind, say (2.96), then we obtain, at a certain stage of construction, a DRS of the form (2.103) which then has to be completed by processing **Fred owns it** inside K_2. In the present case the addition of $\neg K_3$ to K_2 will not help us, however, to interpret the pronoun **it**, for the discourse referent **u**, although now occurring on the right-hand side, again occurs there in a position that is not accessible from that of the pronoun. The situation is different when, as in (2.99) and (2.102), the first disjunct is a negated sentence, provided we make the plausible assumption that when this is so, the "other case" is taken to be described by the corresponding unnegated sentence. With this assumption the DRS of (2.102) (and likewise that for (2.99)!) can proceed to the stage which is shown by (2.104).

(2.103)

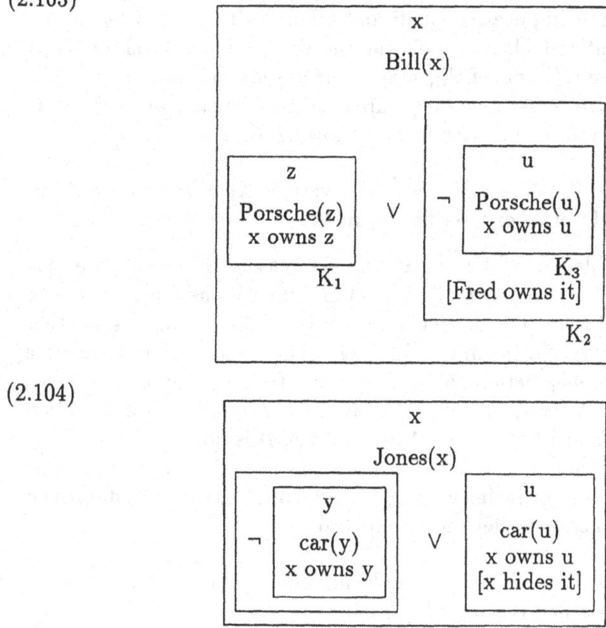

This time u *is* accessible to the pronoun **it** and the right-hand side can be completed. The result is

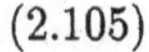

(2.105)

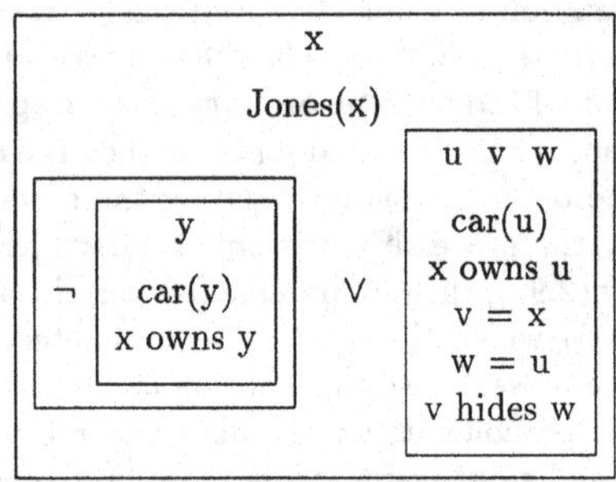

2.3.2 Verification

The next question we have to address is what it is for a disjunctive DRS-condition to be verified. Because there is no relation of accessibility between the member DRSs of a disjunctive condition, the answer to this question is more straightforward than it was in relation to implicative conditions. For, as may be recalled, the complications we encountered when formulating the verification criteria for $K_1 \Rightarrow K_2$ was that the discourse referents of U_{K_1} may occur in the conditions of U_{K_2}. For disjunctive conditions such "cross-references" are excluded. In fact, we might state the verification condition for disjunction in the following form:

(2.106) f *verifies* $K_1 \vee K_2 \vee ... \vee K_n$ *in* M iff f verifies K_1 in M or f verifies K_2 in M or ... or f verifies K_n in M.

However, (2.106) is problematic for a quite different reason. For what, we may ask, does its right-hand side come to? More precisely, what is the force of **or** as it occurs on the right-hand side? The particular problem we have in mind is whether the meaning of **or** is, to use traditional terminology, that of *inclusive* or of *exclusive disjunction*: an inclusive disjunction 'A **or** B' is true if either A is true but not B, or B is true but not A, or A and B are both true. An exclusive disjunction 'A **or** B' on the other hand is true when A is true, but B is not, or alternatively when B is true but A is not, but *not* when A and B are both true. That **or** is sometimes used in the sense of inclusive disjunction can, it seems, be established unequivocally. For instance, consider the conditional

(2.107) If Fred has failed the entire test then he has failed the practical part or he has failed the theoretical part.

Suppose that Fred has failed both the practical part and the theoretical part of the test and that (consequently) he has failed the test as a whole. Then, since the antecedent of (2.107) is true, (2.107) will be true only if its consequent is also true. Now, clearly, if the consequent were an exclusive disjunction then, in the given circumstances, it would be false; and so (2.107) as a whole would be false. But this is clearly absurd: a situation in which Fred fails the entire test because of failing both parts is surely not one in which we would consider the conditional falsified. This shows that the consequent of (2.107) is naturally interpreted not as an exclusive but as an inclusive disjunction.

The most frequently encountered argument that **or** *must* sometimes be understood as used exclusively is a bad one. It goes something like this: consider a disjunction like

(2.108) Jones has been elected president or Smith has been elected president.

What are the circumstances in which (2.108) could be true? Well, they are

(i) Jones has been elected president (in which case evidently Smith has not been elected president)

and

(ii) Smith has been elected president (in which case evidently Jones has not been elected president).

And this is all; (2.108) does not admit the case where both Jones and Smith are elected president. Since only the possibilities (i) and (ii) are compatible with the truth of (2.108), it follows that the **or** of (2.108) represents exclusive, not inclusive disjunction.

This is the argument. Its fallacy should be fairly transparent from the way we have presented it: the circumstance that only (i) and (ii) arise as possibilities for the truth of (2.108) has nothing whatever to do with the question whether **or** functions exclusively or inclusively in (2.108). It is a consequence simply of the fact that the two disjuncts of (2.108) exclude each other; since only one person can be elected president at the same time, the truth of one disjunct automatically carries with it the falsity of the other. Therefore we end up with (i) and (ii) as the only possible circumstances in which (2.108) is true irrespective of whether we assume that **or** functions as exclusive disjunction or that it functions as inclusive disjunction. In other words, the argument proves nothing of the sort it is meant to establish.

In fact, it is not easy to find any conclusive proof that **or** is ever used in an unequivocally exclusive sense. The best indication we know of that **or** is sometimes taken to carry an exclusive meaning is the not infrequent use in English of the locution: '**A or B or both**'. If **or** always unequivocally represented inclusive disjunction, then the addition **or both** would be inexplicable. For if the first **or**, which separates A and B, is inclusive, then the added disjunct is entirely redundant. That we feel it to be sometimes appropriate to add **or both** to a disjunction may therefore be seen as indicative of the speaker's concern to prevent his audience from inferring that he intends to exclude the case where A and B are both true; but this is an inference that the audience could be expected to make only if there was a possibility of taking the **or** of **A or B** as exclusive disjunction in the first place. In our opinion this is a better argument than the previous one. but is still doesn't prove, we think, that **or** really has an exclusive use. For the apparent appropriateness of adding **or both** could also have another explanation: there is a strong tendency to use disjunctive statements in which the disjuncts exclude each other. (We conjecture that there are deep cognitive reasons for this, but this is something we cannot go into here.) Thus, there may well be a tendency, on the part of someone who hears or reads a disjunctive statement, to assume, by default, that the speaker or author thinks of the disjuncts of his statement as mutually exclusive. Therefore, it might be just for the sake of blocking this inference that that speaker may wish to enclude the phrase **or both**.

The absence of any conclusive argument to show that **or** has an exclusive use justifies modern logic in its decision to focus on inclusive disjunction. We adopt the same policy and treat disjunctive conditions as inclusive. To make this fully explicit, eliminating the possible inclusive-exclusive ambiguity that some might associate with the **or**'s on the right-hand side of (2.106), we change (2.106) into (2.109):

(2.109) f verifies $K_1 \vee K_2 \vee ... \vee K_n$ iff f verifies at least one of $K_1, ..., K_n$.

To turn (2.109) into a condition that can serve as a new clause in the verification definition Def. 2.1.4, we need to remember that the DRSs K_1, ..., K_n may have non-empty universes, and thus that the question of verification can only properly be asked relative to embeddings that assign elements of the model to the members of these universes. We must therefore once again talk about appropriate extensions of f. But the modification is straightforward. We get

(2.110) f *verifies* $K_1 \vee K_2 \vee ... \vee K_n$ *in* M iff for some i ($i = 1,...,n$) there is an extension g_i of f such that $Dom(g_i) = Dom(f) \cup U_{K_i}$ and g_i verifies K_i in M.

Since we have once again extended our DRS formalism with a new type of condition – those of the form '$K_1 \vee K_2 \vee ... \vee K_n$' – we must adjust our definitions of an irreducible DRS, a possibly reducible DRS and of accessibility. None of this poses any real problems. The definition of an irreducible DRS has to be extended with the clause

(h) if for some $n \geq 2$, $K_1, ..., K_n$ are (completed) DRSs confined to V and R, then $K_1 \vee ... \vee K_n$ is a *(completed) DRS-condition confined to* V *and* R.

The definition of possibly incomplete DRSs would have to be adjusted similarly.

The definition of immediate subordination, Def. 2.1.2 (i), must be extended with the clause

(c) Con_{K_2} contains a condition of the form $K'_1 \vee ... \vee K'_n$ and for some $i \leq n$ $K_1 = K'_i$.

The definitions of subordination and accessibility, Def. 2.1.2 (ii) and Def. 2.1.3, remain unchanged.

We noted that

(2.97) Jones has borrowed a bicycle or he has rented it.

while it may not be optimally felicitous, seems nevertheless to permit a reading which interprets **it** as anaphoric to **a bicycle**. As indicated, there are in principle two possible explanations for this: either the discourse referents in one of the DRSs that make up a disjunctive DRS-condition are accessible to pronouns occurring in one of the other DRSs; or else the discourse referent for **a bicycle** in the DRS for (2.97) does not belong to the universe of the DRS representing the first disjunct, but occurs in some other position, which is accessible from the position of the pronoun **it** according to the principles of accessibility as we have stated them. The first of these explanations we have already rejected; it would entail general anaphoric accessibility between disjuncts, and this, we saw, would in many instances allow for readings of disjunctive sentences which they do not have. So we were led to an account according to which **a bicycle** gets a "specific" interpretation, which places its discourse referent within the universe of the main DRS. The possibility of anaphoric reference is then a consequence of the general principle that discourse referents from the main DRS are accessible to pronouns processed in any of its sub-DRSs – the same principle, in other words, which explains the anaphora in (2.87) or (2.91). Thus the completed DRS for (2.97) will look as follows:

(2.111)

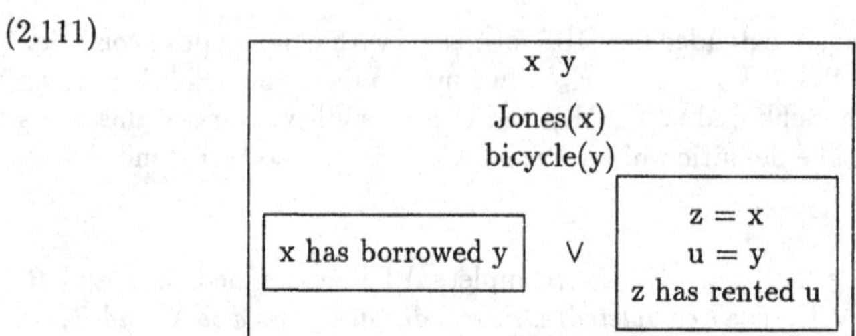

and is reached via the intermediate stages:

(2.112)

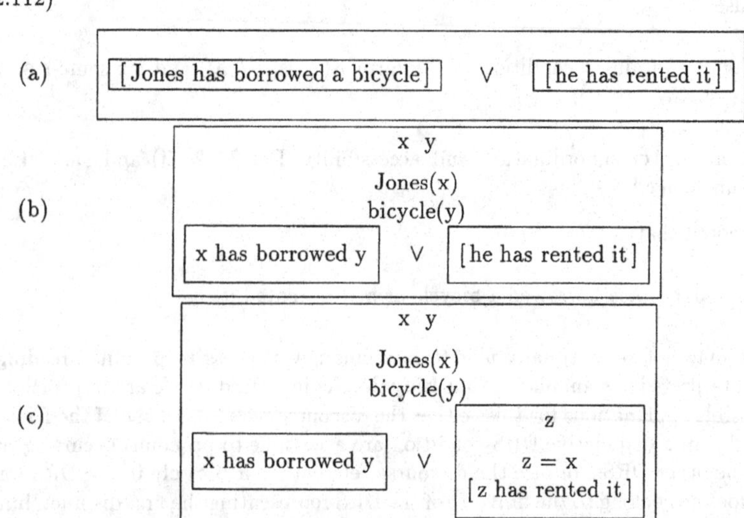

We conclude this section with a word of warning. In our discussion of example (2.97) we have spoken of a "specific" interpretation of the indefinite NP **a bicycle**. Our use of the term was motivated by the assumption that the correct construal of (2.97) involves entering the discourse referent for this indefinite NP not at the level at which the NP occurs at the stage when it is processed, but at some higher level. As we mentioned once or twice before, the possibility of entering the discourse referent that represents an indefinite NP at a higher level arises also in contexts which do not involve disjunction; and we promised that specific indefinites would be discussed at some greater length in 3.7.3. Our caution here is against throwing together, without careful consideration the "specificity" involved in the interpretation of disjunctive sentences such as (2.97) and the "specific" indefinites we encountered earlier, with which the discussion in 3.7.3 will be primarily concerned. For all we know, the kind of "specificity" exemplified by (2.97) is a different phenomenon from that illustrated by the earlier examples and is in need of a quite different explanation. If this is so, it is an explanation we will not supply in this book.

2.3.3 Non-Sentential Disjunctions

We have argued that

(2.97) Jones has borrowed a bicycle or he has rented it.

has a reading where **it** is anaphoric to **a bicycle**. But as we already observed, the sentence does not seem to be the most felicitous expression of that reading. A more natural way of expressing it is given by the sentence

(2.113) Jones has either borrowed or rented a bicycle.

(2.113) illustrates an important property of **or** to which we already referred at the start of this section, viz. that it can occur between expressions of syntactic categories other than sentences. Thus, in (2.113) **or** is used to combine two verbs, **borrowed** and **rented**.

As a matter of fact there are virtually no constraints on what kinds of constituents can be combined by **or**. Here are just a few more examples.

(2.114) Jones or Smith loves Lady Hermione.

(2.115) Mary loves Bill or hates Fred.

(2.116) Every man, woman or child admires Martina.

The only constraint on these combinations is that the combined expressions are of the *same* grammatical category. This common category is then also the category of the combination. We find this constraint obeyed in each of the examples above: in (2.113) the expressions are, as we saw, both transitive verbs; in (2.114) they are noun phrases; in (2.115) verb phrases; and in (2.116) they are common nouns.

Syntactically, the principles can be described as follows. For any syntactic category X, if ξ_1, ..., ξ_n are expressions of category X then so is the expression 'ξ_1, ..., ξ_{n-1} **or** ξ_n'.

Sentences which contain disjunctions of categories other than the category S can as a rule be paraphrased by disjunctive sentences of the type on which we have concentrated so far, i.e. sentences that involve only sentential disjunction. These paraphrases can be obtained by, as it were, "multiplying the disjunction out". For instance, (2.114) can be paraphrased as

(2.117) Jones loves Lady Hermione or Smith loves Lady Hermione.

and (2.115) as

(2.118) Mary loves Bill or Mary hates Fred.

This is not always possible, however. For instance, (2.116) cannot be paraphrased as

(2.119) Every man admires Martina, every woman admires Martina or every child admires Martina.

Nevertheless there is a sense in which most occurrences of **or**, among them those of the examples (2.113)–(2.116), can be reduced to the sentential **or** we have so far studied. The nature of this reduction is easily recognizable when we extend the analysis of disjunctive sentences we have so far given to non-sentential disjunctions in what appears to be the most natural and straightforward way. The one new principle we need is the following: when, in the course of constructing a DRS, we encounter a condition $\overline{\gamma}$ that has a subtree of the form[17]

(2.121)

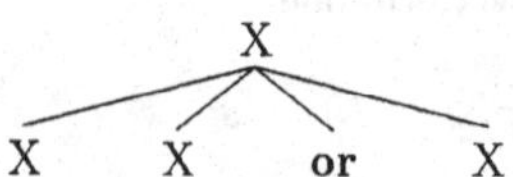

– where the expression associated with the mother node is the disjunction 'ξ_1, ..., ξ_{n-1} **or** ξ_n' of the expressions ξ_i associated with its n daughters – then we introduce a

[17] As some of our earlier formulations of construction rules this is not entirely accurate. For instance, DRS construction for (2.115) will after one step produce the structure

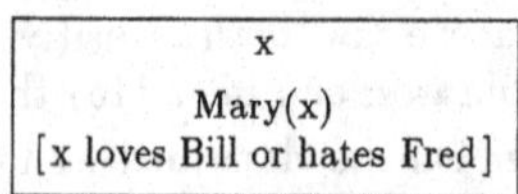

x
Mary(x)
[x loves Bill or hates Fred]

where the second condition is a shorthand for the syntactic structure disjunctive condition $K_1 \vee K_2 \vee \ldots \vee K_n$, with each K_i consisting of an empty universe and having as its only condition the result γ_i of replacing '$\xi_1, \ldots, \xi_{n-1}$ **or** ξ_n' in $\overline{\gamma}$ by ξ_i:

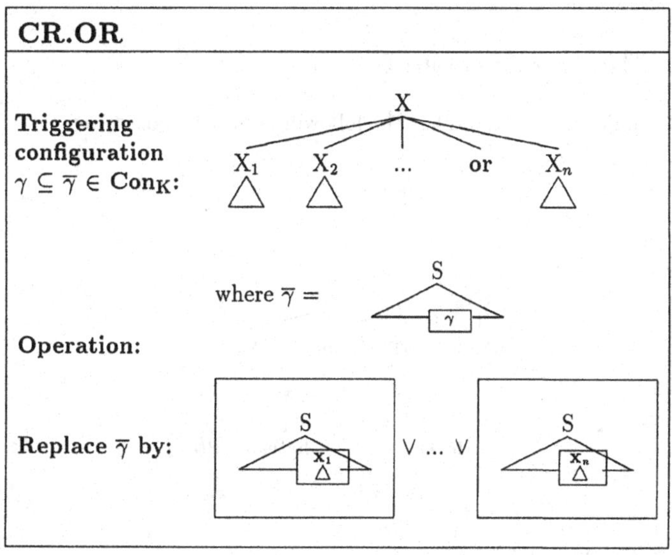

(2.120)

S
x VP′
VP
VP **or** VP
V NP V NP
loves PN **hates** PN
Bill **Fred**

This condition is not itself of the form (2.121). Rather, the part of it that is dominated by the node which triggers the needed application of the rule for **or**, here the highest VP node of (2.120), has the form represented in (2.121).

CR.OR has the effect of "translating" the disjunction between the expressions 'ξ_1, ..., ξ_n' of the category X into a sentence-like disjunction between the new conditions γ_1, ..., γ_n, represented by the DRS-condition $K_1 \vee K_2 \vee ... \vee K_n$. To see how this works let us construct DRSs for some of the sentences we have given, (2.114), (2.115) and (2.116).

The construction of a DRS for

(2.115) Mary loves Bill or hates Fred.

is unproblematic. The sentence has the following syntactic structure:

(2.122)

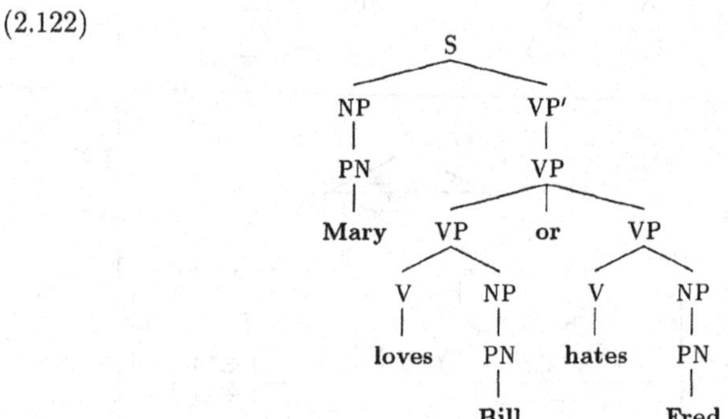

The first step yields a DRS

(2.123)

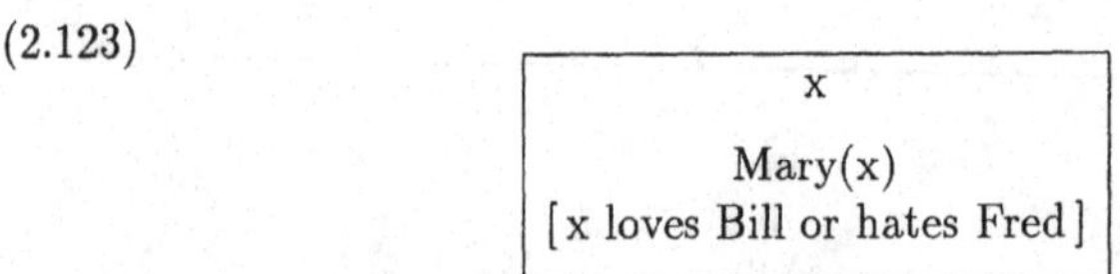

the second condition of which has the syntactic form given as (2.120) in footnote 17. Application of the new principle to this condition yields:

(2.124)

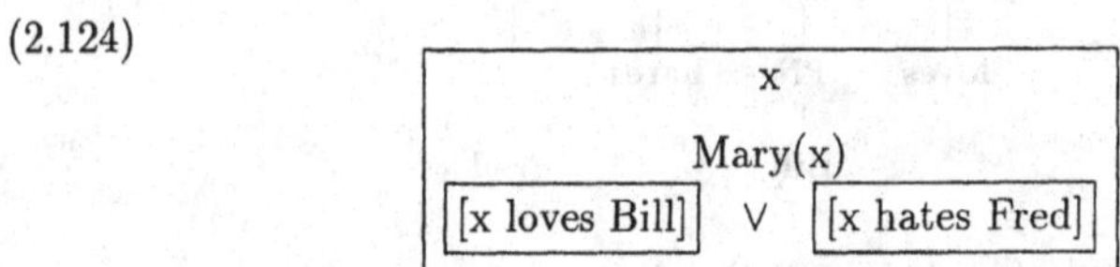

Treatment of the proper names in the disjunctive DRSs then yields, as final DRS,

(2.125)

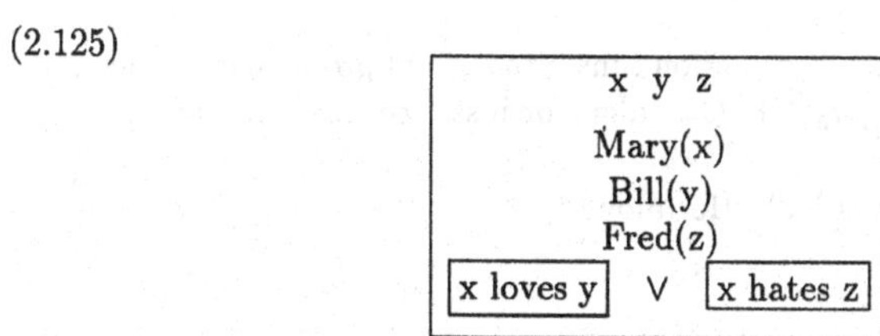

The DRS-construction for (2.116) is a little more interesting. The first step gives

(2.126)

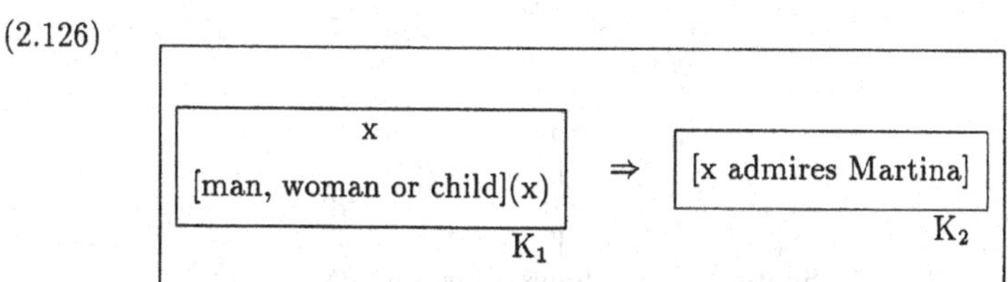

Applying CR.OR to the condition in K_1 and the proper name rule to the condition in K_2 we get

(2.127)

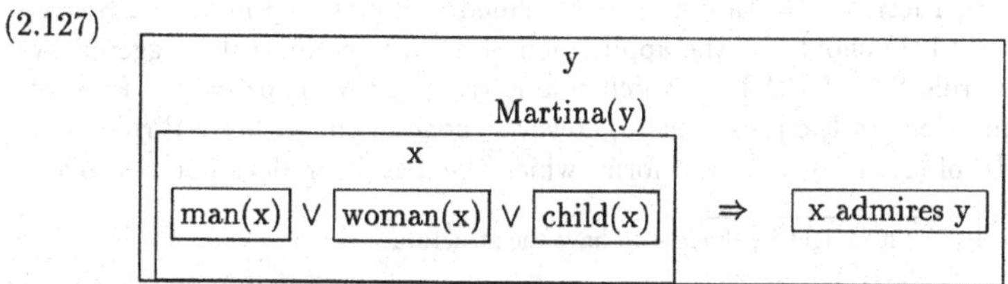

Comparing (2.125) and (2.127) we are able to recognize why it should have been possible to paraphrase (2.115) by means of a disjunctive sentence, whereas no such paraphrase seemed to be forthcoming for (2.116). The difference is that in the DRS for (2.115), the disjunctive condition is a condition of the main DRS, whereas in that for (2.116) it occurs inside the left-hand side DRS of an implicative condition. As a matter of fact, a paraphrase which brings out the ultimately sentential character of **or** can be given also for (2.116), provided we are prepared to depart a little further from the actual words which (2.116) contains:

(2.128) Everyone who is a man, who is a woman or who is a child admires Martina.

2.3.4 Disjunctive NPs

Our treatment of non-sentential disjunction runs into a slight problem in connection with disjunctions of the category NP. Consider, for instance, the sentence

(2.129) Smith or Jones loves Lady Hermione.

Let us assume that this sentence has the syntactic structure[18]

(2.131)

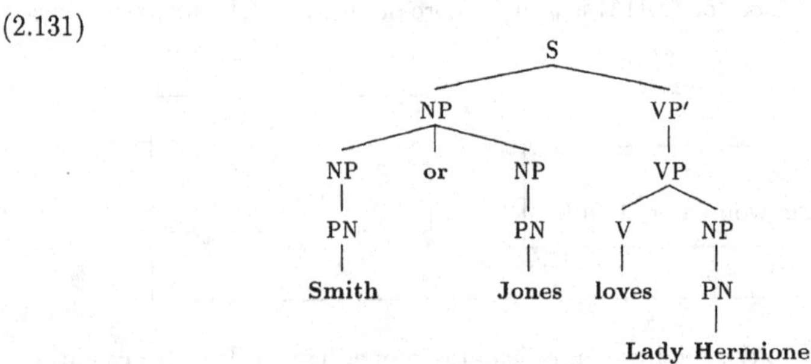

As the construction algorithm has been defined, the first step in the DRS construction for (2.131) should be the application of a construction rule triggered by the syntactic rule S $\rightarrow$ NP VP′ – which rule is triggered depends on the form of the NP in question. In the present case, however, none of our earlier NP rules will do, as the NP of (2.131) is of a new form, which the algorithm does not yet cover.

[18] Alternatively, (2.129) might be thought to have the structure

(2.130)

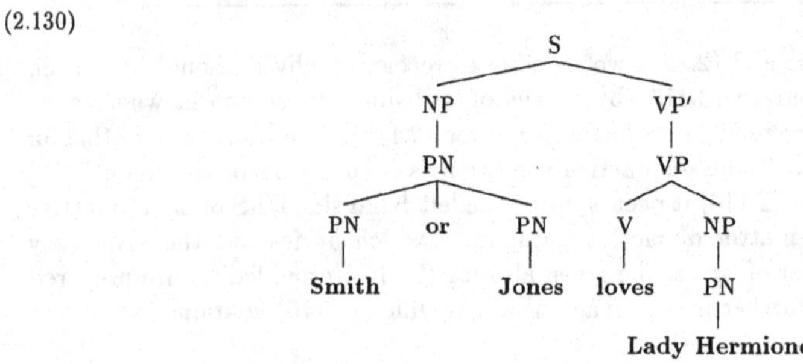

We will not pursue this alternative any further.

In fact, intuitively it is the rule CR.OR that ought to be applied here. However, as we have stated CR.OR, it – or more precisely the version of it we get when taking **X** to be the category NP – does not have the right triggering configuration for an NP rule. The triggering configuration which should enable the rule to act as a rule of that sort, and to get, in particular the DRS-construction for (2.131) off to a start, is:

(2.132)

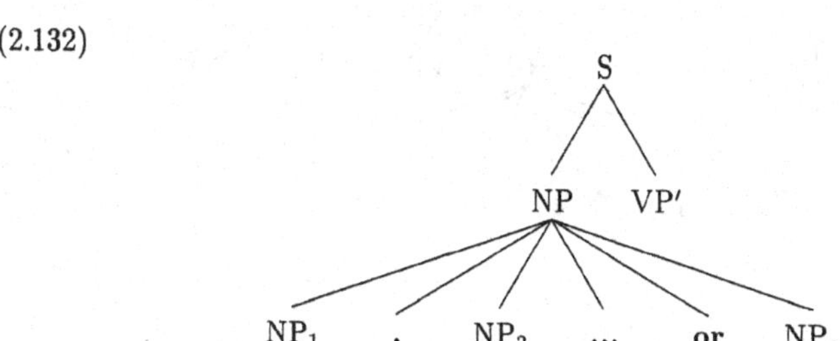

rather than the triggering configuration we get from the definition of CR.OR on page 197, which is

(2.133)

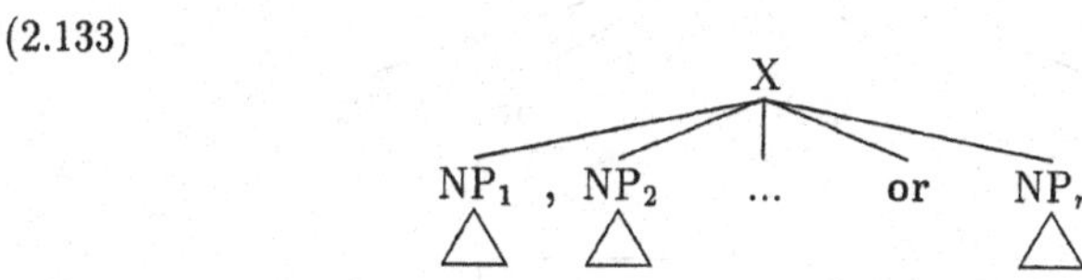

The difference between the rule we need and what CR.OR gives us is evidently very slight; indeed, CR.OR will give us just what we want provided only that we change, for the case where X is NP, its triggering configuration from (2.133) to (2.132).

Though the change is minor it is a change nonetheless. So formally we are forced to distinguish the NP case of CR.OR from those where X is some other category of our fragment. Thus our final formulation of the disjunction rule must take the form of a disjunction of cases:

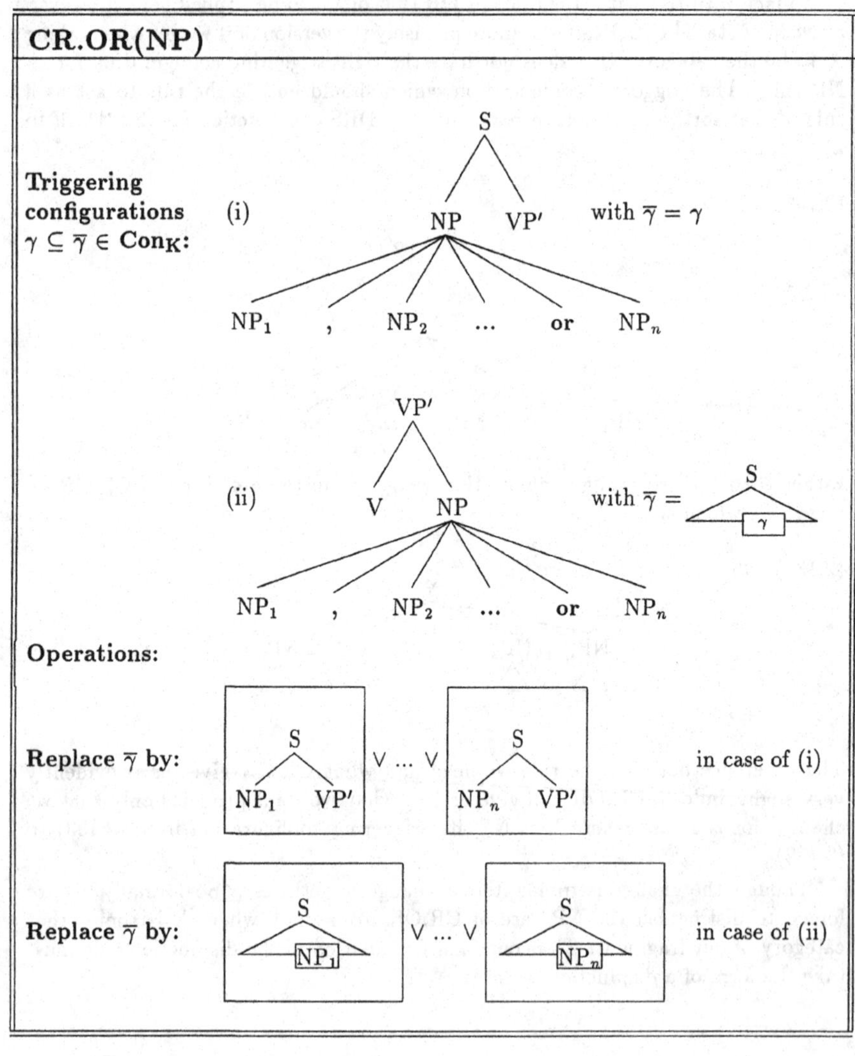
CR.OR(NP)
Triggering configurations $\gamma \subseteq \overline{\gamma} \in \text{Con}_K$:
(i)
S
NP
VP′
with $\overline{\gamma} = \gamma$
NP1 , NP2 ... or NPn
(ii)
VP′
V
NP
with $\overline{\gamma} =$
S
γ
NP1 , NP2 ... or NPn
Operations:
Replace $\overline{\gamma}$ by:
S
NP1 VP′
∨ ... ∨
S
NPn VP′
in case of (i)
Replace $\overline{\gamma}$ by:
S
NP1
∨ ... ∨
S
NPn
in case of (ii)

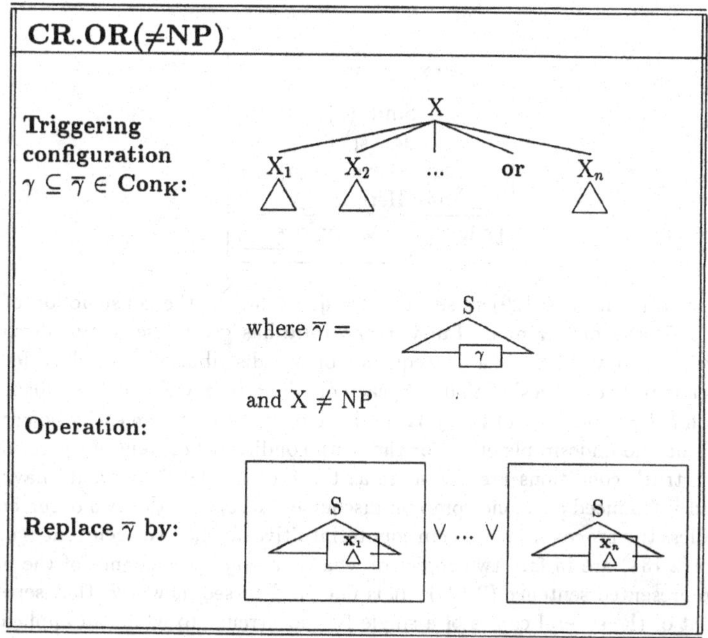

The result of applying CR.OR(NP) to (2.130) is

(2.134)

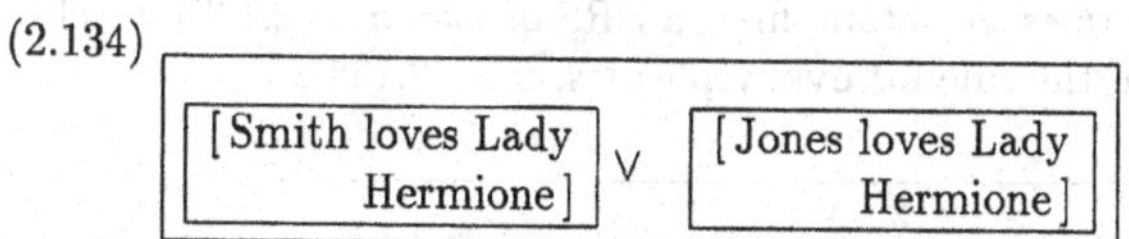

Note that processing of each of the disjuncts of (2.134) requires another application of an NP rule, this time of the rule CR.PN. But this is fully in accordance with the construction algorithm as we have it. Applying the rule CR.NP to the subject NPs **Jones** and **Smith** of the conditions in the two disjuncts of (2.134) and then applying it to the two occurrences of **Lady Hermione** gives us as final result

(2.135)

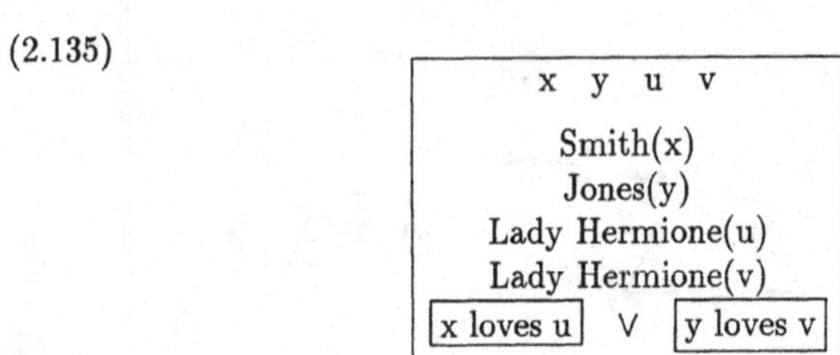

Our treatment of (2.129) raises another question. In the construction of the DRS (2.135) the proper name **Lady Hermione** has given rise to two discourse referents, **u** and **v**. This is a consequence of our distribution procedure for **or**, which leads to two 'copies' of that NP, each of which then yields its own discourse referent for the occurrence of **Lady Hermione** it contains. It can easily be verified that this has no undesirable effect for the truth conditional content of the resulting DRS: its truth conditions are the same as those of the DRS we would have got if we had introduced only one common discourse referent for the two occurrences. Nonetheless the procedure may seem counterintuitive, as the two occurrences of the name in (2.134) are in fact two copies of what is a *single* occurrence of the name in the represented sentence (2.129). It is not hard to see, however, that separate treatment of the several copies of a single NP occurrence to which an application of CR.OR(NP) may give rise is not only harmless, but sometimes even necessary. Consider

(2.136) Fred or Bill has solved every problem which Mary has assigned.

Proceeding according to our rules we obtain, first, a DRS of the form (2.137) which turns, by two applications of the rule for **every**-phrases, into (2.138)

(2.137)

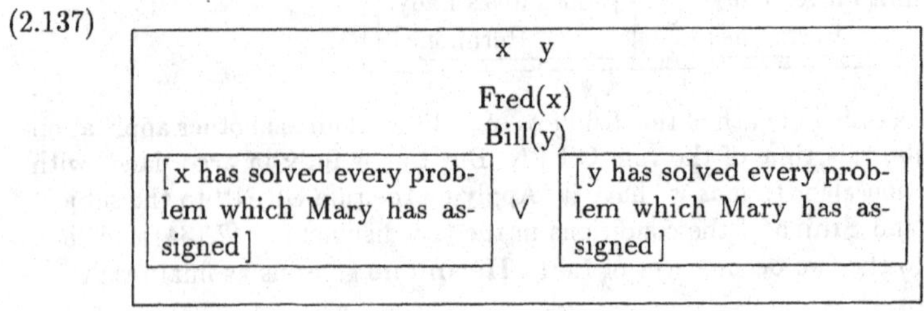

(2.138)

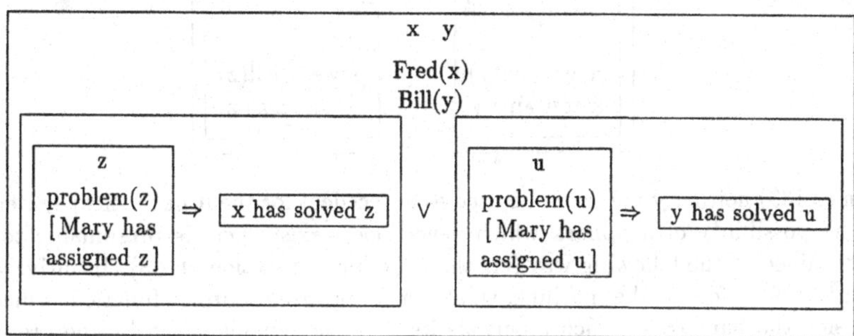

(2.138) represents the reading according to which either Fred has solved all the problems or Bill has solved all the problems. This, it seems to us, is not only a possible reading for (2.136), it is, for all we know, the only possible one. But we do not see any natural modification of the construction algorithm which would treat the NP **every problem which Mary has assigned** only once and yet would produce a DRS representing this reading.

The processing rule CR.OR for disjunctions is unable to provide the basis for the apparently possible anaphora in

(2.139) The barn contains a chain saw or a power drill. It makes an ungodly racket.

or

(2.140) If a commuter owns a car or a motorcycle, he drives it to work.

For instance, the first sentence of (2.139) gives, when processed with the help of CR.OR, rise to the DRS[19].

[19]We have treated **the barn** here in analogy with proper names – **the barn(x)** should be understood as meaning that x represents the object denoted by the form **the barn** (on the relevant occasion of use). For more on this subject see Section 3.3.

(2.141)

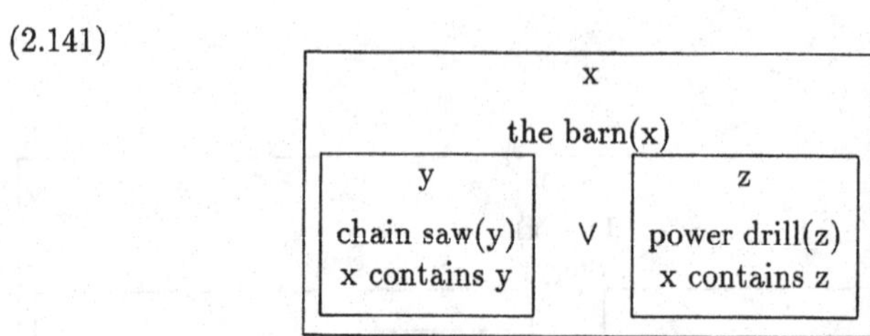

In (2.139) neither **y** nor **z** can be used as antecedent for the **it** of the next sentence. The possibility of anaphora which nevertheless exists here is presumably to be explained in the following way (cf. the introductory section of 2.3). Intuitively, **it** in (2.139) refers to the machine, whatever its precise nature or function, which is inside the barn (and which manifests itself to the outside world by the dreadful noise it produces). In other words, one interprets the two disjuncts **an electric saw** and **a power drill** as alternative characterizations of one and the same thing. It is the discourse referent for this thing that should act as antecedent for **it**. Thus the first sentence of (2.139) should be represented by a DRS like:

(2.142)

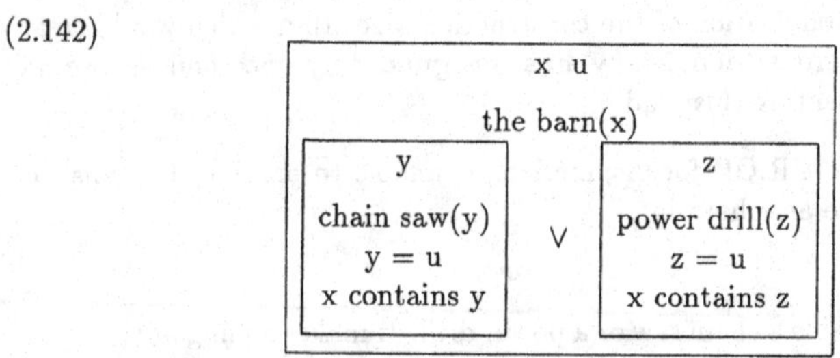

The discourse referent for the **it** of the next sentence can then be identified with **u**. We leave the problem of formulating a suitable construction rule which transforms a DRS like (2.141) into one like (2.142) as a topic for further investigation.

Exercises

1. Give DRSs for

   (a) If a woman fascinates a man then he likes her or she likes him.

   (b) Every gardener or butler loves or abhors Princess Caroline.

   Are these DRSs true in the model M of Exercise 7 of Section 1.4?

2. We noted that English allows the formation of disjunctions of arbitrary (finite) length. If we want to incorporate disjunctions of arbitrary length into our grammar, we have two options. The first involves introducing a *rule schema.* A rule schema is a (typically infinite) set of rules, which share a certain common form (the schema) but are nevertheless distinct from each other. Often the rules can be enumerated in a natural way. In the present case the rules could be represented schematically as

$$X \rightarrow X_1, X_2, ..., \textbf{or } X_n$$

The precise meaning of this is that we have for each number $n \geq 2$ and each syntactic category X a separate rule $R_{X,n}$ which permits us to rewrite any category label X as a sequence consisting of n copies of this label, where the last and one but last copy are separated by **or** while in all other cases (of any) two successive copies are separated by a comma.

The second possibility is to generate disjunctions *recursively.* Note that whenever α and β are expressions of category X and β is a disjunction, then the sequence 'α, β' is also a disjunctive expression of category X. A slight complication arises from the fact that the last two disjuncts of the disjunctions we admit are separated by the word **or**. This requires a separate phrase structure rule. Also, since the statement of the rule requires the distinction between expressions which are disjunctions and expressions which are not, we need a new feature which draws this distinction. We call the feature *Dis.* It has two values, '+' and '−'; *Dis* = + means that the expression in question *is* a disjunction, *Dis* = - that it is not. '−' is the default value. (Thus any syntactic description of an expression in which no value for *Dis* is specified is the description of a non-disjunctive expression.)

With the help of the feature *Dis* we can reduce the production of arbitrary disjunctions of the type X to a couple of rules. However, it will, strictly speaking, still be necessary to state a separate rule for each of the syntactic categories. Here we state the two rules for the case where X is NP.

$$NP_{Dis=+} \rightarrow NP_{Dis=-} \;\; \textbf{or} \;\; NP_{Dis=-}$$
$$NP_{Dis=+} \rightarrow NP_{Dis=-} \;\; , \;\; NP_{Dis=+}$$

Derive each of the following sentences both with the help of the disjunction rules of the first type and those of the second type.

(i) John, Bill or a girl who Bill likes, owns a house which Fred admires.

(ii) John loves, respects or admires Mary.

(iii) Fred loves Ella or hates every man whom Ella loves.

(iv) If a man does not own, lease or rent a car, Mary does not respect him.

In each case state explicitly the disjunction rules used in the derivation.

2.3.5 The Standard Version of Predicate Logic

Our next task is to determine how disjunctive conditions should be translated into formulas of predicate logic. We already saw, in Section 2.1, that there is a close connection between (our analysis of) conditionals and disjunctions. In particular, the material conditional $\varphi \rightarrow \psi$ of predicate logic is satisfied, we said, iff either ψ is satisfied or φ is not. This suggests that binary disjunctive conditions – i.e. conditions of the form $K_1 \vee K_2$ – may be translated as conditions with negated antecedents: $K_1 \vee K_2$ would go into $\neg\varphi_1 \rightarrow \varphi_2$ where φ_1 is the translation of K_1 and φ_2 the translation of K_2. It isn't immediately evident perhaps how disjunctive conditionals with more than two disjuncts could be translated into implicational formulas; but we will see below that it is possible to do this for disjunctive conditions with three or more constituents as well as for those which have just two disjuncts.

As it is, however, the standard versions of predicate logic make things easier for us, for they contain a sign that is made for the purpose of representing disjunctions. Predicate logic uses as a rule the same symbol that we have been using also, viz. '$\vee$'. '$\vee$' forms, like '&', a formula out of two or more others, and its meaning is just what we should expect from the counterpart of our DRS connector '$\vee$':

$\varphi_1 \vee ... \vee \varphi_n$ is true if at least one of the φ_i is.

Adding '$\vee$' yields a still more comprehensive language of predicate logic, a language which we obtain by adding to Def. 1.3.6 the clause

if $\varphi_1, ..., \varphi_n$ are formulas (with $n \geq 2$), then $(\varphi_1 \vee \varphi_2 \vee ... \vee \varphi_n)$ is a *formula.*

The definition of satisfaction, Def. 1.5.8, must be correspondingly extended. But this is unproblematic:

if φ is of the form $(\varphi_1 \vee \varphi_2 \vee ... \vee \varphi_n)$, then f *satisfies* φ *in* M iff for some $i \leq n$ f satisfies φ_i in M.

It ought to be clear how disjunctive DRS-conditions should be translated. To cover such conditions, the translation definition, Def. 1.5.5, must be extended with the clause if γ is of the form $K_1 \vee ... \vee K_n$, then the translation of γ is the formula $(\varphi_1 \vee ... \vee \varphi_n)$, where for $i = 1, ..., n$ φ_i is the translation of γ_i.

It will hardly be necessary to give examples of translations that involve disjunction, but for good measure let us give one. The DRS for

(2.87) Lady Hermione thrives. Either Jones loves her or Smith loves her.

is, as we saw above,

(2.90)

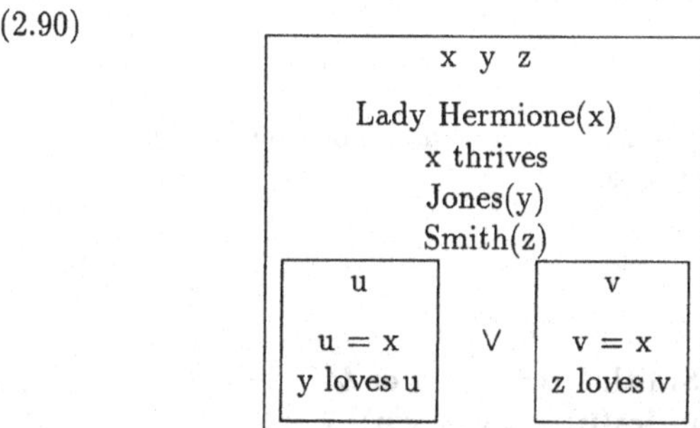

Proceeding in the intuitively obvious way (or, equivalently, following the directions of the extended Def. 1.5.5) we get the translation

(2.143) $\exists$**xyz(x = Lady Hermione & thrives(x)**
& y = Jones & z = Smith &
($\exists$u(u = x & loves(y,u)) $\vee$ $\exists$v(v = x & loves(z,v))))

We conclude this section with a few remarks about predicate logic. We already noted in passing that the languages of predicate logic we have defined here are, even after the changes we adopted in Section 2.2, still idiosyncratic in a couple of ways. The principal remaining differences are two. First, in the usual formulations of predicate logic '&' and '$\vee$' always combine just two formulas into a new formula. To express conjunctions or disjunctions with three or more constituents it is necessary to group these constituents in some way – how they are grouped is immaterial, since the translations which result from the different groupings are all equivalent. For instance, the DRS

(2.144)

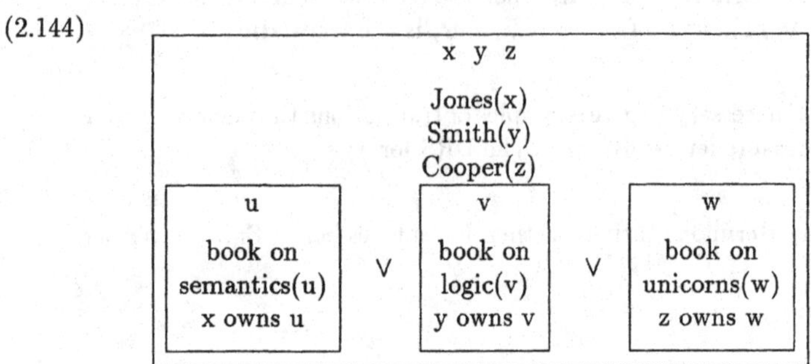

which represents the sentence

(2.145) Jones owns a book on semantics, Smith owns a book on logic or Cooper owns a book on unicorns.

can be translated either as[20]

(2.146) $\exists$**xyz(x = Jones & y = Smith & z = Cooper &**
(($\exists$**u(book on semantics(u) & owns(x,u))** $\vee$
$\exists$**v(book on logic(v) & owns(y,v)))** $\vee$
$\exists$**w(book on unicorns(w) & owns(z,w))))**

or as

(2.147) $\exists$**xyz(x = Jones & y = Smith & z = Cooper &**
($\exists$**u(book on semantics(u) & owns(x,u))** $\vee$
($\exists$**v(book on logic(v) & owns(y,v))** $\vee$
$\exists$**w(book on unicorns(w) & owns(z,w)))))**

The difference between (2.146) and (2.147) will become more clearly visible if we abbreviate the three disjuncts that make up the last conjuncts of these formulas as φ, ψ and χ. Then the last conjunct of (2.146) becomes

(2.148) $((\varphi \vee \psi) \vee \chi)$

[20]In (2.146) and (2.147) we have left '&' as a connective that can combine any finite number of conjuncts. If we treat '&' also as a binary connective, we get of course many more possible translations. Question: How many?

and the last conjunct of (2.147)

(2.149) $(\varphi \vee (\psi \vee \chi))$

Note, however, that (2.146) and (2.147) are both equivalent to

(2.150) ∃**xyz(x = Jones & y = Smith & z = Cooper &**
(∃**u(book on semantics(u) & owns(x,u))** ∨
∃**v(book on semantics(v) & owns(y,v))** ∨
∃**w(book on semantics(w) & owns(z,w))))**

and thus are equivalent to each other: each of the three formulas is satisfied iff at least one of φ, ψ or χ is.

The second difference between our version of predicate logic and the standard version concerns the quantifiers '∃' and '∀'. In the standard versions these quantifiers can bind only one variable at a time. The quantifier prefix of, e.g., (2.147) is thus inadmissible in these versions. Instead one should write

(2.151) ∃**x**∃**y**∃**z (x = Jones & y = Smith & z = Cooper &** $((\varphi \vee \psi) \vee \chi))$

(using the abbreviations φ, ψ and χ introduced above).[21] Again it is very easy to see from the definition of satisfaction that (2.147) and (2.151) are satisfied by the same assignments in the same models. (For instance, saying that there is an **x** such that there is a **y** such that **R(x,y)** is equivalent to saying that there are **x** and **y** such that **R(x,y)**.) The universal quantifier of standard predicate logic is subject to the same restriction. Thus the sentence

(2.46) Every farmer who owns a donkey beats it.

of Section 2.2 would translate not as

(2.152) ∀**xy ((farmer(x) & donkey(y) & owns(x,y))** → **beats(x,y))**

but as

[21]Note in this connection that in predicate logic we can add quantifier prefixes to formulas which begin with a quantifier themselves. This too is a difference between predicate logic and the languages of DRT.

(2.153) ∀x∀y ((**farmer(x)** & **donkey(y)** & **owns(x,y)**) → **beats(x,y)**)

Again the two formulas are obviously equivalent.

Because of these equivalences it is common practice to simplify formulas of the standard versions so that they come to look like the formulas we have been using. Thus one will often write '$(\varphi \vee \psi \vee \chi)$' instead of '$(\varphi \vee (\psi \vee \chi))$' (or of the equivalent '$((\varphi \vee \psi) \vee \chi)$'), and '**∃xyz**' in lieu of the official '**∃x∃y∃z**'. But in the standard version of predicate logic these notations are to be understood as informal substitutes for the official notation, which we tolerate for reasons of convenience or greater orthographic transparency, whereas in the version of the predicate logic we have been using up to now they are the real thing itself.

It should be clear from what we have said that formulas of standard predicate logic form a subclass of the formulas of the logic of Def. 1.5.2 to Def. 1.5.4 and Def. 1.5.6 to Def. 1.5.8. In fact, we obtain a formal definition of the standard versions if in the clauses for '&' and '∨' we restrict n, which in those definitions was allowed to be any number ≥ 2, to the special case '$n = 2$', and restrict n in the quantifier clauses to the case '$n = 1$'.

As a rule predicate logic does not use predicate symbols and individual constants which are – or, if one prefers, 'look like' – English words. Thus instead of '**farmer**' one would use, say, the capital letter '**F**', and instead of '**Jones**' the letter '**j**'. This is strictly a matter of cosmetics. But as it is helpful – viz. when one is trying to prove results about a formal system – to be able to refer to a definition of the language in which everything, including its non-logical vocabulary, is standardized, we conclude this section with an explicit definition of a standard system, partly for our own later use. This language has a fixed non-logical vocabulary, which however is so comprehensive that all applications of predicate logic which we will ever need can be accomodated within it.

Definition 2.3.1

The *non-logical vocabulary* V_0 consists of the following symbols:

(i) An infinite sequence of individual constants, c_1, c_2, ..., c_n, ...

(ii) For each $m \geq 0$ an infinite sequence of m-place predicate constants P_1^m, P_2^m, ..., P_n^m, ...

Definition 2.3.2

The *logical vocabulary* of PL_1 consists of the following symbols:

(i) *Variables*: **x**, **y**, **z**, **u**, **v**, ..., x_1, x_2, x_3, ...

(ii) *Logical constants*:

(a) the connectives: $\neg$, &, $\rightarrow$, $\vee$

(b) the identity sign: =

(f) the quantifiers: $\exists$ and $\forall$

(iii) Parentheses: (,)

Definition 2.3.3

(a) If Π is an m-place predicate and $\mathbf{x}_1, \ldots, \mathbf{x}_m$ are variables or individual constants, then $\Pi(\mathbf{x}_1, \ldots, \mathbf{x}_m)$ is a *formula of* PL_1.

(b) If each of σ and τ is either a variable or an individual constant, then $\sigma = \tau$ is a *formula of* PL_1.

(c) If φ is a formula of PL_1, then $\neg\varphi$ is a *formula of* PL_1.

(d) If φ_1 and φ_2 are formulas of PL_1, then $(\varphi_1 \ \& \ \varphi_2)$, $(\varphi_1 \vee \varphi_2)$ and $(\varphi_1 \rightarrow \varphi_2)$ are *formulas of* PL_1.

(e) If α is a variable and φ is a formula of PL_1, then $\exists\alpha\varphi$ and $\forall\alpha\varphi$ are *formulas of* PL_1.

Definition 2.3.4

(i) Let K be a DRS $\langle$U,Con$\rangle$ confined to V and R

(a) Suppose U = { }.
Then φ is *a translation of* the DRS K *into* PL_0 iff φ is of the form $(\varphi_1 \ \& \ \varphi_2 \ \& \ \ldots \ \& \ \varphi_n)$, where for $i = 1, \ldots, n$ φ_i is a translation of γ_i and $\langle\gamma_1, \gamma_2, \ldots, \gamma_n\rangle$ is some ordering of Con.

(b) Suppose U = $\{\alpha_1, \ldots, \alpha_n\}$.
Then φ is *translation of* the DRS K *into* PL_0 iff φ is of the form $\exists\alpha_1 \ldots \alpha_n \ (\varphi_1 \ \& \ \varphi_2 \ \& \ \ldots \ \& \ \varphi_n)$, where $\varphi_1, \ldots, \varphi_n$ are as under (a) and $\langle\alpha_1, \ldots, \alpha_n\rangle$ is some ordering of U.

(ii) Suppose γ is a DRS-condition confined to V and R.

(a) Suppose γ has the form $\nu(\alpha)$, where α is a discourse referent in R and ν is a proper name in V, then φ is a *translation of* γ *into* PL_0 iff φ is the formula $\alpha = \nu$.

(b) Suppose γ has the form $\nu(\alpha)$, where α is a discourse referent in R and ν is a common noun in V, then φ is a *translation of* γ *into* PL_0 iff φ is the formula $\nu(\alpha)$.

(c) Suppose γ has the form $\nu\alpha$, where α is a discourse referent in R and ν is an intransitive verb in V, then φ is a *translation of* γ *into* PL_0 iff φ is the formula $\nu(\alpha)$.

(d) Suppose γ has the form $\alpha\nu\beta$, where α and β are discourse referents in R and ν is a transitive verb in V, then φ is a *translation of* γ *into* PL_0 iff φ is the formula $\nu(\alpha,\beta)$.

(e) Suppose γ has the form $\alpha = \beta$, where α and β are discourse referents in R, then φ is a *translation of* γ *into* PL_0 iff φ is the formula $\alpha = \beta$.

(f) Suppose γ has the form $\neg$K, where K is a DRS confined to V and R, then φ is a *translation of* γ *into* PL_0 iff φ is the formula $\neg\psi$, where ψ is a translation of K.

(g) Let $K_1 \Rightarrow K_2$ be an implicative condition, where $K_1 = \langle U_1, Con_1\rangle$, U_1 consists of the discourse referents $\alpha_1,...,\alpha_n$ and Con_1 consists of the conditions $\gamma_1,...,\gamma_m$. Then φ is a *translation* of $K_1 \Rightarrow K_2$ iff φ is a formula of the form $\forall\alpha_1...\alpha_n((\psi_1 \& \psi_2 ... \psi_m) \rightarrow \psi)$ where for $i = 1,...,m$ ψ_i is a translation of γ_i and ψ is a translation of K_2.

(h) Suppose C is of the form $K_1 \vee ... \vee K_n$, then the translation of C is the formula $(\varphi_1 \vee ... \vee \varphi_n)$, where for $i = 1,...,n$ φ_i is the translation of C.

2.4 Conjunction

From a syntactic point of view there is a close similarity between **or** and **and**. It is twofold. First both **or** and **and** can combine any finite number of expressions into a new compound expression; and second, they can combine expressions of all grammatical categories, provided only that all the component expressions are of one and the same category. Also, for **and** as well as for **or** the treatment of compound expressions of categories other than S can be reduced to the sentential case - although in the case of **and** there is one important exception to this principle, that where the conjuncts are NPs. We will consider that case separately in Chapter 4.

As we did when dealing with **or**, we will concentrate on the sentential use of **and** first. We adopt syntactic principles which allow the construction, from any n sentences S_1, ..., S_n (with $n \geq 2$), of a single sentence of the form S_1, S_2, ..., S_{n-1} **and** S_n. Sentences of this form are called *conjunctions* or *conjunctive sentences* and their components are called the *conjuncts of* the conjunction in question. The truth conditions for conjunctions are entirely straightforward: S_1, S_2, ..., S_{n-1} **and** S_n is true if each of S_1, ..., S_n is true. This suggests a very simple processing principle for DRS-conditions in conjunctive form: If γ is a condition of the form $[\gamma_1, \gamma_2, ..., \gamma_{n-1}$ **and** $\gamma_n]$, simply replace γ by the conditions γ_1, ..., γ_n. For any DRS which contains all the γ_i as conditions requires for its verification that each of the γ_i be verified, and intuitively this is just the constraint imposed by the single condition $[\gamma_1, \gamma_2, ..., \gamma_{n-1}$ **and** $\gamma_n]$.

Unfortunately this won't do. The reason is connected with anaphora. For note that the procedure we have been following in constructing DRSs allows the conditions γ_1, ..., γ_n, to act, once they have been introduced as separate members of the condition set of a given DRS, as if they were "accessible" to each other. In particular, it would allow pronouns in an earlier conjunct to be anaphorically linked to NPs occurring in a later one. But this is something that is not, or only marginally, possible. By way of example compare

(2.154) She owns it and Maria loves a donkey.

and

(2.155) Maria owns a donkey and she loves it.

In (2.155) interpretation of **she** and **it** as anaphoric to **Maria** and **a donkey** is unproblematic. In (2.154) on the other hand these interpretations of the pronouns are questionable. In fact, it seems that the anaphoric connection between **it** and **a donkey** is well-neigh impossible; interpreting **she** as anaphoric to the subsequent proper name **Maria** is not natural either, but perhaps just possible – compare

(2.156) She owns a donkey and Maria loves it.

Whatever the exact explanation of the difference in acceptability between (2.154) and (2.155), it is clear that the relationships between the successive conjuncts of a conjunction are not symmetrical and that these asymmetries have something to do with the order in which the conjuncts reach the hearer or reader, and in which they are therefore, inevitably, processed. We should remind ourselves in this connection that the difference between (2.154) and (2.155) has its immediate parallel in that between the two-sentence texts. Thus, of (2.157) and (2.158)

(2.157) She owns it. Maria loves a donkey.

(2.158) Maria owns a donkey. She loves it.

(2.158) is formally identical with our very first example (1.1) – and we saw already in Chapter 1 how its anaphoric pronouns can be dealt with – while (2.157) cannot be converted into a DRS which represents **she** and **it** as anaphoric to **Maria** and **a donkey**. The reason is that, as we have set up the construction algorithm, the first sentence of (2.157) must have been fully processed before processing of the second sentence may begin. If this is the right explanation in the case of a succession of separate sentences, one would expect it to be the correct account also for the apparently similar difficulty that is illustrated by (2.154). In other words, we would expect that the prohibition against anaphora in (2.154) is the effect of a principle according to which processing of the first conjunct must be completed before that of the second can start.

If this is the right way of accounting for the difference between (2.154) and (2.155), and if the construction algorithm is to follow its lead, then the algorithm should be modified in such a way that processing of the second conjunct is effectively blocked until the first conjunct has been fully converted into irreducible conditions. However, to formally implement this principle is, as we will see, not entirely trivial. The main tool we need for the implementation is a device which we have not yet used – that of blocking the processing of certain conditions until other conditions have been processed fully. There are various ways in which such a device can be realized. The one for which we opt is that of assigning to certain DRS-conditions an *index*, and to insist that conditions with a given index be processed only when no reducible conditions with a smaller index remain. Formally this means that the members of the condition sets of DRSs will now be indexed conditions, that is pairs $\langle\gamma, i\rangle$ consisting of a DRS-condition and an index.

What is an index? This is a matter we may decide in any way we like. Probably the simplest kind of index is an integer. So let us see where taking our indices to be integers will get us.

The crucial point of our indices is that the later conjuncts of a conjunction end up with higher indices than the earlier ones, and that this prevents the later ones from being processed before processing of the earlier ones is completed. Thus suppose we have a condition of the form

(2.159)

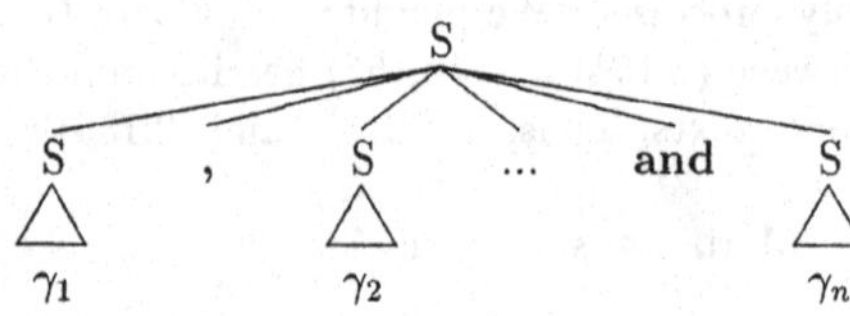

with index m. This condition should be decomposable into two indexed conditions $\langle\gamma_1, k\rangle$ and $\langle\gamma', l\rangle$ where γ' is the structure

(2.160)

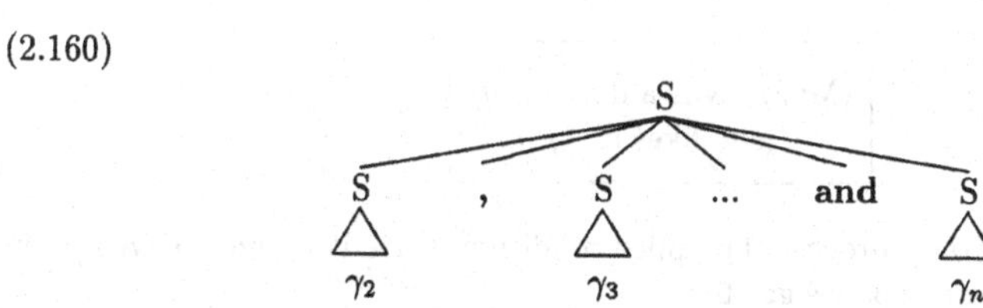

and where $k < l$.

The application of other construction rules should not affect the indices, i.e. application of any of the rules we have formulated in the preceding chapter and sections should pass the index of the condition to which they are being applied on to the conditions which result from the application. Thus, for instance, applying CR.PN to the indexed condition ⟨**Jones owns Ulysses**, m⟩ will yield indexed conditions ⟨**Jones(x)**, m⟩ and ⟨**x owns Ulysses**, m⟩.

Given that no construction rule other than CR.AND alters indices, what can we say about the relation between the numbers l and k, which according to our proposal should come in place of the index m of a processed conjunction? We can say at least this: γ may have got its index m because it results from some already processed conjunction, in which case m will have to secure that γ be fully processed before the construction algorithm tackles any of the later conjuncts of that conjunction (if any). The same should be true of the conjuncts γ_1 and γ' of γ: γ_1 should have been fully processed before we may start with γ'. To make sure that these constraints will be observed we should make neither k nor l greater than m. One way to secure this is to put l equal to m and k equal to $m-1$. This admittedly entails that, as we go on, each of the conditions $\gamma_1, ..., \gamma_{n-1}$ will get the index $m-1$. But this would not matter because the first conjunct that has got index $m-1$ will be completely reduced before the conjunct $\langle[\gamma_2, ... \text{ and } \gamma_n], m\rangle$ will be reduced to $\langle[\gamma_2], m-1\rangle$ and $\langle[\gamma_3, ... \text{ and } \gamma_n], m\rangle$.

We need one further provision concerning the index of a sentence when it gets first introduced into the DRS. As it turns out it is immaterial what index we choose for this; but let us be explicit and use the number 1 for this purpose.

With these stipulations the difference between (2.154) and (2.155) comes out just as it should. First (2.155). We start with the DRS

(2.161)

⟨Mary owns a donkey and she likes it, 1⟩

The first step, an application of the new rule CR.AND, turns this into

(2.162)

⟨Mary owns a donkey, 0⟩
⟨she likes it, 1⟩

At this point we can only process the upper condition, since it is the one with the lower index. After two steps we get to

(2.163)

x y
⟨Mary(x), 0⟩
⟨donkey(y), 0⟩
⟨x owns y, 0⟩
⟨she likes it, 1⟩

(2.163) no longer contains any reducible conditions of index < 1, so now the second conjunct of (2.155) can be processed in the usual way, giving us

(2.164)

x y u v
⟨Mary(x), 0⟩
⟨donkey(y), 0⟩
⟨x owns y, 0⟩
⟨u = x, 1⟩
⟨v = y, 1⟩
⟨u likes v, 1⟩

Note that if we ignore the indices, (2.164) is equivalent with the DRS which our earlier algorithm allows us to construct from (2.158).

(2.154), on the other hand, does not permit completion. The first steps produce

(2.165)

⟨She owns it, 0⟩
⟨Mary loves a donkey, 1⟩

This time we are not permitted to process the condition **Mary owns a donkey** until we have dealt with the lower-indexed condition **She owns it**, which would require finding antecedents for **she** and **it**; but these we do not yet have, and so the construction cannot proceed any further.

Unfortunately the present algorithm does not give the desired results in more complicated cases. For instance, it doesn't when applied to conditionals which have conjunctions for their antecedents. Consider for instance

(2.166) If Mary likes him and she owns a tape recorder, Fred will get it.

The first few steps in the DRS-construction for (2.166) give rise to the DRS

(2.167)

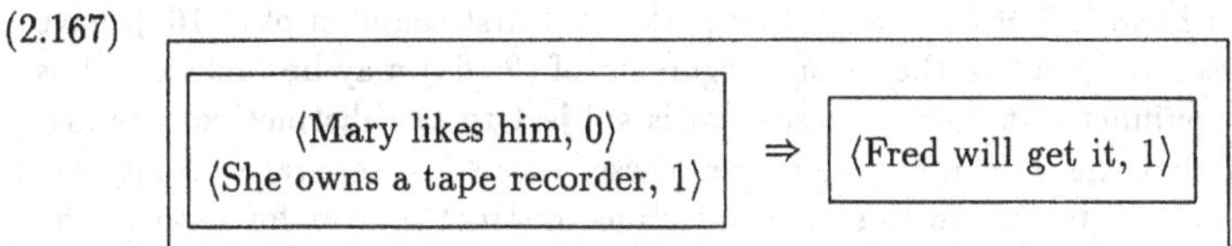

According to our stipulations we must first completely process **Mary likes him** before we may process **Fred will get it**. But this will not be possible, for we won't then have a discourse referent representing Fred, which we would want to use as antecedent for **him**. Of course, our reasons for going from $\langle S_1$ **and** $S_2, m\rangle$ to $\langle S_1, k\rangle$ and $\langle S_2, l\rangle$ with $k = m-1$ and $l = m$ were less than compelling, and we might wonder if another choice of indices k and l for S_1 and S_2 would not remove the problem. It is easily seen, however, that no other choice will do. For on the one hand we want to be able to treat the consequent before dealing with the pronoun **him**; this implies that $k \not< 1$. On the other we should be able to process **a tape recorder** in the second conjunct of the antecedent before processing the pronoun **it** in the consequent; this entails that $l \not> 1$. Finally, for reasons already explained, it ought to be the case that $k < l$. So we have $l \leq 1 \leq k < l$, which is clearly impossible.

Another possible solution might be to leave certain conditions without indices: if the consequent of (2.166) were without index, and only the conjuncts of the antecedent had indices indicating in which order they are to be processed, the particular conflict we just discovered in our discussion of (2.167) would not arise. However, this will not work either. For the entire conditional (2.166) might be a conjunct of some larger sentence, as in

(2.168) If Mary likes him and she owns a tape recorder, Fred will get it and if Mary doesn't like him and she owns a tape recorder, Fred will not get it.

In such cases the consequent of the first conjunct must have an index that tells the algorithm that the second conditional cannot be subjected to rule application before all parts of the first conjunct, including in particular its consequent, have been fully processed.

The conclusion must be that we cannot identify indices with numbers. The problem we are facing can informally be described as follows. In general a reducible DRS-condition can come from a conjunction which is itself a subexpression of a conjunct of some other (larger) conjunction. This would be true for instance of the conjuncts of the antecedent of the first conjunct of (2.168). Consider in particular the second conjunct of that antecedent. On the one hand this conjunct may be processed only after the first conjunct of this antecedent has been processed already. On the other hand it must, like any other part of the first conjunct of (2.168), have been processed fully before the second argument of (2.168) may be tackled. Thus the second conjunct of the first antecedent is subject to two distinct constraints. It is crucial that the indexing system keep these constraints separate. It appears that the best way to ensure this is to introduce distinct indices for each of the constraints.

This means, first, that in general a condition will have to come with a *set* of indices and, second, that the indices carry information that determines which are the indices of other conditions with which they are to be compared. The mechanism we will use to realize this second purpose is to label indices with the very conjunctions whose sequential processing they are meant to ensure. In other words, we now take - and this then is our definitive proposal - an *index* to be a pair $\langle \delta, m \rangle$ consisting of a DRS-condition δ and a number m. The members of condition sets will now be pairs of the form $\langle \gamma, \mathrm{I} \rangle$ where γ is a DRS-condition and I is a set of indices. (As we will see, I will often be empty.)

As before, all construction principles other than CR.AND leave the index sets invariant. (Thus CR.PN applied to ⟨**Jones owns Ulysses**, I⟩ gives rise to ⟨**Jones(x)**, I⟩ and ⟨**x owns Ulysses**, I⟩.) The effect of the new rule CR.AND is that of *adding* new indices. Thus the result of applying CR.AND to $\langle \gamma, \mathrm{I} \rangle$, where γ is the sentence structure (2.159), is the couple of conditions $\langle \gamma_1, \mathrm{I} \cup \{\langle \gamma, 1 \rangle\} \rangle$, $\langle \gamma_2, \mathrm{I} \cup \{\langle \gamma, 2 \rangle\} \rangle$, where γ_1 is as indicated in (2.159) and γ_2 is (2.160).

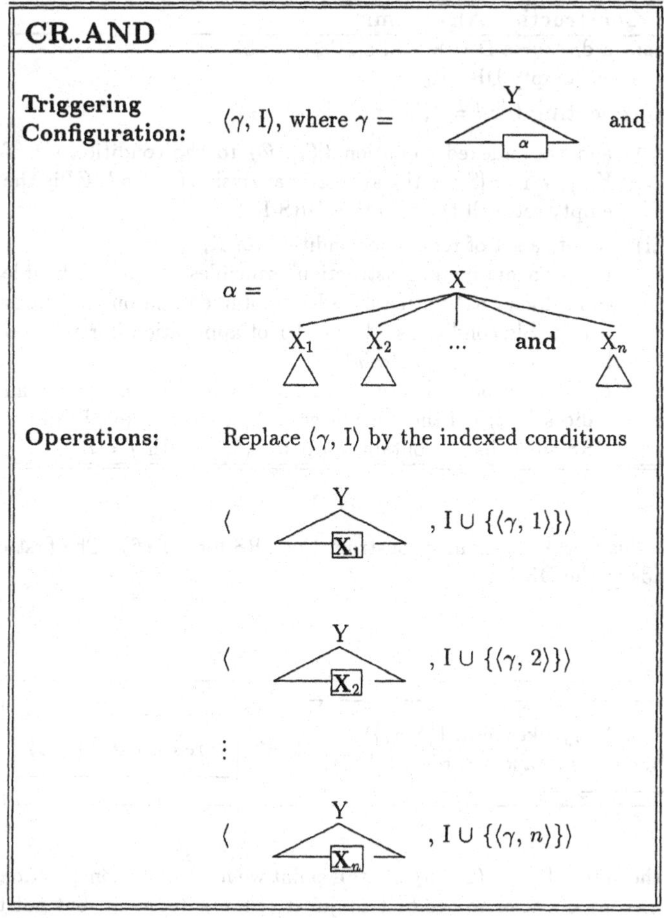

CR.AND
Triggering Configuration:
⟨γ, I⟩, where γ =
Y
α
and
α =
X
X1
X2
...
and
Xn
Operations:
Replace ⟨γ, I⟩ by the indexed conditions
⟨
Y
X1
, I ∪ {⟨γ, 1⟩}⟩
Y
X2
, I ∪ {⟨γ, 2⟩}⟩
Y
Xn
, I ∪ {⟨γ, n⟩}⟩

The constraint on rule application is now as follows: Before $\langle\gamma, \text{I}\rangle$ may be subjected to rule application, it must be the case for all indices $\langle\delta, i\rangle$ in I that there is no reducible condition γ' such that $\langle\gamma', \text{I}'\rangle$ is in the DRS and I′ contains an index $\langle\delta, j\rangle$ with $j < i$. Finally, where the old algorithm introduces a new sentence (more exactly: its syntactic analysis γ) to the DRS, we now add instead the indexed condition $\langle\gamma, \emptyset\rangle$ (where '∅' is the empty set).

DRS-Construction Algorithm	
Input:	a discourse D = $S_1, \ldots, S_i, S_{i+1}, \ldots, S_n$ the empty DRS K_0
Keep repeating for $i = 1, \ldots, n$:	
(i)	add the indexed condition $\langle[S_i], \emptyset\rangle$ to the condition set of K_{i-1}, where $[S_i]$ is the syntactic analysis of S_i and '$\emptyset$' is the empty set; call the resulting DRS $K_i{}^*$
(ii)	Input: a set of reducible conditions of $K_i{}^*$ Keep on applying construction principles to each reducible condition of $K_i{}^*$ until a DRS K_i is obtained that only contains irreducible conditions. The order of application is restricted by the following *constraint*: $\langle\gamma, I\rangle$ may be subjected to a processing rule only if for all indices $\langle\delta, i\rangle \in I$ there is no reducible condition $\langle\gamma', I'\rangle$ in the DRS such that I' contains an index $\langle\delta, j\rangle$ with $j < i$.

To see how this works, let us first construct the DRS for (2.166). The first couple of steps leads to the DRS

(2.169)

⟨Mary likes him, $\{\langle\delta, 1\rangle\}$⟩ ⟨She owns a tape recorder, $\{\langle\delta, 2\rangle\}$⟩	⇒	⟨Fred will get it, $\emptyset$⟩

where δ is the antecedent of (2.166). At this point we may apply construction rules either to the consequent or to the first conjunct of the antecedent, but not to the second conjunct, since its index $\langle\delta, 2\rangle$ is matched by the lower index $\langle\delta, 1\rangle$ of the first conjunct, which therefore needs to be reduced first. Note how crucial it is that we can first process part of the consequent, and thereby obtain a discourse referent for **Fred**, before we complete processing of the first conjunct; at the same time processing of the first conjunct needs to be completed before we can finish processing of the consequent. For processing its pronoun **it** requires that we first deal with its intended antecedent **a tape recorder**, and according to our proposal that NP, since being part of the second conjunct, can be processed only after processing of the first conjunct is complete. For the sake of explicit illustration we give all the remaining construction stages:

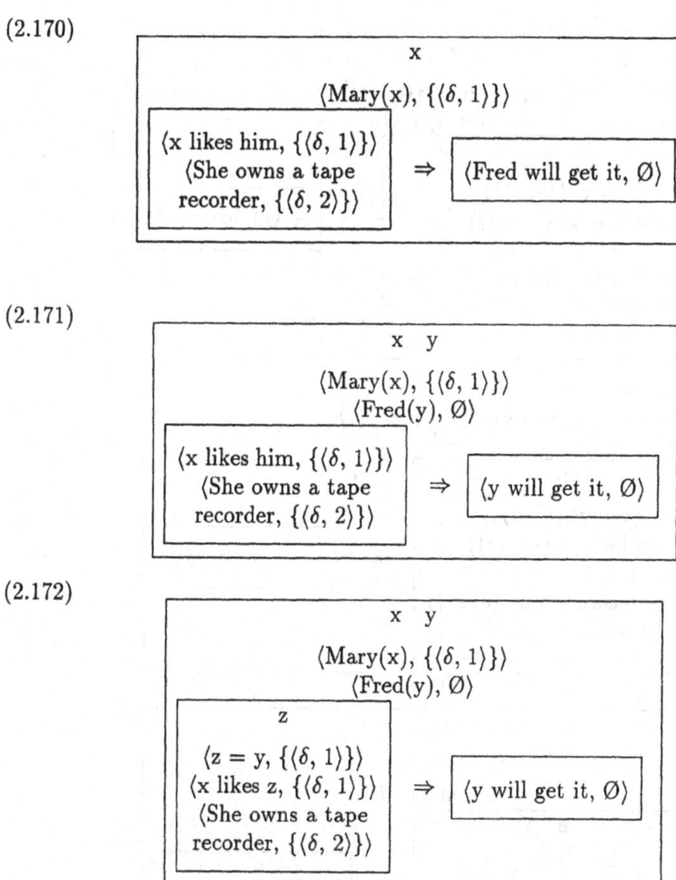

At this point all conditions with index $\langle \delta, 1 \rangle$ are irreducible. So we can now process the condition with index $\langle \delta, 2 \rangle$.

(2.173)

(2.174)

(2.175)

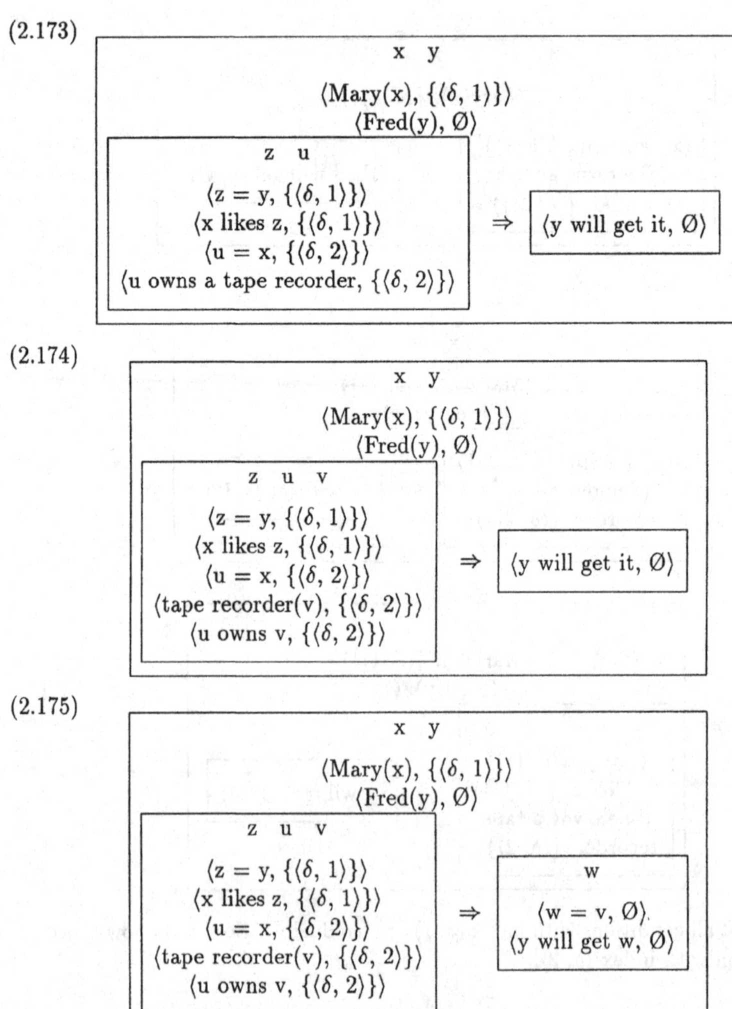

The DRS-construction for (2.168) is a good deal more involved. This is to be expected, since (2.168) was designed to illustrate one aspect of our indexing system that did not show up in the last example, viz. the need for multiple indices. We will carry out only a few steps of the construction, just enough to make the use of multiple indices plain. The first step yields

(2.176)

⟨If Mary likes him and she owns a tape recorder, Fred will get it, $\{\langle\delta, 1\rangle\}$⟩ ⟨If Mary doesn't like him and she owns a tape recorder, Fred will not get it, $\{\langle\delta, 2\rangle\}$⟩

where δ is the syntactic structure of (2.168). From this we get

(2.177)

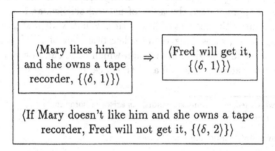

⟨Mary likes him and she owns a tape recorder, $\{\langle\delta, 1\rangle\}$⟩	⇒	⟨Fred will get it, $\{\langle\delta, 1\rangle\}$⟩
⟨If Mary doesn't like him and she owns a tape recorder, Fred will not get it, $\{\langle\delta, 2\rangle\}$⟩		

and then

(2.178)

⟨Mary likes him, $\{\langle\delta, 1\rangle,\langle\eta, 1\rangle\}$⟩ ⟨she owns a tape recorder, $\{\langle\delta, 1\rangle,\langle\eta, 2\rangle\}$⟩	⇒	⟨Fred will get it, $\{\langle\delta, 1\rangle\}$⟩
⟨If Mary doesn't like him and she owns a tape recorder, Fred will not get it, $\{\langle\delta, 2\rangle\}$⟩		

where η is the syntactic structure of the antecedent of (2.166). We will not carry the construction further, for (2.178) makes clear already what constraints on order of processing the conditions of (2.178) impose. Thus all conditions that are part of the complex conditional condition in (2.178) must be fully processed before processing can start of the condition with index $\langle\delta, 2\rangle$. Moreover, the condition with index $\langle\eta, 1\rangle$ must be processed before that with index $\langle\eta, 2\rangle$.

One problem with our revised construction algorithm is that it has the effect that the mentioned reading of (2.156) is now blocked altogether. Thus, whereas our earlier algorithm appeared to be too liberal with regard to (2.156), the revised one seems to be too severe.

The difficulty with which sentences such as (2.156) present us is of a fundamental methodological kind – here we take up a remark at the end of Exercise 4, Section 2.1. In fact, it is a difficulty not just for the theory presented here, but for all other rigorous accounts of syntax and/or semantics which have been proposed to date. All those theories, including the one developed here, are designed to paint pictures in black and white: all concepts they analyse or define are assumed to be sharp; they apply either unreservedly or not at all. In this they follow the methodological canons inherited from the natural sciences. However, the natural sciences do have techniques to deal with shades of grey, for example techniques involving probability theory or perturbation theory. Such techniques are intimately connected with the quantitative character of natural science, and they do not appear to be applicable to the subject of linguistics. What is ultimately but urgently needed – for linguistics, as well as many other branches of the human or social sciences – is a new methodological foundation which can deal, in a scientifically respectable way, with gradations as well as with concepts that are strictly 'yes/no'.[22]

---

[22]The problem which led us to indexed conditions arises in some form also in connection with disjunction. Thus, just as

(2.179) She loves Bill and he admires Maria.

and

(2.180) She loves him and Bill admires Maria.

are less natural than

(2.181) Maria loves Bill and he admires her.

so

(2.182) She loves Bill or he admires Maria.

and

(2.183) She loves him or Bill admires Maria

seem less felicitous than

(2.184) Maria loves Bill or he admires her.

However, just like their conjunctive counterparts, (2.182) and (2.183) do permit readings that link **him** with **Bill** and **she** with **Maria**. The more severe form of the problem, viz. that no anaphora is possible between **it** and **a donkey** in

(2.154) She loves it and Maria owns a donkey.

while it is possible in

(2.155) Maria owns a donkey and she loves it.

We noted that **and**, like **or** can be used to connect not only sentences but also expressions of other syntactic types. In Section 2.3 we sketched how the semantics of these other uses of **or** reduces, through the adoption of a natural processing principle for non-sentential disjunction, to its use as a sentence connector. Virtually all of what we said there is directly transferable to the case of **and**. Thus consider, as a simple illustration, the sentence

(2.187) Maria owns and loves a donkey.

After two steps we arrive at the DRS

(2.188)

x y
⟨Maria(x), ∅⟩ ⟨donkey(y), ∅⟩ ⟨[x owns and loves y], ∅⟩

Applying CR.AND to the last condition of (2.188) we obtain

(2.189)

x y
⟨Maria(x), ∅⟩ ⟨donkey(y), ∅⟩ ⟨x owns y, $\{\langle\delta, 1\rangle\}$⟩ ⟨x loves y, $\{\langle\delta, 2\rangle\}$⟩

---

does not arise with disjunction. For there, as we saw, the anaphoric link is impossible not only in

(2.185) Maria owns it or she loves a donkey.

but also in

(2.186) Maria owns a donkey or she loves it.

Here there is no asymmetry, and the account we gave of the impossibility was, for both (2.185) and (2.186), in terms of inaccessibility. Since the truly impossible cases could be accounted for along those lines, to let the not-so-good-not-so-bad cases involving proper names get by did not seem such a serious offence. However, now that we have introduced the indexing mechanism, the question whether it should not be employed for disjunctions as well as for conjunctions cannot be ignored. It is a question, however, which we will not try to answer here, as its answer appears to involve a number of concepts that go well beyond what has been developed (or, for that matter, will be developed) in this book.

We saw in Section 2.3 that the construction rule CR.OR works fine for all grammatical categories except that of NP. The same is true for conjunctions. Here too we need a separate rule to deal with conjunctive NPs. One might have thought that an analogue of the rule CR.OR(NP) should be what is needed here. But this turns out not to be so. A first suggestion that there might be important differences between disjunctive and conjunctive NPs is that, whereas the former are singulars, the latter are plurals. Thus grammar requires that we say, not

(2.190) Smith and Jones loves Lady Hermione.

but

(2.191) Smith and Jones love Lady Hermione.

In itself this purely syntactic difference need not have been a sufficient reason why an analogue of CR.OR(NP) could not work for conjunctive NPs. The deeper reason that speaks against such a rule is the existence of the *collective* readings which we often find for sentences with conjunctive NPs. For instance,

(2.192) John and Mary own a house.

has an interpretation according to which there is a single house which is owned by John and Mary together. Reducing (2.192) to

(2.193) John owns a house and Mary owns a house.

destroys this reading, for the first conjunct of (2.193) asserts John to be the sole owner of some house and the second conjunct makes a similar claim about Mary. Even more strikingly, reducing

(2.194) John and Mary love each other.

to

(2.195) John loves each other and Mary loves each other.

produces gibberish. Predications which do not allow such reductions are called *collective* as they can only be understood as predications of the *collections* of objects designated by the argument NP. The analysis of such predications, and of plural constructions generally is a large and complex topic. It will be taken up in Chapter 4.

We conclude this section with an explicit statement of the main definitions for the system of DRSs we developed in the first two chapters of this book. However, as the indices needed in the construction of DRSs for conjunctions tend to complicate and obscure DRS notation, we will return in the next chapters to the notation used up until the end of Section 2.3.

Definition 2.4.1

(i) A *DRS* K *confined to* V *and* R is a pair, consisting of a subset U_K (possibly empty) of R and a set Con_K of indexed DRS-conditions confined to V and R;

(ii) An indexed DRS-condition confined to V and R is a pair $\langle \gamma, I \rangle$, where γ is a DRS-condition confined to V and R and I is an Index.

(iii) An index is a pair $\langle \delta, m \rangle$, where δ is a DRS-condition and m is a natural number.

(iv) A *DRS-condition confined to* V *and* R is an expression of one of the following forms:

(a) $\mathbf{x} = \mathbf{y}$, where **x**, **y** belong to R

(b) $\pi(\mathbf{x})$, where **x** belongs to R and π is a name from V

(c) $\eta(\mathbf{x})$, where **x** belongs to R and η is a unary predicate (corresponding to a common noun) from V

(d) $\mathbf{x}\zeta$, where **x** belongs to R and ζ is a unary predicate (corresponding to an intransitive verb) from V

(e) $\mathbf{x}\ \xi\ \mathbf{y}$, where **x**, **y** belong to R and ξ is a binary predicate from V

(f) $\neg$K, where K is a DRS confined to V and R

(g) $K_1 \Rightarrow K_2$, where K_1 and K_2 are DRSs confined to V and R.

(h) $K_1 \vee \ldots \vee K_n$, where for some $n \geq 2$, $K_1, \ldots, K_n$ are (completed) DRSs confined to V and R.

To be consistent with our earlier terminology we will use phrases like 'Con_K contains a DRS-condition γ' or, 'a DRS-condition γ belongs to Con_K' in the sense that Con_K contains an indexed DRS-condition (or, an indexed DRS-condition $\langle \gamma, I \rangle$ belongs to Con_K), which has γ as its first member, i.e. is of the form $\langle \gamma, I \rangle$.

Definition 2.4.2

Let K be a DRS confined to V and R, $\langle \gamma, I \rangle$ be an indexed DRS-condition, and let f be an *embedding from* R *into* M, i.e. a function whose Domain is included in R and whose Range is included in U_M.

(i) f *verifies* the DRS K in M iff f verifies each of the indexed conditions belonging to Con_K in M

(ii) f *verifies* the indexed condition $\langle \gamma, I \rangle$ in M iff

(a) γ is of the form $\mathbf{x} = \mathbf{y}$ and f maps $\mathbf{x}$ and $\mathbf{y}$ onto the same element of U_M

(b) γ is of the form $\pi(\mathbf{x})$ and f maps x onto the element a of U_M such that $\langle \pi, a \rangle$ belongs to $Name_M$

(c) γ is of the form $\eta(\mathbf{x})$ and f maps $\mathbf{x}$ onto an element a of U_M such that a belongs to $Pred_M(\eta)$

(d) γ is of the form $\mathbf{x}\zeta$ and f maps $\mathbf{x}$ onto an element a of U_M such that a belongs to $Pred_M(\zeta)$

(e) γ is of the form $\mathbf{x}\xi\mathbf{y}$ and f maps $\mathbf{x}$ and $\mathbf{y}$ onto elements a and b of U_M such that $\langle a, b \rangle$ belongs to $Pred_M(\xi)$

(f) γ is of the form $\neg K'$ and there is no embedding g from R into M which extends f, such that $Dom(g) = Dom(f) \cup U_{K'}$ and g verifies K′ in M

(g) γ is of the form $K_1 \Rightarrow K_2$ and for every extension g of f such that $Dom(g) = Dom(f) \cup U_{K_1}$ which verifies K_1 in M there is an extension h of g such that $Dom(h) = Dom(g) \cup U_{K_2}$ and h verifies K_2 in M.

(h) γ is of the form $K_1 \vee K_2 \vee \ldots \vee K_n$ and for some i ($i = 1,\ldots,n$) there is an extension g_i of f such that $Dom(g_i) = Dom(f) \cup U_{K_i}$ and g_i verifies K_i in M.

Definition 2.4.3

(i) K_1 is *immediately subordinate* to K_2 iff either

(a) Con_{K_2} contains the condition $\neg K_1$; or

(b) Con_{K_2} contains a condition of the form $K_1 \Rightarrow K_3$ or one of the form $K_3 \Rightarrow K_1$ for some DRS K_3.

(c) Con_{K_2} contains a condition of the form $K'_1 \vee \ldots \vee K'_n$ and for some $i \leq n$ $K_1 = K'_i$.

(ii) K_1 is *subordinate* to K_2 iff either

(a) K_1 is immediately subordinate to K_2; or

(b) there is a K_3 such that K_3 is subordinate to K_2 and K_1 is immediately subordinate to K_3.

(iii) K_1 is *weakly subordinate* to K_2 iff either $K_1 = K_2$ or K_1 is subordinate to K_2. We write $K_1 \leq K_2$ for weak subordination.

Definition 2.4.4

Let K be a DRS, **x** a discourse referent and γ a DRS-condition. We say that **x** is *accessible from* γ *in* K if **x** belongs to U_{K_1} where

(i) $K_1 \leq K$, and

(ii) for some K_2, γ occurs in Con_{K_2}, and either

(a) $K_2 \leq K_1$; or

(b) there is a DRS K_3 and a DRS $K_4 \leq K$ such that $K_1 \Rightarrow K_3$ is in Con_{K_4} and $K_2 \leq K_3$.

Exercises

1. Complete the DRS (2.178).

2. The construction algorithm which ensures that earlier conjuncts are processed before the later ones, runs into trouble with examples quite similar to (2.166). Consider for instance

   (1) If Maria likes him and she owns a tape recorder, Fred uses it.

   If we insist that in the processing of **Fred uses it, it** must be processed before **Fred**, then we cannot construct a DRS for (1) in which **him** is anaphoric to **Fred** and **it** is anaphoric to **a tape recorder.**

   (i) Show this!

   It should be pointed out, however, that the difficulty which (1) presents parallels the one we encountered in Exercise 4 of Section 2.1. Indeed, the relaxation we there proposed of the constraints on processing order will permit us to construct also for (1) a DRS which realizes the mentioned anaphoric connections.

   (ii) Show this!

   (iii) Construct, using this relaxation of processing order, a DRS for

   (2) If she likes Fred, Maria loves him and if she doesn't like him, she doesn't admire him and she doesn't love him.

3. (i) State phrase structure rules which generate complex NPs of the form α's β where α is an NP and β an expression of N. (Hint: formulate a rule to the effect that expressions of the form α's are of the category DET.)

(ii) State phrase structure rules which generate complex NPs of the form $\gamma\beta$ where β is of the category N and γ is **his, her** or **its**.

(iii) State the construction principles for conditions of the form α's $\beta(\xi)$ and for those of the form $\gamma\beta(\alpha)$ where α, β, γ are as above and ξ is a discourse referent.

4. (A) The present fragment, with its rules for disjunction and conjunction, permits the formation of disjunctions of (i.e. whose disjuncts are) conjunctions, conjunctions of disjunctions, and so on. Some of these complex expressions are syntactically ambiguous. For instance, the sentence

(1) Mary admires and respects or fancies Bill.

has two distinct syntactic analyses which, moreover, are not logically equivalent.

(i) Give the two analyses.

(ii) Construct DRSs for each of these two analyses.

(iii) Show that these DRSs are not logically equivalent. (Hint: define a model in which one of them is verifiable and the other is not.)

(iv) Show that one of the DRSs is a logical consequence of the other. (Hint: Show that every model which verifies the latter also verifies the former.)

(B) The two possible readings of (1) can be paraphrased by sentences that are unambiguous. Then, one reading is expressed by the unambiguous sentence.

(2) Mary admires Bill and respects or fancies him.

Give a similar unambiguous paraphrase of the other reading.

5. Which of the following sentences are ambiguous, and which unambiguous?

(a) Mary admires Bill or she respects and fancies him.

(b) Mary admires Bill or respects him and fancies him.

(c) Mary admires Bill or she respects him and fancies him.

(d) Mary admires and fancies or hates and loathes Bill.

(e) Mary admires, respects and fancies or hates, loathes and despises Bill.

Chapter 3

Loose Ends

In this chapter we discuss a number of phenomena which the previous chapters ignored, but which are closely connected with the issues to which we have been paying attention. The phenomena fall into two categories. On the one hand there are those which directly affect the theory we have presented and which, strictly speaking, invalidate it as it stands. The remaining phenomena do not constitute a similar threat to the account we have so far given; but having at least an approximate way of dealing with them will allow us a greater freedom in the choice of examples when we come to discuss plurals and temporal reference in Chapters 4 and 5.

None of these phenomena will be treated in a more than preliminary manner; this is especially true of those in the second category. Most will be the subject of more probing discussions in Volume 2.

3.1 Reflexives

The phenomenon we consider in this section belongs to the first category. It is one that has been of central importance in syntactic accounts of pronominal anaphora. Its essence is contained in the evident semantic difference between the sentence pairs:

(3.1) John supports Peter. He admires him.

and

(3.2) John supports Peter. He admires himself.

Assuming that in both (3.1) and (3.2) **he** is interpreted as referring to John, the second sentence of (3.1) can only be understood as saying that John admires Peter, whereas the second sentence of (3.2) only has the interpretation that John admires John. The second sentence of (3.2) is not within the fragment of English that we have so far treated. So the fact that we cannot yet deal with it does not invalidate our proposals. The second sentence of (3.1), on the other hand, does belong to our fragment. And inasmuch as our construction algorithm contains no check against the construction of a DRS in which **him** is represented as anaphoric to **he**, it constitutes a counterexample to that algorithm.

In first analysis the missing constraint is easily identified: A third person non-reflexive pronoun which occupies the position of object in a given clause cannot be understood as anaphoric to the subject of that clause. This is a strictly syntactic constraint, which we will have to build into the construction rule for anaphoric pronouns in some way or other. There are a number of different ways in which this could be achieved. If the constraint we had just observed were the only one of its kind it would be hard to choose between them, but also the choice would be of little importance.

As a matter of fact, however, the prohibition against an object pronoun being interpreted as anaphoric to the corresponding subject is not the only one of its kind. Some other instances of the contrast between reflexives and non-reflexives that (3.1) and (3.2) exemplify are

(3.3) (a) John wants to shave him.
(b) John wants to shave himself.

(3.4) (a) John talked to him.
(b) John talked to himself.

(3.5) (a) John compared Mary to her.
(b) John compared Mary to herself.

In each of (3.3) and (3.4) not **him**, but only **himself** can be taken as anaphoric to the subject **John**. And in (3.5) it is only **herself**, not **her**, that can be anaphoric to **Mary**. And yet the relations between pronoun and (putative) antecedent are different in each of these cases. In (3.3) the pronoun is not the object of the clause which has **John** for its subject, but rather of the infinitival complement **to shave him** of the verb **wants**. In (3.4) **him** is not in the position of object but part of a prepositional phrase. And in (3.5), not only is the pronoun part of a prepositional phrase, but also the intended antecedent **Mary** is the object rather than the subject. A further taste of the complexity involved in the use of reflexive and non-reflexive pronouns is provided by

(3.6) (a) John found a snake near him.
(b) John found a snake near himself.

where anaphora to the subject is possible both for **himself** and for **him**.

It is not our purpose here to develop a theory that explains all these facts. In any case, all but those manifest in (3.1) and (3.2) fall outside the English fragment which we have so far developed, as they involve either infinitival constructions (as in (3.3)) or prepositional phrases (as in (3.4) and (3.5)). All we have wanted to demonstrate by these examples is that the constraints relating to the contrast between reflexives and non-reflexives are subtle and complex and that presumably they are capable of systematic explanation only within a theory that involves a syntax of a much higher level of sophistication than we are using in this book. In such a theory the syntactic structure should display, in an explicit and explanatory way, what anaphoric connections are possible between antecedent NPs on the one hand and reflexive and non-reflexive pronouns, respectively, on the other.

In our present fragment, however, the problem arises only with pronouns that occupy object positions in simple clauses with transitive verbs. Here the constraint we need does indeed reduce to the simple observation we made above: A pronoun in object position cannot be interpreted as anaphoric to the subject of its own clause. But even this principle must be implemented with some care in a theory such as ours, where anaphoric connections are mediated by discourse referents. The care we must take is illustrated by (3.1); the need for it becomes clearly visible when we construct its DRS up to the point where the pronoun rule is to be applied to **him**:

(3.7)

$$\begin{array}{|c|}\hline \text{x y z} \\ \\ \text{John(x)} \\ \text{Peter(y)} \\ \text{x supports y} \\ \text{z = x} \\ \text{z admires him} \\ \hline\end{array}$$

As we stated the prohibition on pronoun interpretation the discourse referent that will now be introduced for **him**, **u** say, cannot be linked to **z**. But in fact it may not be linked to **x** either, for that discourse referent has already been identified with **z** via the condition **z** = **x**. What this shows is that it is not only the discourse referent which has been introduced for the subject NP itself that cannot be used as antecedent for the pronoun, but that those which are linked with it via identity conditions cannot serve this purpose either.

To make this principle precise we introduce the notion of the *class of discourse referents identified with a given discourse referent* **x**, *relative to* a DRS K, $[\mathbf{x}]_K$. The simplest way to define $[\mathbf{x}]_K$ is as the smallest class Y such that (i) $\mathbf{x} \in Y$, and

(ii) if $\mathbf{z} \in Y$ and either $\mathbf{z} = \mathbf{u}$ occurs somewhere in K (i.e. belongs to Con_K or to $Con_{K'}$ for some subDRS K′ of K) or $\mathbf{u} = \mathbf{z}$ occurs somewhere in K, then $\mathbf{u} \in Y$.

We can now state the constraint on the application of the construction rule for anaphoric pronouns:

(3.8) Suppose that the pronoun rule is being applied to a pronoun α belonging to a condition γ which occurs somewhere in a DRS K, that α occupies the position of syntactic object in γ and that γ's subject has been represented by the discourse referent **y**. Then the discourse referent **x** which the rule introduces for α may not be linked to any of the discourse referents in $[\mathbf{y}]_K$.

It is important to note that the prohibition stated in (3.8) is not a prohibition against actual *coreference* of pronoun and subject. For instance, in

(3.9) Oscar is a popular guy. Fred likes him. Mary likes him. Elaine likes him. Even Oscar likes him.

The last **him** can be understood as coreferential with the first occurrence of **Oscar**. Nevertheless, the two occurrences of **Oscar** will be understood as referring to the same man, so that **him** and the second occurrence of **Oscar** will be understood as referring to the same man as well. The construction of a DRS which represents this reading is possible because the discourse referent which is introduced for the first occurrence of **Oscar** does not belong to the class of discourse referents identified with the one introduced for its second occurrence.

Where two occurrences of the same name are involved, such uses of pronouns, in which they are linked to one occurrence of the name in spite of the fact that that name also occurs in the subject position of the clause which contains the pronoun as object, are comparatively rare, and special contextual conditions appear to be necessary to make the discourse sound felicitous. Specifically, it seems to be necessary that the occurrence of the name to which the pronoun gets linked and its occurrence as subject in the pronoun's own clause should represent the named individual from distinct perspectives. This is so in particular in (3.9), where the first occurrence presents Oscar as the person whom everyone likes while the second represents him as one of those liking him.

Another example of a similar sort is

(3.10) The man in the mirror was on the point of being attacked from behind. When Bill saw him, he cried out in order to warn him. Had he realized he himself was that man, he would have turned around instead and would have tried to defend himself.

Here the two occurrences of **him** are naturally interpreted as anaphoric to **the man in the mirror**. That, as the next sentence reveals, this man is in fact Bill himself, and thus the referent both of the subject of the clause containing the first occurrence of **him** (viz. **Bill**) and that of the clause containing the second **him** (viz. **he**), does not affect the possibility of so interpreting the two **hims**.

(3.8) suffices to block the impossible interpretations of sentences and texts that our syntax already generates. But since the impossibility with which we are now concerned is so intimately connected with the difference between non-reflexives and reflexives, it seems natural to seize the opportunity and incorporate reflexives into our English fragment. On one way of doing this – and this is the way for which we have opted – this is a simple matter. All we need to add to our syntactic rules are new lexical rules that permit the category label PRO to be rewritten as **himself**, **herself** or **itself**. However, since the distinction between reflexive and non-reflexive pronouns is one to which the construction algorithm has need to refer, we must, so as to remain consistent with our earlier policy, introduce a feature which draws this distinction. We call this feature $Refl$. It has two possible values, '+' and '−'; $Refl = +$ means that the pronoun is a reflexive one and $Refl = -$ means that it is not. We make '−' into the default value, so that there is no need to rewrite our earlier rules for non-reflexives. The new rules can then be stated simply as:

(LI 23) PRO $\begin{bmatrix} Num = sing \\ Gen = male \\ Case = -nom \\ Refl = + \end{bmatrix}$ → **himself**

(LI 24) PRO $\begin{bmatrix} Num = sing \\ Gen = fem \\ Case = -nom \\ Refl = + \end{bmatrix}$ → **herself**

(LI 25) PRO $\begin{bmatrix} Num = sing \\ Gen = -hum \\ Case = -nom \\ Refl = + \end{bmatrix}$ → **itself**

We can now state the construction rules for reflexive and non-reflexive pronouns as follows:

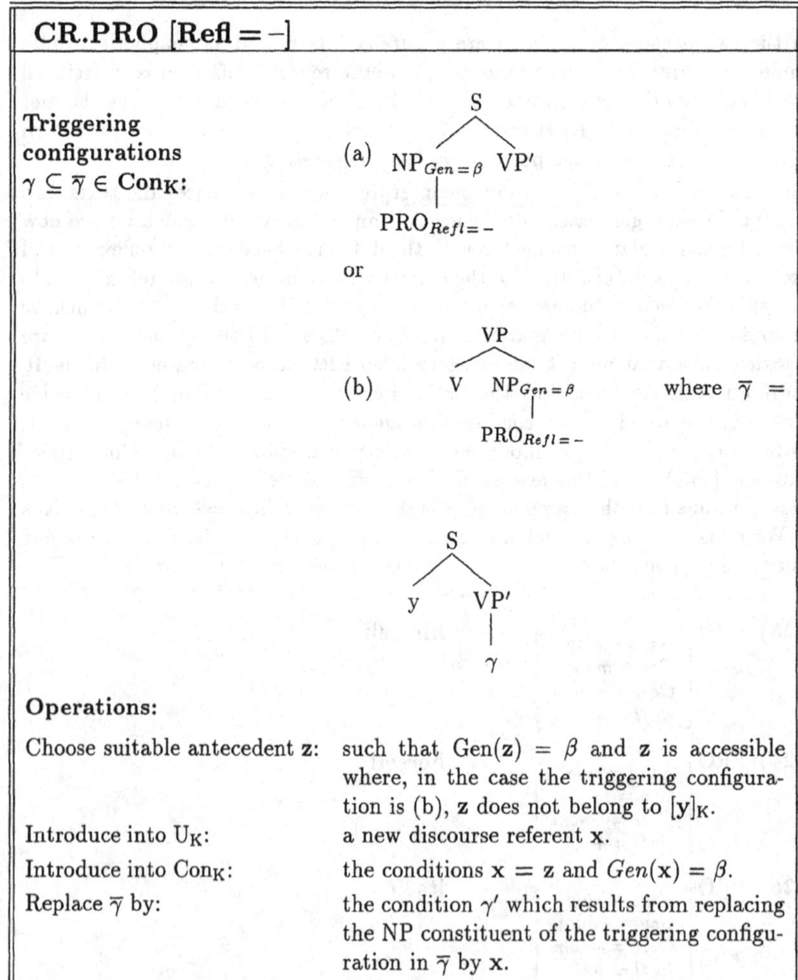

CR.PRO [Refl = –]

Triggering configurations $\gamma \subseteq \overline{\gamma} \in \mathbf{Con_K}$:

(a) $[_S\ NP_{Gen=\beta}[PRO_{Refl=-}]\ VP']$

or

(b) $[_{VP}\ V\ NP_{Gen=\beta}[PRO_{Refl=-}]]$ where $\overline{\gamma}$ = $[_S\ y\ [_{VP'}\ \gamma]]$

Operations:

Choose suitable antecedent **z**:	such that Gen(**z**) = β and **z** is accessible where, in the case the triggering configuration is (b), **z** does not belong to $[\mathbf{y}]_K$.
Introduce into U_K:	a new discourse referent **x**.
Introduce into Con_K:	the conditions **x** = **z** and *Gen*(**x**) = β.
Replace $\overline{\gamma}$ by:	the condition γ' which results from replacing the NP constituent of the triggering configuration in $\overline{\gamma}$ by **x**.

CR.PRO [Refl = +]	
Triggering configuration $\gamma \subseteq \overline{\gamma} \in$ **Con**$_K$:	$[_{VP}\ V\ [_{NP_{Gen=\beta}}\ PRO_{Refl=+}]]$ where $\overline{\gamma} = [_S\ y\ [_{VP'}\ \gamma]]$ and $Gen(y) = \beta$.
Operations:	
Introduce into U_K:	a new discourse referent **x**.
Introduce into Con_K:	the conditions **x** = **y** and Gen(**x**) = β .
Replace $\overline{\gamma}$ by:	the condition γ' which results from replacing the NP constituent of the triggering configuration in $\overline{\gamma}$ by **x**.

Exercises

1. Construct all possible DRSs for (3.1) and (3.2). Explain why according to the new construction algorithm, each of (3.1), (3.2) has only two readings.

2. Construct a DRS for (3.9).

   (Treat **is a popular guy** as an unanalysed intransitive verb.)

3. Construct all possible DRSs for

   (a) Mary loves every woman who she likes.

   (b) Mary likes Susan. She loves her.

   (c) If she loves Susan, then Mary likes her.

   (d) If Susan loves her, then she likes Mary.

   (e) If Susan loves her, then Mary likes her.

   (f) If she loves Susan, then she likes Mary.

4. Construct DRSs for (3.11) and (3.12).

5. Extend the syntax rules and the construction algorithm to deal with verbs like **talk ... to ... about** (compare page 277). Analyse the following sentences.

(1) * Olga talked to him_1 about John_1.

(2) * Olga talked to John_1 about him_1.

(3) * Olga_1 talked to her_1 about John.

(4) Olga_1 talked to John about herself_1.

(5) Olga talked to John_1 about himself_1.

3.2 Possessive Noun Phrases

A subject closely related to that discussed in the last section is that of the possessive pronouns **his**, **her** and **its**. This is therefore the natural place to discuss them if we are to discuss them at all. Our decision to include a brief discussion of possessive pronouns and other possessive NPs has been inspired not so much by theoretical considerations as by the desire to have, in the next two chapters, greater flexibility in the choice of examples.

In the last section we discussed the contrast between reflexive and non-reflexive pronouns. A first comparison between the pronouns we dealt with there and the possessive pronouns might suggest that the latter are immune to the constraints restricting the interpretation of reflexive pronouns on the one hand and to those restricting that of non-reflexive pronouns on the other. Compare, for instance (3.11)–(3.13)

(3.11) Bill employs a man who hates him.

(3.12) Bill employs a man who hates himself.

(3.13) Bill employs a man who hates his wife.

Both (3.11) and (3.12) are unambiguous. **him** in (3.11) can be understood as referring to Bill but not to Bill's employee, whereas **himself** in (3.12) can be understood only as referring to the man Bill employs. In contrast, (3.13) can be understood both in the sense that the employee hates Bill's wife and in the sense that he hates his own wife.

However, possessives are subject to their own constraints. For instance,

(3.14) Bill hates his employee.

can only mean that Bill hates Bill's employee, not that Bill hates some person who is self-employed. In other words, the possessive pronoun in (3.14) cannot be construed as anaphorically linked to the discourse referent representing the NP of which it is an immediate constituent. This is an absolutely general constraint on possessive pronouns. It is a constraint which resembles that for the non-reflexive pronouns, rather than that for the reflexive ones, inasmuch as it excludes as anaphoric antecedents discourse referents that have been introduced for NPs which are "too close" to the pronoun, not discourse referents stemming from NPs which are too "far away". (Indeed, it has been argued that possessives belong to the same category as the non-reflexives, because both are constrained by the principle that they cannot be anaphoric to elements in their "minimal domains". The only difference between the two is that for a possessive pronoun this minimal domain is the smallest NP that contains it as a constituent, whereas for the non-possessive pronouns it is the smallest clause containing the pronoun.)

From this observation it is already largely clear what the construction principle for possessive pronouns should say. First, as with all other NPs, processing a possessive pronoun should involve the introduction of a new discourse referent; secondly, this discourse referent should be identified with some other discourse referent, subject to the constraint just stated; and finally, the discourse referent should supplant the pronoun in the processed DRS-condition γ.

But how precisely should the discourse referent be inserted into γ? To answer this question let us consider possessive phrases that are not pronouns. By a (non-pronominal) possessive phrase we understand an expression of the form α's where α is an NP. Possessive phrases act syntactically as determiners - we find **Bill's donkey, every farmer's donkey** and **her donkey** besides **a donkey** and **every donkey** - and the positions the possessive NPs of these examples occupy, immediately before a common noun phrase, are the only grammatical positions in which possessive phrases can occur. In other words, possessive phrases always occur in configurations of the form α**'s** β, where the entire complex α**'s** β is an NP, whose DET constituent is α**'s** and whose N constituent is β. Therefore it is enough to add the following rule to our syntax

$$\mathrm{Det}_{Num=\alpha} \quad \rightarrow \quad \mathrm{NP}\begin{bmatrix} Num=\beta \\ Gen=\gamma \\ Case=+nom \end{bmatrix} \quad \text{'s}$$

From a semantic perspective expressions of the form α's β are best looked at as consisting of three constituents – α, β and the "genitival" s. The function of **s** is to represent some relation between the thing referred to by the entire NP α**'s** β and that referred to by the embedded NP α. What this relation is varies from case to case. One of the relations the **s** can stand for is that which the term "possessive" surmises, viz. that of possession or ownership. The phrase **Bill's donkey**, for instance, can be understood as meaning "the donkey which Bill owns". But it need not be understood this way. In suitable contexts it can also mean "the donkey Bill is riding", "the donkey Bill has hired", "the donkey Bill has been told to take care of" and so on. In fact, there appears to be no limit to the variety of relations between Bill and the donkey that **Bill's donkey** can be used to express.

For an NP like **Bill's donkey** the relation represented by **'s** must be guessed from the context in which the expression is used. But there are also NPs of the form **α's** β where it is not so much the wider context that determines the relation but rather the noun β. This is so when β is what is called a *relational* noun, such as e.g. **father**, **friend** or **weight**. **Bill's father**, for instance, is rarely if ever interpreted as "some father owned, or taken care of, or ... by Bill"; its natural and by far its most common interpretation is: "the person who stands to Bill in the relation of father to son".

In the brief discussion of possessives we are giving here we do not want to get involved with the quite complicated question of how the relation expressed by **'s** can be recovered from its linguistic and/or contextual environment. Therefore we will adopt a neutral representation, in which **'s** and β are treated as a single unit. Thus, for instance, the DRS (3.15) will have the form (3.16)

(3.15) Mary likes Bill's donkey.

(3.16)

x y z
Mary(x) Bill(z) z's donkey(y) x likes y

In (3.16) **z's donkey(y)** expresses the relation between the discourse referent **y** which represents the donkey and the discourse referent **z** which represents Bill. In this particular case we would be entitled to decompose this condition into two conditions: the first one, **donkey(y)**, which says that **y** represents a donkey, and a second condition, **z's y**, which says that the individuals represented by **y** and **z** stand in a certain relation (either that of ownership or some other). But as we have just seen in connection with the phrase **Bill's father**, such decompositions are not possible in general. To keep the technicalities as simple as is consistent with our needs, we will not bother to carry the decomposition out even in those cases where it would be semantically justified.

Let us look a little more closely at the steps by which (3.16) is constructed. The first step deals with the subject NP, and is of no particular interest here. The second step which deals with the object NP **Bill's donkey**, is one we have not yet encountered, for NPs of this type were not part of our fragment until now. As always, processing of the NP must involve the introduction of a new discourse referent. However, it is not immediately obvious into which DRS universe this discourse referent should be introduced. In fact, this is a fairly complex question, to which we return in Section 3.4. For now it will do, however, to assume that the discourse referent is always introduced into the universe of the DRS whose condition set contains the processed condition. So we get, after these first two steps:

(3.17)

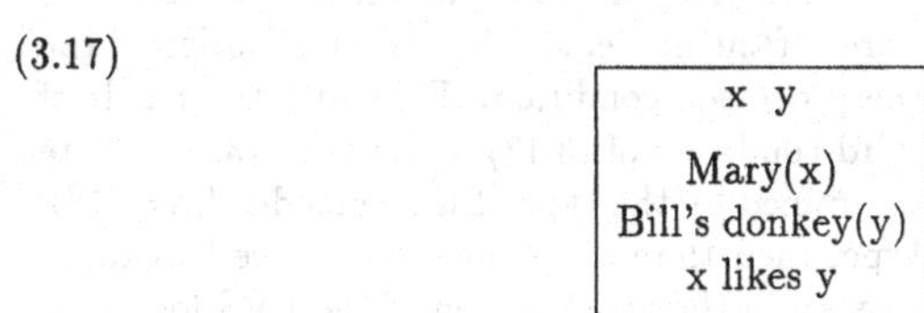

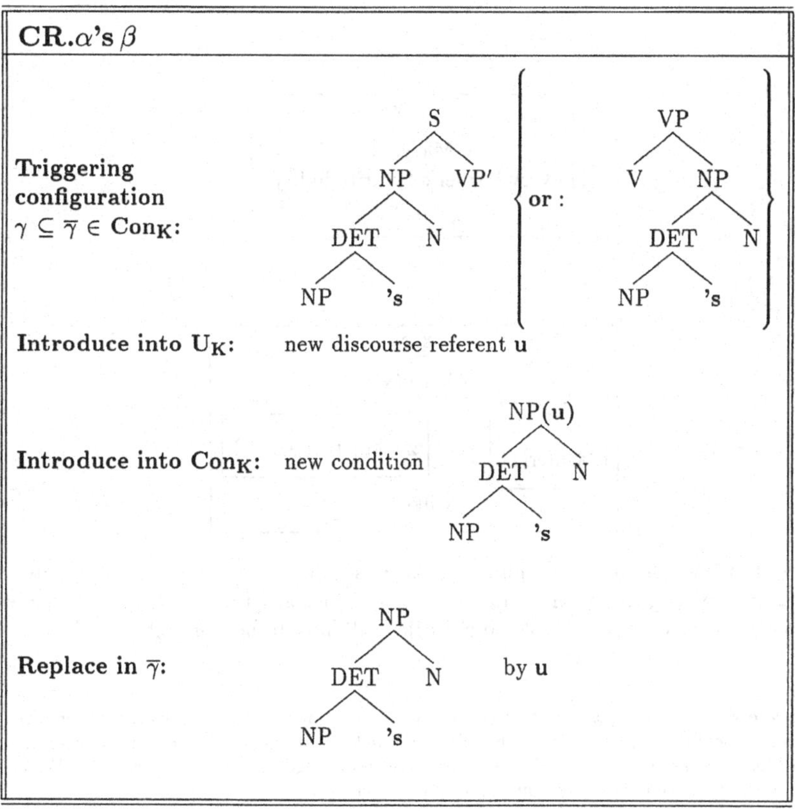

The next and final step deals with the occurrence of the NP **Bill** inside the condition **Bill's donkey(y)**. This too is a step of a sort we have not yet encountered. But here it is not a new construction principle that is needed but rather a new triggering configuration for the familiar principle CR.PN for proper names. The operation of the rule remains otherwise unaffected: Introduction of a new discourse referent into the universe of the main DRS, together with the condition stating that this discourse referent stands for the bearer of the name, and finally substitution of the discourse referent for the NP in the processed condition. Evidently the result of applying these operations to the third condition of (3.17) is the DRS (3.16). Note that this last rule application is determined by the type of the embedded NP **Bill**. Had this NP been of a different type, then the processing would have had to be different also. For instance, the last step in the construction of the DRS for

(3.18) Mary likes every farmer's favorite bull.

will go from

(3.19)

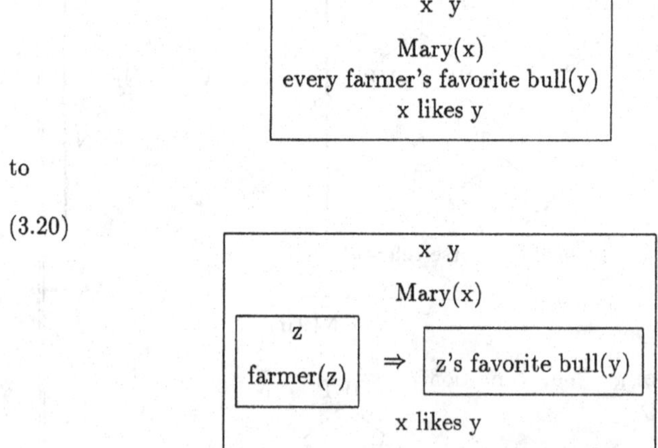

Here it is the rule for **every**-phrases that gets applied. It too must be equipped with the new triggering configuration. In fact, since any type of NP can be made into a possessive phrase, all of the NP rules will have to be thus extended.[1]

[1]Note well that (3.20) is not the only reading of (3.18); in fact, it is not its most prominent reading. The first interpretation which springs to mind is that for each farmer it is the case that Mary likes his favourite bull. This is a reading which our algorithm does not generate. For an extensive discussion of this phenomenon see [May 1985].

CR.α's

Triggering configuration $\gamma \in$ **Con**$_\mathbf{K}$:

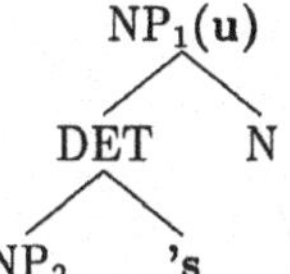

Consider the construction principle which is associated with the triggering configuration:

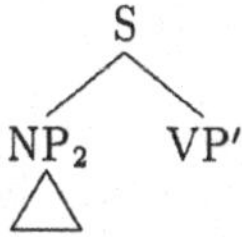

Apply the operations of this principle with S replaced by $\mathrm{NP}_1(\mathbf{u})$ and VP′ replaced by N.

Let us now return to possessive pronouns. From a semantic point of view they are best viewed as combinations of a third person pronoun and the genitival **s**, an analysis which is also suggested by their morphology, most notably that of **its**. This would seem to imply that we can take the construction principle for possessive pronouns to be simply the existing rule CR.PRO, with the new triggering configuration thrown in, just as we have stipulated for the other possessive phrases.

It would indeed be possible to account for the processing of possessive pronouns in just this way. But this would require us to define the notion of a "minimal domain", in the spirit of what was said about this notion above[2] (so that the minimal domain for a possessive is the smallest noun phrase of which it is a proper constituent and the minimal domain of other pronouns is the smallest clause containing them). To do this in a satisfactory manner would involve us in a variety of syntactic problems which we have systematically avoided in this book, and with which it would be unwise to get involved now. Therefore we are forced to introduce the construction principle for possessive pronouns as a separate rule. How this rule is to be stated ought to be clear from what we have said. The actual formulation is left as an exercise.

---

[2]See the parenthetical remark on page 241.

Exercises

1. State the DRS Construction rule for the possessive ponouns **his, her, its.**
2. Construct DRSs for (3.13) and (3.14).
3. Construct DRSs for
   (a) Zebedea loves her cousin's husband.
   (b) Every farmer's favorite bull is worth his price.
   (c) Max does not like his neighbour's daughter's boy-friend.

3.3 Proper Names

The treatment we proposed for proper names in Chapter 1 involves the introduction of a discourse referent **x** to represent the name's bearer together with a condition of the form $\beta(\mathbf{x})$, where β is the proper name in question, whose function it is to specify **x** as the representative of this bearer. But what is it for an individual to be the bearer of a name? In certain cases, where the name is *univocal*, i.e. has one bearer only, this question is unproblematic. But more often than not a name is not univocal. This is true in particular of first names of persons, but it is true of other names as well. For instance, there are many John Smiths of this world, and many a state of the Union has its own Springfield or its own Lafayette.

When a given name is *ambiguous*, what does it refer to when it is actually used? A priori there would seem to exist two possibilities: (a) the name stands for any object that bears it. Thus assuming that there are exactly two persons, call them a and b, who bear the name Zebedea, the sentence

(3.21) Zebedea loves a stockbroker.

could be paraphrased as:

(3.22) Either a or b loves a stockbroker.

(b) the second possibility is that on any particular occasion of use the name refers to some one of its bearers – which bearer depending on the context in which it is being used.

Little reflection suffices to realize that names are never used in the sense of possibility (a). Or, to put the point in different words, a name β is never used as synonymous with the complex NP **someone called** β. Thus any proper use of an ambiguous name involves unique reference to one of the name's possible bearers. But how, one is compelled to ask, is this possible? How is the one bearer of the name to which it is referring on this occasion determined by the properties of this particular utterance? The debate over this question has been particularly lively since the appearance of Kripke's highly influential lecture series 'Naming and Necessity'.[3] In large part the discussion which developed in its wake has turned on how Kripke's proposals should be worked out in detail and how the insights associated with the earlier views he opposes might be integrated into it.

In a nutshell Kripke's theory of proper names comes to this. Proper names do not refer to their bearers by virtue of describing them, but because of a certain non-descriptive connection which holds between a name and its bearer, a connection reminiscent of that which holds between a label and the object to which it is attached. (Of course, a label may carry descriptive information about the object to which it is attached, but what *makes* it the label of whatever it labels is not that, but the fact that it is that object to which it *is* attached.) The treatment of proper names which we proposed in Chapter 1 does not appear to fit this account very well. Consider for instance the DRS for (3.21) as constructed according the principles of Chapter 1:

(3.23)

x y
Zebedea(x) stockbroker(y) x loves y

The one part of (3.23) which serves to insure that **x** acts as a representative for (the relevant) Zebedea is the condition **Zebedea(x)**. We already saw that this condition cannot be synonymous with "x is a person whose name is Zebedea." However, Kripke's theory seems to imply that the condition cannot be regarded as imposing a descriptive constraint of any kind; and, not being a descriptive condition of any kind, it would be unlike all other DRS-conditions we have so far introduced.

Not only does this look like an odd exception; more importantly, there are good reasons for holding that DRS-conditions should always be descriptive in character. The reasons for this position cannot be explained here. They will be explained in Volume 2 (see also [Kamp 1990]). But let us accept that such reasons exist. Then no DRS-condition, whether it be the condition **Zebedea(x)** or any other, could correctly capture the way in which, according to Kripke, a particular use of the name **Zebedea** is connected with the relevant Zebedea. Rather, the linkage must be represented in some other way, involving some device that differs fundamentally

[3]See [Kripke 1980]. These lectures first appeared as part of a collection on semantics of natural language ([Kripke 1972]).

from anything provided by our present machinery for DRS construction. The device which DRT has adopted for this purpose is that of an *(external) anchor.* An *external anchor for* a discourse referent **x** is a function which maps **x** onto some (real) individual **a**. For instance the DRS for (3.21) will have an anchor just for the discourse referent **x** introduced for the proper name **Zebedea**. This will be a function whose domain consists of **x** only and which maps **x** onto the relevant Zebedea, say **a**. Using the familiar set theoretic representation of functions we represent this anchor as $\{\langle x,a \rangle\}$. The result of processing (3.21) will be what we call an *anchored* DRS, i.e. a pair consisting of DRS K (in the sense in which we have been using the term so far) and an anchor for one or more discourse referents in U_K:

(3.24)

x y
$\{\langle x,a \rangle\}$
stockbroker(y)
x loves y

The significance of the external anchor is that it constrains the embedding functions that may be used in DRS-verification. Thus, if M is any model, (3.24) is true in M iff there is a function f from $\{x,y\}$ into U_M such that f agrees with the anchor (formally: $\{\langle x,a \rangle\} \subset f$) and f verifies all the DRS-conditions of (3.24) in M. (Note that this definition makes sense only on the assumption that the values of the anchor – in the present case the object **a** – belong to the universe of M.)

We will have a good deal more to say about anchored DRSs in Volume 2. In the present volume, however, we will continue to do without them. This decision entails that we will have to make do with conditions such as **Zebedea(x)**. In fact, we will leave the processing principle for proper names as it is, and simply ignore the two problems to which we have just seen that it gives rise: first, that the descriptive status of conditions such as **Zebedea(x)** is in doubt; and, secondly, that for ambiguous names such a condition could not be enough, but would have to be supplemented with additional contextual information.

3.4 Definite Descriptions

As we will understand the term, definite descriptions are noun phrases beginning with the definite determiner **the**. This definition captures one widespread use of the term, but unfortunately this use is neither universal nor has it been, among those subscribing to it, altogether unequivocal. First, phrases beginning with **the** can be plural as well as singular. Our definition characterizes both the plural and the singular **the**-phrases as definite descriptions, but the term is sometimes used as referring exclusively to the singular NPs. Secondly, one sometimes includes among the definite descriptions not only phrases whose determiner is the word **the** but also those which have possessive NPs for their determiners. As we shall see below, there are fairly good semantic reasons for this inclusion. Yet, we will argue, these reasons are not conclusive and it is important to consider the NPs with possessive determiners as a distinct semantical category.

Although our definition of the term includes plural **the**-phrases among the definite descriptions, we will in this section only be concerned with singular descriptions. Plural descriptions will be considered in Chapter 4. Moreover, we will exclude from the discussion below certain phrases which, although they begin with **the**, are nevertheless from a semantic point of view simply proper names. Examples are phrases such as **the sun** and **the earth**, names for rivers (**the river Thames, the Mississippi**, etc.) and names for certain other geographical items (**The Grand Canyon, The Great Divide**).

Definite decriptions have played a central role in the development of logic, semantics and philosophy of language during the early part of this century. In particular, Russell's so-called "Theory of Descriptions" (the name he gave to his account of the logical function of descriptive phrases)[4] is pivotal to his views on logic, on its relation to natural language and on the connection between logic and knowledge. Largely because of the enormous influence of Russell's work on these subjects, definite descriptions have continued to be an important topic for logicians and philosophers of language to this day.

According to Russell, the function of a definite description is to supply a uniquely identifying specification of a certain individual. When the description succeeds in this (when it is, as the term goes, a *proper* description), the specified object may be regarded as the description's *referent.* Thus **the first emperor of the Roman empire** can be said to have Augustus for its referent, as Augustus is the one and only individual that satisfies the condition of having been emperor of Rome and of not having been preceded by other Roman emperors. Similarly, **the capital of Spain** has for its referent the city of Madrid, since that is the one and only Spanish capital, and **the number of planets** may be said to denote the number nine, because that is how many planets there are.

However, it is crucial to Russell's theory that speaking of the description as referring to the individual it uniquely specifies is only a *façon de parler.* The logically correct analysis of descriptions can be given only within the context of the full sentences in which they typically occur in actual use. Consider, for instance, the sentence

[4]See in particular [Russell 1905].

(3.25) The first emperor of Rome knew Cleopatra.

According to Russell, its logical analysis is that given by the following formula of predicate logic:

(3.26) $\exists$x(**first emperor of Rome(x)** & $\forall$y(**first emperor of Rome(y)** $\rightarrow$ **y = x**) & **knew(x, Cleopatra)**)

which says that there is an individual **x** which satisfies the condition of being first emperor of Rome, that any **y** satisfying this condition is identical with this individual (so that **x** is the only individual satisfying the condition) and that this individual satisfies the condition of having known Cleopatra. It would seem that this analysis can be paraphrased by saying that the referent of the phrase **the first emperor of Rome** satisfies the condition of having known Cleopatra. But such a paraphrase, if acceptable at all, is possible only in those cases where the description succeeds in specifying some object uniquely. When a description is *improper*, i.e. when it fails to uniquely specify some object, the paraphrase makes no sense, for then there is – this is one of the central tenets of Russell's account – no object that can be invoked as referent.

Russell's theory proves its mettle with particular clarity in relation to sentences which explicitly deny that the descriptions they contain give (unique) specifications of existing objects, such as

(3.27) The golden mountain does not exist.

According to Russell, this sentence has two possible analyses, one in which the negation has "wide scope over" the quantificational complex which represents the contribution of the description, and one in which the negation has "narrow scope".[5] The second analysis is the intuitively less plausible of the two. It is given by the formula

(3.28) $\exists$x(**golden mountain(x)** & $\forall$y(**golden mountain(y)** $\rightarrow$ **y = x**) & $\neg$**exists(x)**)

This formula says that some object, the unique golden mountain, has the property of non-existence. This is surely a very odd reading for (3.27), a sentence which seems to say little more than that there is no such thing as a (unique) golden mountain. This intuitive reading is represented (or at least closely approximated; there

[5]For a discussion of questions of wide and narrow scope see Section 3.7.

may be some quarrel over whether (3.27) carries any information about uniqueness) by the first analysis, in which the negation has wide scope. This analysis is given by the formula

(3.29) $\neg\exists x(\mathbf{golden\ mountain}(x)\ \&\ \forall y(\mathbf{golden\ mountain}(y)$
$\rightarrow y = x)\ \&\ \mathbf{exists}(x)\ )$

If we make the plausible assumpnion that **exists** is the *universal predicate*, i.e. the predicate which is true of everything, then it can be simulated by any formula which is satisfied by every object, e.g. by the formula $x = x$. Adopting this simulation we may replace (3.29) by the formula

(3.30) $\neg\exists x(\mathbf{golden\ mountain}(x)\ \&\ \forall y(\mathbf{golden\ mountain}(y)$
$\rightarrow y = x)\ \&\ x = x)$

or, equivalently, as the universally valid conjunct $x = x$ does not affect truth conditions, by

(3.31) $\neg\exists x(\mathbf{golden\ mountain}(x)\ \&\ \forall y(\mathbf{golden\ mountain}(y)$
$\rightarrow y = x)\ )$

Note that this last formula says something which corresponds closely to the intuitive content of (3.27), viz. that there is no such thing as a (unique) golden mountain. Note also that any account which maintains that definite descriptions have referents whether they uniquely specify objects or not, would have to analyse (3.27) as saying that some mysterious object, viz. the referent of the phrase **the golden mountain**, has the property of non-existence. Such an account would thus have to acknowledge the existence of non-existent objects. But if this is a commitment that we are to make at all, it should not be one into which we are forced by such apparently innocent sentences as (3.27).

When an improper description occurs as part of a simple unnegated sentence, the sentence will, according to Russell's theory, be plain false. Russell's own, most often quoted, example is the sentence

(3.32) The king of France is bald.

According to Russell this sentence has for its logical form the formula

(3.33) $\exists x(\mathbf{king\ of\ France}(x)\ \&\ \forall y(\mathbf{king\ of\ France}(y)$
$\rightarrow y = x)\ \&\ \mathbf{bald}(x)\ )$

which says that there is a unique individual satisfying the predicate **king of France** and that that individual is bald. Since there is no king of France, i.e. no individual satisfying the predicate **king of France**, (3.33) is false. This is an implication that many have found objectionable. The first to protest against it in writing was Strawson[6], who observed that someone who knows that there is no king of France will typically not consider (3.32) false, but rather as failing in some other, arguably more fundamental way. (3.32) suffers, Strawson argued, from failure of *presupposition*. It is a typical presupposition of the use of definite descriptions, he maintained, that they be proper. When that presupposition is not satisfied, the question whether the sentence containing the description is true or false cannot even arise, for under such circumstances the sentence cannot be regarded as expressing a well-defined proposition. Strawson's proposal has far-reaching consequences for the theory of logic for it implies among other things that when a sentence contains an improper description, both that statement and its negation fail to be true. Thus it forces us to give up one of the central principles of symbolic logic as it had been developed by Frege, Russell and others – the so-called *Principle of Bivalence*, according to which for any statement either it or its negation is true.

In proposing his alternative account of improper descriptions Strawson took up a doctrine of Frege[7] which in fact antedated Russell's 'Theory of Descriptions' by more than a decade. But it was only in conjunction with Strawson's critique of Russell's theory that this doctrine came to be recognized for the importance which it has subsequently had. Following Strawson, many philosophers and linguists have developed the theory of presuppositions further, and tried to solve the problems that any theory of presuppositions introduces into logic. The theory of presuppositions is now a subject of extensive research in its own right, and one which is far too complex to permit treatment in this chapter, in which brevity has been among the central concerns. Presuppositions will be the subject of one of the chapters of Volume 2.

Despite their differences Russell and Strawson agreed on one important point. They both held that a definite description is proper only if the common noun phrase following the word **the** is a predicate which is true of exactly one thing. However, as soon as we look at the ways definite descriptions are actually used this requirement appears to be highly unrealistic. There are many instances in which a description apparently succeeds in picking out a unique individual, but where its common noun phrase is satisfied by many individuals besides the one that is picked out. This is true in particular of anaphoric uses of descriptions. Consider, for instance, the two-sentence discourse

---

[6][Strawson 1950].

[7][Frege 1967].

(3.34) A man and a woman entered The Golden Eagle. The man was wearing a brown overcoat.

The description **the man** serves to pick out the man, whoever he may have been, who is mentioned in the first sentence in much the way the pronoun **he** would have picked out that man had it stood in the same position. That the description succeeds in this, even though the common noun **man** is not satisfied by just one individual (as we all know, it is satisfied by billions), is because all the noun needs to accomplish in this given context is to select a unique satisfier from a very restricted set of individuals, viz. those represented by the two discourse referents that are present in the DRS which acts as context for the description's interpretation.

The description of (3.34) is a striking instance of a phenomenon which manifests itself in a variety of different forms: definite descriptions often manage to select a unique referent through the combined forces of their own descriptive content and information supplied by the context in which they occur. To give another example of this phenomenon: In

(3.35) Mary went to the bank and then to the post office.

the descriptions **the bank** and **the post office** would normally be understood as referring to the local bank and post office, i.e. to the bank and post office in the town or neighbourhood or vicinity of Mary's point of departure. Yet another use, which is related on the one hand to that of **the man** in (3.34) and to that of **the bank** and **the post office** in (3.35) on the other, is exemplified by the description **the carburettor** in a context such as

(3.36) My car isn't running. The carburettor malfunctions.

Here **the carburettor** is naturally understood to refer to the carburettor of the car mentioned in the first sentence. So in a sense its use is anaphoric, and in this regard it resembles that of **the man** in (3.34). However, the description **the carburettor** is not coreferential with its antecedent but rather refers to something functionally related to it; in this respect the description of (3.36) is more like those of (3.35).

This is not meant to be an exhaustive list of all the anaphoric ways in which definite descriptions can be used. Indeed, we consider it a non-trivial task to identify and describe all the different purposes to which singular **the**-phrases can be put. And we see it as even more difficult to develop workable criteria that determine for each individual occurrence of a definite description which type of use it instantiates.

Our decision to refrain from tackling these tasks here entails that any processing principle for definite descriptions we can offer must be provisional. In fact, the rule which we propose is nothing more than a stopgap which leaves all the hard questions to be dealt with later. It provides simply for the introduction of a condition of the form $\beta(\mathbf{x})$, where β is the processed definite description and $\mathbf{x}$ the discourse referent introduced for it, which may be interpreted as saying that $\mathbf{x}$ represents the individual denoted by β. A proper processing rule would tell us how $\beta(\mathbf{x})$ is to be reduced further, in a way that varies with the particular use of the processed definite description. (In Section 3.7.5 we will have to consider briefly one such reduction – see also Exercise 2, p. 255.)

As matters stand, failure of the verification conditions associated with $\beta(\mathbf{x})$ will affect the truth value of the DRS, but it will not register as a failure of presupposition. To recast our framework in such a way that failure of $\beta(\mathbf{x})$ amounts to presupposition failure, so that the DRS does not receive any truth value at all, is a non-trivial undertaking, which will have to wait until Volume 2.

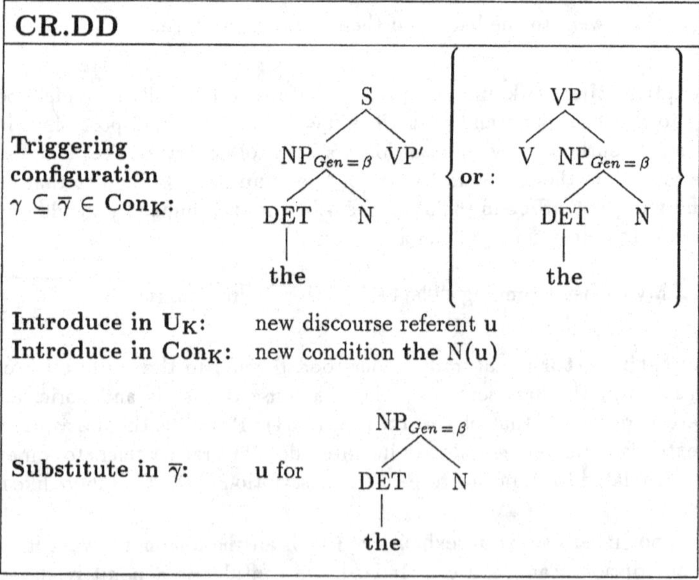

The construction algorithm which results from combining CR.DD with those we already have treats the condition **the** N(x) as irreducible. As we remarked above, this is not really satisfactory. A proper account of definite descriptions will have to provide additional processing principles corresponding to the different types of use of definite descriptions, which reduce such conditions further.

Exercises

1. (a) Give a DRS-construction principle for the determiner **exactly one.**

   (b) Construct DRSs for the following discourses:

   (1) Every woman who owns a Mercedes is rich. Exactly one woman owns a Mercedes. She is rich.

   (2) Exactly one woman owns a Mercedes. She is rich.

   and translate them into formulas of predicate logic.

   (c) Show that these translations are equivalent to Russell's analysis of

   (3) The woman who owns a Mercedes is rich.

2. Grammar distinguishes between two kinds of relative clauses, *restrictive* and *non-restrictive* relative clauses. The first thing to be said about this distinction is that it is not so much a distinction between different expression *types*, but between two different *uses* of the expressions of a single syntactic category: Many relative clauses can be used both in a restrictive and a non-restrictive mode. Roughly speaking, a restrictive relative clause contributes to the determination of the semantic value of the noun phrase of which it is part, whereas a non-restrictive relative clause acts, rather, as a separate assertion about what offers itself as semantic value for the remainder of the NP (i.e. the NP one obtains by excising the relative clause). The difference between the two uses is most easily seen in connection with definite descriptions. Compare for instance

   (1) The son who attended a boarding school was insufferable.

   (2) The son, who attended a boarding school, was insufferable.

   (1), in which the relative clause is used restrictively, suggests that there is more than one son, but only one who is boarding. In (2), where the relative clause is used non-restrictively, the suggestion is rather that there is only one son, of whom it is said not only that he was insufferable but also, parenthetically as it were, that he attended a boarding school. ((1) and (2) illustrate the familiar rule of English orthography that non-restrictive clauses are set apart from the surrounding text by commas, but that restrictive clauses are not. If we adopt the principle that a definite description selects from a given (often contextually determined) set X the unique individual satisfying its descriptive content, we are led to assign to (1) and (2) interpretations that are captured by the following DRSs:

(3)

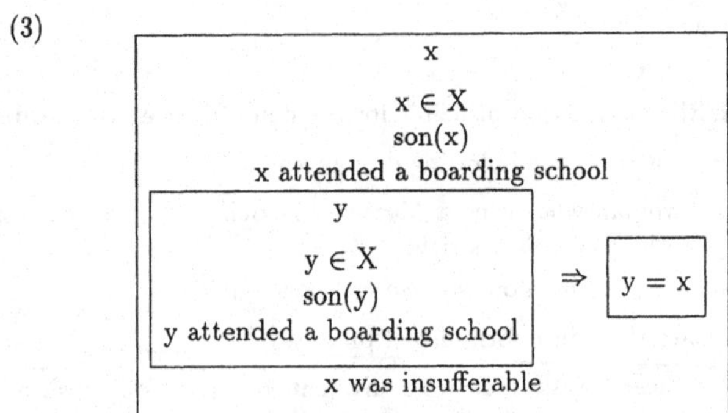

(4)

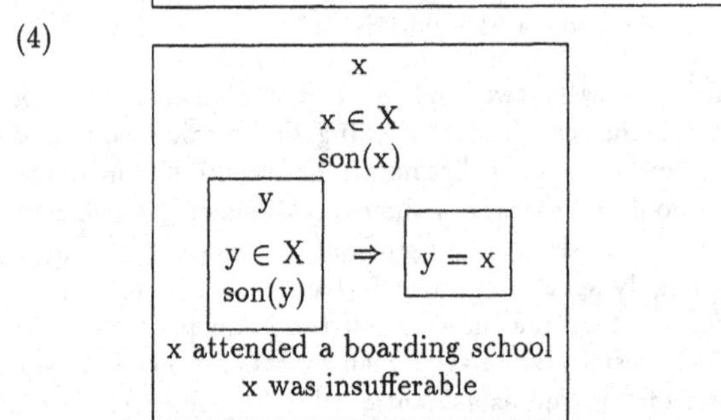

(i) Formulate a processing rule for non-restrictive relative clauses which, together with a rule which processes singular definite descriptions as selecting the unique entities satisfying their descriptive contents, enables us to convert (2) into (4). Make sure to formulate the rule in such a way that it is also capable of producing the natural interpretation for a sentence like

(5) Every American film producer pays the lead actress, who hates his guts, a fortune.

and use the rule to construct a suitable DRS for (5).

(ii) Relative clauses which attach to proper names are always non-restrictive. Explain why this should be so.

3. For relative clauses that are part of indefinite descriptions the distinction between restrictive and non-restrictive use is not as clear-cut as it is for

relative clauses that occur as part of definite descriptions (See Exercise 2). Inasmuch as a distinction can be drawn at all, it is closely connected with that between the specific and the non-specific interpretation of the indefinites. What is this connection?

3.5 Stipulated Identity and Asserted Identity

One function of the verb **to be** is to express identity. Thus the sentence

(3.37) Fred is the manager of the Silver Griffin.

says that the bearer of the name **Fred** is identical with the individual who manages the Silver Griffin: **is** serves to express[8] that the noun phrases flanking it have the same referent. In the DRS (3.38), which (3.37) yields when processed according to our rules, (and where **is** is treated as a 2-place verb),

(3.38)

x y
Fred(x) the manager of the Silver Griffin(y) x is y

this claim is expressed by the condition **x is y**, which asserts that the individuals represented by **x** and **y** coincide.

Identity conditions such as **x is y** in (3.38) should be distinguished from the conditions $\alpha = \beta$ that can be found in many of the DRSs we have so far constructed. Recall one of the first DRSs we presented in this book, viz.

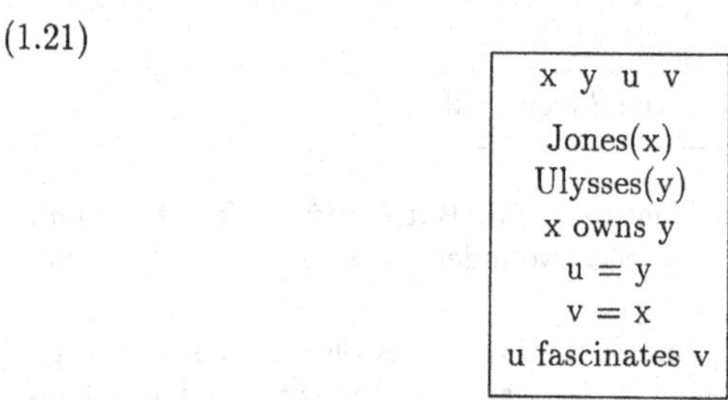

[8]This is not the only use of the verb **to be**. In Section 3.6 we discuss another important function, that of predication. Moreover, in Chapter 5, we will encounter **be** as an auxiliary verb.

with its conditions **u** = **y** and **v** = **x**. From the point of DRS-verification the condition **x is y** of (3.38) and the conditions **u** = **y** and **v** = **x** amount to the same thing: they are verified by just those embeddings which map the two discourse referents onto the same object. But there is nevertheless an important difference between the function of **x is y** in (3.38) on the one hand and that of **u** = **y** and **v** = **x** in (1.21) on the other. Informally speaking, the condition **x is y** embodies the substance of the claim (3.37) which (3.38) represents, whereas the conditions **u** = **y** and **v** = **x** in (1.21) arise as consequences of the particular way in which we have chosen to process anaphoric noun phrases. In fact, we could have phrased the rule for anaphoric pronouns in such a way that no conditions are necessary: instead of introducing a new discourse referent **x** for the pronoun α, choosing an appropriate discourse referent **y** from among those that are accessible from the position of the pronoun, adding **x** = **y** and replacing the processed condition γ by γ[**x**/α], we could simply choose **y** and replace γ by γ[**y**/α]. (1.21) would in that case have produced the DRS

(3.39)

x y
Jones(x) Ulysses(y) x owns y y fascinates x

But there seems to be no intuitively satisfactory way to implement a similar elimination of the condition **x is y** in (3.38). For suppose we adopted a rule for the verb **be** which replaces any condition of the form **x is** α by the condition α(**x**). This would assign to (3.37) the DRS

(3.40)

x
Fred(x) the manager of the Silver Griffin(x)

This DRS is truthconditionally equivalent to (3.38). But it entirely fails to convey the intuition that what (3.37) asserts is that two independently identified individuals are in fact one and the same.

The point can be amplified if we observe that sentences such as (3.37) are typically used in situations where the recipient is already familiar with the individuals referred to by the two noun phrases flanking the verb **be**, but is as yet ignorant of their identity. The context DRS reflecting the background information of such a recipient will already contain discourse referents representing Fred and the manager of the Silver Griffin. Thus its relevant part will look like:

(3.41)

x y
Fred(x) the manager of the Silver Griffin(y)

Suppose now that the recipient interprets (3.37) relative to this DRS and he understands the NPs **Fred** and **the manager of the Silver Griffin** which occur in it as referring to the individuals already represented as **x** and **y**. Thus he will process the NPs as anaphorically linked with these discourse referents. In this way (3.37) will be expanded to a DRS of the form

(3.42)

x y u v
Fred(x) the manager of the Silver Griffin(y) u = x v = y u is v

or, if the alternative "substitutional" way of representing anaphoric connections is used, to

(3.43)

x y
Fred(x) the manager of the Silver Griffin(y) x is y

We could go one step further and eliminate the condition **x is y** altogether in (3.43). We could, that is, substitute **x** for all occurrences of **y** in DRS-conditions of (3.43) and then drop **y** from the universe. But now the particular *contribution* which (3.37) makes to the interpreter's information would no longer have any identifiable representation. In particular, suppose that the interpreter correctly understands (3.37), but doubts that what he has been told is true. Then he certainly will not want to conflate the discourse referents **x** and **y**. A representation such as (3.42) or (3.43), in which no such conflation has taken place, and in which the doubted condition **x is y** (or **u is v**) is in some way marked as "dubious", would reflect this interpreter's epistemic conditions much more accurately.

To pursue this line of thought further we would have to say a good deal about the psychological significance of our theory and of its expansion into a more fully fledged account of verbal communication. These are topics to be dealt with at length in Volume 2 and we will say no more about them here. We hope, however, that the little we have said has made sufficiently clear the difference in status between a condition like **x is y** in (3.38) and one like **u = y** in (1.21). A condition of the form **x is y** is an essential part of what is being *asserted* by the processed sentence. One of the form **u = y** embodies an interpretative *stipulation*, to the effect that a certain anaphoric NP is being used as a means for picking up a certain element introduced into the discourse by independent means. We refer to conditions of the former type as representations of *asserted* and to those of the latter type as representations of *stipulated identity*. To ensure that the distinction is formally recognizable, we will, as we have been doing already, use the identity sign '=' for stipulative identity conditions while using the English verb **be** in conditions of asserted identity.

3.6 Identity and Predication

Not all uses of the verb **be** express identity. For instance,

(3.44) John is unhappy.

and

(3.45) The post office is near the church.

do not claim the identity of the referents of two NPs flanking **is**. Rather, these sentences each assert that the individual referred to by the subject term has a certain property - the property of being unhappy in (3.44), and that of being located in the vicinity of the church in (3.45). Attributions of properties to individuals are often called *predications*, and the expressions that stand for properties - such as **unhappy** or **near the church** - are called *predicates*. In sentences like (3.44) and (3.45), the function of the verb **be** is to express the predicational link between subject term and predicate; accordingly, this use of **be** will be called its *predicational* use.

The predicates of natural language cover a variety of word classes. Arguably the most prominent among them are nouns and verbs, the two categories of predicates we dealt with in Chapters 1 and 2. Besides nouns, verbs, and the two categories exemplified in (3.44) and (3.45), adjectives and prepositions, there are still others - for instance, adverbs, like **quickly, deliberately**, etc. Moreover, certain morphemes, such as those used to express tense, can arguably also play a predicate-like role. (In fact, the treatment of tense and aspect in Chapter 5 may be seen as an extensive plea for a predicative view of tense morphemes.) However, in the following remarks we will limit ourselves to the four classes just mentioned.

The logical conception of a predicate is that of an expression which yields a well-formed sentence when combined with the right number of singular terms, and which denotes a function assigning a truth value to any combination of values for such terms. This is the conception we have been using in the preceding chapters, both in the context of Predicate Logic and in that of DRT. As both formalisms make clear, the syntactic relations which such a predicate bears to each of its arguments are all essentially the same: To turn the predicate into a semantically complete and syntactically well-formed whole, each of its argument places must be filled by a separate argument-denoting term.

For natural language predicates this is not so. From a semantic point of view they function by and large like logical predicates, i.e. as functions from tuples of arguments to truth values. But their syntax is quite different. Each natural language predicate has one argument – its so-called *referential argument* – which is never expressed by an argument phrase that is disjoint from the predicate; though if the predicate takes additional arguments besides, then these – the *non-referential arguments* of the predicate – always *are* expressed by terms that are disjoint from it, just as with any logical predicate. The difference between referential and non-referential arguments is easiest to explain in the case of relational nouns, such as **father** or **friend**. There is an intuitively clear sense in which such words stand for binary relations. It is also intuitively clear how the two arguments of a relational noun are expressed and what the difference between these two modes of expresson is.

As an example, take **friend**, as it occurs in

(3.46) A friend of Carol Rayner teaches physics.

In this sentence the predicate **friend** has two arguments. One of these is expressed by the NP **Carol Rayner**, which is disjoint from the noun **friend** and with which it forms the compound constituent **friend of Carol Rayner**. This is pretty much the way things are done in predicate logic too. The other argument, however – the person who *is* Carol Rayner's friend – is not expressed by a noun phrase that is disjoint from **friend**. The NP which expresses that argument is the entire phrase **a friend of Carol Rayner**, which *contains* the predicate **friend**. It is this second argument, the referent of the NP that has the predicate as one of its syntactic constituents, which is its referential argument.

Presumably referential and non-referential arguments are expressed in these different ways for the following reason. The non-referential argument places of a natural language predicate are just that – slots to be filled by arguments which must come from somewhere else if the predicate is to be turned into a well-defined sentence; in this respect, the non-refential arguments of natural language predicates behave in the same way as any argument of a predicate of formal logic. In contrast, the referential argument of a natural language predicate *is introduced by the predicate itself*; more precisely, the predicate comes with a variable (or, in our terminology, a discourse referent) which itself fills the referential argument slot; at the same time the predicate passes the variable on to the larger expression of which it is a constituent. We will refer to this variable as the *referential argument* of the (given occurrence of the) predicate.

After the predicate has passed its referential argument on to the larger expression of which it is a constituent, one of several things may happen to the argument. Thus, if, as in (3.46), the predicate is a noun, the fate of its referential argument is determined by the NP of which the noun is the principal constituent, or "head". When the determiner is **every**, the argument ends up as a quantificationally bound variable; when the determiner is the word **the**, the variable typically gets linked to some discourse referent that was introduced elsewhere, and on independent grounds. When the NP is an indefinite description, as in (3.46), it will get bound existentially, usually by the first operator it meets when percolating upwards in search of a place where a binder can put it to rest. Each of these possibilities is familiar from our treatment of singular NPs in Chapters 1 and 2. Besides these there are other possibilities as well which we haven't discussed.

Relational nouns are comparatively rare. It is much more common for a noun to function as a 1-place predicate. In fact, all nouns which we dealt with in Chapters 1 and 2 are of this common variety. It should be clear from what we have said that such nouns only have a referential argument. For adjectives the story is largely similar. There are some, such as **devoted to**, which are relational; these have a referential and a non-referential argument. Thus, in **devoted to Carol Rayner**, the non-referential argument is denoted by the subordinate NP **Carol Rayner** while the referential argument can only be the referent of a noun phrase which contains the adjectival phrase, such as **the man devoted to Carol Rayner**, say. Again, most adjectives are non-relational and, like the ordinary noun, have just a single, referential, argument.

What happens to the referential argument of an adjective when it is passed on to the phrase containing the adjective as a constituent is not quite the same as what happens to the referential arguments of nouns. Here we will consider only two cases: (i) that where the adjective directly combines with a noun, as in **old book** or **man devoted to Carol Rayner** and (ii) that where the adjectival follows a copular verb, as in (3.44). In the first case the referential argument of the adjective gets identified with that of the noun and thus comes to share its fate. The second case will be taken up below.

For nouns and adjectives, we said, a single argument is the norm – relational nouns and adjectives are comparatively rare. In contrast, prepositions always have a non-referential argument as well as a referential argument. Thus in **near the church**, **near** expresses a relation between the referent of **the church** and its referential argument, which the phrase does not mention explicitly.[9, 10]

Prepositional phrases differ from adjectives in that they may enter into a wider range of syntactic constructions. By and large, prepositional phrases can be used both adjectivally, as in **the pub near the church**, and adverbially, as in **she stood near the church**. Here we will only consider their adjectival uses. When a prepositional phrase is used adjectivally, the fate of its referential argument is essentially the same as that of any other adjectival phrase in the same construction. For instance, in **pub near the church** the referential argument of **near the church** gets identified with that of **pub**.

Although we will have no more to say about the adverbial uses of prepositional phrases, it is worth noting that they closely parallel the adjectival uses. (Actually, this is true not just for prepositional phrases but also for adjectives and the adverbs that are derived from them, such as **quick** and **quickly**, etc.) The parallelism concerns in particular the fate of the referential argument. Thus, when

[9]It is a matter for debate whether there are prepositions expressing relations of more than two places. An example that comes to mind is the English preposition **between**, which is naturally analysed as a three-place relation, "**x** is between **y** and **z**". Note, however, that it is in principle also possible to see **between** as relating **x** to the two-membered set {**y**,**z**}. That this analysis corresponds more closely to the grammar of **between** is indicated by the fact that if we want to refer explicitly to the arguments **x** and **y** by means of two distinct NPs, then these two NPs must be conjoined into a single complex noun phrase, as in:

(3.47) The pub is between the church and the post office.

[10]The theory of prepositional phrases is complicated by an issue we have left out. Often prepositions seem to function as *case markers*, or as part of such. Thus in a language with morphologically explicit case marking, such as German, the preposition **mit** of

(3.48) Sie verglich ihn mit seinem Köter. (She compared him to his dog.)

invites an analysis according to which **mit** indicates the kind of argument relation in which the referent of **seinem Köter** stands to the other arguments of the verb. (There is historical evidence for such an analysis. In many languages case morphemes seem to have originated as prepositions which eventually got incorporated into the accompanying nouns. Sometimes the functional shift which accompanies such a transformation from relational expression to case marker takes place even when, from a morpho-syntactic perspective, the preposition retains its status as a separate word.) The same account suggests itself for certain English prepositions, including the **to** of (3.48), even if in general English case is not overtly expressed.

When a preposition functions as a case marker it does not act as a predicate, and so it does not have any arguments, referential or otherwise. But where a preposition acts as a predicate it always has both a referential and some other argument.

a prepositional phrase combines with a verb – as does **near the church** in **she stood near the church** – its referential argument gets identified with that of the verb in precisely the same way as the referential argument of a prepositional phrase which is combined with a noun is identified with the referential argument of that noun.

This brings us to the subject of verbs. Verbs have referential arguments too, but this is less easily seen than in the case of nouns. For the larger expressions which contain verbs as constituents do not in any obvious way refer to something that presents itself unequivocally as an argument of the constituent verb. Nevertheless there are many strong considerations supporting the view that verbs have referential arguments (none of which will be presented here), and it is now widely accepted. But note that the referential argument of a verb is not among what are identified as its arguments in more traditional discussions of verb semantics. For instance, in a sentence like

(3.49) John met Fred.

the referential argument of **met** is neither John nor Fred. Rather it is the event of John meeting Fred, an event of which the sentence as a whole says that it occurred at some time previous to the moment of speech. In (3.49) it is the past tense marker which determines what happens to the referential argument of the verb **meet**. (Roughly speaking, it causes the argument to be existentially bound; for details see Chapter 5.) The verb **meet** itself tells us what kind of event the referential argument represents, by relating this event to its non-referential argument phrases **John** and **Fred**.

For verbs this is the general pattern. The referential argument is always an event (or a process, state of affairs or situation). The verb describes this argument by relating it to its other, non-referential arguments. And operators elsewhere in the sentence – such as tense markers, temporal adverbs and the like – ensure its binding.

Note that this analysis conflicts with the way we have been treating verbs up to now. Take a verb verb like **own**. So far we have represented it as a 2-place predicate, whose arguments are specified by the grammatical subject and the grammatical object, not as a 3-place predicate. To this extent we have toed the traditional line that the arguments of a verb are those, and only those, which can be realized by accompanying argument phrases. In Chapter 5 we will abandon this approach for the one just advocated. However, in order to avoid complexities orthogonal to the problems we will study in the remainder of the present chapter and throughout Chapter 4, we will continue to deal with verbs as if they didn't have a referential argument until Chapter 5.[11]

We may sum up the discussion of the last four pages as follows. Natural language predicates fulfill two functions:

(i) they introduce their own referential arguments; and

(ii) they act as predicates, which either assert of their referential argument that it has a certain property or relate it to their remaining arguments.

Before we return to the copular sentences which prompted this long excursion into natural language predication, it will be useful to have a closer look, from our new perspective, at those verbs to which we have so far limited our attention – present tense forms of stative verbs such as **own** or **love**. Consider the verb **loves** as it occurs in

(3.50) John loves Mary.

The first function of **love** in (3.50) is to introduce as its referential argument a discourse referent **s** which represents a state of affairs. This argument is then bound by the finite present tense, which asserts that a state of the given description holds over some period of time which includes the moment of speech (for details see Chapter 5).[12] The second function of the verb is to provide a descriptive characterization of the state represented by **s**; this it does by relating **s** to the referents of its argument phrases **John** and **Mary** – describing it as a state consisting in John's loving Mary. We will represent this descriptive information as a condition of the form **s**: **x love y**, where **x** and **y** represent John and Mary. In this way we arrive for (3.50) at a representation of the following form:

[11]We said a few paragraphs ago that verbs "typically" have at least one non-referential argument besides their referential argument. This is hardly surprising if we keep in mind the relationship between the present perspective and the traditional one. The present claim that a verb has at least one non-referential argument amounts to nothing more than the traditional observation that verbs are predicates of at least one place. This is in fact a claim we have implicitly endorsed all along, insofar as we have assumed that verbs are either intransitive or (simply) transitive or have even more argument places than that.

As a matter of fact, there are a few verbs which have only a referential argument. These are the so-called "weather verbs", such as **rain** and **snow**. Thus the grammatical subject **it** of the sentence **it rained** is not an argument phrase in the semantic sense of the word, but a so-called *expletive*: it does not contribute any discourse referent; its presence is required for purely syntactic reasons.

[12]Here we are forced to run ahead to a few things which will be discussed at length in Chapter 5. We must ask the reader either to take these things at face value or to save the remainder of this section until after that chapter.

(3.51)

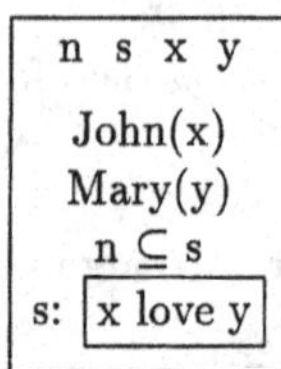

Here **n** represents the utterance time; the condition **n** $\subseteq$ **s** asserts that **s** holds at **n**.

(3.51) bears witness to both functions of the verb **love**. The presence of s results from its capacity to introduce its own referential argument, whereas the condition **s**: **x love y** represents the contribution which the verb makes as a predicate.

The second, predicating function of a natural language predicate can in some cases be virtually devoid of content. This is true of nouns like **thing**, **individual** and **entity**, and of the dummy noun **one** as found in NPs like **that one**. Noun phrases which have such nouns as heads typically serve the purpose of introducing an argument without saying much about what sort of entity it is. Any information about the argument which is conveyed by a sentence involving such an NP comes from elsewhere.[13]

Similar cases, where a predicate makes little if any descriptive contribution but is important because of its other, argument-introducing function, can also be found in the realm of verbs. The copular verb **be** is a case in point. Consider, for instance, the first sentence of this section:

(3.44) John is unhappy.

If we analyse this sentence along the same lines as (3.50), we are led to a referential argument **s** representing the state of affairs described by the verb together with its arguments. What sort of state is **s**? Intuitively, the answer seems clear enough: s should consist in the subject John satisfying the predicate **unhappy**. If we represent this intuitive gloss in the same format as we represented (3.50) in (3.51), what we get is something like:

---

[13]For instance, if I say

(3.52) I have just thought of something.

you will be able to infer that the something is a plan, or a solution to some problem. You are able to infer this because in (3.52) **something** occurs as direct object of **thought** and the only entities that can stand as second arguments in the relation expressed by **think** are thoughts, plans, ideas and the like.

(3.53)

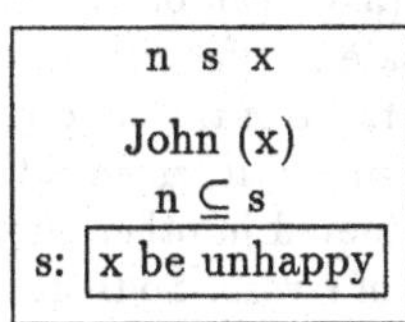

But exactly how do we get to a representation with this content from the syntactic form of a sentence like (3.52)? To answer this we must attend more closely to the form of the verb phrase, which here consists of copula followed by an adjective. And so we return to a matter which we mentioned, but did not pursue on p. 262: What happens to the referential argument of an adjective when the adjectival phrase is combined with a copular verb?

Here is our answer (we give it without the argumentation): The copula **be** has, besides its referential argument, two further and non-referential arguments. One of these is supplied by the grammatical subject; the other comes from the "grammatical predicate", i.e. the constituent which combines with the copula into a complete VP; in the present example this is the adjective **unhappy**. The copula "binds" the referential argument of this constituent by identifying it with its other non-referential argument, in other words, with the referential argument of the subject.[14] The only part which the adjectival phrase plays in this is that it makes its referential argument available for identification with the referential argument of the subject. This contribution is essentially the same as the one which an adjective makes when it combines directly with a noun (as in our examples **old book** and **man devoted to Carol Rayner**).

The comparison of these two modes of adjective interpretation is of interest also

[14]In fact, since this identification fully fixes the value of the referential argument of the grammatical predicate, the combination of copula and grammatical predicate has the effect of genuinely binding its referential argument. It is for this reason that the grammatical predicate may not contain any other independent binding instructions of its own. This is the reason why the NPs that can complement the copular **be** cannot be either definite or quantificational. Indeed, by far the most common type of NP in this position are the indefinites, which supply their referential arguments without any binding instructions which conflict with the binding effected by the copula. There are, it is true, some cases where what follows the copula is a definite description, as in

(3.54) He is the president of Exxon.

But these cases do not refute the analysis proposed here: rather, in an NP like that of (3.54) the does precisely what the classical analyses of the definite article said. It claims unique satisfaction of the common noun phrase that follows it. (See in particular [Russell 1905].) In fact, the use of a definite description in predicative position is one of the rare cases in which the classical analysis appears to be literally true.

from the perspective of the copula **be**. The descriptive contribution which **be** makes to the meaning of a sentence like (3.50) can be glossed as follows: **be** describes its own referential argument **s** as a state of affairs that consists in the identification of its other two arguments. The substance of this description evidently consists in the identification of those two arguments. But, as adjective-noun combinations show, argument identification can be achieved in other ways as well. It is an operation which does not seem to be in need of a verb. So there is a sense in which the copula appears to be descriptively redundant.[15]

In the light of the remarks we made in the previous section about stipulated identity, it might be expected that a DRT implementation of the analysis we have just sketched for the English copular construction should result not in (3.53), but rather in the following DRS for (3.44)

(3.55)

n s x y
John(x)
unhappy(y)
$n \subseteq s$
s: [x = y]

As it turns out, however, (3.55) cannot be the structure we want. Although the evidence we have against (3.55) is somewhat indirect, we nonetheless consider it to be persuasive enough to refute this representation. The evidence is this.

As has been observed by E. Doron[16], in languages like Hebrew which mark gender morphologically (and where e.g. feminine nouns bear other affixes or combine with other articles than male nouns) it seems impossible to refer anaphorically to the noun phrase following the verb **be**. Thus in sentence pairs of the form

(3.56) The *N* is (a) *N'*. He ... / *She ...

where *N* is masculine and *N'* feminine, only the masculine pronoun can be used to pick up the individual mentioned in the first sentence. If the part after **is** were to introduce its own discourse referent **y**, it would no longer be explicable why the

[15] In the light of this last observation one may wonder why the copula is needed at all: Could the copular connection not be more economically expressed by means of simple juxtaposition of subject and grammatical predicate? We conjecture that the answer to this question has to do with the requirements that every declarative sentence of English must contain a finite tense; that this tense acts as an operator which must bind some variable; and that it can only bind a variable introduced by the verb bearing the tense. So it is, one might say, the argument introducing rather than the predicative function of **be** which requires its presence in the copular construction.

[16] See [Doron 1983].

feminine pronoun, which fits the gender constraints on y, could not be used in this context. If, however, the part following **is** functions as a predicate, no such discourse referent will get introduced, and the impossibility of using the feminine pronoun is explained by the fact that its only possible antecedent, the discourse referent for the subject NP, does not come with the right gender constraints. Admittedly this evidence is oblique, as it pertains to languages other than English (Hebrew in Doron's case). Even so we consider it a sufficient reason to reject (3.55).

In the last section we observed that the construction rule for anaphoric pronouns can be stated in two different ways, which, however, produce fully equivalent results for the fragment developed in Chapters 1 and 2. An anaphoric pronoun can be processed in either of two ways. One can let it introduce its own discourse referent and then stipulate identity between that discourse referent and the one selected as antecedent. Alternatively, one can replace the pronoun by the discourse referent that is chosen as antecedent. If we choose this second alternative in the DRS-construction for (3.53) the result will not be (3.55) but rather

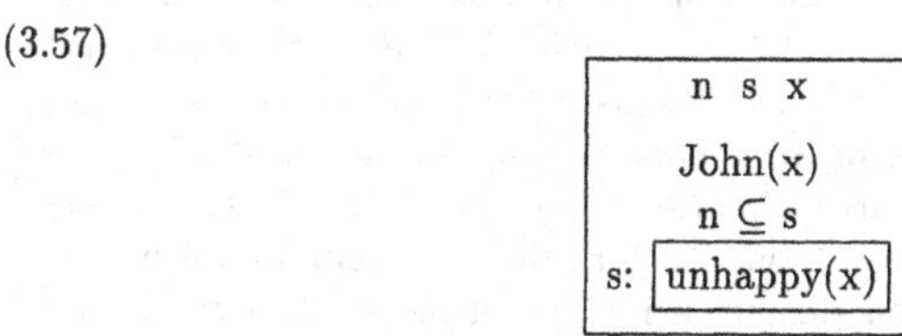

In (3.57) the referential argument of the adjective is no longer represented by its own discourse referent. Instead it is *absorbed*, as we will say, through identification with the subject. As a consequence, (3.57) is not open to the objection which led us to reject (3.55).

The conclusion we draw from this is that the DRS-construction rule which deals with the combination of copula and grammatical predicate must use absorption rather than stipulation of identity. A secondary conclusion is that, contrary to the impression that still seemed valid in the last section, absorption and stipulated identity are not entirely equivalent after all.[17]

[17]Now that we have found, in connection with the copular construction, an argument in favour of absorption as opposed to stipulated identity, we should wonder whether absorption should not also be preferred in connection with anaphoric pronouns. This appears to be a quite difficult question, which depends on certain theoretical commitments as well as on data of remarkable subtlety. One possibility that should be mentioned here has been suggested by [Roberts 1987a], who, building on earlier work of Reinhart's (see [Reinhart 1983b]) subdivides cases of pronominal anaphora, which in the account developed here are all treated the same, into cases of *syntactic binding* and cases of *stipulated coreference*. The former cases trigger a construction rule which uses absorption and the latter a version of our rule for anaphoric pronouns, in which the anaphoric link is established through stipulated identity. The matter will not be pursued here. The interested

Besides (3.55) and (3.57) there is a third DRS which captures the truth conditions of (3.44) well enough, viz.

(3.58)

n s x y
John(x)
unhappy(y)
n $\subseteq$ s
s: [x is y]

Evidently, (3.58) suffers from the same objection as (3.55).[18] Its inadequacy implies an answer to a perennial question in the philosophy of language and logic: Is there only one verb **to be**, with one unitary meaning, which can be used both as copula and in identity statements? Or are the "**is** of identity" and the "**is** of predication" (as the copular use of **be** is often called) two distinct concepts, which happen to be realized by one and the same word? The considerations of this section show that strictly speaking the "**is** of identity" and "**is** of predication" express two distinct concepts, the difference between them is manifest as the difference between the two processing rules which the two uses of **be** apparently require. Yet it also appears from our analysis that the two uses are intimately related. For after all, (3.58) does assign (3.44) the right truth conditions. Inasmuch as this representation is wrong, it is so only in that it assigns some element a referential independence which it does not seem to have. But this is a quite subtle failure, which will cause trouble only when the copular sentence in question is considered as part of a wider lingistic context. Thus the difference between the two rules is one of considerable delicacy, and it is easy to see how the one rule could give rise to the other by what seems to be a very slight adjustment. This observation goes some way, it seems to us, towards explaining how it is that while the "**is** of identity" and the "**is** of predication" are strictly speakling distinct, they are nevertheless expressed by what appears to be a single verb – not only in English, but in many other languages as well.

Since we will not deal with the referential arguments of verbs until Chapter 5, the type of representation for copular sentences which we have chosen – that exemplified by (3.55) – does not quite fit the present mode of representation, in which those arguments are ignored. So for the time being we will make use of "reduced" versions of representations like (3.55), in which the state discourse referent **s** and the temporal information involving it have been suppressed. In particular, (3.55)

reader should consult the cited works.

[18]In fact, its inadequacy might be thought worse, since the discourse referent **y** in (3.58) is supposed to enjoy a status of greater independence from **x** than it does in (3.55); thus in relation to (3.58) it is if anything harder than in the case of (3.55) to see why **y** should not be available as an antecedent to subsequent anaphoric pronouns.

will be reduced to the DRS

(3.59)

To turn the reflections of the last ten pages into a formal theory, one would have to build on a level of syntactic sophistication well above that of the simple grammar of Chapter 0. But since it is this grammar of Chapter 0 which we have chosen to make do with, we should have a quick look at how the lessons we have learned can be adapted to the simple-minded syntactic structures which this grammar allows.

We begin with the adnominal use of adjectives and prepositional phrases, as exemplified in

(3.60) an unhappy donkey

and

(3.61) a bar near the church

As indicated above, we assume that when an adjective occurs prenominally or a PP postnominally, it combines with the head noun to form a complex common noun phrase, which then joins forces with the determiner to produce an NP.

Thus the relevant NP of (3.60) has the structure

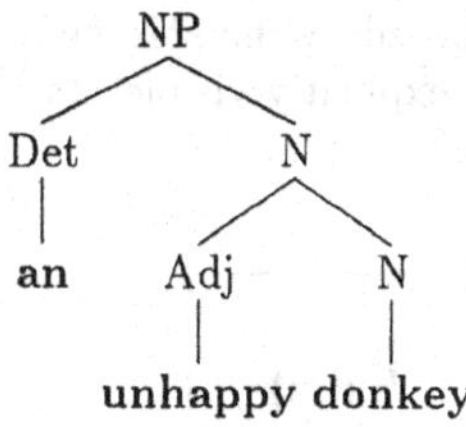

and that of (3.61) the form

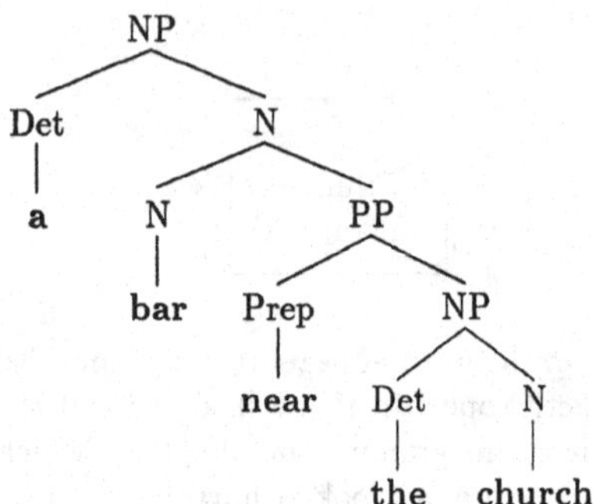

It seems clear that the complex noun phrase **unhappy donkey** expresses a predicate which is true of precisely those things which are (i) a donkey and (ii) unhappy. To arrive at this analysis of **unhappy donkey** we must, once again, identify the referential argument of the adjective with that of the noun. In the context of DRS-construction this amounts to the following. Suppose, for instance, that we want to construct the DRS for **Bill owns an unhappy donkey**. The first two steps are familiar and lead to the structure

(3.62)

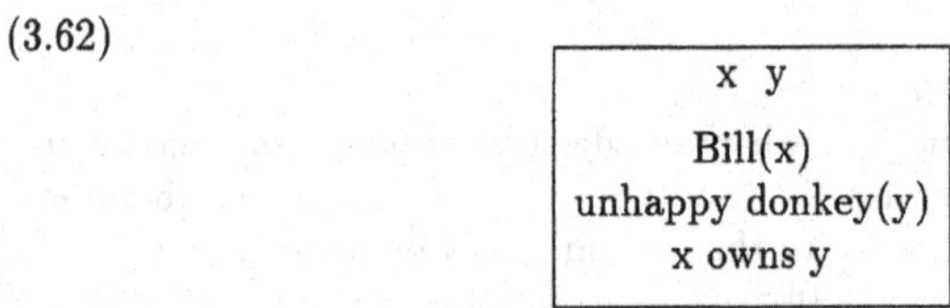

There is only one step remaining, which identifies the (referential) argument of **unhappy** with that of **donkey**. In the present case this means no more than that we treat **y** as the argument of both the adjective and the noun – the referential argument of the adjective gets absorbed by the argument of the noun as soon as it is introduced; so it never becomes explicitly visible. In this way, (3.62) is turned into

(3.63)

Just as the condition **unhappy donkey(y)** reduces to the pair of conditions

(3.64) donkey(y)
unhappy(y)

so a condition like **bar near the church(y)** reduces to the pair

(3.65) bar(y)
near the church(y)

in which the referential argument of **near** has been absorbed by that of **bar**. Applying the rule for definite descriptions to the second condition of (3.65) will reduce this further to

(3.66) the church(z)
bar(y)
near z(y)

with **z** some new discourse referent.

About the semantics of the copular use of adjectival and prepositional phrases we have said enough already. About the syntax of the copular construction there isn't very much that needs (or, for that matter, can) be said within the simple-minded phrase structure framework employed in this book. What can be said comes to no more than this: the copula combines with a "predicate" - which can be a PP, and AP or, for that matter, an NP - and the result is a VP. We won't bother to define the relevant syntactic rule or to display an example of the kind of syntactic structure it generates. In view of our remarks about the semantics of the post-copular construction, the reader should have no difficulty in formulating the corresponding construction rule.

The processing of adjectives and prepositional phrases we have sketched in this section ignores a number of major problems. The first concerns adjectives. More often than not an adjective in prenominal position must be interpreted in relation to the noun it precedes. Thus the criteria for **small** are very different when it occurs in **small mouse** and when it occurs in **small elephant**. And the criteria for **skillful** in the context **skillful dart player** are quite different from what they are when the word occurs in the combination **skillful cobbler**. Such dependencies of the adjective on the noun it accompanies are lost when the complex phrase is represented in the manner proposed above, viz. as a simple conjunction:

(3.67) mouse(x)
small(x)

This difficulty is, moreover, not restricted to prenominal adjectives. When an adjective such as **small** occurs after **is**, we feel a need to ask the question 'small for what?'; and to answer that question we must recover some reference class from the context. Sometimes the class is given by the noun of the subject NP. For instance

(3.68) This mouse is small.

is naturally interpreted as 'This mouse is small for a mouse'. In other cases this is not the right interpretation. For instance

(3.69) Mice are small.

would not normally be understood as the trivially false claim that as a rule mice are small for mice.

The proper analysis of these properties of adjectives is a very complex and difficult business, which could easily fill a thick book. Here we will proceed as if these problems did not exist.

Prepositional phrases present two different (and less momentous) problems. The first problem is one of ambiguity. This problem arises also in connection with the lexical categories of verb and noun with which we have been dealing from the outset. But with prepositions it seems to be more pronounced: Consider, for instance, the different meanings of the preposition **on** in the following phrases:

(3.70) (a) This book is on the table.
(b) Bill's picture is on the wall that is opposite the front door.
(c) This book is on Greek sculpture.
(d) The meeting is on Wednesday.

In the first two examples **on** expresses a spatial relation; but the relation expressed in (3.70.b) seems to be somewhat different from the one expressed in (3.70.a), answering to different application criteria (an observation that is supported by the fact that in certain other languages there isn't a single preposition covering both cases. For instance, in German one says **Das Buch liegt auf dem Tisch** but **Das Bild hängt an der Wand.**) The third example concerns the temporal use of **on**, whereas the fourth illustrates an abstract use, one which expresses the relation between a text and its topic. Presumably there are systematic connections between these different senses. For instance, it would have been much more surprising if a preposition which denotes the spatial relation referred to in (3.70.a) were to mean **after** when combined with an NP denoting a time. But even so it is as a rule not possible to predict one sense of a preposition with any degree of certainty from of its other senses. Thus the French preposition **sur**, which is the correct translation of **on** in the context of (3.70.a), cannot be used with a temporal meaning at all.

Explicit semantic representations ought to disambiguate prepositions to the extent that this is done by a human interpreter. Often disambiguation is possible on the strength of quite simple clues, such as the semantic category of the NP that complements the preposition. (Is it an NP for a place, for a time, for a surface, for a three-dimensional object, for a person ...?) But often other factors enter into the disambiguation process as well; and there appears to be little hope at present of developing detailed accounts of how disambiguation works in these more complex cases. Here we sidestep the problem (as we have sidestepped it in relation to other lexical categories such as nouns and verbs), and treat conditions such as **on x(y)** as not further reducible.

The second problem with prepositional phrases concerns their syntactic "attachment". This is a problem that does not arise for prepositional phrases which occur as complements to predicational **be**. Nor does it arise for PPs following the head noun of a subject NP in sentence-initial position. But it does arise in sentences such as

(3.71) John discovered a girl with a telescope.

Here the prepositional phrase **with a telescope** can be understood either as modifying the act of discovering the girl or as qualifying the object of discovery – it was a girl *with* (e.g. carrying, or standing next to) a telescope. We take it that such ambiguities are syntactic – a sentence like (3.71) has two distinct syntactic readings, each corresponding to one of the two interpretations mentioned. One of these analyses is the tree (3.72) while the other analysis, (3.73), has the PP as part of the VP. Only the first of these two syntactic structures, (3.72), is such that our semantic representation formalism can deal with it. The DRS for this structure should be of the form (3.74) (Here the one but last condition means that **y** was "with" **z** – i.e. was equipped with **z** or had **z** with her or something like that.)

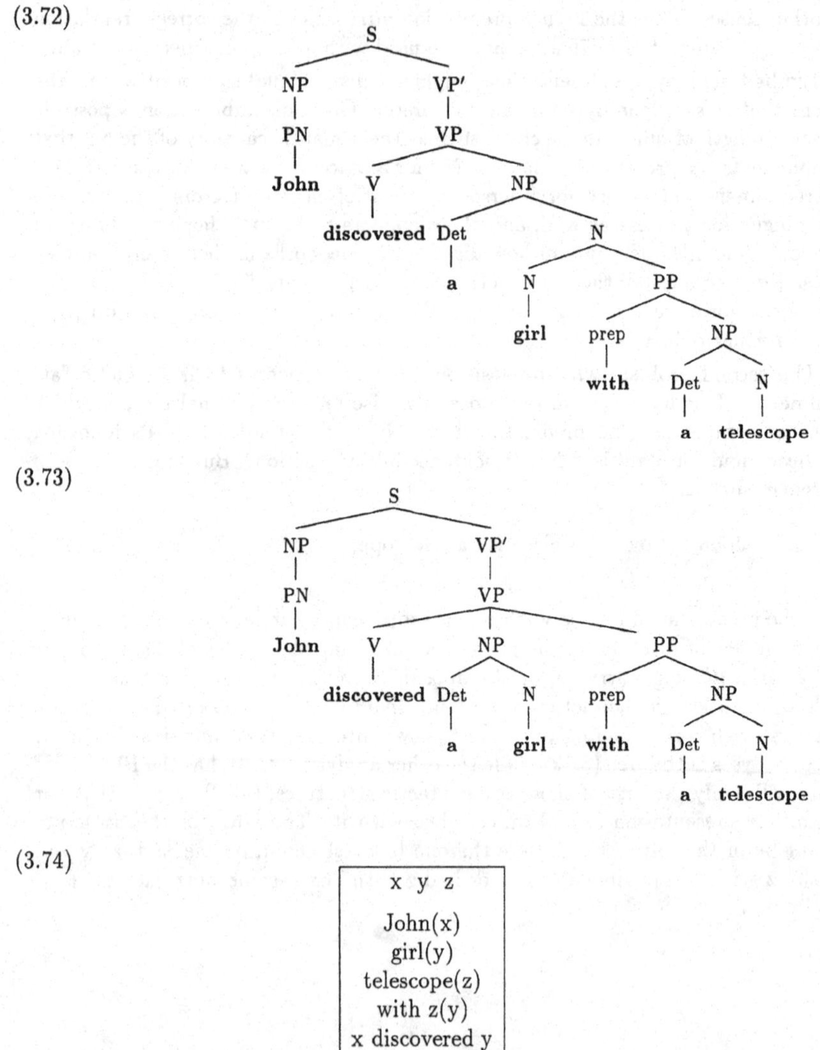

(3.73) cannot be represented with the resources we have. Its semantic import is that the telescope was used as an instrument in the discovery of which the sentence speaks. Here the prepositional phrase relates its non-referential argument to the referential argument of the verb, i.e. the event of discovering the girl. In view of its syntactic position the prepositional phrase of (3.73) belongs to the category of *adverbials* – expressions whose semantic function is to give additional information about the events or states described by the verb phrases to which they are subordinate. It is clear that a representation which does justice to our informal gloss must provide an explicit representation of this event. As we have said already, the representational resources needed for this will be developed only in Chapter 5. Even there, however, only a very limited class of adverbials will be considered, consisting exclusively of expressions whose function is to determine the temporal location or duration of events and states. In fact, it would have been hard to do much better than that. In spite of all the attention it has received in recent years, the semantics of adverbs is still in its infancy. In this book, nothing will be said about this topic (apart from the treatment of temporal adverbs in Chapter 5).

We noted earlier that prepositions sometimes act as case markers (see footnote 9 on page 263), and that where this is so, the NPs following them should be treated as argument phrases of the VPs or NPs which contain the prepositional phrase as a constituent. In the next two chapters we will sometimes make use of examples which contain such prepositional phrases. These will always be constituents of verb phrases, and thus function as argument phrases to some verb. In such cases we will treat the verb as a predicate with argument places corresponding to these preposition phrases, without bothering to comment on the matter explicitly. By way of example, the verb **talk** as it occurs in

(3.75) Olga talked to Mary about Bill.

will be treated as a three-place relation which holds between **x**, **y** and **z** in case **x talks to y about z**. On this assumption, (3.75) yields the DRS

(3.76)

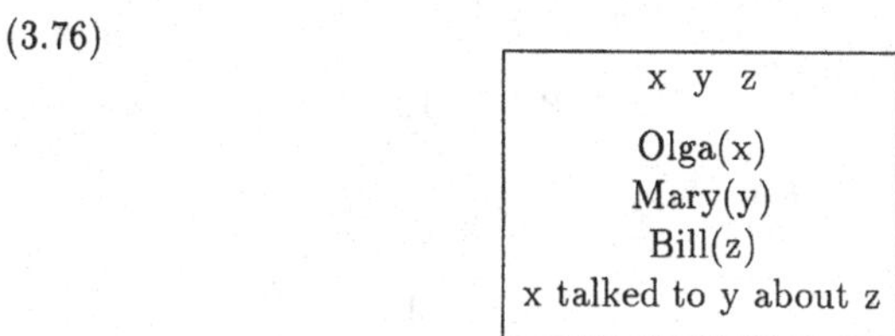

where ... **talked to** ... **about** ... is treated as an irreducible three-place relation. It is straightforward to alter the construction algorithm so that it yields DRSs like (3.76) from syntactic analysis trees such as (3.73).

Exercises

1. (a) Extend the syntax so that it covers uses of the copula **be** in which it is followed by (i) an adjective or (ii) a prepositional phrase.

   (b) Extend the construction algorithm with a rule or rules which handle the semantics of the syntactic constructions mentioned under (a).

2. If we try to extend the construction algorithm to deal with verbs like **talk to ... about ...** we first have to decide on the syntactic representation of such verbs and their arguments.

   Because there is no assymmetry between the two PPs (**Olga talked about Bill to Mary** is as good as (3.75)) we assume that the VP of sentences containing such verbs has the following structure.

   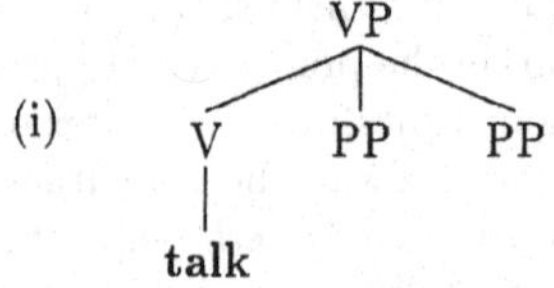

   This structure, however, does not fit with the overall specification of the DRS-Construction Algorithm as given in Section 1.1. Remember that the construction rules have to be applied to the *highest* triggering configuration in the syntactic configuration of the conditions to which they are applied. For the ternary branching configuration no priority between the two PPs is given directly: Both triggering configurations

   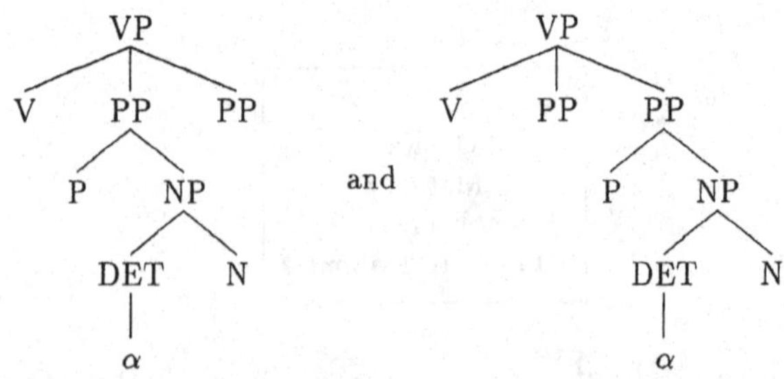

   have the same top node.

On page 88 we stipulated that the correct processing of conditions containing incomparable triggering configurations should be the following: The condition may be reduced either via one of these configurations or via the other. This element of order indeterminacy has the effect that each of the following sentences can be turned into two distinct DRSs.

(1) Dov talked about every theorem to a student.

(2) Dov talked about a theorem to every student.

Construct these DRSs. Do they correspond to your intuitions about the possible interpretations of (1) and (2)?

3.7 Scope Ambiguity

3.7.1 Scope

Like Section 3.1 this one is devoted to phenomena that are covered by the fragment we have studied in Chapters 1 and 2, and which strictly speaking invalidate the account of that fragment. This time the problem is not that our theory generates readings which do not exist, but that it fails to generate certain readings which are generally judged possible. An example is presented by the sentence

(3.77) A problem about the environment preoccupies every serious politician.

On one reading this sentence means that there is some particular environmental problem that has the attention of every serious politician. But (3.77) is generally thought to also have another interpretation, according to which every serious politician is concerned with some environmental problem or other but where not all politicians need be concerned with the same problem.

The ambiguity between these two readings is a case of what is called *scope ambiguity*. Scope ambiguity, as the term suggests, is ambiguity as to the scope of scope-bearing constituents of a sentence. The notion of scope is most easily explained in connection with a formal language such as the predicate calculus. In predicate logic the scope-bearing elements are the quantifiers and the sentential connectives. The scope of a quantifier, '$\forall$' or '$\exists$', is, logically speaking, the (simple or complex) predicate of which the quantifier says that it is satisfied by everything or something. The scope of a two-place sentential connective is just the two formulas it connects, while the one-place connective '$\neg$' has as its scope just the formula which it is used to negate. Thus, in

(3.78) $\forall x((W(x) \& D(x)) \rightarrow \exists y((M(y) \& \neg\exists z(W(z) \& L(z,y))) \& L(y,x)))$

'$\forall$' has as its scope the entire formula following it: $(W(x) \& D(x)) \rightarrow \exists y((M(y) \& \neg\exists z(W(z) \& L(z,y))) \& L(y,x))$. Similarly, the first occurrence of '$\exists$' has as its scope the formula $((M(y) \& \neg\exists z(W(z) \& L(z,y))) \& L(y,x))$, while the scope of the second occurrence is limited to $(W(z) \& L(z,y))$; '$\neg$' has as its scope the formula $\exists z(W(z) \& L(z,y))$; the scope of '$\rightarrow$' is the pair of formulas $\langle W(x) \& D(x), \exists y((M(y) \& \neg\exists z(W(z) \& L(z,y))) \& L(y,x))\rangle$; finally, the scopes of the four occurrences of '&' are, in order of appearance, $\langle W(x), D(x)\rangle$, $\langle M(y), \neg\exists z(W(z) \& L(z,y))\rangle$, $\langle W(z), L(z,y)\rangle$ and $\langle(M(y) \& \neg\exists z(W(z) \& L(z,y))), L(y,x)\rangle$.

The close connection between predicate logic and the representational formalism of DRT (the formal "language" whose formulas are the DRSs) makes it possible to transfer the notions of scope and of scope-bearing elements straightforwardly from the one to the other. In the DRS language, the scope-bearing elements are (i) the signs used in the different types of complex conditions '$\neg$', '$\Rightarrow$' and '$\vee$'; and (ii) the discourse referents. For the symbols '$\neg$', '$\Rightarrow$', '$\vee$' the definition of scope is remarkably simple. Where '$\neg$' occurs as part of a DRS-condition $\neg K'$, its scope is the DRS K'; similarly, an occurrence of '$\Rightarrow$' as part of a complex condition $K_1 \Rightarrow K_2$ has as its scope the pair $\langle K_1, K_2\rangle$; and the scope of '$\vee$', as it occurs in a complex condition $K_1 \vee K_2 \vee ... \vee K_n$, is the n-tuple $\langle K_1, K_2, ..., K_n\rangle$. (We may take this to be the scope of each of the occurrences of '$\vee$' in $K_1 \vee K_2 \vee ... \vee K_n$.) Finally, the scope of a discourse referent occurring in the universe of the DRS K' is a set of conditions. In all cases except that where K' is the antecedent of a condition $K' \Rightarrow K''$, this set is $Con_{K'}$. In the case where K' is part of the condition $K' \Rightarrow K''$, it is $Con_{K'} \cup Con_{K''}$.

In relation to natural language the concept of scope is more problematic. Discussions of the scope of natural language constituents rely on more or less explicit correlations between the natural language and some formal language such as, say, a language of first order predicate logic. The scope-bearing constituents of natural language are then those constituents which, when translated into the formal language, give rise to at least one scope-bearing element there. In the typical case there is just one such element which can be seen as reflecting the scopal properties of the natural language constituent. In that case one takes the scope of the natural language constituent to be that part of the natural language sentence or text which converts upon translation into the scope of that scope-bearing formal counterpart. Consider, for instance, (3.77). It has the syntactic structure

(3.79)

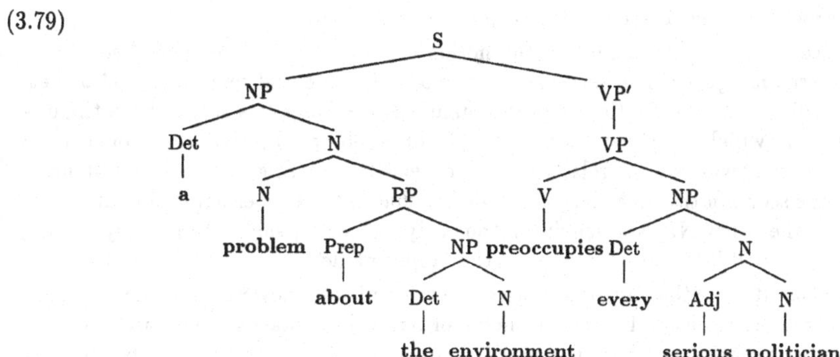

One of its interpretations corresponds to the predicate logic formula

(3.80) $\exists$y(**problem about the environment**(y) & $\forall$x(**serious politician**(x) $\rightarrow$ y **preoccupies** x)

The scope-bearing constituents of (3.77) are those which give rise to the quantifiers in (3.80), i.e. the NPs **a problem about the environment** and **every serious politician.** According to (3.80), the former has the entire sentence for its scope while the scope of the latter is the verb phrase **preoccupies every serious politician.** According to the other interpretation of (3.77), given by

(3.81) $\forall$x(**serious politician**(x) $\rightarrow$ $\exists$y(**problem about the environment**(y) & y **preoccupies** x))

it is the **every**-phrase which has the entire sentence for its scope; the scope of the subject consists in this case of the subject itself together with the verb **preoccupies.**

Having committed ourselves not only to a formal representation language but also to an explicit mechanism for translating natural language into that formalism, the notion of a scope-bearing natural language constituent and of its scope can be defined more rigorously. First, the scope of a constituent introducing a discourse referent. This can be identified with the set of constituents which furnish the material of the DRS-conditions constituting the scope of the discourse referent it introduces. More precisely, suppose that α is such a constituent (in the fragment of English we have studied so far these are always NPs) of a given sentence or text, that K is a DRS representing that text or sentence and that the discourse referent **x** represents α in K. Then *the scope of* α, *in* the given text or sentence and *according to* K, consists of all those constituents which provide predicates occurring in conditions that belong to the scope of **x** in K.

Note that in this definition the notion of scope has been extended so that it concerns not just single sentences but also multisentential texts. Note also that, according to this definition, a proper name always has as its scope the entire discourse in which it occurs. This entails the often observed fact that a proper name always has "wide scope" relative to any other NP occurring in the same sentence – i.e. the scope of the other NP is included in that of the proper name. In particular, when the other NP is a genuinely "quantifying" NP[19], such as an **every**-phrase, its scope will be included in that of the proper name.

Constituents that introduce discourse referents are, however, not the only ones that qualify as scope-bearing elements of natural language. There are a variety of other types of expressions, among them conjunctions, auxiliary verbs and various kinds of adverbs and abverbials. The only such elements that belong to the fragment considered in this chapter are the connective **or**, the adverb **not** and the sentential combination **if ... then**. The last three of these give rise to complex DRS-conditions containing an equivalent sign ($\vee$, $\neg$, or $\Rightarrow$). As we have already defined the scopes of these signs, we can, just as in the case of noun phrases, characterize the scope of one of the mentioned English constituents as the set of constituents which provide the predicates of the conditions in the scope of the particular sign "translating" the given occurrence.

With **and** the matter is a little different since it does not translate into an operator, but is represented implicitly: the constituents it conjoins give rise to conditions that belong to the same condition set. To obtain a characterization of scope that harmonizes with the one just given for **or**, **not** and **if ... then**, we must stipulate that the scope of **and** consists of the constituents that are conjoined by it.

3.7.2 'Every'-Phrases and Indefinites

We said that, according to the judgement of English speakers, (3.77) is ambiguous. It has a reading in which the object NP includes the subject NP in its scope (or in which it "has scope over" the subject NP, as one also says) as well as one in which the subject has scope over the object. These two scope relations would be represented by the DRSs (3.82) and (3.83). Of these two DRSs only the second can be derived from (3.77) by the construction algorithm as stated in Chapters 1 and 2. If we want the algorithm to be able to transform (3.77) into (3.82) as well, it must be modified. But how?

---

[19]See Chapter 4.

(3.82)

(3.83)

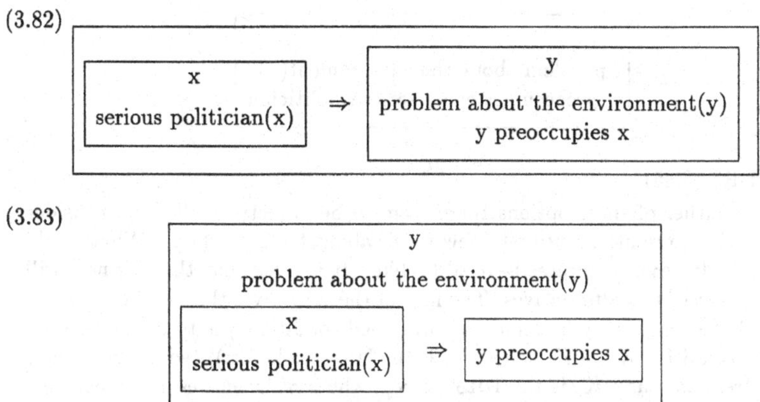

Two options suggest themselves. The first is to loosen the constraints on the order of application of the construction rules, so that in the processing of a transitive clause the object NP may be treated before the subject. If we are allowed to proceed in this way when constructing a DRS for (3.77) we can get, first, the DRS

(3.84)

and then from (3.84)

(3.85)

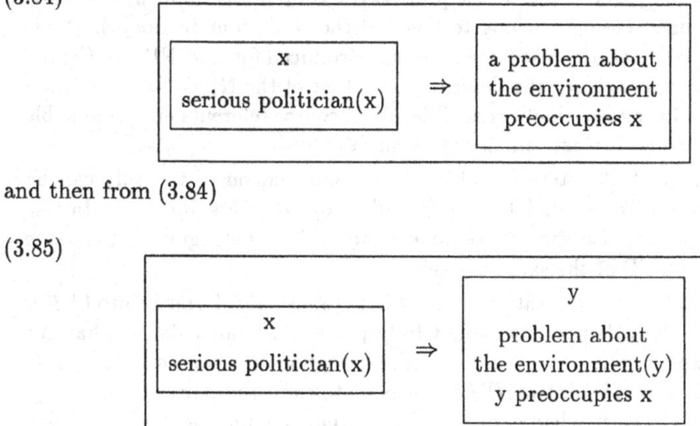

This gives us the reading we were after.

The second option is to leave the constraints on the order of rule application intact, but to restate the rule for NPs of the form **every** α so that it is able to transform the DRS

(3.86)

y
problem about the environment(y) y preoccupies every serious politician

into the DRS (3.85).

Against either of these options there seem to be objections. We will consider the first option presently. But first a few words about the second one. What would the new rule for **every**-phrases have to be like? It is clear that the rule now will have to consist of two alternatives. The first of these involves the set of operations with which we are already familiar: the processed condition γ is to be replaced by a complex condition $K_1 \Rightarrow K_2$, where K_1 is the DRS $\langle\{\mathbf{x}\}, \beta(\mathbf{x})\rangle$ (with **x** some new discourse referent) and K_2 is the DRS $\langle\emptyset, \gamma'\rangle$, where γ' is the result of replacing the processed **every**-phrase in γ by **x**. The second alternative differs from the first in that some of the material already in the DRS K' which contains γ as one of its conditions, is to be "incorporated" into the DRS K_2. Here by "incorporation" we mean that the relevant part of the DRS is taken out of K' and added to K_2. What is to be incorporated into K_2 is easily expressed in informal terms: it is to be the collection of discourse referents and conditions which (i) "stem from" one or more NPs belonging to the same clause as the processed **every**-phrase and (ii) belong to K' (i.e. the discourse referents belong to $U_{K'}$ and the conditions to $Con_{K'}$). What "stems from" an NP is (i) the discourse referent introduced for that NP and (ii) the condition $\beta(\mathbf{x})$ which captures the descriptive content of the NP, if that condition is irreducible, or, if the condition is reducible, all discourse referents and irreducible conditions to which its further reductions eventually lead.

In the fragment of Chapters 1 and 2, the second version of the rule can be applied is only where an object NP is given wide scope over a subject NP. In this special case we can replace the phrase "one or more NPs belonging to the same clause" by "subject NP of the same clause".

It should be clear that application of the rule to (3.86) transforms it into (3.85). Our statement of the rule is of course not fully precise. In particular, we haven't made formally explicit what it is for a discourse referent or condition to "stem from" a certain NP, nor what it is for two NPs to "belong" to the same clause, even though it may be intuitively clear what is intended. It is not our purpose here to arrive at a fully explicit and correct formulation of the rule. It ought to be obvious that, whatever its details, the rule requires a more elaborate DRS format than we have been using so far. For we must be able to tell, at the point where the rule is applied, which conditions come from which natural language constituents. It is, of course, not difficult to carry such information along in the DRS that is being constructed. However, to do so would mean introducing an additional element of complexity into our representational formalism, and this might be seen as a reason for preferring an alternative solution to the problem.

The first option, that of allowing the object NP to be processed before the subject NP appears to be open to a more serious objection: if we permit objects to be processed before subjects, then we will end up with impossible interpretations for sentences like

(3.87) He loves a girl who does not like Bill.

Evidently, this sentence cannot mean that Bill loves a girl who doesn't like him. Yet, if we are allowed to process the sentence starting with the object NP **girl who does not like Bill**, then nothing will stop us from also treating the embedded NP **Bill** before we finally turn to the subject **he**. At that point a discourse referent representing **Bill** will be available as antecedent for the pronoun, and so we get, successively (3.88)–(3.90)

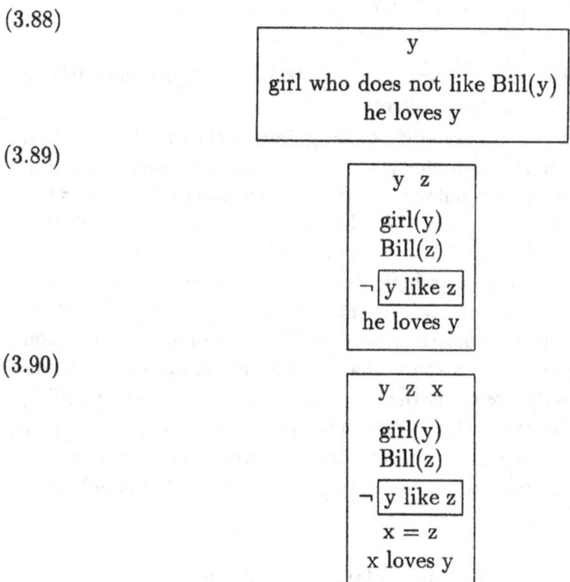

This last objection appears to be much more serious than the drawback of having to enrich DRSs with information about the sources of the discourse referents and conditions they contain. So it might seem that our first option, which avoids this

complication of DRS-structure, would be preferable after all. However, this looks much less obvious once we notice that the construction algorithm in its presently given form gets into trouble with a type of sentence which we have not so far scrutinized. An example is

(3.91) Bill employs a man who he doesn't like.

In (3.91) **he** cannot be understood as anaphorically connected with **a man**. Nevertheless our algorithm permits the construction of a DRS which countenances that connection. After three steps we get:

(3.92)

x y
Bill(x)
man(y)
he doesn't like y
x employs y

In our present version of the algorithm there is no constraint which prevents linking the pronoun in (3.92) with the discourse referent **y**.

It might be thought that the impossibility of assigning (3.91) an interpretation in which this connection is being made derives from a prohibition relating to the difference between reflexives and non-reflexives. After all, **who** in (3.91) acts as the object of the verb in the relative clause. Shouldn't we, then, see the prohibition against linking **he** with the discourse referent representing the referent of **who** as being of the same making as those which we discussed in Section 3.1? The constraint we need here is not captured by the revision of the pronoun rule which we proposed in Section 3.1. But a comparatively small extension of that revision would capture it: We only need to specify that a pronoun in subject position cannot be linked to a discourse referent that already occurs in a corresponding object position (in addition to the earlier constraint that a pronominal object may not be linked with a discourse referent representing the corresponding subject).

That this cannot be the solution to the problem presented by (3.92) is indicated by the following example:

(3.93) Bill employs a man who he thinks Mary does not like.

This sentence contains a construction – involving the verb **think** with its subordinate clause **Mary does not like** – which is not covered by our syntax, so that there can be no question of actually constructing a DRS for it with the tools available to us.[20] Even so, it will serve to make the point we are concerned to establish. Compare (3.93) with

(3.94) (i) Bill thinks Mary does not like him.

(ii) Bill thinks he does not like Mary.

(3.94) shows that a pronoun which occurs as part of the complement clause of a verb like **think** is "sufficiently distant from" the subject of that verb to be understood as anaphoric to it. Indeed, the "distance" is such that a reflexive pronoun could not be used in these examples.

(3.95) Bill thinks Mary does not like himself.

for instance, does not have the same meaning as (3.94.i). (Inasmuch as we refuse to link **himself** with **Mary** because of the apparent gender conflict between them, (3.95) is simply ungrammatical.)

The sentences in (3.94) thus suggest that in (3.93) the impossibility of linking **he** with **who** cannot be a simple consequence of the restrictions on pronoun interpretation which explain the opposition between reflexives and non-reflexives. On the other hand, the opposition must have something to do with the relationship between the position of **he** and of the 'source' of **who** (in (3.93): the object position of **like**). For depending on how we vary this relationship the connection may or may not become possible. Thus

(3.96) Bill employs a man who Mary told him Susan does not like.

does not permit the linking of **him** with **who**.

(3.97) Bill employs a man who Susan says courts a woman he does not like.

on the other hand is fine on the interpretation that Susan said of the man, **x**, whom Bill employs that **x** courts a woman who does not like **x**. These examples should convince the reader that the interpretation of plural pronouns is subject to constraints which go well beyond those formulated in Section 3.1. But to state these additional constraints we need a much more refined syntactic framework than

[20] In fact, the analysis of indirect discourse constructions – in which a verb of saying or thinking is combined with a complement clause – is notoriously hard. It is a subject that will be discussed at length in Volume 2. At this point even a preliminary treatment of it (like, say, that which we have offered in the preceding section for definite descriptions) is out of the question.

the one we have been using. So, as we are reluctant to switch to a different syntax in midstream, we will leave this matter for another occasion.[21]

The same constraints which allow the derivation of just those DRSs for (3.91), (3.95) and (3.96) that we want will also block the unwanted DRS for (3.87) even if we allow the object phrase of a transitive clause to be processed before the subject. (This is an assertion, for which we cannot argue here, and which the reader will have to take on faith.) Thus, in a revised version of the theory in which the needed constraints are implemented, loosening the order of rule application no longer constitutes a problem. Since, as we have argued, such a revision is necessary in any case, weakening the order constraints appears to be the right way of accounting for scope ambiguities of the type exemplified in (3.77).

3.7.3 Specific and other Wide Scope Indefinites

The scope ambiguity of (3.77) has its counterpart in that of a sentence like

(3.98) Every boy in Mary's class fancies a girl who Mary does not know.

Besides the reading which our theory generates, and which is represented by the DRS,

(3.99)

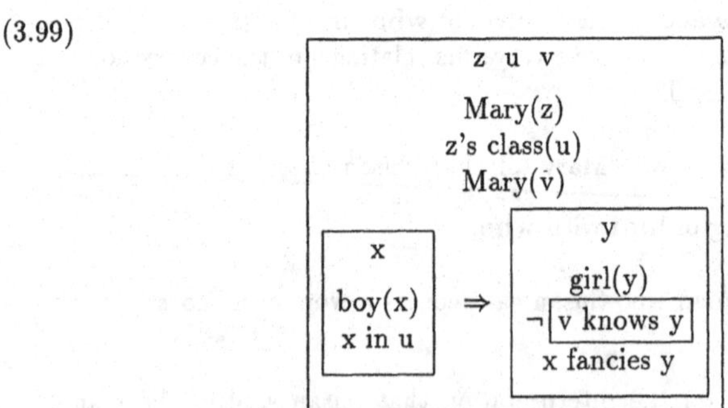

(3.98) also has a reading according to which there is some specific girl unknown to Mary such that every boy in Mary's class fancies her. This second reading, which is represented by the DRS (3.100),

[21] Although the development of a theory which combines the semantic approach of DRT with a syntax of the needed degree of sophistication is now under way, very little has so far been published on this subject. For discussion of some of the issues involved see [Roberts 1987a] and, especially, [Frey 1989].

(3.100)

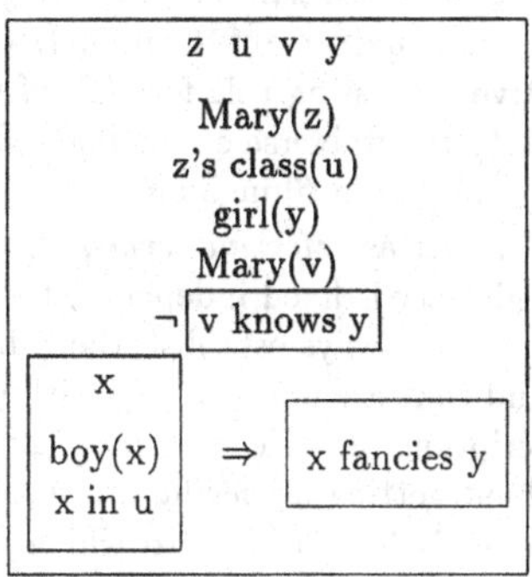

can be obtained if we modify the construction algorithm in either of the two ways we suggested in Section 3.7.2. Relaxing the constraints on order of rule application will give us the derived DRS without further modification. The other option means that this time we must introduce an alternative version to the rule for indefinite descriptions. It is clear what this alternative version must be like: The discourse referent **x** which the NP **a** β introduces (and with it the condition $\beta(\mathbf{x})$ that capture its descriptive content) is to be introduced, not into the DRS K′ of the processed condition, but into some "higher" DRS.

In (3.100) the only higher DRS is the main DRS itself. But in more complicated examples there may be several DRSs higher than K′. In such cases placing **x** and $\beta(\mathbf{x})$ in one rather than another of these higher DRSs will produce different results. Each of the resulting DRSs assigns the object NP in question scope over the corresponding subject; but in general no two of them will be equivalent. So it is an important question precisely which of the higher DRSs are available for adjunction of **x** and $\beta(\mathbf{x})$. The question is, it turns out, not easy to answer and it is not entirely clear to us what the answer should be. But at least we can give a partial answer.

It is a widely accepted view among linguists that indefinite descriptions admit of a use in which the speaker employs them to refer to some particular object he has in mind and which he could, if he wanted to, describe in uniquely identifying terms. (The use of the indefinite article serves, in these as in other cases, to signal to the hearer that the speaker takes the object to which he is referring to be new to the hearer. But this does not prevent the hearer from assuming that the speaker has uniquely identifying information about the object.) Indefinite noun phrases used in this way are sometimes referred to as *specific* indefinites. We will follow this terminology obliquely, speaking of *specific* as opposed to *non-specific* uses of indefinite NPs.

In our terms, interpreting an indefinite NP as used specifically means that the discourse referent it introduces must be seen as representing some particular object, and thus that it must belong to the universe of the main DRS. This suggests that we adopt the following alternative processing rule for NPs of the form **a** β: Introduce a new discourse referent **x** into the universe of the main DRS K and add $\beta(\mathbf{x})$ to Con_K. Furthermore replace γ by $\gamma[\mathbf{x}/\mathbf{a}\ \beta]$ in $Con_{K'}$.

Specifically used indefinites act as *referring terms*, terms that are used to refer to particular things, whose identity is fixed independently of the context in which the term occurs. Referring terms always establish their discourse referents in the universe of the main DRS and thus are not properly within the scope of any other NP. But can indefinite descriptions in object position also have scope over their corresponding subjects without getting a specific interpretation? In other words, are there readings of indefinite NPs according to which their discourse referents occupy some intermediate position between the universe of the main DRS and that directly containing the processed condition? It appears that the answer is 'yes'. For instance, the sentence

(3.101) Every student to whom every professor recommends a certain book which the student has already read is lucky.

has, it seems to us, an interpretation captured by the DRS[22]

(3.102)

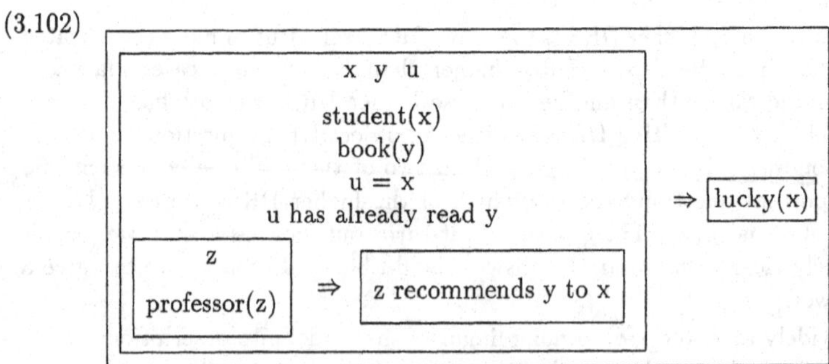

To account for a reading such as (3.102) we need yet a third alternative for processing indefinite NPs. This alternative must permit that the new discourse referent **x** be placed neither in the universe of the DRS K_2 containing the processed condition nor in that of the main DRS, but in the universe of the DRS containing the complex condition $K_1 \Rightarrow K_2$ of which K_2 is the consequent part. Similarly, in relative clauses

[22]The definite NP **the student** is dealt with as if it were a pronoun. This is a use of definite descriptions which we briefly discussed in Section 3.4. For further discussion see page 299 below.

with four or more arguments we would expect an indefinite to be able to take scope over two of the other three arguments which would normally be processed before it, but not over the third. For instance

(3.103) Every student to whom every professor recommends during every private consultation a certain book which the student has already read is lucky.

has, it seems to us, the reading given by

(3.104)

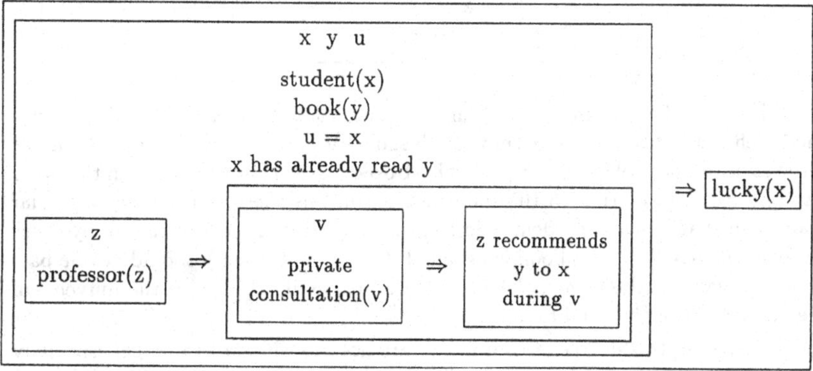

Furthermore, there appears to be the possibility that x may end up even higher than its having scope over the other arguments of the clause in which it stands requires. Thus

(3.105) If every student to whom every professor recommends a given book passes then the book is useful.

has, we believe, as one of its interpretations that given by

(3.106)

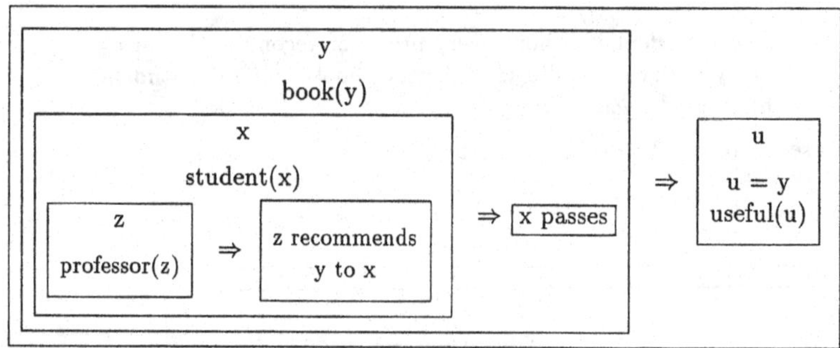

Even if **y** had been a member of the universe containing **x**, it would still give the indefinite NP scope over **every professor**. However, in that case it could not serve as antecedent of the description **the book**[23] in the **then** clause. On the other hand, it seems to us that (3.105) does not commit us there being some particular book such that *if* every student who has that book recommended to him by every professor passes *then* that book is useful. If this is right, then **y** should not be part of the universe of the principal DRS, but rather, as in (3.106), of the universe of the antecedent of the conditional.

Sentences of this degree of complexity are notoriously hard to judge, especially when it is a question of how many different interpretations they allow, and not simply whether they are interpretable at all. So we are reluctant to draw any definite conclusion from the examples above. Nevertheless, we are inclined to infer from these and other examples that the processing of indefinite noun phrases must allow for a considerable spectrum of alternatives if it is to cover the full range of interpretations that indefinites allow; and that perhaps no universe that is superordinate to the DRS of the processed condition can be categorally excluded.

There is, however, a further consideration which a satisfactory processing principle for indefinite descriptions should take into account. Not only do the possibilities exemplified in (3.101), (3.103) and (3.105) seem to be quite rare, they also seem to be severely restricted by the actual form of the indefinite noun phrase in question. For instance, in (3.105) the possibility of reading the indefinite as having scope over **every professor** seems to depend on the presence of **certain** – when **certain** is eliminated it becomes, in our judgement, virtually impossible to read the sentence as having the meaning given by (3.106); the indefinite noun now appears firmly within the scope of **every professor** as well as within that of **every student**.

[23]Cf. footnote 22 on page 290.

If, on the other hand, we eliminate the relative clause **which the student has already read** in (3.101), it is no longer necessary to assign the indefinite a scope within that of **every student**; as a consequence the specific reading, according to which the sentence is about just one book, becomes a possibility, although even here the scope assignments given by (3.102) appear to fall within the range of possibilities too.

We do not understand the precise effect of the presence of adjectives such as **certain, particular, given** etc. nor that of relative clauses which attest a dependence of the head (i.e. of the discourse referent representing the NP to which the relative clause is attached) on some other NP. It seems to us that these effects are fairly systematic and therefore that a good processing rule for indefinites would have to take them into account, but we do not know how such a rule should be stated.

The distinction between specific and non-specific indefinites is also constrained by certain other aspects of their form. Short and descriptively uninformative indefinite NPs admit as a rule only a non-specific interpretation, and in fact one which assigns them the smallest possible scope (as reflected by the processing rule for indefinites which we formulated in Chapter 1). Thus, if we strip the object NP of (3.98) of its relative clause, which transforms the sentence into (3.107), only the "narrow scope reading" of **a girl**, given by (3.108) seems to be available.

(3.107) Every boy in Mary's class fancies a girl.

(3.108)

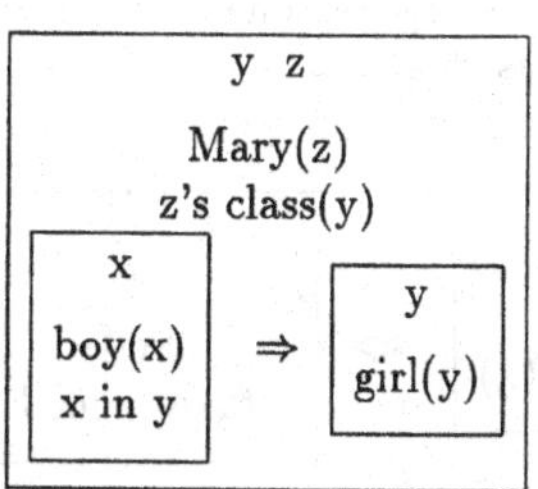

Even if the person who utters (3.107) has a particular girl in mind, and even if her interlocutor is disposed to think that she does, **a girl** still resists interpretation as a specific indefinite. The distinction between "long" and "short" indefinites is thus one which a good processing rule for such noun phrases should also take into account. But once again we find ourselves in a predicament. Where is the dividing line between long and short? We do not know, and so long as we do not know, we can do no better than restate the rule for indefinite NPs as a disjunction of processing options, leaving the choice between these options to the discretion of those applying the rule.

3.7.4 Generics

There is a further use of indefinite NPs which no discussion of their possible interpretations can afford to ignore. This is their so-called *generic use.* It is exemplified by the indefinites of (3.109) to (3.111).

(3.109) A wolf takes a mate for life.

(3.110) An honest man doesn't cheat on his wife.

(3.111) A good neighbour is worth more than a distant friend.

As we understand these sentences they each express a *generic* proposition – (3.109) the proposition that basically the typical wolf mates for life, (3.110) the proposition that basically no man truly deserving the predicate 'honest' is an adulterer, (3.111) the proposition that, as a rule, the comparison between any good neighbour and any distant friend favours the former. Our construction algorithm assigns quite different interpretations to (3.109)–(3.111), in fact, it assigns them interpretations that they do not seem to have. For instance, (3.109) is assigned the reading that there exists a wolf which takes a mate for life, but that is clearly not what the sentence means.

How would the meaning of, say, (3.109) be represented? In the light of the theory we have so far developed it seems reasonable to demand that the representation should have some such form as this:

(3.112)

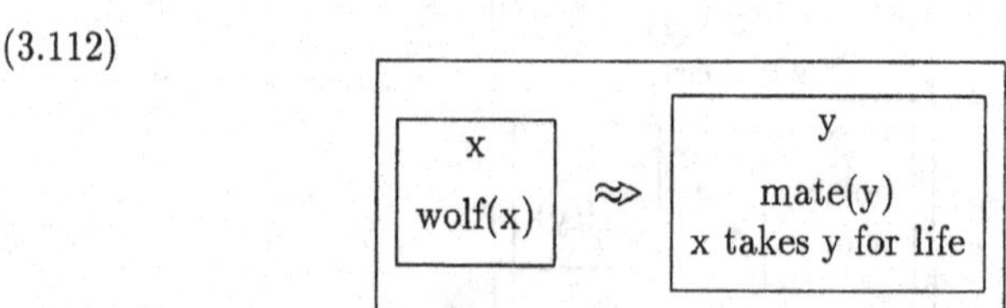

Here the wavy arrow is meant to indicate that the conditional connection between being a wolf and taking a mate for life need not hold with strict universality, but only that it does for all the "typical" or "normal" cases. One of the most difficult problems that generic statements pose is to explain exactly what this conditional connection is (or, if you prefer, of articulating the precise meaning of the wavy arrow). But this is an issue which will not be our concern here. The issue that does concern us is where a complex condition such as that of (3.112) could come from and why the discourse referent **x** should end up in that part of this condition in which it does end up.

There is as yet no general agreement over what the correct account of sentences like (3.109)–(3.111) is. But it must be something along the following lines. The verb of such a sentence carries a certain generic *operator*.[24] When the verb is in the present tense and is an action verb (such as, for instance, **take**), the presence of this operator is indicated by the fact that the tense form is that of the simple present, and not that of the present progressive.[25] For instance, it is the generic operator carried by the verb form **takes** in (3.109) which is responsible for the complex condition displayed in (3.112). Evidently the generic operator has, according to this analysis, much in common with the conditional operator **if ... then.** (It is noteworthy in this connection that a large percentage of present tense conditional sentences have action verbs in the simple present too.) But there is one important difference: a conditional sentence makes plain what is to be put into the antecedent box and what into the consequent box of the complex condition it introduces, but for generic sentences the partition between what goes into the left and what goes into the right box is not derivable in any simple way from the syntactic form of the sentence. There appears to be in general a strong pressure to put at least something into the left-hand box and at least something into the right-hand one; but according to what principles generic sentences are to be separated into these two halves is still a topic of research. In particular, there is as yet no fully satisfactory explanation why the indefinite subjects of (3.109)–(3.111) are all understood as contributing their discourse referents to the universe of the left-hand and not to that of the right-hand side box of the main DRS.

Whatever the principles according to which the partition is carried out, once it is accepted that generic sentences trigger the introduction of complex condition such as in (3.112), it becomes understandable how indefinite NPs in such sentences can take on the apparent force of (roughly) universal quantifiers. It is not the indefinite itself which carries this universal force; rather, it "rides along", just as the indefinites which occur in the antecedents of conditionals, with the universal,

---

[24]See in particular [Heim 1982].

[25]In statements that describe particular events a verb like **take** cannot occur in the simple present tense except in quite special contexts. For instance

(3.113) This wolf takes a mate for life.

cannot be understood as referring to a particular event of the wolf in question making a bond for life with some particular other wolf, but only in a spirit akin to that of (3.109), viz. that this wolf has the disposition to mate for life – compare in this respect

(3.114)

$$\text{This wolf} \left\{ \begin{array}{c} \text{is mating} \\ \text{has mated} \\ \text{will mate} \end{array} \right\} \text{for life.}$$

all of which can be understood as referring to some particular (present, past or future) mating event.

or quasi-universal, quantifier that is part of the meaning of the operator that has the indefinite NP in its scope.

It should be noted in this connection that an indefinite NP in a generic clause doesn't always introduce its discourse referent into the left-hand side box. For instance, the natural interpretation of

(3.115) A self-respecting German businessman drives a Mercedes.

is that in which the subject contributes its discourse referent to the left-hand side box and the object contributes its discourse referent to the right-hand side one. And it seems possible (if only just possible) to interpret

(3.116) A pond occupies the centre of a proper English park.

in such a way that it is the object NP **a proper English park** which contributes its discourse referent to the left-hand side box while the discourse referent of the subject goes into the box on the right.

We have done no more here than to identify the generic use of indefinite noun phrases. To present a proper account of this use we would have to develop a general theory of genericity; this is a major undertaking, which requires more resources than are developed in this book. The main conclusion that we draw from the few conclusions we have made is that generic uses of indefinites are not as different from the other uses we had previously looked at as might appear from the superficial description of a generic indefinite as a kind of universal quantifier. Even generic indefinites can be processed in accordance with the principle that we have found confirmed by all other uses of indefinites we have considered: the discourse referent which an indefinite NP introduces always goes either into the universe of the DRS of the processed condition, or else into that of some superordinate DRS.

Unlike **every**-phrases, an indefinite NP *never* introduces a position for its discourse referent that is *sub*ordinate to the condition as part of which it is being processed. In order to maintain that generic indefinites obey this constraint it is necessary to assume that generic sentences contain a separate constituent which is responsible for the complex DRS-condition whose left-hand side can then act as recipient for the discourse referent which the indefinite noun phrase introduces. This assumption may at first look rather *ad hoc*, since this constituent is not present as an overt element of the generic sentence. However, there appears to be some independent evidence for the presence of such a constituent, viz. the occurrence of action verbs in the simple present tense, rather than the present progressive. The force of such evidence is hard to appreciate if it is not placed within the proper context of tense, aspect and temporal quantification. We briefly return to the subject of generics in Sections 4.2.7 and 5.5.2.

Exercise

1. Give DRS representations for (3.110), (3.111), (3.115), (3.116) and for
   (1) A good student appreciates a good book.
   (2) A good student owns a good book.
2. (a) What are the accessibility relations for conditions of the form $K_1 \approx\!> K_2$?
   (b) How does the analysis of generic indefinites explain that the indefinite NP in (1) cannot have a generic reading, whereas a generic reading is possible in (2)?
   (1) If a spider has eight legs then a spider has more legs than a donkey.
   (2) If a spider has eight legs then it can run fast.

3.7.5 The Scope of Definite Descriptions

To conclude our discussion of scope ambiguities involving interactions between NPs we must return to a question concerning definite descriptions which is still outstanding from Section 3.4. The examples of descriptions which we considered in that section set up their discourse referents in the universe of the main DRS. But this is not true of all definite descriptions. Consider, for instance,

(3.117) Every student fears the professor who supervises his dissertation.

This sentence is understood as speaking not of a single professor, but of different professors in relation to different students. Thus its representation should be like this:

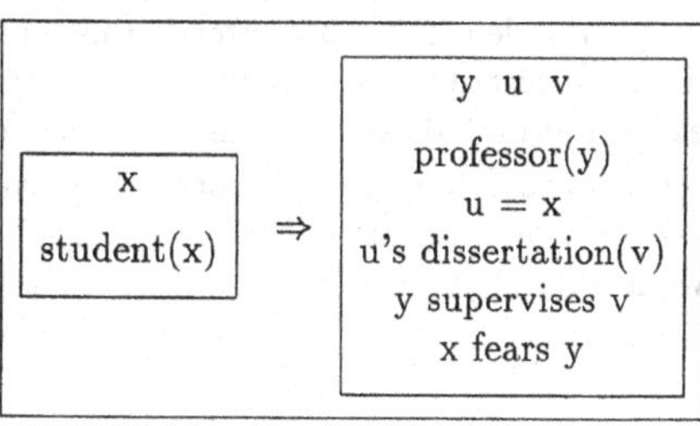

(3.118) is inadequate insofar as it ignores the difference between **the** and **a**, but at least it places the discourse referent **y** in the correct universe, and that is, in the case at hand, not the universe of the main DRS. In fact, **y** cannot be placed within the universe of the main DRS if the pronoun **his** is to be interpreted as anaphoric to **every student**. This follows from a principle that applies to all noun phrases and has already been built into the processing rules for indefinite NPs. This is the principle that the conditions which determine or constrain the possible referent(s) of a noun phrase must always be entered into the *same* DRS as the discourse referent representing the NP.

The intuition behind this principle is easily explained: the individuals that are assigned to a discourse referent **x** representing an NP α in the course of evaluating the DRS which contains **x** should always satisfy the constraints which α imposes. It is easy to see that in general this condition is fulfilled only if these constraints are represented at the same DRS the universe of which contains **x**. Applied to the definite description of (3.117) this principle entails that if the discourse referent **y** had been introduced into the main DRS then the constraint **professor who supervises his dissertation(y)** would have had to be put there also. It would then have been impossible to link **his** with **every student**, as the discourse referent **x** would not have been accessible from the position occupied by the pronoun.

(3.118) shows that definite descriptions can introduce their discourse referents at subordinate levels. As with indefinites this raises two questions: (i) Do definite descriptions introduce their discourse referents at a level different from the one originally assumed (in this case, that of the main DRS)? And (ii) which other levels are possible? Again, we have no definite way of answering these questions, and the reader will have to be content with a few informal remarks. One difference between definite and indefinite descriptions is that while indefinites tend towards narrow scope (i.e. introduce their discourse referents at the lowest possible level) and can as a rule be given a wide scope interpretation only when they contain special constituents – such as the adjective **certain**, or a relative clause like **who Mary doesn't know** – definite descriptions tend in the opposite direction: In order that a definite description be interpretable as introducing its discourse referent into a subordinate universe it is often necessary that it includes a relative clause in which there is an anaphoric element whose intended interpretation forces this subordinate position. Definite descriptions without such dependent elements must in the majority of cases be interpreted as having maximal scope.

Exceptions to this principle are those descriptions which can be understood as having an implicit dependency on some other NP, as in (3.119) or in (3.120) (See, for instance, [Asher/Wada 1988]).

(3.119) When a Mercedes runs into a wall, the steering column collapses.

(3.120) In every small Midwestern town the post office is next to the church.

In (3.119) **the steering column** is understood as referring to the steering column of the Mercedes in question. Similarly, **the post office** and **the church** in (3.120) are understood as taking on values which vary from one small midwestern town to the next. A good processing rule for descriptions, which tells us for each description at which level or levels its discourse referents may be introduced, will have to be able to recognize such implicit dependencies.

Definite descriptions pose a further problem, which was discussed at some length in Section 3.4. Such NPs, we said there, presuppose some sort of referential uniqueness. Rather than trying to determine the precise nature of this presupposition (a task to be left to Volume 2), we have decided to adopt the expedient of simply leaving the conditions $\beta(\mathbf{x})$ that are introduced by definite descriptions β unanalysed. It is true that in this way we fail to make the uniqueness implication transparent. But at least we keep our options open; we can still, at some later time, introduce construction rules that will decompose such conditions in a manner that their uniqueness implications become explicit.

In our representation of (3.117) we went on to reduce the condition $\beta(\mathbf{x})$ further, in spite of earlier injunction against it. We had to, for it was only by breaking the condition **professor who supervises his dissertation(y)** up that we were able to show why it is necessary that **y** be introduced into some other DRS than the principal one. As regards the uniqueness presupposition, however, this move is a step in the wrong direction. For (3.118) clearly fails to capture this presupposition. In fact, it gives **the professor who supervises his dissertation** a representation that is indistinguishable from the one which our construction algorithm assigns to the corresponding indefinite description **a professor who supervises his dissertation(y)**, a representation which, rightly, mentions no such presupposition. To correct this defect of (3.118) we would have to find a way to make the uniqueness presupposition explicit after all. But, as we said before, that is precisely what we are not in a position to do with the limited resources at our disposal.

From now on we will stick to the injunction not to process definite descriptions β beyond the introduction of the condition $\beta(\mathbf{x})$. Only in exceptional cases, where a definite description contains a pronoun which makes further reduction especially desirable, we will proceed as in the construction of (3.118); in those cases we will just put up with the fact that the resulting representation falls short of what it ought to be.

3.7.6 Scope Ambiguities involving Sentential Connectives

The scope ambiguities we have discussed so far all involved pairs of noun phrases. But noun phrases are not the only scope bearing constituents of natural languages. In fact, even within the small English fragment we have so far studied there are a number of other such constituents: the "sentence operators" negation, implication, disjunction and conjunction. We may expect that there exist also scope ambiguities which arise through the interactions between these sentence operators, or through the interaction of sentence operators and NPs.

In our treatment the scope ambiguities that arise through interaction between two sentence operators are all resolved at the level of syntactic representation. Consider, by way of an example, the ambiguities in (3.121) and (3.121).

(3.121) John likes Mary and Mary likes Fred or Alice doesn't like John.

(3.122) If John likes Mary then Susan doesn't like Mary and Fred doesn't like John.

(3.121) is ambiguous between a conjunction whose second member is a disjunction and a disjunction whose first member is a conjunction. The ambiguity of (3.122) is between a conjunction whose first conjunct is a conditional, and a conditional the consequent of which is a conjunction. Each of these ambiguities is resolved at the point when the sentence is assigned a syntactic analysis.[26] As syntax is not a

[26]In the present fragment there turn out to be no ambiguities arising through the interaction of negation and other sentence operators. But in the larger fragments which we will study in Chapters 4 and 5 this will no longer be so. Thus both (3.123) and (3.124f) are ambiguous.

(3.123) The men do not love or envy the women.

(3.124) John will not invite Mary and invite Bob.

These ambiguities too are resolved at the level of syntax. That such ambiguities have no counterparts in sentences that involve singular subjects and main verbs in the present tense is an accident of English morphology. Thus (3.123) has two singular counterparts

(3.125) (a) The man does not love or envy the woman.
(b) The man does not love or envies the woman.

each of which corresponds unambiguously to one of the two interpretations of (3.123). The ambiguity of (3.123) is made possible by the fortuitous circumstance (fortuitous both from a semantic and from a structural syntactic perspective) that the 3rd person plural present tense form **envy** is indistinguishable from the infinitive **envy**. When (3.124) is transposed from the future into the present tense its ambiguity disappears for similar accidental reasons: We get two distinct sentences, each with only one reading.

(3.126) (a) John does not invite Mary and invite Bill.
(b) John does not invite Mary and invites Bill.

central concern in this book, we will say no more about these or other syntactic ambiguities.

Ambiguities between a sentence operator and an NP are a different matter. For example

(3.127) Every student doesn't know the answer.

appears to be ambiguous between the readings

(3.128)

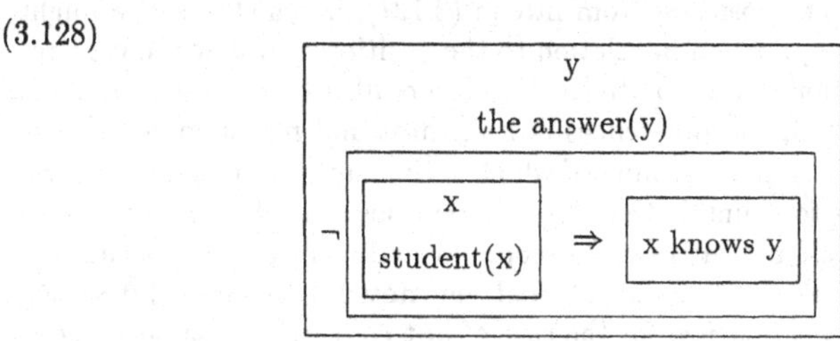

and

(3.129)

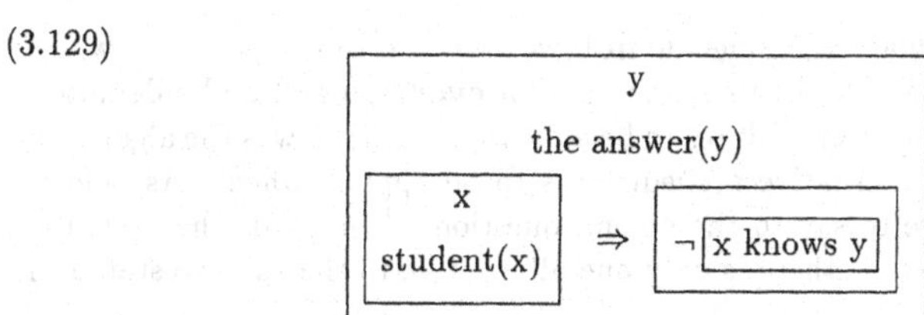

Of these readings our algorithm is able to generate only the second. In fact, this reading seems to be the less preferred one, and some English speakers even doubt that it is a possible reading for (3.127). To obtain the first reading would require, once again, one of two possible changes to the construction algorithm. Either we relax the constraints on order of rule application or we add an alternative to the rule which is triggered by the second scope bearing element (here: negation). Again it is not easy to make a motivated choice between these options. But there is one consideration that appears to favour the second. Consider

(3.130) (a) Every girl who Bill invited almost made it to his party.
(b) Everyone of Bill's friends never comes to his parties.

Neither (3.130.a) nor (3.130.b) has a reading in which the adverb has scope over the subject. Thus (3.130.a) cannot be paraphrased as 'almost every girl who Bill invited made it to his party'. And (3.130.b), which admittedly is a little awkward, can only mean that no friend of Bill's ever comes to his parties, not that there is always at least one friend missing. These observations speak against relaxing the constraints on rule order application, for presumably such a relaxation would run afoul of the facts just noted: it would assign to (3.130.a/b) the same ambiguity as to (3.127), although it is only (3.127) which is ambiguous in this way.

We hasten to say that as it stands this argument is not conclusive, as we have said nothing about the nodes which the words **almost** and **never** occupy in the syntactic analyses of (3.130.a) and (3.130.b). It is certainly conceivable that they could be assigned different positions from **not** in (3.127), in which case we might relax the order of rule application in relation to the position of **not** without introducing a similar relaxation in relation to the position of **almost** or **never**. Indeed, there are various distributional differences between **not** and **never** in contemporary standard English, the most striking of which is that **not** requires **do**-support. So perhaps it is possible to maintain that the apparent position which **not** occupies within the sentence is less indicative of its scope possibilities than this position is for other adverbs (such as in particular **almost** and **never**). However, lifting the restriction on order application *just* for the case of **not** comes to the same thing as introducing new alternatives in the processing rule for **not**. So let us turn to this second alternative.

In trying to reformulate the rule for **not** we face the same questions which confronted us when we tried to diversify the rules for **every**-phrases and indefinites: (i) Which are the alternative procedures to be added? and (ii) How is the algorithm to decide which of the alternative procedures is to be applied when? As before, there is nothing we have to say to the second question. As regards the first, the answer we conjecture is that there is only one alternative to the rule we stated in Chapter 1:

> When the negation is processed as part of a condition γ belonging to the right-hand DRS K_2 of a complex condition $K_1 \Rightarrow K_2$, then replace $K_1 \Rightarrow K_2$ by $\neg \boxed{K_1 \Rightarrow K_2'}$, where K_2' is obtained from K_2 by replacing γ in Con_{K_2} by its unnegated counterpart γ'.

The claim that this is the only alternative can be rephrased informally by saying that the **do**-supported negation of a verb can take scope over the subject of its clause, but not over anything external to that clause.

Just as there is scope ambiguity between negation and subject NP, so we may expect there to be ambiguity of scope between negation and other arguments of the clause in which it appears, in particular between negation and the direct object. Apparently, this relation is different from that between negation and subject. For instance, there seems to be no ambiguity of scope between **not** and an **every**-phrase in object position. Thus

(3.131) Bill didn't invite everyone of his friends.

and

(3.132) Bill doesn't know every answer.

only have the readings that not all friends were invited, or not all answers known; the sentences cannot be understood as saying that no friend was invited or no answer known (or if they can be so understood, this seems to involve considerable strain).

With negation and indefinite objects the situation is different. Some indefinite objects can be understood as having scope over the negation of the clause in which they occur, as witnessed by

(3.133) Bill doesn't know a book which I have at home and which is essential to his research.

The preferred reading of this sentence appears to be one according to which there is some particular book which I have at home and which is essential to Bill's research, but which he does not know. On the other hand, there are many other indefinites in the same position whose preferred or even only reading assigns them narrow scope. This has been true in particular of the sample sentences we have met in the preceding chapters, such as e.g.

(3.134) Bill doesn't own a car.

There seems to be no way of reading (3.134) as meaning that there exists a car which Bill does not own (in the sense in which it is compatible with his owning some other car). Other sentences appear to be sitting on the fence. Thus

(3.135) Bill doesn't know a book that I have read during the past four weeks.

seems genuinely ambiguous between the two interpretations under consideration.

That this type of ambiguity should exist, and that, as our examples suggest, it is constrained by the form of the indefinite NP, is exactly what should have been expected in the light of what we have been saying about specific versus non-specific uses of indefinite noun phrases. When an indefinite is understood as specific, it will establish its discourse referent in highest possible position, and so it will not be subordinate to the scope of any other constituent. An indefinite such as **a car**, in contrast, which, we have maintained, is difficult to understand as a specific indefinite, will introduce its discourse referent at the level at which it is processed, and so in particular will remain within the scope of negation, provided the DRS-condition as part of which it is processed belongs to that scope already.

We have been able to do little more in Section 3.7 than to point out a number of difficult problems, all of which our theory will have to confront eventually. Again and again we have found that the questions which must be answered before we can adjust the construction algorithm transcend our present explanatory powers. This is not satisfactory.

While we have not been able to offer definitive solutions to any of the scope problems we have discussed, we hope that our discussion has left no doubt on one point: Scope ambiguities arise in a number of different ways and for a variety of different reasons; consequently scope ambiguity is not something to be dealt with by a single cure applicable to all cases. In the past, discussions of scope have often been guided by the forms which sentences with scope ambiguities typically take when the ambiguous sentences are represented in the notation of predicate logic. In this notation scope ambiguities always manifest themselves as a choice between alternative orderings of two or more scope bearing elements. Since little or no attention was being paid to the processes by which predicate logic representations could be derived from the natural language sentences they were claimed to represent, the variety of procedural possibilities which our discussion has begun to unveil remained obscured from view. In this way, scope phenomena appeared to have a uniformity which, we are convinced, they do not really have.

FROM DISCOURSE TO LOGIC

Studies in Linguistics and Philosophy

Volume 42

The titles published in this series are listed at the end of this volume.

FROM DISCOURSE TO LOGIC

Introduction to Modeltheoretic Semantics of Natural Language, Formal Logic and Discourse Representation Theory

Part 2

by

HANS KAMP
and
UWE REYLE

Institute for Computational Linguistics,
University of Stuttgart

KLUWER ACADEMIC PUBLISHERS
DORDRECHT / BOSTON / LONDON

Library of Congress Cataloging-in-Publication Data

ISBN 0-7923-2402-1 (Part 2)
ISBN 0-7923-1027-6 (Part 1)
ISBN 0-7923-2403-X (Set)

Published by Kluwer Academic Publishers,
P.O. Box 17, 3300 AA Dordrecht, The Netherlands.

Kluwer Academic Publishers incorporates
the publishing programmes of
D. Reidel, Martinus Nijhoff, Dr W. Junk and MTP Press.

Sold and distributed in the U.S.A. and Canada
by Kluwer Academic Publishers,
101 Philip Drive, Norwell, MA 02061, U.S.A.

In all other countries, sold and distributed
by Kluwer Academic Publishers Group,
P.O. Box 322, 3300 AH Dordrecht, The Netherlands.

Printed on acid-free paper

Printed in the Netherlands

Contents

PART 1

PART 2

Chapter 4

The Plural

4.1 Introduction

This chapter is devoted to the plural. One of our principal concerns will be with plural pronominal anaphora – anaphora, in other words, which involves the pronominal forms **they**, **them** and **their**. This is a topic that arises naturally in the context of the theory developed in Chapters 1 und 2. Recall that singular pronoun anaphora played an important part in the development of our theory – in fact, the desire to account for some of the known facts about singular anaphoric pronouns was among its central motivations. It might have been hoped that such a theory, which appears to deal satisfactorily with certain aspects of singular pronoun anaphora, would be equally successful in accounting for the corresponding anaphoric properties of plural pronouns. For there is no obvious reason why plural pronouns should behave according to different principles than those governing singular pronouns. And indeed, a superficial look at the facts could easily suggest that singular and plural pronoun anaphora are largely parallel phenomena.

But this impression disappears on closer inspection. As it turns out, there are striking differences between the anaphoric properties of plural and singular pronouns, and this means that the principles we have invoked in our account of singular pronouns do not, or only partially, apply to their plural counterparts. A more general account of pronominal anaphora, which includes the plurals as well as the singulars, must explain how and why the old principles fail for plural pronouns, and supplement them with alternatives that capture their anaphoric properties correctly. This is one of the tasks we will tackle in this chapter.

In trying to solve this problem we will find that plural anaphora involves a number of complexities that we did not encounter in our study of singular pronoun anaphora. Many of these complexities are connected with the properties of plural expressions other than pronouns. Therefore, a satisfactory account of plural pronoun anaphora can only be given within the wider context of a theory that deals with those other expressions as well. For instance, the question which plural NPs can serve as the antecedents of plural pronouns, and under what conditions, forces us to look at these NPs not only as potential anaphoric antecedents, but also from a more general perspective. The study of those NPs then leads naturally to further plural expressions and constructions, such as the reciprocal **each other**, adverbs like **together** and **respectively**, "collective" verbs like **gather** and "floating quantifiers", exemplified by the particle **each** in a sentence like

(4.1) The boys were each given an ice cream cone.

To provide adequate treatment of all these different words and constructions is a major undertaking that would require a separate monograph. What we offer in this chapter can therefore be no more than a selection from the large spectrum of questions and issues to which plural constructions give rise. By and large we will restrict attention to plural noun phrases, but even their analysis will be far from exhaustive.

4.1.1 Summation

Before we proceed with a formal analysis of those phenomena with which we will deal in this chapter, it is well to give a brief informal survey of the problems we will address. The first is one of those that specifically concern plural anaphora. The treatment of singular anaphoric pronouns we offered in Part I came to this: The discourse referent introduced by the pronoun must be set equal to a discourse referent that belongs to the DRS already, and which occupies a position accessible from that of the pronoun. The remainder of our DRS-construction algorithm entailed that this other discourse referent was always introduced through the earlier processing of some singular NP. In other words, only singular NPs had the power to introduce new discourse referents.[1] One might have thought that a similar principle obtains for plural pronouns: Processing a plural pronoun involves equating the

[1]Admittedly our treatment of singular pronoun anaphora has been far from exhaustive. However, a more thorough study of what is possible with singular pronouns reveals that for the pronouns **she** and **he** the principle has very few exceptions. With **it** the matter is different. First, **it** is often used to refer to abstract entities such as propositions, events, facts, actions etc.; and such abstract entities are typically given not by earlier noun phrases, but by entire clauses or sentences – as in

(4.2) Bill passed the exam. It astonished everyone.

where **it** is naturally understood as referring to the fact that Bill passed the exam. Secondly, **it** can be used to refer to a *kind*, which has been indicated earlier in the text by a mass noun that occurs as a proper part of an NP, but is not an NP in its own right. An example:

discourse referent it introduces with one introduced earlier through the processing of some other plural NP. But in general this is not so. Consider for instance:

(4.4) (i) John took Mary to Acapulco. They had a lousy time.
(ii) Last month John took Mary to Acapulco. Fred and Suzie were already there. The next morning they set off on their sailing trip.

In these sentences **they** does not have a single NP for its antecedent. Rather, the "antecedent" has to be "constructed" out of various parts of the preceding text.

Such examples, in which a plural pronoun is understood as referring to a set whose existence is entailed by the antecedent text but is not denoted by any one NP which that text contains, are very common. They might seem to suggest that while the antecedents of singular pronouns have to be supplied by particular noun phrases, **they** can pick up any antecedent that can be obtained from antecedent information by means of logical deduction. However, the deductive principles that are permitted in this context are, it turns out, subject to surprising restrictions. For instance, compare the following three sentence pairs:

(4.5) (i) Two of the ten balls are not in the bag. They are under the sofa.
(ii) Eight of the ten balls are in the bag. They are under the sofa.
(iii) Freddy took one ball out of the bag. Andy took out another one. They are under the sofa.

The **they** of (4.5.i) can be understood as referring to the two balls that are missing from the bag. In contrast, no such interpretation is possible for the **they** of (4.5.ii). Nevertheless we can infer from the first sentence of (4.5.ii) that there must be such a set – it is the difference between sets that are explicitly mentioned, viz. the set of eight balls that are in the bag and the larger set of ten balls of which this first set is said to be a subset. But, apparently, subtracting one set from another is not a permissible operation for the formation of pronominal antecedents. The **they** of (4.5.iii), finally, can be understood to refer to the set of the two mentioned balls, although there is no antecedent NP that refers to that set all by itself.

Indeed, this last case is just like the examples in (4.4). In particular, there appears to be a close analogy between (4.5.iii), where **they** can be taken to refer

---

(4.3) All right, you may have more money than I do. But then, it means so much more to you than it means to me.

which has an interpretation according to which **it** means "money".

to the set consisting of the two mentioned balls, and (4.4.i), where the pronoun is interpretable as referring to the set consisting of John and Mary. In both those examples, as in (4.4.ii), the processs which supplies the intended antecedent must involve some kind of inference. But, as (4.5.ii) shows, in the context of pronominal anaphora not every type of deduction is permitted. One of the questions which we will have to address, therefore, is which inferential processes are available for the construction of antecedents for pural pronouns.

The examples in (4.4) exemplify one such process. We will refer to this process as *summation.* It consists in combining the referents of a number of different NPs into a single set, or, in our terminology, in introducing a new discourse referent which represents the "union" of the individuals and/or sets represented by discourse referents that are already part of the DRS. By way of illustration let us consider the DRS which, according to the construction rules we will detail below, will result from processing (4.4.i):

(4.6)

u v y Z U
John(u) Mary(v) Acapulco(y) u took v to y Z = u ⊕ v U = Z U had a lousy time

Some preliminary comments on this DRS are in order. First, (4.6) contains discourse referents of two different types, discourse referents which we graphically represent as lower case letters (**x**, **v**, **y**) and which stand, as before, for individual objects; and discourse referents which we represent as upper case letters (**Z**, **U**) and which stand for sets of individuals. We refer to discourse referents of the first kind as *individual discourse referents*, or *atomic discourse referents*, and to discourse referents of the second kind as *non-individual discourse referents*, or *non-atomic discourse referents.*[2] In (4.6) the atomic discourse referents all come from singular NPs. Of the non-atomic discourse referents one, viz. **U**, is introduced by a plural NP, **they**, while the other, **Z**, is created through an application of the principle of Summation. In this instance the application serves to form a representation of the set consisting of John and Mary from the available representation of John and the available representation of Mary.

[2]The meaning of the terms "atomic discourse referent" and "non-atomic discourse referent" will be explained in 4.3.1.

4.1.2 Abstraction

A related but nevertheless distinct process of antecedent formation is exemplified by the following discourse.

(4.7) Susan has found every book which Bill needs. They are on his desk.

The first sentence of (4.7) yields the following DRS:

(4.8)

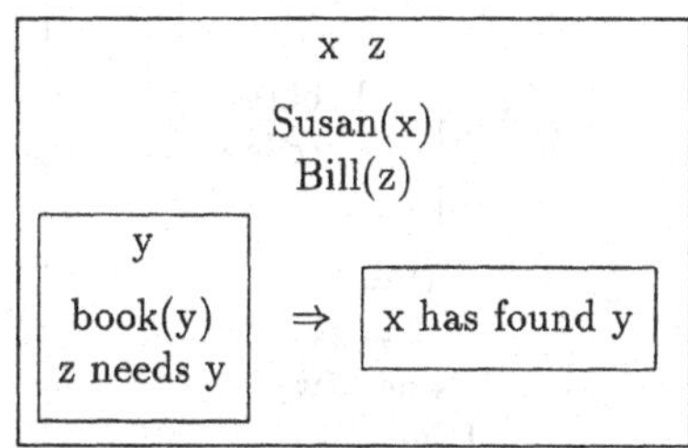

The first step required for the interpretation of the second sentence involves finding an antecedent for the pronoun **they**. According to the definition of accessibility[3] the discourse referent **y** is not accessible to the position occupied by **they** (which is that of the main DRS of (4.8)). Moreover, **y** itself would not do as antecedent in any case, for what it represents is an individual and the referent of **they** in (4.7) ought to be not an individual but a set. The discourse referent we need as antecedent should be a non-atomic discourse referent and such a discourse referent is clearly not present in (4.8). So it has to be created from what is present in (4.8), and, more specifically, from that part of (4.8) which has something to say about the set we want, the set of those books that Bill needs. This part is the complex condition contained in (4.8). The principle which enables us to form, on the basis of this condition, the non-atomic discourse referent we want is called *abstraction.* We will discuss this pinciple in detail later; for the moment we only want to give a rough idea of how it works, and for this it is best to first show what its application looks like in the case at hand. The complete DRS for (4.7) is as follows:

[3]See Def. 2.4.4, p. 231.

(4.9)

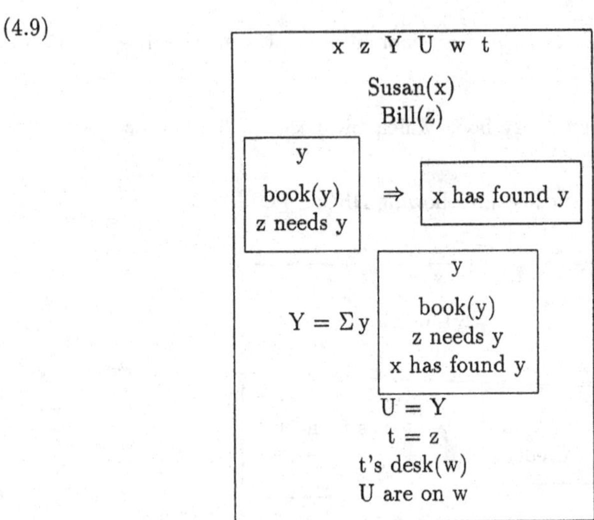

The application of Abstraction in (4.9) is represented by the equation

(4.10) Y = Σy [y | book(y), z needs y, x has found y]

This condition says in essence that the newly introduced discourse referent **Y** stands for the set consisting of all individuals **y** which satisfy the conditions of the DRS behind the summation sign 'Σ'.

A general description of the principle of Abstraction must state explicitly to what type or types of DRS-condition the principle applies. As implied by our example, the complex conditions that are introduced by NPs beginning with **every** are of the required kind, and, as it turns out, they are the only conditions suitable for Abstraction that are part of the DRS language of Chapters 1–3. However, there are many plural NPs which yield conditions to which Abstraction is also applicable. Consider for instance

(4.11) Susan has found most books which Bill needs. They are on his desk.

Here **they** can be understood as referring to the books that Bill needs and Suzie has found. Intuitively this interpretation appears to depend on the information contained in the first sentence of (4.11) in much the same way as the interpretation of **they** in (4.7) depends on the information contained in its first sentence. We will assume, in accordance with this intuition, that the interpretation of **they** in (4.11) involves, like that of **they** in (4.7), an application of Abstraction, and that the first sentence of (4.11) makes available to the Abstraction rule a structure closely resembling the complex condition of (4.8). We will represent this condition as in the DRS below:

(4.12)

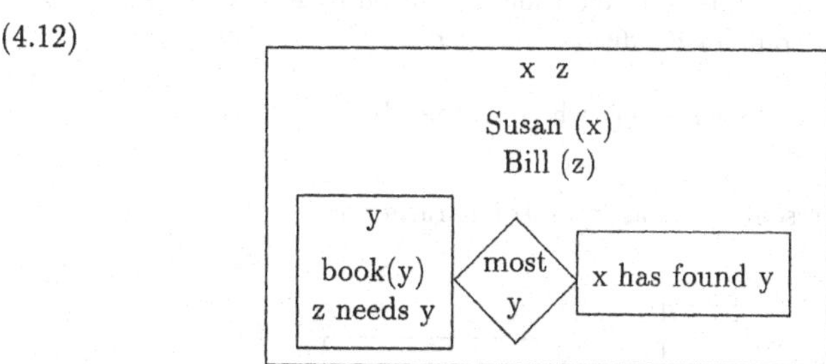

The intuitive meaning of this condition should be transparent: For most **y** which satisfy the conditions on the left it is true that they satisfy the condition on the right.

DRS-conditions like the complex condition of (4.12) consist of three parts: The DRS on the left, the DRS of the right and the part in the middle, consisting in the present case of the symbol **most** and the discourse referent **y**. Conditions of this general tripartite form are called *duplex conditions.* We will refer to the left DRS of a duplex condition as its *restrictor*, to the right DRS as its *(nuclear) scope* and to the middle part as its *quantifier.* The discourse referent occurring in the middle part (here: **y**) will be called the *principal* discourse referent of the duplex condition. There are many different plural NPs which give rise to duplex conditions – **many books, few books, at least seven books** are only a few examples. Evidently the conditions that these NPs yield will differ in particular in regard of their quantifiers. For instance, the sentence

(4.13) Susan has found few books which Bill needs.

will yield the condition

(4.14)

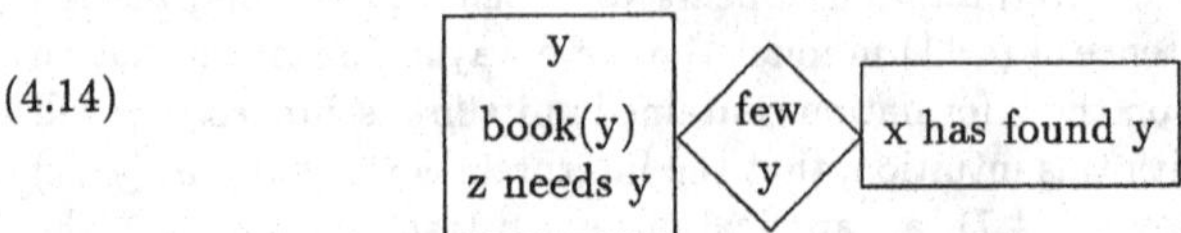

There are also singular NPs that produce such conditions, among them **many a book, almost every book** and **at most one book**. Indeed, NPs beginning with **every** also belong to this group, and now that we have introduced duplex conditions it is natural to adjust the conditions produced by **every**-phrases to this general format. So the complex condition produced by

(4.15) Susan has found every book which Bill needs

will henceforth be represented not as in (4.9) but rather as

(4.16)

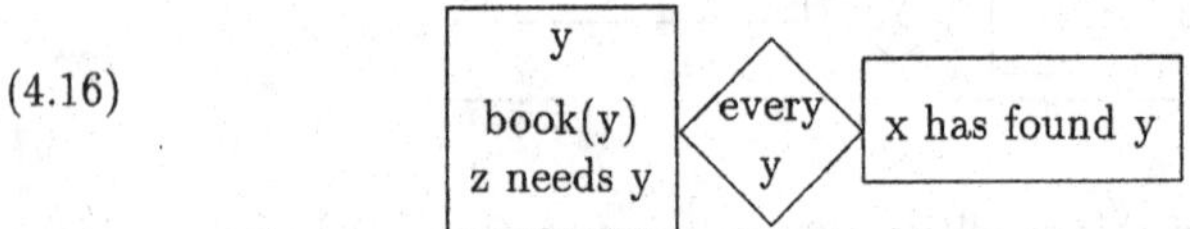

(DRS-conditions arising through the processing of conditional sentences we will continue to represent with the help of the double arrow.)

Having represented the first sentence of (4.11) as in (4.12) we can then complete the DRS for (4.11) in much the same way in which we completed that for (4.7):

(4.17)

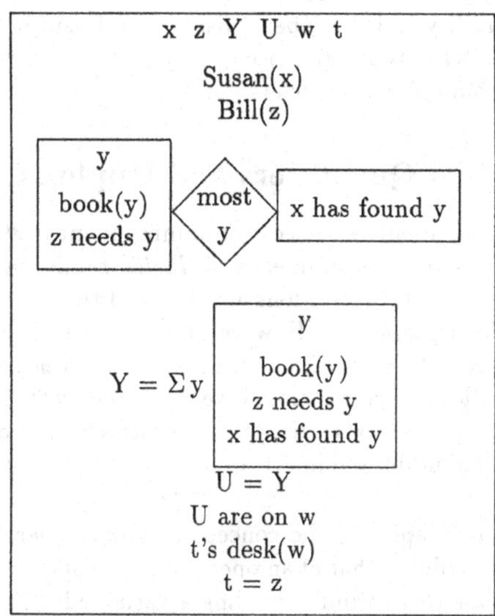

Note that the application of Abstraction in (4.17) cannot dispense with the condition **x has found y**, which stems from the nuclear scope of the duplex condition to which Abstraction is being applied. For if that condition were omitted, then the summation condition in (4.17) would make **Y** into the representative of the set of all books that Bill needs, not of the set of those books that he needs and Susan has found. This is a general feature of Abstraction: if it is to give the intuitively correct interpretations of plural pronouns, it has to be applied to the union of restrictor and nuclear scope. All examples in which the duplex condition to which Abstraction is being applied have a quantifier distinct from the universal quantifier bear this out. In cases where the duplex condition has a universal quantifier, applying Abstraction to restrictor and nuclear scope together and applying it to the restriction alone produce indistinguishable results. By parity, however, the general principle should apply in these cases as well. Therefore we have included the condition from the nuclear scope also in the Application of Abstraction in (4.9), even though there its omission would have made no tangible difference.

Plural NPs like **most books**, and the DRS-conditions to which they give rise, illustrate an important point, which, as we will see below, is responsible for many of the complications that a systematic treatment of the plural has to cope with. The point is this: Although **most books** is syntactically a plural, the discourse referent it introduces – **y** in the case of (4.11) and (4.12) – is an individual discourse referent. In this respect plural NPs such as **most books** and singular ones such as **every book** are on a par. As a consequence we cannot hope for a simple correlation between syntactic plurality and the type of discourse referent involved – we cannot maintain that singular NPs always give rise to atomic discourse referents and plural NPs always to non-atomic discourse referents.

4.1.3 Generalized Quantifiers and Duplex Conditions

We said that we will represent sentences containing quantificational NPs such as **every book** or **most students** by means of *duplex conditions.* We already described informally what duplex conditions are like, and there is nothing that needs to be added to that description here. However, the concept of quantification which duplex conditions represent derives from an important development in contemporary semantics and philosophical logic, and we wish to devote a few words to that development before we proceed with the formal articulation of our own treatment of plurals, in which, as adumbrated in 4.1, duplex conditions will play their crucial part.

As we have seen in Chapter 2, the concept of a quantifier that can be found within the predicate calculus is that of an operator that applies to a single formula, out of which it forms another formula, binding a variable in the process. Thus

(4.18) Bill owns a cat

can be represented within predicate logic as

(4.19) ∃x (**cat**(**x**) & **owns**(**Bill**,**x**))

where the existential quantifier '∃' operates on the formula (**cat**(**x**) & **owns**(**Bill**, **x**)), producing (4.19). In the process '∃' binds the variable **x**.

This quantifier concept originated with Frege. As we noted earlier, however, it is not the notion that fits in most naturally with the way things are done in natural language, whose quantifier phrases, such as **every book** or **some woman**, do not simply translate into a Fregean quantifier, but into a complex structure in which the descriptive content of the NP and that of the remainder of the sentence are somehow combined. In the notation of predicate logic this structure can sometimes be represented with the help of a Fregean quantifier and a sentential connective. Thus the translation of (4.18) involves not only the existential quantifier '∃' but also the conjunction sign '&', which is needed to combine the formulas **cat**(**x**) and **owns**(**Bill**,**x**) into a single formula, to which the quantifer is then applied. But such a representation is not only somewhat indirect; more often than not it is not available at all. Take for instance the determiner **most**. It is not altogether clear what the truth conditions are for sentences in which this word occurs. For instance, how many planets would have to be further from the sun than the earth is in order that the sentence

(4.20) Most planets are farther from the sun than the earth.

be accepted as true? It is hard to say for sure. But one reasonable stipulation is that the asserted property – being farther from the sun than the earth – must be true of more than half of the planets – in other words, (given that the number of planets is equal to nine) at least five. On this stipulation, that **most** means the same as "more than half", it is possible to prove that no formula of the predicate calculus can capture the meaning of **most**. In fact, it wouldn't be possible to introduce into predicate logic a new quantifier which, like '∃' and '∀', applies to single formulas and which would capture this sense of **most**, even if we were free to fix the meaning of this new quantifier in any other way that is consistent with firm intuitions about what **most** means.[4] The problem is that as we have stipulated the meaning of **most** (actually this would be so for any plausible way in which its meaning could be fixed), the truth of a sentence in which **most** occurs depends upon the *comparison* between (the sets of objects satisfying) *two* formulas, not on the property of (the set of objects satisfying) some one single formula. Thus, (4.20) is true iff the size of the set of planets that are farther from the sun than the earth is more than half the size of the set of planets. More generally, 'Most Ps are Qs' will be true if the set of Ps that are Qs contains more than half as many objects as the set of Ps.

This, it turns out, is a property of many quantifiers of natural language: A sentence of the form '$\mathcal{Q}$ Ps are Qs', where $\mathcal{Q}$ is the quantifier in question, is true provided a certain relation, determined by $\mathcal{Q}$, obtains between the set of Ps that are Qs and the set of Ps simpliciter. This is true in particular of the quantifiers **all** and **some**. Thus 'All Ps are Qs' is true if the set of Ps that are Qs exhausts the set of Ps; and 'Some Ps are Qs' is true if the set of Ps has something in common with the set of (Ps that are) Qs. In these particular instances the comparison turns out to be reducible to a property of a single compound formula, formed with the help of '&' or '→', but this is, from the present perspective, a logical accident.

These observations have led to the concept of a *generalized quantifier*:

A *generalized quantifier* is a relation between two sets.[5]

---

[4]A proof of this is given in [Barwise/Cooper 1981].

[5]See for instance [Mostowski 1968]; [Barwise/Cooper 1981]; [van Benthem & ter Meulen 1985]; [Gärdenfors 1987].

According to this definition a generalized quantifier is not a symbol of a (formal or natural) language, but a semantic counterpart of such a symbol (It is more like an individual, one might say, than like a variable or a name!). In order that a (simple or complex) symbol would qualify as a generalized quantifer, it would have to be *interpreted* as a generalized quantifier in the sense just defined. And in order that it can be so interpreted, it has to combine syntactically with two expressions that can be interpreted as defining sets. Thus (4.20) could be represented by a formula of the form:

(4.21) $\overset{\textbf{Most}}{\mathbf{x}}$ **(planet(x), x is farther from the sun than the earth)**

Not surprisingly, in the light of the above discussion, in (4.21) the two set-defining expressions are formulas with one free variable, the first stemming from the quantified NP and the second from the rest of the sentence.

Duplex conditions relate to the sentences they represent in a similar way. They too connect two set-defining "expressions", given in the form of the two subordinate DRSs that are connected by the quantifier sitting between them – recall the duplex condition that we used in the representation of the first sentence of (4.11), **Susan has found most books which Bill needs:**

(4.22)

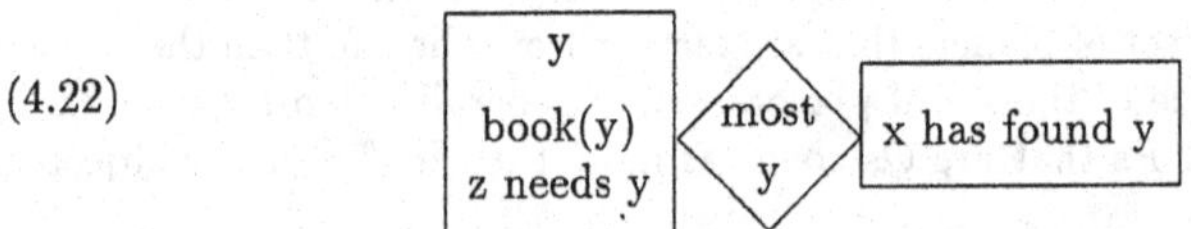

In (4.22) each of the two DRSs which are connected by the diamond containing **most** can be interpreted as determining a set, roughly the set of all possible values for **y** which can be extended to a proper embedding of the DRS in question. So, the condition in (4.22) is verified (by a suitable embedding function f, i.e. one which assigns objects to the discourse referents **x** and **z**) iff most of the objects a such that there is an extension g of f ∪ {⟨y, a⟩} which verifies the left-hand side DRS are such that some extension h of g verifies the right-hand side DRS as well. More generally, let

(4.23)

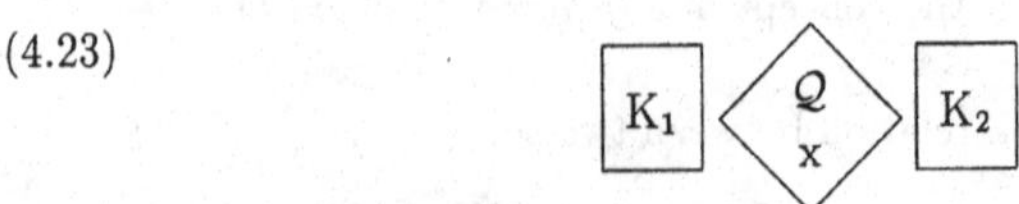

be a duplex condition, and suppose the quantifier symbol $\mathcal{Q}$ is interpreted by the generalized quantifier R. Let M be a model, as defined in Chapter 1, p. 93, and let f be a function which maps the free discourse referents of K_1 and K_2 onto elements of U_M. Then[6]

(4.24) f *verifies* (4.23) *in* M iff R holds between the sets A and B, where
(i) $A = \{a: \exists g\ (g \supseteq_{U_{K_1}} (f \cup \{\langle x, a\rangle\})\ \&\ g \text{ verifies } K_1 \text{ in } M)\}$,
and
(ii) $B = \{a: \exists g\ (g \supseteq_{U_{K_1}} (f \cup \{\langle x, a\rangle\})\ \&\ g \text{ verifies } K_1 \text{ in } M)$
$\&\ \exists h\ (h \supseteq_{U_{K_2}} g\ \&\ h \text{ verifies } K_2 \text{ in } M)\}$

Note that our representation of quantifiers by means of duplex conditions, together with the semantics for such conditions contained in (4.24), implies that the generalized quantifier R interpreting such a condition can always be chosen in such a way that it satisfies the following property:

(4.25) For any sets A and B, $R(A, B)$ iff $R(A, A \cap B)$

For suppose that the verification conditions for (4.23) are given as in (4.24) and let R' be the relation defined by:

(4.26) For any sets A and B, $R'(A, B)$ iff $R(A, A \cap B)$

Then (i) (4.24) is equivalent to the condition which we get by replacing R by R'[7]; and (ii) R' satisfies (4.25) (For $R'(A, B)$ iff $R(A, A \cap B)$ iff $R(A, A \cap (A \cap B))$ iff $R'(A, A \cap B)$).

[Barwise/Cooper 1981] have called generalized quantifiers satisfying this property quantifiers which *live on* their first argument A[8] (the term is motivated by the observation that the question whether such a quantifier is fulfilled in any situation involving the set A as first argument depends only on elements belonging to A), and hypothesized that all natural language quantifiers obey this constraint. Our analysis of quantification brings out why this should be so. As we argued when discussing conditionals and universal quantification in Chapter 2, the material that goes into the right-hand DRS of the complex condition which represents a conditional or universal sentence should be seen as an additional description of a situation that has already been partly described by the left-hand DRS. (This was our intuitive explanation of why the discourse referents from the left-hand DRS are available on the right, though not vice versa). These same considerations are

[6]For a detailed discussion and a refinement of this condition see Section 4.3.2.1.
[7]See Exercise 3, p. 319.
[8]Quantifiers which live on their first arguments are also called *conservative*.

equally valid for the larger class of quantifying constructions in natural language which we represent by means of duplex conditions. In all these cases the right-hand DRS should be seen as an elaboration of the situation description provided by the DRS on the left-hand side; a claim which is generally confirmed by the behaviour of anaphoric pronouns in sentences containing such quantifiers. This view of quantified sentences and of the duplex conditions representing them entails that the verification conditions of such structures relate the set of those situations which verify the DRS-conditions from the left-hand side as well as those from the right-hand side DRS to the superset consisting of all situations that only need to answer to the conditions of the DRS on the left. It is easily verified that such verification conditions can always be cast in the form of (4.24), with R satisfying (4.25).

We conclude this section with a statement of the construction rule for the "true" quantifying determiners (i.e. those determiners which have the feature value *Quant* = +). Because this rule will be slightly modified in Section 4.2.4 we present it in a box which is framed with a *single line* only:[9]

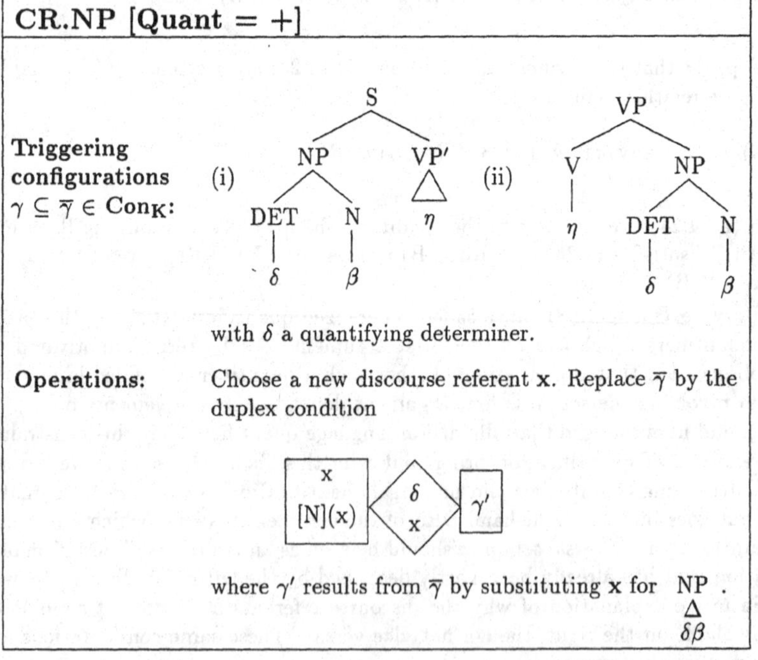

Note that this rule applies also to the singular determiner **every** and thus allows

[9]The final version of this rule can be found on page 347.

us to do away with the rule CR.EVERY.

Exercises

1. Apply the new processing rule for generalized quantifiers to the following sentences.

   (i) Most women who own a dog are in love with it.

   (ii) A woman who owns many dogs feeds them .

   (iii) Few men who admire her know Jane.

   (iv) At least two boys who fell in love with her dated a girl.

   (v) Paula doesn't like many dogs that live in her vicinity.

   (vi) Every professor recommends many books which most students don't read.

2. Beneath the property of 'living on' [Barwise/Cooper 1981] discuss further conditions on quantifiers R.

   Among these are

   Monotonicity: for any sets A, B and B′, if R(A, B) and $B' \supseteq B$ then R(A, B′)

   Persistence: for any sets A, A′ and B, if R(A, B) and $A' \supseteq A$ then R(A′, B)

   (i) Classify the determiners of our extended fragment according to these properties.

   (ii) The property of downward Monotonicity (Persistence) results from that of being (upward) monotone (persistent) by replacing the assumption $B' \supseteq B$ ($A' \supseteq A$) by $B \supseteq B'$ ($A \supseteq A'$).
   List the determiners which are downward monotone (persistent).

3. Show that (4.24) is equivalent to the condition which we get by replacing R by R′, where R′ is defined by (4.26)

4. (a) Suppose we define

   (i)

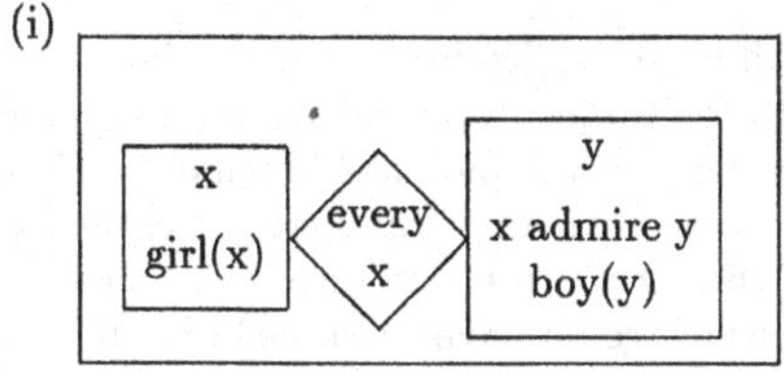

to be true in any model M iff $A \subseteq B$, where

$$A = \{a \in U_M \mid a \in Pred_M(\mathbf{girl})\}$$

and

$$B = \{a \in U_M \mid a \in Pred_M(\mathbf{girl}) \text{ and for some } b \in Pred_M(\mathbf{boy}) \text{ and } \langle a,b\rangle \in Pred_M(\mathbf{admire})\}$$

Show that according to this definition (i) is equivalent to

(ii)

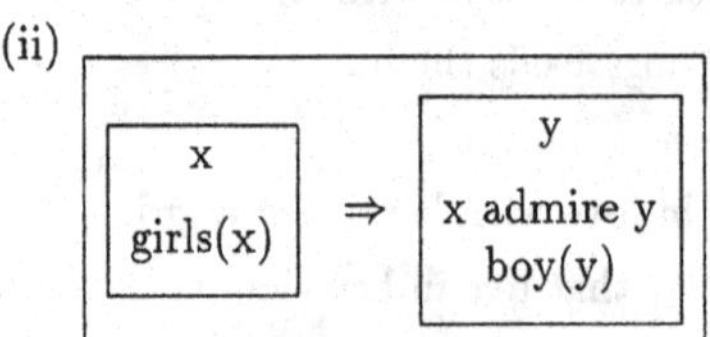

(b) Generalize the definition given in (a) to a verification condition for duplex conditions of the form

4.1.4 Collective Readings and Distribution

So far we have encountered several types of plural NPs that give rise to atomic discourse referents, but only one, viz. the pronoun **they**, which triggers the introduction of non-atomic discourse referents. There are however also other types of plural NPs that must also be treated as giving rise to discourse referents of this second type. This can be seen by looking at sentences involving so-called *collective predicates.* Here are some examples:

(4.27)
(i) The men carried the piano upstairs.
(ii) The lawyers hired a secretary.
(iii) The inhabitants built a town hall.
(iv) Martin interconnected the computers.
(v) The newspaper tycoon left his children a huge fortune.

The verb phrases of (4.27.i–iii) all have a collective reading in the sense that what they say about the set denoted by the subject term cannot be paraphrased exhaustively as a conjunction of predications of the individual members of this set. For instance, (4.27.i) says, on one of its possible readings, that the men carried the piano upstairs by a joint effort, something to which each, or at any rate most, of them made a contribution, but which could have succeeded only by virtue of the synergetic effect of their concerted action. No paraphrase that does not somehow refer to the way in which their individual efforts *combine* can render this reading correctly. Similarly, (4.27.ii) has a reading according to which the lawyers jointly hired a secretary, one who is to be a secretary to them all and who stands in a relation of employment to the group as a whole. Similarly for (4.27.iii). (4.27.iv) and (4.27.v) illustrate the same phenomenon, except that the argument with respect to which the verbal complex has a collective interpretation is not the grammatical subject of the sentence, but the direct object (in (4.27.iv)) or the indirect object (in (4.27.v)).

In some cases, as in (4.27.iv), the collective reading is obligatory. In other cases, such as (i), (ii), (iii) and (v), it appears to be optional, although even in these examples a collective reading seems to be preferred. But the non-collective reading can be brought to prominence by suitably manipulating the context. For instance, in

(4.28) Both the professors and the lawyers decided to get private secretaries. But there was a difference. The lawyers hired a secretary they liked. The professors hired a secretary they could afford.

the sentence **The lawyers hired a secretary they liked** is more readily interpreted as saying that each of the lawyers hired his own private secretary. But whether they be optional or obligatory, the important point now is that collective readings exist and that they cannot be represented by means of duplex conditions. They cannot be so represented, because the principal discourse referent of a duplex condition is an atomic discourse referent, whereas a correct representation requires, as we have just seen, the representation of a set. Indeed, a DRS for, say, (4.27.i) should look something like this:

(4.29)

X y
the men(X) the piano(y) X carried y upstairs

where the condition **the men(X)** expresses that **X** stands for the (set consisting of the) men and **X carried y upstairs** asserts that a certain set (the set of men) and an individual (the piano) stand in the relation expressed by the verb **carry upstairs.**[10]

[10]In this form the DRS for (4.27.i) is strictly speaking not yet complete. In fact each of

The examples we have just looked at showed that plural definite descriptions such as **the men** or **the lawyers** must sometimes be analysed as introducing a non-atomic discourse referent. But there are also cases where their representation must nonetheless involve an atomic discourse referent. For instance, if (4.27.ii) is to receive the reading according to which each lawyer hired his own secretary, then it must be represented as some kind of duplex condition, which has an atomic discourse referent **x** ranging over the set of lawyers. The representation we adopt for such cases, where the interpretation "distributes over" the value of a definite plural NP, is as follows:

(4.30)

X		
the lawyers(X)		
x x ∈ X	every x	y secretary(y) x hired y

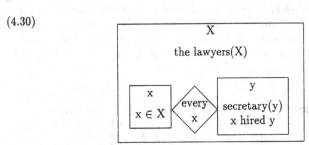

Our reasons for adopting this particular representation will become clear below.

Not all plural NPs permit just any kind of collective predication. Note for example the following contrasts:

(4.31)
- (i) The lawyers hired a secretary.
- (ii) Few lawyers hired a secretary.
- (iii) The villagers built a town hall.
- (iv) Many villagers built a town hall.

---

the conditions it contains is in need of further elaboration. The problem connected with the condition **the piano(y)** which is meant to express that **y** stands for the referent of the definite description **the piano** we touched upon in 3.4. In accordance with the policy declared in that section, we will continue to make use of such 'stop-gap' DRS-conditions for definite NPs, and we will do so henceforth not only for singular but also for plural definite descriptions. The condition **X carried y upstairs** with its past tense also requires further elaboration, in which the semantic contribution made by the past tense becomes fully explicit. (The same is true of the conditions **u took v to y** and **U had a lousy time** in (4.6) and the condition **x has found y**, among others, in (4.9)). This is a problem we have tried to circumvent in Chapters 1 and 2 by confining our attention to stative (or habitual) verbs in the present tense. However, in giving plausible illustrations of the phenomena discussed in this section we have found this restriction too confining. The representational problems relating to the past tense, the perfect and other tenses will be discussed in the next chapter. Until then we will leave conditions like **x carried y upstairs**, in which the contribution of the tense morpheme is not separated from that of the main verb, unanalysed.

Whereas in (4.31.i) and (4.31.iii) the collective reading appears to be clearly preferred, in (4.31.ii) such a reading is impossible and in (4.31.iv) it seems marginal at best. For instance, (4.31.ii) can only mean that the number of lawyers **x** such that **x** hired a secretary was small. This fact suggests that NPs beginning with **many** or **few** cannot introduce non-atomic discourse referents or at best do so only reluctantly. For now we will, simplifying somewhat, assume that they do not introduce set discourse referents at all. More precisely, we will assume that such NPs are genuine quantifiers, in the sense that their processing always yields a duplex condition immediately. Thus, for instance, the DRS for (4.31.ii) will be:

(4.32)

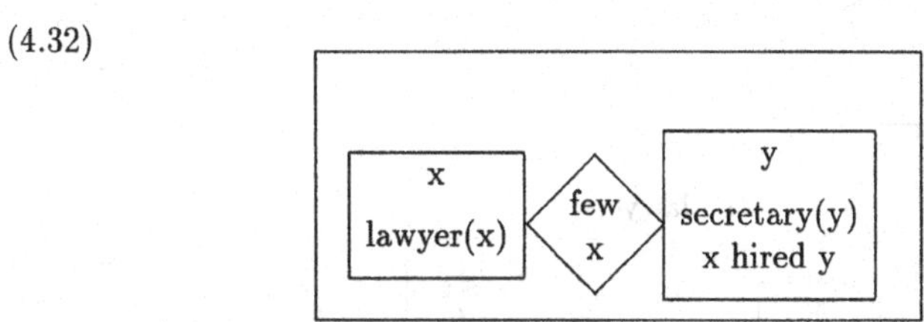

We should, however, note right away that the data are more complicated than (4.31) might suggest. For there are other collective predicates which can be combined with NPs such as those of (4.31.ii) and (4.31.iv). A well-known example is the verb **gather**. That **gather** is collective seems clear enough. For one, the only subjects with which it can combine are either plurals or else singular NPs which denote collections, such as **the crowd** or **the workforce**. Thus, we can say (4.33.i) and (4.33.ii), but not (4.33.iii):

(4.33) (i) The crowd gathered in the square.
(ii) The men gathered in the square.
(iii) The man gathered in the square.

Nevertheless NPs beginning with **many** or **few** go well with **gather**:

(4.34) (i) Many men gathered in the square.
(ii) Few men gathered in the square.

For the analysis of plural NPs that we will propose this is a recalcitrant fact. We return to the issue in 4.4.6.

The question when a plural NP introduces an individual and when it introduces a non-individual discourse referent is one of the major complications that a theory of the plural has to disentangle. As we will see, plural pronouns are particularly problematic in this connection. In the few examples we have thus far considered pronouns were treated as introducing non-atomic discourse referents. But this cannot be right in all cases. For instance, we noted that the sentence

(4.35) The lawyers hired a secretary they liked.

has a non-collective, or *distributive*, as well as a collective reading. The DRS that represents its distributive reading should, in analogy with (4.30), look at one stage of its construction like this:

(4.36)

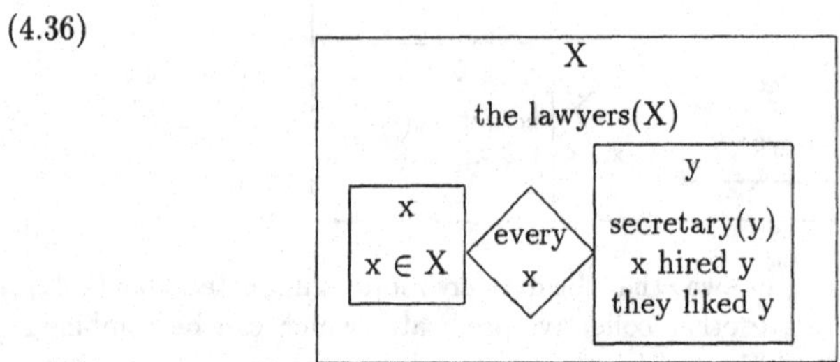

One intuitively right way of processing **they** in the condition on the right in (4.36) is to let it introduce a new atomic discourse referent, which then gets identified with the "antecedent" discourse referent x:

(4.37)

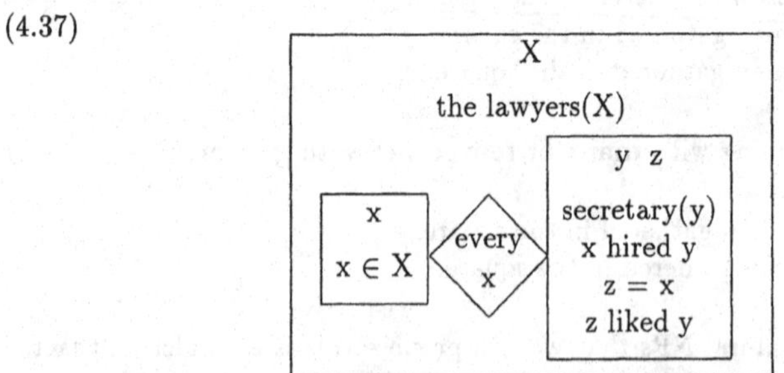

(4.37) should be contrasted with the interpretation of (4.35) in which the verb phrase **hired a secretary** is taken to be collective and the pronoun **they** as referring to the set of lawyers denoted by the subject:

(4.38)

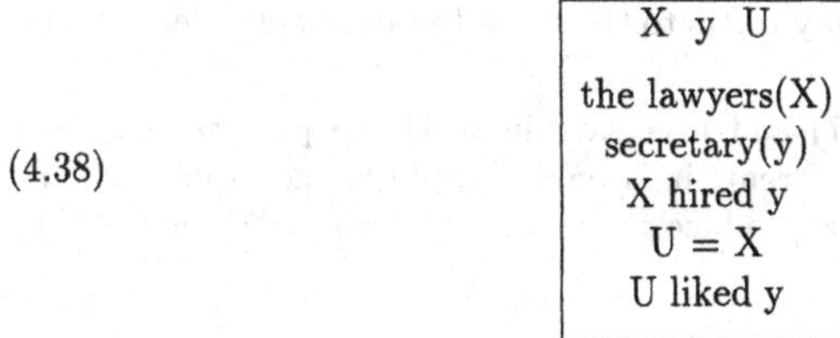

It is arguable that (4.35) also has a reading in which the predicate **hired a secretary** is interpreted non-collectively, but where nevertheless **they** is understood as referring to the set of lawyers, a reading represented by the following DRS[11]

(4.39)

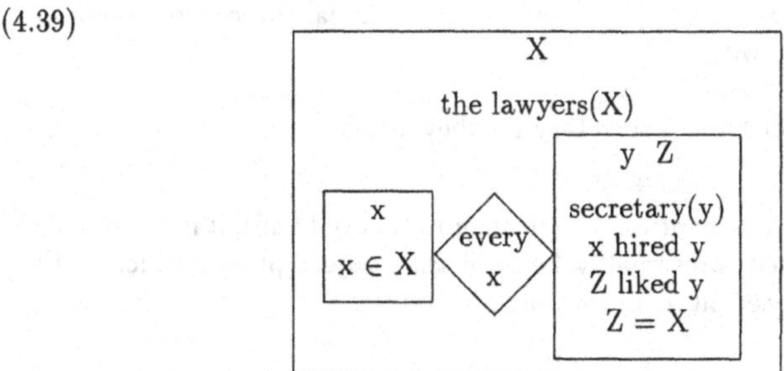

In this regard it is interesting to compare (4.35) with

(4.40) Few lawyers hired a secretary they liked.

This sentence has only one reading, which is given by:

(4.41)

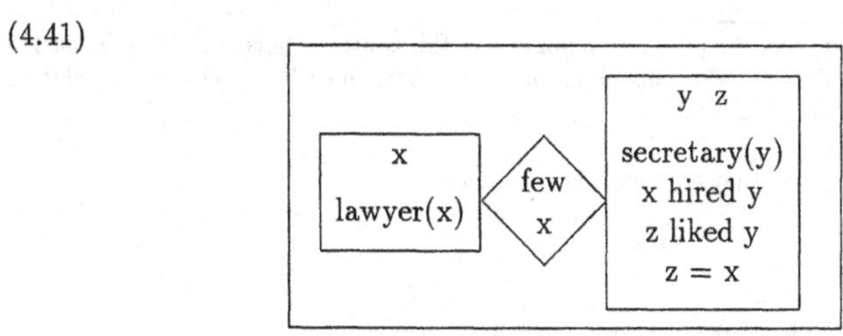

[11]See pp. 353 for discussion.

(4.40) not only lacks the collective reading. It also does not have a reading corresponding to (4.39), one in which **they** refers to the set of these (few) lawyers which each hired a secretary.

Not only is it possible in (4.37) and necessary in (4.41) to process **they** as introducing an atomic discourse referent, it is only the plural, not the singular pronoun that can, in these contexts, produce the readings which (4.37) and (4.41) identify. Thus, in (4.42)

(4.42) $\left\{ \begin{array}{l} \text{Few} \\ \text{The} \end{array} \right\}$ lawyers hired a secretary he liked.

he cannot be interpreted as anaphoric to **few/the lawyers**. The obligatory plurality of the pronoun appears to be in such cases a primarily syntactic phenomenon, of number agreement between the pronoun and its grammatical antecedent. Compare in this connection (4.40) with

(4.43) Many a lawyer hired a secretary he/they(?) liked.

In (4.43), whose subject is semantically equivalent to that of (4.40), it is the singular pronoun that is preferred, presumably because the subject phrase which is the intended anaphoric antecedent, is in the singular too.[12]

4.1.5 Distributive Readings of Non-quantifying NPs

In the preceding section we represented sentences with non-quantifying NPs as subjects by DRSs in which the verb phrase is analysed as a predication of the set to which the subject NP refers. We noted that such sentences are sometimes ambiguous. Thus

(4.46) Three lawyers hired a new secretary.

---

[12]Some English speakers accept the plural pronoun also in this context. This appears to be part of a growing tendency to allow plural pronouns in positions where in earlier days only singulars were judged correct. Compare

(4.44) $\left\{ \begin{array}{l} \text{Everyone} \\ \text{No one} \end{array} \right\}$ said that they enjoyed themselves.

as a paraphrase of

(4.45) $\left\{ \begin{array}{l} \text{Everyone} \\ \text{No one} \end{array} \right\}$ said that he enjoyed himself.

can mean either that a group consisting of three lawyers jointly hired a single secretary or that each lawyer in the group hired a new secretary on his own. It would seem natural that the second distributive reading should receive a representation similar to those of sentences whose subject is a quantifying NP and which only have the distributive reading. (We already followed this intuition in our representations (4.37) and (4.39) for (4.35).) There are two ways in which we could achieve this. The first involves an alternative construction rule for non-quantifying NPs that treats them just like quantifying NPs. This rule would transform for instance (4.46) in one step into

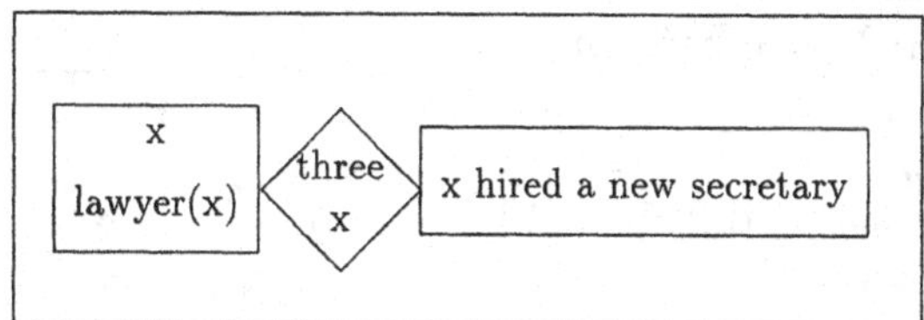

The second possibility is to start the construction process, as for the collective reading, with the introduction of a discourse referent representing a set of three lawyers:[13]

(4.47)

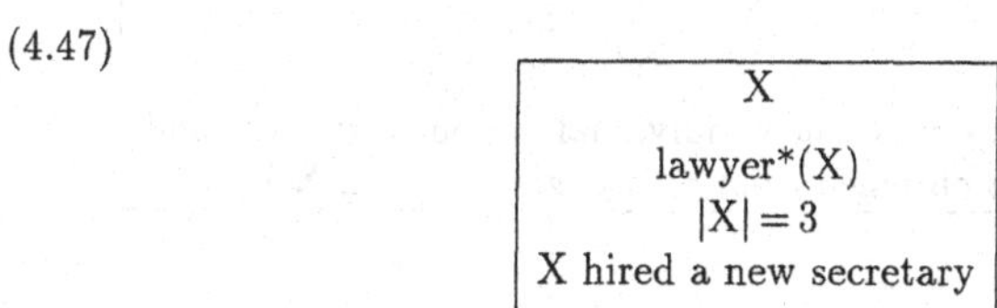

but then subject the condition **X hired a new secretary** to a further rule of *distributive expansion*, which converts it into the duplex condition

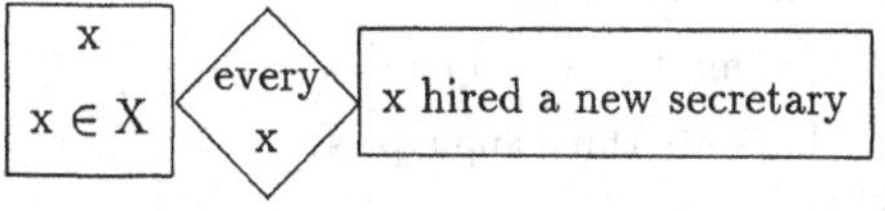

It may not seem obvious how we should choose between these two options. But in fact some relevant data have already come to light. We argued that (4.35) has one reading, given in (4.39), in which the VP **hired a secretary they liked** is

[13] **lawyer*** is a predicate which is true both of single lawyers and of collections of lawyers. See 4.2.2, p. 338 and 4.3.1, p. 406.

interpreted distributively, but where the pronoun **they** is interpreted as referring to the same set as the subject term **the lawyers**. If, as it would seem reasonable to assume, the pronoun can get this interpretation only because a discourse referent for the set of lawyers is available at the time when it, the pronoun, is processed, then the second option would allow us to construct this interpretation, but the first one would not. So it seems that the second construction method is needed in any case. Since the first cannot produce any readings that are also obtainable via the second method, it is, barring further evidence to the contrary, the second option that ought to be preferred. Indeed, it is that one we have chosen. A preliminary statement of the rule is as follows:[14]

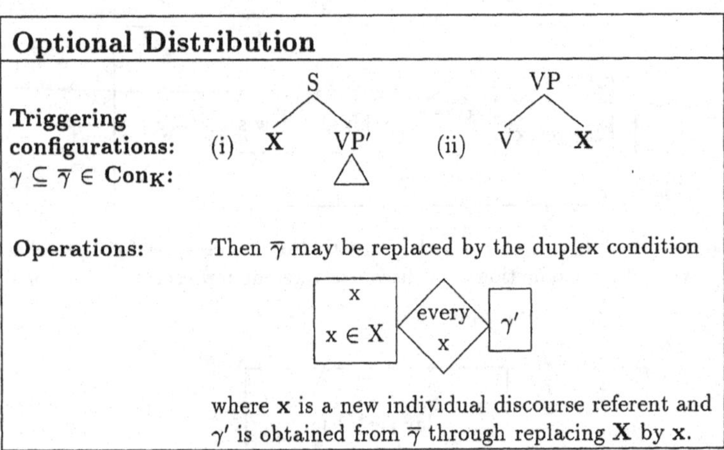
Optional Distribution
Triggering
configurations:
γ ⊆ γ̄ ∈ Con_K:
(i)
S
X
VP′
(ii)
VP
V
X
Operations:
Then γ̄ may be replaced by the duplex condition
x
x ∈ X
every
x
γ′
where x is a new individual discourse referent and
γ′ is obtained from γ̄ through replacing X by x.

Exercises

1. Construct DRSs for all possible readings of the following discourses:

   (i) Five boys ate three apple pies.

   (ii) Five boys ate at most three apple pies.

   (iii) At most five boys ate three apple pies.

   (iv) At most five boys ate at most three apple pies.

2. Compare

   (i) Three boys ate five cherry pies.

[14]The final statement can be found on page 347.

with

(ii) Most boys ate five cherry pies.

(i) has an ambiguity that (ii) lacks. Show this by constructing the DRSs for (i) that exhibit the different readings. Why is this ambiguity not present in (ii)?

3. Like singular definite descriptions (see 3.4), plural definite descriptions have an absolute as well as a contextual/anaphoric use. An example of the former is

(1) The inhabitants of Greenland know Danish.

Here the description denotes the set of all those who inhabit Greenland.

The second type of use is instantiated in the following examples.

(2) Bill invited ten girls to his party. The girls did not come.

(3) Bill invited ten girls to his party. The girls who came enjoyed themselves.

(4) The inhabitants gathered in the square. The women screamed.

In (2) **the girls** is most naturally understood as referring to the set of ten girls Bill invited. In (3) we see a slightly different phenomenon. **The girls who came** refers, in its most natural interpretation in this context, to the set of those girls Bill invited and who, moreover, turned up. In (4) **the women** is naturally understood as referring to that part of the set mentioned in the first sentence which consists of satisfiers of the noun **women**.

These examples indicate what seems to be true of a large proportion of occurrences of plural definite descriptions:

(a) the NP **the** β refers to the subset Y, consisting of *all* satisfiers of the (simple or complex) noun β of the NP (i.e. of the part following **the**), of some set X.

(b) Sometimes, as in (1), the set X is not constrained by the context: X can be taken to be everything, and so Y is the set of those things satisfying β. But, as often as not, X is itself a restricted set, to be retrieved from context.

(c) Where X is contextually restricted, it is typically a set already available in the context that can easily be recognized as consisting wholly or partly of satisfiers of β. Sometimes, as in (2), where β is the noun **girls**, X, the set of girls invited by Bill, consists entirely of individuals that satisfy β –

here X = Y. In other cases, such as (3), X will consist entirely of satisfiers of the head noun of β – in (3), where β is **girls who came**, the head noun is simply **girls**. Here we have that $Y \subset X$, assuming that not all of the girls Bill invited came.

(4) presents yet another case. Here the set X is a set which we readily recognize (on the basis of our general knowledge that the inhabitants of a place typically consist of men, women and children) as containing satisfiers of β. In this case too Y will be a proper subset of X.

The last of these three cases is difficult to capture in terms of a precise construction rule for "anaphoric" plural descriptions as such a rule would have to give precise content to the loose phrase "readily recognizable". But the first two cases can be made precise without going beyond the terminology in which construction rules have been stated so far.

(i) Formulate one or more construction rules which make it possible to interpret each of the descriptions in (1–3) in the way described above.

(ii) Construct DRSs for (1), (2) and (3) using your construction rule(s).

(iii) Construct all possible DRSs for the text:

(5) Five boys invited twelve girls. The boys had fun. The girls who did not come had fun. The girls who came did not have fun.
(Treat **have fun** as an intransitive verb.)

4.1.6 Dependent Plurals

The obligatory plural morphology of the pronoun in (4.40) constitutes one instance of the interference of syntactic considerations with a straightforwardly semantic account of the difference between plural and singular NPs. Another instance is given by the so called *dependent plurals*. These are bare plurals, i.e. plural NPs without overt articles, which need not be understood as denoting sets. Thus, in

(4.48) Most of my friends own cars.

the plural NP **cars** does not signify that for each **x** where **x** is one from a majority of my friends, **x** owns more than one car: The sentence will be true so long as a majority of my friends own at least one car each. Thus the discourse referent for the NP **cars**, which will have to occupy a position that is dependent on that of **x**, should not be a non-atomic discourse referent. On the other hand, and here lies a difference with the case of (4.40), (4.48) does not mean either that each of the relevant friends owns one car. To see this more clearly, consider (4.49)

(4.49) Most students bought books that would keep them fully occupied during the next two weeks.

Suppose that there were five students, that of these the first two didn't buy any books and that of the remaining three, Alan, George and Miriam, Alan bought one book, George three and Miriam four, and that in each case the book or books bought were all its or their buyer would be able to read in the course of the following fortnight. So, where for Alan the one book he bought was all he was going to be able to read, in the case of George it was the three books he bought (and not any one book he bought, for during the two weeks in question he will be able to read two more); and similarly for Miriam it was the four books bought by her. Intuitively (4.49) is a correct statement in this situation. This means that the bare plural **books that would keep them fully occupied during the next two weeks** must be interpretable as denoting a single book in relation to Alan, a collection of three books in relation to George and a collection of four books in relation to Miriam. For it is only those denotations which will satisfy the description **books that would keep them fully occupied during the next two weeks**. To put the same point in different words, (4.49) can be paraphrased as

(4.50) Most students bought one or more books and that book or those books would keep its or their buyer fully occupied during the next two weeks.

while neither

(4.51) Most students bought a book that would keep them fully occupied during the next two weeks.

nor

(4.52) Most students bought several books that would keep them fully occupied during the next two weeks.

would be a fully adequate rephrasing. ((4.52) is not right for the situation we described because Alan bought only one book, (4.51) because George and Miriam bought more than one book.)

The moral of this example is that the discourse referent introduced by the bare plural **books that would keep them fully occupied during the next two weeks** must be capable of representing, depending on the value of the discourse referent introduced by **most students**, sometimes a single book and sometimes a set of books. So far we do not have discourse referents which allow this: A discourse referent is either an atomic discourse referent, whose value could not be a set consisting of two or more books; or it is a non-atomic discourse referent, in which case the value cannot be a single book. So we need a more general kind of discourse referent, whose values may be individuals as well as non-individuals. We will use Greek letters for this purpose. Thus the DRS for (4.49) will look as follows:

(4.53)

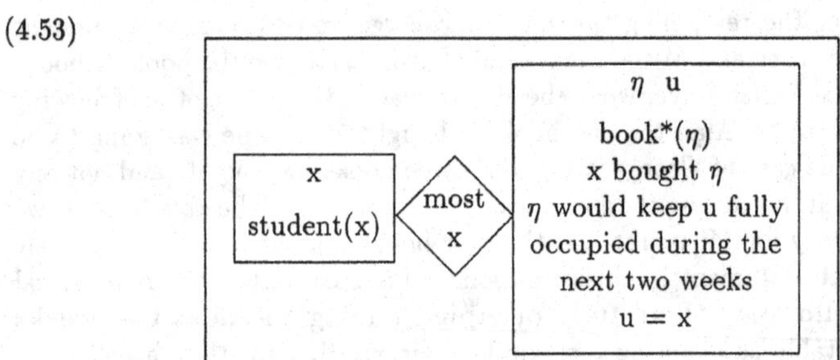

We will refer to such discourse referents as η as *neutral* discourse referents.

Now that we have introduced neutral as well as atomic and non-atomic discourse referents, it seems that we have more than we strictly speaking need. Evidently it should be possible to make do with the neutral discourse referents only, which we might then, whenever we want to, restrict to atomic or non-atomic values by an accompanying DRS-condition. This is indeed exactly what we will do in 4.2.2 (p. 334). We will still make use of lower and upper case letters, but only as convenient shorthands for neutral discourse referents with one or the other of these conditions attached.

This completes our informal overview of the central phenomena we will deal with in this chapter. Our next task is to define the syntax of the extended English fragment in which these phenomena can be found.

4.2 DRS-Construction for Plurals I

4.2.1 Syntax

The basis for much of what we need for our new fragment was already established in Chapter 0. There we introduced in particular the feature *Num*, with its two values *Sing* and *Plur*. In fact, the phrase structure rules given there allow for the generation of plural as well as singular sentences. The only reason why the fragments we have considered so far do not contain any plural sentences is that up to now our lexicon has been without plural nouns, verbs, pronouns or determiners.

But this lacuna is easily filled. As plural nouns and verbs we introduce all plurals of those nouns and verbs which already figure in our lexicon in the singular. We will not bother to write these new entries out as lists of lexical rules, trusting that the reader can supply these himself if he feels so inclined.[15] We do however specify the plural pronouns and determiners we will consider in this chapter:

(LI 23) PRO $\begin{bmatrix} Num = plur \\ Gen = \beta \\ Case = +nom \\ Refl = - \end{bmatrix}$ → **they**

(LI 24) PRO $\begin{bmatrix} Num = plur \\ Gen = \beta \\ Case = -nom \\ Refl = - \end{bmatrix}$ → **them**

(LI 25) DET $\begin{bmatrix} Num = plur \\ Quant = + \end{bmatrix}$ → **most, many, few, no, all, at least two, at least three, ..., at most two, at most three, ..., exactly two, exactly three, ...**

(LI 26) DET $\begin{bmatrix} Num = sing \\ Quant = + \end{bmatrix}$ → **every**

(LI 27) DET $\begin{bmatrix} Num = plur \\ Quant = ind \end{bmatrix}$ → **some, several, two, three, ..., Ø**[16]

(LI 28) DET $\begin{bmatrix} Num = sing \\ Quant = ind \end{bmatrix}$ → **a**

(LI 29) DET $\begin{bmatrix} Num = sing/plur \\ Quant = def \end{bmatrix}$ → **the**

The rules for DET make use of a new feature, *Quant*. It distinguishes between determiners that normally require distributive readings (*Quant* = +) and among the remaining ones between the definite determiners (*Quant* = *def*) and the indefinite ones (*Quant* = *ind*).[17] We will discuss the criteria that led us to this subcategorization in the next sections.

---

[15]Except for the verb **be**, plural verb forms we want here – i.e. the third person plural of the present tense – are identical with the infinitival forms, which we already have (They were needed for negation). Plural nouns are, of course, usually formed by tacking an **s** onto the singular form of the noun, with the familiar regular exceptions (**oxen, feet**, etc.) and with the proviso that when a noun ends on an **-s**, **-x**, **-sh**, **-ch** or **-z**, in which case the suffix is not **-s** but **-es**.

[16]We assume that bare plurals are analysed by NPs with empty DETs.

[17]One would also have done this with the two binary features $\pm Quant$ and $\pm Def$; but the one three-valued feature saves a little writing!

4.2.2 NPs that Denote Collections

We observed that some plural NPs combine happily with collective predicates. Thus

(4.54) a. The lawyers / b. Three lawyers } hired a new secretary

have readings according to which what happened was a collective hiring of a single secretary; in fact, for many speakers this is the salient reading. In such readings the verb acts as a predicate of a set that is made available by the subject NP. In terms of semantic representation this means that the subject contributes to the DRS of the sentence a discourse referent whose values are sets or collections.[18]

As announced in 4.1, we use capital letters for discourse referents which represent sets of individuals, while continuing to use lower case letters for discourse referents representing individuals. However, as we stated at the end of Section 4.1, this usage will be a matter of convenient abbreviation, and not the official notation. Let us make this official notation, as well as our abbreviatory conventions, explicit once and for all. As before, we assume that discourse referents are subscripted lower case letters. (We continue to use unsubscripted letters, e.g. **x, y, z, u, v, w** to avoid spurious clutter of subscripts.) We introduce two types of DRS-conditions, **at(v)** (short for 'v is an atom'; this means that v is an individual) and **non-at(v)** (read: 'v is a collection of 2 or more individuals').[19] Thus, in official notation the DRS for a sentence such as (4.55) will now look like (4.56).

(4.55) Bill owns a car.

(4.56)

x y
at(x) Bill(x) at(y) car(y) x owns y

Similarly, (4.57) has the official DRS (4.58).

[18]Here and in the title of this section we have spoken of 'collections', not of 'sets'. In fact, we will argue in Section 4.3 that the denotations of plural NPs should not be taken to be sets in the precise sense of Set Theories such as those of Zermelo-Fraenkel or Gödel-Bernays. Until then we will nevertheless occasionally speak of the denotations of plural terms informally as 'sets', simply because the term is short and comparatively unpretentious.

[19]The precise meaning of the terms 'atomic' and 'non-atomic' will be explained in 4.3.

(4.57) Many students are poor.

(4.58)

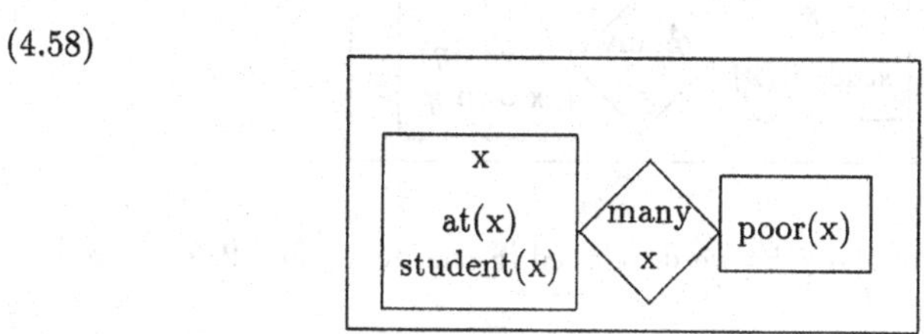

On the other hand, the official DRS for (4.59) which captures its collective interpretation is in official notation (4.60). (The condition $|\mathbf{x}| = \mathbf{3}$ expresses that the set represented by **x** is to have three elements; more about this later.)

(4.59) Three lawyers have hired a new secretary.

(4.60)

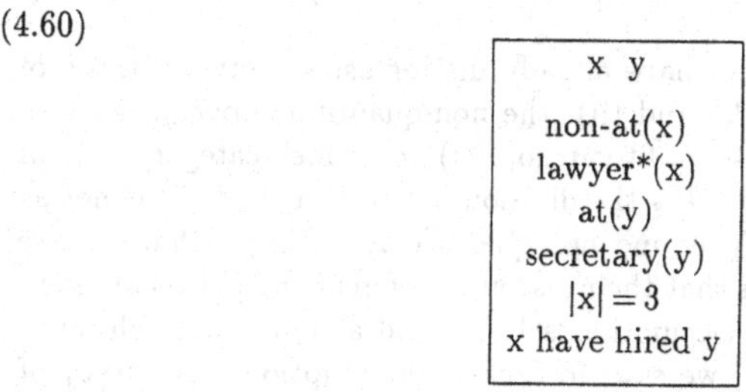

In practice, we adopt the following conventions. It will be a default assumption that a discourse referent **v** is "accompanied by" the condition '**at(v)**', i.e. that when, for any DRS K, U_K contains the lower case letter **v**, Con_K contains the condition '**at(v)**'. Thus the DRSs for all sample sentences and texts we considered in the preceding chapters will, with this convention, look just as they did before even though they would look different when presented in what is to count henceforth as the official notation. If we want to indicate that **v** is accompanied by the condition '**non-at(v)**', we use an upper case letter. Finally, to indicate that neither '**at(v)**' nor '**non-at(v)**' accompanies **v** we use a lower case greek letter, so that the DRS for (4.57) takes the form (4.58).

(4.61) Many students own books.

(4.62)

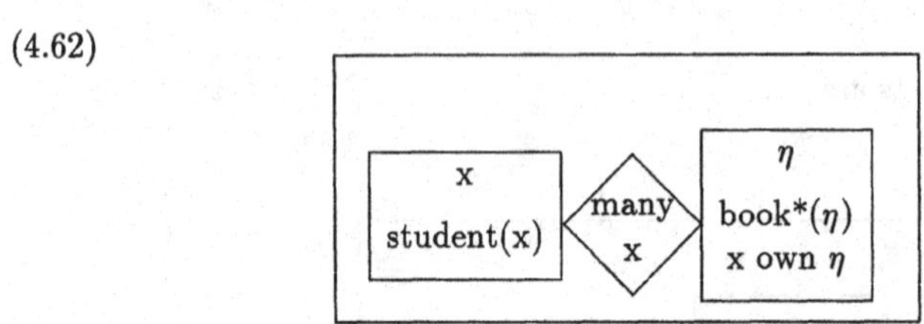

The treatment of singular NPs we developed in chapters 1 and 2 makes a tripartite distinction between:

(i) NPs which introduce their discourse referents into the main DRS (e.g. proper names)

(ii) NPs which introduce their discourse referents at the level at which they are processed (e.g. indefinite descriptions); and

(iii) NPs which introduce their discourse referents at a level subordinate to that at which they are processed (NPs beginning with **every**).

Within the realm of plural NPs we have already distinguished between those of category (iii) (the quantifying NPs) and (ii) (the non-quantifying ones). But we have not yet considered which of them fit category (i) and which category (ii). In Chapter 3 we saw that for singular NPs the division between (i) and (ii) is not as clear-cut as that between quantifying and non-quantifying NPs. Indefinites have uses whose representation requires that their discourse referents be placed at levels superordinate to that where they occur themselves. And a comparable plurality of processing possibilities obtains, we saw, for definite descriptions. A survey of the facts concerning plural NPs reveals that the same range of possibilities exists for them too. Thus the plural counterparts of **a**-phrases, viz. bare plurals, behave much like the singular indefinites, and the same is true for plural and singular **the**-phrases.

By and large we will ignore these complications here. We will, that is, return to the simplifications adopted in Chapters 1 and 2 and treat plural proper names and definite descriptions (such as **The Beatles** or **the students**) as belonging to category (i) and plural indefinites (These are, in our fragment, the bare plurals, the plural NPs beginning with **some** and those that begin with a simple cardinal, i.e. **two**, **three**, etc.) as being of category (ii) (cf. page 333). With this simplification we come to the following two construction rules for *definite* and *indefinite* plural NPs.[20]

[20] We remind the reader that the phrase "Introduce a new plural discourse referent **X** into the

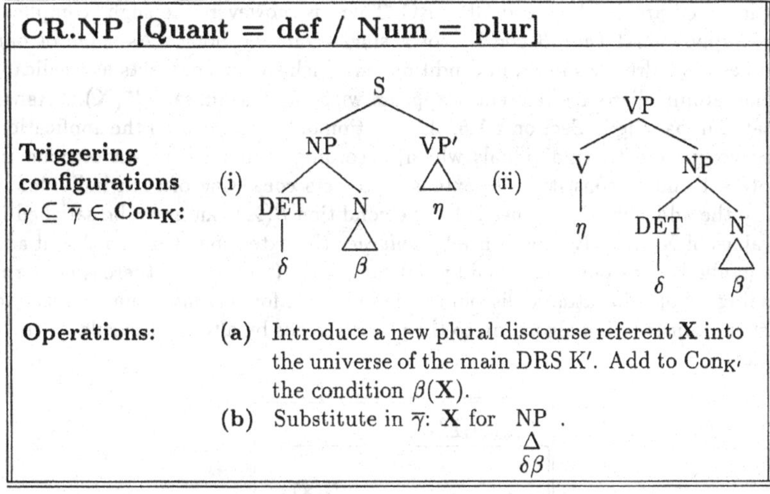
CR.NP [Quant = def / Num = plur]
Triggering
configurations
γ ⊆ γ̄ ∈ ConK:
(i)
S
NP
VP′
DET
N
η
δ
β
(ii)
VP
V
NP
η
DET
N
δ
β
Operations:
(a) Introduce a new plural discourse referent X into the universe of the main DRS K′. Add to ConK′ the condition β(X).
(b) Substitute in γ̄: X for NP δβ .

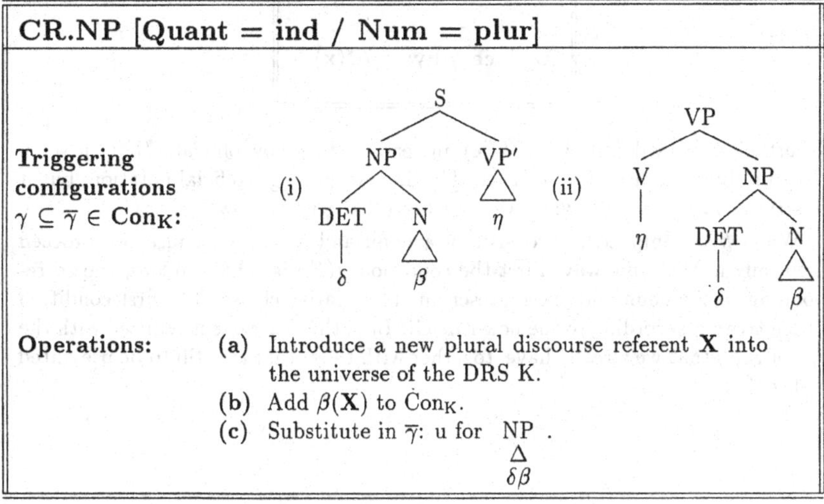
CR.NP [Quant = ind / Num = plur]
Triggering
configurations
γ ⊆ γ̄ ∈ ConK:
(i)
S
NP
VP′
DET
N
η
δ
β
(ii)
VP
V
NP
η
DET
N
δ
β
Operations:
(a) Introduce a new plural discourse referent X into the universe of the DRS K.
(b) Add β(X) to ConK.
(c) Substitute in γ̄: u for NP δβ .

The reduction of conditions of the form $\beta(\mathbf{X})$, where β is an expression of category N, runs along the same lines as conditions of the form $\beta(\mathbf{x})$. As before the

universe of K" is an abbreviation for "Introduce a new discourse referent **x** into the universe of K, and introduce into Con_K the condition **non-at(x)**."

rules involved are CR.LIN and CR.NRC. There is, however, one slight complication. Suppose first that β consists of a single common noun. As some of our examples have already shown, in conditions in which such a noun acts as predicate of a non-atomic discourse referent it appears with an '*' as in, say, $\beta^*(\mathbf{X})$.[21] As we indicated in passing in Section 4.1.5, the function of '*' is to extend the application of the noun from the individuals which, according to our treatment of noun in Chapters 1 and 2, constitute its extension to sets consisting of such individuals. Clearly the addition of '*' is needed – the condition $\beta(\mathbf{X})$ can never be satisfied if the values of $\mathbf{X}$ are only sets. Since '*' *enlarges* the extension of β – so that if a is an individual of the kind described by β it satisfies $\beta^*(\mathrm{x})$ as well – there is no harm in adding '*' also for atomic discourse referents. So, for reasons of uniformity, we adjust the construction algorithm to the present needs by altering the rule CR.LIN as follows.

CR.LIN	
Triggering configuration:	N(x) | β
Replace γ by:	$\beta^*(\mathrm{x})$

Nevertheless, we will still write '$\beta(\mathrm{x})$' instead of the – now official – '$\beta^*(\mathrm{x})$' when x is an individual discourse referent. This is now no longer official notation, but it preserves continuity with what we have been doing up to now.

When β is complex, i.e. consists of a noun and a relative clause, we proceed essentially in the same way. First the condition $\beta(\mathbf{X})$ is split into two, one corresponding to the noun and one representing the relative clause. The first condition is then treated according to the new rule CR.LIN, the other one is reduced with the help of rules that we already have, together with those that are still to be presented in this chapter.

[21]See, e.g., (4.47).

Exercises

1. Rewrite the DRSs (4.9), (4.37) and (4.53) in "official notation". Note that a strict application of our conventions to (4.37) produces a DRS that does not make sense in that we would get both **at(x)** and **non-at(x)**.

   Extend the conventions accordingly.

2. Construct DRSs (in "official notation") for the following sentences.

   (i) The men who carried pianos gather.

   (ii) Most men who carry pianos are tired.

   Rewrite these DRSs in abridged form.

4.2.3 Set-denoting Anaphoric Plural Pronouns

Often the fact that an anaphoric pronoun is in the plural indicates that its semantic value must be a set. Thus in

(4.63) Fred bought two donkeys. They are unhappy.

they can be understood as referring to the two donkeys, and perhaps also as referring to the set consisting of the two donkeys together with Fred. But it can't be understood as referring just to Fred. It is on such cases, where the morphological plurality of the pronoun demands that its semantic value be a collection, that we will concentrate in this section.

The simplest instances of the anaphoric process we will look at are those where the antecedent of the pronoun is already represented by a discourse referent. Thus consider the first of the two mentioned interpretations of (4.63). The first sentence of (4.63) produces the DRS:

(4.64)

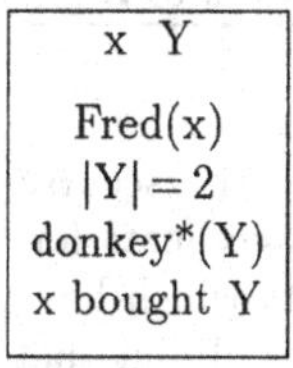

Processing of the second sentence begins with the pronoun **they**. In this case the operation it triggers is simple: Introduce a new plural discourse referent, **Z** say, and set it equal to a plural discourse referent already in the DRS. In (4.64) there is exactly one non-individual discourse referent available; so we get, as DRS for all of (4.63),[22]

(4.65)

x Y Z
Fred(x)
$\|Y\| = 2$
donkey*(Y)
x bought Y
Z = Y
unhappy*(Z)

A preliminary formulation of the construction rule for plural pronouns can be stated as follows:[23]

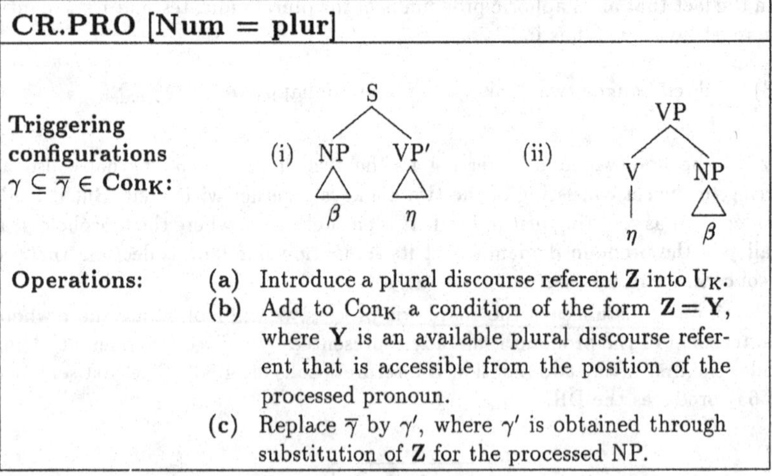

CR.PRO [Num = plur]

Triggering configurations $\gamma \subseteq \overline{\gamma} \in \mathrm{Con_K}$:

Operations:

(a) Introduce a plural discourse referent **Z** into $\mathrm{U_K}$.
(b) Add to $\mathrm{Con_K}$ a condition of the form **Z = Y**, where **Y** is an available plural discourse referent that is accessible from the position of the processed pronoun.
(c) Replace $\overline{\gamma}$ by γ', where γ' is obtained through substitution of **Z** for the processed NP.

Clause (b) speaks of "available" plural discourse referents. The word "available" is to indicate that the possible antecedents for the pronoun are in general not only those plural discourse referents which have already been introduced at the point where the pronoun is interpreted, but that others, to be manufactured out

[22] The condition **unhappy*(Z)** says that the members of **Z** are unhappy, just as **donkey*(Y)** means that the members of **Y** are donkeys.

[23] The final formulation can be found on page 348.

of material already in the DRS, may also serve in this capacity. For instance, as we saw in 4.1, the **they** in a text like

(4.66) Fred admires Susan. They are writing a paper on plurals.

is interpreted as referring to the set consisting of Fred and Susan. (4.63) illustrates the same point insofar as **they** can be interpreted as referring to the set consisting of both Fred and his donkeys. In either case the DRS of the first sentence will not, if it has been constructed according to the principles we have sofar been using, contain a discourse referent representing the intended antecedent. Therefore, if (in keeping with the method we have followed up to now) we want to account for the anaphoric character of the pronoun by way of an equation, we must first construct the discourse referent that is to act as that equation's second term. As indicated in 4.1, the construction principle involved is the one we referred to as *Summation*, which permits combining two or more discourse referents into a single discourse referent that represents the set in which all individuals and/or sets represented by the summands are joined together. Formally:

Summation	
Triggering configurations:	K′ is a sub-DRS of the DRS K (possibly K itself) and $v_1,...,v_k$ $(k \geq 2)$ are discourse referents occurring in K and accessible from K′.
Operation:	Introduce a new non-individual discourse referent **Z** into $U_{K'}$ while introducing into $Con_{K'}$ the condition $\mathbf{Z} = v_1 \oplus ... \oplus v_k$

Using Summation we can construct an appropriate DRS for (4.66) as follows. The first sentence of (4.66) yields the DRS

(4.67)

At this point we may apply Summation to obtain the DRS

(4.68)

Now the rule for plural pronouns can be applied, in the form in which we already have it, yielding

(4.69)

x y Z U
Fred(x)
Susan(y)
x admires y
$Z = x \oplus y$
$U = Z$
U are writing a paper on plurals

(4.69) can then be completed as usual. Similarly, applying Summation to the DRS obtained from the first sentence of (4.63) produces

(4.70)

x Y Z
Fred(x)
donkey*(Y)
$\|Y\| = 2$
x bought Y
$Z = x \oplus Y$

after which the pronoun **they** can be linked either with **Y** or with **Z**.

Note that Summation can be applied at any construction stage at which there are discourse referents that can be summed together. In practice, however, one will want to apply the principle only then when it is needed, i.e. when a suitable antecedent must be created for some anaphoric noun phrase.

Summation is only one of several principles that allow for the construction of pronominal antecedents. Another principle, also mentioned in 4.1, is what we called Abstraction. As we described this principle in Section 4.1, it applies to duplex conditions. We recall the example

(4.11) Susan has found most books which Bill needs. They are on his desk.

and its DRS

(4.17)

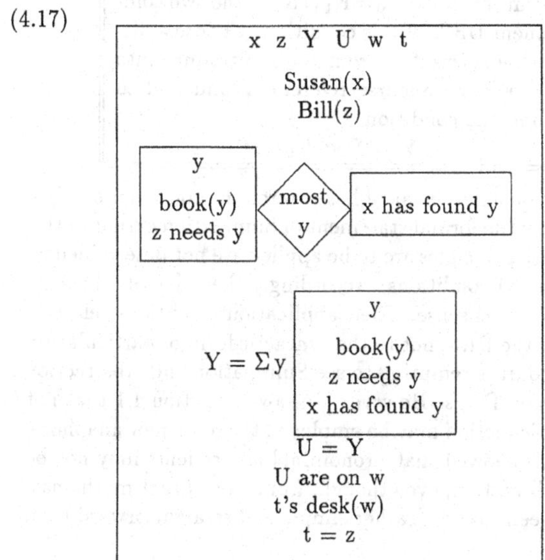

Here Abstraction has been applied to the duplex condition of (4.17), occasioning the introduction of **Y** and the condition

Y = Σy
y
book(y) z needs y x has found y

The application illustrates all the essential features of the principle, which can be stated as follows:

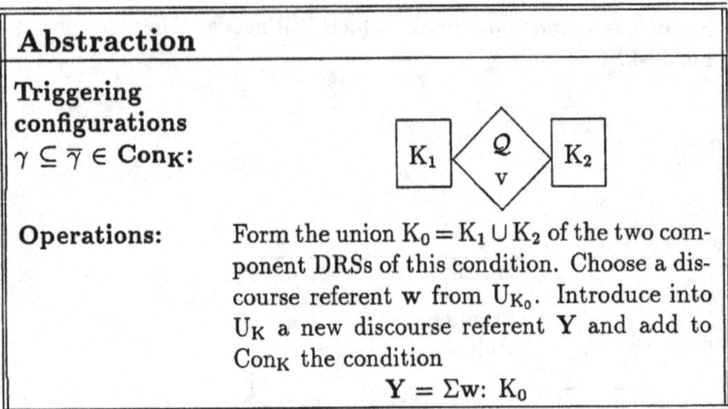

Abstraction
Triggering configurations
$\gamma \subseteq \overline{\gamma} \in Con_K$:
K_1
Q
v
K_2
Operations:
Form the union $K_0 = K_1 \cup K_2$ of the two component DRSs of this condition. Choose a discourse referent w from U_{K_0}. Introduce into U_K a new discourse referent Y and add to Con_K the condition
$Y = \Sigma w: K_0$

With Summation and Abstraction a new element has entered the construction algorithm. As we already noted after the formal statement of Summation earlier in this section, the stages at which these principles are to be applied are not determined by the syntactic form of the processed conditions. Accordingly the principles have no triggering configurations in the usual sense. Their application conditions relate to the DR-theoretical structure of the DRS, not to the syntactic form of particular reducible DRS-conditions. Indeed, it is tempting to see Summation and Abstraction as kinds of inference principles on DRSs. However, we saw in Section 4.1 that not just any kind of logically valid deduction may be employed to create new anaphoric antecedents. For instance, (4.5) showed that pronominal antecedents may not be constructed by means of set subtraction, even though, from an abstract mathematical point of view, this would seem to be a rather simple and straightforward form of inference.

Since not every form of inference is available for antecedent construction, it is natural to ask whether those forms that are available can all be seen as instances of a single overarching principle. At the present stage of research it is not possible to give a definitive answer to this question. But it seems fairly clear that the crucial feature which sets Summation and Abstraction apart from an inadmissible inference pattern such as set subtraction is that the former are both strictly *positive*: Each collects together into a set elements that the DRS presents as existing. (One might say that Abstraction stands to Summation in much the same way in which integration stands to the operation of adding together a finite number of rectangles in the Euclidean plane.)

Exercises

1. Construct DRSs for all possible readings of the following discourses (the phrases in parentheses may be ignored).

(a) John has given Mary a dog. They walk it (in the park). They are (all) happy.

(b) John and Mary live in Paris. Their parents live in Lyon. They rarely meet.

(c) If Fred visits Barbara, they play sonatas. But if he brings a friend who plays the cello, they play trios.

(d) If Suzie gets more than ten cats, they will ruin her living-room.

(e) If Suzie has invited no boys from her class she does not like them.

2. Construct DRSs for all possible readings of the following discourses.

(a) Fred and Lennie went to see Angela. They brought her a bottle of brandy. Angela introduced them to all girls who work for her. Then they drank the brandy.

(b) Ben has an apple tree and a pear tree. If his apple tree carries many apples, he sells them to the jelly factory. If his pear tree carries many pears, he sells them to the store. If his apple tree carries no apples and his pear tree carries no pears, he sells them to the sawmill.

3. Construct DRSs for (i) and (ii):

(i) Bill and Elsa own a poodle. It bites.

(ii) Bill and Elsa own a poodle. They bite.

Add the word **both** to the first sentence and explain the difference between (i) and (ii), and between (iii) and (iv).

(iii) Bill and Elsa both own a poodle. *It bites.

(iv) Bill and Elsa both own a poodle. They bite.

4.2.4 'They' as Individual Variable

In 4.1.4 we saw that **they** sometimes can, and sometimes *must* be understood as a variable ranging over individuals. All such cases, however, involve anaphoric antecedents which exhibit the same tension between syntax and semantics: they too are plural noun phrases which nevertheless introduce individual discourse referents. As noted in 4.1.4 this tension *must* reproduce itself in the pronoun. It must agree with its grammatical antecedent in number even though the discourse referent it picks up, and which originated with that antecedent, is one standing for an individual. Thus, **they** in

(4.71) Few lawyers hired a secretary who they liked.

can pick up the discourse referent **x** in

(4.72)

x lawyer(x)	few x	y secretary(y) x hired y they liked y

But the **he** of

(4.73) Few lawyers hired a secretary who he liked.

cannot be so interpreted. The requirement of morphological number agreement between pronouns and their grammatical antecedents which the pair of (4.71) and (4.73) illustrates poses a slight complication for the kind of processing theory we have been developing up to now. As we have described DRS-construction so far, the information whether an individual discourse referent was introduced by a plural or a singular noun phrase is no longer available after the introduction has taken place. Nevertheless, this is information that may be needed later, when a plural or singular pronoun needs to be interpreted and the given discourse referent is among those accessible to the pronoun. Since we cannot afford to lose the information, we must make a provision for retaining it.

The device we will employ is simple and straightforward: Whenever an individual discourse referent is introduced by a plural NP, it is marked by a superscript *pl*. Discourse referents introduced by singular NPs remain without superscript. Only those individual discourse referents which are marked *pl* can serve as antecedents for plural pronouns.

If all individual discourse referents were directly introduced by NPs, the conventions just introduced would exhaustively identify the cases in which such discourse referents are available as antecedents for **they** and **them**. However, plural NPs can yield individual discourse referents also indirectly, viz. when the plural discourse referent which the NP has yielded in the first instance is then subsequently distributed. With sentences which involve such distributions we find the same contrast as we found with (4.71) and (4.73). Consider for instance

(4.74) The lawyers hired a secretary who they liked.

(4.75) The lawyers hired a secretary who he liked.

As argued in Section 4.1, (4.74) and (4.75) admit a distributive as well as a collective reading. But only the plural pronoun of (4.74) can pick up the discourse referent which distributes over the set denoted by the subject term. We conclude that the individual discourse referents introduced through distribution over sets introduced by plural NPs must be marked *pl* too.

We thus come to the following restatement of the construction rules CR.NP [Quant = +] (p. 318) and Opt. Distr (p. 328).

CR.NP [Quant = +]: as before, except that when the processed NP is in the plural (i.e. the feature *Num* assigns it the value 'plur'), the occurrence of the new discourse referent **x** in the universe of the left-hand DRS of the duplex condition created by the application is marked with the superscript *pl*. Thus the duplex condition has the form

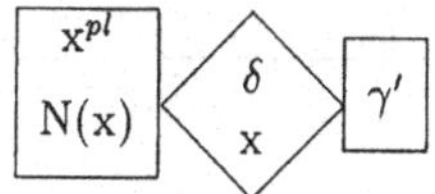

Opt. Distr: As in the restatement of CR.NP [Quant = +] the occurrence of **x** in the universe of the left-hand DRS is marked with *pl*. So the new duplex condition becomes:

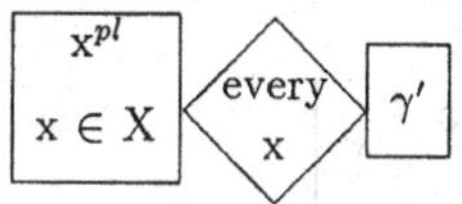

Next we must adjust the construction rule CR.PRO [Num = Plur] for **they** (p. 340) so that it can exploit the anaphoric possibilities which the superscripts are meant to make available. The adjustment is fairly straightforward.

Two changes are needed. (i) we must extend clause (b) so that antecedents of the form $\mathbf{x}^{pl}$ are now allowed as well as non-atomic discourse referents. (ii) The discourse referent ζ introduced by the pronoun need not always be a non-atomic discourse referent; ζ will stand either for an individual or for a set depending on what kind of antecedent (one of the form '**X**' or one of the form '$\mathbf{x}^{pl}$') is chosen for it. The simplest way to achieve this is to let the discourse referent introduced by the pronoun be a neutral one. It will then inherit its intended status (individual, non-individual or neutral) from the discourse referent with which it is identified. Thus, CR.PRO [Num = Plur] must be modified in the following two places:

CR.PRO [Num = plur]:

(i) Clause (a) should now read: Introduce a neutral discourse referent ξ into $U_{K'}$.

(ii) Clause (b) becomes: Add to $Con_{K'}$ a condition of the form $\zeta = \xi$ where either (i) ξ is an available non-individual discourse referent accessible from the position of the pronoun; or (ii) ξ is an individual discourse referent marked *pl*, which, again, is accessible from the position of the pronoun.

In practice we will continue to use **z** or **Z** instead of ζ, depending on whether the discourse referent ξ with which ζ is connected via $\zeta = \xi$ stands for an individual or a set. We present the new versions of these rules in the now familiar schematic form. From now on they are to replace those to be found on pp. 318, 328 and 340.

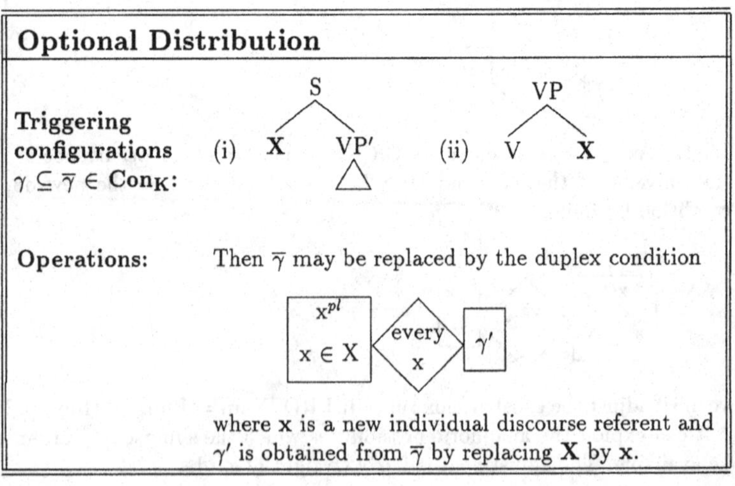

Optional Distribution
Triggering configurations
$\gamma \subseteq \overline{\gamma} \in$ ConK:
(i) S, X, VP'
(ii) VP, V, X
Operations:
Then $\overline{\gamma}$ may be replaced by the duplex condition
x^{pl}
x ∈ X
every x
γ'
where **x** is a new individual discourse referent and γ' is obtained from $\overline{\gamma}$ by replacing **X** by **x**.

CR.NP [Quant = +]

Triggering configurations $\gamma \subseteq \overline{\gamma} \in$ **Con**$_\mathbf{K}$:

(i)

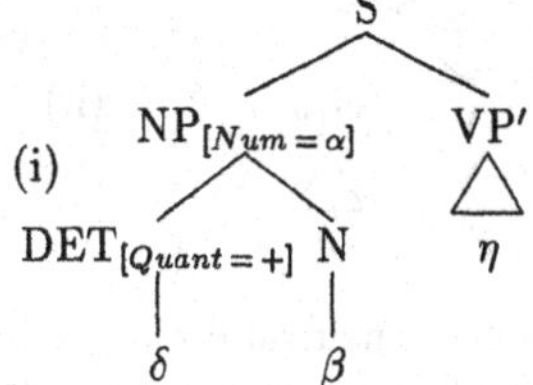

(ii)

VP; V, NP$_{[Num=\alpha]}$; η; DET$_{[Quant=+]}$ N; δ β

with δ a quantifying determiner.

Operations: Choose a new discourse referent **x**. Replace $\overline{\gamma}$ by the duplex condition

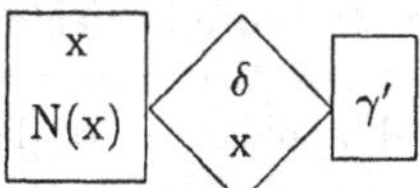

where γ' results from $\overline{\gamma}$ by substituting **x** for NP (Δ $\delta\beta$).

If *Num* = *plur*, then mark **x** with *pl*.

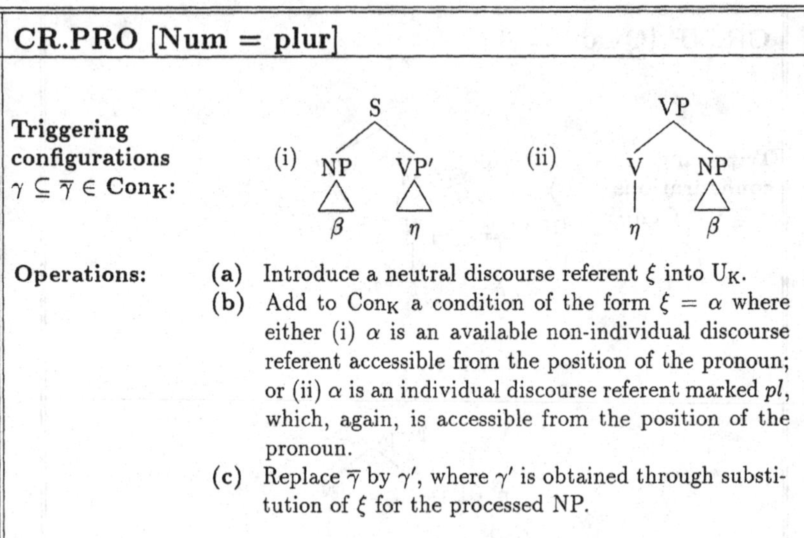

CR.PRO [Num = plur]
Triggering configurations $\gamma \subseteq \overline{\gamma} \in \text{Con}_K$:
(i) S, NP, VP′, β, η
(ii) VP, V, NP, η, β
Operations:
(a) Introduce a neutral discourse referent ξ into U_K.
(b) Add to Con_K a condition of the form $\xi = \alpha$ where either (i) α is an available non-individual discourse referent accessible from the position of the pronoun; or (ii) α is an individual discourse referent marked *pl*, which, again, is accessible from the position of the pronoun.
(c) Replace $\overline{\gamma}$ by γ′, where γ′ is obtained through substitution of ξ for the processed NP.

We saw that discourse referents marked *pl* cannot serve as antecedents to singular pronouns. This means that the rule for singular anaphoric pronouns, also formulated in Chapter 1 (see p. 122 and p. 238), should now be read as allowing only for antecedents that are individual discourse referents without the superscript *pl*. We will not bother to restate the rule so that it makes this restricton explicit; but we will observe the restriction in all applications of the rule henceforth.

For the sake of explicitness let us see how the DRSs for (4.71) and (4.74) are constructed with the help of the new rules. (4.71) yields, after one application of CR.NP [Quant = +], the structure

(4.76)

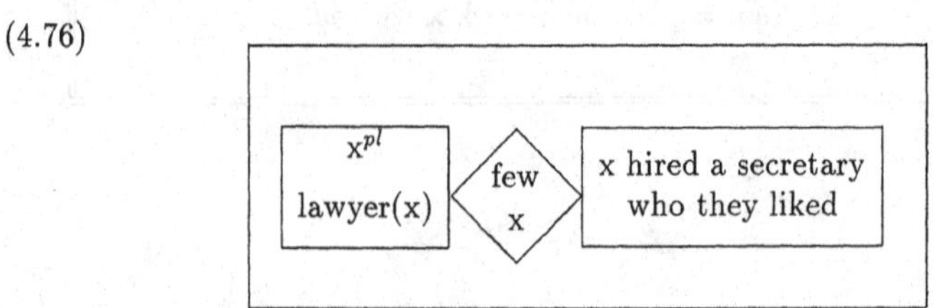

Applications of the familiar rules for (non-specific) indefinites and of the rule for nouns with relative clauses transform (4.76) into

(4.77)

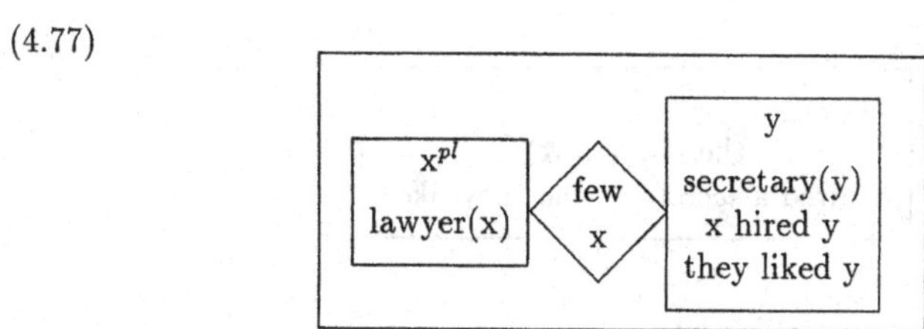

At this point we must apply the rule for plural pronouns. The new version of the rule permits us to use **x** as antecedent for **they**, since **x** is accessible and also is marked *pl*. So we get

(4.78)

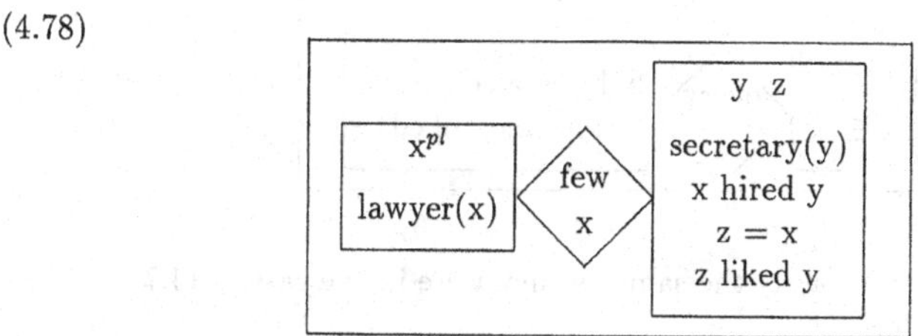

This is what we wanted.

A brief comment on the types of discourse referents introduced by the new rules. The discourse referent **x** is, as before, an individual discourse referent. Thus, in official notation the left-hand DRS of the duplex condition has the form

(4.79)

ξ^{pl}

at(ξ)
lawyer(ξ)

The discourse referent ζ introduced by the pronoun is itself neutral – that is, we introduce neither of the conditions **at**(ζ), **non-at**(ζ) – but of course it inherits the predicate **at** through identification with ξ. (In (4.78) we have followed the convention, announced on p. 334, of choosing a new discourse referent of the same type as the one with which it is set equal.)

The DRS-construction for (4.74) coincides for the most part with that for (4.71). There is a difference only with regard to the first couple of steps. The first construction step for (4.74) produces

(4.80)

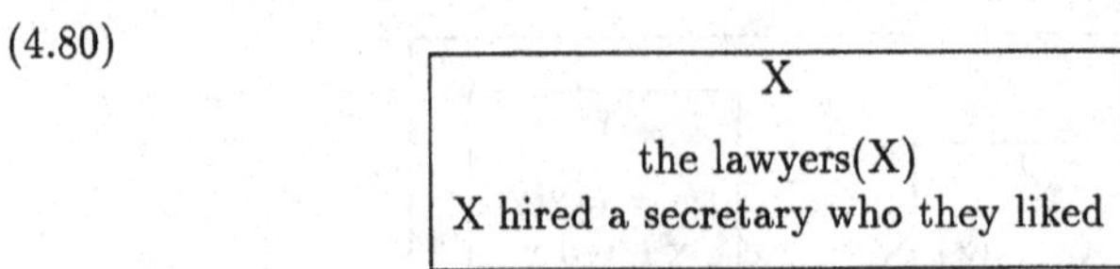

Optional Distribution converts this into

(4.81)

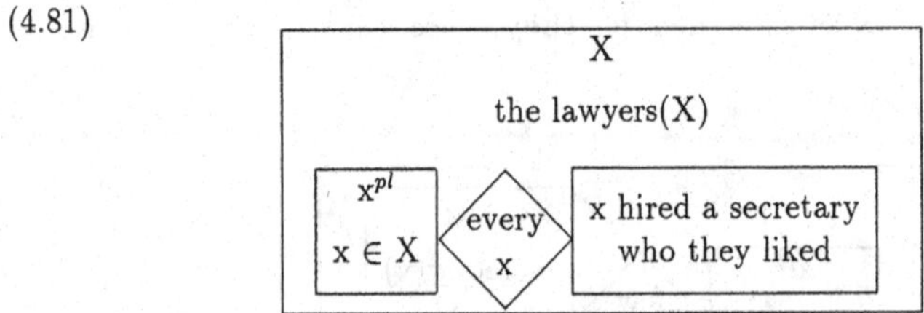

The remaining steps are exactly the same as they were in the case of (4.71).

Our analysis points towards a difference between (4.71) and (4.74) which we already noted in 4.1.4. It relates to the options available for the anaphoric pronoun **they**. In (4.77) there is only one possible antecedent for the pronoun, viz. the discourse referent $\mathbf{x}^{pl}$. At the corresponding stage of the DRS-construction for (4.74), viz.

(4.82)

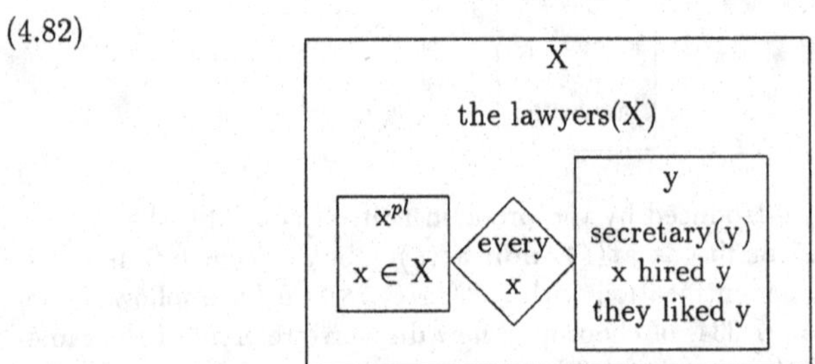

there are two candidates, $\mathbf{x}^{pl}$ and **X**. Choosing the first, we obtain a DRS paralleling (4.78):

(4.83)

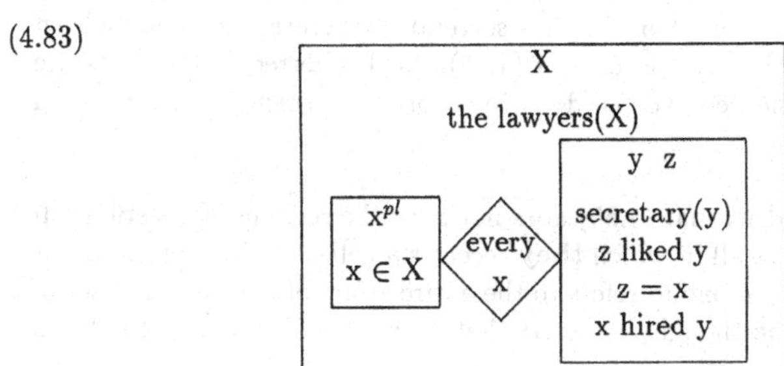

The alternative option leads to

(4.84)

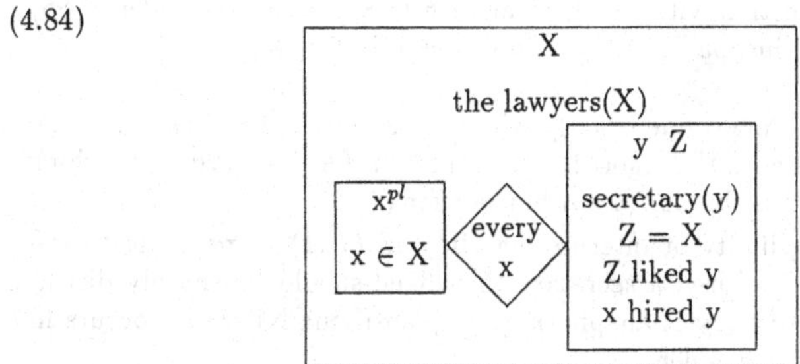

(4.83) and (4.84) differ in meaning. Whereas (4.83) says that each of the lawyers hired a secretary that he liked, (4.84) says each of the lawyers hired a secretary that the lawyers liked. According to our theory only (4.74), with its non-quantifying subject, allows for this alternative interpretation. (4.71), with its quantifying subject NP, never introduces a set discourse referent; consequently the second option is not available there. In 4.1.5 we briefly addressed the question, whether this difference accords with speaker's intuitions. We now want to look at this matter more closely.

To focus more clearly on the problematic readings, compare the following two sentences, in which the verb phrase of the relative clause has a preferred collective interpretation:

(4.85) Few lawyers hired a secretary who they had discussed.

(4.86) The lawyers hired a secretary who they had discussed.

To repeat, our present account predicts that in (4.85) **they** cannot refer to the (small) set of lawyers each of whom hired a secretary; whereas it claims such an interpretation to be possible in the case of (4.86). Is this correct? The facts are hard to ascertain, and the best we can do is to report our present appreciation of the relevant data:

(i) We are fairly confident that (4.85) does not have the reading in question. (If it has any reading at all in which **they** receives a collective interpretation, it is that on which the pronoun refers to the entire group of lawyers, that set of which (4.85) may be thought to assert that only a small fraction of it hired new secretaries.)

(ii) We are less firmly convinced that the relevant reading exists in the case of (4.86). Although some speakers appear to find such a reading more readily accessible in connection with (4.86) than with (4.85), others consider (4.85) and (4.86) equally incapable of being interpreted in this way.

More work is needed to determine exactly what the empirical facts are. For the time being, we will stick with the algorithm in its present form, according to which the disputed reading is possible for (4.86) but not for (4.85).

The apparent impossibility of interpreting **they** in (4.71) as referring to the (small) set of lawyers who hired a secretary they liked should be sharply distinguished from cases where **they** is anaphoric to a quantifying NP which occurs in an earlier sentence. Thus consider

(4.87) Few lawyers hired a secretary who they liked. They had discussed the applicants beforehand.

The second sentence of (4.87) can be interpreted as saying that the few lawyers who hired a secretary they liked had discussed the applicants beforehand.

At this point it may look as if we have arrived at an inconsistency – on one occasion a quantifying NP acting as an anaphoric antecedent can only provide an individual discourse referent for this purpose, on the next it *must* provide a discourse referent representing a set. The conflict, however, is only apparent. The reason why we can get the set interpretation for the second **they** in (4.87) is that once the first sentence has been processed, and the duplex condition it introduces fully established, it becomes possible to apply abstraction to this completed duplex condition. Thus, having obtained from the first sentence of (4.87) the DRS (4.78),

(4.78)

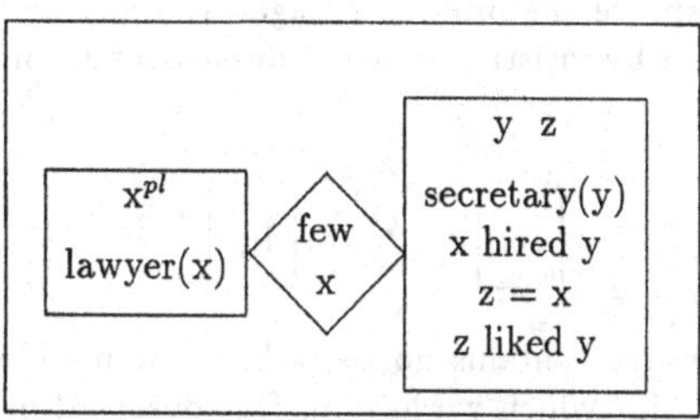

we can then process the subject of the second sentence of (4.87) in the following way:

(4.88)

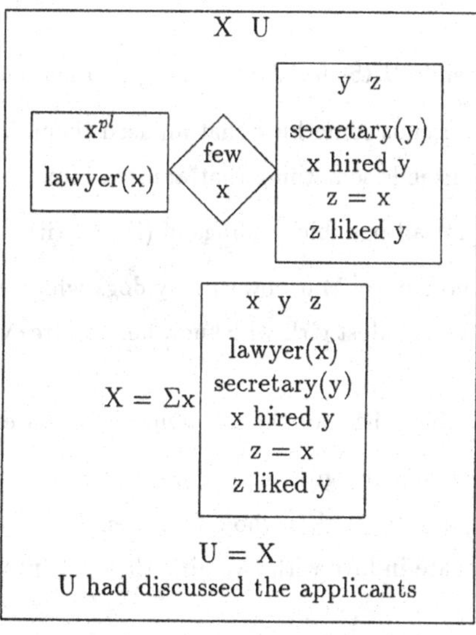

This explains how (4.87) could have the reading in question. But why could the same principle of abstraction not be used to yield a similar interpretation to the **they** of (4.71)? The answer to this last question is implicit in our informal description of Abstraction as it is used in (4.88). Abstraction may only be applied once the duplex condition to which it is being applied has been completed. The application of Abstraction needed to provide the intuitively impossible interpretation of **they** in (4.71) does not fit this description. For here the pronoun is itself part of the duplex condition to which Abstraction should be applied. This duplex condition is still under construction; in fact, it could not have been completed, for that would require that the pronoun had been interpreted already.

Formally we can capture the prohibition against applying Abstraction in this "self-referential" manner by insisting that the duplex condition

on which the rule operates contains no reducible (but unreduced) conditions as parts. This is a constraint which we have in fact observed in all applications of Abstraction so far, but up to this point there was no need for making that constraint explicit.

Exercises

1. Construct all possible DRSs for the following two sentences.

   (i) Bill told his friends something that amused them.

   (ii) Bill told his friends something that amused him.

2. Construct DRSs for all possible readings of (i) and (ii):

   (i) The boys who admire Mary own many dogs which cannot stand them.

   (ii) Mary owns a dog. Most girls who know her admire every boy who cannot stand them.

3. Construct all possible DRSs for the following three sentences:

   (i) Few boys amuse many girls who adore them.

   (ii) Five boys amuse three girls who adore them.

   (iii) If three boys are in love with two girls they get into a fight.

4.2.5 Dependent Plurals

In 4.1.6 we briefly discussed the phenomenon of dependent plurals, illustrated by the object NPs of sentences such as

(4.48) Most of my friends own cars.

and

(4.49) Many students bought books that would keep them occupied during the next two weeks.

We noted that it is a peculiarity of such phrases that they are neutral with regard to the distinction between individual and set discourse referents. For instance, the discourse referent introduced by **books** in (4.49) should be able to take a set of books as value in relation to one student while taking a single book as value in relation to some other student. In fact, it was this observation which led us to introduce neutral discourse referents **x**, which are accompanied neither by the condition **at(x)** nor by **non-at(x)**. (We will stick with the convention of using Greek letters for discourse referents that are constrained by neither of these conditions.)

We have said that dependent plurals show a superficial similarity with those instances of anphoric **they** in which the pronoun picks up an individual discourse referent: In both cases the plurality of the noun phrase seems to be required for syntactic reasons, and it doesn't carry the semantic import – that of requiring sets rather than individuals for semantic values – which we have found to attach to plural NPs in many other contexts. There are, however, also important differences between dependent plurals and the pronouns discussed in 4.2.4. Perhaps the most important of these is the fact that dependent plurality is a more "local" phenomenon than **they**-anaphora to individual discourse referents. Specifically, the dependence of bare plurals is clause-bound, whereas the **they**-anaphora of the last section is constrained, like any other kind of anaphora, by accessibility. This difference may not be immediately apparent, as individual discourse referents marked *pl* are invariably introduced into the universes of subordinate DRSs. This has the effect that **they**-anaphora to such discourse referents is more restrictive than other kinds of pronominal anaphora. (With relatively few exceptions the plural pronoun and the NP that gave rise to the individual discourse referent which the pronoun may pick up are part of one and the same sentence.) That plural pronoun anaphora to individual discourse referents is nevertheless less severely restricted than dependent plurality of the sort illustrated in (4.48) and (4.49) is shown by the following examples:

(4.89) a. The women bought cars which had automatic transmissions.

b. The women bought a car which had automatic transmissions.

c. The women bought cars which they liked.

d. The women bought a car which they liked.

(4.89.a) can be read as involving two dependent plurals, with **cars** depending on **the women**, and **automatic transmissions** depending on **cars**. As a consequence the sentence would count as true if each of the women bought one car and that car was equipped with an automatic transmission. (4.89.b) cannot be so interpreted. It only has the somewhat absurd reading that the women bought cars each one of which was equipped with several automatic transmissions. The reason for this difference is that the NP **automatic transmissions** cannot be interpreted as dependent on the main clause subject **the women**. Consequently its plural morphology can only be interpreted as signifying that the discourse referent it introduces represents a set. In other words, (4.89.a) is capable of generating a DRS of the form

(4.90)

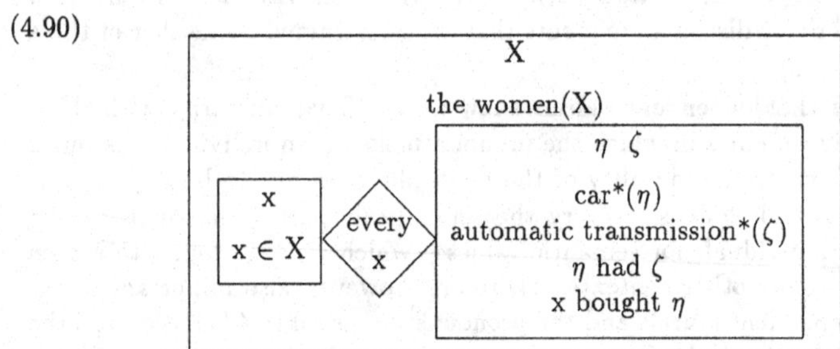

while (4.89.b) only yields the DRS

(4.91)

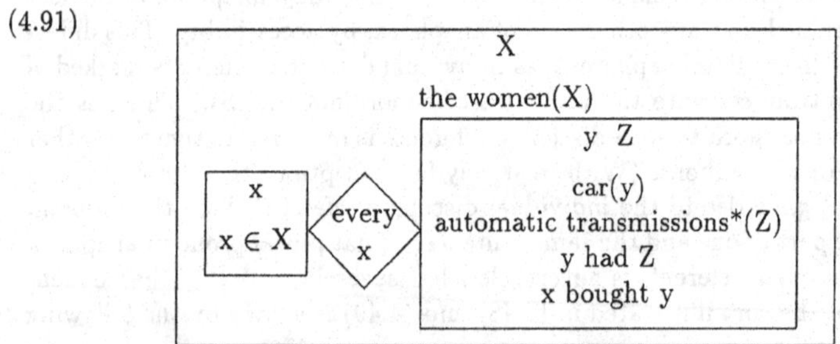

The fact that automatic transmissions can be interpreted as a dependent plural in (4.89.a) but not in (4.89.b) is explained by the following principle:

(4.92) A bare plural NP can be interpreted as a dependent plural only if it can be interpreted as dependent on some other plural NP which occurs in the same clause.

(4.92) allows for an interpretation of **automatic transmissions** as dependent on the plural NP **which** in (4.89.a), whereas the relative clause of (4.89.b) contains no plural NP on which it could be dependent.

(4.92) limits the possible instances of dependent plurality to those in which the dependent plural and the plural NP on which it depends belong to one and the same clause. It leaves open whether the phenomenon is further restricted by additional constraints, operating within a clause. One such constraint, which is suggested by the examples we have so far considered, might be that the licensing NP always be the subject. However, that this is not the only possibility is shown by the following sentences[24]

(4.93) German civil defence workers spotted those two planes.

(4.94) The boys gave the girls nickels.

(4.93) has an interpretation according to which it is true in a situation where each of two given planes was spotted by a different civil defence worker. This reading is possible only because the subject **German defence workers** can be taken to depend on the object phrase **two planes**. Similarly (4.94) has a reading according to which the boys, as a group, may have given each of the girls no more than one nickel. This reading construes the direct object **nickels** as dependent not on the subject **the boys** but on the indirect object **the girls**.[25]

When a clause contains several bare plurals, the question may arise which of them should be taken as dependent on which. Consider the following sentences

(4.95) a. Weak men tend to drive strong cars.

b. Strong cars tend to be driven by weak men.

c. It is weak men who tend to drive strong cars.

In relation to both (4.95.a) and (4.95.b) there is a preference for taking the direct object as dependent on the subject. But if we read these sentences with the right intonation, i.e. with a strong emphasis on the subject phrase, it is rather the reverse dependence, with the subject depending on the object, which becomes the more prominent of the two. The construction in (4.95.c) – one that is known in the syntactic literature as *pseudo-clefting* – has an effect similar to that of stressing the subject in (4.95.a): the more prominent reading is that on which

[24]Both (4.93) and (4.94) are from [Roberts 1987b]. Roberts attributes (4.94) to B. Partee.

[25]Of course (4.94) also has a reading on which **nickels** is dependent on **the boys**; and we may wonder if it doesn't have a third one, in which the object phrase is dependent on both **the boys** and **the girls** at the same time. This third reading would mean that each of the boys gave each of the girls one or more nickels. But since the truth conditions of this reading are indistinguishable from those which emerge when we for instance interpret **the girls** as dependent on **the boys** and distribute not only over **the boys** but also over **the girls**, there are no good tests for this third possibility. We will proceed on the assumption that it does not exist. Even so, the total number of different readings for (4.94) is greater than 2, because of the option to distribute both over the set of the boys and the set of the girls.

weak men – or, more precisely, the relative pronoun **who** – is dependent on **strong cars**. These examples suggest that the question which bare plurals can be taken as dependent on which, is intimately connected with a semantic distinction the importance of which is generally acknowledged, but which is nonetheless still far from well-understood. This is the distinction between *topic* and *comment*: It is thought that many linguistic utterances can be divided into two parts. The first part, the topic, identifies an element (it could be an individual, several individuals, an event, a situation etc.) about which the utterance must be taken as saying something, while the remaining part, the comment, identifies what the utterance says about the topic. The distinction between topic and comment is complicated by at least two problems. First, it is still unclear what informal glosses of the distinction – such as that "the comment is used to describe the topic", "the topic constitutes the old, the comment new information" come to when one tries to apply them rigorously. In much of the relevant literature the use of the terms "topic" and "comment" is intuitive and loose, and it appears that different authors use the term in different ways, sometimes without seeming to realize, or at any rate without explicitly noting the fact, that they are doing so. Secondly, and as an almost inevitable consequence of the first problem, no clear and precise analyses exists of how particular sentences, or particular utterances of them, are to be separated into topic and comment. In view of these unclarities there can be no question of incorporating a viable topic-comment distinction into our theory at the present time. As a consequence we lack the means of analysing the correlation between plural dependence and topic-comment structure.

We conclude this brief fact-finding mission with two further facts concerning dependent plurals which fall outside the scope of the formal theory developed in this chapter, but which we think are worth mentioning nevertheless, as they point towards some of the additional complexities with which a comprehensive account of dependent plurals should be prepared to deal. The first fact concerns complex noun phrases which contain another NP as part of some prepositional complement. Consider

(4.96) a. The women bought cars with automatic transmissions.

b. The women bought a car with automatic transmissions.

(4.96.a) and (4.96.b) constitute a direct parallel to (4.89.a) and (4.89.b): Only (4.89.a), where the head noun of the object NP is in the plural, allows for a sensible interpretation, which does not require cars with several transmissions. This suggests that the complex NPs **cars with automatic transmissions** and **a car with automatic transmission** act as syntactic units, which define their own locality domains. If we assume that an embedded bare plural may not depend on an NP outside this domain, the contrast between (4.96.a) and (4.96.b) falls into line with that between (4.89.a) and (4.89.b). However, as prepositional phrases are not part of the fragment we treat explicitly, the issue has no consequences for our formal theory.

The second aspect of plural dependence relates to the temporal properties of natural language (see Chapter 5). Dependent plurals are not always licensed by some other plural NP. They may also be licensed by adverbial quantifiers or by the kind of generic quantification discussed in Section 3.7.4. (4.97.a) and (4.97.b) illustrate the first possibility, (4.97.c) the second:[26]

(4.97) a. Trains are regularly leaving from here for Amsterdam.

b. Strange voices were to be heard everywhere.

c. Fred wears loud neckties.

(4.97.a) represents the most common form of this kind of plural dependence, in which the quantification that licenses the dependent bare plural is over time. However, (4.97.b) shows that the quantification does not have to be over time; apparently plural dependence is also possible if the quantification is over parts of space.

The analysis of temporal quantification we will offer in the next chapter suggests a unifying principle underlying both the cases illustrated by the sentences in (4.97) and those in which another noun phrase is the licensing element: In all these cases it is the occurrence of the dependent NP within a quantificational structure (in our terminology: inside the right-hand DRS of some duplex condition) introduced by a constituent belonging to the same local domain as the dependent NP. But there is nevertheless one important difference between the two types of licencers: where the licensing element is an NP, it must agree in number with the dependent NP, and thus be a plural; that the NP introduces a quantificational structure does not seem to be sufficient. For instance,

(4.98) Every student bought books.

does not seem to have an interpretation according to which it is true when each of the students bought one book only.[27]

As we have said, we will incorporate only those instances of dependent plurality into the construction algorithm in which the licensing element is a plural NP

[26] (4.97.a) is from [de Mey 1981]; (4.97.b) from [Roberts 1987b].

[27] We are not altogether certain that such an interpretation is totally excluded. If it is not, this would provide further evidence that the decisive conditions for dependent intepretation of bare plurals are (i) locality and (ii) quantificational structure, with number agreement being an additional constraint which, though important, is not absolutely indispensable.

belonging to the same clause as the dependent plural. To keep the complexities within bounds we also will ignore further constraints on plural dependencies of this type, in particular those relating to topic-comment structure. This entails that the construction algorithm will somewhat overgenerate.

To see how the processing rule for dependent bare plurals might be stated we should observe (i) that the NP which acts as a licencer for the dependent interpretation must itself be interpreted distributively not only when it is a quantifying NP (in that case a distributive interpretation is automatic!), but also when it is non-quantifying. Thus the relevant discourse referent that derives from this NP will always be an *individual* discourse referent marked *pl*. (ii) It is not hard to verify that within the limited fragment of English for which we are trying to provide a precise formal treatment the locality constraint on plural dependence will be satisfied if and only if this discourse referent occurs as a constituent of the condition $\overline{\gamma}$, which also contains the bare plural that we want to interpret as dependent on the NP from which this discourse referent stems.

In the light of these last two observations we can give a (preliminary) formulation of the construction rule for dependent plurals, CR.NP(Dep), as follows[28]:

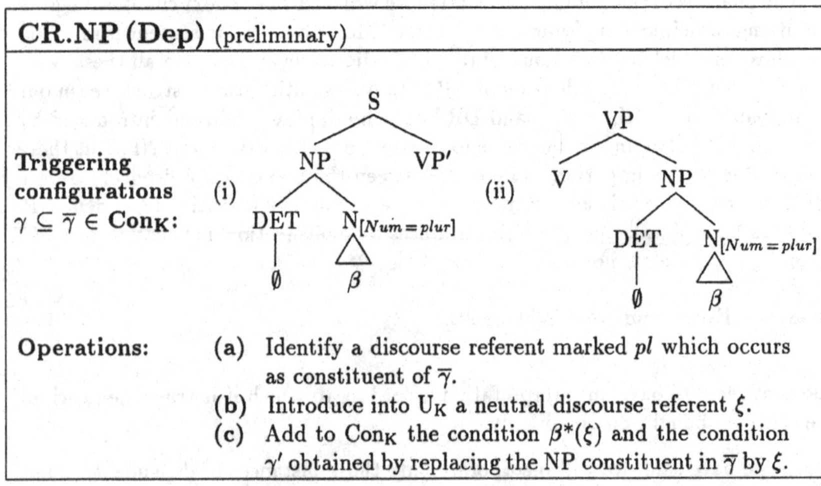

CR.NP (Dep) (preliminary)
Triggering configurations
$\gamma \subseteq \overline{\gamma} \in Con_K$:
(i)
S
NP
VP'
DET
$N_{[Num=plur]}$
∅
β
(ii)
VP
V
NP
DET
$N_{[Num=plur]}$
∅
β
Operations:
(a) Identify a discourse referent marked pl which occurs as constituent of $\overline{\gamma}$.
(b) Introduce into U_K a neutral discourse referent ξ.
(c) Add to Con_K the condition $\beta^*(\xi)$ and the condition γ' obtained by replacing the NP constituent in $\overline{\gamma}$ by ξ.

To see how the rule works in some simple cases, we construct DRSs for the next two sentences.

---

[28] A slightly modified formulation of this rule can be found on page 388. That version constitutes the last word on this rule we give in this book.

(4.99) Most students bought books.

(4.100) Most students who bought books were content.

The first construction step for (4.99) produces the DRS

(4.101)

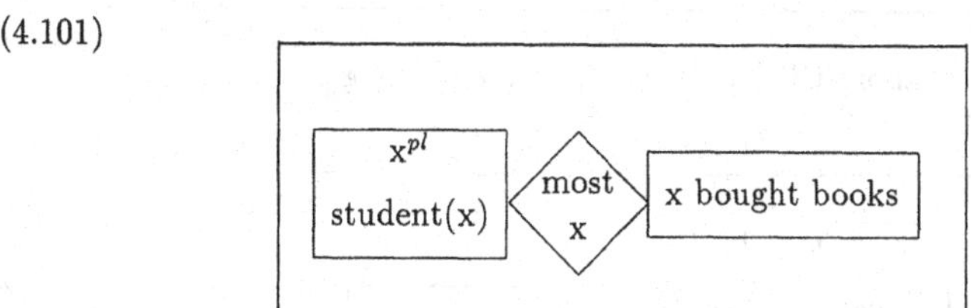

Now the precondition for the application of CR.NP(Dep) is fulfilled: The condition containing the bare plural **books** also contains the discourse referent **x**, which is marked *pl*. Application of the rule produces

(4.102)

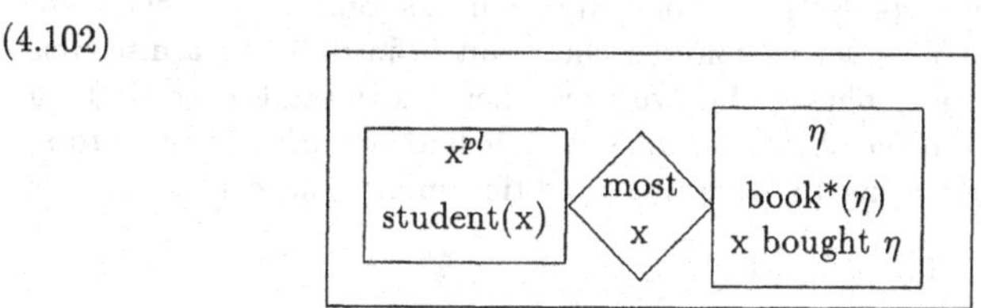

The first construction step in the DRS construction for (4.100) gives

(4.103)

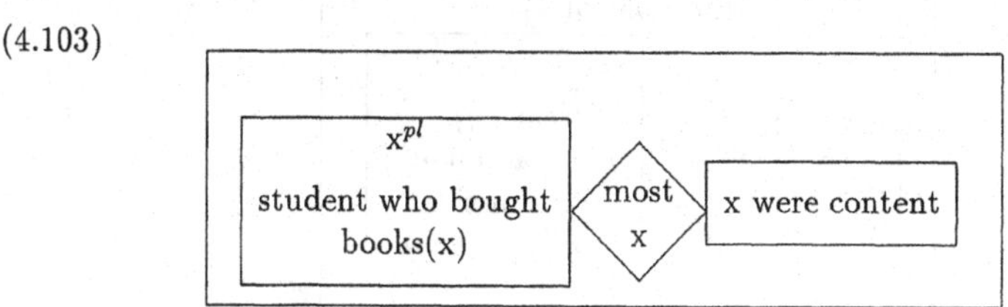

Decomposing the complex condition **student who bought books(x)** turns (4.103) into

(4.104)

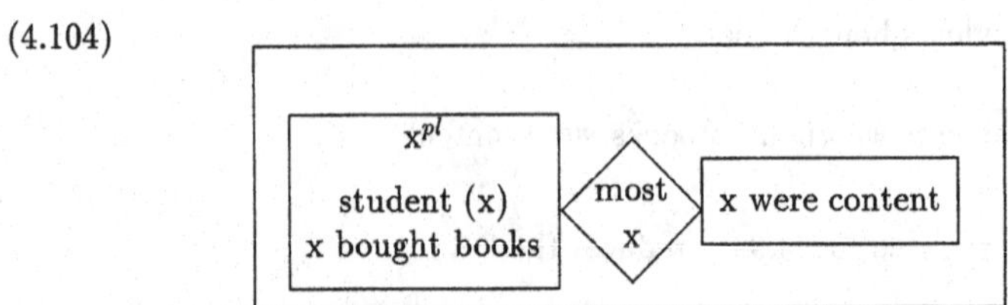

Again it is possible to apply CR.NP(Dep), this time yielding

(4.105)

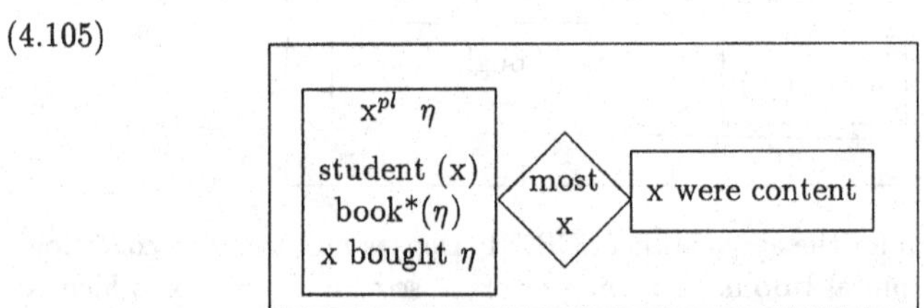

The DRS-construction of (4.90) runs along similar lines. But there is one complication. To see what it is, let us consider the result of introducing a discourse referent **X** for the subject phrase **the women**, then distributing over **X**, then applying CR.NP(Dep) to the object NP **cars which had automatic transmissions**, and, finally, separating the resulting condition into its head noun and its relative clause:

(4.106)

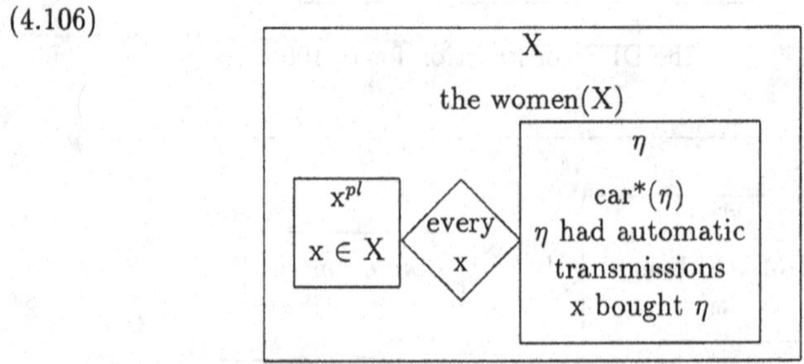

The discourse referent η in (4.106) presents two distinct problems. First, it ought to be possible to arrive at a reading where each of the cars bought has its own automatic transmission. In particular, if one of the women, call her Ella, bought three cars, then the interpretation of (4.89.a) should allow for the possibility that each of these cars had its own transmission rather than that the three cars have a single transmission in common. To obtain this reading we must allow for the possibility of distributing over the neutral discourse referent η. The simple-minded way of solving this problem is to simply extend the applicability of the rule of optional distribution from non-individual to neutral discourse referents. Since neutral discourse referents always come from plural NPs, the individual discourse referent which an application of the rule introduces is to be marked again as *pl*. Applying Optional Distribution in this extended form to (4.106) we obtain

(4.107)

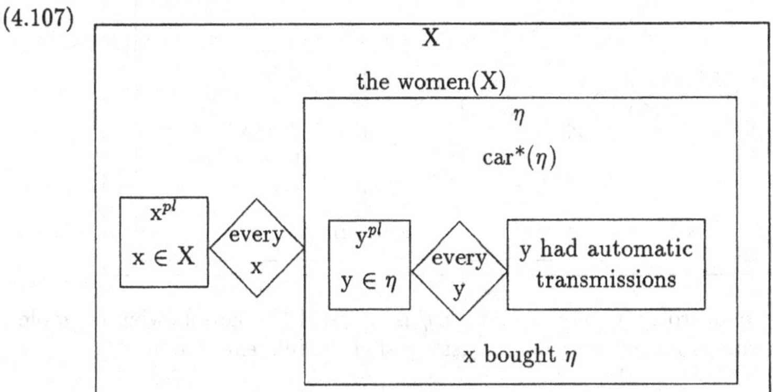

There is a slight complication relating to the condition $\mathbf{y} \in \eta$. What are the verification conditions for $\mathbf{y} \in \eta$? The point of neutral discourse referents, we saw, is that they can take both sets and individuals as values. When the value is a set, the verification conditions are as before and unproblematic:

if $f(\eta)$ is non-atomic, then $M \models_f \mathbf{y} \in \eta$ iff $f(\mathbf{y})$ is an atomic part of $f(\eta)$

But what are we to make of $\mathbf{y} \in \eta$ in case $f(\eta)$ is atomic? A look at (4.107) makes clear what is wanted: Of those women who bought one car (4.89.a) should be saying that *that* car had an automatic transmission. Extrapolating in the obvious way we conclude that if $f(\eta)$ is atomic then $\mathbf{y} \in \eta$ should count as satisfied just in case $f(\mathbf{y}) = f(\eta)$. However, as this is the case if and only if $f(\mathbf{y})$ is an atomic part of $f(\eta)$, we can retain our original formulation of the verification conditions for $\mathbf{x} \in \mathbf{Y}$. For they already settle the new possibility, which arises if we no longer insist that $\mathbf{Y}$ be a plural discourse referent, in just the way we want.[29]

[29]It is perhaps preferable to write in general not $\xi \in \eta$ but rather something like $\xi \subset \eta$. In those, but only those, cases in which ξ comes with the condition $\mathbf{at}(\xi)$ and η with the condition $\mathbf{non\text{-}at}(\xi)$, $\xi \subset \eta$ would be replaced with the set-theoretically suggestive $\mathbf{z} \subseteq \mathbf{Y}$. However, leaving matters as they are seemed to cause the least notational disruption. For more discussion of these matters see 4.3.

Having reached the structure (4.107) we can once again apply CR.NP(Dep), this time to the object phrase **automatic transmissions** of the relative clause. The result is

(4.108)

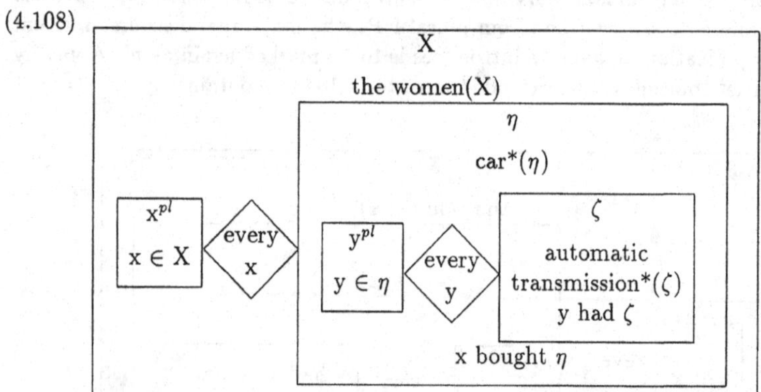

The second problem associated with η is revealed by the following example, which is formally like (4.89.a) but suggests a slightly different reading.

(4.109) The linguistics professors have assistants who share offices.

Proceeding by the same steps which generated (4.106) from (4.89.a) we get

(4.110)

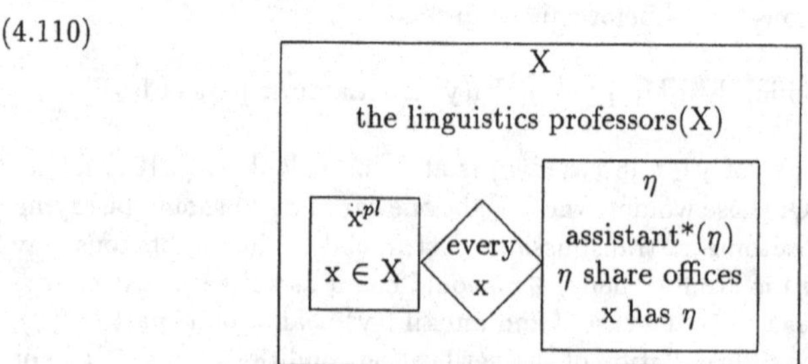

To arrive at a plausible reading in this case we should *not* distribute over η. A single assistant cannot share an office (with himself). So the only way in which the right-hand DRS could be satisfied is for η to be assigned a set of assistants who share an office between them. As a matter of fact, for all (4.109) says the assistants to any one professor might share several offices between them. But, crucially, the cases where they share just one office should be included. This means that **offices** can be interpreted as dependent on **assistants**. In order that a DRS representing this reading be forthcoming we need to make a slight adjustment to the rule CR.NP(Dep). We could do this either by allowing neutral discourse referents as licencers or by marking neutral discourse referents with *pl*. We take the second option. Thus we revise the second operation of CR.NP(Dep) as:

(b) Introduce a new neutral discourse referent ξ and mark it with *pl*.

This change implies in particular that the DRS which we presented above as (4.110) is strictly speaking of the form[30]

(4.111)

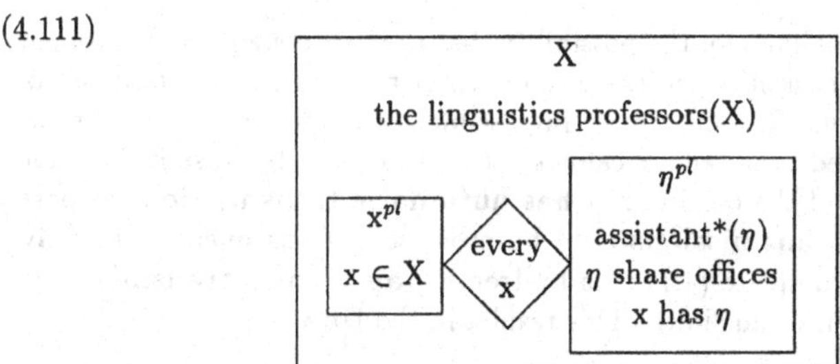

Application of CR.NP(Dep) to **offices** is permitted, and yields the DRS

(4.112)

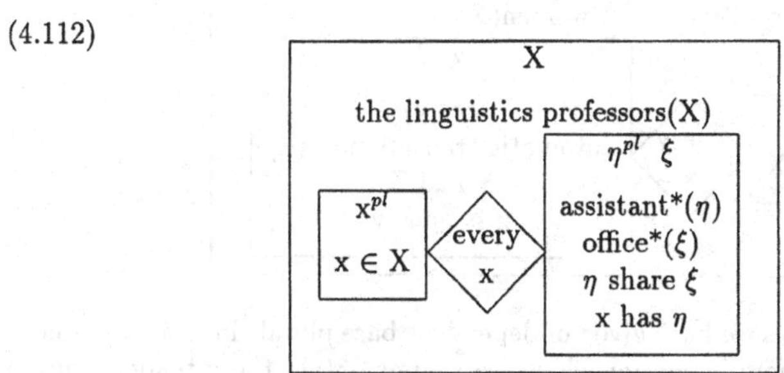

Formally a DRS similar to (4.112) is available also for (4.89.a), though the particular combination of nouns and verbs in (4.89.a) militates against such an interpretation for extragrammatical reasons. For (4.89.b), however, neither this interpretation is possible, nor the one represented by (4.106). To see that neither interpretation is generated by our rules, consider the DRS that we get from (4.89.b) after having processed subject and direct object of the main clause:

[30](4.109) has a further reading according to which offices are shared by assistants to different professors. This reading our rules are not able to capture.

(4.113)

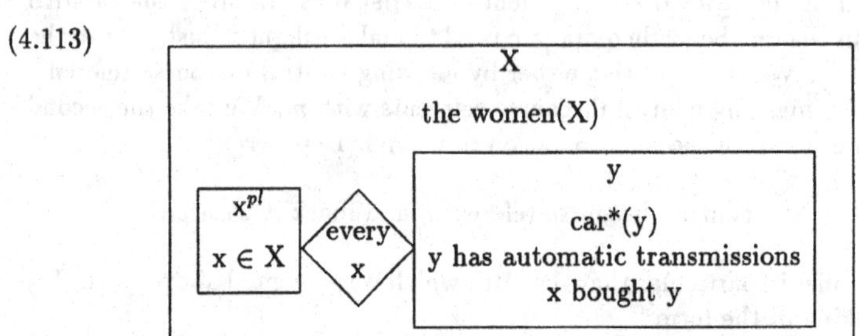

To obtain a DRS which allows for the possibility that the cars bought by the women have one transmission each it is necessary to interpret **automatic transmissions** as a dependent bare plural. But this is impossible. **y** cannot act as a licenser, because it is not marked as *pl*; and **x** cannot act as a licenser, because it does not occur as a constituent of the condition **y has automatic transmissions** as part of which **automatic transmissions** is to be processed. Consequently the only way in which we can complete (4.113) is by treating **automatic transmissions** as a non-dependent plural indefinite. This results in the DRS

(4.114)

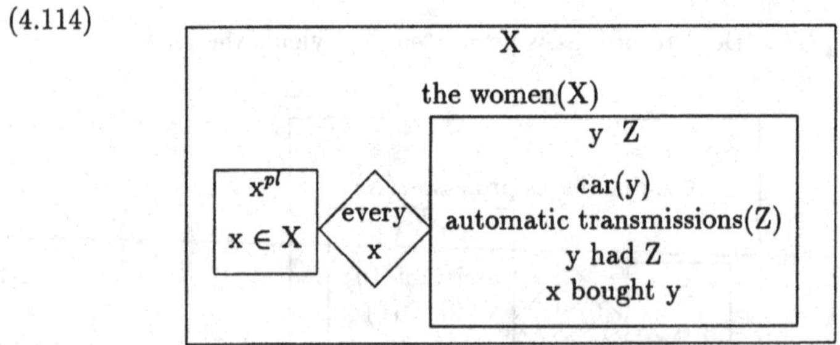

Among the examples we have given of dependent bare plurals licensed by other plural noun phrases there is one for which we cannot obtain the intended representation even with the help of the rule CR.NP(Dep). This is (4.93). In order to process the subject of (4.93) as dependent plural we must at that point have a discourse referent in object position. This is possible only if we have the option to process the direct object before the subject. And this is an option of which we have not explicitly availed ourselves.[31] The existence of a reading for (4.93) in which subject is dependent on object might constitute a further argument for permitting processing of the object before the subject.

[31] Compare the discussion in 3.7.

We conclude this subsection with a second though still preliminary version of the rule CR.NP(Dep).[32]

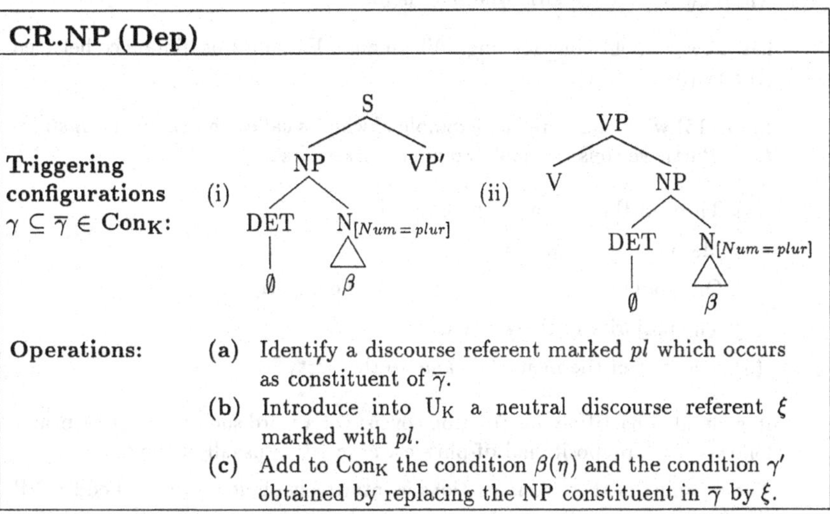

CR.NP (Dep)
Triggering configurations $\gamma \subseteq \overline{\gamma} \in \mathrm{Con_K}$:
(i)
S
NP
VP′
DET
N[Num = plur]
∅
β
(ii)
VP
V
NP
DET
N[Num = plur]
∅
β
Operations:
(a) Identify a discourse referent marked pl which occurs as constituent of $\overline{\gamma}$.
(b) Introduce into U_K a neutral discourse referent ξ marked with pl.
(c) Add to $\mathrm{Con_K}$ the condition $\beta(\eta)$ and the condition γ' obtained by replacing the NP constituent in $\overline{\gamma}$ by ξ.

Exercises

1. Construct DRSs for all possible readings of the following sentences and texts (the phrases in parentheses may be ignored).
   (a) Most women who own a dog are in love with it.
   (b) Most women who own dogs are in love with them.
   (c) The women who own a dog are in love with it.
   (d) The women who own dogs are in love with them.
   (e) Many students bought records. (Then) they pooled them.
   (f) Many students bought records. (Then) they sold them (again).

2. The sentence

   (i) The boys know girls who like them.

[32] A slightly modified formulation of this rule can be found on page 388. That version constitutes our last word about this rule.

has three different readings. Construct the DRSs.

The sentence

(ii) Few boys know girls who like them.

has, however, only one reading. Which one? Explain this difference between (i) and (ii).

3. In (4.115) we encountered an example of what is called the *partitive construction*. Partitive constructions are noun phrases like

   (1) Three of the five men who applied.

   (2) Many of the women who came.

   (3) One (out) of five men responded to the advertisement.

   (4) The majority of the women.

   (5) The first of the men who came to the party.

   In general, a partitive construction consists of a word such as **three** or **many** followed by a prepositional **of**-phrase whose NP is usually definite.

   The meaning of these constructions is intuitively obvious: the embedded NP provides a set which is exploited by the head of the construction – that is the determiner – in one of two ways: Either it is the domain over which the head quantifies or it is a set which contains the set that acts as value of the head as a subset. Which of these two roles is appropriate depends on the form of the head: if it is a determiner of the quantifying type, only the first possibility arises; if it is indefinite, we have both possibilities.

   This informal description makes clear how the processing of partitives should go.

   Extend the syntax to deal with the partitive constructions under (1)–(5) and state the processing principles. Apply them to (6) and (7):

   (6) Few of the girls who came to the party were smart.

   (7) Few of the boys who dated a girl bought a present.

4. Construct DRSs for all possible readings of the following discourses:

   (a) The women own dogs which they show at exhibitions.

   (b) Most women own dogs which they show at exhibitions.

   (c) The women own a dog which they show at exhibitions.

5. The *cardinals* **one**, **two**, **three**, etc. behave syntactically much like adjectives. In fact, we can treat them as genuine members of the class of adjectives if we assume that noun phrases such as **two donkeys**, **three books**, etc. are like bare plural NPs in having an empty determiner, which in these phrases is followed by a compound noun consisting of a common noun together with a cardinality adjective in prenominal position. Such an analysis is supported by the fact that cardinals can be combined with the definite article, as in **the two donkeys**. In such combinations the cardinal would have to be analysed as an adjective in any case.

   (i) Change the syntax so that it treats cardinals as adjectives.

   In Chapter 3 we briefly discussed the distinction between restrictive and non-restrictive relative clauses (See in particular Excercise 2 of Section 3.4). Recall: Sentences such as

   (1) The members of the Secret Police who have systematically subverted the course of justice will all be deprived of their jobs.

   (2) The members of the Secret Police, who have systematically subverted the course of justice, will all be deprived of their jobs.

   differ in that (2) makes an assertion about all members of the Secret Police while (1) tells us something only about those members who systematically subverted the course of justice. The semantic contributions that are made by prenominal adjectives vary in a way which matches the distinction between restrictive and non-restrictive relatives. Thus, in

   (3) The entire female population was rounded up. The fair-haired women were all sold as slaves.

   the second sentence can be taken to tell us something about those among the women mentioned in the first sentence that were fair, while saying nothing about the fate of those who were not fair. Alternatively, the sentence can be taken as an assertion that all the women who were rounded up were sold as slaves, implying in addition that they were all fair.

   (ii) State two construction rules C_1 and C_2 for anaphoric definite descriptions of the form **the** $\alpha\beta$**'s**, where α is an adjective and β**'s** a plural count noun such that C_1 treats the adjective α restrictively and C_2 treats it non-restrictively. Apply these rules to (3) to get the two different interpretations indicated.

When a cardinal is part of a definite description, as in **the two donkeys**, it almost always acts as a non-restrictive adjective. (Question: Why is this?) This fact is illustrated in (4):

(4) John, Bill and Robin entered the room.
  (i) The three men were wearing greatcoats.
  (ii) The two men were wearing greatcoats.

In both (4.i) and (4.ii) the subject noun phrase of the second sentence can only be understood as referring to *all* the men mentioned in the first sentence. This has the effect that when hearing (4.i) the interpreter will infer that there were three men, and so that Robin (as well as John and Bill) was a man. If the interpretation gets (4.ii) instead, he will be led to infer rather that Robin must have been a woman. (Question: What does this have to do with the non-restrictive character of cardinals?)

(iii) Formulate construction rules for (a) indefinite and (b) definite NPs with pronominal cardinals. Use the second rule to construct suitable DRSs for the following texts.
  (5) John likes Bill. Bill admires John. The two men do not get on.
  (6) Joan plays the violin and Ella plays the piano. If Alice visits them, the three women play trios.
  (7) Joan plays the violin and Ella plays the piano. If a girl friend who plays the cello visits them, the three women play trios.

(iv) Extend the treatment of the words **two, three, ...** as adjectives to cover the word **one**.

6. [33] In Exercise 4. we noted that **two, three** etc. occur in definite descriptions and that when occurring in these positions they may be viewed as non-restrictive adjectives. The same seems to be true of **many** and **few** (as well as a few similar words). Consider for instance

(1) The inhabitants had all come to the town square. The many women who had brought their children did not speak.

Here the phrase **the many women who had brought their children** must be understood as conveying that the set consisting of those women among the inhabitants who brought their children was large; **many** does not assist the definition of this set.

[33] N.B. This exercise is hard in that it involves a number of issues we have hardly touched upon. The reader may want to postpone it until he has reached Section 4.4.2.

(i) Formulate a construction rule for **many** and **few** in definite descriptions which allows for the construction of a DRS that captures the intuitive interpretation of (1).

(ii) In Exercise 4. it was suggested that if NPs like **two men** are analysed as bare plurals, with **two** an adjective, then the same rule for **two** can serve both in connection with **two men** and with **the two men**. Is it possible to state the rule for **many** in such a way that it too will serve for **many men** and **the many men**?

7. Plural definite descriptions can be interpreted, like plural indefinite descriptions, as dependent on some other plural NP. This can be seen, for instance, from sentences like

(1) Three students hate the teachers who instruct them.

(2) Most men do not forget the women whom they loved first.

To focus on (1), the **teachers who instruct them** can be understood as denoting, for each of the three students, the teacher or teachers who instruct(s) that student. Thus the plurality of **teachers** is neutralized in that (1) can be true even if each of the students is being instructed by only one teacher. As with bare plurals this neutralization must be licensed by an element within the same local domain – i.e., for our purpose, the same clause. Once again we restrict attention to those cases where the licensing element is another plural NP.

Another similarity with the dependent bare plurals is that the discourse referent for the dependent description must occupy a position that qualifies as "dependent" on that occupied by the discourse referent representing the licensing NP. That is, the discourse referent representing the licensing NP must be accessible from the universe containing the one representing the dependent one. In connection with bare plurals this was a point on which we did not think it was necessary to insist, as it is the default assumption anyway that they, as indefinites, introduce their discourse referents at the level at which they are processed, in which case the accessibility constraint is automatically satisfied.

With definite descriptions, however, the default assumption goes rather in the opposite direction: There is a strong tendency for definites to be interpreted as establishing their discourse referents at the highest level; only when the description betrays a clear dependency on some other element will it be possible to assign its discourse referent to some subordinate level, in particular that at which the description is being processed. As we saw in Section 3.4 the clearest way in which such a dependency can be conveyed is through the presence of a pronoun that is anaphoric to the NP on which the description then comes to depend.

Indeed, it seems very hard to come up with examples in which the dependent definite description does not contain such a pronoun. What we have said implies that the DRS for (1), in which the plural definite description is interpreted as depending upon the subject phrase, should have the form:

(3)

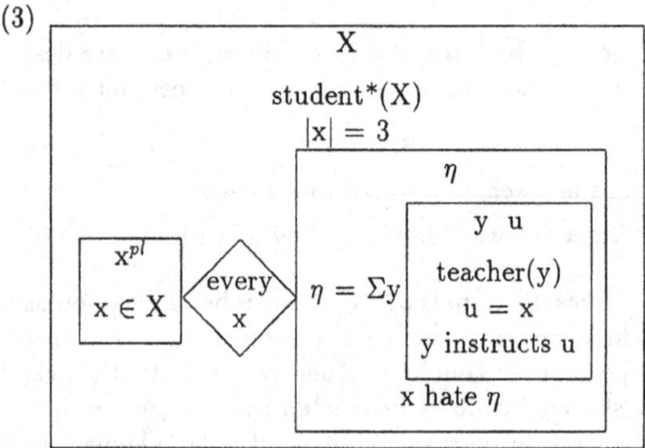

(i) Formulate the construction rule for dependent definite descriptions, which, in combination with the construction rules we already have, is able to transform (1) into (3).

(ii) Use this rule to construct a DRS for (2).

There is one further complication. Consider the phrase **the teachers who instruct Bill**. This phrase denotes the set of all the teachers from whom Bill receives instruction. In principle, some of these teachers might teach Bill jointly, while others teach him singly. Thus, in the definition of the set or individual η, abstraction should involve a variable which is itself neutral. In other words, the abstraction equation in (3) should not have the form

(4) $\eta = \Sigma y$

y u
teacher(y)   u = x   y instructs u

but rather

$$(5)\ \eta = \Sigma\xi \boxed{\begin{array}{c} \xi \ \ \mathrm{u} \\ \hline \mathrm{teacher}^*(\xi) \\ \mathrm{u} = \mathrm{x} \\ \xi \text{ instructs u} \end{array}}$$

(iii) Restate the rule for dependent plural definite descriptions so that the DRS for (1) is not (3) but one which contains (5) instead of (4).

4.2.6 Dependent Plural Pronouns

The phenomenon we discuss in this section combines some of the features of the type of pronominal anaphora discussed in 4.2.4 with certain properties of plural dependence as discussed in the last subsection, 4.2.5. It is illustrated in the following passage.

(4.115) Every director gave a present to a child from the orphanage.
They opened them right away.

The second sentence of (4.115) has, if we set plausibility aside, a great many readings, as each of the pronouns **they** and **them** can refer to each of the sets that can be obtained by Abstraction from the duplex condition introduced by the first sentence.[34] Of all possible readings the most plausible one is that where **they** refers to the children who received a present from some director and **them** to the presents received. For good measure we give the DRS represented by this reading:

[34]Of course with the premise that **them** cannot pick up the same set as **they**, that **them** cannot be coreferential with **they** follows from the principles discussed in 3.1. Although we there restricted attention to singular NPs, exactly the same principles obtain for plurals, where the non-reflexive **them** contrasts with the reflexive **themselves**.

(4.116)

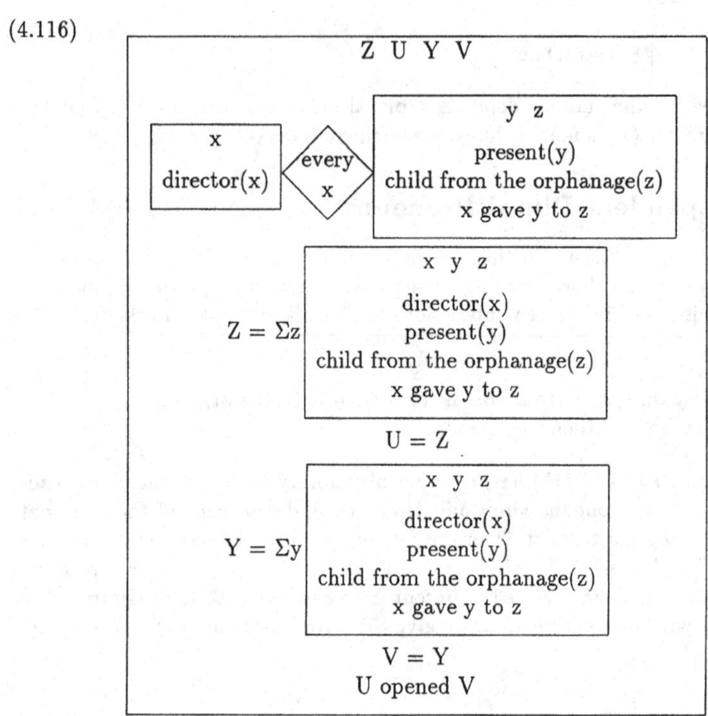

The reading on which we want to focus here is close to that represented by (4.116); but it is not quite that. (4.116) represents the children who got presents as having, as a group, opened the presents that were given to them. The reading in which we are interested is that according to which each child opened the present that was given specifically to him or her.

But are we really entitled to regard this as a separate *reading* of (4.115), distinct from the one represented in (4.116)? After all, it might be argued that each child opening her or his present is just one of the many ways in which the children as a group could go about opening the entire collection of presents the directors bestowed upon them? That there really is a separate reading according to which each child opens her or his own present is not so easy to see in relation to (4.115). However, the situation changes when we modify the example, as in

(4.117) Every director gave a present to a child from the orphanage.

(a) Two of them opened them.
(b) Few of them opened them.

(4.117.a) has a reading according to which two of the children opened all the presents. But it also has one according to which two children each opened their own presents, while all the other presents remained unopened. And for (4.117.b) the reading according to which few of the children opened their own presents seems to be the only reasonable one. (The alternative, according to which it was true of not many a child that it opened the presents, seems to imply that the presents could be opened repeatedly.)

Although these considerations do not strictly prove that a similar reading also exists for (4.115), we regard them as providing sufficient evidence. For it is hard to see how the strategies that yield such readings for (4.117.a) and (4.117.b) could be unavailable in connection with (4.115), which appears to be similar in all relevant respects.

In a DRS representing either of these readings the discourse referent introduced by **them** must be able to pick up different presents as values *in relation to* the corresponding children. For instance, the relevant reading of (4.117.a) is given by the DRS[35]

[35]The condition $\mathbf{V} \subseteq \mathbf{U}$ represents the *partitive* use of the preposition **of**: **two of them** means a set consisting of two elements drawn from the set denoted by **them**. We have decided not to include an explicit treatment of such partitive constructions in this book. (See Exercise 1 in Section 4.2.5.)

(4.118)

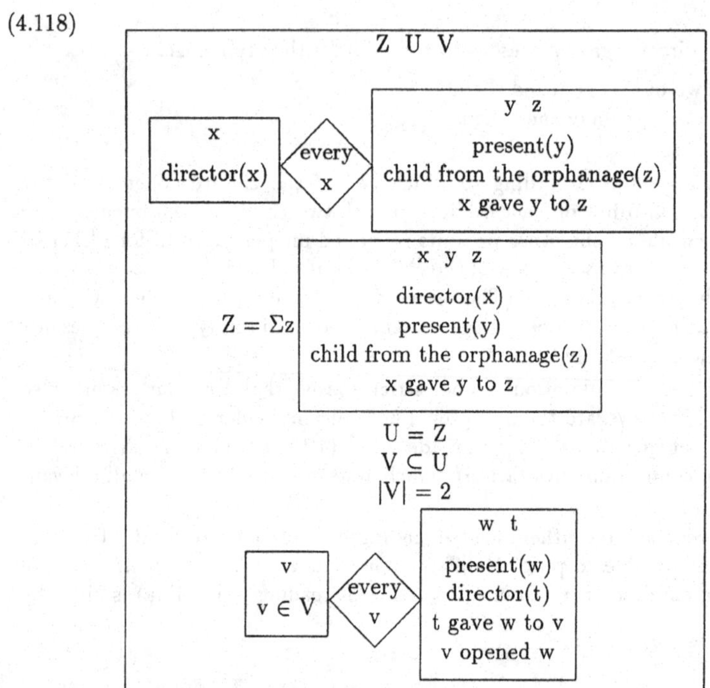

The DRS for the parallel reading of (4.115) is very much like (4.118), the only difference being that it does not contain a discourse referent like **V** and that the last duplex condition arises not through distribution over **V** but over **U**:

(4.119)

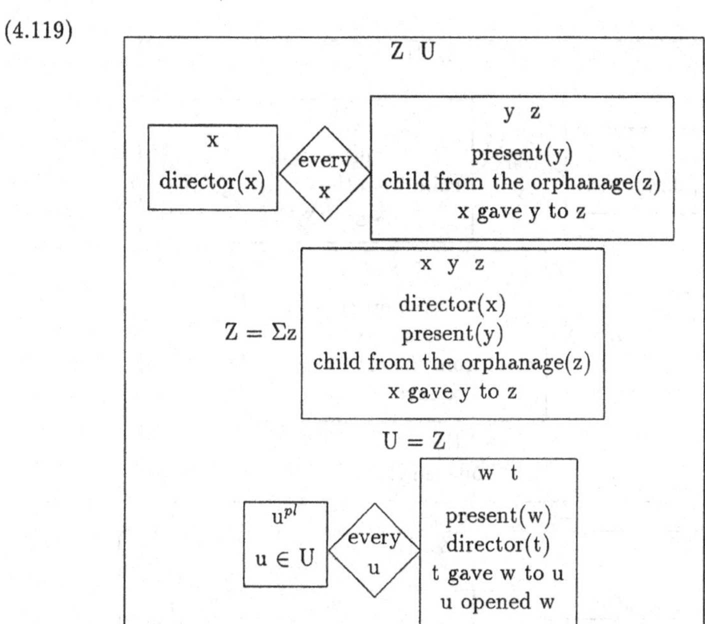

What construction principles could be responsible for the construction of DRSs such as (4.118) or (4.119) (or of other DRSs capturing these same readings)? Our proposal has several parts. The first is this:

When a set is introduced via Abstraction over some duplex condition δ, then the information contained in the constituent DRSs of δ is available as information concerning the members of that set. This means that when we distribute over such a set, the DRS occurring on the right-hand side of the Abstraction equation may be "copied" into the left-hand DRS of the duplex condition which the distribution operation introduces. Thus, having arrived at the stage, shown by (4.120) in the DRS-construction for (4.115), we may copy the DRS occurring on the right of the equation that begins with **Z** into the left-hand side of the new duplex condition. In this way we obtain a structure like (4.121).

(4.120)

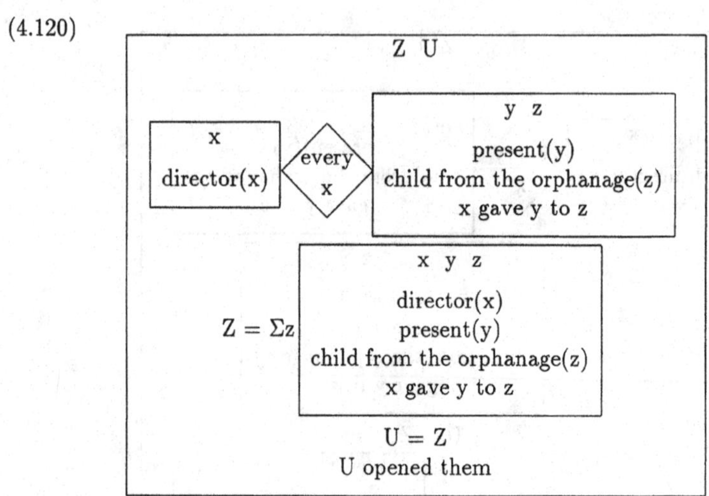
Z U
x
director(x)
every
x
y z
present(y)
child from the orphanage(z)
x gave y to z
x y z
director(x)
present(y)
child from the orphanage(z)
x gave y to z
Z = Σz
U = Z
U opened them

(4.121)

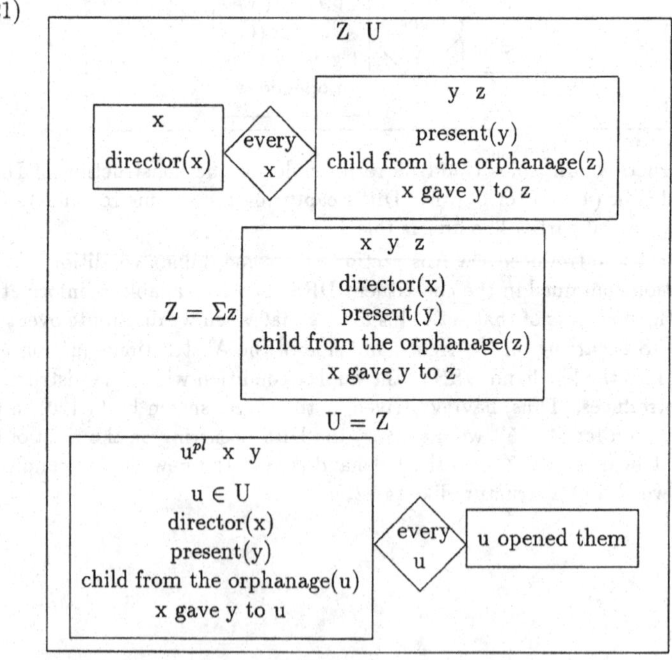
Z U
x
director(x)
every
x
y z
present(y)
child from the orphanage(z)
x gave y to z
x y z
director(x)
present(y)
child from the orphanage(z)
x gave y to z
Z = Σz
U = Z
u^pl x y
u ∈ U
director(x)
present(y)
child from the orphanage(u)
x gave y to u
every
u
u opened them

We now have a discourse referent – viz. **y** – which stands in the right relationship to **u**. So we obtain the intended reading provided we can use **y** as antecedent for the pronoun **them**. Unfortunately, however, we have no license to use **y** for this purpose. For, as it stands, **them** can pick up an individual discourse referent only when it is marked *pl*, and the **y** of (4.121) is not marked in this way. (Note in this connection that all NPs of the first sentence of (4.115) are singulars!)

Should **y** be so marked? To focus on this question, let us consider the following variants of (4.115):

(4.122) Every director gave a present to a child from the orphanage.

(a) Two of them opened it.
(b) One of them opened it.
(c) One of them opened them.

(4.122.a) and (4.122.b) both have a reading according to which the child or children in question opened the one present it or they were given. (4.122.c), however, cannot be so interpreted. Though it does have an interpretation according to which the value of the object NP **them** is a function of the value of the subject **one of them**, (i.e. where the object NP denotes the present or presents given to the child that acts as value for the subject), the pronoun is not neutral in this case; the child could not have received just one, but must have got several presents. Thus the plural morphology of the object NP **them** in (4.122.c) has the familiar semantics, that of representing a set with at least two members. That the object phrases of (4.115) and (4.117.a/b) do not have this impact must be related to the fact that in each of these texts the subject of the second sentence is in the plural and not in the singular.

If one assumes that it is indeed this which "neutralizes" the plurality of the pronoun **them** in these examples, the dependencies involving bare plurals which we studied in the preceding section may tempt us to suppose that the apparent dependence of object on subject in (4.115) and (4.117.a/b) is of the same making. For although there are evident differences between the bare plurals of the last section and the pronouns under discussion now, these differences seem explicable in terms of what we have learned about indefinite NPs and pronouns in the earlier chapters: Indefinites tend to convey that their values are *new* to the context in which they are used, whereas pronouns must take their values via identification with elements already established as part of the context. If these respective properties are also true of the pronouns and indefinite noun phrases discussed in this and the preceding section, then one would expect precisely what our examples seem to confirm: Both for the pronoun and for the indefinite NPs the semantic connotation of plurality is neutralized. In the case of the indefinite this means that the new entity introduced can be either an individual or a set; for the pronoun it means that either an individual or a set may be represented by the discourse referent with which it is linked.

Persuasive though this analogy may appear at first sight, this should not blind us to a crucial feature of the pronouns under discussion: They cannot pick up just any discourse referent, but only those which are themselves dependent on the discourse referent introduced for the NP on which the pronoun is taken to depend. Thus, to make an obvious point fully explicit, the second sentence of

(4.123) Every director gave a present to a child from the orphanage.
Two hated them.

could not possibly be interpreted as saying that two of the children hated the orphanage. So we must restrict the individual discourse referents which the pronoun in question can pick up and which do not come with the mark *pl* already to those that stand in some appropriate relation to the discourse referent for the individuals to which the values of the pronoun stand in the depending relation (in (4.121) this is the discourse referent **u**). It appears that the only discourse referents that qualify are those which stem from the universe of the copied DRS – in (4.121) these are **x** and **y**.

Having decided that this is how the new class of additional pronominal antecedents is to be restricted, we can, it would seem, round off the interpretation mechanism we need by stipulating that the individual (and neutral) discourse referents which get copied into a duplex condition when the defining part of an Abstraction equation is incorporated into its left-hand side, are all provided with the mark *pl*. The rule CR.PRO[Num = plur] will then permit the intended interpretation of the problematic pronouns.

Unfortunately this would let in too much, or so at least it seems to us. For consider

(4.124) Every director gave a present to a child from the orphanage.
Two of them found a teacher who opened them.

The question to be asked in relation to (4.124) is whether it has a reading on which it is true in case there were two children, Alice and Bennie, say, who found different teachers to open their respective presents. We do not think that (4.124) allows for such a reading.[36] If it doesn't have this reading, then the strategy just proposed which permits us to construct this very reading will give us more than it should.

The difference between (4.124) on the one hand and (4.115), (4.116) and (4.122) on the other is that in each of the latter passages **them** occurs in the same clause

[36]It does have a reading according to which one teacher opened both childrens' presents. See Exercise 1 in Section 4.2.6.

as the plural NP represented by the earlier *principal*[37] discourse referent of the duplex condition. (**They** in (4.115), **two of them** in (4.116)).

This is only part of the story. For consider

(4.125) Every director gave a present to a child from the orphanage.
Two found teachers who opened them.

Here it does seem possible to interpret the last sentence as saying that each of two children found a teacher who opened *its* present. The difference between (4.124) and (4.125) is that in (4.125) the plural of **them** is licensed by a plural NP in the same clause (viz. the relative pronoun **who**) which itself is dependent, via its connection with the object NP **teachers** of the main clause, on the NP represented by the principal discourse referent of the duplex condition.

The facts we have noted in relation to (4.124) and (4.125) imply:

(i) that we cannot simply mark the copied discourse referents (i.e. **x** and **y** in (4.121)) as *pl*; for this would make for instance **y** a possible antecedent for **them** in (4.124), something that ought to be avoided. We propose to mark those discourse referents *pl*(**u**) instead, indicating in this way that if a plural pronoun is to use such a discourse referent as antecedent, then it must stand in a special relationship to the discourse referent **u**, or to the NP α which **u** represents.

(ii) The relationship between pronoun and α may be direct, as it is in (4.115), (4.116) or (4.122), where α and the pronoun occur within the same clause; or it may be mediated, as in (4.125), by a plural NP on which the pronoun can be taken to depend and which itself is dependent on α. However, in either case the licencer must belong to the same clause.

To allow for the second possibility, we mark the neutral discourse referents introduced by intermediate NPs as *pl*(**u**), too. (They also receive, as neutral discourse referents introduced by plural NPs, the mark *pl*!) These new conventions lead to the following DRSs for (4.115) and (4.125), just before the final step – that of processing the relevant occurrence of **them** – is to occur. First, instead of (4.121) we now get

---

[37]See page 311.

(4.126)

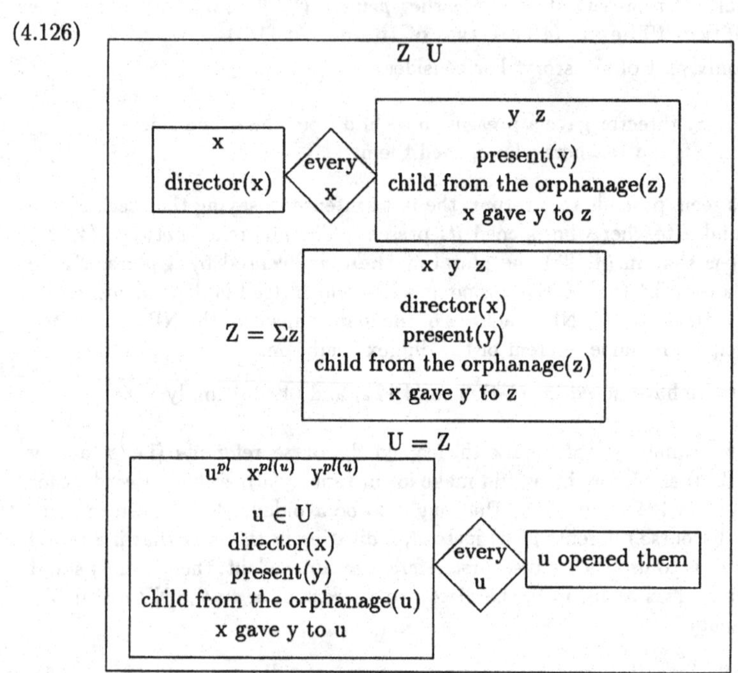
Z U
x
director(x)
every
x
y z
present(y)
child from the orphanage(z)
x gave y to z
x y z
director(x)
present(y)
child from the orphanage(z)
x gave y to z
Z = Σz
U = Z
u^pl x^pl(u) y^pl(u)
u ∈ U
director(x)
present(y)
child from the orphanage(u)
x gave y to u
every
u
u opened them

Similarly, (4.125) yields the DRS

(4.127)

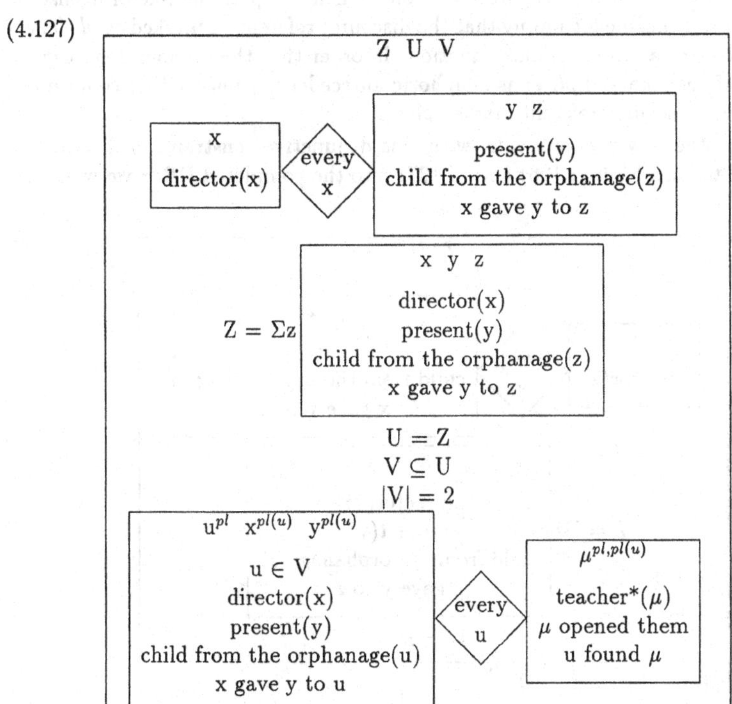

The contents of the left-hand DRSs of the lower duplex conditions in (4.126) and (4.127) show the effects of the new copying rule. Moreover, on the right-hand side of the duplex condition in (4.127) we find the neutral discourse referent μ introduced through processing **teachers** as a dependent plural. (The feature $pl(\mathbf{u})$ which decorates μ shows that CR.NP(Dep), the rule for dependent bare plurals, must be adjusted too: the discourse referent introduced must be marked not only as *pl*, but also as $pl(\alpha)$, where α is the discourse referent for the NP on which the bare plural is taken to depend.)

At last we are in a position to state the construction rule for plural pronouns that will give us the readings we have been after. The rule must enable us to process the pronoun in the intended way, with **y** serving as its antecedent, both in (4.126) and in (4.127). As in our statement of CR.NP(Dep), we express the constraint that the dependent plural and the NP on which it depends belong to the same clause, by requiring that the condition γ as part of which the pronoun is processed also contains the discourse referent representing the licensing NP. This discourse referent must be recognizable as one which can play the role of licenser. In CR.NP(Dep) this meant simply that the discourse referent be marked as *pl*. The present rule faces a more complex situation: In order that the pronoun may use a discourse referent marked $pl(\alpha)$ as anaphoric antecedent, γ must either contain α itself or else a discourse referent marked $pl(\alpha)$.

Applying the new pronoun rule, with this disjunctive constraint on licencers, we are able to turn both (4.126) and (4.127) into the completed DRSs we want:

(4.128)

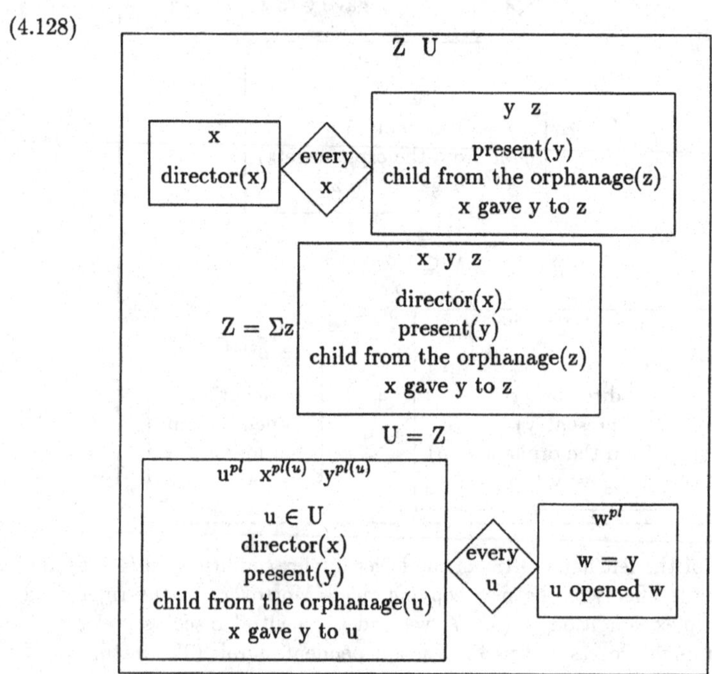

(4.129)

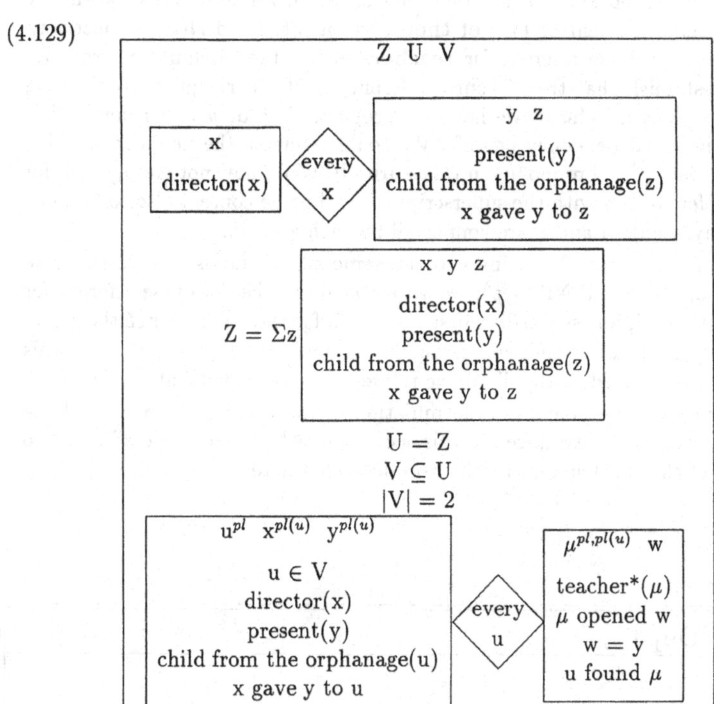

There is one further complication we should mention. The phenomenon we have studied in this section is not limited to cases such as (4.125), where there is one intermediate NP; it also occurs in cases with two or more such intermediaries. Examples of such cases become a little strained because of the cumulation of subordinate clauses. But they can be constructed, and do seem to allow for the relevant readings. Here is one.

(4.130) Every director gave a present to a child from the orphanage. Two of them found teachers who had knives which were sharp enough to cut the strings with which they were tied.

In (4.130) there are no less than three intermediaries, **teachers, knives, the strings.**[38] The procedure we have stated has the effect of marking the discourse

[38]Definite plurals can act as dependent plurals, too. This is a matter we do not want to

referents for the second and third of these not as $pl(\mathbf{u})$, where $\mathbf{u}$ is once again the discourse referent representing **two of them**, but as $pl(\mu)$ and $pl(\nu)$, respectively, where μ is the discourse referent for **teachers** and ν the discourse referent for **knives**. To establish that the discourse referent for **the strings**, π say, licenses $\mathbf{y}^{pl(\mu)}$ as antecedent for **them**, we have to recognize that $\mathbf{u}$, μ and ν form what might be called a "dependency chain". We could rephrase the new construction rule for dependent plural pronouns in this spirit: It would now not simply look for a discourse referent in γ with the superscript $pl(\mathbf{u})$, but be content also to find one with $pl(\nu)$, say, where $\mathbf{u}$ and ν are connected by such a chain.

We opt for a solution that comes to the same thing, but is a little easier to state: When applying CR.NP(Dep), we attach $pl(\mathbf{u})$ to the discourse referent for the dependent plural, unless the discourse referent $\mathbf{u}$ for the NP on which the plural is taken to depend bears itself a superscript of the form $pl(s)$. If it does, then this superscript is transferred to the discourse referent for the dependent plural.

We conclude this section with a formulation in the familiar format of all the rules which were either introduced in this section, or which had to be adjusted to fit the needs of the construction mechanism described here.

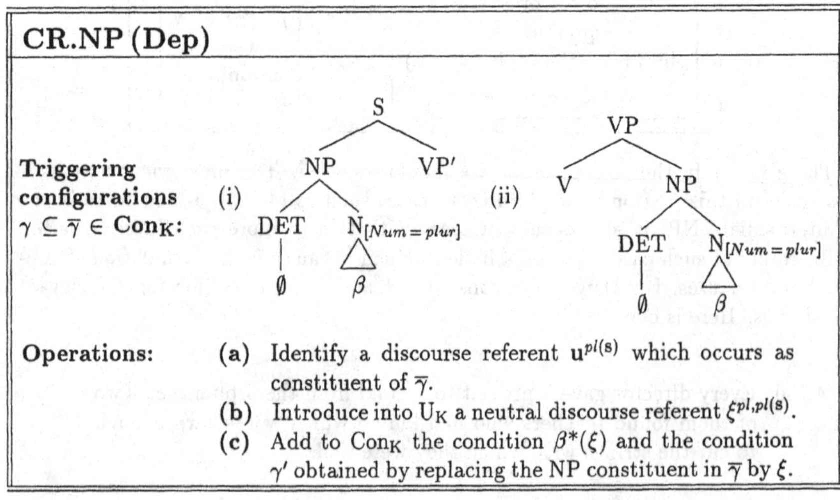

elaborate here. But see Exercise 7 in Section 4.2.5.

CR.NP (Dep)
Triggering configurations $\gamma \subseteq \overline{\gamma} \in \mathrm{Con_K}$:
(i)
S
NP
VP'
DET
$N_{[Num=plur]}$
$\emptyset$
β
(ii)
VP
V
NP
DET
$N_{[Num=plur]}$
$\emptyset$
β
Operations:
(a) Identify a discourse referent $\mathbf{u}^{pl(s)}$ which occurs as constituent of $\overline{\gamma}$.
(b) Introduce into U_K a neutral discourse referent $\xi^{pl,pl(s)}$.
(c) Add to $\mathrm{Con_K}$ the condition $\beta^*(\xi)$ and the condition γ' obtained by replacing the NP constituent in $\overline{\gamma}$ by ξ.

CR.DA (Rule for distribution over a set obtained by Abstraction)

Triggering configuration $K' \subseteq K$:

$Z \ Z_1 \ \dots \ Z_n \ U$

$Z = \Sigma z$: [$z \ \xi_1 \ \dots \ \xi_m$ | γ_1 ⋮ γ_n]

$Z_1 = Z \ ; \ Z_2 = Z_1 \ ; \ \dots \ ; \ U = Z_n$

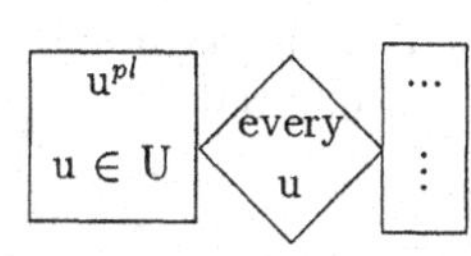

Operations: Then the duplex condition

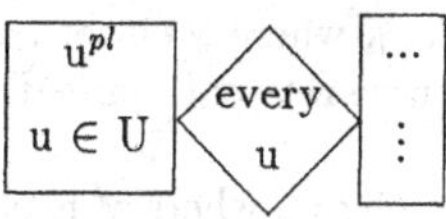

may be replaced by

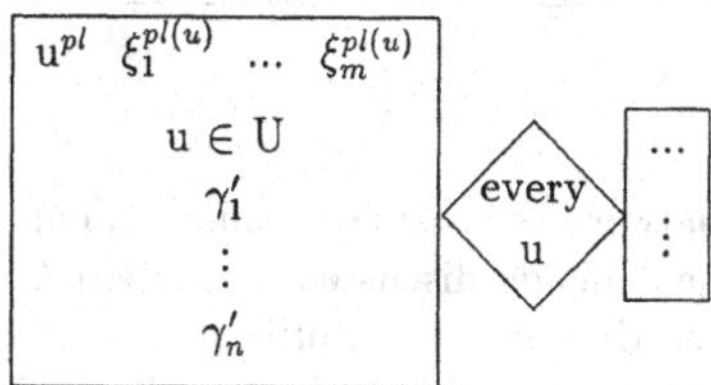

where γ_i' results from γ by replacing **z** throughout by **u**.

CR.PRO [Num = plur]

Triggering configurations $\gamma \subseteq \overline{\gamma} \in \text{Con}_K$:

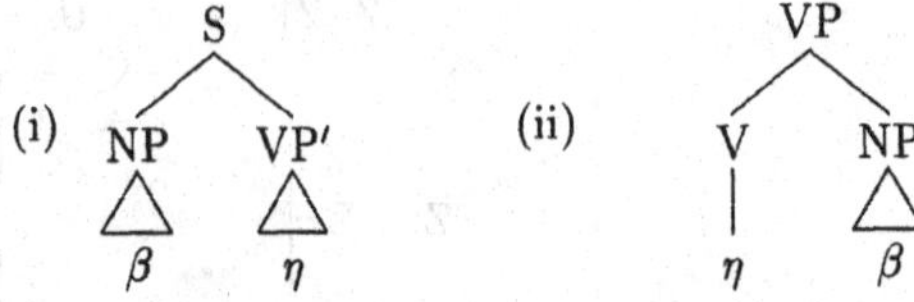

Operations:

(a) Introduce a plural discourse referent ξ into U_K.

(b) Add to Con_K a condition of the form $\xi = \alpha$ where α is a discourse referent accessible from the position of the pronoun and either

(i) α is an available non-individual discourse referent;

or

(ii) α is an individual discourse referent marked *pl*;

or

(iii) α is an individual discourse referent marked $pl(u)$, where $\overline{\gamma}$ either contains **u** itself or a discourse referent marked $pl(u)$

(c) Replace $\overline{\gamma}$ by γ', where γ' is obtained through substitution of ξ for the processed NP.

Exercises

1. One difference between the cases of pronominal anaphora studied in this section and the phenomenon discussed in Section 4.2.4 is that the latter only involves pronouns that are obligatorily plural, whereas this is not generally the case for the instances of pronominal anaphora discussed in the present section. This is shown for instance, by (4.122): To the plural **them** of (4.122.c) (4.122.b) offers **it** as an alternative.

   (i) Show, by constructing appropriate DRSs, that (4.122.a) and (4.122.b) both admit of readings that are parallel to the reading of (4.117.a) which is given by the DRS (4.119). Describe in detail how the relevant construction rule is applied to **it**, and how this application differs from the processing of **them** in (4.122.c).

2. We observed that (4.124) does not have the reading which (4.127) assigns to (4.125). However, it does have at least two other readings. According to the first, two of the children who received a present found a teacher who opened all the presents; according to the second, two of the children who received a present found a teacher who opened the two presents those two children had received.

   (ii) Construct for each of these two readings a DRS that captures it.

   (iii) Does (4.124) have any additional readings? If so, construct DRSs for these too.

4.2.7 Generic Interpretations of Plural Pronouns

The principles of Summation and Abstraction are not the only possible means of creating antecedents for plural pronouns. We won't try to give an exhaustive list of those means. But there is one construction principle besides the two we have already considered which merits a brief discussion. It is illustrated by the following example.

(4.131) Few women from this village came to the feminist rally. No wonder.
They don't like political rallies very much.

According to our present rules the only available interpretation for **they** in (4.131) would be the (small) set of women from the village who came to the rally. But this is not the interpretation that naturally comes to mind. The sense in which one is inclined to interpret (4.131) is that where **they** refers to women in general, or perhaps to the women of this village. Thus, **they** is interpreted as referring to a certain 'genus', explicitly mentioned in the text by a simple or complex noun (here: either the simple **women** or the complex **women from this village**). Such nouns act much like names, not proper names of persons, cities, etc (such as **Susan** or **New Orleans**) but as "common names", i.e. as names of genera or species. That they do act as names is indicated among other things by their behaviour as anaphoric antecedents. Consider, for instance, the following two-sentence discourse.

(4.132) If at least one chicken which Ottilie owns has laid an egg, she had
a nice breakfast. They are very good to eat.

The first sentence of (4.132) gives rise to a DRS of the form:

(4.133)

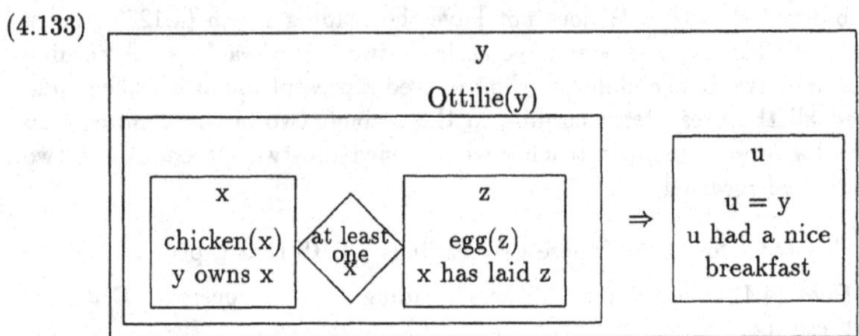

If we apply Abstraction to the duplex condition of (4.133), we obtain a new discourse referent – representing the set of eggs laid by Ottilie's chickens – in the universe of the antecedent of the ⇒ condition. This discourse referent is not accessible from the position of the subject **they** of the next sentence. Indeed, this impossibility appears to agree with intuition: **they** cannot be understood as referring to the set of eggs laid. Nor is this surprising, for after all (so intuitive reasoning would go) the last sentence does not tell us that any eggs were laid; it only speaks about the *possibility* of some having been laid. The interpretation of **they** which *is* available is that where it refers to eggs in general or perhaps to eggs of the kind laid by Ottilie's chickens, or by that kind of chicken. Let us focus on the first of these interpretations, according to which **they** refers to eggs in general. This interpretation is possible because the noun **egg** names the genus 'egg'. Translated into the terms in which we have been dealing with proper names in Chapters 1 and 3, the noun establishes a discourse referent for the genus within the universe of the main DRS. For the sake of simplicity we will represent genera by non-individual discourse referents.[39]. However, we are in no position to discuss the complex issues connected with the question what sorts of entities genera, or 'kinds' really are. Thus (4.133) can be extended to the DRS

[39]Such a representation is not really tenable, as genera are not simply sets

(4.134)

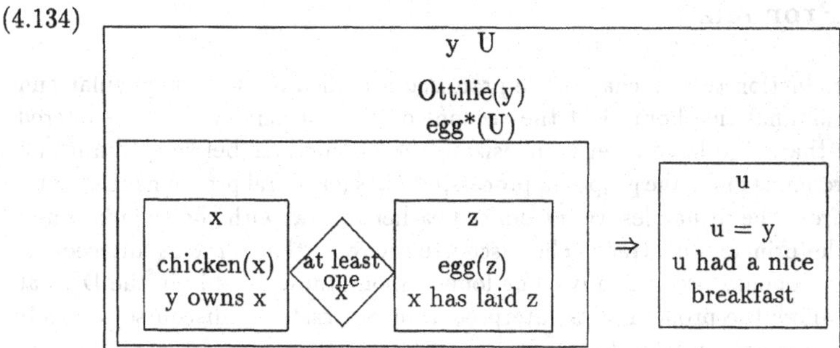

The discourse referent **U** can then be exploited in the processing of the pronoun **they** of the following sentence. We leave the completion of the DRS to the reader.

Constructing representations for the other interpretations of (4.131), such as the one where **they** is interpreted as 'eggs laid by Ottilie's chickens' is more complicated. For the first sentence of (4.132) does not contain any single phrase of category N which can be so paraphrased. Rather, a complex predicate to this effect has to be constructed from bits of the sentence which do not all belong to one and the same noun phrase. It is no easy question – and it is one we will not further pursue – precisely when a discourse referent may be created from material scattered throughout a sentence or text. The rule below ignores the possibility of such constructions, and further research will have to determine how it should be modified so that it also covers the more complex cases exemplified by (4.132).[40]

Explicit Representation of Genera	
Triggering configurations $\gamma \in \mathbf{Con_K}$:	Suppose γ is of the form $\beta(\mathrm{x})$, where β is of category N.
Operations:	Introduce into the universe of the main DRS K a new non-individual discourse referent **U** while introducing into $\mathrm{Con_{K'}}$ the condition $\beta^*(\mathbf{U})$.

[40]We have not yet explained what – in the following rule – β^* means when β is complex. Intuitively the meaning of the '$*$' here is the same as when it is applied to a lexical predicate such as **book** or **unhappy**.

4.2.8 A Uniform Theory of Singular and Plural Pronouns?

In the introduction to this chapter we promised a unified account of singular and plural pronominal anaphora. But the account of plural pronouns we have offered is not like that. We have been emphasizing the distinctions between plural and singular pronouns and have proposed processing rules for plural pronouns that differ markedly from the principles we introduced earlier to deal with the singular ones. To recall the principal contrast: The discourse referents that serve as antecedents to singular pronouns are typically to be found among those already in the DRS at the point where the pronoun gets interpreted; in contrast, the discourse referents needed in the interpretation of plural pronouns are often not present when they are required, and so must be "synthesized" from other discourse referents which can be found in the DRS at that point. Connected with this distinction is another one. The discourse referents that act as antecedents for singular pronouns represent almost invariably the semantic values of other NPs (viz. those which introduced those discourse referents). Consequently, it is possible (or almost possible) to describe singular pronoun anaphora as a relation between pairs of noun phrases. In contrast, since the antecedents of plural pronouns are often synthesized from the discourse referents of several NPs, describing plural anaphora as a binary relation between NPs is out of the question.

Is there any way of reconciling the apparently diverging behaviour of singular and plural anaphoric pronouns? There would seem to be no hope of doing this as long as one holds on to the conception that anaphora is a relation between an anaphoric expression (i.e. plural or singular pronoun) and another one of similar type (viz. another NP). But if we are prepared to abandon that conception, and to take our clues from the plural rather than the singular case, then the road is free towards a more unified account. The key is the observation that all the rules which create antecedents for plural pronouns out of other discourse referents are "cumulative" in the following sense: The newly created discourse referent represents an entity of which the discourse referents used in the application of the rule represent (atomic or non-atomic) parts. These parts, moreover, are *proper* parts of the collection, either by logical necessity (as in the case of Summation) or as a matter of presupposition (as in the case of Abstraction and of anaphoric reference to kinds). In other words, the entity represented by the new discourse referent is, by necessity or implication, non-atomic. The grammatical fact that only plural pronouns can pick up such synthesized discourse referents as antecedents follows therefore from the principle that was our starting point in this chapter:

(4.135) Only plural pronouns can refer to non-atomic entities.

To put the matter differently, the rules of Summation, Abstraction and Kind Introduction are as readily available in the case of singular as in that of plural pronoun anaphora, but the very nature of what these rules introduce makes them otiose in connection with the interpretation of singular pronouns. The semantic constraint that (4.135) imposes on singular pronouns makes that only a discourse referent which has been introduced as representative of another NP can serve as antecedent to a singular pronoun (and then only if what this NP is taken to represent is atomic also).

Attractive though this way of accounting for both the similarities and differences between singular and plural pronouns may be, we have become acquainted with too broad a spectrum of anaphoric data to embrace it unhesitatingly. There is in particular one salient fact about plural pronoun anaphora which does not fit the account just outlined. This is the fact, discussed at length in Section 4.4, that plural pronouns can be used to represent individuals; in such cases, we argued, the pronoun's plurality is licensed (in fact, it is required) by the plurality of its grammatical antecedent.

But isn't there perhaps another way of looking at such cases of plural pronoun anaphora? It is tempting to try and explain the use of morphologically plural pronouns in such cases also in terms of principle (4.135). This might not appear unreasonable at first sight, for there is a sense in which even such pronouns can be considered to refer to entities obtained by abstraction over the discourse referent that our treatment of such cases identifies as its antecedent. Consider, for instance, the sentence

(4.136) If the lawyers have won, they go on holiday.

This sentence has a reading according to which each of the lawyers goes on holiday if he has won. Our algorithm obtains this reading by first introducing a discourse referent **X** to represent the set of lawyers, then distributing over **X** - an operation which introduces an individual discourse referent **x** to represent the individual members of the set - and then using **x** as antecedent for the pronoun **they**. Let us remind ourselves of the result of these operations:

(4.137)

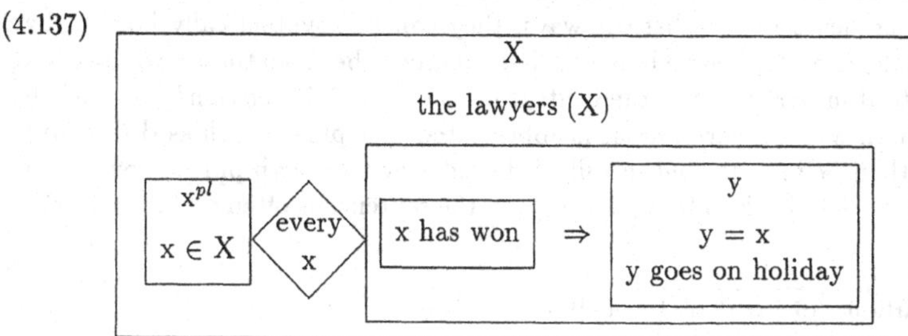

We might restate the principle behind the last step in the construction of (4.137) – which leads to the introduction of the duplex condition – as follows. Strictly speaking, we might say, the pronoun **they** refers to the set of lawyers, and its plurality is thus explained by the fact that it refers to a set and not to an individual. However, the intended interpretation entails that we distribute over this set, and moreover that this distribution "covaries" with the distribution over the set of lawyers that is represented by the discourse referent **X**. This last requirement is reminiscent of what we saw in Section 4.2.6, where we discovered the need for enriching the distributive interpretation of a set that was obtained by abstraction by adding the DRS over which Abstraction was carried out.

But how could a similar strategy work out in the present case? In order to make it work, we would need a rule that would allow us to do Abstraction on the very DRS-condition in which the pronoun we want to interpret occurs. But Abstraction in this context would violate the non-circularity principle, that was invoked in 4.2.4 (p. 354) to explain the impossibility of interpreting **they** in

(4.138) Few lawyers hired a secretary they liked.

as referring to the small set of lawyers who hired secretaries they liked. In the light of this difficulty the possibility of giving a truly uniform account of plural pronoun anaphora, in which all plural pronouns are analysed as having sets for their semantic values, evaporates. The requirement of number agreement which governs those plural pronouns that act as individual variables (i.e. that must be interpreted as introducing individual discourse referents) appears to be a constraint that cannot be reduced in any plausible way to something like principle (4.135).

The problem we have just discussed has to do with plural pronouns. However, even within the exclusive domain of singular pronouns there may be difficulties for a uniform account; or so at least some linguists have argued. The view of singular pronoun anaphora which causes problems for such a uniform theory is one we have not yet mentioned so far, even though it relates closely to one of the central topics of this book. According to this view[41] singular pronouns can relate to their antecedents in two distinct ways; they can be "syntactically bound" by their antecedents or "discourse bound". The difference between these two relations manifests itself in particular in the context of so-called "VP-deletion", an English construction in which a verb phrase is abbreviated by a phrase such as **did** or **did so**, rather than being repeated in full. If the abbreviated verb phrase contains a pronoun that refers back to the subject, then the sentence is often ambiguous. For instance,

[41] See in particular [Reinhart 1983a] and [Roberts 1987a].

(4.139) Bill bought a present for his aunt and so did Fred.

has two interpretations, one according to which Fred bought a present for Bill's aunt and one according to which he bought a present for his own (i.e. Fred's) aunt. For reasons that do not matter here these two readings have become known as the "strict" and the "sloppy" reading, respectively. The proposal of [Reinhart 1983a] is that the strict reading of (4.139) results when the pronoun in the first conjunct is interpreted as discourse bound by **Bill** and the sloppy one when the pronoun is construed as syntactically bound. Syntactic binding, but not discourse binding, is supposed to be subject to quite strict constraints on the positional relationship between pronoun and antecedent, a claim which predicts that sloppy readings are often not available where strict readings are.

We decided against discussing this view of pronominal anaphora in depth because it would have meant going into a quantity of syntactic detail, which we have made it our policy to avoid. Nonetheless we felt the position should be mentioned in the context of the present discussion. For if it is correct, then there is no hope for a uniform treatment of anaphoric pronouns irrespective of how we may want to deal with the specific problems of plurality.

4.3 Model Theory

There are many problems relating to plural anaphora that still await discussion. But before we tackle these it is advisable to first consider another question: What are the truth conditions for the DRSs we have been constructing in this chapter so far.

As in Chapters 1 and 2 the question has two parts:

(a) What are the models like, relative to which these DRSs should be evaluated?

and

(b) What are the verification conditions for the different types of conditions which may occur in these DRSs?

We start with question (a), which will occupy us throughout Section 4.3.1.

4.3.1 Models

4.3.1.1 Set Theory and Lattices

The DRSs of this chapter differ from those of Chapters 1–3 in that they may contain discourse referents of different *semantic types* – discourse referents that represent individuals, discourse referents that represent collections of individuals and discourse referents that could represent either. When such a DRS is embedded in a model, the discourse of the second kind must, and those of the third category may be mapped onto collections of individuals. So our models must now make collections available as targets for the embedding functions.

But what is a collection? One way in which this notion could be made precise is in terms of the mathematical concept of *set*. To clarify the concept of a set has been one of the central concerns of formal logic. In the second half of the last and the first half of the present century mathematical logicians developed a variety of theories of the concept of a set, theories which not only try to answer the question 'What is a set?', but also to ascertain in detail how the universe of sets is structured and how many sets there are.[42] Among these set theories there is one which has come to be widely acknowledged as the most satisfactory analysis of the set concept as it is used within mathematics. It was developed by the German mathematician Ernst Zermelo in the early years of this century, and subsequently developed further by the German-Israeli mathematician Abraham A. Fraenkel. In honour of these two parents it is known as *Zermelo-Fraenkel Set Theory*, or simply as ZF. Nowadays ZF (or alternatively an extension of it developed by Kurt Gödel and Paul Bernays usually called GB) is the theory of sets that is presupposed in almost all mathematical discourse in which sets play a role.

It is a notable feature of ZF and GB that they distinguish sharply between sets and the objects those sets contain as members. In particular, they treat an object a and the set $\{\mathsf{a}\}$ that has a for its one and only member as different objects. Thus, starting with a universe U_0 of individuals, one gets, first, a second universe U_1, consisting of all sets whose members are individuals and which contains, among others, the singleton set $\{\mathsf{a}\}$ for each a in U_0. At the next level matters become more complex, as here we will have not only sets whose members are sets of individuals but also "mixed" sets, some of whose members are individuals while other members are sets themselves – a simple example is the set $\{\{\mathsf{a}\}, \mathsf{a}\}$, which has as members (i) the object a and (ii) the set whose only member is a.

Thus the full theories of ZF and GB give us far more than corresponds to our present needs.[43]

[42] To this second question no fully satisfactory answer has yet been given, and it seems increasingly unlikely that a conclusive answer ever will be given.

[43] The situation changes when one moves to the study of natural language fragments which

It has been argued that a theory of sets such as ZF not only gives us far more than we really need, but that moreover it gives us what we do need in not quite the right form. There are two points on which the account that ZF offers of sets and of how they are related to the individuals contained in them does not seem to be with the ways in which ordinary singular and plural NPs function. On both points the tension arises from the strict typological distinction between individuals and sets which the set-theoretical conception of ZF regards as central. The first point concerns the neutral discourse referents, which we found we needed in order to account for dependent plurals. As we saw, such discourse referents must sometimes be allowed to be mapped onto sets and sometimes onto individuals. This seems to imply that natural language does not treat individuals and sets of individuals as irreconcilably distinct categories, but rather as subcategories of a single overarching category. The second point has to do with the distinction between individuals and singleton sets on which, we noted, ZF insists. If we consider the range of denotations of non-quantifying singular and plural NPs, we do not find any evidence for this distinction: A singular NP such as **this table** denotes a single table, **the two tables** denotes some set consisting of two tables, and the NP **the tables** will denote a set consisting of some number n of tables where $n \geq 2$. But no NP involving the noun **table** – whether it be plural or singular – appears to denote a set consisting of a single table, as opposed to simply denoting that table. So, if we think of what there is in terms of what can be denoted by singular and plural NPs, we are led to conclude that there are no singleton sets.

It was partly for such reasons that [Link 1983] proposed a semantics for singulars and plurals which is not based on a settheoretical universe such as the one described by ZF. Instead he proposed that individuals and sets be seen as entities of the same type, which differ from each other only in that individuals are *indivisible* or *atomic* members of this single domain, while the "sets" of two or more members are *non-atomic* or *divisible* entities. Roughly an entity counts as divisible if it can be decomposed into parts which answer the same description. Thus consider an entity that satisfies the predicate **sand** – in other words, some quantity of sand, such as a heap of sand. This entity can be divided into smaller portions which will also qualify as **sand**: they will be smaller quantities – smaller heaps – of sand. Much the same applies to entities we usually describe as sets, groups or collections. Consider for instance a collection of books. It too can be decomposed into smaller

---

include not only plural NPs, but also singular NPs denoting groups or sets, such as, say, **the committee to elect the President**, or **a set of natural numbers**. The plurals of such NPs – e.g. **all sets of natural numbers**, **several committees** etc. – denote collections of collections. A closer look, moreover, shows that along these lines we can form terms denoting entities from a complex hierarchy, of which the individuals and the sets of individuals only form the bottom tiers. These more comprehensive fragments will not be considered in this book. Their model theory has been studied by a number of people – see in particular [Hoeksema 1983], [Link 1984], [Lasersohn 1988], [Lønning 1989].

parts, which answer to the description **book** – they will either be collections of books or individual books from the original collection.

It is a widely accepted view that the denotations of plural count nouns (**books, stones, clouds, words, ...**) differ from those of mass nouns (**sand, water, money, information, ...**)[44] in that the former, but not the latter, can be decomposed into indivisible parts of the same description. Thus, a collection of books has a (unique) decomposition into the individual parts, viz. the books that make up the collection, but there is no obvious way in which the water in the glass on the table in front of you could be divided into "minimal" portions of water. Evidently this is not a distinction that holds in a strict and literal sense. For instance, a heap of sand would appear to have a unique decomposition into atomic parts no less than a heap of stones – viz. that which decomposes it into grains of sand that make up the heap. Even the denotations of a noun like **water**, i.e. quantities of water such as, say, the water in the glass – seem to allow for a unique partition into smallest parts that are water, viz. the water molecules which constitute the given quantity.

Such examples show the claim that the denotata of plural count nouns can be decomposed into indivisible parts, while those of mass nouns cannot, to have only a *conceptual* validity. We language users tend to think of the denotata of plural count nouns as divisible in this sense, and of the denotata of mass nouns as resisiting such a decomposition, although we know (through common sense or natural science) that for the denotata of mass nouns division must eventually come to an end, too.[45]

One way of articulating this difference is to say that the denotata of NPs containing count nouns are composed of *atoms* – "minimal" elements that cannot be partitioned into smaller elements of the same kind – whereas the denotata of NPs involving mass nouns are not so composed. The model proposed in the paper [Link 1983] which we cited above provide a semantics for mass as well as count nouns. In these models the extensions of (singular and plural) count nouns are distinguished from the extensions of mass nouns precisely in that the former are

---

[44]Mass nouns and count nouns differ syntactically in that only the former occur in the singular without an article. Thus we can say **Water was in short supply** or **Money talks**, but we can't say **Book was interesting** or **Sentence was grammatical**. In **Water was in short supply** and **Money talks water** and **money** have the grammatical status of NPs (they are the subjects of their respective sentences). Such NPs show striking similarities with bare plurals, such as **dollars** in **Dollars no longer buy everything** or **potatoes** in **Potatoes were in short supply**.

[45]That the distinction between mass and count nouns cannot be an absolute one is also demonstrated by pairs of count and mass nouns such as **pebbles** and **gravel** or nouns such as **beliefs** or **knowledge**, as much as by the fact that some languages express by means of a plural count noun what others denote with the help of a mass noun. (Compare German **Gemüse** with English **vegetable**.)

built out of atoms, while the latter are not. In the present chapter we ignore mass nouns. Accordingly we retain from Link's model only the parts that correspond to count nouns. These parts are "atomic" in the sense just alluded to: Each count noun α has an extension which exists (i) of atoms - i.e. things that belong to the extension of α but cannot be subdivided into parts that also belong to the extension of α (these are the entities in the extension of the singular form of α); and (ii) non-atoms, entities that - again in the sense just alluded to - belong to the extension of the plural form of α and which can be decomposed, in a unique way, into atoms all of which belong to the extension of α. Thus the atoms are what we earlier termed the indivisible entities, and the non-atoms are the divisible ones. Henceforth we shall use these terms interchangeably, but with a preference for *atom* (or *atomic*) and *non-atom* (or *non-atomic*).

We will see below that the parts of Link's models that we will use are quite easily converted into models based on the first two tiers of the hierarchy described by ZF. So there is, from a formal point of view, not too much to choose between these two approaches. Nevertheless we have opted for Link's approach as it does seem to correspond more naturally to the way we speak, and because it promises a smoother integration into a semantic analysis which takes mass nouns as well as count nouns into account.

Domains of entities structured by a part-whole relation belong to a class of abstract mathematical structures known under the name of *upper semilattices. Lattice theory*, the mathematical theory which studies the class of structures to which these belong, has grown into a complex branch of modern algebra, but we will need only the rudiments of this theory here.

Definition 4.3.1

An *upper semilattice* is a structure $\mathcal{A} = \langle \mathsf{A}, \subset \rangle$, where A is a set of entities and '$\subset$' is a partial order of A - i.e. a binary relation such that for all $\mathsf{a}, \mathsf{b}, \mathsf{c} \in \mathsf{A}$:

(A1) $\mathsf{a} \subset \mathsf{a}$ (**REF**lexivity)

(A2) $\mathsf{a} \subset \mathsf{b}\ \&\ \mathsf{b} \subset \mathsf{c} \rightarrow \mathsf{a} \subset \mathsf{c}$ (**TRANS**itivity)

(A3) $\mathsf{a} \subset \mathsf{b}\ \&\ \mathsf{b} \subset \mathsf{a} \rightarrow \mathsf{a} = \mathsf{b}$ (**ANTIS**ymmetry),

with the following additional property that for all $\mathsf{a}, \mathsf{b} \in \mathsf{A}$

(A4) $(\exists \mathsf{c} \in \mathsf{A})\ (\mathsf{a} \subset \mathsf{c}\ \&\ \mathsf{b} \subset \mathsf{c}\ \&\ (\forall \mathsf{d} \in \mathsf{A})\ ((\mathsf{a} \subset \mathsf{d}\ \&\ \mathsf{b} \subset \mathsf{d}) \rightarrow \mathsf{c} \subset \mathsf{d}))$
(**L**east **U**pper **B**ound)

The first postulate, (A1), says that every entity is a part of itself. This may seem counterintuitive in view of the way in which we have been using the term 'part' so far, a part of something always was a "proper" part of it, and thus distinct from the entity of which it is a part. (A1) stipulates that the part relation represented in upper semilattices is one which also holds between any entity and itself. Thus the "parts" of any entity e are the proper parts of e as well as e itself.

(A2) says that a part of a part of e is again a part of e. (A3) expresses the intuition that if a is a proper part of b then b cannot at the same time be a proper part of a: the combination of 'a is part of b' and 'b is part of a' is possible only when the part relation is improper in both directions, i.e. when a and b are identical. (A4), finally, says that for any two entities a and b there is an entity c, of which both a and b are parts and which, moreover, is itself a part of precisely those entities that both a and b are part of. Each of these postulates is clearly true of the part-whole relation which concerns us, a relation involving only individuals and collections of individuals and according to which individuals have no proper parts, and collections of individuals have as parts only those individuals themselves and the subcollections that can be formed from them.

In lattice theory the object c postulated by (A4) is called *the supremum.* In the application we intend here, it corresponds to what we have already been calling 'the sum of a and b' and have denoted as '$a \oplus b$'. The use of the definite description (c.q. *the* supremum) is justified, because (A3) guarantees that the c is unique: For suppose c and c′ both satisfy the condition of (A4). Then, since $a \subset c$ and $b \subset c$ and c′ has the property $(\forall d)\,(a \subset d \;\&\; b \subset d) \rightarrow c' \subset d)$, it follows that $c' \subset c$. Similarly, $c \subset c'$, and so by (A3) $c = c'$. The uniqueness of the supremum c of a and b permits us to think of the association of c with a and b which (A4) establishes as a function, which maps pairs of elements a, b to their corresponding sums. The next definition makes this explicit.

Definition 4.3.2

Suppose $\mathcal{A} = \langle A, \subset \rangle$ is an upper semilattice. For all $a, b \in A$ the element denoted by $a \oplus b$ is the unique c such that

(i) $a \subset c$,
(ii) $b \subset c$ and
(iii) $(\forall d)\,(a \subset d \;\&\; b \subset d \rightarrow c \subset d)$

The concept of supremum is applicable not only to pairs a, b of lattice elements, but more generally to sets of them.

Definition 4.3.3

Suppose $\mathcal{A} = \langle A, \subset \rangle$ is an upper semilattice. Suppose B is a subset of A. b *is the supremum* of B (*in* $\langle A, \subset \rangle$) iff

(i) $(\forall x \in B)\,(x \subset b)$ and
(ii) $(\forall d \in A)\,(((\forall x \in B)\, x \subset d) \rightarrow b \subset d)$

By the same reasoning as above one shows that when such a b exists, it is unique. When b exists, we denote it as $\oplus$ B.

It is easily shown that $\oplus$ B always exists when B is finite. But if B is infinite, this need not be so (Exercise 1, p. 417).

An upper semilattice $\langle A, \subset \rangle$ such that $\oplus$ B exists for all $B \subseteq A$ is called *complete*. A complete upper semilattice $\mathcal{A}$ always has a largest element, viz. $\oplus$ A. Such a largest element a – with the property that $x \subset a$ for all $x \in A$ – is also called a *one* (*of* the upper semilattice). Similarly, by a *zero of* $\mathcal{A}$ we mean an element z of A such that for all $b \in A$, $z \subset b$. Completeness does not guarantee the existence of a zero. However, by the same reasoning we used to show that suprema are unique, we easily establish that each upper semilattice has at most one zero. Thus we have:

Theorem 1: Each upper semilattice has at most one one and at most one zero.

We denote the one of $\mathcal{A}$ (if it exists) as $1_{\mathcal{A}}$, and its zero (if it exists) as $0_{\mathcal{A}}$.

In our analysis of singular and plural we will be making use of upper semilattices which are complete and thus are guaranteed to have a one. We will also assume that each of these upper semilattices has a zero. Henceforth then, each upper semilattice A we will consider has elements $1_{\mathcal{A}}$ and $0_{\mathcal{A}}$.

Let $\mathcal{A}$ be an upper semilattice. By an *atom of* $\mathcal{A}$ we understand any element $a \neq 0_{\mathcal{A}}$, such that $\forall x\,(x \subset a \rightarrow (x = a \vee x = 0_{\mathcal{A}}))$. Thus atoms are "minimal non-zero elements". When a is an atom, we write At(a). $\mathcal{A}$ is said to be *atomic* if for every $a, b \in A$ such that $a \not\subset b$ there is an atom c such that $c \subset a$ and $c \not\subset b$.

Theorem 2: If $\mathcal{A}$ is atomic and complete, then for each non-zero element a of $\mathcal{A}$
$$a = \oplus\{b \in A : \mathrm{At}(b)\ \&\ b \subset a\}$$

Proof: Let us write At[a] for $\{b \in A : \mathrm{At}(b)\ \&\ b \subset a\}$.

(i) Since $\mathcal{A}$ is complete, $\oplus$ At[a] exists for each a.

(ii) $\oplus$ At[a] $\subset$ a, since for each $b \in$ At[a] $b \subset a$.

(iii) Suppose $a \not\subset \oplus$ At[a]. Then, since $\mathcal{A}$ is atomic, there is an atom b such that $b \subset a$ and $b \not\subset \oplus$ At[a]. But if $b \not\subset \oplus$ At[a], then $b \notin$ At[a]. But $b \subset a$ and At(b): Contradiction.

The last property of upper semilattices we will need is that of a *free* upper semilattice. $\mathcal{A}$ is *free* iff for all $a \in A$ and $X \subseteq A$, if At(a) and $a \subset \oplus X$, then $(\exists b \in X)\ a \subset b$. We will from now on focus on upper semilattices which are complete, atomic and free. We repeat the definitions of these properties, and of the notions needed to define them, in

Definition 4.3.4

(i) An upper semilattice $\langle \mathsf{A}, \subset \rangle$ is called *complete* if for all $\mathsf{X} \subseteq \mathsf{A}$ the supremum $\oplus \mathsf{X}$ exists.

(ii) If a is the "largest" element of A – i.e. for all $\mathsf{x} \in \mathsf{A}$, $\mathsf{x} \subset \mathsf{a}$ – then a is called the *one of* A and denoted as $1_{\mathcal{A}}$. Similarly, if a is the "smallest" element of A – i.e. for all $\mathsf{x} \in \mathsf{A}$, $\mathsf{a} \subset \mathsf{x}$ – then a is called the *zero of* A and denoted as $0_{\mathcal{A}}$.

(iii) By an *atom of* $\mathcal{A}$ we understand any element $\mathsf{a} \neq 0_{\mathcal{A}}$, such that $\forall \mathsf{x} (\mathsf{x} \subset \mathsf{a} \rightarrow (\mathsf{x} = \mathsf{a} \vee \mathsf{x} = 0_{\mathcal{A}}))$.

(iv) $\mathcal{A}$ is said to be *atomic* if for every $\mathsf{a}, \mathsf{b} \in \mathsf{A}$ such that $\mathsf{a} \not\subset \mathsf{b}$ there is an atom c such that $\mathsf{c} \subset \mathsf{a}$ and $\mathsf{c} \not\subset \mathsf{b}$.

(v) $\mathcal{A}$ is *free* if for all $\mathsf{a} \in \mathsf{A}$, $\mathsf{X} \subseteq \mathsf{A}$ if $\mathrm{At}(\mathsf{a})$ and $\mathsf{a} \subset \oplus \mathsf{X}$ then $(\exists \mathsf{b} \in \mathsf{X})\ \mathsf{a} \subset \mathsf{b}$.

Upper semilattices with zero that are complete, atomic and free have a remarkably simple structure. In fact, each such upper semilattice $\langle \mathsf{A}, \subset \rangle$ is isomorphic to a structure $\langle \mathcal{P}(\mathsf{B}), \subseteq \rangle$ where $\mathcal{P}(\mathsf{B})$ is the set of all subsets of some given set B and '$\subseteq$' is the relation of set-theoretical inclusion.[46] In particular, we can take B to be the set of all atoms $\mathrm{At}(\mathcal{A})$ of $\mathcal{A}$:

Theorem 3: Let $\mathcal{A} = \langle \mathsf{A}, \subset \rangle$ be a complete, atomic, free upper semilattice with zero, and let $\mathrm{At}(\mathcal{A})$ be the set of atoms of $\mathcal{A}$. Then $\mathcal{A}$ is isomorphic to the structure $\langle \mathcal{P}(\mathrm{At}(\mathcal{A})), \subseteq \rangle$.

Proof: Define F: $\mathsf{A} \rightarrow \mathcal{P}(\mathrm{At}(\mathcal{A}))$ by: $\mathrm{F}(\mathsf{a}) = \{\mathsf{c}\colon \mathrm{At}(\mathsf{c})\ \&\ \mathsf{c} \subset \mathsf{a}\}$.

1. F is onto: For let $\mathsf{X} \subseteq \mathrm{At}(\mathcal{A})$. We have to find an $\mathsf{a} \in \mathsf{A}$ with $\mathrm{F}(\mathsf{a}) = \mathsf{X}$. Take $\mathsf{a} = \oplus \mathsf{X}$. Then:
   - $\mathrm{F}(\mathsf{a}) \subseteq \mathsf{X}$:
     Suppose $\mathsf{b} \in \mathrm{F}(\mathsf{a})$. Then $\mathsf{b} \in \{\mathsf{c}\colon \mathrm{At}(\mathsf{c})\ \&\ \mathsf{c} \subset \oplus \mathsf{X}\}$. So, by freedom there exists an atom $\mathsf{d} \in \mathsf{X}$ such that $\mathsf{b} \subset \mathsf{d}$. By Atomicity and ANTIS we get $\mathsf{b} = \mathsf{d}$. Thus $\mathsf{b} \in \mathsf{X}$.
   - $\mathsf{X} \subseteq \mathrm{F}(\mathsf{a})$:
     This holds by definition of $\oplus \mathsf{X}$.
2. F is 1–1:
   Suppose $\mathsf{a} \neq \mathsf{b}$. Then either $\mathsf{a} \not\subset \mathsf{b}$ or $\mathsf{b} \not\subset \mathsf{a}$. If $\mathsf{a} \not\subset \mathsf{b}$, then by atomicity

[46] $\langle \mathsf{A}, \subset \rangle$ is ***isomorphic to*** $\langle \mathsf{A}', \subset' \rangle$ if there exists a 1–1 function f from A onto A′ such that for all $\mathsf{a}, \mathsf{b} \in \mathsf{A}$ $\mathsf{a} \subset \mathsf{b}$ iff $\mathrm{f}(\mathsf{a}) \subset' \mathrm{f}(\mathsf{b})$.

there is a d such that At(d), $d \subset a$ & $d \not\subset b$. So $d \in \{c\text{: At}(c) \;\&\; c \subset a\}$ and $d \notin \{c\text{: At}(c) \;\&\; c \subset b\}$, and so $\{c\text{: At}(c) \;\&\; c \subset a\} \neq \{c\text{: At}(c) \;\&\; c \subset b\}$, i.e. $F(a) \neq F(b)$. If $b \not\subset a$, the argument is the same.

3. For $a, b \in A$, $a \subset b$ iff $F(a) \subseteq F(b)$:
   Clearly, if $a \subset b$, then for each atom $c \subset a$, $c \subset b$. So $F(a) \subseteq F(b)$. Conversely, suppose $F(a) \subseteq F(b)$. Since $\mathcal{A}$ is complete, both $\oplus F(a)$ and $\oplus F(b)$ exist. It is easily inferred from the definition of '$\oplus$' that, as $F(a) \subseteq F(b)$, $\oplus F(a) \subset \oplus F(b)$. Since A is atomic, $a = \oplus F(a)$ and $b = \oplus F(b)$.[47] So $a \subset b$.

Theorem 3 shows that the choice between a lattice-theoretic and a set-theoretic approach towards the model theory of singular and plural count nouns is not crucial from a strictly formal point of view: models based on the one approach can be readily converted into equivalent models based on the other. Even so, there are considerations of naturalness which clearly favour the lattice-theoretic approach. For on this approach singular NPs denote – as one can't help feeling they should – individuals; but in the set-theoretic models that are obtained from these lattice-theoretic models by the conversion procedure described in the proof of the theorem they denote singleton sets; and as we have argued earlier this is counterintuitive. (Of course we can, as noticed before, stipulate that the denotation of a singular NP in a set-theoretic model is always an individual; but then there is no semantic role left for the singleton sets and they should be eliminated. Evidently this can be done, but that too is not a natural move.) It is for these reasons that we adopt the lattice-theoretic approach. However, it will be convenient to use the familiar set-theoretic terminology informally. Thus we will continue to speak of non-atomic entities as "sets" and of their parts as the "members" or "elements" of the sets.

4.3.1.2 The Function Pred_M

A *model* M, then, will be a structure based on some complete, free and atomic upper semilattice $\mathcal{U}_M$ with zero. As before, M will have to provide interpretations for the names and predicates of our language. And, also as before, we separate these interpretations into two functions, Name_M and Pred_M. Thus M will be a triple $\langle \mathcal{U}_M, \mathsf{Name}_M, \mathsf{Pred}_M \rangle$, where $\mathcal{U}_M = \langle U, \subset \rangle$. We refer to U and $\subset$ as U_M and $\subset_M$, respectively.

Since the universe of such a model has a certain structure (induced by '$\subset$') which was absent from the models used in Chapters 1–3, the functions Name and Pred ought to obey a number of constraints which have no counterparts in relation to the earlier models. The function Name_M is unproblematic in this regard. As before, names of individuals are to be mapped onto individuals of $\mathcal{U}_M$ (i.e. on

[47]Show this!

atomic members of U_M). Names of groups of individuals should be mapped onto non-atomic members of U_M. However, as our fragment does not contain such names, this is an issue we can ignore.

The function $Pred_M$ presents us with greater problems. These problems are all connected with the semantic relationship between singular and plural predicates. We have already caught a few glimpses of this problem in connection with verbs: when a verb is used in the plural, i.e. in combination with a plural subject, its meaning can relate to that of its singular uses in more than one way: certain verbs permit *collective* as well as *distributive* readings. Similar problems also arise with nouns and adjectives. Those concerning adjectives we will ignore here; but a few remarks on nouns are in order, and we will begin with those.

Plural Nouns

First a preliminary observation. We have seen that some occurrences of plural nouns act as predicates of individuals. This is true, to be precise, of those occurrences which are part of quantifying NPs. The DRS-construction rule for such NPs makes this explicit by converting the plural noun β in the NP into a condition of the form $\beta'(\mathbf{v})$ with β' the singular form of β and $\mathbf{v}$ a discourse referent representing an individual. Thus the words **books** as it occurs in **many books** and **book** as it occurs for instance in **every book** act as the very same predicate.

But this is not true of all plural noun occurrences. We saw that what we have called non-quantifying plural NPs must often be interpreted as expressions that denote sets. Where this is so the (plural) noun acts as a definition of the set denoted. For example, **books** in the NP **the books** acts as a characterization of the set of books the NP refers to (on the given occasion of use). What **books** says of that set is that it consists of books – that is a non-atomic entity each of whose atomic parts is a book.

For nouns this is the normal situation: When the plural of a noun acts as the description of a set, then the noun describes that set as one whose members all satisfy the predicate represented by the corresponding singular. We follow Link in using the operator '$*$' to transform a predicate P of individuals into one which is true not only of those individuals, but also of all collections consisting exclusively of such individuals. In other words, if X is a set of atoms of some upper semilattice $\mathcal{U}$, X^* will be the set of all elements a of U such that $(\forall b \subset a)\ (At(b) \rightarrow b \in X)$. So, if X is the extension of the predicate **book**, then X^* is the extension of the predicate **book or books** (and **books,** as a predicate of sets of two or more elements, has for its extension the non-atomic part of X^*).[48]

---

[48]As the function '$*$' has been defined, the value it returns for the set X apparently depends not only on X but also on the semilattice $\langle U_M, \subset_M \rangle$ within which X^* is computed. However, as this lattice will always be unequivocally determined in the context, there is no need to explicitly

We use '$*$' not only to denote this function from extensions to extensions, but also to modify predicates into other predicates. In fact, it is in this second sense that '$*$' has been used already, e.g. to form the predicate **book*** out of the predicate **book**. The correspondence between these two uses of '$*$' should be obvious: whenever $\mathsf{Pred}_{\mathsf{M}}$(**book**) is the set X, $\mathsf{Pred}_{\mathsf{M}}$(**book***) is the set X*.

Plural nouns that act as set predicates in the way just outlined may be said to be *strictly distributive*. For (i) they characterize the sets denoted by the non-quantifying NPs of which they are part as sets consisting of individuals all of which have a certain property P; and (ii) this property P is not a "relational" property: it can be characterized without reference to other individuals, and in particular without reference to any other members of the given set. We could make the strict distributivity of a set predicate such as **books** more clearly visible if we represented it by the duplex condition

(4.140)
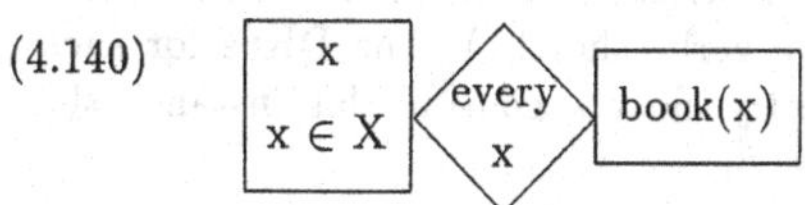

rather than by the shorter **book*(X)**. We will stick however with the latter condition. You may regard it as an abbreviation of (4.140) if you want to.

Not all plural nouns act as set predicates that can be analysed in the manner of (4.140). Among the exceptions are plurals of so-called *relational* nouns,[49] such as **friend** or **relative**. The phrase **three friends**, for instance, as we find it in the sentence

(4.141) Three friends bought a sailboat.

is typically understood as denoting not a set each member of which is 'a friend' (in the sense of being someone or other's friend), but rather a set each member of which is a friend of the set's other two members. Thus the extension of the plural noun **friends** is defined in terms of the relation **x is a friend of y**, and is not computable from the set of those people who are a (i.e. somebody's) friend in the way that the extension of **books** is computable from the set of things that are books. Even in the case of relational nouns it is possible to characterize the denoted set in terms of its members, but here the characterization is relational. Thus the DRS-condition **friends(X)** could be expanded to

mention it as an additional argument of '$*$'.

[49]See Section 3.2.

(4.142)

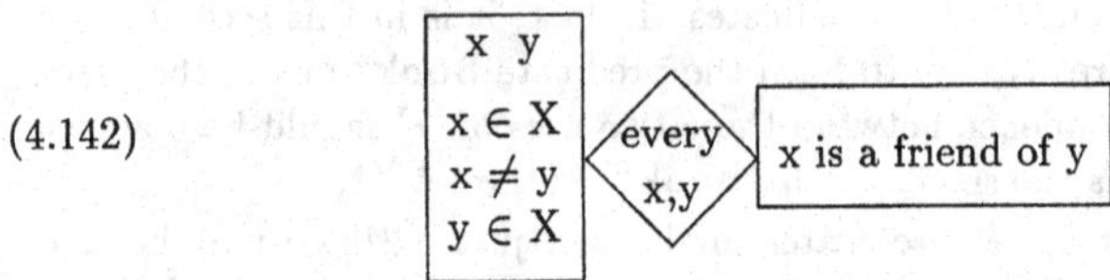

As we haven't included any relational nouns in the English fragment treated in this chapter we need not worry about this complication any further.

Intransitive Verbs

We now turn to plural verbs. Like plural nouns, plural verb forms often act as predicates of individuals. This is so, for instance, whenever an intransitive verb combines with a quantifying subject NP. (We restrict attention to intransitive verbs for the moment. We will turn to transitive verbs shortly.) The DRSs for such subject-verb combinations make this perfectly clear – consider for instance the DRS for

(4.143) Few students thrive.

which according to the construction rules for quantifying NPs has the form

(4.144)

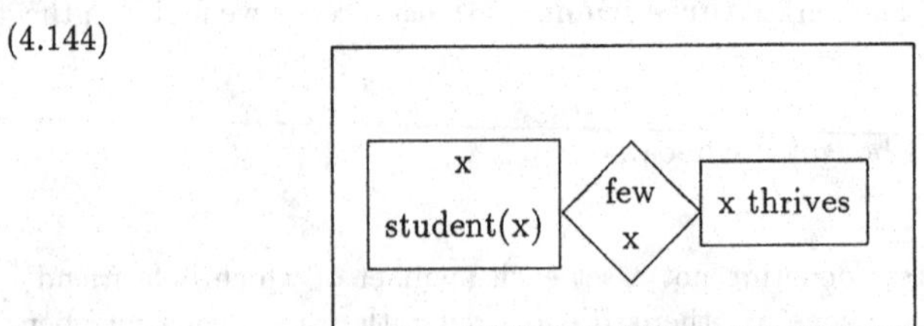

Here the condition which derives from the verb phrase, viz. **x thrives**, combines the verb with an individual discourse referent. According to what we said in Section 4.1.5, plural verbs permit the same interpretation when they follow non-quantifying subjects, as in

(4.145) Two students thrive.

which has a distributive reading, represented by the DRS

(4.146)

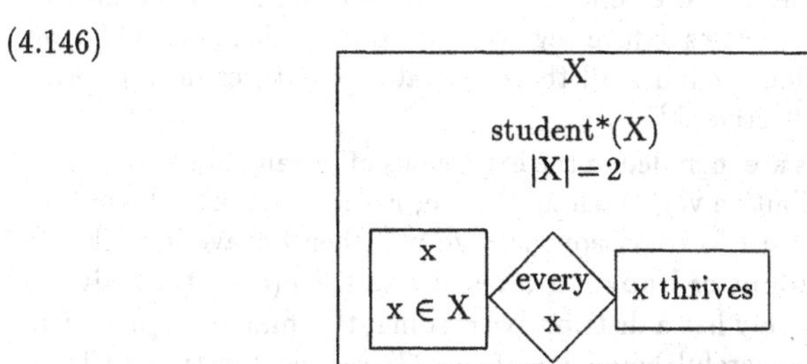

As it stands, our construction algorithm, in which the rule of distribution over a non-individual discourse referent is optional, also gives rise to another DRS, in which the rule has not been applied

(4.147)

X
student*(X) $\|X\| = 2$ X thrives

Before we address the question what truth conditions (4.147) might represent, let us compare (4.145) with the sentence

(4.148) Two bottles suffice.

As opposed to (4.145), this sentence has a collective reading: that two bottles suffice does not mean that there is a set of two bottles each one of which suffices on its own – it is only together that the two bottles suffice for the purpose at hand. This reading evidently cannot be represented by a DRS like (4.146), but only by one in which no distribution over the subject has taken place, as in

(4.149)

X
bottle*(X) $\|X\| = 2$ X suffice

In order that (4.149) comes out as verified by those situations where (4.148) is true, the extension which Pred assigns to **suffice** should include sets of bottles which suffice collectively. For otherwise the condition **X suffice** could not be verified in any situation in which the bottles suffice together but not by themselves. So we stipulate that Pred_M(**suffice**) includes all those non-atomic entities in U_M which satisfy the predicate as collectives.[50]

If only those collections are included in the extensions of intransitive verbs, then for an (obligatorily) distributive verb such as **thrive**, Pred_M(**thrive**) will contain only individuals. With regard to collections **thrive** will then behave just like an ordinary noun such as **student** or **book**. As a result, the DRS (4.147) will always come out false. As (4.145) only has a distributive reading, this may seem just what we want. But we must be careful here. For if (4.147) can be constructed from (4.145), then by the same token it would be possible to convert

(4.151) Two students do not thrive.

into

(4.152)

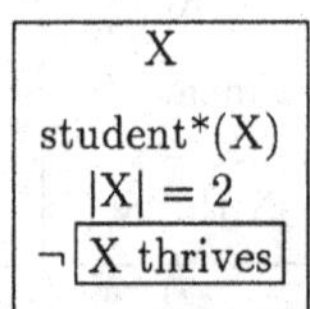

which would come out true even in a situation in which all students do thrive. If we are to avoid such misrepresentations we must either admit into Pred(**thrive**) those sets all of whose members thrive, or else prevent the construction of DRSs such as (4.147) and (4.152) altogether. Having already decided against the first option, we are forced to find a way of blocking the construction of such DRSs. We may accomplish this by stipulating that

the distribution rule is obligatory for all distributive verbs.

If non-distributive interpretations were all of the kind exemplified by (4.148), we could end our discussion of intransitive verbs right here, and conclude the section with a few unsurprising remarks on the collective readings of transitive verbs. But unfortunately the phenomena are more complicated. Even a distributive verb such as **thrive** enters into plural sentences the truth conditions of which are not correctly captured by a distributed DRS such as (4.146). Consider for instance the sentence

[50](4.148) also has a distributive reading, one that it is easier to get for a sentence like

(4.150) The large bottles suffice for a party of six people, but the small ones do not.

This distributive reading can be obtained by distributing, as in (4.146), over the subject term.

(4.153) The children in this city thrive.

This sentence can be accepted as true even when there are a few children in the city who do not thrive. There may be special children, children born with some debilitating malformation, say, who don't thrive. But that does not really threaten the global generalization that (4.153) means to express.

To capture the intention of sentences such as (4.153) correctly, one might proceed in one of two ways.

(i) Modify the distribution rule so that it produces a duplex condition involving a generic instead of a strictly universal quantifier (see 3.7.4). This would lead, in the case of (4.153), to the DRS

(4.154)

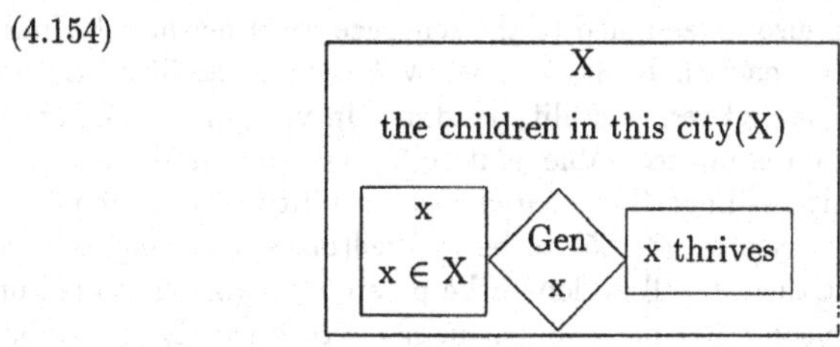

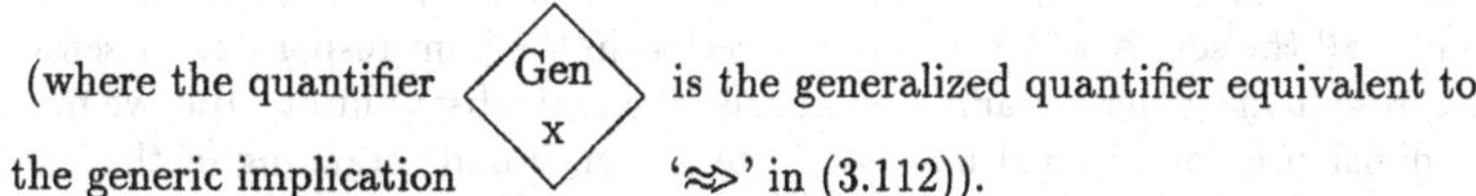

(where the quantifier [Gen x] is the generalized quantifier equivalent to the generic implication '$\approx\!>$' in (3.112)).

(ii) Include within $\mathsf{Pred}_{\mathsf{M}}$(**thrive**) those sets A such that all the "typical" or "representative" members of A thrive. As this strategy would entail that in particular all those A are put into Pred(**thrive**) it would constitute a reversal of our earlier decision to keep such sets out of the extension of **thrive**.

Before we try to compare these options we must mention one further fact. (4.153) could only be true, one feels, if a substantial proportion (presumably a majority) of the city's children thrive. However, there are other sentences that are superficially like (4.153), but which are not subject to this kind of constraint. For instance

(4.155) The guys in 5b have been cheating on the exam again.

can be accepted as correct even when only a small number of the guys cheated; the sentence is acceptable in such a situation to the extent that it makes sense to hold the class as a whole responsible for the acts of some, perhaps even only one, of its members. It seems that the interpretational schema that we apply when assigning this reading to (4.155) differs from the "generic" schema involved in interpreting (4.153) in the way we described above. In fact, (4.155) too permits a generic interpretation. On this interpretation (4.155) would be true only if it was true of most of the students in 5b, excepting only those who qualify as exceptions for some special reason, e.g. the one who walked out after 15 minutes because he thought that, cheating or no cheating, the problems were impossible; or the two who were sitting directly opposite the teacher, exposed to the scrutiny of his watchful eye, but who would have cheated too had they only been given a chance. We will assume that these two interpretations of (4.155) do indeed constitute genuinely distinct readings and should be given distinct DRS representations.

If the "shared responsibility reading" of (4.155) is indeed distinct from a generic interpretation that can also be assigned to the sentence, then neither the first nor the third option will be enough by itself - we will need in addition a kind of DRS-condition for the shared responsibility reading. In view of the ambiguity of (4.155) the second option is unacceptable as it collapses the shared responsibility reading and the generic reading: The shared responsibility reading requires the set A denoted by the subject of (4.155) to be in Pred(**cheat**) as long as some of its members cheat; but then it will no longer be possible for (4.155) to fail on its generic reading in case some but not enough members of A satisfy the verb.[51] If indeed we want our construction algorithm to be able to yield distinct DRSs for the generic and the joint responsibility reading, then it would seem best to include in Pred(α) all the sets A which satisfy the verb α in the joint responsibility sense, and to represent the generic reading by means of generic distribution. But we must see this division as provisional until we have a deeper understanding of the different ways in which the plural uses of intransitive verbs may be semantically related to their singular uses.[52]

[51]These conclusions are premissed on the assumption that the distinction between the generic and the joint responsibility interpretation of a sentence such as (4.155) involves a genuine ambiguity between two different readings that demand two distinct semantic representations. We expect that many linguists would see this position as contentious. Unfortunately this is an issue that cannot be discussed here in the depth and detail it deserves. (The methodological questions relate to the concept of *ambiguity* which will be discussed at length in Volume 2).

[52]A further complication is the following. Generic and shared responsibility readings are possible only when the set-introducing NP is definite, not when it is indefinite. Thus

(4.156) 37 children slept.

cannot be accepted as true if in fact only 36 children slept: the existence of a set of 37 children almost all members of which did sleep is not good enough, not even when the few exceptions may be considered as atypical. Similarly,

Transitive Verbs

Transitive verbs point up much the same spectrum of distributive and non-distributive interpretations as intransitive verbs; but there is one major complication. First some simple points. A transitive verb has two arguments, and each of these may give rise to an ambiguity between collective and distributive interpretations. Ambiguity with regard to the subject position we already observed in Section 4.1, where we considered sentences of the type

(4.158) Three lawyers hired a new secretary.

A sentence like (4.158), we noted, could be taken to mean that the three lawyers hired one new secretary together or that each of them hired his own secretary. Once again, the second reading is obtained by application of the distribution rule, whereas the first reading is got by refraining from applying the rule. The resulting DRS will capture the truth conditions associated with this reading correctly on the assumption that $\mathsf{Pred}_{\mathsf{M}}(\textbf{hire})$ contains only those pairs of the form $\langle \mathsf{A}, \mathsf{b}\rangle$ for which it is the case that A collectively hires b. Much the same is true of the object position of transitive verbs. Thus

(4.159) Fred hired five cleaners.

can be understood as saying that Fred hired each of the cleaners separately, or that he hired a crew of five cleaners on a collective contract (so that, for instance, it would have been impossible for him to fire one cleaner without also firing the others). Admittedly, the distinction between distributive and collective interpretation is less clear in this case, and on the whole this seems to be true for the object positions of transitive verbs. There are certain verbs, however, which show a fairly clear distributive-collective ambiguity vis-à-vis their objects. One of such verbs is **connect**. The sentence

(4.160) Fred connected five computers.

(4.157) Three children cheated.

cannot be accepted when only two children cheated (out of a class of 25, say), not even in a situation in which "The children cheated" would be acceptable in its shared responsibility sense. These facts show that the construction rules which create the DRSs that represent generic and shared responsibility interpretations would be applicable only where the non-individual discourse referent in question is introduced by a definite NP, but not where the introducing NP is indefinite.

for instance, can mean that Fred connected each one of the computers to some already given network or that he connected the five computers to each other.

When a transitive verb is flanked by non-quantifying plural NPs on both sides, we may find the distributive-collective ambiguity in both arguments at once. For example,

(4.161) Three lawyers hired five cleaners.

is four-ways ambiguous in this respect. In addition, however, (4.161) has an interpretation that is captured by none of the four DRSs which can be generated by the construction algorithm in its present form, and which is also distinct from the generic and the shared responsibility interpretations that we decided to ignore. This is the reading that allows us to accept (4.161) as true in a situation in which there is a set of three lawyers and a set of five cleaners such that, say, lawyer 1 hired cleaner 1 and hired cleaner 2, lawyer 2 hired cleaner 3 and hired cleaner 4, and lawyer 3 hired cleaner 5. More generally, a sentence of the form

(4.162) n Ps γ m Gs.

is true on this type of reading provided that

(4.163) there is a set A consisting of n Ps and a set B consisting of m Gs such that

(i) $(\forall a \in A)\,(\exists b \in B)\,(a\ \gamma\ b)$ and

(ii) $(\forall b \in B)\,(\exists a \in A)\,(a\ \gamma\ b)$

Note in particular that these conditions do not agree with the truth conditions of the doubly distributive reading represented by the DRS

(4.164)

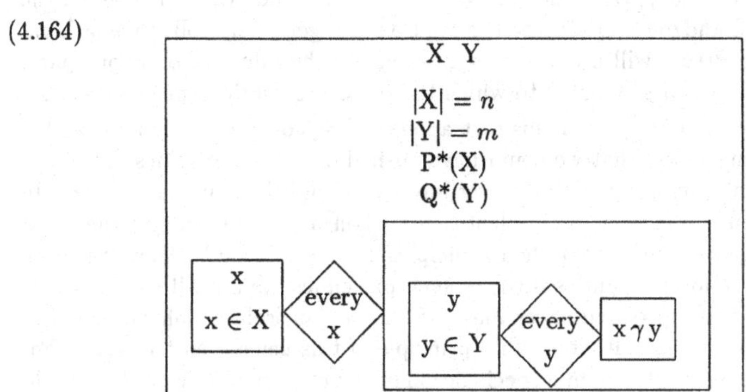

The interpretation on which (4.161) is true in the described situation has been discussed in the literature as a distinct *reading* of the sentence – one which in our theory would require a separate DRS that would make the conditions in (4.163) explicit. This reading has become known as the *cumulative reading*[53]. The intriguing fact about the cumulative reading is that it appears to involve an irreducible relation between the sets represented by the discourse referents for subject and object (the relation is irreducible inasmuch as it is impossible to find seperate interpretations for subject and object which yield the cumulative reading when combined). For the construction algorithm this has the following implication. To obtain the cumulative reading we would first have to convert the clause into a DRS-condition of the form $\mathbf{X}\, \gamma\, \mathbf{Y}$, where γ is the verb and **X** and **Y** are the non-atomic discourse referents representing subject and object. A special construction rule would then convert this condition into one or more others to make the cumulative reading explicit.

While we believe that something like the cumulative reading must indeed be treated as a distinct reading, we wish to point out that there are situations resembling the one we have just described but which do not fit the condition (4.163). For instance, suppose that the first lawyer hired cleaners 1, 2 and 3 on a joint contract and also hired cleaner 4 on a separate contract; and finally that the three lawyers together hired the remaining cleaner. (4.161) would still count as true in such a situation, but the "distributive" conditions (i) and (ii) of (4.163) do not hold for it. Thus it seems that (4.163) captures a special case of a more general principle, according to which (4.162) is true provided the parts of A which are γ-related to some part of B exhaust all of A and the parts of B to which some part of A is γ-related exhaust all of B. It is possible to state the truth conditions for this generalization of the cumulative reading correctly provided we stick to the already agreed policy

[53]See [Scha 1981].

of putting into $\mathsf{Pred}_\mathsf{M}(\gamma)$ only those pairs $\langle \mathsf{C}, \mathsf{d}\rangle$ $\langle \mathsf{c}, \mathsf{D}\rangle$ and $\langle \mathsf{C}, \mathsf{D}\rangle$ for which the respective sets C and/or D enter into the relation in a genuinely collective fashion. For in that case Pred_M will provide us with precisely the information about parts of A being γ-related to parts of B to which those truth conditions need to refer.

Interpretational principles of this sort appear to be comparatively rare, and it should not be surprising that we could have pushed our own semantics project as far as we have at this point without ever having to appeal to such principles. In fact, it has been the explicit or implicit assumption of more than one theory of natural language semantics that such principles are not needed.[54] However, even if constructions whose semantics involves such principles are not all too common, the cumulative reading of sentences like 4.161 is not an isolated phenomenon in this respect. We will encounter another principle of this general sort in 4.4.6. For reasons of space we omit a formal specification of the construction rule that would enable us to construct representations of cumulative readings.

Exercises

1. (a) Give examples of upper semi-lattices that are
   (i) not complete, but atomic
   (ii) not atomic, but complete
   (iii) not complete and not atomic

   (b) Consider the structure $\mathcal{U} = \langle \mathsf{U}, \subset\rangle$ with $\mathsf{U} = \{\mathsf{Peter}, \mathsf{Paul}, \mathsf{Mary}\}$ and $\subset$ $= \{ \langle \mathsf{Peter}, \oplus\{\mathsf{Peter}, \mathsf{Paul}, \mathsf{Mary}\}\rangle, \langle \mathsf{Paul}, \oplus\{\mathsf{Peter}, \mathsf{Paul}, \mathsf{Mary}\}\rangle, \langle \mathsf{Mary}, \oplus\{\mathsf{Peter}, \mathsf{Paul}, \mathsf{Mary}\}\rangle \}$.
   (i) Show that $\mathcal{U}$ is an upper semi-lattice that is not free.
   (ii) Show that the following holds in $\mathcal{U}$:
   $\mathsf{Peter} \oplus \mathsf{Paul} = \mathsf{Peter} \oplus \mathsf{Mary} = \mathsf{Peter} \oplus \mathsf{Paul} \oplus \mathsf{Mary}$.

2. Let $\mathcal{A} = \langle \mathsf{A}, \subset\rangle$ be an upper semilattice.

   (a) Show that the following hold for any $\mathsf{a}, \mathsf{b}, \mathsf{c} \in \mathsf{A}$
   (L1) $\mathsf{a} \oplus \mathsf{a} = \mathsf{a}$
   (L2) $\mathsf{a} \oplus \mathsf{b} = \mathsf{b} \oplus \mathsf{a}$
   (L3) $\mathsf{a} \oplus (\mathsf{b} \oplus \mathsf{c}) = (\mathsf{a} \oplus \mathsf{b}) \oplus \mathsf{c}$

   (a) Suppose that $\mathcal{A}$ satisfies the additional axiom

[54] This assumption is central to Montague Grammar, especially in the form in which it was developed by Montague himself. (See [Montague 1974], [Partee 1973b], [Partee 1984a].) It has been reaffirmed in recent "dynamic" modifications of Montague's approach, as in [Groenendijk/Stokhof 1990], or [Groenendijk/Stokhof 1991].

(A5) $(\forall\, a, b \in A)\,(\exists\, c \in A)\,(c \subset a \wedge c \subset b \wedge (\forall\, d \in A)\,((d \subset a \wedge d \subset b) \rightarrow c \subset d))$

which allows us to define the *infimum* $a \odot b$ of two elements a and b of A to be the unique greatest lower bound of a and b. Show:

(L1′) $a \odot a = a$

(L2′) $a \odot b = b \odot a$

(L3′) $a \odot (b \odot c) = (a \odot b) \odot c$

(L4′) $a \odot (a \oplus b) = a$

(L4) $a \oplus (a \odot b) = a$

(c) Define a *lattice* to be a structure $\langle A, \oplus, \odot\rangle$, where A is a non-empty set and $\oplus$, $\odot$ are binary operators on A, such that for all a, b, c $\in$ A (L1) – (L3) of page 416 and (L1′) – (L4′) of page 417 hold.

Define a relation '$\leq$' on A by

$$a \leq b \leftrightarrow_{def} a \oplus b = b$$

Show that T1 to T8 are provable from (L1) to (L4′)

(T1) $a \leq a$

(T2) $a \leq a \odot b;\ b \leq a \odot b$

(T3) $a \oplus b \leq a;\ a \oplus b \leq b$

(T4) $(a \leq b\ \&\ b \leq c) \rightarrow a \leq c$

(T5) $(a \leq b\ \&\ b \leq a) \rightarrow a = b$

(T6) $a \leq b \leftrightarrow a \oplus b = a$

(T7) $a \leq b \rightarrow a \odot c \leq b \odot c$

(T8) $a \leq b \rightarrow a \oplus c \leq b \oplus c$

(d) Show that $\mathcal{A} = \langle A, \leq\rangle$ is an upper semi-lattice such that (L5) holds. (Therefore $\langle A, \leq\rangle$ is also called a lattice.)

3. Suppose $\mathcal{A} = \langle A, \subset\rangle$ is an upper semilattice.

(i) Show that for any $B \subset A$, $\oplus B$ exists, if A is finite.

(ii) Give an example of an upper semilattice $\mathcal{A}$ with infinite A such that there is a $B \subset A$ for which $\oplus B$ does not exist.

4. A *lattice* $\langle A, \oplus, \odot\rangle$ is called *distributive* if for all a, b, c $\in$ A:

(L5) $a \oplus (b \odot c) = (a \oplus b) \odot (a \oplus c)$
$a \odot (b \oplus c) = (a \odot b) \oplus (a \odot c)$

Give an example of a lattice that is not distributive.

5. In Exercise 3 on page 329 we observed that a plural description **the** β denotes that subset of a given set X which consists of all members of X which satisfy β. Thus **the students who pass (the exam)** will denote that subset Y of a given set X of students which Y consists of those members of X who pass. A construction rule for plural definite descriptions which does justice to this intuition must lead to a representation of this NP which involves

   (a) the selection of a set X from context (we ignore here how X is to be selected)

   (b) the introduction of a new discourse referent **Y** together with the defining clause

   (1) **Y** = Σx

x
x ∈ X student(x) x passes

   (i) Formulate a construction rule for plural descriptions which has this effect. (To repeat, you may ignore the problem how X is to be selected.)

When discussing the cumulative reading of clauses with two plural arguments such as

(2) Three lawyers hired five cleaners.

we noticed that such clauses are true if the relation expressed by the verb holds between *non-atomic* parts of the sets denoted by subject and object. Thus, for instance, (2) would be accepted as true if there is a set of three lawyers a, b and c and a set of five cleaners so that a and b jointly hired the first three cleaners and c by himself hired the fourth and the fifth.

A similar complication also arises in connection with plural definite descriptions. For instance

(3) The lawyers who hired a cleaner.

can, in our judgement, be used to refer to the set of all lawyers who hired a cleaner, even when some cleaners were hired by a single lawyer while others were hired by two or more lawyers jointly. This means that the discourse referent **Y** representing (3) should not have the defining equation (1), but rather

(4) $\mathbf{Y} = \Sigma\xi$

ξ z
$\xi \in$ X
lawyer*(ξ)
cleaner(z)
ξ hired z

(ii) Restate the construction rule for plural definite descriptions so that it takes this into account. Use it to construct DRSs for the following sentences:

(5) The students who fail loathe the students who pass.

(6) The lawyers who hired a cleaner own the building which Ella abhors.

(7) The lawyers who hired consultants live in Darmstadt.

4.3.2 Verification of DRS-Conditions

We begin this subsection with an enumeration of the different types of DRS-conditions which we have introduced in this chapter.

1. The conditions **at(x)**, **non-at(x)** needed to distinguish between neutral, atomic and non-atomic discourse referents.

2. The conditions arising in connection with summation and abstraction.

   (i) $\mathbf{x} = \mathbf{y}_1 \oplus \ldots \oplus \mathbf{y}_n \ (n \geq 2)$

   (ii) $\mathbf{x} = \Sigma\mathbf{z}\ \mathbf{K}$

3. Conditions of the form $|\mathbf{x}| = \nu$, where ν is a cardinal number term, i.e. one of the expressions **1**, **2**, **3**, **...**

4. The condition $\mathbf{x} \in \mathbf{y}$, which arises in the context of distributions.

5. Duplex conditions, i.e. conditions of the form

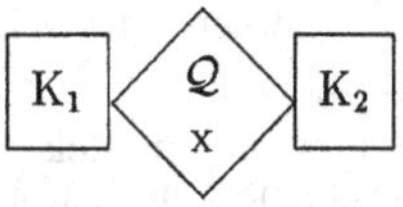

$$\boxed{K_1} \left\langle \begin{matrix} \mathcal{Q} \\ x \end{matrix} \right\rangle \boxed{K_2}$$

For conditions of types **1**, **2**, **3** and **4** the verification conditions follow straightforwardly from our earlier informal glosses. Thus

1.a $\mathsf{M} \models_f \mathbf{at}(\mathbf{x})$ if f(x) is an atom of M,

1.b $\mathsf{M} \models_f$ **non-at(x)** if f(x) is a non-atomic entity of M

2.a $\mathsf{M} \models_f \mathbf{x} = \mathbf{y}_1 \oplus ... \oplus \mathbf{y}_n$ iff $f(\mathbf{x}) = f(\mathbf{y}_1) \oplus_{\mathsf{M}} ... \oplus_{\mathsf{M}} f(\mathbf{y}_n)$;

2.b $\mathsf{M} \models_f \mathbf{x} = \Sigma \mathbf{z}\ \mathbf{K}$ iff $f(\mathbf{x}) = \oplus_{\mathsf{M}}\{\mathsf{b} : \mathsf{b} \in \mathsf{U}_{\mathsf{M}}\ \&\ \mathsf{M} \models_{f \cup \{\langle z,b \rangle\}} K\}$;

3. $\mathsf{M} \models_f |\mathbf{x}| = \nu$ iff $|\{\mathsf{b} \in \mathsf{U}_{\mathsf{M}}$: b is an atom of M & $\mathsf{b} \subset_{\mathsf{M}} f(\mathbf{x})\}| = \nu$

4. $\mathsf{M} \models_f \mathbf{x} \in \mathbf{y}$ iff $f(\mathbf{x}) \subset_{\mathsf{M}} f(\mathbf{y})$.

Duplex conditions are more problematic. In fact, as there is quite a bit to be said about them, we devote a separate subsection to this topic.

4.3.2.1 The Semantics of Duplex Conditions

A fair number of plural determiners, we have seen, are generalized quantifiers. In a comprehensive coverage of English there should be a type of duplex condition for each such determiner. And with each of these types should come a specification of the generalized quantifier (that is, relation between sets) which determines its verification conditions.

Which quantifying determiners shall we include? Up to now we have been rather cavalier on this point. We have used determiners in examples as it suited our purposes, without ever committing ourselves to a definite list. Perhaps now should have been the time to make up our minds precisely which to include and to state fully explicit verification rules for each of the corresponding types of duplex conditions. But we have decided against this. Rather, we will deal with quantifying determiners as we have been dealing with nouns and verbs: We assume that the vocabulary of our fragment includes a certain number of them without committing ourselves to a fixed, explicitly specified list once and for all. As with verbs and nouns, it is possible to proceed in this way because we have a general concept of how quantified determiners are to be interpreted, viz. as generalized quantifiers or binary relations between sets.

We implement this decision by assuming that the DRS vocabulary V contains a certain set of quantifying determiners and that each model M relative to V has an additional component, $\mathsf{Quant}_{\mathsf{M}}$, which assigns a relation between subsets of U_{M} to each of the quantifying determiners in the DRS vocabulary V.

It seems reasonable to impose some general constraints on such models. Most quantifying determiners have a kind of "logical" meaning, which is fixed independently of the contingencies of the world or situation about which we happen to be speaking, and which, therefore, ought to be the same for all models. The determiners **every** and **all**, for instance, should always be interpreted as universal quantifiers. That is, for every model M we should have

$$\text{Quant}_M(\textbf{every}) = \text{Quant}_M(\textbf{all}) = \{ \langle A,B\rangle : A \subseteq U_M \text{ and } B \subseteq U_M \text{ and } A \subseteq A \cap B\}$$

With other determiners this issue is more delicate. It is often said that the meaning of **most** is given by the generalized quantifier

$$\{ \langle A,B\rangle : |A \cap B| > |A \setminus B|\}$$

But a closer look on how the word **most** is used throws doubt on this. For instance, the sentence **Most natural numbers are not prime** would come out as false on this definition, although there seems to be a good sense of **most** which makes the sentence true. If we want to avoid such conflicts we should impose weaker constraints on $\text{Quant}_M(\textbf{most})$, e.g. by insisting that $\langle A,B\rangle \in \text{Quant}_M(\textbf{most})$ iff $|A \cap B| > |A \setminus B|$ only in the case where A is finite.

With determiners such as **many** and **few** the issue is even more complicated. Even though the semantics of these words has received a considerable amount of attention, there still is no clear consensus on the general constraints that the meanings of these words should obey.

We will not pursue these matters further. Instead we turn to a second problem about the semantics of quantified sentences. This is the so-called *proportion problem*, which was briefly discussed in 4.1.3. Consider the duplex condition

(4.165)

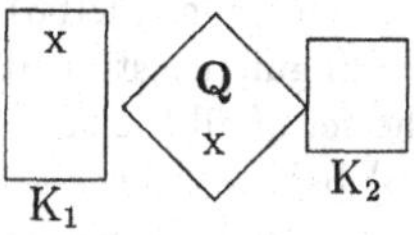

where **Q** denotes the generalized quantifier $\mathbf{R_0}$. In 4.1.3 we stated the verification conditions for (4.165) as in (4.166) (which is essentially the same as (4.24)).

(4.166) $M \models_f (4.165)$ iff $\langle A,B\rangle \in \mathbf{R_0}$, where

$$A = \{b : b \in U_M \;\&\; (\exists g)\ (f \cup \{\langle x,b\rangle\} \subseteq_{U_{K_1}-\{x\}} g \;\&\; M \models_g K_1)\}$$

and

$$B = \{b : b \in U_M \;\&\; (\exists g)\ (f \cup \{\langle x,b\rangle\} \subseteq_{U_{K_1}-\{x\}} g \;\&\; M \models_g K_1 \;\&\; \exists h\ (g \subseteq_{U_{K_2}} h \;\&\; M \models_h K_2))\}$$

Recall our reason for mentioning the discourse referent **x** in the central component of (4.165) (that is, underneath the symbol **Q**). Its presence there is to indicate how the sets A and B are to be defined. There is, however, also another reason for mentioning the variable in the central diamond. Consider

(4.167) Most linguistics students who are taking a course in semantics are miserable.

Suppose that there are 100 linguists 70 of whom are taking one course in semantics and are miserable and that the remaining 30 are each taking three courses in semantics and that these students are perfectly happy. In such a situation it is intuitively clear that (4.167) is true. The DRS (4.168) for (4.167)

(4.168)

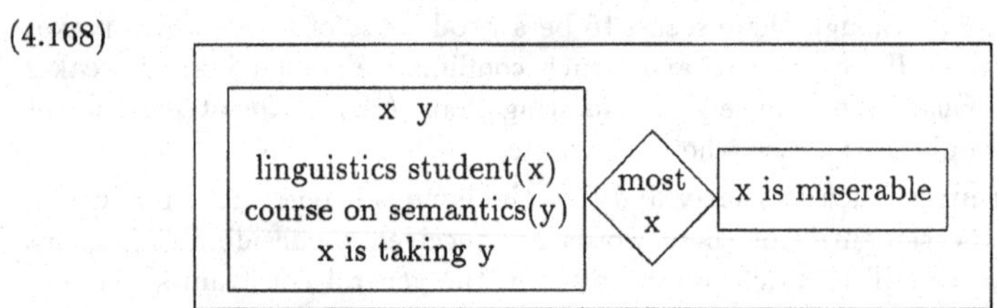

correctly reflects this intuition: according to (4.166) (4.168) will indeed be true with respect to the situation we have described. Note that the presence of **x** in the central component of the duplex condition in (4.168) is crucial. It is needed, because only in this way are we certain to "count the right objects". Let us go through the argument one more time:

When we apply the verification conditions (4.166) to the special case of (4.168), we obtain for A the set of all those linguistics students who are taking one or more courses in semantics, and for B the set of all the students in the set A who are miserable. (4.168) will be true if ⟨A,B⟩ belongs to the generalized quantifier expressed by **most**; given what **most** means, this will be the case iff B is more than half the size of A. So the numbers relevant to the truth of (4.168) are the cardinalities of A and B. (4.166) yields the right truth conditions for (4.167), because in using the cardinality of A it counts the different possible instantiations of the discourse referent **x**. It does *not* count instantiations of the discourse referent **y**, nor does it count all the pairs ⟨b,c⟩ such that b is a linguistics student, c is a course in semantics and b is taking c.

So far, so good. For a sentence such as (4.167) (4.166) appears to give the right truth conditions. But now consider the sentence

(2.46) Every farmer who owns a donkey beats it.

In Chapter 2, where we discussed this sentence, we noted that our theory assigns it the truth conditions given in (4.169):

(4.169) for all **x** and all **y** if **x** is a farmer and **y** a donkey and **x** owns **y** then **x** beats **y**.

It is to be remembered that these truth conditions come from the DRS for (2.46) we were then using

(4.170)

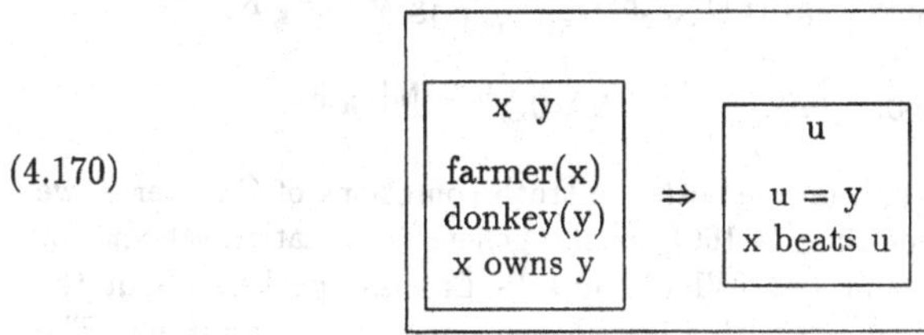

in which the ⇒ binds both **x** and **y**, without making any distinction between them. It was precisely because of the proportion problem that we decided to represent quantifying determiners by means of duplex conditions, so that (2.46) would henceforth get a representation of the form

(4.171)

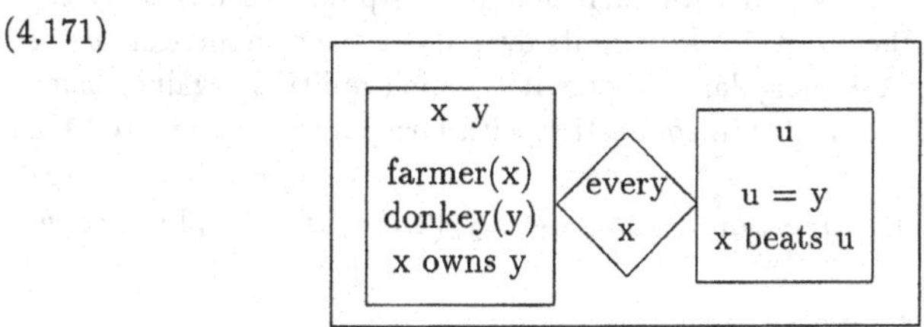

But now we have a problem. For according to (4.166) (with the universal quantifier instantiating **Q**, i.e. $\mathbf{R}_0 = \{\langle A,B\rangle : A \subseteq A \cap B\}$) (4.171) is true iff the set A of farmers who own a donkey is included in the set of farmers who own a donkey which they beat. This is different from (4.169), and, indeed, it seems wrong. For it predicts that (2.46) would be true even in a situation in which every farmer who owns at least one donkey owns more than fifty, but beats only one of the donkeys he owns. Thus, for "donkey sentences", in which a discourse referent introduced by an indefinite in the left-hand DRS of a duplex condition serves as antecedent for a pronoun occurring in the right-hand DRS, the verification conditions given in (4.166) are not right. If the truth conditions of such sentences are indeed those given by (4.169), then (4.166) should be replaced by

(4.172) $M \models_f$ (4.165) iff $\langle A,B\rangle \in \mathbf{R}_0$, where
$A = \{b : b \in U_M \ \&\ (\exists g)\ (f \cup \{\langle x,b\rangle\} \subseteq_{U_{K_1}-\{x\}} g \ \&\ M \models_g K_1)\}$
and
$B = \{b : b \in U_M \ \&\ (\exists g)\ (f \cup \{\langle x,b\rangle\} \subseteq_{U_{K_1}-\{x\}} g \ \&\ M \models_g K_1)$
&
$\forall g\ (f \cup \{\langle x,b\rangle\} \subseteq_{U_{K_1}-\{x\}} g \rightarrow (\exists h)\ (g \subseteq_{U_{K_2}} h \ \&\ M \models_h K_2))\}$

Thus, if we want to remain in line with the truth conditions of Chapter 2, we should adopt (4.172), rather than (4.166), as the general verification schema for duplex conditions. But should we? When one asks English speakers about the truth or falsity of (2.46) one meets with a bewildering spectrum of intuitions. The data are, if possible, even more confusing with regard to the sentence

(4.173) Most farmers who own a donkey beat it.

We ourselves have found it diffcult to draw any clear moral from the reactions we have got, other than that judgements become instable and inconsistent as soon as the situation includes farmers who own more than one donkey. Apparently there is a "uniqueness effect" connected with such sentences – produced either by the syntactic singularity of the NP **a donkey** on its own, or by the combination of the indefinite and the anaphoric singular pronoun **it** – which militates against using sentences such as (4.173) or (2.46) in connection with farmers who own more than one donkey.[55]

It is interesting in this connection to compare, say, (4.173) with its plural counterpart

(4.174) Most farmers who own donkeys beat them.

which is not subject to the abovementioned constraint that appears to be associated with the singular **a donkey**. Unfortunately, the truth conditions of this last sentence are not very clear either, but presumably for a different reason: Here it is the possibility of interpreting the relation expressed by **x beat Y** where **Y** is the set of donkeys owned by **x** collectively, so that it doesn't require that **x** beat each of the donkeys in **Y**.

It should be emphasized that we are not arguing that there are no situations at all in which some of the farmers own more than one donkey and in which (4.173) strikes English speakers as nevertheless having a definite truth value. If for instance

[55] On this topic see [Kadmon 1987a], [Kadmon 1990], [Heim 1990] and [Chierchia 1991].

every farmer who owns one or more donkeys either beats all the donkeys he owns or else beats none, (4.173) will be recognized as clearly true or false depending on whether the donkey-beating farmers constitute a majority among the donkey owners. Note, however, that in this situation (4.166) and (4.172) predict the same truth values. This is so in particular when each of the farmers in question has at most one donkey. For in that case, beating all the donkeys one has and beating just one of them evidently comes to the same thing.

To sum up, (i) it is not clear that the truth conditions which we assumed in Chapter 2 for sentences such as (2.46) are really the ones which normal speakers associate with these sentences; and (ii) it is therefore not clear either whether one should adopt the revised verification conditions (4.172), stick with the somewhat simpler earlier conditions (4.166) or opt for some third, as yet unexplored possibility, which envisages truth conditions that vary with the context.

Although it is clear from this discussion that (4.172) fails to do justice to all intuitions that speakers associate with quantificational sentences such as (4.173), we have nonetheless decided to adopt this condition in our summary of the formal theory in the next section. In this way the continuity with our earlier treatment of **donkey** sentences is preserved; and at least the semantics we get is consistent with that opinion on the meaning of **donkey**-sentences which, justifiably or not, has long prevailed among logicians and philosophers as well as many linguists.

4.3.2.2 Summary of Definitions

Definition 4.3.5

A model M for DRL_{Plur} is a triple $\langle \mathcal{U}_M, \mathsf{Name}_M, \mathsf{Pred}_M, \mathsf{Quant}_M \rangle$ consisting of

(i) a complete, free, atomic upper semilattice $\mathcal{U}_M = \langle U_M, \subset \rangle$ with zero.

(ii) a function Name_M mapping each name **a** of DRL_{Plur} to its bearer in U_M such that

$\mathsf{Name}_M(\mathbf{A}) \in At(U_M)$ if **a** names an individual.
$\mathsf{Name}_M(\mathbf{A}) \in U_M \setminus (At(U_M) \cup \{0_M\})$ if **a** names a group.

(iii) a function Pred_M mapping predicates **P** to their extensions in M.

Definition 4.3.6

(i) A *DRS* K *confined to* V *and* R is a pair consisting of a subset U_K (possibly empty) of R and a set Con_K of DRS-conditions confined to V and R;

(ii) A *DRS-condition confined to* V *and* R is an expression of one of the following forms:

(a) **at(x), non-at(x)**, where **x** belongs to R
(b) $\mathbf{x} = \mathbf{y}_1 \oplus ... \oplus \mathbf{y}_n$ $(n \geq 2)$
(c) $\mathbf{x} = \Sigma \mathbf{z}$ K
(d) $|\mathbf{x}| = \nu$ where $\nu \in \{1, 2, 3, ...\}$
(e) $\mathbf{x} \in \mathbf{y}$
(f) $\pi(\mathbf{x})$, where **x** belongs to R and π is a name from V
(g) $\eta(\mathbf{x})$, $\mathbf{x}\eta$, where **x** belongs to R and η is a unary predicate from V[56]
(h) $\mathbf{x}\xi\mathbf{y}$, where **x**, **y** belong to R and ξ is a binary predicate from V
(i) $\neg$K, where K is a DRS confined to V and R
(j) $K_1 \Rightarrow K_2$, $K_1 \vee ... \vee K_2$ where K_1 to K_n ($n \geq 2$) are DRSs confined to V and R.
(k) K_1 ⟨Q x⟩ K_2, where K_1 and K_2 are DRSs confined to V and R, and Q is a quantifying determiner from V.

Definition 4.3.7

Let K be a DRS confined to V and R, γ a DRS-condition and f an embedding from K into M, i.e. a function whose Domain equals U_K and whose Range is included in U_M

(i) f *verifies* the DRS K in M iff f verifies each of the conditions γ belonging to Con_K in M

(ii) "f *verifies* the condition γ in M" is defined by cases, depending on the form of γ:

(a) (i) $M \models_f$ **at(x)** if f(x) is an atom of M
(ii) $M \models_f$ **non-at(x)** if f(x) is a non-atomic entity of M
(b) $M \models_f \mathbf{x} = \mathbf{y}_1 \oplus ... \oplus \mathbf{y}_n$ iff $f(\mathbf{x}) = f(\mathbf{y}_1) \oplus_M ... \oplus_M f(\mathbf{y}_n)$
(c) $M \models_f \mathbf{x} = \Sigma \mathbf{z}\ \mathbf{K}'$ iff $f(\mathbf{x}) = \oplus\{b : b \in U_M\ \&\ M \models_{f \cup \{\langle z,b \rangle\}} \mathbf{K}'\}$
(d) $M \models_f |\mathbf{x}| = \nu$ iff $|\{b \in U_M\text{: b is an atom of M } \&\ b \subset_M f(\mathbf{x})\}| = \nu$
(e) $M \models_f \mathbf{x} \in \mathbf{y}$ iff $f(\mathbf{x})$ is an atom of M and $f(\mathbf{x}) \subset_M f(\mathbf{y})$
(f) $M \models_f \pi(\mathbf{x})$, where π is a name iff $\langle \pi, f(\mathbf{x}) \rangle \in Name_M$
(g) (i) $M \models_f \eta(\mathbf{x})$, where η is a noun iff $f(\mathbf{x}) \in Pred_M(\eta)$
(ii) $M \models_f \mathbf{x}\zeta$, where ζ is an intransitive verb iff $f(\mathbf{x}) \in Pred_M(\zeta)$
(h) $M \models_f \mathbf{x}\xi\mathbf{y}$, where ξ is an intransitive verb iff $\langle f(\mathbf{x}), f(\mathbf{y}) \rangle \in Pred_M(\xi)$
(i) $M \models_f \neg\mathbf{K}$ iff there is no extension g of f to $U_{K'}$ such that $M \models_g \mathbf{K}$

[56] Recall our practice to write '$\eta(\mathbf{x})$' when η is an English common noun and '$\mathbf{x}\eta$' when η is an English verb. For present purposes the difference is of course immaterial.

(j) (i) $M \models_f K_1 \Rightarrow K_2$ iff for every extension g of f to U_{K_1} such that $M \models_g K_1$ there is an extension h of g to U_{K_2} such that $M \models_h K_2$

(ii) $M \models_f K_1 \vee ... \vee K_n$ iff for some i with $1 \leq i \leq n$ $M \models_f K_i$

(k) $M \models_f$ 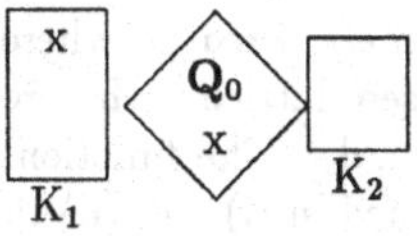

iff $\langle A,B \rangle \in Quant_M(Q_0)$, where

$A = \{b : b \in U_M \ \& \ (\exists g)\ (f \cup \{\langle x,b \rangle\} \subseteq_{U_{K_1}-\{x\}} g \ \& \ M \models_g K_1)\}$

and

$B = \{b : b \in U_M \ \& \ (\exists g)\ (f \cup \{\langle x,b \rangle\} \subseteq_{U_{K_1}-\{x\}} g \ \& \ M \models_g K_1) \ \&$
$\forall g\ (f \cup \{\langle x,b \rangle\} \subseteq_{U_{K_1}-\{x\}} g \rightarrow (\exists h)\ (g \subseteq_{U_{K_2}} h \ \& \ M \models_h K_2))\}$

Exercises

1. (a) Construct the DRSs for all possible readings of (i) and (ii):

   (i) The boys who admire Mary own dogs which cannot stand them.

   (ii) Mary owns a dog. Most girls who know her admire every boy who cannot stand them.

   (b) Let M be the model $\langle \mathcal{U}_M, Name_M, Pred_M \rangle$, where $\mathcal{U}_M = \langle U, \subset \rangle$ is an atomic, free, complete upper semilattice with zero. The atoms of $\mathcal{U}_M$ are: $g_1, ..., g_5, b_1, ..., b_5, d_1, ..., d_5$. The functions $Name_M$ and $Pred_M$ have for the predicates mentioned in (i) and (ii) the following values:

   $Name_M$(Mary) $= g_1$;
   $Pred_M$(girl) $= \{g_1, ..., g_5\}$;
   $Pred_M$(boy) $= \{b_1, ..., b_5\}$;
   $Pred_M$(dog) $= \{d_1, ..., d_5\}$;
   $Pred_M$(know) $= \{\langle g_2, g_1 \rangle, \langle g_2, d_1 \rangle, \langle g_3, g_1 \rangle, \langle g_4, g_1 \rangle, \langle g_2, g_3 \rangle, \langle g_3, g_2 \rangle, \langle g_5, g_2 \rangle, \langle g_5, d_1 \rangle\}$;
   $Pred_M$(own) $= \{\langle g_1, d_1 \rangle, \langle g_1, d_2 \rangle, \langle b_1, d_3 \rangle, \langle b_2, d_4 \rangle, \langle b_3, d_5 \rangle$;
   $Pred_M$(admire) $= \{\langle g_1, b_1 \rangle, \langle g_2, b_2 \rangle, \langle g_3, b_1 \rangle, \langle g_3, b_2 \rangle, \langle g_3, b_3 \rangle, \langle b_1, g_1 \rangle, \langle b_1, d_1 \rangle, \langle b_2, g_2 \rangle\}, \langle b_2, d_2 \rangle, \langle g_4, b_3 \rangle, \langle b_3, g_1 \rangle, \langle b_3, d_2 \rangle\}$;
   $Pred_M$(can stand) $= \{\langle b_1, g_1 \rangle, \langle b_1, d_1 \rangle, \langle b_2, d_2 \rangle, \langle b_3, g_1 \rangle, \langle b_3, d_2 \rangle, \langle d_1, b_1 \rangle, \langle d_2, b_2 \rangle, \langle d_3, b_3 \rangle\}$;

   Determine for each of the DRSs derived from (i) and (ii) of part (a) whether or not it is verified in M.

2. (a) Construct DRSs for all possible readings of (i) and (ii).

   (i) Mary admires Bill. Bill admires Sue. Mary owns every dog which likes them.

   (ii) Bill owns three dogs. Most girls who like him admire them.

   (b) Let M be the model $\langle \mathcal{U}_M, \mathsf{Name}_M, \mathsf{Pred}_M \rangle$, where $\mathcal{U}_M = \langle \mathsf{U}, \oplus \rangle$ is an atomic, free, complete upper semilattice with zero. The atoms of $\mathcal{U}_M$ are: $g_1, ..., g_5, b_1, ..., b_5, d_1, ..., d_5$. The functions Name_M and Pred_M have for the predicates mentioned in (i) and (ii) the following values:

$$
\begin{aligned}
&\mathsf{Name}_M(\textbf{Mary}) &&= g_1;\\
&\mathsf{Name}_M(\textbf{Bill}) &&= b_1;\\
&\mathsf{Name}_M(\textbf{Sue}) &&= g_2;\\
&\mathsf{Pred}_M(\textbf{girl}) &&= \{g_1, ..., g_5\};\\
&\mathsf{Pred}_M(\textbf{boy}) &&= \{b_1, ..., b_5\};\\
&\mathsf{Pred}_M(\textbf{dog}) &&= \{d_1, ..., d_5\};\\
&\mathsf{Pred}_M(\textbf{know}) &&= \{\langle g_2, g_1\rangle, \langle g_2, d_1\rangle, \langle g_3, g_1\rangle, \langle g_4, g_1\rangle,\\
& && \quad \langle g_2, g_3\rangle, \langle g_3, g_2\rangle, \langle g_5, g_2\rangle, \langle g_5, d_1\rangle\};\\
&\mathsf{Pred}_M(\textbf{like}) &&= \{\langle g_1, b_1\rangle, \langle g_2, b_2\rangle, \langle g_2, b_1\rangle, \langle g_3, b_3\rangle,\\
& && \quad \langle g_3, b_2\rangle, \langle g_3, b_1\rangle, \langle d_1, g_1\rangle, \langle d_1, g_2\rangle,\\
& && \quad \langle d_1, b_1\rangle, \langle d_2, b_1\rangle, \langle d_2, g_2\rangle\};\\
&\mathsf{Pred}_M(\textbf{own}) &&= \{\langle g_1, d_1\rangle, \langle b_1, d_2\rangle, \langle b_1, d_3\rangle, \langle b_1, d_4\rangle,\\
& && \quad \langle (b_3 \oplus b_4 \oplus b_5), d_5\rangle\};\\
&\mathsf{Pred}_M(\textbf{admire}) &&= \{\langle g_1, b_1\rangle, \langle g_2, b_2\rangle, \langle g_3, b_1\rangle, \langle g_3, b_2\rangle,\\
& && \quad \langle g_3, b_3\rangle, \langle b_1, g_1\rangle, \langle b_1, d_1\rangle, \langle b_2, g_2\rangle,\\
& && \quad \langle b_2, d_2\rangle, \langle b_3, g_1\rangle, \langle b_3, d_2\rangle\};
\end{aligned}
$$

   Show for each of the DRSs derived from (i) and (ii) of part (a) whether or not it is verified in M.

3. Choose two of the DRSs you have constructed in 2. so that one of them is verified in M and the other is not. Change M to a new model M′ by altering the function Pred_m in such a way that the first DRS is not verified in M′ but the second one is.

4. Show that the following arguments are valid.

   (i) Bill owns books which quote him. $\models$ Bill owns at least two books which quote him.

   (ii) Bill owns five books which quote him. $\models$ Bill owns books which quote him.

   (iii) Bill owns books which quote him. $\models$ Bill owns a book.

(iv) Bill owns five books which quote him. $\models$ Bill owns at least three books which quote somebody.

5. Show that Summation always preserves truth or falsity, i.e.:
If K is a DRS and K′ results from K by an application of Summation then we have for all models M

$\mathsf{M} \models \mathrm{K}$ iff $\mathsf{M} \models \mathrm{K}'$

4.4 DRS-Construction for Plurals II

In this last part of Chapter 4 we briefly review a few problems which we think should be included even in a first survey of the English plural, but which we do not want to treat in detail. Not that with these problems the list of issues arising in connection with the plural will be complete. For one thing, there are many problems which are related to the interaction of plurals with other linguistic constructions, which have not been treated in these first four chapters. (Among them are the English devices for referring to time, in particular tenses and adverbs. They will be the subject of the next chapter, which ends with some of the questions arising from their interaction between plural NPs.) And even within the narrower limits determined by the constructions we have considered up to now, our treatment has been anything but exhaustive. The choice of topics for the present chapter has been guided by our desire to focus on those problems which our framework seems especially well equipped to handle, or which bring out most clearly how construction algorithm and model theory can be adapted to deal with a larger linguistic repertoire.

4.4.1 Collective vs. Distributive Readings and Ambiguity of Scope

This section is a short interlude, in which we elaborate one of the themes we touched upon in Section 4.3.1.1. There we noted that sentences with plural "cardinal" NPs (i.e. NPs in which the name is preceded by a plural cardinal – **two**, **three**, ...) in both subject and object position are multiply ambiguous. In the next few paragraphs we discuss again what readings such sentences have, and consider what processing principles are needed to generate those (and only those) readings.

We will concentrate once more on the sentence we considered at some length in Section 4.3.1.1.

(4.175) Three lawyers hired five cleaners.

As we saw, the first processing step transforms (4.175) obligatorily into the DRS

(4.176)

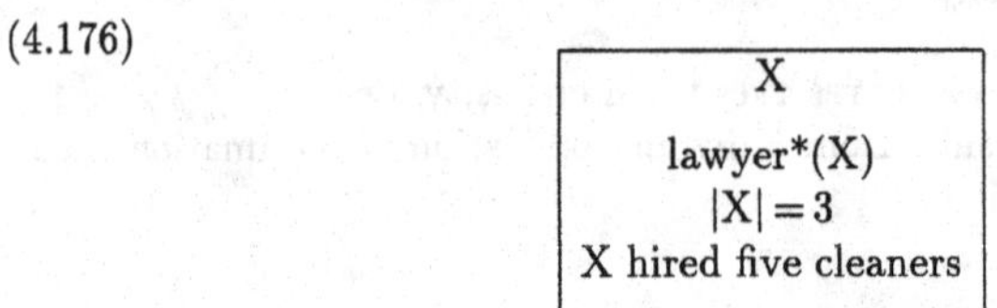

This is then transformed into (4.177) or into (4.178).

(4.177)

(4.178)

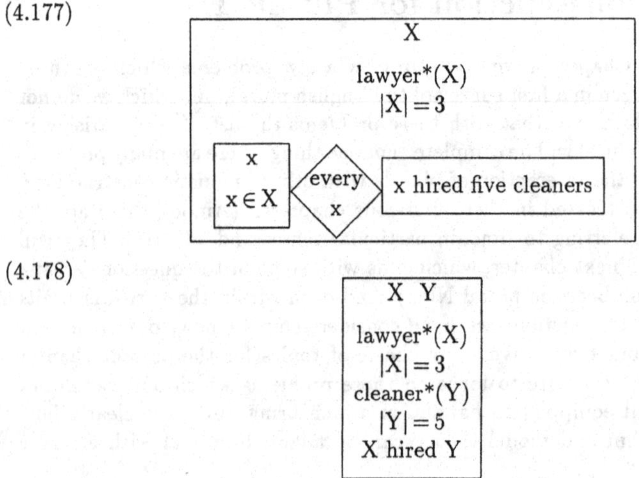

depending on whether or not we take the option of distributing over the discourse referent **X**. One of the two possible continuations of (4.177) is (4.179), which can then be optionally reduced to (4.180).

(4.179)

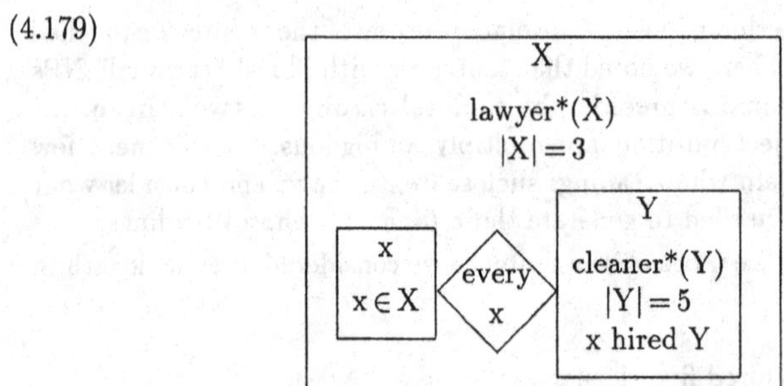

(4.180)

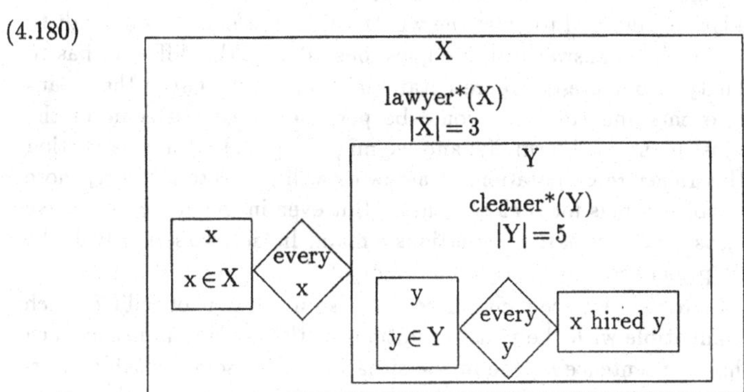

Both (4.179) and (4.180) assert that each one from a certain set of three lawyers hired five cleaners, so the total number of cleaners hired could have been as high as fifteen. The difference is that (4.179) speaks of collective hirings (hirings of 'crews'), whereas (4.180) talks of each cleaner being hired individually.

Parallel to (4.179) and (4.180) there are two further DRSs for (4.175). The first is (4.178) itself, the second is the result of distributing in (4.178) over **Y**:

(4.181)

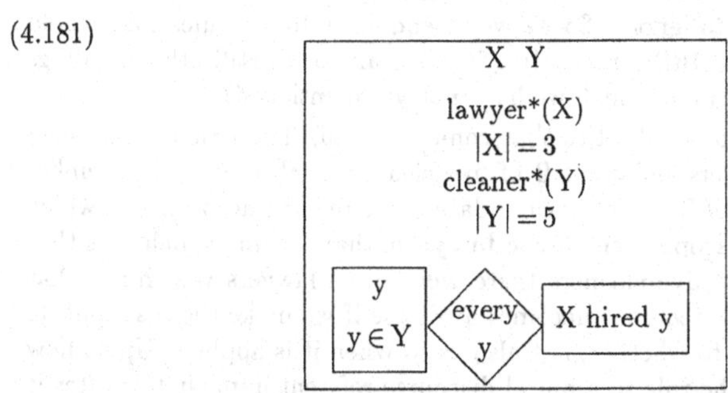

Of these last two DRSs (4.181) represents the reading according to which three lawyers acted collectively in five different instances, in each case hiring one cleaner. (4.178) (considered as completed DRS) differs from (4.181) in saying not only that the lawyers acted collectively but also that the cleaners were hired as a group.

Described in this way the difference between (4.178) and (4.181) may at first seem clear enough. But is it? How separate must the hirings of the individual cleaners be, in order that we have a case as described in (4.181), rather than (4.178)? Should the hirings have taken place at different times? Or would it have been enough if each cleaner got his own contract, although they all received their contracts at the same time (perhaps even on the strength of the same interview, after which the lawyers decided to "hire the whole lot")? It seems very difficult to come up with a principled answer to these questions. Partly, the difficulty has to do with the paucity of our present representational framework. Given the means for representing events and times, it would be possible to express some of the distinctions we just mentioned formally; and we might expect that a construction algorithm for this richer representational framework will generate a larger, more refined repertoire of readings for such sentences. But even in this more expressive framework, it turns out, some of these questions remain. In fact, we seriously doubt that there is any principled way of resolving them all.[57]

Note that the problem we are facing here is not so much that of telling which situations are compatible with the truth conditions of the given sentence as such (in the sense that the sentence is true in the situation under some suitable interpretation), but rather how to distinguish between possible readings – that is, to tell which situations fall under the one reading and which under the other. We will come back to this point at the end of the section.

We argued in the last section that the readings so far discussed are not the only ones that (4.175) has. There is also the cumulative reading, according to which there are a set of three lawyers and a set of five cleaners, such that each of the lawyers played a part in the hiring of at least one of the cleaners and each of the cleaners was, singly or jointly with others, hired by one or more of the lawyers. This reading we decided to ignore. So we won't enquire into the rules that would be needed to construct a DRS representing it. But are there still other readings besides the cumulative reading which we have not yet mentioned?

There are at least two possibilities that come to mind. The first is that there are a set A of three lawyers and a set B of five cleaners such that every member of A hired every member of B. Another candidate is the reading according to which **five cleaners** "has wide scope over" **three lawyers**, that reading which says that for each of a given set of five cleaners there were three lawyers who hired that cleaner. The first of these readings becomes available if we make the distribution rule optional not only as to whether, but also as to when it is applied: Up to now we have always applied the rule to a plural discourse referent immediately after it was introduced. But perhaps this constraint need not be observed invariably. If it is dropped, we can get the reading in question by distributing over **X** and over **Y** (in either order) in (4.178), obtaining, say,

---

[57]Since a representational framework involving times and events will be introduced in Chapter 5, there would seem to be little point in pursuing the problem any further in this section. As a matter of fact, since even the framework of Chapter 5 does not seem capable of providing a truly satisfactory solution to the problem, we have decided not to return to again.

(4.182)

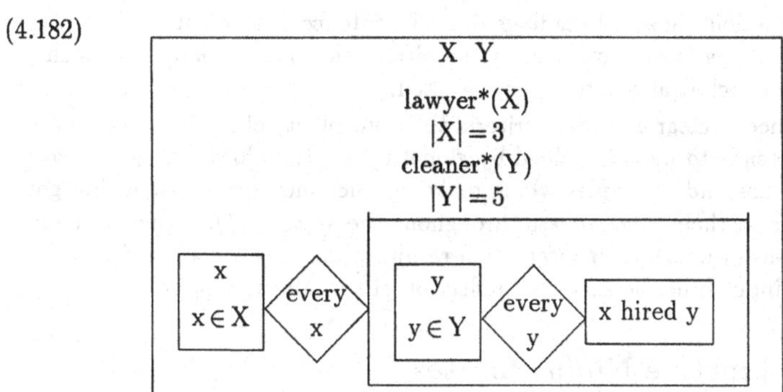

To obtain the second of the two readings mentioned it isn't enough to permit the distribution rule to apply at any time. What we need is the option of dealing with the object NP **five cleaners** before we introduce a discourse referent for the subject NP. If we proceed in this way and then distribute right away over the discourse referent for the object phrase, we get

(4.183)

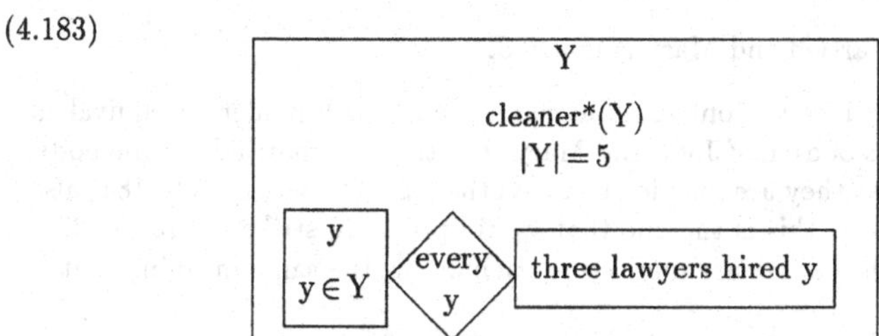

(4.183) can then be turned either into a DRS asserting that each of the cleaners was hired by three lawyers jointly, or into one saying that each cleaner was hired three times, each time by a different lawyer. The question whether object NPs may be treated before subject NPs was touched upon in 3.7. Though we did not propose a definite answer there, we conjectured that this is not a real possibility. Our own intuitions concerning (4.175) confirm this conjecture, as we find it virtually impossible to assign such a reading to this sentence.

The reflections of this section ought to have made plain not only that sentences with two or more cardinal NPs admit of a surprising spectrum of possible interpretations, but also that it is often not easy to see what is to count as a separate reading of a given sentence or text. This presents a special predicament for a theory like ours, which sharply distinguishes between the construction of semantic representations and their truth-conditional evaluation. For such a theory cannot avoid assigning a definite set of readings to each sentence or text within its scope: the different readings it predicts are, by definition, the (not trivially equivalent) representations which it allows to be constructed.

In the absence of clear empirical criteria the multiplicity of readings which the theory assigns tends to be determined by global rather than local considerations: The different rules and principles which make up the construction algorithm get their support from their effectiveness throughout the system. Thus the spectrum of interpretations in which their interaction results when they are applied to some one particular input must be seen as a reflection of this global support too.

4.4.2 Conjunctive Noun Phrases

In Section 2.4 we offered a general treatment of the word **and** which acknowledges the fact that **and** may occur between expressions of any syntactic category, as long as the two or more expressions it conjoins belong to the same category. In particular, the analysis allowed **and** to occur between two NPs. What the analysis did not allow for are uses of conjunctive NPs with collective predicates.

(4.184) John and Mary are married.

(4.185) John is married and Mary is married.

For instance, (4.184) received only one interpretation, which renders it equivalent to (4.185) which says of each of John and Mary that they are married to somebody, without insisting that they are married to each other. Surely, however, (4.184) also has a reading – in fact, this is the one that would probably strike the reader first – according to which the two are married to each other, the same meaning that is conveyed by

(4.186) John is married to Mary.

It is clear what is missing from our earlier analysis of conjunction. A conjoined NP such as **John and Mary** can be understood as denoting the set consisting of John and Mary, which may serve as argument to a collective predicate. (Note again in this connection that conjoined NPs always act as plurals: if they occur in subject position, the inflected verb must have plural morphology.) The processing algorithm for conjunctive phrases which we defined in Chapter 2 does not capture this interpretation of conjoined NPs. So we need a new construction which treats them as we have treated other non-quantifying plural NPs, viz. as introducing a discourse referent representing a set.

The NP **John and Mary** tells us that this set consists of two individuals, John and Mary. More generally the set denoted by a conjunctive NP is the summation of the denotations of the conjuncts. It must be kept in mind here that the conjuncts of complex NPs can also be plurals and thus denote sets themselves, as in

(4.187) a. The Montagues and the Capulets

b. Hannah and her sisters

c. Bill, Fred and seven girls they had met

In the examples we have considered so far all conjuncts were non-quantifying NPs.[58] This is no accident – only when the conjuncts are non-quantifying does it make sense to think of the conjunction as denoting the sum of the denotations of its parts. So it is only for conjunctive NPs the parts of which are non-quantifying that the new construction rule is needed. What we have just observed about conjunctive NPs suggests the following statement of the rule:

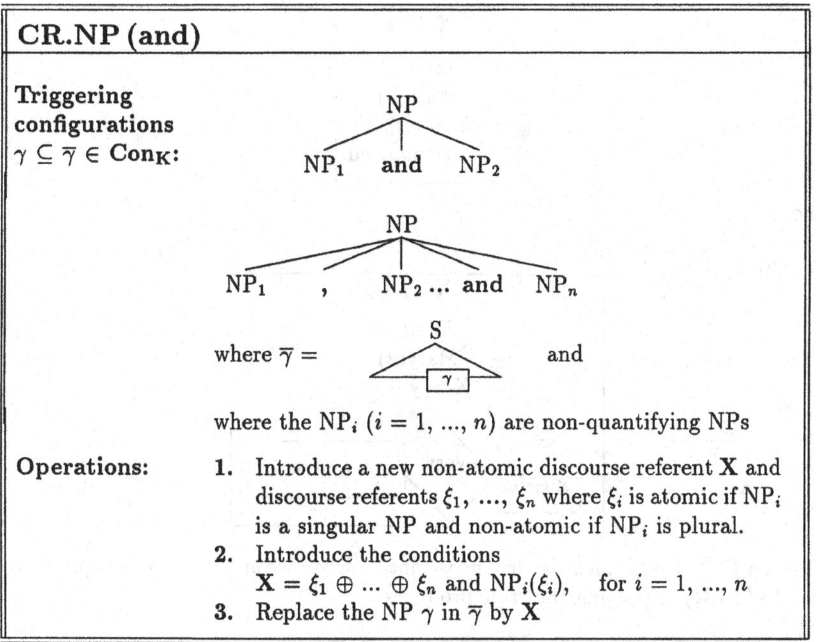

CR.NP (and)
Triggering configurations
$\gamma \subseteq \overline{\gamma} \in \mathrm{Con}_K$:
NP
NP$_1$ and NP$_2$
NP
NP$_1$, NP$_2$ ... and NP$_n$
where $\overline{\gamma}$ =
S
γ
and
where the NP$_i$ (i = 1, ..., n) are non-quantifying NPs
Operations:
1. Introduce a new non-atomic discourse referent X and discourse referents ξ_1, ..., ξ_n where ξ_i is atomic if NP$_i$ is a singular NP and non-atomic if NP$_i$ is plural.
2. Introduce the conditions
$\mathbf{X} = \xi_1 \oplus \ldots \oplus \xi_n$ and NP$_i(\xi_i)$, for i = 1, ..., n
3. Replace the NP γ in $\overline{\gamma}$ by X

Formulated in this way the rule fails to cope with the data that were discussed

[58] We recall that quantifying NPs are those whose processing leads (obligatorily) to duplex conditions, and that non-quantifying NPs are those which do not. The fragment of English we treat in this book contains only one type of singular quantifiying NP, that where the determiner is every.

in Chapter 2: The earlier conjuncts of a conjunction can provide antecedents for pronouns in the later conjuncts, but hardly ever the other way round. To account for those facts the rule should record the sequential order in which the arguments appear. We could achieve this by proceeding along the lines of Section 2.4. However, since questions of pronominalisation within conjunctive NPs are orthogonal to those on which the present section means to concentrate, we will not go into the technical complications that refining the rule along these lines would bring with it.

CR.NP(and) permits us to interpret sentences with conjunctive NPs collectively. Note however that it does not *force* such an interpretation upon us. For after having applied the rule to interpret the NP as denoting a set, we are still free to distribute over this set. Thus for (4.184) we can, with the help of CR.NP(and), obtain two DRSs, viz.

(4.188)

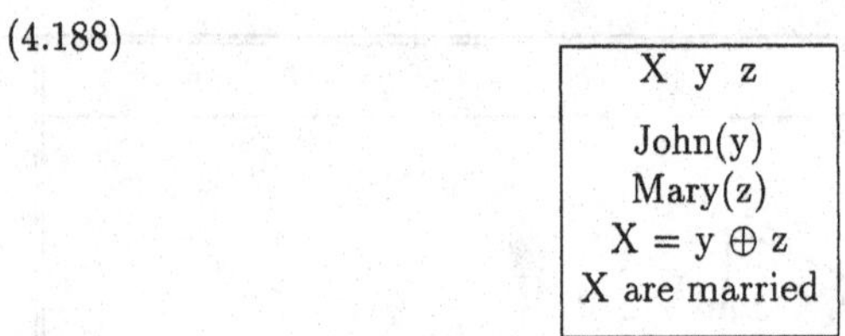

and

(4.189)

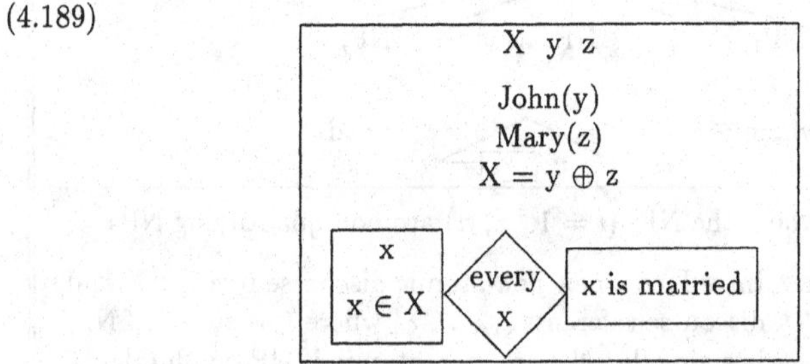

The last DRS is equivalent to the one we obtain when we apply our old conjunction rule to (4.184). Applying that rule produces

(4.190)

$\langle$John is married, $\{\delta, 1\}\rangle$
$\langle$Mary is married, $\{\delta, 2\}\rangle$

where δ is the syntactic analysis of the sentence (4.184). This gets further reduced to

(4.191)

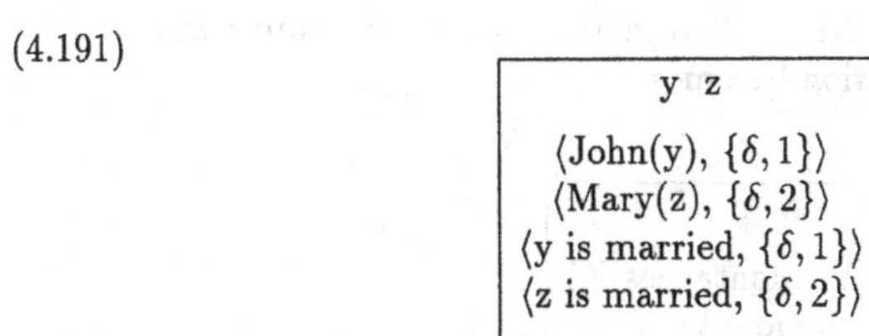

or, after dropping the sequential information,

(4.192)

y z
John(y) Mary(z) y is married z is married

Evidently, (4.189) and (4.192) carry the same truth conditions.

This example may seem to suggest that the option of distributing after applying CR.NP(and) makes our earlier rule CR.AND redundant for the category of NP. However, in general this is not so. Consider, for instance,

(4.193) The Montagues and the Capulets own a large estate.

One reading of this sentence is that where the Montagues own (as a family) a large estate and where the same is true for the Capulets. Introducing first a discourse referent for the set consisting of the Montagues and the Capulets together and then distributing over that set will not give that reading. Instead it produces the one according to which each Montague owns a large estate and the same is true of each Capulet. Not distributing, on the other hand, gives rise to the reading according to which the Montagues and the Capulets jointly own a large estate, a particularly implausible interpretation if one thinks of Shakespeare's play. However, we get the intended reading if we first apply the old conjunction rule, obtaining

(4.194)

⟨The Montagues own a large estate, $\{\delta, 1\}$⟩ ⟨The Capulets own a large estate, $\{\delta, 2\}$⟩

where δ is the syntactic analysis of the sentence (4.193). Two applications of the rule for non-quantifying plural NPs will turn this into a structure which upon dropping the sequential information becomes

(4.195)

X u Y v
the Montagues(X)
large estate(u)
X owns u
the Capulets(Y)
large estate(v)
Y own v

As we have formulated the rule CR.NP(and) it applies only to those conjunctive NPs whose conjuncts are non-quantifying NPs. Indeed it seems that only such conjunctions are capable of the collective readings that the rule is meant to capture. NPs such as

(4.196) Bill and most of his friends

seem to admit only of an interpretation which distributes the predicate over their conjuncts. Thus

(4.197) Bill and most of his friends bought a new car.

has the interpretation on which Bill bought a new car and so did each one from a majority of his friends; and this interpretation appears to be the only one.[59] We get this reading by applying first the old conjunction rule to (4.197), which gives us

(4.199)

⟨Bill bought a new car, $\{\delta, 1\}$⟩
⟨Most of his friends bought a new car, $\{\delta, 2\}$⟩

[59]It may be just possible to give a collective interpretation to sentences like

(4.198) Bill and many of his colleagues hired a new secretary.

Inasmuch as this possibility exists, it shows that under certain circumstances an NP beginning with **many** can be given a non-quantifying reading. The question if and when the NPs which we have thus far classified as quantifying may allow for non-distributive interpretations will be raised in Section 4.4.4.

where δ is the syntactic analysis of the sentence (4.197). The remaining steps are all familiar; they lead eventually to

(4.200)

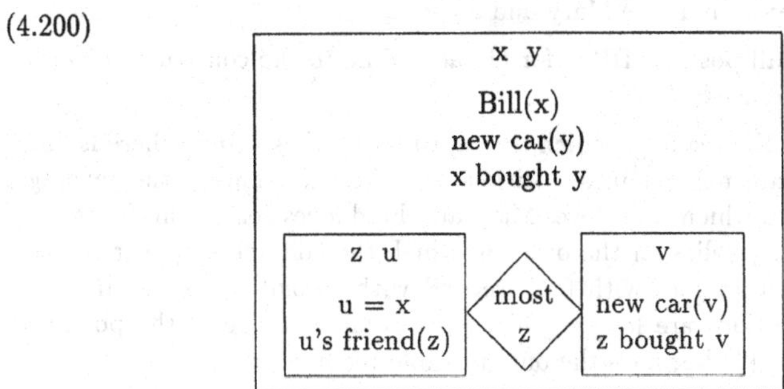

Although our new rule for conjunctive NPs allows us to represent many readings that were not represented before, it unfortunately does not enable us to represent them all. For instance,

(4.201) The Montagues and the Capulets are on bad terms.

has a reading according to which the Montagues, as a group, are on bad terms with another group, the Capulets. In other words, **are on bad terms** in (4.201) functions not only as a collective predicate which is true of a set {a,b} if a and b are on bad terms, but also as a collective predicate applying to a *pair of groups*, a predicate that is satisfied by the pair consisting of the group of Montagues and the group of Capulets. This last interpretation, however, eludes us not only because of a lacuna in the construction algorithm that we have put together so far; more fundamentally, it requires a more sophisticated model theory than the one stated in Section 4.3, a model theory which allows for the formation of pairs (or, more generally, sets of groups) and not only for their mereological sum.

In fact, a proper analysis of (4.201) would require a much more sophisticated mathematical foundation for the treatment of plurals than we offered here, one in which the set-theoretic and the lattice-theoretic approaches, which in Section 4.3.1 we presented as competing treatments of the same concepts, are combined into a single theory. For reasons of space we have decided not to present this theory and its linguistic applications here.[60]

[60]Detailed discussions of the matter can be found in [Landman 1989], [Link 1991], [Lønning 1989], [Hoeksema 1983] and [Lasersohn 1988].

Exercises

1. (a) Consider

   (1) John and Fred love Mary and Joan.

   Construct all possible DRSs for (1) according to the construction rules so far introduced.

   (b) Besides all the readings which are captured by those DRSs there is one which we are not yet in a position to represent. This is the reading according to which John loves Mary and Fred loves Joan. This interpretation clearly relies on the order in which the conjuncts appear in the two NPs – first goes with first, second with second and so on in case the conjunctions are longer. What is available as one of the possible readings for (1) becomes the only possible reading for

   (2) John and Fred love Mary and Joan, respectively.

   (i) Formulate a construction rule which allows for construction of the missing DRS for (1).

   (ii) Formulate a construction rule for **respectively**. (N.B. be careful about the constraints under which this rule operates.)

   (iii) Using the new rule construct DRSs for the following sentence:

   (3) John, Bill and Fred love Mary, Joan and Alice, respectively.

   (4) John, Bill and Fred and Gerald love Ella, Jennifer and Mathilda, respectively.

   (5) The Donovans and the Bakers own a Daimler and a Rolls Royce, respectively.

   (iv) How could the rule for **respectively** be extended to cover conjunctions of other syntactic categories than that of NP, so that the right DRS can be constructed for

   (6) Johnson and Berkowitz own and lease a PC, respectively.

2. We saw that our old rule for conjunctions and the new rule CR.NP(and) get us all the apparently available readings for (1) and (2).

   (1) [=(4.193)] The Montagues and the Capulets own a large estate.

   (2) John and Bill hired a new secretary.

   But there is a complication that arises with sentences which are like (1) and (2) except for having plural object phrases.

   (3) The Montagues and the Capulets own large estates.

(4) John and Bill have hired new secretaries.

In both (3) and (4) the object NPs can be understood as dependent plurals. In the case of (3) this enables us to assign a reading to the effect that the Montagues own one or more large estates and the Capulets likewise. This reading is represented by the following DRS.

(5)

X Y μ ν
the Montagues(X)
the Capulets(Y)
large estate*(μ)
large estate*(ν)
X own μ
Y own ν

As the construction rules have been stated, such a DRS cannot be constructed from (3).

(i) Why not?

(ii) Modify one or more rules so that (5) can be constructed from (3) and carry out this DRS construction.

(iii) Does your modification generate any new readings for (4)?

4.4.3 Floating Quantifiers

This section is devoted to so-called *floating quantifiers.* Here are some examples:

(4.202) The men all own a Renault.

(4.203) The men each own a Renault.

(4.204) John and Mary both own a Renault.

The floating quantifiers in (4.202), (4.203) and (4.204) are the words **all, each** and **both**, respectively. They have been called 'floating quantifiers'[61] because they do not occur in what is supposed to be their standard position, i.e. that of a noun phrase determiner, but are "adrift" from that position, apparently figuring

[61] Floating quantifiers are also sometimes called 'floated' quantifiers.

as constituents of the predicate of which the relevant NP is an argument. Indeed, the semantic contributions that floating quantifiers make to sentences seem to be no different from when they occupy determiner positions. For instance (4.202)–(4.204) appear to be equivalent in meaning to

(4.205) All men own a Renault.

(4.206) Each man owns a Renault.

(4.207) Both John and Mary own a Renault.

The function of **all**, **each** and **both** in (4.202)–(4.204) is to distribute over the set denoted by the subject term. This function is consistent with – though according to our theory of quantifying NPs it is not identical with – that of **all** and **each** in (4.205) and (4.206), where the words occur as determiners of quantifying NPs. We will treat this function – that of making distribution over a given set explicit – as the decisive feature of "floating quantifiers".

This informal characterization of the notion of a floating quantifier indicates quite clearly which DRS-construction principles should be associated with floating quantifiers. Before we formulate these principles, however, we want to draw attention to a few additional facts. First an observation which supports the semantic characterization we just proposed. Floating quantifiers combine at best marginally with those NPs we have classified as 'quantifying'. Thus the sentences in (4.208) are infelicitous; those in (4.209)

(4.208) $\left\{\begin{array}{l}\text{Few}\\ \text{Many}\\ \text{Most}\end{array}\right\}$ men $\left\{\begin{array}{l}\text{all}\\ \text{each}\end{array}\right\}$ own a Renault.

(4.209) $\left\{\begin{array}{l}\text{At least}\\ \text{At most}\\ \text{Exactly}\end{array}\right\}$ five men $\left\{\begin{array}{l}\text{all}\\ \text{each}\end{array}\right\}$ own a Renault.

seem somewhat better, but, according to our own judgement and that of our informants, not much. If, as we have proposed in the earlier parts of this chapter, quantifying NPs differ from non-quantifying ones in that they do not introduce sets, then our characterization of floating quantifiers predicts these infelicities. For it implies that the floating quantifier has a set over which it distributes, and a quantifying NP fails to make such a set available.[62]

[62] That the sentences in (4.208) and (4.209) have any degree of acceptability at all suggests that the set interpretation we have so far excluded for quantifying NPs can be forced on them by the floating quantifier, which requires a set on which it can operate.

The second set of facts concerns the precise positions of floating quantifiers. Often floating quantifiers occur between the subject and the main verb. But when other material intervenes between those two constituents, its positional relation to the floating quantifier is not always fixed. For instance, both (4.210) and (4.211) are fine, and even (4.212) is acceptable.

(4.210) The men may all have bought a Renault.

(4.211) The men may have all bought a Renault.

(4.212) The men all may have bought a Renault.

Precisely where floating quantifiers may occur is a question on which we have nothing to say, and which, as a primarily syntactic issue, lies outside the scope of this book. For simplicity we will assume that the floating quantifier occurs as the initial part of the VP (thus ignoring occurrences like those in (4.210) and (4.211)).

There is another indeterminacy in the position of floating quantifiers which arises when (a) the verb has at least two arguments and (b) there is some sentence material following the second argument. One kind of sentence in which this situation arises is that where the verb takes more than two arguments.

Consider, for instance, a ditransitive verb such as **give**. One can say not only (4.213) but also (4.214).

(4.213) The boys $\left\{\begin{array}{c}\text{all}\\ \text{each}\\ \text{both}\end{array}\right\}$ gave the girls a present.

(4.214) The boys gave the girls $\left\{\begin{array}{c}\text{all}\\ \text{each}\\ \text{both}\end{array}\right\}$ a present.

(4.214) also illustrates a further point. While each of its three sentences has a reading which matches that of the corresponding sentence of (4.213), it also has one which is not available for those sentences, viz. one according to which the floating quantifier distributes with respect to the set denoted by **the girls**, rather than that denoted by **the boys**. The relevant empirical generalization appears to be that a floating quantifier must follow the NP over which it distributes. But again, this is a matter for syntax and we will not go into it here.

The interpretation of a floating quantifier must, we have seen, associate it with some NP occurring in the same clause as the floating quantifier, and this NP must be (a) plural, (b) non-quantifying and (c) in a position that dominates the floating quantifier. (We will refer to this NP as the *licencing* NP (of the floating quantifier).) The construction rules for the different floating quantifiers must reflect this in that they provide for the selection of such an NP – or, more accurately, of the non-atomic discourse referent introduced by it. The factors that enter into the selection of this NP are, like those that enter into the selection of anaphoric antecedents for pronouns, varied. They include considerations of plausibility as well as strictly grammatical constraints (such as, we just saw, linear precedence). As with "pronoun resolution" (i.e. the selection of the antecedents of anaphoric pronouns) only some of those factors can be adequately described within the framework of the theory we have developed. However, even the role of those factors cannot be made fully explicit without a formal treatment of the syntax of floating quantifiers. As such a treatment would involve us in issues that are extraneous to the purpose of this book, and especially of the present, largely explorative section, the best we can offer is an approximate statement of the relevant construction rules.

These rules – one for floating **all**, one for floating **each** and one for floating **both** – are very similar, differing only in the presuppositions they carry concerning the cardinality of the set over which they distribute. In the case of **both** the cardinality must be 2, whereas in the case of **all** there is a strong presumption that it is greater than 2. **Each** appears to be neutral in this regard, with perhaps a slight presumption that the cardinality exceeds 2.

We describe the rule for **each**. In order to state the rule in the familiar format we must specify in particular its triggering configuration. This is something we cannot do, however, as we have not articulated the constituent structure of verb phrases in which floating quantifiers occur. All we can say is that the triggering configuration has the form of a condition γ of category S which contains a floating occurrence of **each** and in which one or more argument NPs may already have been replaced by discourse referents. The operations of the rule involve, firstly, the selection of a non-atomic discourse referent **X**, which represents a plural non-quantifying NP α, where α is one of those argument NPs which precede the given occurrence of **each**. (The fact that the NP must be an argument to the triggering VP is tantamount to **X** occurring in the condition γ that is being processed; cf. Section 4.2.6). Secondly, γ must be replaced by a duplex condition expressing distribution over **X**. In the English fragment to which our formal treatment applies (recall that the extensions discussed in Chapter 3 are not part of it) we have only intransitive and simple transitive verbs, and the object phrase of a transitive verb will always be the last constituent of its clause (so that, in particular, the occurrence of floating **each** will precede it). Consequently, in this fragment the floating quantifier must always distribute over the subject NP; and so we may identify the triggering configuration as

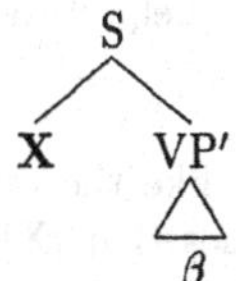

with β containing the floating occurrence of **each** and **X** the discourse referent selected by that occurrence. Here the only operation is that of replacing γ by the appropriate duplex condition. We present this special case of the rule in the familiar format:

CR.Fl Qu (each)

Triggering configuration $\gamma \in Con_K$:

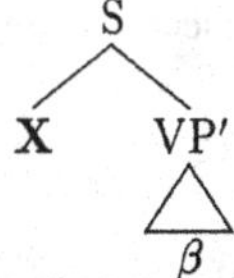

where β contains the floating quantifier **each**, and **X** is a plural discourse referent.

Operations: Replace the condition γ containing the triggering configuration by the duplex condition

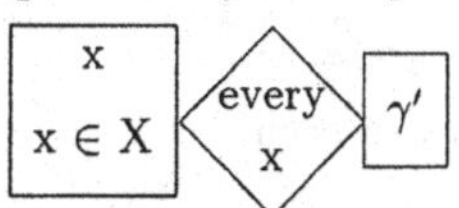

where γ' is the condition

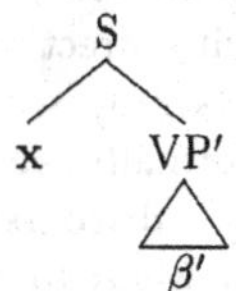

with β' the result of deleting the floating quantifier from β.

(It should be clear how this rule alllows us to construct an intuitively adequate DRS for, say, (4.203). An example of a DRS constructed with the help of the rule can be found on p. 447 below, i.e. (4.220) as DRS for (4.222).)

We noted that the construction rules for **all** and **both** are like the one for **each**, except that the application of the rule for **both** presupposes that $|\mathbf{X}| = \mathbf{2}$, whereas application of the rule for **all** presupposes $|\mathbf{X}| > \mathbf{2}$. We cannot hope to give a precise formal statement of these extra constraints in the absence of a general discussion of presupposition, a topic which we have reserved for Volume 2. So we must leave the matter at that.

The word **each** has a use that reminds us of the floating quantifiers we have discussed in this section, but which nevertheless has its own distinctive properties. It is illustrated in

(4.215) The boys received an apple each.

Superficially the meaning of this sentence may seem to be just like that of

(4.216) The boys each received an apple.

However, (4.215) and (4.216) differ in that the occurrence of **each** in (4.215), where it stands at the end of the sentence, requires that the NP which immediately precedes it be indefinite. Thus, while

(4.217) The boys each went into the garden.

is fine,

(4.218) The boys went into the garden each.

is ungrammatical.

This is not just a syntactic curiosity without semantic import. When **each** occurs sentence-finally it must be interpreted with direct reference to the indefinite NP directly preceding it. Thus the meaning of (4.215) is, informally put, that each of the boys received "his own apple". More formally, **each** selects, like ordinary floating quantifiers such as the **each** of (4.216), a discourse referent **X** for a plural non-quantifying argument phrase occurring somewhere to its left; and like any other floating quantifier it forces distribution over **X**, thus yielding a duplex structure which binds an individual discourse referent x (restricted by the left-hand box condition $\mathrm{x} \in \mathbf{X}$). At the same time **each** acts in association with the discourse referent **y** for the indefinite NP immediately preceding it, making this discourse referent functionally dependent upon the individual discourse referent **x**. Sentences with this type of occurrence of **each** seem to carry in addition a fairly strong implication that there is a 1–1 correspondence between the dependent variable (**y** in our example) and the independent variable (in our example: **x**). In the case of (4.215) this is not remarkable, for it would be odd for reasons that have nothing to do with linguistics if the same apple was given separately to two different boys. But consider the following sentence

(4.219) The students solved one simple problem each.

The truth conditions of (4.219) clearly entail those of the DRS

(4.220)

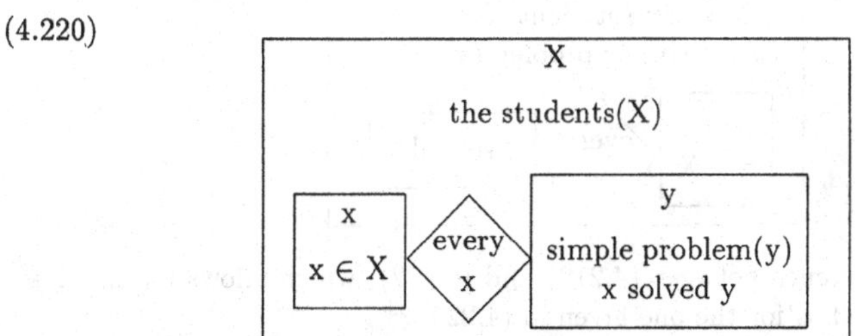

But arguably they entail something more than this, viz. that different students solved different problems, as in

(4.221)

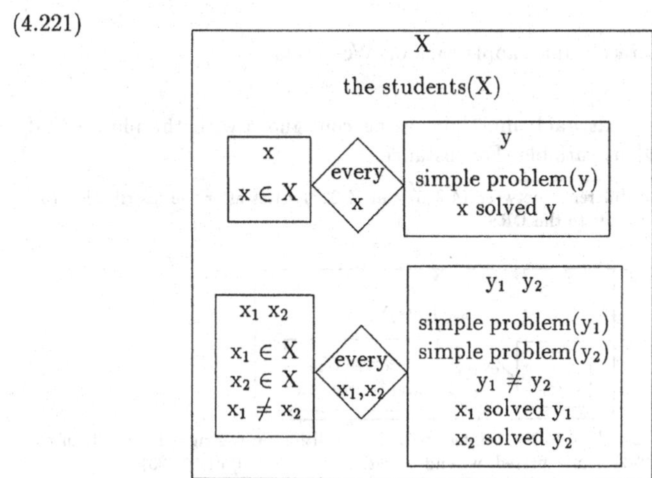

If this is correct, then (4.219) differs from

(4.222) The students each solved one simple problem.

which (on the narrow scope reading of **one simple problem**) means just what is given in (4.220). We are ourselves unsure, however, if the last condition of (4.221) should be considered an actual part of the content of (4.219). The reader is invited to make up his own mind.

Whether the semantic content of (4.219) is given by (4.220) or by (4.221), it seems clear that 4.219 does *not* have the specific interpretation given in

(4.223)

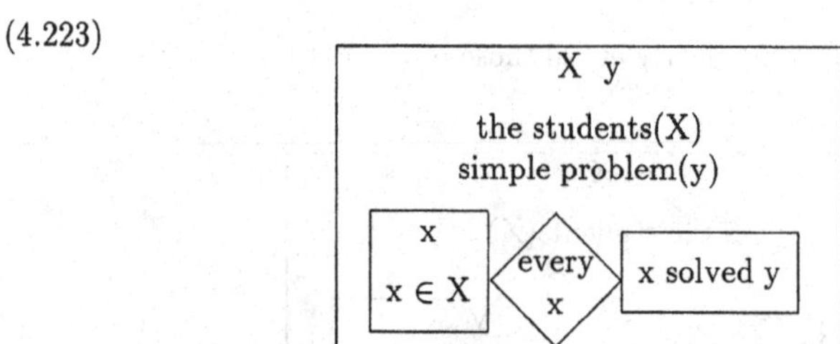

This is another difference between (4.219) and (4.222), which allows for this last interpretation as well as for the one given in (4.220).[63]

In (4.215) and (4.219) **each** is sentence final. This is not a necessary feature of this use of **each**. In (4.225), for instance, **each** is not the last word of the clause to which it belongs, but semantically it functions in the same way as the **each** of, say, (4.225).

(4.225) The boys received an apple each on Wednesday.

However, it appears that **each** must always be contiguous with the phrase that furnishes the dependent variable. For instance,

[63]We assume that the difference between (4.220) and (4.223) arises after the distribution rule has been applied, which leads to the DRS

(4.224)

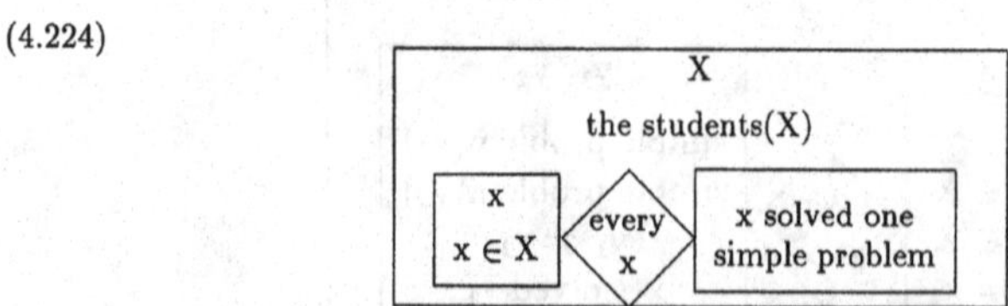

Depending on how the indefinite NP belonging to the condition on the right-hand side of the duplex condition in (4.224) is interpreted, we end up either with (4.220) or (4.223).

(4.226) The boys received an apple on Wednesday each.

is ungrammatical. This suggests that when used in this way, **each** is actually a constituent of the dependent noun phrase itself.[64] On this assumption the triggering configuration for the contribution rule dealing with such occurrences of **each** must have some such form as

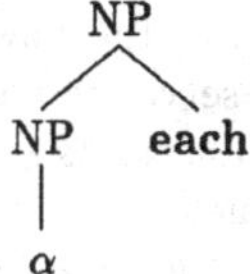

where α is the NP which introduces the dependent discourse referent. The operations of this rule will include, as for the other **each** rule, (i) selecting a non-atomic discourse referent **X** introduced for an NP belonging to the same clause; and (ii) replacing the processed condition γ by the appropriate duplex condition; in the present case we introduce into the right-hand DRS of this duplex condition a new discourse referent η for the indefinite NP α (η will be atomic or non-atomic depending on whether the NP is singular or plural) together with the conditions (a) δ(y), where δ is the N-part of α, and (b) the result γ' of substituting **x** for **X** and η for α in γ. In the limited fragment of English which we have developed so far formally the non-atomic discourse referent **X** will once again always be the one introduced by the subject NP, so that the rule can be simplified in analogy with **CR.Fl Qu (each)**.

[64]Syntactic evidence that **each** is part of the NP comes from the impossibility of relativizing on the NP:

(4.227) (i) * The apple(s) which the boys received each

(ii) The apple(s) which the boys each received

(4.227.ii) is fully grammatical, both with the singular **apple** and the plural **apples**. (4.227.i) in contrast, is neither. The impossibility of extracting from the NP position immediately to the left of **each** in (4.227.i) would be inexplicable if **each** were not part of the NP. In fact, it is possible to extract the NP with **each** included, as in

(4.228) The one apple each which the boys received could not possibly sustain them for more than a couple of hours.

One of the questions that floating quantifiers raise is why only the words **each**, **all** and **both** can occur in floated positions. For note that none of the sentences in (4.229) is grammatical.

(4.229) The men $\left\{\begin{array}{l}\text{many}\\ \text{most}\\ \text{few}\\ \text{at least three}\end{array}\right\}$ own a Renault.

A possible explanation is that a floating quantifier does not have the power of introducing a quantifying (=duplex) structure itself, but rather serves as a signal that of the two interpretative options which would have been available in its absence (the collective and the distributive option) only the distributive one is a live option. In other words, the floating quantifier would serve as a device to *block* a certain interpretation which would otherwise have been possible.[65]

According to this hypothesis, the rule which is responsible for the duplex condition of, say, (4.222) would strictly speaking not be the rule **CR.Fl Qu (each)** we gave on p. 445, but the distribution rule which was also involved in the construction of the DRSs (4.179) and (4.180) in Section 4.4.1. The effect of the floating quantifier is to render this rule obligatory instead of optional.

We said that the use of **each** which we have just been studying requires its occurrence as part of an *indefinite* noun phrase. The examples we have considered so far involved singular indefinites only. But the same construction is possible also with plural indefinites, as in

(4.230) The boys received $\left\{\begin{array}{l}\text{two}\\ \text{several}\end{array}\right\}$ apples each.

This is what we might have expected. In the sentence in (4.230), **each** marks the same kind of functional dependence as in (4.219); the only difference is that the dependent variable now denotes a set rather than a single individual. What seems to fit our account not so nicely is that the given use of **each** is also possible with certain quantifying NPs such as

(4.231) The boys received $\left\{\begin{array}{l}\text{few}\\ \text{at least two}\\ \text{at most three}\end{array}\right\}$ apples each.

[65] Note that this does *not* explain why **every** can't function as floating quantifier. We suspect that this is a purely syntactic phenomenon. It is not something for which we can offer an explanation.

Other quantifying NPs, however, e.g. these beginning with **all** or **most**, are not possible in this construction; as shown by the difference between (4.232.i) and (4.232.ii):

(4.232) i. * The board members read $\left\{\begin{array}{c}\text{most}\\ \text{all}\end{array}\right\}$ application dossiers each.

ii. The board members each read $\left\{\begin{array}{c}\text{most}\\ \text{all}\end{array}\right\}$ application dossiers.

The NPs with **all** or **most** thus behave in relation to NP-final **each** more like the definite than the indefinite NPs.

That different quantifying NPs should pattern in these markedly distinct ways is unexpected from the theory so far developed. But it patterns with a distinction familiar from the literature on natural language quantifiers, that between *weak* and *strong* quantifiers. In the next section, we will briefly discuss this distinction, together with the related distinction between *proportional* and *cardinality* quantifiers.

Exercises

1. (i) Modify the syntax of Chapter 0 so that it admits floating quantifiers.
   (ii) Formulate DRS-construction rules for the floating quantifiers **all** and **each**.
   (iii) Use your syntax and construction rules to construct DRSs for the following sentences and texts:
   (a) The boys each carry a briefcase.
   (b) Five boys and three girls each carry a briefcase.
   (c) The boys all carried the trunk upstairs.
   (d) The boys each carried the trunk upstairs.
   (e) The students each play a piano which occupies their basement. They own it.
   (f) The students own a piano. They all play it.
   (g) Fred knows two professors who each own a piano.
   (h) Every professor who knows ten students who all own a computer teaches computer science.

2. Extend the construction rules you were asked to state in 1. so that they also cover ditransitive verbs such as **give**. Use the extended rules to construct the possible readings of the sentences:

(a) The boys gave the girls each an apple.
(b) The boys all gave the girls an apple.
(c) The boys gave the girl each an apple.
(d) The boys each gave the girl an apple.
(e) The boy gave the girls all an apple.
(f) Fred knows three girls whom the boys each gave an apple.
(g) Fred knows three girls whom the boy each gave an apple.

3. (i) State an extension of the syntax which includes sentences like (a)–(c):

(a) The boys receive an apple each.
(b) The boys give the girls an apple each.
(c) The boys receive several/two apples each.

(ii) Give an explicit statement of a DRS construction rule for NP-final **each**. Use this rule to construct DRSs for these sentences, as well as for:

(a) Fred knows three girls whom the boys gave two apples each.
(b) Fred knows three girls whom the boy gave two apples each.

4.4.4 Cardinality Quantifiers

The division between quantifying NPs we noticed towards the end of the last section matches one that is well-known and has been much discussed within the literature on natural language quantification. As noted explicitly in [Milsark 1974], so-called "existential **there-insertion**" sentences are possible with indefinite NPs as well as with the quantifying NPs occurring in (4.231); but not with definites or with quantifying NPs beginning with **all** or **most**:

(4.233) i. There is $\left\{\begin{array}{l}\text{an}\\ \text{one}\end{array}\right\}$ apple in the basket.

ii. There are $\left\{\begin{array}{l}\text{two}\\ \text{several}\\ \text{many}\\ \text{few}\\ \text{at least two}\\ \text{at most three}\end{array}\right\}$ apples in the basket.

iii. * There is $\left\{\begin{array}{l}\text{the}\\ \text{this}\\ \text{every}\end{array}\right\}$ apple in the basket.

iv. * There are $\left\{\begin{array}{l}\text{all}\\ \text{most}\end{array}\right\}$ apples in the basket.

[Barwise/Cooper 1981] account for this difference by distinguishing between what they call *weak* and *strong* quantifiers. A *weak* quantifier is an NP of the form $\delta\nu$ – where δ is the determiner and ν a simple or complex expression of type N – such that the sentence

(4.234) $\delta\nu$ is a ν.

is contingent (that is, it could in principle be either true or false). In contrast, when $\delta\nu$ is a *strong* quantifier, then (4.234) is either necessarily true or necessarily false. On this criterion indefinites such as **an apple** or **two apples** qualify as weak. For **Two apples are apples** can be either true or false (it is true if there are at least two apples, false otherwise); and the same goes for **An apple is an apple**, when this sentence is read existentially and not generically (thus, as we would normally interpret **Some apple is an apple**; admittedly, for **An apple is an apple** this reading is not prominent). Similarly, **at least two apples, at most three apples, many apples** and **few apples** all qualify as weak. On the other hand, **every apple, all apples** and **most apples** come out as strong; for when one of these NPs occurs in the subject position of (4.234) the sentence is true irrespective of how many apples there are. Arguably the same conclusion follows for definite NPs such as **the apple** or **this apple**. For these NPs, it might be said, presuppose the existence of some (contextually salient) apple – unless this presupposition is fulfilled, the question whether a sentence like **The/This apple is an apple** is true would not even arise. So it seems natural to interpret the criterion for strong quantifiers – (4.234) is necessarily true – in this case as "(4.234) is necessarily true whenever it has a truth value at all". And if we do, then **the apple** and **this apple** come out as strong too.

The reader will have noted that this classification is orthogonal to those we have proposed so far in this chapter, not only in that it cuts our category of quantifying NPs in half, but also in that it characterizes those NPs as (weak or strong) quantifiers which by our light are not quantifying NPs at all – those which we have classified as definite and indefinite NPs.[66] Insofar as the present division does justice to the grammaticality judgements concerning the sentences in (4.233)

[66]Barwise and Cooper worked on the assumption central to classical Montague grammar according to which all NPs, including even proper names, are semantically speaking quantifiers – they are all quantifiers in the sense that they denote (without exception) sets of properties. Thus **some apple** denotes the set of all those properties which are true of at least one apple, **every apple** denotes the set of properties that are true of each and every apple and **Fred** denotes the set of all properties that are true of Fred. Thus, the sentence **Every apple is a fruit** is true iff being a fruit is a property that is true of all apples, **Some apple is green** is true iff the property of green is true of some apple and **This apple is green** is true iff the property holds of the particular apple the speaker is pointing at. We saw already in Chapters 1 and 2 that the

and (4.234), one might consider adopting it in conjunction with the classification we have already adopted. The construction with NP-final **each** might be an additional reason; for as was implied at the end of the last section the NPs that can and cannot play the role of dependent noun phrases in that construction correspond quite closely to the weak and strong quantifiers too. Unfortunately however, the distinction between weak and strong quantifiers does not quite do the work for which it was introduced in the first place. For instance, the sentence

(4.235) There are zero or more apples in this basket.

while perhaps a little odd, is certainly a grammatical sentence, even though the NP **zero or more apples** is by the Barwise & Cooper criterion strong rather than weak (**Zero or more apples are apples** is evidently true no matter what!). The same difficulty arises in connection with NP-final **each**:

(4.236) The boys received zero or more apples each.

is grammatical – even if it is, like (4.235), a little odd for extra-grammatical reasons.

These observations suggest that the strong-weak distinction cannot be the final explanation of what it is that makes an NP acceptable in the constructions exemplified in (4.235) and (4.236). A distinction which seems to us to come much nearer to what lies at the bottom of these grammaticality facts is made in work by B. Partee ([Partee 1988]). She distinguishes between *proportional quantifiers* and *cardinality quantifiers.* The analysis of quantifying NPs we have so far offered – as phrases which introduce the tripartite structure of duplex conditions at the level of semantic representation – makes them all into what are in Partee's sense proportional quantifiers. Cardinality quantifiers do not induce such structures. Rather, they are assertions to the effect that a certain set satisfies certain cardinality conditions – i.e. certain conditions which say something about the size of the set (e.g. whether it consists of no elements, of one element, of two elements, of more than two elements, etc.). For instance, if we assume that **exactly three Beethoven string quartets**, as it occurs in

(4.237) Fred likes exactly three Beethoven string quartets.

acts as a cardinality quantifier, the sentence as a whole might be paraphrased as: "The set of Beethoven string quartets which Fred likes consists of exactly three

distinct behaviour of definite, indefinite and quantifying NPs in anaphoric contexts requires a more refined noun phrase typology.

elements." Similarly, making the same assumption about **more than two apples**, we can paraphrase

(4.238) There are more than two apples in the basket.

as "The set of apples in the basket has more than two elements"; and so on.

To capture the concept of a cardinality quantifier at the level of discourse representation is fairly straightforward. We make use of the notation for set abstraction which we have already used in connection with the abstraction principle. In addition we use notation familiar from set theory to denote the cardinality of a given abstract – two vertical bars flank the abstract denoting term – together with certain self-explanatory ways for specifying cardinalities (such as $\leq \mathbf{1}$, $\geq \mathbf{2}$, $> \mathbf{3}$, $= \mathbf{3}$, etc.). With this notational machinery we can represent (4.237) as

(4.239)

x η

Fred(x)

$\eta = \Sigma$y: [y | Beethoven string quartet(y), x likes y]

$|\eta| = 3$

and that of (4.238) as

(4.240)

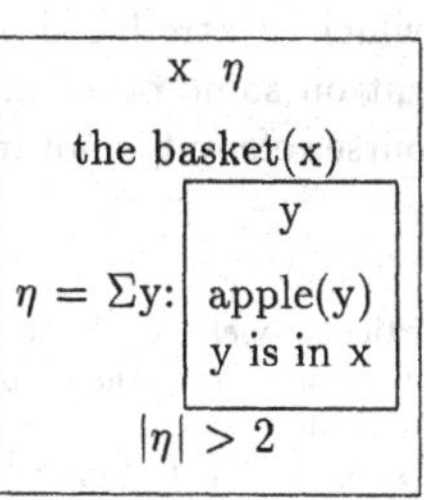

It should be fairly clear how one might state the construction rule for cardinality quantifiers which produces such representations: The NP in question introduces (i) a neutral discourse referent η; (ii) a cardinality specification C[η], such as $\eta = \mathbf{3}$, $\eta > \mathbf{2}$, etc. – depending on the determiner of the given NP; (iii) a condition of the form $\eta = \Sigma$**y**: **K**. In conditions of this last form **y** is a new discourse referent and K is a DRS whose universe consists of **y** and which contains two DRS-conditions, one which says that **y** satisfies the descriptive content of the quantifying NP and one which results from replacing the NP by **y** in the condition that is being processed.[67]

Part of the point of distinguishing between proportional quantifiers and cardinality quantifiers is that only the latter can appear in **there**-insertion sentences. More precisely, the NPs that can appear in these sentences are (a) the cardinality quantifiers and (b) the indefinite NPs. This is what we would expect given what has been said about definites, indefinites, proportional quantifiers and cardinality quantifiers, provided only that we make the additional and quite reasonable assumption that the semantic function of **there**-insertion sentences is to asssert that an individual, or set of individuals, with certain specified properties exists. In order that the sentence – or, more precisely, its distinctive constituent **there** – can make such a claim, the remainder of the sentence must provide a discourse referent (together with certain constraining conditions) to represent the individual or set whose existence is being asserted; and for this it is crucial that this discourse referent is not bound already, or anaphorically linked to some discourse referent outside the representation of the sentence itself. Because of this last requirement both proportional quantifiers and definite NPs are unusable in **there**-insertion sentences – the former because the discourse referents they introduce are bound by the duplex conditions which they themselves introduce, and the latter because they come with the presumption that the discourse referents which they introduce can be linked to some other discourse referent. Cardinality quantifiers and indefinites, on the other hand, both deliver "free" discourse referents, which can then be bound by the existential operator of the **there**-insertion construction.

A similar argument supports the fact that only indefinites and cardinality quantifiers can occur in the NP-final **each**-construction we explored in the last section. According to what we have said, the function of **each** in this construction is to represent the discourse referent which is introduced by the NP of which it is a constituent as functionally dependent on some other discourse referent. Again, this only makes sense if the first discourse referent is not independently bound or linked already.[68]

---

[67]This construction rule will in particular yield a DRS equivalent to (4.240) for a "**there**-insertion" sentence such as (4.238), if we assume that the verb phrase of this sentence, expressed by the words **there are**, expresses the condition that what is mentioned by the subject term "exists". In view of the cardinality specification C that is part of the representation of the sentence as a whole, the DRS-condition which the verb phrase contributes will have no effect on the truth conditions of the resulting DRS. Thus we can leave it out, as we have done in (4.240), without affecting the logical content of the DRS.

[68]The NPs that can occur with NP-final **each** are more restricted than those one finds in **there**-insertion sentences. Among the NPs that can occur in the second but not in the first context are those beginning with **no**. The reason for this difference is, we suspect, that NPs of the form **no** α are a conflation of (i) an NP that is equivalent to **an** α and (ii) a morpheme which semantically

Since the grammaticality facts we have been discussing in this and the preceding section seem to fall into place when quantifiers are divided into proportional quantifiers and cardinality quantifiers, and since we do not know of any other hypothesis that succeeds in explaining them, we will assume that certain NPs are to be analysed as cardinality quantifiers, and so that the clauses in which they occur give rise to DRSs which look like (4.239) and (4.240). Assuming this, however, means that we must review some of the commitments which we already made in earlier parts of this chapter. For up to now we have been analysing quantifying NPs uniformly in a manner which makes them all into proportional quantifiers. This is true in particular of NPs such as **at least two/more than three/many/few apples**, which, we have seen, must be interpretable as cardinality quantifiers if the facts about **there**-insertion and NP-final **each** are to come out right. Are we to conclude, then, that at least where those NPs are concerned, we have been wrong all along?

Not quite. Consider, for instance, the sentence

(4.241) Fred knows at least two senators.

On the assumption that **at least two senators** is a cardinality quantifier, this sentence gets the representation

---

is not part of the NP but acts as negation over the clause which contains it. (Such an analysis of "negated NPs" imposes itself for languages like German or Dutch, where such NPs – e.g. **kein Student** or **geen student** – are very common and where negation of a sentence containing an indefinite NP often cannot be naturally expressed in any other way; the English data, though perhaps somewhat less compelling, point in the same direction.) The inadmissibility of **no** α with NP-final **each** should then be explained in terms of the inability of the negation morpheme to take scope over the entire clause in which the NP-final **each**-construction is embedded. Two other types of NPs that can occur in **there**-insertion sentences but not with NP-final **each** are bare plurals and bare mass terms. (Friederike Moltmann, p.c.). Here the difference must have some other explanation, which presumably involves some requirement associated with the NP-final **each**-construction that the NP followed by **each** contains some phrase indicating the size of the represented atomic or non-atomic individuals it represents. At this point we have no detailed explanation of the difference. A third category of NPs which can occur in **there**-insertion sentences but not with NP-final **each** are those involving compound determiners such as **more apples than pears**, etc. (see [Keenan 1987a].) Here too we give no account of the difference. In fact, there is much of interest to be said about such compound determiners generally, something that is evident in particular from Keenan's work (including the paper just cited but much more besides). Compound determiners form a topic which we have decided to ignore.

(4.242)

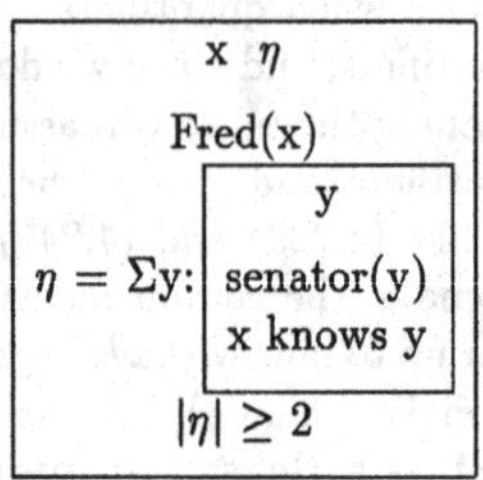

On the earlier assumption that the NP is a proportional quantifier, the DRS has the form familiar from preceding sections:

(4.243)

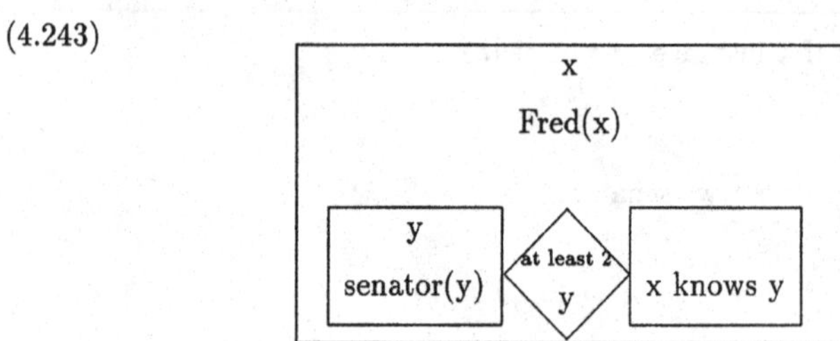

How are we to choose between these two representations? The usual semantic considerations won't help us. For what are the truth conditions associated with (4.243)? As we said in Section 4.3, (4.243) is true if the generalized quantifier "at least two" holds between the set defined by the left-hand side DRS of the duplex condition and that defined by the left- and the right-hand side DRSs taken together. But this relation holds precisely when the set defined by the two sets together has two or more elements – and this is precisely the truth condition associated with (4.242). So the duplex structure of (4.243) is from a truth-conditional perspective unnecessary – the generalized quantifier holds between the two sets just in case the second set has a certain property. Or, to put it in more general terms, there is a certain set property P – that of having at least two members – such that the quantifier "at least two" holds between two sets A and $A \cap B$ iff $A \cap B$ has P. A generalized quantifier Q for which there is such a property P may be called *(intersectively) reducible* to P.

Much the same appears to be true of **many** and **few** – they too are arguably reducible. Consider **many**, as it occurs, say, in the sentence

(4.244) Fred knows many senators.

Compare the DRS which we get when we treat **many senators** as a cardinality quantifier:

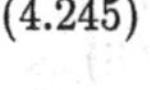

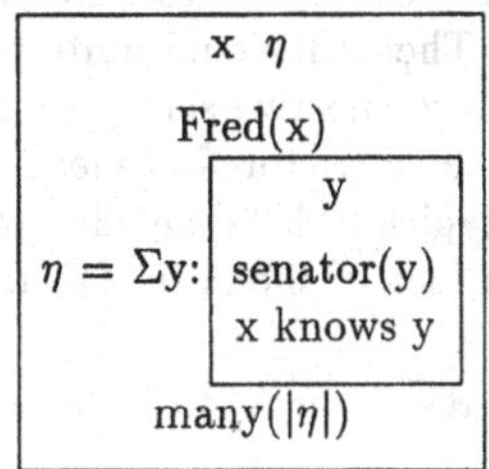

with the one which results on our earlier assumption that it is a proportional quantifier:

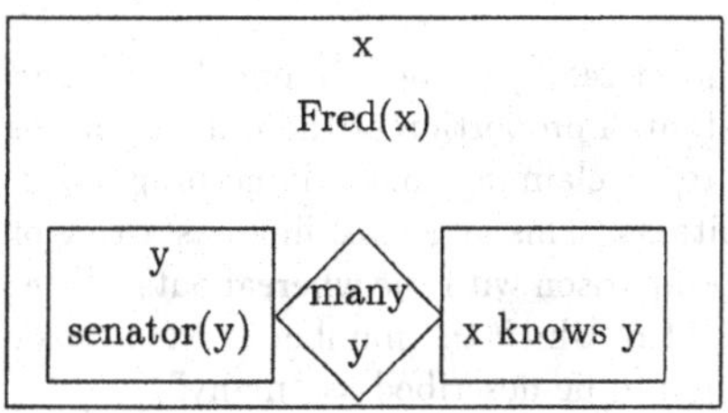

(4.245) is true when the set of senators Fred knows has the property expressed by **many**; (4.246) is true when the set defined by its left-hand side DRS and the one defined by left-hand and right-hand side DRSs taken together stand in the relation indicated by the central diamond of the duplex condition. Note, however, that the relation described by **many** is vague and context-dependent. Whether two sets stand in the relation depends on a variety of factors and may remain undecidable even when all clues have been taken account of. One factor, which does play an important part in the interpretation of many occurrences of **many** is the set A which acts as the restrictor of the duplex representation. But it is by no means the only factor. That other forces may be at work as well is shown by the following pair of sentences

(4.247) (i) Many houses in this city were insured against fire last year.

(ii) Many houses in this city burnt down last year.

Assume that both (4.247.i) and (4.247.ii) are used with reference to a typical western European city in the twentieth century. In such a context most speakers would want a much larger number of houses that were insured before they would accept (4.247.i) as true than they would require in connection with the second sentence. In fact, suppose that five percent of the houses were insured and that all and only the insured ones burnt down. Then one could quite plausibly regard (4.247.ii) as true and (4.247.i) as false. Since the two sentences have identical subjects, the difference cannot be due to the restrictor A. Indeed, it is not hard to see what is responsible for it: People typically have an idea of what is the norm for fire insurance just as they have an idea of the norm for fires, and the second tends to be much lower than the first.

This is not to deny that the restrictor A often plays an important role. Compare for instance the sentences

(4.248) (i) Many inhabitants of this town are Mexicans.

(ii) Many Mexicans live in this town.

Intuitively, (4.248.i) and (4.248.ii) mean different things. The preferred reading of (4.248.i) is that a substantial proportion of those living in this town are Mexicans, while (4.248.ii) seems to be claiming that a large proportion of the Mexicans are among the local inhabitants. This latter reading has a ring of implausibility, inasmuch as it suggests a comparison with the whereabouts of the remaining Mexicans, a comparison in the light of which the number of Mexicans living in this town is likely to appear too small to be described as "many".

Examples such as (4.248.i,ii) may suggest that the proportional interpretation of **many**, in which the norm is determined exclusively by the predicate A, is sufficiently distinct to warrant treatment as a separate reading, with an irreducible duplex representation. Whether this is so is not crucial to the argument. For the present purpose it suffices if there is at last one use of **many** in which it functions semantically as a (parameterized) cardinality quantifier, for which (4.245) is an adequate representation.

In this regard the quantifiers we have just been discussing (i.e. **many** and **at least three**) differ clearly from quantifiers such as **all** and **most**. The latter quantifiers are irreducibly and unambiguously proportional. **All** always asserts that the set A is included in the set of As that are B. Clearly this cannot be stated as a condition on the second set alone. A similar observation clearly applies to **most**.

The upshot of this section may be summarized as follows. We have found a semantic distinction among the generalized quantifiers – between those quantifiers which can be reduced to a property of the intersection of the two sets they relate and those which cannot. Only the former admit representations as cardinality quantifiers. In many cases it appears immaterial whether such a quantifying NP is represented in the new manner of cardinality quantifiers or, old style, by means of a duplex condition. But there are contexts in which the new mode of representation is essential, since it, but not the old form, makes a discourse referent available that, as far as the NP is concerned, is free; **there**-insertion sentences and the construction with NP-final **each** are examples of such contexts.

Thus we have arrived at a four-way distinction among noun phrases: (i) definites, (ii) indefinites, (iii) cardinality quantifiers and (iv) proportional quantifiers. These pair up according to two orthogonal criteria:

(a) Indefinites and cardinality quantifiers introduce discourse referents that are free, and thus may be bound by a sentence constituent unrelated to the introducing phrase; the discourse referents introduced by proportional quantifiers and definite NPs are not free in this sense.

(b) Both cardinality quantifiers and proportional quantifiers introduce into the argument positions which they occupy always an *individual* discourse referent and thus allow only for distributive interpretations of (plural) verbs. The difference between them is that cardinality quantifiers introduce in addition another discourse referent, which, contrary to the individual discourse referent, is not bound by the NP itself. Definites and indefinites are not subject to the restriction that the introduced discourse referent stands for an individual; though, of course, when a definite or indefinite NP is in the singular, then the discourse referent it introduces will be an individual one because of a separate constraint, imposed by its number feature.

Exercises

1. Formulate a construction rule for cardinality quantifiers which have one of the following determiners: **exactly** n, **at least** n, **at most** n, **more than** n, (where n is any numeral), **zero or more, many** and **few**. Use this rule to construct DRSs for all sample sentences and texts that can be found in this chapter and which involve the determiners just mentioned. (That is, assume that the NPs beginning with these determiners are cardinality quantifiers!)

2. As noted, floating quantifiers are not particularly felicitous when the licensing NP is a quantifier. Nevertheless, when the NP is a cardinality quantifier, the presence of the floating quantifier does not seem all that bad (compare the sentences (a)–(k) below). So there may be a case for extending the construction rule of Exercise 2 of Section 4.4.3 so that it applies not only to definite and indefinite NPs but also to cardinality quantifiers.

(i) Extend the rule in this sense.

(ii) Construct DRSs for the following variants of the sentences of Exercises 1 and 2 of Section 4.4.3:

(a) At least five boys each carry a briefcase.

(b) At least five boys and more than three girls each carry a briefcase.

(c) At least ten students each play a piano which occupies their basement. They own it.

(d) At least ten students own a piano. They all play it.

(e) Every professor who knows more than ten students who all own a computer teaches computer science.

(f) At least five boys gave at most three girls each an apple.

(g) At least five boys each gave at most three girls an apple.

(h) At least five boys gave the girl each an apple.

(i) At least five boys each gave the girl an apple.

(j) Fred knows more than three girls who the boys each gave an apple.

(k) Fred knows more than three girls who the boy each gave an apple.

3. (i) Adapt the construction rule of Exercise 3 of Section 4.4.3 so that it can deal with sentences such as:

(a) The boys receive many apples/at most one apple/exactly five apples each. (i.e. so that the NP with which **each** is associated can be a cardinality quantifier as well as an indefinite.)

(ii) Use this rule to construct DRSs for the sentences represented in (i.a). Do the same for the sentences:

(a) Fred knows three girls who the boys gave at least two apples each.

(b) Fred knows three girls who the boy gave at least two apples each.

4. (i) Formulate a construction for **there**-insertion sentences which accommodates both indefinite NPs and cardinality quantifiers as subjects.

(ii) Use this rule to construct DRSs for the following:

(a) There is a unicorn which Mary loves.

(b) There is no unicorn which Mary loves.

(c) There are ten apples in this basket.

(d) There are less than ten chocolates which Freddy has not eaten. There are more than ten chocolates which he has eaten.

(e) If there are ten chocolates which Sue has not eaten, then there are at least ten chocolates which Freddy has eaten.

5. For each of the plural determiners you can think of, classify it according to the four-fold schema (definite, indefinite, proportional quantifier, cardinality quantifier) discussed in this section. Motivate each of the classifications you propose.

4.4.5 Reciprocals

Floating quantifiers, we saw in 4.4.3, distribute a predicate over the members of a certain set, the set represented by the discourse referent introduced by the licensing NP. This is so in particular for the floating quantifier **each**, the word to which most of the section was devoted. Some of the properties of **each** we studied in that section are also displayed by those of its occurrences which are conjoined with **other**, as in

(4.249) The two students admire each other.

In particular, **each other** requires, like the cases of floating **each** considered in Section 4.4.3, a plural NP that belongs to the same clause as the licensing NP. Indeed, it is tempting to see **each other** as a special case of floating **each**, a case where the floating quantifier is juxtaposed to an argument phrase, **other**, distinct from the licensing NP.

Looking at **each other** from this angle we arrive quite naturally at the semantics of a sentence such as (4.249), which clearly means that of the two students denoted by the subject term, call them a and b, a admires b and b admires a. Proceeding from the suggested "analysis" of **each other**, the "floating" **each** of **each other** has the effect of making the sentence assert of each of the members of the set denoted by the two students that it satisfies the predicate of "admiring other". The interpretation of this predicate must assign to the phrase **other** an individual distinct from some individual already mentioned – or, in DRT terms, **other** must be represented by a discourse referent that is presented as distinct from some discourse referent already introduced into the DRS. If we choose for this latter discourse referent the one used to express distribution over the set denoted by the subject term, we have almost arrived at the correct interpretation for (4.249):

(4.250)

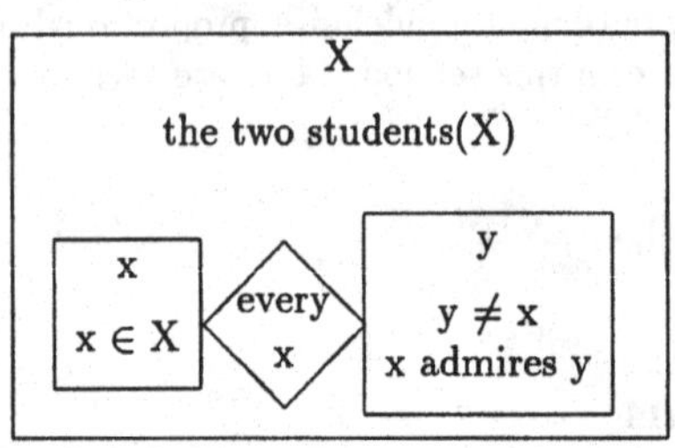

What is missing from (4.250) is that **y**, like **x**, must be a member of **X**. It is here that the suggested "analysis" of **each other** breaks down. It is a general property of **each other** that the referent of **other** belongs to the set defined by the licensing NP; but there seems to be no way of deriving this constraint from a general understanding of the meaning of the word **other**.[69]

This is one of the reasons why **each other** must be treated as a single, essentially indivisible constituent with its own syntactic and semantic properties. In fact, in most treatments of **each other** the possibility of a compositional analysis is not even entertained. This is true especially of syntactic treatments, which usually speak of the expression **each other** as a "reciprocal" and then proceed to deal with it jointly with reflexive pronouns such as **himself**, **herself**, etc. – treating all these expressions as lexical items without a syntactically or semantically significant internal structure.[70] Although syntactic considerations are not decisive for us here – we will leave virtually all the syntactic problems which reciprocals pose aside – the semantic complications we have just noted seem sufficient reason to abandon our attempts to find a compositional account of the semantics of **each other**. So we too will be striving for an analysis based on the assumption that **each other** is

[69]It might be thought that in **each other**, **other** stands for "the other". In that case the interpretation of **each other** should make clear how the referent of **other** is uniquely determined in the given context. In the case of a sentence like (4.249) the pressure to see the referent as uniquely determined might be thought to yield the constraint that **y** belongs to **X** in the following way: the referent must be a unique individual distinct from the individual **x**; this condition is satisfied if one assumes that the domain in which the referent is to be found is circumscribed by **X**; for in that case there will be – since **X** has only two elements – only one possible value for the referent, viz. the one element of **X** that is distinct from **x**. Unfortunately, this argument works at best for those cases where the licensing NP refers to a set of two elements. But the constraint that the referent of **other** must be an element of that set is fully general – it applies equally when the set has more than two members.

[70]An exception is the important recent article by [Heim, Lasnik & May 1991]. The treatment of reciprocals as lacking significant internal structure is encouraged not only by the considerable degree of similarity that exists between them and the reflexives, but also by the fact that in many languages, among them French and German, reflexives and reciprocals are represented by the very same words (cf. French **se**, German **sich**).

a single word. Nevertheless, the informal considerations that derive from looking into its internal structure – in the way we just did – will continue to play a heuristic role.

We noted in passing that **each other** can occur not only in contexts in which its licensing NP denotes a set of two elements, but also when that set is bigger. However, the meaning of reciprocal sentences which involve larger sets is more difficult to describe – in fact, it appears to be much less clearly defined – than is the case when the licensing NP denotes a set of two individuals. Therefore we will split our discussion into two parts, beginning with cases where the set has cardinality 2, and then looking at cases involving larger sets.

When the set defined by the licensing NP has two members, the semantic effect of **each other** usually follows the pattern of (4.249): **each other** is possible only in clauses whose main verb is a predicate of at least two places (otherwise the clause could not contain both the **each other** phrase and its licensing NP). In the simplest case, where the verb is a simple transitive verb α and the set defined by the licensing NP β consists of two members **a** and **b**, the meaning of β α **each other** is typically that **a** α **b** and **b** α **a**. But there appear to be exceptions. When I say to you:

(4.251) Would you put those two chairs on top of each other.

I am not asking you to perform the impossible task of creating a situation in which chair **a** is on top of chair **b** and at the same time chair **b** is on top of chair **a**. All I want you to do, you may reasonably assume, is to bring it about that one of the two chairs is stacked on top of the other, no matter which one ends on top and which underneath.[71] That (4.251) can be understood in this way is curious. It certainly does not seem consistent with the informal principle that the **each** of **each other** forces universal quantification over the set denoted by the licensing NP. But it is nonetheless an interpretation which the sentence seems to have according to some speakers. Indeed, it is the only reasonable interpretation.

To produce the interpretation which (4.251) appears to have, **each other** must transform the clause in which it occurs into a disjunction, not a conjunction, of two parallel clauses: β α **each other** becomes equivalent to "**a** α **b** or **b** α **a**". As far as we know, this disjunctive interpretation arises (insofar as it arises at all) only when the predicate α is asymmetric – i.e. where, for arbitrary **a** and **b**, **a** α **b** excludes that **b** α **a** – but even where there is such exclusion, the disjunctive interpretation of reciprocals is not always possible. For instance, you can't say of a father and

[71] Not all speakers seem to share this intuition. For some (4.251) is just odd. It cannot really be assigned the reading that would make it reasonable, while the other, clearly grammatical interpretation is logically absurd.

son

(4.252) Those two $\left\{ \begin{array}{l} \text{are fathers} \\ \text{fathered} \end{array} \right\}$ each other.

Inasmuch as (4.249) and (4.251) have the interpretations we ascribed to them, the reciprocal **each other** is ambiguous. However, as the disjunctive interpretation seems to us rather marginal, we will ignore it.

We now turn to examples where the set defined by the licensing NP has more than two elements. Consider:

(4.253) The members of this club know each other.

Let us assume that the club in question has 50 members. What must be the case for (4.253) to be true? A clearly sufficient condition is that for every two distinct members a and b, a knows b. But is this condition also necessary? Here we find the same phenomenon which we already encountered when discussing predications of sets denoted by definite plural NPs. The practice of such predications seems to allow for a certain looseness: In order that the claim is accepted as true, the predication must be true of an overwhelming number of the set's members, but need not be true without exception. So it seems to be also in the case of (4.253). And as with other such set predications, the looseness disappears when we add the floating quantifier **all**, as in

(4.254) The members of this club all know each other.

(The looseness has disappeared from (4.254) because **all** introduces a universal quantifier over the set and this quantifier does not admit of exceptions.)

Of greater importance to the account of plurals we have been developing in this chapter are sentences such as (4.255):

(4.255) Exactly ten members of this club know each other.

Assume again that the club has 50 members in all. When is (4.255) true? If there is a set M of club members such that (i) any two persons in M know each other, while (ii) there are no other pairs ⟨a,b⟩ of club members such that a knows b, and moreover M has exactly 10 members, then (4.255) is clearly true; and if M satisfies (i) and (ii) but has a cardinality different from 10, then (4.255) is false. The sentence is also surely false in case there are fewer than 10 club members who know any other club member at all. But as we contemplate other possible settings for

(4.255) we soon get into murky water. Suppose, for instance, that there are three "clusters" of club members, of 5, 10 and 15 members, respectively, such that within each cluster everyone knows everyone and there are no further cases of anybody knowing anyone. Is (4.255) true in this situation? Probably not. For if it were, then the assertion that exactly 5 members know each other would have an equal claim to truth, as would the assertion that exactly 15 members know each other. But any two of these three assertions seem to contradict each other. So what *is* true in this situation? That exactly 30 members know each other? This does not seem right either. In fact, we confess that we have no clear idea how sentences like (4.255) are to be assessed in this setting. Our intuitions leave us even more at sea when we consider scenarios in which acquaintance between the club members does not partition them into clusters, for instance because on the given set the relation "x knows y" is not transitive.

From such considerations it seems that the truth conditions of reciprocal sentences are not very clearly defined when the licensing NP denotes a set of three individuals or more. Any proposal that we could come up with can not therefore be expected to be more than an approximation, which accords with speakers' intuitions where these are clear, but which also makes definite predictions for cases where actual speakers waver.

Incomplete as it may be, intuition appears to eliminate certain proposals for the truth conditions of (4.255) that naturally come to mind. In particular, it follows from our observations that the following proposal (which might occur to one on first sight) cannot be right:

(4.256) (4.255) is true iff the/a maximal set A is such that: for every two distinct members a and b of A, a knows b, has 10 members.

For the theory of this chapter the inadequacy of (4.256) (both on the "the"- and on the "a"-version) is a matter of special significance. For the truth condition given in (4.256) is essentially a condition on *sets*, not a condition on individuals; more explicitly: There is no condition C on individuals which is expressible within the logical framework we have been using and which defines "the/a set A" of (4.256) as the set of all individuals satisfying C. In other words, there is no DRS K containing only discourse referents for individuals and whose universe contains the individual discourse referent x such that A is the set of all a such that the assignment $\{\langle x,a\rangle\}$ can be extended to a verifying embedding of K. (The proof of this fact, which is not straightforward, is omitted.)

The moral of this: If (4.256) captured the truth conditions of (4.255), then it could no longer be maintained that **exactly ten members of this club** is a quantifier in the technical sense in which we have been using the term – it could neither be a proportional quantifier nor a cardinality quantifier, for in either case the set A would be definable as the set of all individuals that satisfy both the content of the nominal and the predication expressed by the VP. If we were forced to acknowledge other types of quantifiers besides the two we distinguished in the last section this would mean a non-trivial revision, the implications of which are not easy to estimate in advance. As things stand, however, the need for such a revision is not yet proven.

In fact, the problem which (4.255) might pose for our account of plurals as a whole takes on a very different complexion if we assume that semantically (4.255) is well-defined only under quite special circumstances. Suppose for instance that the use of (4.255) presupposes that the "know"-relation is symmetric and transitive on the set of club members and moreover that it generates only one cluster (of two or more elements). Given this assumption the set A of (4.256) can be defined by abstraction, as in

(4.257) Σx:

x y
member of this club(x) member of this club(y) x ≠ y x knows y

and thus is "first order definable" (viz. by the DRS following "Σx:")

Quite probably, however, this presupposition is too restrictive and it might well be that a weaker, more reasonable presupposition would no longer guarantee that the set A can be characterized in some such way as (4.257). So the question whether reciprocal sentences allow us to hold on to our hypothesis that NPs like **exactly ten members of this club** are cardinality quantifiers has not been settled. We leave the question as a matter for further research.

The semantical problems posed by reciprocal sentences with licensing NPs that are not definite NPs is brought out further by sentences such as those in (4.258).

(4.258) Most members of this club know each other.

Once again, our own intuitions about the truth conditions of these sentences are hazy. What, for instance, does the truth of (4.258) precisely require? We will briefly look at three possibilities that come to mind, without implying that the list is exhaustive: (a) the largest set A of club members such that for any two distinct elements a and b of A, a knows b and b knows a, consists of more than half of the members of the club; (b) the set of club members a for which there is some other member b such that a knows b and b knows a consists of more than half of the members of the club; (c) the set of pairs of distinct club members a and b such that a knows b and b knows a consists of more than half of the total number of pairs of distinct club members. The first of these conditions is apparently too strong. For suppose again that the club has 50 members and compare the following two situations: (A) there is one cluster of five people such that the people within this cluster know each other while otherwise no-one knows anyone; (B) there are besides the cluster of case (A) seven additional clusters of four people each, such that all and only the people within one and the same cluster know each other. In situation (A) (4.258) is clearly false. But in (B) it is, in our judgement, arguably true. As the set specified in possibility (a) is the same in situation (A) and in (B), (a) cannot, it seems, be right. In fact, the example indicates that it is not the size of a single cluster which decides whether (4.258) is true; it also matters how many clusters there are.

This consideration would rule out possibility (a), but it does not decide between (b) and (c). It has been pointed out (see e.g. [Roberts 1987a]) that the number of pairs cannot be the criterion for truth of (4.258). For, it is argued, the sentence would certainly be considered true in a situation in which there is a set consisting of more than half of the members of the club such that any two members in that set know each other. But even in such a situation the number of pairs of distinct a and b such that a knows b and b knows a may be less than half the total number of pairs of distinct individuals. For instance, suppose that there are 10 members in all and that there is a subset of 6 members which all know each other, while otherwise noone knows anyone. In this situation (4.258) may, we surmise, legitimately be regarded as true. But the number of pairs ⟨a,b⟩ such that a knows b is 30 while there are 36 pairs for which this is not so. So requiring a majority of pairs of mutual knowers, as (c) has it, would be too strong.

So, only possibility (b) remains: That is, for (4.258) we are left with

(4.259) (4.258) is true iff the set of members a for which there is at least one other member b such that a and b know each other consists of more than half of the members.

But are (4.259) the right truth conditions for (4.258.i)? We are not sure. In order to make sure one would have to analyse many more examples than we have considered here. But it is not certain that the matter could ever be settled, no matter how many sentences and scenarios we look at. It may well be that sentences of the type exemplified in (4.258) do not *have* well-defined truth conditions, which apply to all situations in which the sentence can be used – that all that can be ascertained of them is that they are true in some situations and false in certain others, but that there are many other situations in which their truth values are not determined.

Nor do we believe that having partially defined truth conditions is an isolated phenomenon, found only with reciprocal sentences. On the contrary. Semantic partiality is found throughout natural language – in this regard the semantic theory we have been developing in this book, in which we have systematically side-stepped the complications to which partiality gives rise, might easily be misleading. Nor should this be thought of as surprising. In fact, it is what ought to be expected if one believes, with Chomsky and the many syntacticians he has formed or influenced, that the syntax of natural languages has a large degree of *autonomy* – that the syntactic principles that govern a language form a self-contained system of rules, so that the speakers of this language who have internalized these principles, will recognize expressions as grammatical and will be able to parse them according to these rules – i.e. assign them the kind of structure in virtue of which they are grammatical. When the syntax of a language has attained this kind of independence, it should be quite possible for certain combinations of words to present themselves as grammatical sentences in the sense that they satisfy all syntactic constraints, while yet failing to fit together in a way that is semantically well-defined: There is no way of combining the interpretation rules associated with these words so as to arrive at a fully transparent interpretation for the sentence as a whole. In such cases the language user, who is faced with the problem of attaching a meaning to the sentence, will have to do the best he can. And so he may come up with an interpretation which is to a greater or lesser extent ad hoc, forcing the interpretation rules to take the Procrustean frame which syntax has laid down; or alternatively, the interpretation may be left incomplete, excluding certain situations and admitting certain others while remaining ambivalent with respect to many others.

In the past there has been comparatively little systematic work on semantic partiality, especially on its empirical aspects. Here lies without doubt one of the major challenges for natural language semantics in the years ahead of us.

Let us summarize the tentative conclusions of this section. We found that reciprocal sentences have comparatively well-defined truth conditions when the licensing NP is a definite or indefinite plural whose semantic value is a set with exactly two members. Even with regard to such sentences we found a problem which we did not solve, connected with sentences like "The two chairs are stacked on top of each other", which seem to favour a "disjunctive" as opposed to a "conjunctive" interpretation. The semantics of reciprocal sentences becomes considerably more problematic when the licensing NP stands for a set of more than two elements or when it is a quantifier. In part the difficulties one encounters here are instances of the problems which arise through a general lack of definiteness that relates the semantics of verbs with plural arguments to their uses with singular arguments. But in addition reciprocal sentences present special problems, which apparently arise because the interpretation principles that govern simple reciprocal sentences (in which the value of the licensing NP is a two-membered set) cannot be straightforwardly extended to cases where this set is bigger or where the licensing NP is quantificational.

If this is the way things are, then obviously we cannot hope to find an extension to our construction algorithm which covers all reciprocal sentences and which at the same time is also demonstrably correct. At best we can hope for construction principles which cover the simpler, unproblematic sentences. Beyond that, we can still use the method of DRS-construction to explore the available options for an algorithm that deals with additional reciprocal sentences – and eventually for a complete semantics of reciprocals. But if we wish to remain faithful to the intuitions of normal speakers, it is at the comparison of possible options for such an extension that we shall have to stop.

Exercise

1. Formulate a DRS-construction rule for reciprocal sentences in which the licencing NP stands for a set of two elements. Use this rule to construct DRSs for the following sentences and texts:

   (a) Two students admire each other.

   (b) Three students admire each other and three students do not admire each other.

   (c) Exactly ten members of this club know each other.

   (d) If ten club members know each other, then twenty club members do not know each other.

4.4.6 Gather, The Same and Together

Consider the following sentences:

(4.260)	(a) Most		(i) gathered in the square
	(b) Many	students	(ii) saw the same film
	(c) Few		(iii) went to the cinema together
	(d) At least five		

These sentences are problematic of our analysis of the determiners **most, many, few, at least five** and others as generalized quantifiers. For their verb phrases are unequivocally collective: they combine only with subjects that denote groups or sets; when the subject denotes an (atomic) individual, the sentence is either plainly ungrammatical, as in

(4.261)	(a) John	(i) gathered in the square
	(b) A student	(ii) went to the cinema together

or else it is more restricted in its interpretation. Thus,

(4.262) John saw the same film.

can only mean that John saw the same film as some other individual which the context makes available. Such a reading is also possible for the sentences (4.260.a–d.ii), but these have in addition the interpretation – the one intended in (4.260) – according to which the students mentioned in the subject each saw the same film, irrespective of any further, contextually salient individuals.

Recall the reason which led us to assume that determiners like **most**, **many**, etc. are generalized quantifiers. With verb phrases like **hired a new secretary**, which allow for a collective as well as a distributive interpretation when their subject is some NP like **the lawyers** or **five lawyers**, only the distributive interpretation is available when the subject NP begins with a determiner like **most** or **many**. This difference is accounted for if we assume that NPs headed by such determiners introduce only a (quantified) individual discourse referent, and no discourse referent representing a set. But then how do we explain that the sentences in (4.260) have the meanings they clearly have?

Compare the availability of collective readings of the sentences in (4.260) with the lack of collective readings for sentences such as

(4.263) Most lawyers hired a new secretary.

The contrast between them has the appearance of paradox, irrespective of one's theoretical predilections or commitments. How can an NP prohibit the collective interpretation of some predicates, which are readily understood collectively when combined with other NPs, and yet allow for perfectly good collective interpretations with other, strictly collective predicates?

A simple solution to this puzzle would be to assume that the semantics of NPs like **most students** is governed by a default principle to the effect that they always select a distributive interpretation where there is one to be had, but permit a collective interpretation if no distributive reading is available. Perhaps some such principle does indeed play a role. But it cannot be the whole story. For one thing, we just noted that verb phrases such as **saw the same film** can also be read distributively. Nevertheless, they can be read collectively with subjects like **most students**, and this is so even in contexts which offer an external element to support the distributive reading. Thus, in

(4.264) Fred went to see Citizen Kane, but his girl friend insisted on going to Children of Paradise. Most of their friends saw the same film.

the last sentence is genuinely ambiguous between the collective reading, which leaves open whether the film seen by most of their friends was Citizen Kane, Children of Paradise or some third film, and the distributive reading according to which most of the friends saw Children of Paradise. (The third reading, according to which most friends saw Citizen Kane, seems hard to get here; but this is, presumably, due to some rhetorical and not a grammatical constraint.)

A second, more delicate observation which argues against the default solution concerns sentences such as

(4.265) Most professors voted for the same candidate they had interviewed the week before.

If the subject of (4.265) were to directly introduce, under the pressure exerted by the exclusively collective verb phrase, a discourse referent representing a set – viz. some majority of the professors – then it ought to be possible to interpret the **they** of the relative clause as referring to that same set. Suppose, for instance, that many candidates were interviewed during the preceding week and that each interview was conducted by a group of professors. One group, a majority, interviewed several candidates and for one of these candidates, say Jones, all members of that majority later voted. Then it should be possible to understand (4.265) as saying about this majority (i) that it collectively interviewed some candidate and (ii) that each of the professors belonging to that majority later voted for him. In our judgement the **they** of (4.265) cannot be interpreted in this way.

So we need a different explanation. As the one we will propose is clearest in connection with verb phrases of the type **saw the same film**, we will for the time being stick to those. We will turn to **gather** and **together** afterwards.

We concentrate on (4.260.a.ii):

(4.260.a.ii) Most students saw the same film.

We begin by noting that the truth conditions of this sentence (on its collective reading) are captured well enough by the following DRS:

(4.266)

y
film(y)
[x / student(x)] ⟨Most x⟩ [x saw y]

If some majority of the students saw the same film, then there was some film they all saw, and conversely. It is our contention that this equivalence is not accidental; that it is not like a case where two natural language sentences happen to yield the same truth conditions by distinct interpretational mechanisms. Rather, it is the element which the seeing events of the different students have in common, the "same" film which they all went to see, which groups these individual seeings into an event that can be described as relating to the group consisting of all those students. Insofar as (4.266) represents that element explicitly, it succeeds in capturing this intuition.

To make the suggestion of the last paragraph precise we would have to be explicit about the actions and events of which the suggestion speaks. This is done in the next chapter, which deals with the semantics of tense and aspect. There we will argue that all tensed sentences should be analysed as descriptions of states or events and thus that the DRSs of such sentences must all contain discourse referents for such entities. (Thus according to what we will propose, all the DRSs we have been considering so far need modification. We will see, however, that for the vast majority of DRSs considered in Chapters 1–4 the modification is straightforward.) As Chapter 5 deals with these matters, it might have been better to present our proposal there. In fact, there are many issues in the semantics of both plural and singular NPs which require the consideration of the states and events described by the sentences in which those NPs occur (see e.g. [Reyle 1986]); in this regard the present problem is just one among many. Ideally, those problems should have been addressed in an additional chapter, but considerations of space firmly spoke against this and so we have decided to leave them for some other occasion. We have decided to make an exception, however, for the problem presented by the sentences in (4.260), since it is too plain to be overlooked: In the absence of some account of those sentences our quantificational treatment of **most**, etc. would in all likelihood have come across to most readers as an elementary fallacy.

Our decision to deal with the matter here requires that we take for granted many of the points that are discussed in detail in Chapter 5. So the reader may want to return to this section after that chapter.

According to the treatment of Chapter 5, every tensed sentence is the description of some state or event and the DRS of the sentence will contain a discourse referent representing that state or event. For instance,

(4.267) John saw a film.

has the DRS

(4.268)

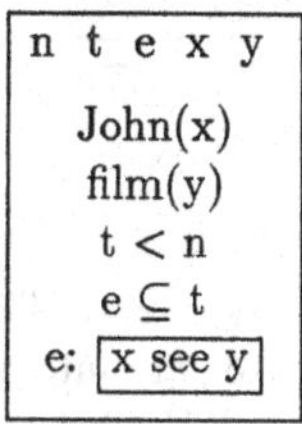

Here **n** represents the time of utterance and **t** the time at which the described event **e** is situated; the last condition expresses that **e** is an event of **x** seeing **y**; the other conditions are self-evident.

For the remainder of this section we will suppress the specifically temporal information, involving **n** and **t**. With this simplification

(4.269) Most students saw a film.

gets a representation of the form:

(4.270)

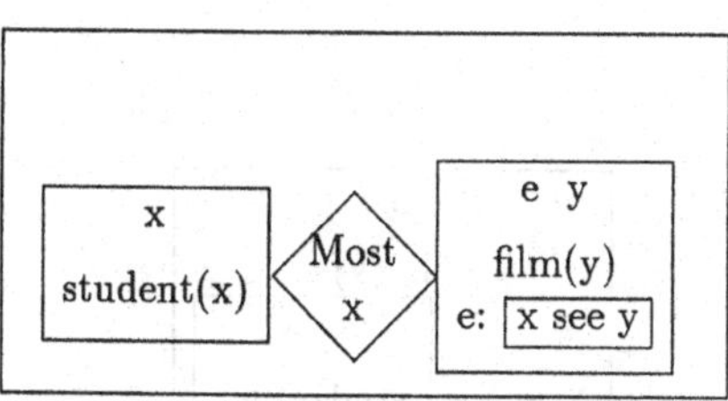

With reference to representations such as (4.268) and (4.270) our proposal for

(4.260.a.ii) Most students saw the same film.

takes the following form. We treat the expression **the same** as operating on (i) the remainder **film** of the NP **the same film** which contains it, (ii) the 1-place predicate **saw the same film** of which this NP is a part and (iii) the nominal part **student** of the NP which serves as argument of this predicate. The predicate can be represented in DRS-like fashion as

(4.271)

where **x** represents the predicate's argument. The effect of the operation which **the same** triggers is to turn this predicate into a collective one, which is true of the set **X** iff there is a collective event **E** whose constituent events are all of the type of the event **e** of (4.271) and which are connected to each other by being all seeings of the same **y**.

A formal representation of this predicate which reflects this informal description closely would need to have, among other things, a dicourse referent for the collective event **E**; and it would have to express that **E** "consists", in some appropriate sense, of all the seeings of the given film by individual students. To do this properly would be quite involved, and out of place in the present context. Fortunately, we can preserve the essence of our analysis of **the same** without representing the collective event explicitly:

(4.272)

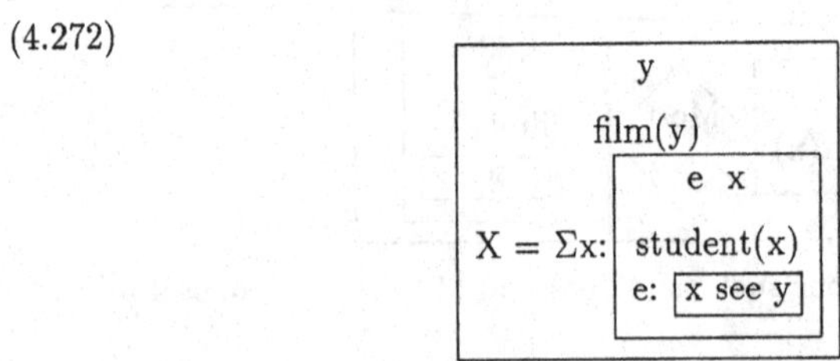

The sentence (4.260.a.ii) can then be analysed as saying that most of the students participated in the collective event **E**, or, what comes to the same thing, belong to the corresponding set **X** of participants:

(4.273)

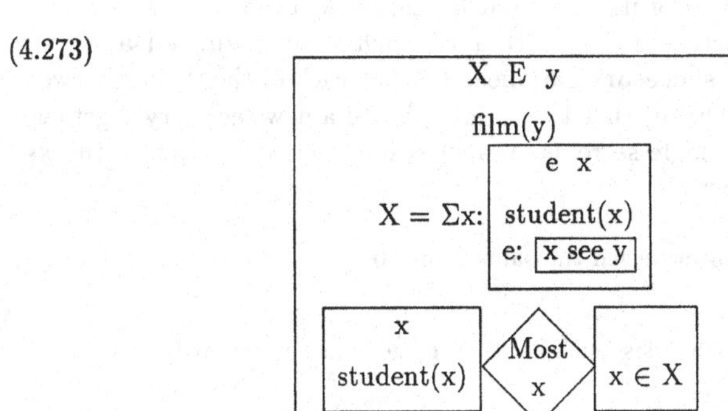

With predicates which owe their collective character to the presence of **the same**, representations like (4.273) could be simplified to DRSs in which the mention of events is suppressed, as in

(4.274)

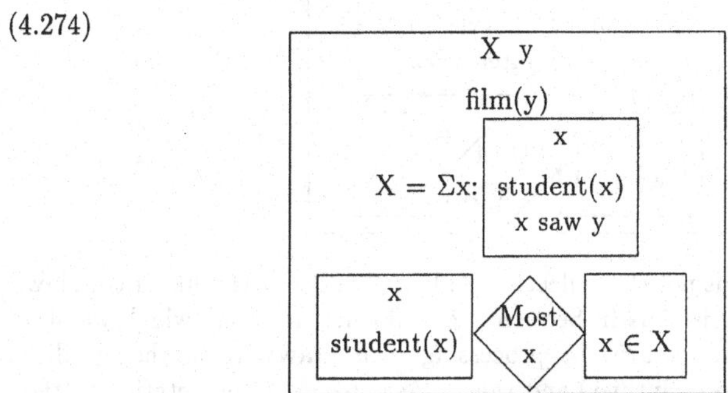

Evidently (4.274) represents the same truth conditions as the DRS (4.266) which we presented at the outset of this discussion.

Before leaving **the same**, we want to deal with what would seem an obvious objection. If the compatibility of **saw the same film** and **most students** can be explained along the lines we have sketched, why doesn't the same explanation apply equally to a sentence like

(4.275) Most lawyers hired a secretary.

and thus make the false prediction that it too has a collective reading? Our answer is as follows. Note that predicates such as **hired a secretary** are strictly speaking not two-ways but three-ways ambiguous. With a verb like **hire** the third interpretation is, for reasons of its particular lexical content, not very prominent. But the three-way distinction is clear with a VP such as **interviewed a secretary**. **X interviewed a secretary** can mean (i) that each of the **x**s interviewed a new secretary on his own; (ii) that the **x**s interviewed a new secretary together, or (iii) that there was a single secretary that was interviewed by each of the **x**s individually. Consider now

(4.276) Most lawyers interviewed the same secretary.

We could, following the analysis outlined above, get the (necessarily collective) interpretation given in

(4.277)

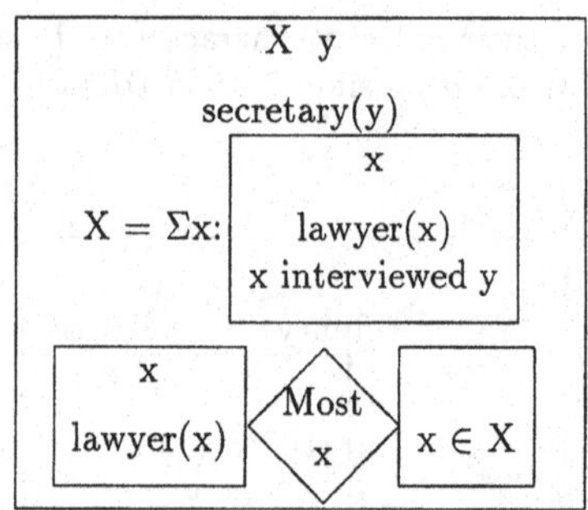

Note, however, that this is not the collective reading of verb phrases like **interview a secretary** which exercised us in Section 4.2.4. Rather, it is one which we also obtain when we interpret (4.275) by processing **most lawyers** in the familiar way (i.e. as a generalized quantifier) and then give a specific interpretation to the indefinite **a secretary**. In fact, (4.277) stands to the DRS resulting in this way exactly as (4.274) stands to (4.266).

The prediction implicit in this analysis of (4.276) strikes us as correct: (4.276) only means that the same secretary was interviewed by most of the lawyers, with no commitment to its having been a joint interview. Thus the collectivity of (4.276), like the "collectivity" which results in (4.275) when **a secretary** is given a specific interpretation, is of a comparatively "modest" sort. It arises through a process of abstraction over the condition **x interviewed y**, which expresses a relation between individuals. The collective interpretations of plural verbs that motivated the treatment of **most**, etc. as generalized quantifiers relate to the uses of those verbs as relations between individuals in a different and more dramatic way. With verbs such as **hire** and **buy** this is particularly clear: As we noted before, when a group of people acts as the buyer of something, then strictly speaking no individual member of the group can be said to have bought the thing. Precisely how the plural uses of such verbs are related to their singular uses is a problem for lexical semantics and one about which we have nothing more to say. All that matters in the present context is that the relation is not one that permits reducibility of the kind we have relied upon in our analysis of (4.260.a.ii). Thus our account of the acceptability of (4.260.a.ii) does not carry over to sentences such as (4.275) and the danger of overgeneration has proved illusory.

It is interesting to compare constructions with **the same** with those containing the complementary expression **different**. Consider

(4.278) Most students saw different films.

Such sentences are a potential problem for the account we have sketched. If (4.278) has like (4.260.a.ii) a reading to the effect that there was some majority of students such that no two students from that majority saw the same film, then we are in trouble. For how could the set **X**, which was instrumental in our analysis of (4.260.a.ii) (see (4.273) and (4.274)) be defined in this case? We have found no way of doing this and although we have no formal proof of the matter, we are prepared to conjecture that such a proof exists. If, however, the set **X** cannot be obtained through definition over predicates of individuals, then the only way of arriving at the mentioned reading would be to let the NP **most students** introduce a set discourse referent from the outset, and that would amount to giving the game away.

But does (4.278) have such a reading? We are inclined to doubt it. In fact, the truth conditions of sentences like (4.278) seem extremely difficult to ascertain and the intuitions we have been able to confirm are quite fragmentary. If a majority of the students saw the same film, then it seems quite clear that (4.278) is false. If, on the other hand, there is a majority such that each member of that majority saw a film while none of the films he saw was seen by any other student, then the sentence seems true. But note that there are truth conditions which capture these two cases and which can be defined on the basis of relations between individuals. For instance, we might define **X** to be the set of those students **x** such that (i) there was some film **y** which **x** saw and (ii) for any student **x′** such that **x′** $\neq$ **x** and films **y** and **y′** such that **x saw y** and **x′ saw y′ y** $\neq$ **y′**; and then represent (4.278) as saying that most students belong to **X**. We do not seriously propose this as the correct semantic analysis of (4.278). Its sole purpose is to convey our impression that so long as the semantics of sentences like (4.278) is not better understood, it remains unclear how they bear on the proposal of this section.

We now turn to the remaining two items that appear in the title of this section, **gather** and **together**. First **gather**. As shown in (4.260), **gather** is just as tolerant of subjects beginning with **most**, etc. as predicates involving **the same**. In fact, a very similar analysis offers itself for sentences involving this verb, as **gather** is quite naturally paraphrased as "come to the same place". In other words, we may interpret the collective predication which **gather** expresses as arising through summation over a family of individual comings to some place **y**, which are connected through their all being directed towards this same final location. Applying this analysis to, say,

(4.260.a.ii) Most students gathered in the square.

we get a DRS of something like the following form

(4.279)

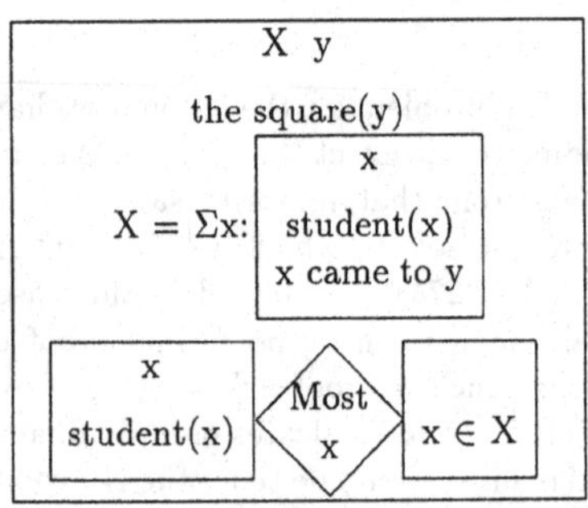

It should be acknowledged that the extension of our earlier proposal to the case of **gather** is a non-trivial one, as it involves a kind of "lexical decomposition" of the verb, in the spirit of our paraphrase "come to the same place". It would be nice if there were independent evidence for such a decomposition. At the moment we know of no such evidence.

There are other verbs besides **gather** whose collective use invites a similar treatment. An example is **collect**, which allows for collective interpretations with respect to its direct object position. Here too the analysis presupposes a lexical decomposition, in the sense of some such paraphrase as "put in the same place".

There is another paraphrase of **gather** – "come together" – which naturally comes to mind when we think about a semantic analysis of this verb. In fact, we might with equal plausibility have tried to acccount for **gather** as a special case of predicates whose collective character is due to the presence of **together**, instead of assimilating it to collective predicates involving **the same**. With good reason. For **together** is, of all the terms and constructions we have looked at in this chapter, the one which causes our theory the most trouble.

Like predicates which owe their collective character to the presence of **the same**, those whose collectivity stems from **together** invite an analysis according to which an underlying predicate of individuals is transformed into one which is applicable only to sets. In some cases the meaning of the resulting predicate relates to the underlying predicate just as we saw in the case of predicates involving **the same. Go to the cinema together**, the example represented in (4.260), is a case in point. This predicate is true of a set X iff there is some particular cinema to which each of the members of X went. But not all **together**-predicates are like this. **Buy a house together**, for instance, clearly is not. Its salient interpretation is that where it describes collective purchases, where the buying group as a whole becomes the owner, and its members only become partial owners. This reading is synomymous with the salient collective reading of the simple **buy a house** and that reading, we went out of our way to argue not many paragraphs ago, cannot be analysed as being true of a set just in case each member **x** of it stands to one and the same house **y** in the relation we can describe as **x bought y**.

To give a systematic account of how the meaning of a verb phrase with **together** is related to the predicate without it is no simple matter. In fact, the synonymy just observed, between **buy a house together** and the collective reading of **buy a house**, shows that this will be very tricky: At least as tricky as saying just how the application of a verb to a set-denoting argument depends on how it is applied to individuals in that set. But this is not the serious trouble to which we were alluding in the concluding sentence of the preceding paragraph. The real trouble is this: From what we have been saying, here and earlier in the present chapter, it seems to follow that (4.280.i) only has the distributive reading, whereas (4.280.ii) only has a collective one – that one which, we have argued, is not available in the case of (4.280.i):

(4.280) (i) Most lawyers hired a secretary.

(ii) Most lawyers hired a secretary together.

If this is the way things are, then appealing to a default principle seems unavoidable:

(4.281) When the argument is of the form **most** α, interpret the predicate distributively if you can; if you really can't, then, as a last resort, interpret the argument phrase as a set introducer.

We ourselves are not convinced that (4.280.ii) can mean that a majority of the lawyers was involved in a joint hiring. However, those who really think it can mean this, may well be forced to accept that they are committed to some such principle as (4.281). We should add that we would find it surprising if principles like (4.281) were constitutive of natural language semantics. But if you are among these that read (4.280.i) distributively but (4.280.ii) collectively, it is the best we have to offer.

It should be clear that in this section we have done no more than to scratch the surface of a problem of very considerable complexity. First, we have confined our attention to examples involving the determiner **most**. And the facts which we are able to ascertain about them were often quite tentative. Other sentences, in which **most** is replaced by such determiners as **many**, **few**, **at least n** or **at most n**, or, alternatively, in which the predicate is varied by a change in verb and/or object NP, show that collective interpretations are sensitive to a host of as yet only very incompletely understood factors. In addition, the context in which such sentences are placed tends to affect our judgements about them as well.

Much more empirical work is needed here than we have done. But it may well turn out at the end of the day that this is an area where there are few significant generalizations to be had. As we ventured to say in relation to reciprocal sentences in Section 4.4.5, we suspect that the semantic discrimination needed to support further generalizations simply isn't there. This too is a hunch that only careful further research can confirm or refute.

Chapter 5

Tense and Aspect

5.1 The Semantics and Logic of Temporal Reference

The theory we have developed in the preceding chapters ignores all questions of reference to time. In view of this one might have thought that it cannot possibly by right. For in natural languages such as English reference to time is ubiquitous. Virtually every English sentence involves an element of temporal reference because of the tense of its verb: as a first approximation, a sentence in the past tense locates the episode it describes before the utterance time, sentences in the future tense serve to describe episodes later than the time of utterance and a present tense sentence is typically used to present a condition as holding over some period which surrounds the utterance time. Since our theory paid no heed to any of this, how could it possibly be correct?

As a matter of fact, the theory is not quite as inadequate as these observations make it seem. For up to now we have concentrated on sentences in the present tense, sentences which could all be understood as describing the way things are at some single fixed "utterance" time and thus as being about the world at that one time only; and where only one time is involved time requires no special attention. Consider, for instance, an example much like the very first we considered in Chapter 1:

(5.1) Peter owns a Peugeot. It doesn't run.

The construction rules of Chapter 1 assign to this a DRS of the form:

(5.2)

x y z
Peter(x)
Peugeot(y)
x owns y
z = y
¬: [z runs]

When interpreting such DRSs, we made use of models in which predicates such as **owns** and **runs** are assigned extensions consisting of a set of individuals (in the case of **runs**) or a set of pairs of individuals (in the case of **owns**). The implicit assumption behind this was that the intended model gives the extensions of those predicates at the time that the discourse (5.1) is about. Which time this is depends on when and how the discourse is being used. Thus the present tense sentences that make up (5.1) will, given that the discourse is uttered at time **t**, both be taken to describe the situation at **t**.

This strategy works properly, however, only for so long as we confine ourselves to sentences in the present tense. It becomes problematic as soon as we consider past or future tense sentences; and it fails dramatically for discourses in which there is a mixture of tenses, e.g. when some sentences are in the present and others in the past tense. Thus, consider

(5.3) Peter owns a car. He bought it from Fred.

Proceeding in the manner of the last chapter, where we constructed the occasional DRS for sentences in the past tense, we obtain for (5.3) the DRS

(5.4)

x y z u v
Peter(x)
car(y)
x owns y
z = x
u = y
Fred(v)
z bought u from v

Intuitively, the truth conditions of (5.3) are clear enough: (5.3) is true if there is some car b such that the pair ⟨Peter, b⟩ belongs to the extension of **own** at the time when it is uttered, while the triple ⟨Peter, b, Fred⟩ belongs to the extension of **buy from** at some earlier time. (5.4), which is meant to represent (5.3), ought to have these same truth conditions. But if we apply the truth definition of Chapter 1 to (5.4) we do not get quite what we want. What we get is this: (5.4) is true in a model M, the definition tells us, if there are a, b, c in U_M such that a and c are the bearers in M of the names Peter and Fred, b is a car in M, ⟨a, b⟩ belongs to the extension of **own** and ⟨a, b, c⟩ satisfies the condition **x bought y from z**. This fails to account for how satisfaction of the predicate **x bought y from z** is determined by the extension of the verb **buy from**.

The problem is two-fold. First, a model which determines whether (5.4) is true or false will have to contain information about the extensions of predicates at more than one time; in fact, since the second sentence does not fix the past time at which the car was bought, it will have to provide information about the extension of **buy** not just at one past time, but at arbitrary times preceding the time of utterance of (5.3). We will presently consider the question what the structure of such models ought to be like.

Second, the DRS (5.4) is unsatisfactory as a representation of the content of (5.3) because it fails to make explicit that the present tense **owns** and the past tense **bought** pertain to different times. Our first and central task in this chapter is to reflect on how such information can be made explicit, to define the DRSs which contain this information and to develop a construction algorithm that produces those DRSs.

If tense is to be taken seriously, then both models and DRSs need to be different from what we have assumed them to be up to now. But precisely how either models or DRSs should be structured cannot be determined from the little we have said. As a matter of fact, the problem how to model the temporal structure of the world and the problem how to capture the temporal information that is contained in a tensed discourse are both quite complicated. So we will have to proceed carefully and slowly. In the course of our investigations we will find that neither problem has an unequivocal solution. Consequently, both the DRSs and the models we will propose will have features which reflect our intuitive preferences and are not supported by arguments that we ourselves consider conclusive.

We start with a brief survey of some earlier proposals for the treatment of temporal reference and tense. This will not only permit us to relate our own theory of tense and aspect to the history of the logic and semantics of temporal reference, but will also provide the natural context for a discussion of certain issues concerning the logic of time which must be got out of the way before we address the specific problems of temporal reference in English.

5.1.1 Tense Logics

What would a model have to be like in which a discourse like (5.3) can be meaningfully evaluated? The first idea that comes to mind is that it should specify "extension as a function of time", i.e. that it should give, for each time t, the extensions of all predicates of the language at t. Thus, a model of the kind needed to make sense of passages like (5.3) should be a structure which associates with each time t a model of the kind defined in Chapters 1, 2 and 4. In other words, it should specify a function from times to such models. But what are times? Here we face our first dilemma. Probably the most familiar notion of time is that according to which the constitutive elements of time are *moments*, or *instants* – atomic particles of time with zero duration which yield intervals of non-vanishing duration only when they are combined into very large (non-denumerably infinite) packages. This is the concept of time that lies at the root of theoretical physics, where it has been standard practice at least since the days of Galilei and Newton to identify the basic constituents of time with the real numbers. According to this conception, these basic constituents are indivisible and strictly ordered by the relation of earlier and later: for any two distinct elements t_1 and t_2, either t_1 is earlier than t_2 or else t_2 is earlier than t_1. Formally, such time structures can be represented as pairs $\langle T,<\rangle$ where T is the set of temporal instants and '$<$' is the earlier-later relation; this relation is assumed to be a total ordering of T, i.e. for any t_1, t_2, t_3 in T we have:

(i) $t_1 < t_2 \rightarrow t_2 \not< t_1$

(ii) $(t_1 < t_2 \wedge t_2 < t_3) \rightarrow t_1 < t_3$

(iii) $t_1 \neq t_2 \rightarrow (t_1 < t_2 \vee t_2 < t_1)$

Given such a conception of time we may think of a model $\mathcal{M}$ as a pair consisting of a time structure $\mathcal{T} = \langle T,<\rangle$ together with a function M which assigns to each $t \in T$ a corresponding model M_t. Let us assume, provisionally, that the M_t are models in the sense of Definition 1.2.1. (p. 94) and that any two models M_t and $M_{t'}$ have the same universes, i.e. $U_{M_t} = U_{M_{t'}}$. Where $\mathcal{M} = \langle\langle T,<\rangle, M\rangle$, we will often denote T as $T_{\mathcal{M}}$, $<$ as $<_{\mathcal{M}}$, and $\mathcal{T} = \langle T,<\rangle$ as $\mathcal{T}_{\mathcal{M}}$.

Models of this sort were first used in a treatment of the logic of time known as *(Priorean) tense logic.* The familiar systems of tense logic are extensions of either predicate logic or propositional logic, obtained through the addition of one or more so-called *tense operators.* A particularly well-known system of this kind[1] consists

[1] See [Cocchiarella 1965]. Tense logic of the type discussed here was created by the philosopher Arthur Prior [Prior 1967] (hence the term 'Priorean'). Although Prior concentrated in much of his work on tense logics based on propositional logic, Cocchiarella's system may be considered the natural extension of Prior's conception in the direction of predicate logic.

of standard predicate logic enriched with two tense operators, P and F, which are intended as formal analogues of the simple past and the simple future tense in languages such as English. Formally, P and F are 1-place sentence connectives, just as $\neg$. (Thus, from any given formula ϕ we can form the complex formulas Pϕ and Fϕ in the same way in which we can form $\neg\phi$.) Roughly speaking, Pϕ and Fϕ may be paraphrased as "It was the case that ϕ" and "It will be the case that ϕ". However, we will see presently that these paraphrases are problematic. We will refer to this particular tense logical language as TPL ("Tense Predicate Logic"). Within TPL it is possible to represent a variety of sentences and discourses from natural language which we could not represent hitherto. For instance, (5.3) could be represented as

(5.5) $\exists x \exists y\ (x = \mathbf{Peter} \wedge \mathbf{car(y)} \wedge \mathbf{own(x,y)} \wedge$
$\exists z\ (z = \mathbf{Fred} \wedge P\ \mathbf{buy(x,y,z)}))$

To see what the model-theoretic interpretation of the tense operators P and F ought to be, let us consider two simple sentences in the past and future tense, repectively:

(5.6) Peter was ill.

(5.7) Amelie will live in Boston.

One of the basic assumptions underlying TPL is that such sentences can be represented as Pϕ and Fψ, where ϕ represents the present tense sentence **Peter is ill** and ψ the present tense sentence **Amelie lives in Boston**. The first, Pϕ, is true at a given time **t** iff there is some time **t′** before **t** at which ϕ is true (i.e. such that Peter is ill at **t′**); and similarly Fψ is true at **t** iff ψ is true at some time **t′** later than **t**. The standard semantics for P and F is a direct generalization of these reductions. It is given by the truth clauses

(5.8) Pϕ is *true in* $\mathcal{M}$ *at* t iff $\exists$t′ (t′ < t $\wedge$ ϕ is true in $\mathcal{M}$ at t′)

and

(5.9) Fϕ is *true in* $\mathcal{M}$ *at* t iff $\exists$t′ (t < t′ $\wedge$ ϕ is true in $\mathcal{M}$ at t′).

Besides telling us how the operators P and F are to be interpreted, the clauses (5.8) and (5.9) also show what the truth definition for a language such as TPL should look like in general. They indicate the central feature which distinguishes such a definition from the truth definition for predicate logic that was given in Chapter 2:

the truth value of a formula now depends not only on the particular model relative to which the formula is being evaluated, but also on the time with respect to which this evaluation takes place. Since truth values now generally depend on time, the evaluation time will have to be mentioned explicitly also in those clauses of the definition which have nothing directly to do with this dependency. For instance, the clause for conjunction becomes:

(5.10) $\phi \wedge \psi$ is *true in* $\mathcal{M}$ *at* t iff ϕ is true in $\mathcal{M}$ at t and ψ is true in $\mathcal{M}$ at t.

The clause for atomic formulas will have to make the dependence on time explicit as well. For instance, for an atomic sentence like **R(c,d)**, where **R** is a binary relation symbol and **c** and **d** are individual constants, we now get

(5.11) **R(c,d)** is *true in* $\mathcal{M}$ *at* t iff $\langle \mathsf{Name}_{\mathsf{M_t}}(\mathbf{c}), \mathsf{Name}_{\mathsf{M_t}}(\mathbf{d})\rangle$ belongs to $\mathsf{Pred}_{\mathsf{M_t}}(\mathbf{R})$.

A complete truth definition for the quantifier free part of TPL which incorporates clauses (5.8–5.11) is given in Definition 5.1.1 ('$\|\phi\|_{\mathcal{M},t}$' denotes the truth value of ϕ in $\mathcal{M}$ at t).

Definition 5.1.1

(i) $\|P_i^n(c_1, ..., c_n)\|_{\mathcal{M},t} = 1$ iff $\langle \mathsf{Name}_{\mathsf{M_t}}(c_1), ..., \mathsf{Name}_{\mathsf{M_t}}(c_n)\rangle$ belongs to $\mathsf{Pred}_{\mathsf{M_t}}(P_i^n)$

(ii) $\|\neg\phi\|_{\mathcal{M},t} = 1$ iff not $\|\phi\|_{\mathcal{M},t} = 1$

(iii) $\|\phi \wedge \psi\|_{\mathcal{M},t} = 1$ iff $\|\phi\|_{\mathcal{M},t} = 1$ and $\|\psi\|_{\mathcal{M},t} = 1$

(iv) $\|\phi \rightarrow \psi\|_{\mathcal{M},t} = 1$ iff if $\|\phi\|_{\mathcal{M},t} = 1$ then $\|\psi\|_{\mathcal{M},t} = 1$

(v) $\|\phi \vee \psi\|_{\mathcal{M},t} = 1$ iff $\|\phi\|_{\mathcal{M},t} = 1$ or $\|\psi\|_{\mathcal{M},t} = 1$

(vi) $\|P\phi\|_{\mathcal{M},t} = 1$ iff $\exists t' \; (t' < t \wedge \|\phi\|_{\mathcal{M},t'} = 1)$

(vii) $\|F\phi\|_{\mathcal{M},t} = 1$ iff $\exists t' \; (t < t' \wedge \|\phi\|_{\mathcal{M},t'} = 1)$

On the basis of Definition 5.1.1, we can define what it is for a sentence ϕ of TPL to be valid. The idea is that if ϕ is to be valid, it must be true in every model $\mathcal{M}$ at every time belonging to the time structure of $\mathcal{M}$. In a similar fashion, we define validity of arguments whose premisses and conclusions belong to TPL.

Definition 5.1.2

(i) A (closed) formula ϕ of TPL is *valid* iff for each model $\mathcal{M}$ and each $t \in T_{\mathcal{M}}$ $\|\phi\|_{\mathcal{M},t} = 1$

(ii) A formula ϕ is a *logical consequence* of a set of formulas Γ in TPL iff for each model $\mathcal{M}$ and each $t \in T_{\mathcal{M}}$ if $\|\psi\|_{\mathcal{M},t} = 1$ for all $\psi \in \Gamma$, then $\|\phi\|_{\mathcal{M},t} = 1$.

The question which formulas of TPL are valid has received a great deal of attention. It was especially popular in the early days of tense logic. To get a feeling for the complexities involved consider the formula

(5.12) $\quad P\phi \rightarrow PP\phi$

Let $\mathcal{M}$ be any model and t any element of $T_{\mathcal{M}}$. Suppose that the antecedent of (5.12) is true in M at t. Then there must be an element $t' \in T_{\mathcal{M}}$ such that $t' <_{\mathcal{M}} t$ and $\|\phi\|_{\mathcal{M},t'} = 1$. Can we conclude from this that the consequent of (5.12), $PP\phi$, is also true in $\mathcal{M}$ at t? For this to be so, there must be a $t'' \in T_{\mathcal{M}}$ such that $t'' <_{\mathcal{M}} t$ and $\|P\phi\|_{\mathcal{M},t''} = 1$, and this is the case iff there is a $t'' \in T_{\mathcal{M}}$ such that $t'' <_{\mathcal{M}} t$ and a $t''' \in T_{\mathcal{M}}$ such that $t''' <_{\mathcal{M}} t''$ and $\|\phi\|_{\mathcal{M},t'''} = 1$. We could conclude that such t'' and t''' exist provided we knew that between t' and t there was at least one other time t''''. For then we could let t'' be this time t'''' and t''' the time t', and the conditions required for the truth of $PP\phi$ in $\mathcal{M}$ at t would be satisfied. So, if we could infer the existence of such a time t'''' in general, that would establish the validity of (5.12). But can we be sure that $T_{\mathcal{M}}$ contains such a time? In order that this inference be licenced in general, the time structure $T_{\mathcal{M}}$ would have to be of a special sort: it would have to be, as mathematical terminology has it, a *dense linear ordering*, i.e. an ordering such that between any two of its elements there is a third. This is a property that the standard representation of time – that representation which identifies the moments of time with the real numbers – does have. But it is not a property of all linear orderings. For instance, the linear ordering $\mathbb{Z}$, whose elements are the integers ..., −3, −2, −1, 0, 1, 2, 3, ..., does not have it. If linear orderings such as $\mathbb{Z}$ are admitted among the possible time structures of the models for TPL, then the validity of (5.12) cannot be established; only when all models have densely ordered time structures is its validity guaranteed.

The question which of the formulas (and arguments) of TPL are valid thus depends on another question: What are the logically necessary properties of the structure of time? This second question is a very hard one, and it may well be that there is no unique answer to it. Tense logicians have finessed this difficulty by studying validity relative to certain sets of properties of temporal orders. In particular they have studied validity relative to the property of being just any linear order as well as validity relative to the pair consisting of this property together with the property of being dense. We have just seen that these two sets of valid formulas will not coincide, since (5.12) is valid in the second sense but not in the first.

We must be a little bit more precise. For any class of models $\mathcal{K}$, one may consider the set of formulas (and arguments) *valid with respect to* $\mathcal{K}$. This is the set of those formulas ϕ such that for each member $\mathcal{M}$ of $\mathcal{K}$ and each $t \in T_{\mathcal{M}}$, ϕ is true in $\mathcal{M}$ at t. Tense logicians have been interested in certain classes $\mathcal{K}_{\mathcal{P}}$ consisting of all models whose time structures possess each of the properties in some given property set $\mathcal{P}$; examples are the class consisting of all models $\mathcal{M}$ such that $T_{\mathcal{M}}$ is a dense linear ordering, the class whose only member is the structure of the real numbers, and so on.

Using the notion of validity with respect to $\mathcal{K}_{\mathcal{P}}$, we can state our observations about (5.12) as follows: Let $\mathcal{P}$ be any class of properties of linear orderings and let $\mathcal{K}_{\mathcal{P}}$ be the corresponding class of models for tense logic. Then (5.12) is valid with respect to $\mathcal{K}_{\mathcal{P}}$ iff $\mathcal{P}$ entails the property of being dense. To see this, argue as follows: (i) if $\mathcal{P}$ entails the property of being dense then every model M in $\mathcal{K}_{\mathcal{P}}$ will have a dense time structure, and so for any $t \in T_{\mathcal{M}}$ (5.12) will be true in $\mathcal{M}$ at t by the argument just given. (ii) Suppose that $\mathcal{P}$ does not entail the property of being dense. Then $\mathcal{K}_{\mathcal{P}}$ will contain models $\mathcal{M}$ such that $T_{\mathcal{M}}$ is not dense, i.e. $T_{\mathcal{M}}$ has at least two members t_1 and t_2 such that $t_1 <_{\mathcal{M}} t_2$ and for no $t_3 \in T_{\mathcal{M}}$, $t_1 <_{\mathcal{M}} t_3 <_{\mathcal{M}} t_2$. Among such models it will always be possible to find one which invalidates some instance of (5.12). For instance, let ψ be that instance of (5.12) in which ϕ is the atomic formula Q(c), with Q some one-place predicate of TPL and c some individual constant; and let for $t <_{\mathcal{M}} t_2$ the models M_t be such that $\mathrm{Name}_{M_t}(c)$ belongs to the extension of $\mathrm{Pred}_{M_t}(Q)$ when $t = t_1$ but not when $t <_{\mathcal{M}} t_1$. Then PQ(c) will be true in $\mathcal{M}$ at t_2, but PPQ(c) will be false there. Consequently, $PQ(c) \rightarrow PPQ(c)$ is false in $\mathcal{M}$ at t_2.

Questions of validity will not preoccupy us in this chapter, and TPL is not the system we will use to represent the content of tensed sentences. If we have nevertheless discussed the validity of (5.12) at such length, it is because this seemed the best way to bring out what we take to be a point of primary conceptual importance: once the temporal dimension of natural language is taken into account, questions of "logical validity" can no longer be clearly separated from certain metaphysical questions which concern the nature of time. We should stress that this is a problem which does not just arise for TPL but for any formalism suited to the representation of temporal information expressible in natural language. In particular it arises, just as much as it does for TPL, for the DRS-language which we will develop in the course of this chapter. If we have decided not to pursue questions of validity, it is not because we consider them unimportant but because other, more urgent business had to get priority.

5.1.2 Inadequacies of TPL and Similar Systems

Whatever its interests for the formal logician, as a system for representing natural languages like English, TPL suffers from a number of drawbacks. To begin with, there is much that such a system should be able to express, but which cannot be expressed in TPL. Consider, for instance, the sentence

(5.13) Bill has been watching little Alice ever since Mary left.

This sentence is true at time t iff there is some time t′ preceding t such that (i) the proposition that Mary leaves is true at t′ and (ii) the proposition that Bill is watching little Alice is true at all times from t′ onwards, up to (and including) t. It can be shown that in all cases where the structure of time has certain "natural" properties, this proposition cannot be adequately represented within TPL. In particular, this is so when time is like the real numbers.[2] To be precise, there is no complex formula $\phi(\xi,\eta)$ of TPL built up from formulas ξ and η of TPL such that in every model $\mathcal{M}$ whose time structure is like the real numbers and any $t \in T_{\mathcal{M}}$ $\phi(\xi,\eta)$ is true in $\mathcal{M}$ at t iff there is a $t' \in T_{\mathcal{M}}$ such that $t' <_{\mathcal{M}} t$, ξ is true in $\mathcal{M}$ at t′ and for all $t'' \in T_{\mathcal{M}}$ such that $t' <_{\mathcal{M}} t'' \leq_{\mathcal{M}} t$ η is true in $\mathcal{M}$ at t″.

More powerful systems of tense logic have been developed to repair this defect, systems which differ from TPL in that they have tense operators other than P and F. Notable among these is a system whose tense operators are two binary sentence operators, S and U. $S(\phi,\psi)$ and $U(\phi,\psi)$ can be approximately paraphrased as "it has been the case that ψ since it was the case that ϕ" (or "it had been the case that ψ since it was/had been the case that ϕ" or "it will have been the case that ψ since it was the case that ϕ", depending on the context in which the formula appears) and as "it will be the case that ψ until it will be the case that ϕ" (or "it was the case that ψ until it was the case that ϕ", etc.). But these are only approximations. The "official" semantics of S and U is given by the clauses

(5.14) $\|S(\phi,\psi)\|_{\mathcal{M},t} = 1$ iff
$\exists t' \, (t' <_{\mathcal{M}} t \rightarrow \|\phi\|_{\mathcal{M},t'} = 1 \wedge \forall t'' \, (t' <_{\mathcal{M}} t'' <_{\mathcal{M}} t \rightarrow \|\psi\|_{\mathcal{M},t''} = 1))$

(5.15) $\|U(\phi,\psi)\|_{\mathcal{M},t} = 1$ iff
$\exists t' \, (t <_{\mathcal{M}} t' \wedge \|\phi\|_{\mathcal{M},t'} = 1 \wedge \forall t'' \, (t <_{\mathcal{M}} t'' <_{\mathcal{M}} t' \rightarrow \|\psi\|_{\mathcal{M},t''} = 1))$

[2] What counts as a natural property of time is a matter that cannot be easily decided. However, we regard it as uncontroversial that the natural properties of time, whatever they may be, do not *exclude* the structure of the real numbers.

Our English paraphrases for S and U do not quite capture these formal clauses.[3]

The tense logic with S and U as primitive operators has considerable advantages over its weaker sibling TPL. It is capable of expressing a much larger part of the temporal properties of, and relations between, propositions that are expressible in natural languages. (This claim is formally supported by a theorem to the effect that if time is like the real numbers, or, alternatively, if it is like the integers, then every property or relation that can be semantically characterized by means of quantification over times and reference to the earlier-later relation '$<$' can be rendered by some complex formula built up from atomic formulas with the help of truth functional connectives '$\neg$', '$\wedge$', '$\vee$', '$\wedge$', the quantifiers '$\forall$' and '$\exists$', and no other tense operators than S and U. This implies in particular that it can define a very large class of tense operators in the same sense in which F is defined in footnote 3.) When it comes to providing *natural* representations of tensed sentences from languages such as English, however, the system with S and U is no more satisfactory than the one with P and F. In fact, its ability to provide truthconditionally correct representations for a much wider variety of temporal relations that are expressible in English has, from a linguistic point of view, been none to the good. It has

[3]First, according to (5.14), $S(\phi,\psi)$ does not require that ψ be true at t, whereas our paraphrase seems to imply this. This means in particular that the correct representation of (5.13) is not $S(\phi,\psi)$ (with ϕ short for **Mary leaves** and ψ for **Bill is watching little Alice**), but rather $S(\phi,\psi) \wedge \psi$.

Whether our paraphrase for $U(\phi,\psi)$ corresponds to (5.15) is harder to decide. Past tense sentences, such as, say, **Bill stayed with little Alice until Mary returned** seem to behave in accordance with (5.15). But in present or future tense sentences, e.g. **This regulation will remain in force until revoked by the full assembly**, its preferred interpretation, seems to be a weaker one, one which does not entail that there will be a future time at which the full assembly revokes the mentioned regulation. According to this preferred interpretation **until**-sentences of this latter type should not be represented as $U(\phi,\psi)$ but by a disjunction such as

(5.16) $U(\phi,\psi) \vee (\neg F\phi \wedge \neg F\neg\psi)$.

Note that, strictly speaking, (5.16) is not a formula of the new system, for F is not one of its operators. However, we can *define* F with the help of U. We can, that is, represent the formula $F\phi$ of TPL in the new logic as $U(\phi \vee \neg\phi,\phi)$. According to (5.15), this latter formula says that there exists, in the future of the time t of evaluation, a time t′ at which ϕ is true while $\phi \vee \neg\phi$ is true at all the intervening times. As this last conjunct is trivially satisfied (because $\phi \vee \neg\phi$ is a tautology and thus of necessity true at any possible time) the claim $U(\phi \vee \neg\phi,\phi)$ boils down to there being a future time at which ϕ is true. This matches the truth conditions of $F\phi$.

(5.16), then, may be regarded as a shorthand for

(5.17) $U(\phi,\psi) \vee (\neg U(\phi \vee \neg\phi,\phi) \wedge \neg U(\neg\psi \vee \neg\neg\psi,\neg\psi))$

and this is a formula of the new system. It should be clear from the definition of F in terms of U that a parallel definition can be given of P in terms of S.

encouraged the tendency to ignore how *devious* these representations are and so has stood in the way of our seeing more clearly what the particular mechanisms are which natural languages exploit in order to convey the quite complex temporal information that it is within their power to express.

The first of the several features that TPL and the logic with S and U have in common, and that distinguish them from natural languages like English, is the possibility of iterating tense operators, as in formulas like: $PP\phi$, $PPP\phi$, $FPF\neg P\neg\phi$, $\neg F\neg((\phi \wedge \neg F\neg\phi) \wedge P\neg F\neg\phi)$, etc. Such formulas have no direct natural language counterparts. This is not to say that the temporal relations they express cannot be rendered in English. They can be. But as a rule the correct English paraphrase will not only use tenses and other operator-like devices such as temporal conjunctions, it will also refer to times *explicitly* with the help of nouns such as **time, moment**, etc. Consider, for instance, the comparatively simple formula $PPPQ(\mathbf{c})$, where Q represents the verb phrase **be ill** and the constant **c** stands for the individual Mary. Of course we can paraphrase this formula as 'There was a time before which there was another time before which there was yet another time at which last time Mary was ill'. But what would be a paraphrase which avoids the use of such expressions as 'there was a time'? Here is one with which tense logicians often make do:

(5.18) It was the case that it was the case that Mary was ill.

Does this correctly capture the content of $PPPQ(\mathbf{c})$? It is hard to tell. For one thing, the sentence is so awkward that one has difficulty bringing one's linguistic intuitions to bear on it. But on closer inspection there is a deeper problem as well. As we will argue below, embedded occurences of the English past tense often allow for more than one interpretation. As a consequence (5.18) is ambiguous – its truth conditions *might* be those of $PPPQ(\mathbf{c})$, but it could also be interpreted in some other way.

One reason why English paraphrases for such formulas are hard to come by is that English has no straightforward way of iterating tenses. A tense is always associated with a verb and verbs cannot just be piled one on top of the other. There are, it is true, complex tenses, such as, for instance, the past perfect, which, you might say, "produces" for instance the sentence **Mary had been ill** when applied to **Mary is ill**. It might be thought that this is the natural language paraphrase of $PPQ(\mathbf{c})$, and that, conversely, $PPQ(\mathbf{c})$ would be the correct formal representation of the past perfect English sentence within TPL. As we will see later (cf. Sections 5.3 and 5.4), even this is not quite true. But in any case, the complex tenses of English can at best provide paraphrases for TPL formulas with two layers of tense operators (at the very most, and only in quite special instances, three layers). Beyond that, paraphrases must exploit other resources.

If natural language manages to express complex temporal relationships without the benefit of unrestricted iterability of its "operators", how does it succeed? In part the answer is simple and straightforward. As we have already noted, a language like English (and this, surely, is equally true of most, perhaps all, natural languages) makes frequent use of phrases such as **at some time, when ..., at all subsequent times, when it was the case that ...** and the like, which explicitly quantify over times. But this is not the whole story. First, natural language phrases which explicitly quantify over times often get their specific meaning partly from the particular tense of the verb they contain – compare, for instance, **there will be a time** with **there was a time**. A theory of temporal reference ought to explain how the tenses contribute to the meaning of such quantificational phrases. Another example of how tenses and phrases that explicitly denote times may interact is given by the following pair of sentences.

(5.19) (i) Alvin rang on Sunday.

(ii) Alvin will ring on Sunday.

The phrase **on Sunday** has the property that it refers to the nearest Sunday – in the future or in the past – to some given, contextually salient time (see also Section 5.5.1). In particular, in a context in which no times have yet been made salient, the phrase will refer either to the next Sunday after the day on which the utterance takes place or to the last Sunday before it.[4] Let us assume that (5.19.i) is uttered in a context of this sort. Then it is clear that the token of **on Sunday** which it contains must refer to the last Sunday before the utterance time. For the past tense of **rang** indicates that the described event lies before the time of utterance, thereby selecting one from the two possible referents of the referentially ambiguous prepositional phrase. By the same token, (5.19.ii) will, when uttered in a context of the sort described, be understood as saying that Alvin will come on the next Sunday after the time of speech.[5]

Another device for expressing temporal relationships which does not involve explicit reference to times is one that is easiest to recognize within the context of discourse. The interpretation of tenses (as well as of certain other temporal devices, e.g. of adverbs such as **then, subsequently** or **the day before**) often involves a kind of *anaphora*. Consider the following two-sentence text:

(5.20) Last week Fred bought his ninth cat. He paid 75 ECU for it.

---

[4] See the discussion of **on Sunday** in Section 5.5.

[5] When the utterance time falls itself on a Sunday, (5.19.i) and (5.19.ii) sound strange. It would carry us too far to give an exhaustive explanation of why this should be so.

There is an overriding tendency to take the second sentence of (5.20) as talking about the same time as the first. Similarly, the second sentence of (5.21)

(5.21) Bill left the house at a quarter past five. He took a taxi to the station and caught the first train to Bognor.

is naturally understood as describing two events that directly follow the one described in the first sentence. This phenomenon, that the second of a pair of sentences describes an event that coincides with, or is in the temporal vicinity of, the event described in the first sentence, is a pervasive feature of the use of tense in natural language. We will study this aspect of temporal reference in considerable detail later on. For the moment we only want to point out that it puts natural languages, which have it, at a considerable distance from formal systems such as TPL, which do not.

Not only does temporal anaphora add much to the expressive power and flexibility of natural language; it also makes tenses, because of their anaphoric interaction with the contexts in which they appear, incomparable to the tense operators of TPL and similar systems which are supposed to represent them. In fact, it is this which is responsible for the inadequacy – which we have mentioned, but not yet explained – of (5.18) as a paraphrase of the formula PPPQ(**c**). Temporal anaphora, like pronominal anaphora, works both on an intersentential and on an intrasentential plane. (5.20) and (5.21) are examples of the former, (5.22) illustrates the latter:

(5.22) Mary said that she felt sick.

The second tense of (5.22) is naturally taken as pointing towards the same time as its first tense – it can be interpreted, just as the second tenses of (5.20) and (5.21), as "anaphoric" to the time that the previous tense introduced. But note that this is only one of two ways in which (5.22) can be understood; the sentence can also be seen as describing a situation in which Mary felt sick some time before she said so. This, for instance, is a plausible interpretation for

(5.23) Fred and Mary told us of the horrible scene they had watched earlier that night when coming out of the cinema. Mary said she felt sick.

A similar ambivalence affects the interpretation of (5.18). One could interpret its second tense as pointing to a time before that indicated by the first, and the third as pointing to a time before that indicated by the second. So interpreted, (5.18)

will be equivalent to PPPQ(**c**). But we are under no obligation to interpret (5.18) in this way. We could also take its second and third tense to refer to the same time as the first one. The sentence would then end up with the same truth conditions as the simple **Mary was ill.**[6]

(5.18) is one of many natural language paraphrases of logical formulas which illustrate the tension between natural languages and formal systems like TPL. Another example is the following paraphrase of the formula PQ(**c**):

(5.24) It was the case that Mary is ill.

(5.24) is meant to highlight the idea that a past tense sentence such as **Mary was ill** must be construed as the result of applying the past tense operator (**it was the case that**) to an underlying present tense sentence. However, when we try to make sense of (5.24) just on the strength of our understanding of English (rather than of what we know about the intentions behind TPL), this is not the reading that we get. Present tense sentences have the property that they often refer to the time of utterance even when they occur embedded within some other, non-present tense sentence. Consider, for instance,

(5.25) Fred told me that Mary is pregnant.

This sentence is appropriate only in situations where the state of affairs of which Fred informed the speaker (at some time before the utterance time of (5.25)) still obtains at the utterance time. A similar principle governs the interpretation of (5.24). Its embedded sentence is to be construed as describing what is going on at the time of utterance – as expressing the proposition that at that time Mary is or was ill. Indeed, the matrix clause **it was the case that** seems to make no real contribution to (5.24) which is presumably why the sentence seems so odd. Similar comments apply to an alternative paraphrase for PPPQ(**c**):

(5.26) It was the case that it was the case that it was the case that
Mary is ill.

The tendency of the present tense to relate to the utterance time even when embedded under some other tense is shared by the simple future. For instance,

(5.27) It was predicted that the Messiah will come.

---

[6]Inasmuch as this is the most natural interpretation, it may explain the awkwardness of (5.18): on its default interpretation it is grotesquely redundant. So we try to give it another interpretation which does not fit it comfortably.

reports a past prediction about an event lying in the future of the time at which (5.27) is asserted, not about an event that lies in the future of the time of the prediction but might have taken place before the time of assertion. To make the weaker claim, which leaves the temporal relationship between the utterance time and the event of the Messiah's coming undecided, one would have to say

(5.28) It was predicted that the Messiah would come.

As these examples show, the present tense and the simple future may have to be interpreted in relation to the time of utterance even when they occur within the syntactic scope of other tenses. This, as we will see later, is true of many other tenses as well. In this regard, tenses are like many other natural language expressions which must be interpreted with reference to the utterance context, irrespective of how deeply they are embedded. This phenomenon is known as *indexicality*. The indexical character of natural language tenses is yet another feature that sets them apart from tense operators such as P, F, S or U.

Let us summarize the discussion of the present section up to this point. We have seen that the tenses of natural languages such as English have a number of features that are not represented in tense logics such as TPL:

(F1) The tenses *do not permit nesting or iteration* in the way in which the operators of a formalism like TPL can be nested and iterated.

(F2) Tenses tend to be *indexical*: The times they refer to must often be determined in relation to the utterance time, and this is so even when they occur embedded within other tensed clauses.

(F3) The interpretation of tenses often has an *anaphoric* aspect: the next tense refers to the same time as the one preceding it, or else refers to some time in the vicinity of that time.

(F4) Tenses often determine the time of the described event or state of affairs *in cooperation with other elements* of the sentences in which they occur, in particular with expressions which are naturally and generally understood as explicitly referring to, or quantifying over times.

Could systems such as TPL be adapted so that their operators become endowed with the properties (F1–F4)? We have four questions here; we shall take them one at a time.

(1.) As regards (F1), it is easy enough to define tense logics which conform to this feature of natural language tense systems, viz. by modifying the syntax of, say,

TPL, stipulating that once a formula contains a tense operator it is not possible to place another tense operator in front of it. However, such systems turn out to be extremely limited in what they can express.

(2.) To redesign tense logics so that their operators conform to (F2), it is sufficient to adjust their semantics, and this can be done without too much difficulty. For instance, it is not difficult to change the truth clause for the operator F as follows.

$$(5.29) \qquad \|F\phi\|_{\mathcal{M},t} = 1 \text{ iff } \exists t' \, (t_0 <_{\mathcal{M}} t' \wedge \|\phi\|_{\mathcal{M},t'} = 1)$$

where t_0 denotes the time of utterance of the entire sentence of which the relevant token of $F\phi$ is a part.[7] (5.29) turns F into an operator which has the kind of indexicality which, we saw, attaches to the simple future in English.

(3.) To adapt tense logics in such a way that their operators reflect the anaphoric aspects of the tenses is much harder. In the course of the preceding chapters, we have learned that a proper account of anaphora must allot a central place to context dependence and context change. In a semantic theory built around a truth definition such as Definition 5.1.1 there is no room for the required notion of context, let alone for context modification. Changing the semantics of tense logics so that context and context change can play their part would leave little of the original spirit of these logics intact.

(4.) The most serious difficulty for the tense logical systems we have been discussing arises in connection with (F4). Where tenses cooperate, in the manner we have illustrated, with noun phrases that are naturally interpreted as referring to or quantifying over times, their semantic contributions have the effect of *constraints* on those times. Tense logics of the type of TPL are not equipped to account for such interactions because they have no direct means for representing explicit reference to times. At best, such logics might be used to represent those occurrences of tenses which do not interact with temporal NPs. But to use them in this way would create a highly artificial dichotomy – between the tenses which happen to interact with such NPs and those which happen not to – for which natural language provides no evidential basis whatsoever. If we aim for the uniform analysis of tense which natural language suggests, then the only reasonable option is to analyse the semantic contributions of the tenses *always* as constraints on times, whether or not they visibly interact with devices for explicit temporal reference or quantification.

[7] This formulation has its problems. For a formally correct formulation see Exercise 3 on page 500.

Exercises

1. On pages 489 and 490 we showed that the formula $P\varphi \rightarrow PP\varphi$ is valid only with respect to the class of models $\mathcal{K}_\mathcal{P}$ such that $\mathcal{P}$ contains (or entails) the property of being dense. Consider the properties under (a)–(i) and show which of the formulas (1) to (11) are valid with respect to which property. Does any of the given formulae (1) to (11) express any of the conditions (a)–(i) in the sense in which $P\varphi \rightarrow PP\varphi$ expresses density?[8]

   (1) $P\varphi \rightarrow H(F\varphi \vee \varphi \vee P\varphi)$
   (2) $P\varphi \rightarrow GP\varphi$
   (3) $\varphi \rightarrow HF\varphi$
   (4) $\varphi \rightarrow GP\varphi$
   (5) $F\varphi \rightarrow HF\varphi$
   (6) $F\varphi \rightarrow G(P\varphi \vee \varphi \vee F\varphi)$
   (7) $P\varphi \rightarrow FP\varphi$
   (8) $\varphi \rightarrow FP\varphi$
   (9) $F\varphi \rightarrow FP\varphi$
   (10) $F\varphi \rightarrow FF\varphi$
   (11) $FF\varphi \rightarrow F\varphi$

   (a) $\forall y < x\ \forall z < x\ (z < y \vee z = y \vee y > z)$
   (b) $\forall y > x\ \ x > y$
   (c) $\forall y < x\ \forall z > x\ \ y > z$
   (d) $\forall y < x\ \exists z > x\ \ y < z$
   (e) $\forall y > x\ \exists z > x\ \ y < z$
   (f) $\forall y > x\ \forall z > x\ \ y < z$
   (g) $\forall y > x\ \forall z > x\ \ (y < z \vee y = z \vee z < y)$
   (h) $\exists y\ \ x < y$
   (i) $\forall y > x\ \exists z > x\ \ z < y$

2. Show that the following formulas are not valid with respect to the class of all linear orderings. (Construct for each formula a model **M** such that for some t the formula is false in **M** at t.)[9]

   (a) $\forall x\, (Q(x) \rightarrow G\, (\exists y\, Py \rightarrow \exists y\, (Py \wedge Qx)))$
   (b) $\forall x\, (Q(x) \rightarrow G\, (\exists y\, Py \rightarrow \exists y\, (Py \wedge Qy)))$
   (c) $\forall x\, (Q(x) \rightarrow F\, \Box\, Q(x))$
   (d) $\forall x\, (Q(x) \rightarrow F\, \exists y\, \Box\, Q(y))$

[8] Here $H\varphi$ is defined as $\neg P \neg \varphi$ and $G\varphi$ as $\neg F \neg \varphi$.
[9] G is defined as in 1.

(e) $\exists x\ (\neg Q(x) \rightarrow F\ \exists y\ F\ Q(y))$
(f) $(F\ Q(a) \wedge F\ Q(b)) \rightarrow F\ (Q(a) \wedge Q(b))$

3. In footnote 7 on page 498 we hinted at a certain formal problem connected with clause (5.29):

   (5.29) $\|F\phi\|_{\mathcal{M},t} = 1$ iff $\exists t'\ (t_0 <_{\mathcal{M}} t' \wedge \|\phi\|_{\mathcal{M},t'} = 1)$

   This problem concerns the status of the "utterance time" t_0. Formally, there are two ways we can alter the semantics of tense logic to clarify the status of the expression "t_0". The first is to redefine the notion of a model for tense logic, so that a model reflects not simply a world as it develops through time, but reflects a world as it developed through time up to a given "present", as it is at that present and as it will develop after that present. The simplest way to do this is to define a model to be a structure

   $\langle \mathcal{T}, M, t_0 \rangle$, where $t_0 \in T$.

   Here the third component t_0 represents the model's present. The second way is to leave the notion of a model as we defined it in Section (5.1.1) (see pp. 486ff.), but to alter the truth definition as follows. We now define the concept of a sentence ϕ *being true in a model M at a time* t, *when part-of-an-utterance-made-at-time* t', $\|\phi\|_{\mathcal{M},t,t'}$. Truth of a sentence ϕ at t in M can then be defined as truth of t in M when part of an utterance made at t':

   $\|\phi\|_{\mathcal{M},t} \equiv_{df} \|\phi\|_{\mathcal{M},t,t'}$

   In the context of the new truth definition (5.29) turns into

   (5.29′) $\|F\phi\|_{\mathcal{M},t,t'} = 1$ iff $\exists t''\ (t' < t'' \wedge \|\phi\|_{\mathcal{M},t'',t'} = 1)$

   Task: Give a complete definition of $\|\phi\|_{\mathcal{M},t,t'}$, of which (5.29′) is one of the clauses.

5.1.3 Instants, Intervals, Events and States

There is one further reason why tense logical systems such as TPL and the S,U-logic have been thought unequal to the demands of natural language. The standard models for these systems (those we have discussed in Section 5.1.2) interpret their predicates by assigning them extensions at *instants* of time. The models directly assign truth values to atomic sentences at instants; and the recursive part of the truth definition then specifies, starting from these assignments, the truth values of complex sentences again at temporal instants. This, it has been argued, is not the notion of truth that is needed for the semantic analysis of natural language. Truth, as it pertains to language in the way we use it, relates sentences not to instants but to temporal intervals.

When we think of how natural language is used, we cannot escape the conclusion that a notion of truth which relates sentences to indivisible temporal instants is surely an idealization. In practice, the times **t** with respect to which we have reason to ask whether some statement or other is true are not that finely cut. The standard setting in which such questions arise is that where **t** is the statement's utterance time. But utterances take time; they last through many moments, and not just for a single ('big') indivisible one. So utterance times present themselves as intervals, not instants. By itself this is not much of an objection to instant-based semantics. Typically it won't make any difference to the truth value of a statement which instant we pick from the stretch of time that was needed to produce it. Arguably it is even a requirement for truthful assertion that what one asserts is true irrespective of which particular instant within the utterance time is chosen: the statement counts as unequivocally true at the utterance time **t** only if it is true at each instant included in **t**.

Indeed, if this were the only objection against instant semantics, we need not be worried. Nor do we need to be worried by the objection that often the truth value of some complex sentence at a time **t** depends not on the truth value of some component of the sentence at some other instant, but on the truth value of that component at some extended interval. So long as it is possible to reconstruct this latter relation – that between the component sentence and the interval – from the truth relation between sentences and instants (for instance by the recipe given in the last sentence of the preceding paragraph), truth at instants will be as good as truth at intervals. In fact, if the recipe is right, the two relations are interdefinable; for conversely, truth at an instant can be obtained from truth at an interval provided instants are treated as intervals of a special kind (viz. as those intervals which are minimal in that they contain no other intervals besides the empty interval and themselves).

Interdefinability does not mean, however, that there is nothing to choose between the two approaches. Interval semantics suffers from one very serious drawback. Suppose that i is an interval consisting of two consecutive parts i_1 and i_2, and that Mary is ill during the first interval and healthy during the second. What then is the truth value of **Mary is ill** with respect to i? According to our recipe, the sentence should be false at i, since it is false at some instants contained in i. But if **Mary is ill** is false at i, are we to conclude that **Mary is not ill** is true at i? Certainly not, if truth of a sentence S at i is meant to entail that S is true at all instants i contains. For at some of those instants, those in i_1, **Mary is not ill** is not true. There are a number of things we could do to deal with this problem.

We can alter the truth clause for negation (but then we must be prepared for the need to make corresponding alterations in other clauses of the truth definition); we can try to reassess the meaning of the claim that S is true with respect to the interval i (so that it does not invariably entail that a sentence S is true at every subinterval of i); or we can decide that for many combinations of a sentence S and interval i S is neither true with respect to i nor false with respect to i, and thus make truth into a partial relation. As it stands, none of these options is attractive. Each creates its own problems, some easily forseeable, some hard to discern until the moment they hit you. So, other things being equal, an instant-based semantics seems the better bet.[10]

But are other things equal? We believe not. From the perspective of how the predicates of natural language are used and understood, the instant-based models for tense logic about which we have so far been talking appear to be not just harmless idealizations; it is doubtful that the information which they treat as primitive – i.e. what belongs to the extension of a predicate at an indivisible instant of time – can be considered primitive at all. Let us explain.

Suppose that our semantics is instant-based and that $\mathcal{M}$ is a model in the sense of this semantics (thus $\mathcal{M}$ is a model in the sense of the definition on page 486). What, according to such a model, is it for Mary to be asleep at some instant **t**, or for Mary to be running at **t**, or for her to be writing a letter at **t**? According to what we have been saying (see Definition 5.1.1), Mary was sleeping at **t** iff Mary belongs to the extension of the predicate **asleep** in $\mathcal{M}$ at **t**. Similarly, Mary was running at **t** according to the model iff she belongs to the extension at **t** of **run**, and she was writing a letter at **t** iff there is some letter **b** such that the pair ⟨**Mary**,**b**⟩ belongs to the extension at **t** of the two-place predicate **write**. To begin with the last case, what could it be about the way the world (represented by $\mathcal{M}$) is at the instant **t** that makes it true that **Mary** and **b** stand in the **write** relation at **t**? The fact that her pen touches the paper on which the letter is being written? (We are assuming that Mary is one of those rare, antiquated beings who write letters with pen and ink.) This would clearly be too strong a requirement. For a good deal of the time that you are writing a letter, even if you use pen and ink, your pen is not touching the paper. So perhaps it is not just the fact that Mary's pen is touching the paper which is sufficient ground for her standing in the **write** relation to **b**; perhaps her holding the pen, in the way one holds a pen when one is writing, is good enough? No, it isn't good enough. Perhaps the letter she is writing is a difficult one, and Mary has paused, putting down her pen, to think about the next sentence. Or she has been interrupted by a telephone call, which forced her to put down her pen and stop with the actual writing (which, however, she intends to resume as soon as she has dealt with the caller).

[10]The problem of truth value gaps and partiality in the semantics of time is discussed at length in [Landman 1991], Chapters 3–5.

One could go on, but the moral should be clear. What makes it true that at t Mary stood in the **write** relation to b is, for all one can see, not just what is the case at that very instant, but what is going on over some interval i surrounding t: At the start of i Mary sits down in front of a blank sheet and at the end of it she folds the sheet, covered with her script, into an envelope. What is the case just at the instant t, though not irrelevant to whether she was writing at t, is never going to decide by itself whether she was writing at t or wasn't.

As it stands, this is not a proof that a conceptually plausible instant semantics should be impossible. Perhaps we might succeed in analysing Mary's standing in the relation of writing the letter b at t in terms of what is the case at successive instants of the interval i. But on reflection it appears that such an analysis would be exceedingly far-fetched. Letters can be written in all sorts of ways, at different speeds, with interruptions of varying length, etc. To spell out conditions about series of "snapshots" at instants surrounding t which are both necessary and sufficient for Mary's writing b at t would seem to be a thankless task at best.

Actually, the prospects for such a project are even worse than is implied by what we have said so far. To see this let us consider the other two predicates we have mentioned above, **asleep** and **run**. At first glance, the notion that Mary's belonging to the extension of **asleep** at t could be assessed just on the strength of what is the case at that very moment may seem more plausible than it was for **write a letter**. But on closer inspection the case does not look to be much better. When someone is asleep, he is always asleep for some stretch of time. This is how we tell he is asleep, and in fact, what could it *mean* for someone to be asleep at t without being asleep at some interval (short perhaps, but not instantaneous) of which t is part? By the same token, what could it mean for someone to be running at t if his running doesn't span some interval containing t? Pursuing this line of thought one comes to realize, or at least to suspect, of more and more predicates that they cannot be treated as primitive relations between individuals and instants. Indeed, it becomes doubtful if there are *any* predicates P such that P being true of a at t would not have to be analysed in terms of what is the case at times in t's vicinity. And so the project of analysing truth at t in terms of the series of snapshots surrounding t not only comes to look like it is going to be forbiddingly complex; it actually appears ill-founded in the specific sense that the snapshots in the terms of which we analyse 'P is true of a at t' will themselves involve predications of the form 'Q is true at t′', which demand a series-of-snapshots analysis in their turn, and so on.

We do not consider this argument absolutely conclusive. But it appears to us to have enough force to cast serious doubt on the ultimate viability of an instant-based semantics for natural language. Does this force us into the unattractive alternative of an interval semantics, with the nasty logical problems that come with it? Fortunately not quite. There exists a third option, which shares some of the features of the interval approach but which offers a natural way out of what appears to be its disagreeable consequences. We will refer to this third approach as *event-based.*

5.1.3.1 Events

In the last section, we suggested that Mary was writing a letter at the instant **t** if and only if **t** is one of a series of stages which together constitute a complete letter writing. In slightly different words: Mary was writing the letter at **t** provided that the event of her writing temporally included **t**. Putting the matter this second way accords with a thesis which was originally proposed for reasons unrelated to tense and aspect, the thesis that sentences such as (5.30) are, quite literally, descriptions of events. They are "quite literally" about events in the sense of having logical forms in which the event described is explicitly represented. Thus Davidson, who championed this view into contemporary philosophy, proposes that the sentence (5.30) has a logical form given by the sentence (5.31) of predicate logic:[11]

(5.30) Fred buttered a toast in the bathroom at midnight.

(5.31) **∃e∃x∃p∃t(buttering(e,Fred,x) & toast(x) & bathroom(p) & midnight(t) & in(e,p) & at(e,t))**

Similarly, (5.32) has a logical form which, now using DRS-notation, we can represent as (5.33).

(5.32) Mary wrote the letter on Sunday.

(5.33)

e x y t
Mary(x) the letter(y) Sunday(t) write(e,x,y) Time(e,t)

[11] See [Davidson 1967a]. A central motivation behind Davidson's proposal was to show inferences like that from **Fred buttered the toast at midnight** to **Fred buttered the toast** could be justified by principles of predicate logic. If one adopts his proposal, then the logical forms of these two sentences are related as ∃x∃y(A(x) & B(x,y)) is to ∃xA(x), so that the inference can be seen to involve a simple instance of conjunction reduction (the principle that a conjunction entails each of its conjuncts).

Since the time when Davidson made his case that action-sentences should have logical forms like (5.31), an impressive list of arguments, linguistic as well as philosophical, have been given in support of it. Nevertheless the proposal has met with resistance, mostly because it is so difficult to determine precisely what events are and what general properties they have. Can events be interrupted and then, after a phase of non-existence, start up again? Do all events have a spatial as well as a temporal location? If not, which events do and which don't? And for those that do, how is their spatial location determined? Can there be two events that occupy exactly the same region of space and time? Is the event of A selling his car to B the same as that of B buying A's car, or are they distinct?

It is not easy to answer these questions. In fact, the more we look for answers, the less likely it comes to appear that genuine, non-stipulative answers will ever be found. They won't be found because our pretheoretical conception of what events are is fundamentally underdetermined. In our daily commerce with events this underdeterminateness does not pose too much of a problem. It becomes clearly noticeable only when we start asking the general questions a linguist or philosopher is bound to ask, but which rarely disturb the average citizen.

In the eyes of some, the indeterminacy of our event concept disqualifies it from use in philosophical or semantical analysis. To be legitimate in such analytical contexts a concept should support genuine, non-stipulative answers to questions like those we asked above; if it does not support such answers, then it should be replaced by a concept of our own making, for which these questions can be answered simply because we have decided to answer them this way or that.[12]

There is much to be said for conceptual rigour. Indeed, within philosophy the demand for it has been all to the good. But in natural language semantics the situation is, we think, somewhat different. One of the central tasks of semantics is to articulate the conceptual structures that guide and support our, human, understanding of the languages we use. If that understanding crucially involves concepts which are to some degree underdetermined, then the semanticist has the task of spelling out precisely how and to what extent the concept is underdetermined; it will not do to substitute a fully determinate concept of one's own conception for the underdetermined notion that is in actual use.

This recommendation applies in the first place to the analysis of sentences in which an underdetermined concept is explicitly mentioned – in the present context, these would be sentences which explicitly speak of events. But it should also apply, we think, to sentences whose understanding apparently involves underdetermined concepts, even though they do not actually contain any explicit reference to them. Since we are persuaded (by Davidson's own arguments and those of others) that

[12]Perhaps the best known advocate of this methodological principle is Quine, who has pleaded against the use of ill- or underdefined ontological categories in logic and philosophy. Witness his famous slogan "no entity without identity".

sentences like (5.30) *are* naturally understood as reports of events, an event-based semantics appears to us to be what tensed sentences need.

To adopt an event-based semantics rather than an "instant-based" or "interval-based" one does not mean that instants or intervals can be dispensed with. Natural languages, we have seen, express temporal relations not only through their tenses but also with the help of phrases such as **at 5 o'clock** or **on the first of January**. Intuitively, such phrases refer to times and that is how we propose to analyse them. This means that we will need discourse referents that represent times in our DRSs, and "real" times in our models onto which those discourse referents can be mapped. We will not make any categorical distinction between instants and intervals. Instants will be those times that are, in the appropriate sense, "atomic" and intervals will be the non-atomic times, much as individuals were the atomic and pluralities the non-atomic elements in the Linkian models defined in Section 4.3.

It is another question whether either events or times can be defined in terms of other categories. There have been repeated efforts to define events in terms of times (and some notion of temporally dependent predicate satisfaction). From what we have said in the last section, it should be clear that we doubt if such a reduction could be made to work. For those who, like ourselves, are prepared to accept events as ontologically irreducible entities, there arises the possibility of a reduction in the opposite direction: Could times not be defined in terms of events? As a matter of fact, something along this line appears to be a distinct possibility. The literature contains several formal proposals for defining times in terms of events, with closely comparable if not fully identical results. In Section 5.6 we will look at one such proposal in detail. Whether this reduction (or, for that matter, any of its rivals) is ultimately tenable we will not be in a position to decide. Fortunately, the answer is not decisive for the semantic project to which this chapter is devoted.

5.1.3.2 States

Davidson proposed his analysis as an analysis for "action sentences". But what is an action? Surely buttering a slice of toast and writing a letter qualify. But what about something involuntary like sneezing, or something that does not involve any sentient creature at all, such as the eruption of a volcano or the melting of an ice cube? No matter. All these are, by anyone's reckoning, events. And all available evidence suggests that the sentences we typically use to report such events – **Mary sneezed; The volcano erupted; The ice cube melted** – should be given the same analysis as indubitable action-sentences like **Mary buttered the toast**. So we assume that what Davidson proposed for action-sentences applies to event-sentences generally.

But which sentences are the event-sentences? Here we find that the road towards a clear answer is once again impeded by the indeterminacy of our (pretheoretical) concept of what an event is. In fact, indeterminacy has an aspect we did not note in the last section. It is brought out by a comparison of sentences such as those in:

(5.34) (i) The play delighted Mary.
(ii) Fred was angry.
(iii) Alan was ill.
(iv) The train was standing alongside the platform.
(v) The statue stood in the centre of the square.
(vi) Susan was a pediatrician.

As we go down this list, the suggestion that what is described is an event has an increasingly implausible ring to it. What, for instance, is described in (vi)? It would seem very odd to call it an event. Rather, it is something like a "condition" or a "state", or a "state of affairs". There is a tendency to say the same about (v), (iv) and (iii). In relation to (ii) and (i) we are less certain. Here, saying that what is described is a state strikes us as neither less nor more natural than saying the sentence describes an event.

Reflecting on such sentences we are led to conclude (i) that not every sentence can be treated as the description of an event; (ii) that some sentences must rather be seen as descriptions of states; and (iii) that the division between event-describing and state-describing sentences appears to be gradual rather than sharp.

Insofar as we understand the distinction between events and states it seems to come to something like this. Events involve some kind of change, whereas states do not: that a state obtains over some interval i means that some condition remains in force for the duration of i. The occurrence of an event, in contrast, seems to imply that some condition, which obtains when the event begins, is terminated by the event and gets replaced by another, "opposite" condition.

Putting things this way is no more than a hint at where a clearer distinction between events and states might be found – the actual search is still to be carried out. But it nevertheless brings out one aspect of the distinction which is crucial for the theory of tense and aspect. States differ from events, we said, in that states involve the continuation of some condition whereas events involve its abrogation. But a condition is something conceptual, something that has as much to do with the way in which we choose to see reality as with reality itself. So we should not be surprised to find that the same bit of reality can be conceptualized either as event- or as state-like, depending on how we look at it. This conceptual dimension to the distinction between events and states is reflected by the way we speak. Compare the sentences:

(5.35) (i) Mary wrote a letter.

(ii) Mary was writing a letter.

These sentences can be used to describe the same actual situation (of Mary sitting at her desk and writing). But they describe this situation from different points of view. (5.35.i) presents it as a completed totality – as the process which leads from the state of there being no letter to that in which the letter has been written. (5.35.ii) seems to view the situation "from the inside" – to describe it as something that is going on. From this internal perspective things are not changing just then – Mary was already writing and she continues to do so. So in a sense the sentence may be seen as describing a state, the state that lasts while she is writing the letter.

Sometimes the distinction between state-sentences and event-sentences is recognizable from their form. Thus, the state-describing sentence (5.35.ii) is in the progressive, whereas the event-describing (5.35.i) is not. In other cases form is relevant in a less direct way. Thus verb phrases that describe states have the property that they cannot (or can only marginally) be used in the progressive. By this criterion a sentence like (5.34.vi) will qualify as the description of a state. But there are also sentences for which no formal properties reveal whether what they describe is an event or a state. Consider (5.34.iii). The verb phrase **be ill** might seem to be a particularly clear case of a predicate that ascribes states, both on intuitive grounds and by our formal criterion (the progressive, **is being ill**, seems marginal). Nevertheless, there are contexts in which (5.34.iii) appears to carry a strong implication that what it describes is a kind of event – one which starts when Alan falls ill, has the progress of his illness for its central part and ends with his recovery. Consider, for instance,

(5.36) I only corrected the paper last night. First I had to finish the grant proposal. Then I was ill. Then we had the project review which took three days and more than a week of preparation.

In this context the illness reported in the second sentence is presented as one event among several. But many other contexts do not carry this kind of event-like implication. In

(5.37) I arrived at the Olivers' cottage on Friday night. It was not a propitious beginning to my visit. She was ill and he in a foul mood.

for example, the sentence **she was ill** seems to describe a state of affairs obtaining at the time of the speaker's arrival.

The comparison between (5.36) and (5.37) brings out particularly clearly to what extent the distinction between events and states can be a matter of how a situation is conceptualized. The sentence **I was ill** of (5.36) describes an event insofar as we see the illness as involving change – from health to illness and back – which interrupts the initial condition of health. Inasmuch as the sentence **she was ill** of (5.37) can be seen as describing a state rather than an event, this is because the context of (5.37) enables us to focus just on the condition of illness, ignoring the changes from health to illness and back which are associated with it.

The pair (5.36)/(5.37) shows that the question whether a given sentence describes an event or a state may depend on considerations of considerable subtlety, which have as much to do with its role in the discourse as with its own grammatical form. A theory that would correctly distinguish between state- and event-sentences on the strength of, among other things, their rhetorical role, would have to incorporate a fully developed account of rhetoric and discourse structure. As things are, such a theory is well beyond anybody's reach, and there is no question of our developing even as much as a first approximation to it in this chapter.

All these differences between states and events notwithstanding, there is much that event-sentences and state-sentences have in common. It seems natural therefore to try and analyse event-sentences and state-sentences as expressing essentially the same semantic structures, and this is what we will do. Thus we will analyse state-describing sentences as just that – i.e. as sentences describing states – in much the same way in which we will treat event-sentences as descriptions of events.

Having made the decision to analyse state-sentences and event-sentences in these closely parallel ways, we might hope to by-pass the irksome questions how events and states differ and how event- and state-sentences can be held apart. Why not see events and states as subcategories of one overarching category – of *eventualities*, to use a term that is now widely accepted.[13] Both state-describing and event-describing sentences would then be analysed as describing some eventuality, the temporal location of which is indicated by the tense of the verb as well as, perhaps, by other devices of temporal reference such as temporal adverbs. That the eventuality is sometimes an event and in other cases a state might be of no further consequence.

But this is not quite the way things are. As it turns out, the difference between state-describing and event-describing sentences does matter. The difference matters insofar as it correlates with distinct semantic behaviour: state-describing sentences tend to connect with the discourse of which they are part in a way other than sentences which describe events. (For instance, a state-describing sentence typically situates the described state as surrounding the contextually salient "reference" time; in contrast, there exists a strong tendency to interpret event-sentences as

[13]The term is from Emmon Bach. See in particular [Bach 1981].

describing events that follow the reference point; for details see Section 5.2.) Thus, whatever the distinction between events and states may be, correct interpretation of tensed discourse presupposes at a minimum the ability to tell state-describing and event-describing sentences apart.

So it appears that we need to be able to distinguish between state-describing sentences and event-describing sentences after all. But as we have already said, there can be no question of developing a theory here which draws this distinction accurately. We shall therefore have to treat the distinction in certain cases as simply given.

In the course of this discussion, we have slid from an ontological question – How do events and states differ from each other? – to a linguistic problem – How are we to tell sentences which describe events from sentences which describe states? This second problem, we saw, is directly relevant to the semantic representation of tensed discourse. But the ontological question is important too. It is just that it makes itself felt at a different level. As we said at the end of the last section, the problems of ontology are problems for the model-theoretical component of our theory, not for the component which deals with the form and construction of semantic representations. It is to this second component that we turn first. It will occupy us for the next four sections (5.2–5.5). The ontological questions will be considered only thereafter, when in Section 5.6 we define the model theory for the DRS-language that will be developed in the intervening sections.

5.2 DRS-Construction for Tensed Sentences

5.2.1 DRS-Construction for Single Sentences in the Past Tense

We are at last ready to return to the questions that have been our primary concern throughout this book: how is linguistic information to be represented, and how are the semantic representations to be constructed? We start by having another look at our first try for a DRS for a tensed sentence, the representation (5.33) of (5.32).

(5.32) Mary wrote the letter on Sunday.

(5.33)

e x y t
Mary(x) the letter(y) Sunday(t) write(e,x,y) Time(e,t)

First we must settle some matters of notation. In (5.33) we represented the statement that **e** is an event of **x** writing **y** as **write(e,x,y)**. From now on we will present such conditions in a slightly different form. Insofar as it is right to see such conditions as specifying the type of a given event, the discourse referent for that event has a status different from the other discourse referents in the condition. We make this special status of the event discourse referent explicit by putting it in front of the verb. Thus we will, for instance, write **e: write(x,y)** instead of the condition **write(e,x,y)** of (5.33). Second, the relation between **e** and **t** which (5.33) gives as 'Time(**e**,**t**)' will henceforth be stated as '$\mathbf{e} \subseteq \mathbf{t}$', where '$\mathbf{e} \subseteq \mathbf{t}$' expresses that **e** is temporally included within **t**. Clearly, this is the relation expressed by (5.32): it presents the event of writing the letter as lying entirely within the period denoted by the phrase **Sunday**.

With these notational changes, the DRS for (5.32) will look like (5.33′):

(5.33′)

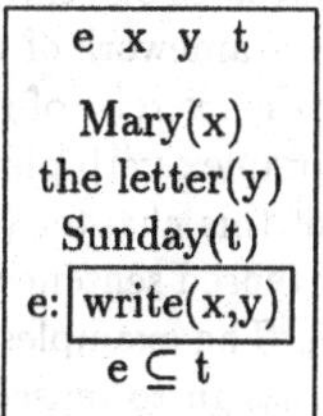

(5.33′) is not yet completely identical with the DRS that will be assigned to (5.32) by the construction algorithm which we will develop later in this chapter. In particular, it still misses some important information about the temporal location of **e**, viz. that it occurred before the time at which (5.32) was uttered. In order to express this condition, we introduce a special discourse referent **n**, which shall always refer to the utterance time of the discourse that the DRS is taken to represent. The past tense of (5.32) can then be analysed as indicating that the eventuality described is located in the past of **n**. Thus, (5.32) receives a representation as in

(5.38)

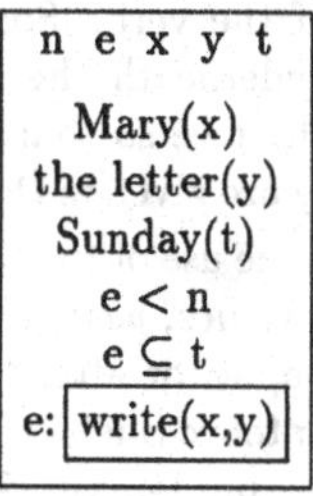

If (5.38) is the DRS for (5.32), how do we derive it from the syntactic form of (5.32)? In fact, what *is* the syntactic form of (5.32)?

To answer this question we could proceed as we did in the earlier parts of this book: present the rules which generate the syntactic structures that serve as inputs to the DRS-construction algorithm and then state the construction rules. For strictly expository reasons we have decided not to follow this strategy here. As it turns out, the kind of syntax we introduced in Chapter 0 is not optimally suited to deal with the complexities which arise for sentences containing complex tenses involving auxiliary verbs – as in **John will come, Mary had been writing** or **Fred would not have been singing.** To capture precisely which verb complexes (consisting of a main verb and zero or more auxiliary verbs) are grammatical by means of the kind of phrase structure rules we have been using proves to be quite awkward. Ideally we should have switched to a syntactic theory that is more attuned to these particular problems. But this would have been a major undertaking, and out of place in a study which focusses on semantics. So we will stick, for better or worse, with the phrase structure framework of Chapter 0. As little of real interest is to be learned, however, from the exercise of getting the phrase structure rules to give us just the right class of complex verb phrases, we will leave the details of the extended syntax till the end of this chapter (see Section 5.7). Until then, we will display syntactic structures of tensed sentences as they are needed, without an explicit grammar to support them. The examples should give a fair impression of what syntactic representations we assign to tensed sentences generally.

The syntactic structures that we will make use of are motivated in large part by the role they have to play as inputs to the construction algorithm. The algorithm must represent the temporal information that is contained in the tense of a sentence and in its temporal adverb (if there is one). In the construction procedure we have adopted, this temporal information is made explicit in the DRS at an early stage of processing, essentially that where the algorithm deals with the S-node. This imposes certain configurational requirements on the syntactic tree, and also entails that the S-node must carry certain bits of information which pertain to nodes deeper down (e.g., it must be possible to recognize from the information attached at the S-node whether the sentence describes an event or a state; often this is determined by the choice of the verb. So, without further provision this information is to be found only underneath the V-node.) We will assume that these aspects can "percolate up" the tree so that they are available at the nodes where they are needed and that they are given in the form of "feature assignments".

In the present section, we will make use of two features. The first one, which we will call *TENSE*, has three possible values, *past, present* and *future*, signifying that the described eventuality lies before, at, or after the utterance time, respectively. The value of *TENSE* for a given sentence S is determined by the tense of the verb of S. When the main verb is in the simple past, *TENSE=past*; when it is in the simple present, *TENSE* = *pres*; and when the verb complex contains the auxiliary **will**, *TENSE* = *fut*. The second feature whose value must be available at the first processing step is called *STAT*. This feature tells whether the eventuality described is a state or an event. It has two values, $+STAT$ for when the eventuality is a state and $-STAT$ for when it is an event. (We write simply + and − for $+STAT$ and $-STAT$ where this cannot lead to confusion. This will be done also for other features F that have the two values $+F$ and $-F$.)

The information provided by *STAT* is especially needed when the sentence contains a temporal adverb, such as, say, **on Sunday**. The contribution which the NP **Sunday** makes to an event-sentence such as (5.32) is that the period it denotes *includes* the event described. If the letter Mary wrote had been started on Saturday or finished on Monday, (5.32) would not have been the right thing to say. This seems to be a general property of event-sentences with temporal adverbs such as **on Sunday, yesterday, tomorrow morning** and many others: they assert that the event falls entirely within the time denoted by the adverb. But with sentences that describe states this is not so. (This is one reason why our algorithm must distinguish between states and events.) For instance,

(5.39) Mary was ill on Sunday.

can be said truly not only when Mary was ill only on Sunday, but also when her illness started earlier and/or went on for longer. In fact, there is a tendency to take (5.39) to imply that Mary's illness went on for the entire day, in other words, that the inclusion relation is the reverse of what it is in the case of event-sentences. However, with sentences that describe states the matter is not cut and dried. Even if Mary's illness did not last throughout Sunday, (5.39) might be an acceptable thing to say, for we can say quite consistently

(5.40) Mary was ill on Sunday. But by Sunday night she had recovered.

The question how a described state can relate to the time denoted by the temporal adverb is complicated by the problem, noted in Section 5.1.3.2, of telling state-describing and event-describing sentences apart. For instance, the sentence

(5.41) Yesterday Mary was in the library.

will be true even if Mary was in the library for only half an hour – that is, for some small portion of the given day. But it is not immediately clear what should be concluded from this. For arguably (5.41) may be taken as an event-describing sentence, even though the verb phrase **be in the library** would normally be used to decribe a state. We do not think, however, that the dividing line between state- and event-describing sentences can be drawn in such a way as to entail that a state always includes the adverb time. (For instance, the first sentence of (5.40) would not seem to qualify as event-describing on any plausible criterion.) We therefore shall have to be content with the condition that state and adverb time overlap. This means that our representation of state-describing sentences with temporal adverbs will be less informative than those for sentences which represent events, since a described event will be represented as actually included in the time of the adverb.

With certain adverbs, however, the relation between designated time and described state is always inclusion. Thus, as far as we can tell,

(5.42) At 10 Mary was in the library.

always means that the time denoted, 10 o'clock, is included in the state of Mary being in the library. Similarly,

(5.43) Mary is now in the library.

means that the state of her being in the library includes the utterance time. This difference between **now** and **at 10** on the one hand and adverbs such as **on Sunday**, **last week**, **next year**, **in the spring of 1989**, on the other is that the former are conceived as *punctual* and the others as temporally extended. For a punctual temporal adverb, i.e. for one which designates an indivisible moment of time, there is of course no difference between inclusion and overlap: overlap with any part of an indivisible moment means overlap with everyone of its parts, and thus inclusion.

It must be stressed that the distinction between punctual and non-punctual adverbs of which we have spoken is one of conceptualization. As we noted when discussing the choice between instant and interval semantics the times relevant to our experience never are punctual in any absolute sense. But we can *treat* certain times as indivisible within a given experiential or conceptual setting. Furthermore, we can commit ourselves to treating a time as punctual by describing or naming it in some particular way. The punctual adverbs are those which have this commitment built into them.

Our informal remarks about what is going to happen during the first step in the construction of the DRS for (5.32) should have made it clear that it must involve the following operations:

(i) Introduction of a new discourse referent for the described eventuality;

(ii) recording the temporal relation between this discourse referent and the utterance time **n**;

(iii) in case the sentence contains a temporal adverb, such as **on Sunday**, introduction of a discourse referent **t** for the time denoted by the adverb;

(iv) recording the temporal relation between this discourse referent and the described eventuality.

In addition we need

(v) Introduction of a DRS-condition **e:** $\boxed{\gamma}$ which specifies the "type" of the described eventuality.

There is an ambiguity in (iii) and (iv). What is the time "denoted by" the adverb **on Sunday**? There are two ways of looking at this question. On the one hand there is the denotation – in the given context – of the noun phrase **Sunday**. This is some particular Sunday – which one will be discussed in Section 5.5.1. On the other hand, the adverb **on Sunday** might be thought of as imposing a constraint on the location time of the described eventuality. In the case of **on Sunday** the difference between these two times is not so easily perceived. But with an adverb like **before Sunday** the distinction is perfectly transparent: here the location time and the time denoted by **Sunday** cannot be the same, because the former must (in view of the meaning of **before**) precede the latter.

We will assume that the interpretation of an adverb such as **on Sunday** involves the introduction of two discourse referents, one representing the location time of the eventuality and one representing the referent of the NP. The adverb will be interpreted as imposing a constraint on the discourse referent for the location time. It is only in elaborating this constraint that the second discourse referent gets introduced. However, we will study such constraints not until Section 5.5. In the meantime we will leave them in the form in which they are first introduced. In the case of **on Sunday** this means that the condition **on Sunday(t)** is kept as it is.

Besides sentences like (5.32), which contain a temporal adverb that constrains the location of the described eventuality, there are those which have no such adverb (e.g. **Mary wrote the letter**). From what we have said so far there would appear to be no need of a location time in the processing of such sentences. We have found it useful, however, to introduce discourse referents for location times also in the representations of these sentences. (Their usefulness will become apparent for the first time in Section 5.2.5 below.) Given that such a time discourse referent is introduced in all cases, there are now two ways of expressing the temporal relation between described eventuality and utterance time: either directly as a relation between the eventuality discourse referent and **n** (as we did e.g. in (5.38)) – or indirectly, by relating the location time of the eventuality to **n** and relating the eventuality to its location time. Again for reasons that will appear only later (see in particular Section 5.2.5), we adopt the second option.

(5.44) Mary wrote the letter.

Let us assume that this sentence is processed in an empty context. Then, proceeding in the way just indicated, we get

(5.45)

n e x y t
e ⊆ t t < n Mary(x) the letter(y) e: [x write y]

which is truth conditionally equivalent to (5.46), from which **t** has been omitted:

(5.46)

n e x y
e < n Mary(x) the letter(y) e: [x write y]

In the light of this decision operations (iii) and (iv) should be revised to:

(iii′) Introduction of a discourse referent t for the location time

(iv′) recording the temporal relation between the discourse referent for the location time and the utterance time n

(iv″) in case the sentence contains a temporal adverb β, introduction of the condition β(t) to record the constraint which the adverb imposes on the location time.

The last condition e:[γ] always stands in need of further reduction. In fact, γ is the same kind of syntactic complex that formed the point of departure for sentence processing in the preceding chapters. We may think of this complex as representing the 'detensed' sentence – something like an infinitival clause. In essence, this syntactic structure is to be processed just as our previous tense-ignoring algorithm processed the syntactic trees of sentences in the present tense. To maximize continuity with the earlier algorithm the syntax has been set up in such a way that the "detensed" sentence structures coincide with the complete sentence structures defined by the grammar of Chapter 0. Thus the syntactic structure of (5.32) will have the following form:[14]

(5.47)

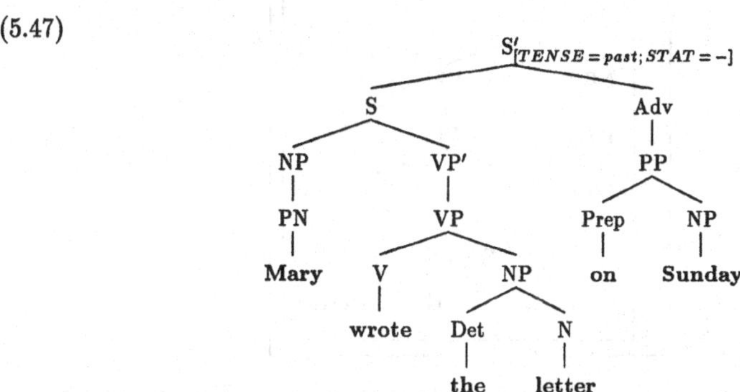

The first step in the DRS-construction for (5.32) is triggered by the S′-node. Its result is (5.48).[15]

[14]There remain certain differences between (5.47) and the "official" syntactic structure generated by the grammar of Section 5.7. The official structure involves additional features. Furthermore, feature values are attached also to nodes other than the S′-node.

[15]The discourse referent **n** will be assumed to be part of the context DRS even before the processing of its first sentence has started. In other words, the initial DRS is never empty. In the example of DRS-construction we present in the remainder of this book, it is always assumed to have the form [n].

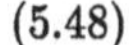

(5.48)

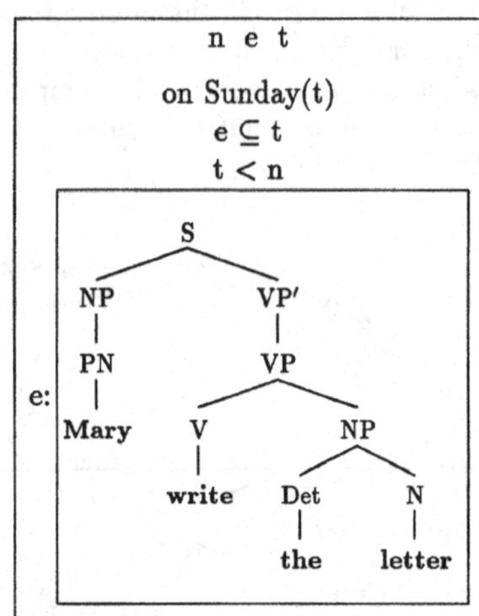

(5.48) contains two conditions which require further reduction. The first is **on Sunday(t)**. This condition looks much like the condition **Sunday(t)** of (5.38), but, as we have just explained, its intended meaning is different: **on Sunday(t)** says that the location time **t** of **e** satisfies the predication expressed by the prepositional phrase **on Sunday**.

The second condition that must be reduced further is the condition **e**:$\boxed{\gamma}$. The first point to note about this condition is that the verb of the syntactic structure γ is not the finite past tense of **wrote** what we find in (5.47), but the infinitive form **write**. The motivation for this change is that finite verb forms such as the **wrote** of (5.47) result from a fusion of the finite past tense with the uninflected verb. The operation which leads e.g. from (5.47) to (5.48) processes the finite tense of the verb and separates it, so to speak, from the uninflected verb. It is this uninflected verb which remains in the syntactic structure representing the "detensed" sentence that we use to characterize **e**.

The second point concerns the further reduction of γ. As we have said, the reduction of this condition follows the line of the preceding chapters. But there is one complication. When we break γ up into its constituent parts, which of these parts are to remain inside the characterization of **e** and which should be placed outside? This question is closely connected with the ontological question what sorts of events there are. Such ontological questions will be discussed (to the extent that we will discuss them at all) in Section 5.6.

As far as the examples are concerned which we will consider in this and the next two sections, it really does not matter how the first question is answered. The answer we adopt is this. We retain within the characterization of the eventuality only the verb, flanked by the discourse referents representing its arguments; all other conditions are to be placed outside the characterization. Thus the result of the first step in the reduction of γ (which applies to its S-node) is the DRS (5.49).

(5.49)

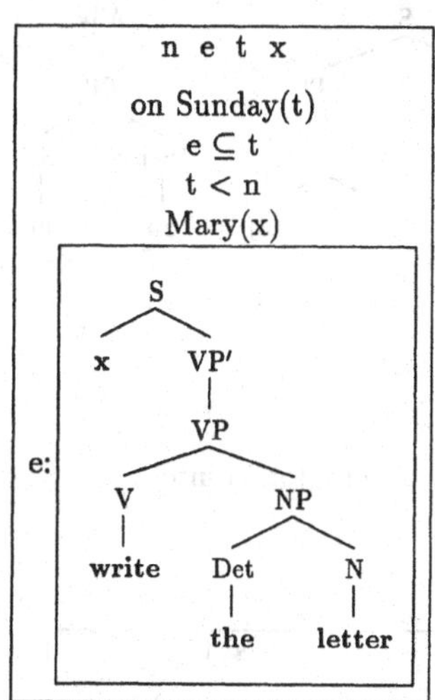

Completion of (5.49) requires one further step, which we leave to the reader.

The next example we consider is a state-describing sentence.

(5.50) Mary was ill on Sunday.

Its syntactic structure has the form represented by (5.51).

(5.51)

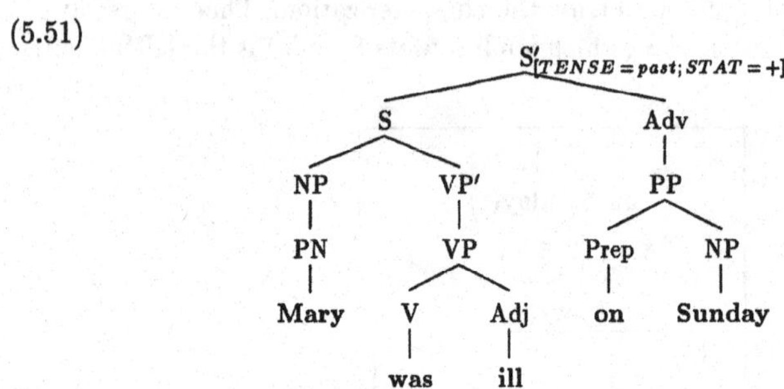

The first construction step converts (5.51) into

(5.52)

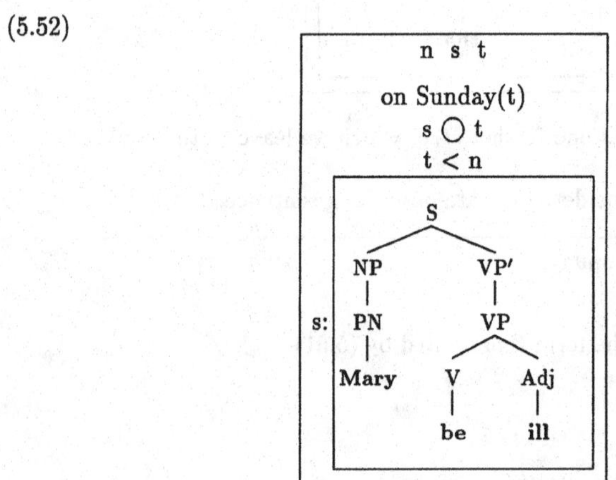

(We use discourse referents **s**, **s'**, **s''**, ..., $\mathbf{s}_1$, $\mathbf{s}_2$, ... to represent states; discourse referents **e**, **e'**, **e''**, ..., $\mathbf{e}_1$, $\mathbf{e}_2$, ... will henceforth be reserved for events.) Further construction steps, which the reader should be able to supply himself, will convert (5.51) into the DRS

(5.53)

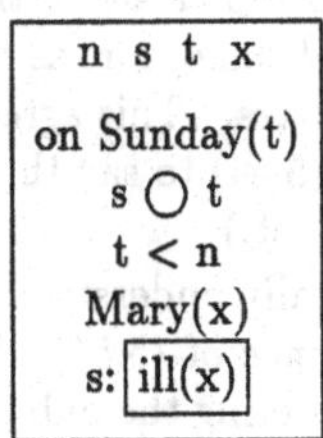

5.2.2 Temporal Anaphora. DRS-Construction for Sequences of Sentences

We noted in Section 5.1.2 that natural languages like English often express temporal relations through temporal anaphora: tensed sentences are interpreted as temporally related to the sentences preceding them. A look at the following example will give us a first glimpse of how temporal anaphora works.

(5.54) A man entered the White Hart. He was wearing a black jacket.
Bill served him a beer.

The first sentence of (5.54) yields the DRS

(5.55)

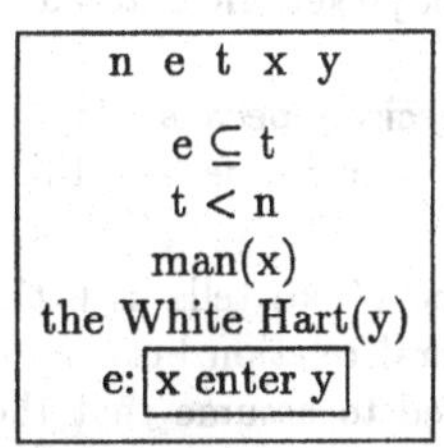

The past tense of the second sentence contributes, just as that of the first sentence, the condition that the described eventuality **e** precedes **n**. But now there is a further relationship that the semantic representation should capture. It is one of the principles governing past tense "narrative" discourse (of which (5.54) is an example) that the eventuality described by a non-initial sentence is interpreted as standing in some specific relationship to some other event **e′** introduced by an earlier sentence (or alternatively to some earlier introduced time **t**). The temporal relation between **e** and **e′** becomes especially important when the new sentence does not contain a temporal adverb, so that the new eventuality **e** can be located only in relation to the antecedent context.

How **e** and **e**′ are related depends on a number of factors. One of these is whether **e**′ is an event or a state. If **e**′ is a state, the relation is almost invariably that of inclusion. This is the case at hand, for, as we mentioned earlier, sentences in the progressive always describe states. (This agrees with intuition – we naturally understand the second sentence of (5.54) to say that the man was wearing a black jacket *as* he entered the establishment.)

If **e**′ is an event, then it is typically understood as following the event **e**. This case is illustrated by the last sentence of (5.54). When this sentence gets to be interpreted, the event of the man entering the pub is still the last mentioned event. And indeed, the new event, that of the publican serving the man a beer, is naturally seen as following the event of his coming in.

It might be thought that our inclination to interpret the state of the man's wearing a black jacket as simultaneous with his entering, and the serving of the beer as following it, is conditioned by "world knowledge". Surely a man would not be expected to change his clothes while or immediately after entering a pub; and surely he would be served a beer only once he is properly inside. But it is not just world knowledge that is involved here. For when plausibility considerations based on world knowledge go against the formal discourse principles we stated in the last two paragraphs, there is a real conflict. This becomes visible, for instance, when we switch the sentences of (5.54) around, as in

(5.56) The publican of the White Hart served a customer a beer. The man was wearing a black jacket. He entered the pub.

This discourse seems strange precisely because its structure implies that the man was first served a beer and then went inside; and this is not the order in which we expect such things to happen.

The comparison of (5.54) and (5.56) tells us little about the role which tense plays in determining the temporal relation between events and states. For both (5.54) and (5.56) we are inclined to assume that the state mentioned – that of the man's wearing a black jacket – obtained throughout the entire episode which included, in whatever order, each of the two events mentioned. To see what the structural constraints might be that govern this kind of combination we must look at an example in which a state-describing sentence does not carry this implication:

(5.57) (i) A man entered the White Hart. He was whistling an Irish jig. Bill served him a beer.

(ii) Bill served a customer a beer. The man was whistling an Irish jig. He entered the pub.

The second sentence of (5.57.i) and (5.57.ii) describes a state which, as far as world knowledge is concerned, might have covered any part of the period spanned by the two events (serving the beer and entering). Nevertheless, (5.57.i/ii) carry different implications about how the state and the events are temporally related. In (5.57.i), the whistling is naturally understood as taking place while the man enters the pub. The discourse implies nothing about the temporal relation between the whistling and the serving of the beer – the whistling could have gone on, but it could just as well have stopped before or when the beer arrived. The implications of (5.57.ii) are, as our discourse principle would predict, just the reverse. The whistling is presented as simultaneous with the serving of the beer; no particular relation is implied between whistling and entering. Evidently, these distinct implications must come from the grammatical properties of (5.57.i) and (5.57.ii), and not from their content.

We conclude that the interpretation of non-initial past tense sentences requires a special processing rule which links the described eventuality to some suitable element of the antecedent discourse. In this we follow Reichenbach, who was the first to recognize what we have been calling the "anaphoric dimension" of the tenses of natural language (see [Reichenbach 1947]). To account for this dimension, Reichenbach introduces the concept of a *reference point.* He defines the meaning of the tenses of the verb as each involving two temporal relations, the relation between reference time and speech time and the relation between described eventuality and reference time. For instance, the English simple past signifies according to him that the reference time lies before the speech time and that the eventuality is located at the reference time. Typically the reference time is given by the context. In particular, when the sentence is part of an ongoing discourse, its reference time often is, as it is in the example we have just looked at, given by a sentence immediately or closely preceding it.

We will not follow Reichenbach in detail, but we adopt his notion of reference time. (We will return to Reichenbach's views in Section 5.4. There we will argue for our own, quasi-Reichenbachian, analysis.) For the purpose of our theory, a Reichenbachian analysis of tense entails that the reference point must be made explicit in the DRS which interprets the sentence. We do this by introducing into the DRS a condition of the form $\mathbf{Rpt} := \alpha$, where α is some discourse referent which represents a time or an event and which is already present in the DRS. Thus, the first step needed to process the second sentence of (5.54) in the context provided by (5.55) involves adding the condition $\mathbf{Rpt} := \mathbf{e}$, meaning that $\mathbf{e}$ is to act as reference point for the second sentence. Since the eventuality denoted by the second sentence is a state, the processing principle we formulated above entails that it includes the reference point. So the first step in the interpretation of the second sentence extends (5.55) as follows:

(5.58)

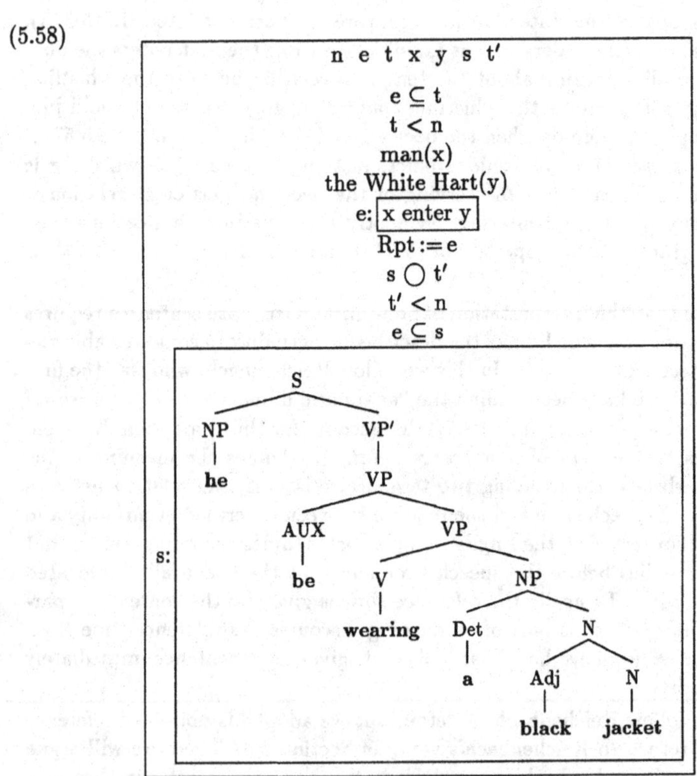

Treating the progressive **be wearing** as a single predicate[16] we can complete (5.58) as in

[16]Treating **be wearing** as an unanalysed predicate is of course not really as things should be: a theory of tense should provide a systematic analysis of how the meaning of a progressive verb phrase depends on the meaning of its main verb. We address this problem in Section 5.3.

(5.59)

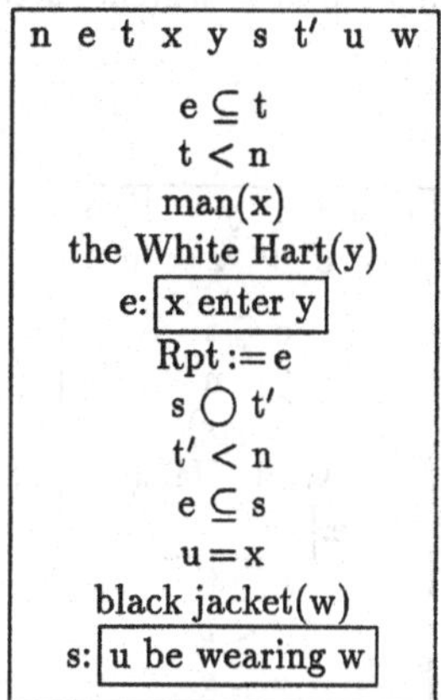

(5.59) serves as context for the interpretation of the third sentence of (5.54). The interpretation of this sentence will again require the choice of a reference point. In other words, the value of Rpt will have to be "reset". (In the present case, **e** remains the reference point, so Rpt is "reset to the same value". But in general this is not so.) To allow for the resetting of Rpt, we adopt the principle that when a sentence whose interpretation required the choice of an Rpt has been fully processed, the equation expressing this choice is eliminated from the resulting DRS. In particular, the final DRS for the first two sentences of (5.54) will not be (5.59), but

(5.59′)

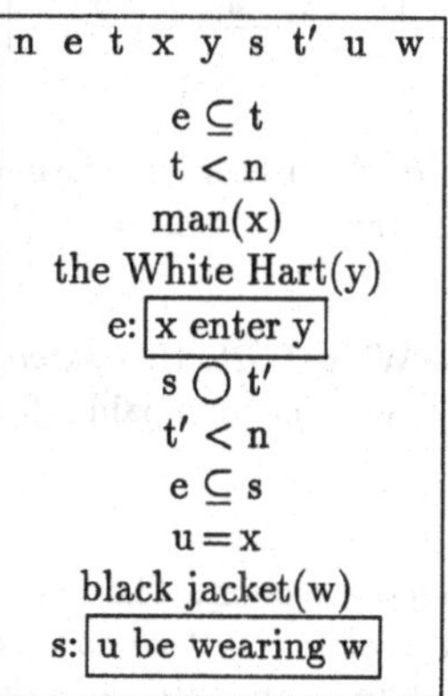

Processing the third sentence poses no new problems. The sentence describes an event and so the relation between this event and the reference point need not be

that of inclusion. In the present case, as in most cases of narrative discourse, the relation is succession. Processing the third sentence accordingly transforms (5.59′) into

(5.60)

n e t x y s t′ u w e′ t″ z r u′
$e \subseteq t$
$t < n$
man(x)
the White Hart(y)
e: [x enter y]
$s \bigcirc t'$
$t' < n$
$e \subseteq s$
$u = x$
black jacket(w)
s: [u be wearing w]
$e' \subseteq t''$
$t'' < n$
$e < e'$
Bill(z)
beer(r)
$u' = x$
e′: [z serve u′ r]

The next few examples provide further illustrations of the principles that govern the choice of reference points. First, suppose that (5.54) is continued as in (5.61)

(5.61) A man entered the White Hart. He was wearing a black jacket. Bill served him a beer. The man paid. He drank the beer. He liked it.

Here we observe a shift in reference point. The reference point for **The man paid** is the last mentioned event **e′** of (5.60), that for **He drank the beer** the event introduced by the sentence **The man paid,** and that for the last sentence is the event introduced by **He drank the beer.** Thus the first processing step for **The man paid** will extend (5.60) to

(5.62)

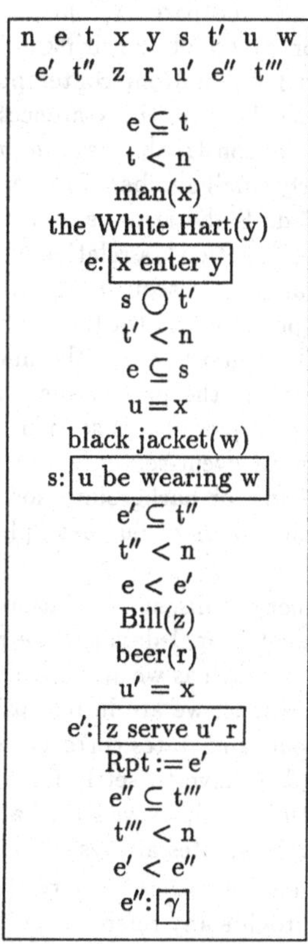

where γ is the syntactic structure of **The man paid** without its S′-node. We leave the completion of the DRS for (5.61) to the reader.

We have argued that event-sentences typically describe eventualities following the contextually given reference point, but that if the described eventuality is a state, then it typically incudes the reference point. That these principles are not without exceptions is shown by the following examples. Suppose we extend (5.61) with the additional sentence

(5.63) Some of it ran down his chin.

This sentence does not seem to describe a state. Indeed, no theories of tense and aspect that we know of would classify it as such. Yet, the eventuality it describes is naturally understood as simultaneous with the drinking of the beer, not as following it. This judgement is part and parcel of our seeing the beer running down the man's chin as a *detail*, or *aspect* of the drinking event – as an *elaboration* of it, to use a technical term familiar from contemporary theories of discourse structure.[17] According to these theories, the sentences that make up a coherent piece of discourse must always be construable as standing to the immediately preceding discourse in one of a fairly small number of *rhetorical relations* – or *discourse relations*, as they are also called. Elaboration is one of these. Another is the one sometimes called "narrative continuation", a relation which holds between two successive event-sentences in a narrative discourse when the event described by the second sentence constitutes a possible and (in the context of the given narration) relevant continuation of the event described by the first. (Narrative continuation was the relation that held between the pair of successive event-sentences which we encountered in the earlier examples of this section.) A third relation is "backgrounding". It holds between an event-sentence and a state-sentence when the latter describes part of the setting, or background, for the event described by the former. The event-state-sentence pairs of our examples all instantiate this third relationship.

At the present time, no theory of discourse relations that we are familiar with has been worked out in sufficient formal detail to be readily incorporated into a theory of discourse interpretation such as we are pursuing here. Lacking a suitably explicit theory of discourse relations, we are in no position to articulate how the temporal relations between events and states correlate with the rhetorical relations between them. We will therefore have to settle for a compromise. So we shall oversimplify and assume that the principles we stated above hold generally: Events always follow their reference point, states always include it.[18]

As shown by (5.54), the first sentence of a narrative may be acceptable even though the context does not provide any reference point. But even for discourse-initial sentences this is not always so. While it is a convention of narrative fiction that the first sentence need not be anchored to some specific reference time, the

---

[17]See [Hobbs 1985], [Mann & Thompson 1986, 1987] and [Reichman 1985]

[18]The principle that the eventualities introduced by state-describing sentences include the reference point is not universally valid either. This is shown by the following example. Suppose we continue (5.54) with

(5.64) The beer tasted awful.

This sentence describes a state. (That **taste** is a stative verb may not be immediately obvious. For instance, the progressive **was tasting**, though not very good, does not seem to be completely out. The strongest indication that the verb is stative is that simple present tense sentences such as **The beer tastes awful** are perfectly acceptable. For the relevant discussion of present tense see Section 5.2.3 below.) Yet, in the context of (5.54), it is naturally construed as referring to a time after that of serving the beer (viz. to the time of the man's presumed drinking of the beer).

first sentence of a discourse concerning the affairs of this world, in particular when it concerns our daily lives, is in general not free of this constraint. Thus, as argued by Partee,[19]

(5.65) I did not turn off the stove.

will typically be understood as pertaining to some contextually salient time, even if no other utterance precedes it. (The situation Partee considers is one where someone says (5.65) to her spouse with whom she has just set off on a trip. It is this time – the time of, or slightly before, their departure – of which (5.65) asserts that it contains no turning-off-the-stove event.)

One of the simplifications we will assume in formulating a construction algorithm for tensed discourse is that the interpretation of a discourse-initial sentence never requires the choice of a reference point; when the sentence contains no temporal adverb, then the time of the eventuality will be represented as unspecified except for the information carried by the tense (i.e. if the tense is a simple past then the eventuality is located before **n**, etc.). When the sentence does contain a temporal adverb, then this adverb will provide a specification of the location and thus obviate the need for a reference point.

Non-initial sentences without temporal adverbs, we have said, need a contextually supplied reference point to determine the location of the eventualities they describe. However, when a non-initial sentence does contain a temporal adverb, then it is the adverb which will supply the location, just as it does for a discourse-initial sentence. In these cases the adverb in fact overrides, as it were, the effect of the antecedent context. Consider, for instance, the following discourse, where the last sentence – which is the one of interest to us – contains the adverbial phrase **the next day**.

(5.66) Fred arrived on the first of January. It was raining continuously. But the next day the sun was shining.

In (5.66), the state described by the third sentence is located at the time designated by the adverb **the next day**. The presence of the adverb deactivates the contextual principle according to which the state described by that sentence would have to include the event of Fred's arrival. (Such an inclusion would produce an inconsistency with the implication, carried by the first two sentences of (5.66), that his arrival also overlaps with a condition of rain, so that there would be rain and sunshine at the same time.) This is precisely what makes the discourse incoherent when the phrase **the next day** is dropped:

[19] See [Partee 1973a].

(5.66′) Fred arrived on the first of January. It was raining. The sun was shining.

Even when a non-initial sentence contains a temporal adverb, the reference point may still have a role to play. Compare, for instance, the sequence

(5.67) Fred left on Wednesday. He arrived on Sunday.

In (5.67), one is naturally disposed to take the event described by the second sentence to come after the one described in the first. This does not follow from the temporal adverb, for **Sunday** might just as well refer to the last Sunday *before* the Wednesday referred to by the adverb **Wednesday** as to the next Sunday *after* that Wednesday. So the reference point mechanism and the referential properties of the terms **Wednesday** and **Sunday** interact in this case to produce the most salient readings that (5.67) seems to have. A further illustration of the same point is provided by a sequence such as

(5.68) The expedition arrived on the 25th of July 1941. It left on the 5th of May of that year.

To us this sounds odd precisely because the second adverb designates an earlier time than the first adverb. To say that the departure preceded the arrival would have been more proper to use the past perfect **had left** instead of the simple past **left**.

Speakers of English seem to vary in how bad they find (5.68). In our formal treatment we assume that (5.68) is ungrammatical. We capture this, as well as the judgements we have reported on (5.67), by stipulating that the relation between described eventuality and reference point holds for sentences with temporal adverbs as well as for sentences without such adverbs. For those speakers who do not share our judgements, this principle would have to be relaxed.

We have been writing the characterizing conditions of eventualities in the form **e**:$\boxed{\gamma}$. We argued for this notation as a way of giving prominence to the event discourse referent: by setting it apart from the discourse referents occurring in γ, we make explicit that the condition is intended as a characterization of the eventuality. Writing eventuality characterizations in this form, however, is at variance with the notation we have been using in comparable cases earlier. Consider complex NPs, e.g., **a book which Mary likes.**[20]

[20] We revert temporarily to the syntactic structure of Chapters 1 and 2, and we will return to relative clauses in Section 5.3.

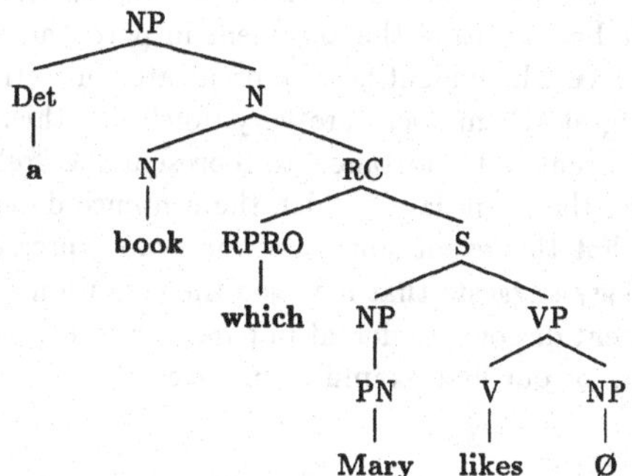

Processing this NP involves, first, the introduction of a new discourse referent, **x** for instance, together with the condition

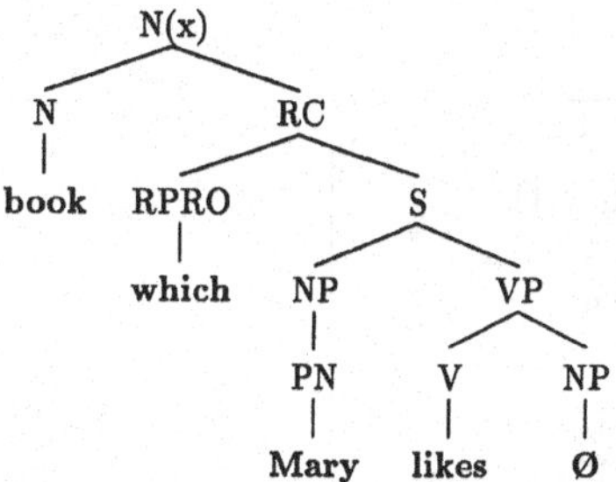

This condition then gets reduced further to the conditions **book(x)** and

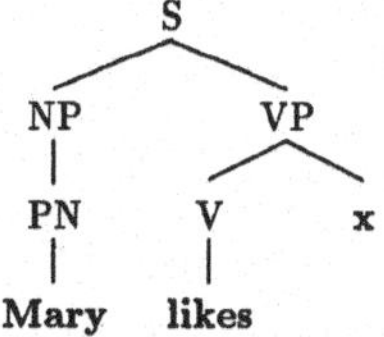

whose latter condition is then processed like any other sentence. The idea behind this and many other sequences of processing steps defined by our construction algorithm is that certain intermediate conditions take the form of predications in which the argument is a discourse referent and the predicate is a complex syntactic structure. In these cases, we have been writing the argument in parentheses behind the top node of the syntactic tree which identifies the predicate. In spirit, the processing steps we are considering at the moment are very much like this. The first step introduces a discourse referent, **e** for instance, to represent the "referential argument" of the sentence, i.e. the eventuality which the sentence describes, together with a condition saying that this eventuality is of the type expressed by the (detensed) sentence. The analogy suggests that here too the condition should be expressed by writing the argument discourse referent in parentheses behind the top node of the "predicate". Thus, for our first example sentence

(5.32) Mary wrote the letter on Sunday.

the DRS obtained after the first step will have the form

(5.69)

```
+--------------------------------------+
|               n e t                  |
|                                      |
|           on Sunday(t)               |
|              e ⊆ t                   |
|              t < n                   |
|                                      |
|              S(e)                    |
|           /        \                 |
|         NP          VP'              |
|         |           |                |
|         PN          VP               |
|         |         /    \             |
|        Mary      V      NP           |
|                  |     /   \         |
|                write  Det    N       |
|                        |     |       |
|                       the  letter    |
+--------------------------------------+
```

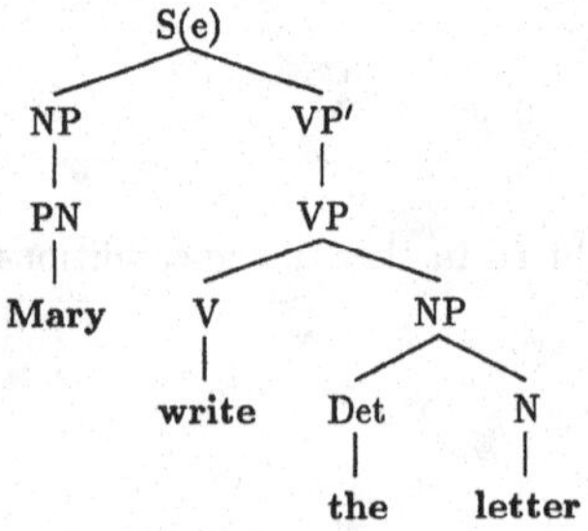

The next step decomposes the condition at the bottom of (5.69) into **Mary(x)** and another condition in which the root of the triggering condition is no longer the S-node but the VP′-node below it. The discourse referent **e** gets passed down to this node. So the resulting DRS – the counterpart to (5.49) of our previous construction – is

(5.70)

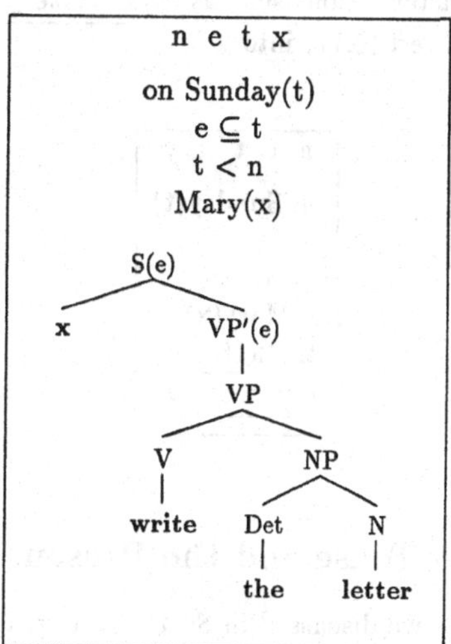

The next step carries **e** down from the VP′-node to the VP-node and the final step carries it down to the V-node. The result of these two steps looks as follows:

(5.71)

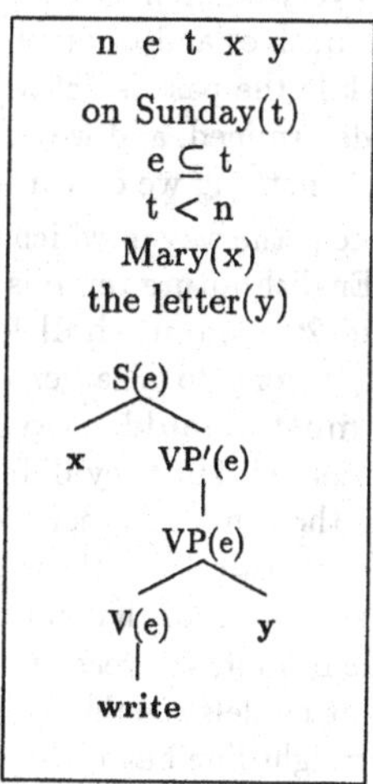

While this is the notation we shall adopt henceforth as the official one, we do not want to give up the graphically suggestive way we have introduced for writing irreducible eventuality characterizations such as e: **x write y**. So by an additional, optional step we may convert (5.71) into

(5.72)

n e t x y
on Sunday(t) e ⊆ t t < n Mary(x) the letter(y) e: [x write y]

5.2.3 The Future Tense and the Present Tense

The tense logical systems we discussed in Section 5.1 treat past tense and future tense as mirror images of each other. We already noted in passing that this is one of the points on which those systems are open to criticism. For our use of the future tense differs in many ways from the uses we make of the past tense. In fact, that the two tenses should be used differently is hardly surprising, given that our attitude towards the future is so very different from our attitude towards the past. It is part of our conception of ourselves and of our role in the world in which we live that the future is "open" while the past is "closed". What the future will be like is to a significant degree undetermined, and we ourselves are among those who can help shape it. As to the past, nothing we do can make any difference.

Symptomatic of this difference is the way in which the future tense is grammatically realized in English. The English future tense is formed with the help of the auxiliary **will** (or, in the 1st and 2nd person, **shall** for certain dialects of British English). But **will** (and **shall**) belong to a larger class of "modal auxiliaries", which also contains words like **must**, **should**, **may**, **might**. All these particles have a meaning that is future-oriented; but they differ in their "modal force". To describe the differences between them model-theoretically, we would need models with a more complex temporal structure than those discussed in Section 5.1. At each point in time, the future, as seen from that point, would have to be open in that several possible futures issue from it, whereas in the opposite direction there is only one past. In other words, our models should not be based on a time structure which can be represented as a straight line but rather on a structure part of which (the part that is relevant from the perspective of the time t) looks something like this:

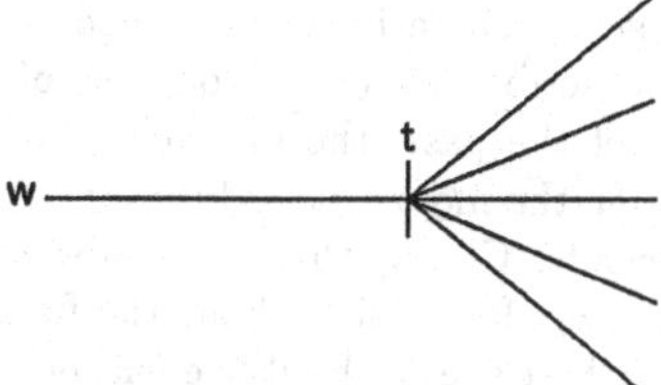

(of course, there would be such ramifications at each time point in each branch!)

With respect to models that have this kind of underlying structure the difference between, say, **must** and **may** (in the sense of necessity, not obligation) could be approximately defined by stating that for any infinitival complement ϕ x **may** ϕ is true in the branch w at t iff ϕ is true of x at some time after t in some branch issuing from w at t, whereas x **must** ϕ is true in w at t iff ϕ is true at some time after t in each of those issuing branches. (This is really no more than a very rough shot. But we do not intend to improve upon it. Modality is not a topic we deal with in this book.)

What about the future tense auxiliary **will**? What are the truth conditions, in w at t, for x **will** ϕ? This is a problem with a long history going back to Aristotle.[21] Aristotle himself seems to have held the position that the simple future tense should be given the analysis that we have just suggested for **must**. We do not believe this is right. Rather, when someone uses the future tense, he is typically referring to whichever way the future will turn out to be, irrespective of whether the aspects of it that are relevant to the truth of his statement are already fixed or not. In other words, the future tense refers to a single continuation of w after t – to that way in which w continues in actual fact. (There may be many other worlds w′ which are indistinguishable from w up to t but diverge from it after that!) Thus, so long as we limit ourselves to **will** and ignore the other modal auxiliaries, we can stick with models based on linear time structures. This is what we will do. So, as far as our models are concerned, past and future are mirror images. For instance, for any model based on the structure $\langle \mathbb{R},< \rangle$ of the real numbers, past and future are mirror images with respect to any time point (i.e. real number) r in the specific sense that the function which maps each real number r′ onto the number $2 \cdot r - r'$ will leave r invariant and map the past and the future of r one-to-one onto each other while reversing the temporal order.

But the *use* people make of the future tense is *not* a mirror image of the use they make of the past tense. One respect in which it is not has to do with what we call *temporal perspective*, a concept that will be discussed in Section 5.4. A second one can be explained with the conceptual apparatus now at our disposal. We have argued that there is a strong tendency in past tense narrative to tell

[21] [Aristotle, De Interpretatione], [Rescher 1967], [Thomason 1984], [Zanardo 1985].

events in the order in which they (are supposed to have) happened: the order of the sentences reflects the order of the described events. If our use of the future tense was the mirror image of our use of the past, the predominant strategy in future tense discourse would be to mention the most distant future events first and then to proceed to ever nearer future events. Clearly this is not how we normally talk. Inasmuch as we have a default strategy for talking about the future at all it is the same as with past tense discourse: first speak about the earlier, then about the later events.

While there are, as we have just seen, certain differences between past and future that are of importance to the problems of semantic representation which this chapter addresses, they are slight when compared with the differences which separate past and future from the present tense. The principal distinction that sets the present tense apart from the two others is what might be called its *token-reflexiveness.* The present tense, in its most common use, is governed by the interpretation principle (5.73).

(5.73) The location time of a present tense sentence is the utterance time **n**.

One consequence of this principle is that present tense sentences have no need of a textually determined reference point. Or, to put it another way, the reference point of a present tense sentence is always the utterance time **n**. So present tense sentences are typically not part of narrative sequences in the way that past tense sentences often are (as well as, to a lesser extent, sentences in the future tense).

(5.73) is also at the bottom of a more important difference that sets the present tense apart from both future and past tense. A present tense sentence describes an eventuality as occurring at the time at which the sentence is uttered, and thus at a time at which the thought is being entertained which the sentence expresses. So the thought must conceive the eventuality as it appears from the perspective of a time at which it is going on. These considerations imply that (5.73) may be strengthened to

(5.74) The eventuality described by a present tense sentence must properly include the utterance time **n**.

In the light of what we have been saying about states and events in Section 5.2.2, (5.74) indicates that the eventuality must have the status of a state and not of an event. For events, we said, are presented as included within their location times, whereas the most common temporal relation between location time and state is the reverse: the state surrounds the location time rather than being included in it. Therefore a sentence which describes something as going on at a time – in the sense of not having come to an end when that time is up – cannot represent that something as an event. For the event would have to be entirely included within the location time and thus would not extend beyond it.

These intuitions are confirmed by the following observation. When we want to assert that right now Mary is ill, then these are the very words we may use

(5.75) Mary is ill.

But if we want to report a current event – say, the writing of a letter – then we cannot use the simple present, as in (5.76.i), but must use the progressive, as in (5.76.ii).

(5.76) (i) Mary writes the letter

(ii) Mary is writing the letter.

On the one hand, these facts support our earlier contention that progressives express states, in contrast to the corresponding non-progressive sentences which are used to describe events. On the other hand, they are evidence for our analysis of present tense assertions as attributing certain states to the utterance time and the resulting interpretation principle (5.74). For they suggest that stative present tense sentences are permitted, but that non-stative ones are not.

We hasten to add that not all uses of the present tense fit the analysis we have just sketched. In particular, there are some which allow for event-sentences as well as sentences that describe states. We can distinguish four types. First, there is the so-called "time-table use" of the present tense, as in

(5.77) The train for Saloniki leaves at 11.35 p.m.

Such sentences can be used either to describe the content of a particular entry of the railway schedule (roughly "Every day at 11:35 a train is due to depart for Saloniki.") or to say of a particular train – the one to leave that evening – that it is due to leave at 11:35 p.m.

Second, there is the generic use of the simple present, as in

(5.78) John drinks tea at breakfast.

which means something like "Normally when John has breakfast, he drinks tea with it."[22]

[22]Closely related to the generic use of the present tense is the one we find in quantified sentences such as **John always (often, never, ...) drinks tea at breakfast**; see Section 5.5.2.

Third, there is a kind of use of the present tense, often referred to as "reportive speech", in which each sentence establishes a new utterance time for itself, with the implication that the described event happens just as the sentence is uttered. The paradigmatic example is that of somebody giving an eyewitness report of an athletic event on radio or television, as in

(5.79) Hoddles passes the ball to Smith. Smith lunges forward, passes Bickerton. He shoots. He scores!

Finally, there is the "historical present". This is a use of the present tense in which it is made to refer to past episodes. It is a stilistic device, employed for the sake of greater vividness – it would seem that the present tense creates an illusion that what is described is going on now, and thus tends to heighten the listener's or reader's sense of participation.

Neither the time table use of the present tense nor reportive speech nor the historical present will be part of the English fragment we will study in this chapter. The generic use of the present tense will be briefly discussed in Section 5.5.2. But the construction algorithm developed here will consider only the 'standard' use of the present tense, in which all present tense sentences describe states.

We conclude this subsection with the DRS-construction for two very simple sentences, one in the present and one in the future tense. The present tense sentence we consider,

(5.80) Mary knows French.

has the syntactic structure

(5.81)

$S'_{[TENSE = pres;\, STAT = +]}$

S

NP VP′

PN VP

Mary V NP

knows PN

French

The DRS this structure should yield is essentially that in (5.82).

(5.82)

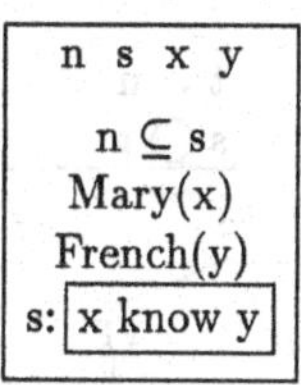

But how do we arrive at such a structure? In particular, which interpretation principles yield the condition **n** $\subseteq$ **s**? We have said that the present tense locates the described state at the utterance time. In the light of our processing strategy for past tense sentences, which always involve the introduction of a location time, it seems reasonable to interpret this as a statement to the effect that utterance time **n** and location time coincide. As it stands, this does not enable us to infer that **n** is included in **s**, but only that the two overlap. We can conclude that **n** is included in **s**, however, as long as it is assumed that the utterance time is indivisible; for then, as we noted in Section 5.5.2, overlap and inclusion come to the same thing. It seems to us that this assumption is indeed correct: the utterance time *is* conceived as punctual, just as the time denoted by the word **now** (see (5.43)!).

By identifying the location time **t** with the utterance time **n**, we also commit ourselves to the punctuality of **t**. So the relation of overlap between **s** and **t** can be recast as inclusion of **t** in **s**. At this point we can proceed in one of two ways. We can either introduce DRS notation to the effect that a certain time is conceived as punctual, and then introduce conditions to the effect that (i) **n** is punctual, (ii) **t** is identical with **n** and (iii) **s** overlaps with **t**. The logical properties of punctuality, overlap and inclusion will then yield **n** $\subseteq$ **s** as an inference.

If (5.80) is processed in this way, we obtain after the first step

(5.83)

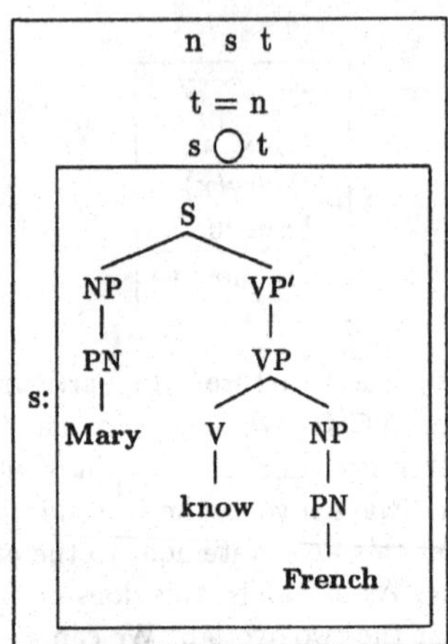

The remaining steps introduce discourse referents for the NPs **Mary** and **French**, resulting in a DRS that is identical to (5.82) but for the presence of **t** and the conditions involving it.

The DRS-construction for sentences in the simple future is comparatively straightforward. Consider, for instance, the future tense counterpart of our old aquaintance (5.32), **Mary wrote the letter on Sunday**:

(5.84) Mary will write the letter on Sunday.

Its syntactic structure is

(5.85)

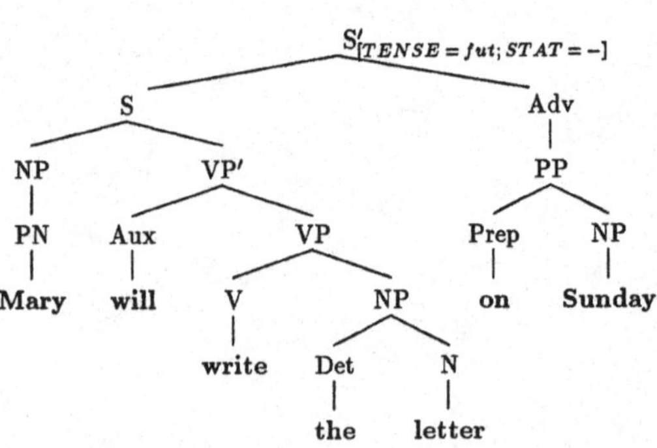

We face a minor technical complication in this case, which has to do with the auxiliary **will**. **Will** makes its semantic contribution via the feature value fut. Once it has made this contribution it can be discarded. We account for this by pruning the auxiliary from the sentence structure that remains after the first construction step, in the course of which the contribution of **will** is explicitly represented, has been performed.

The first step in the construction of a DRS for (5.84) places the described event in the future of **n**, while otherwise things are like they were for (5.32):

(5.86)

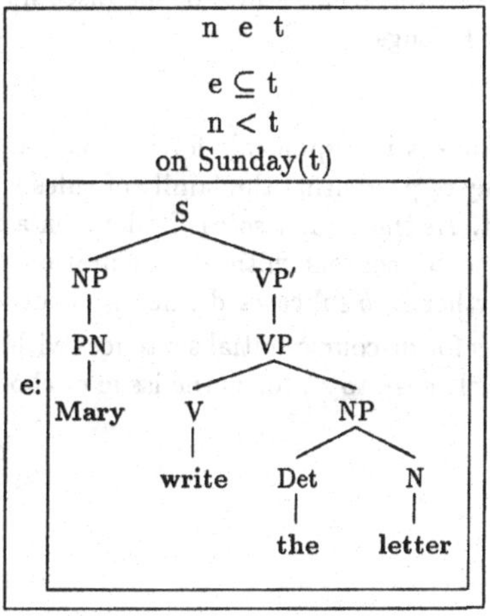

n e t

$e \subseteq t$

$n < t$

on Sunday(t)

e: [S [NP [PN **Mary**]] [VP' [VP [V **write**] [NP [Det **the**] [N **letter**]]]]]

The completion of (5.86) is straightforward.

5.2.4 DRS-Construction Rules for Temporal Reference I

In this section, we state the construction rules that are triggered by syntactic configurations of the form

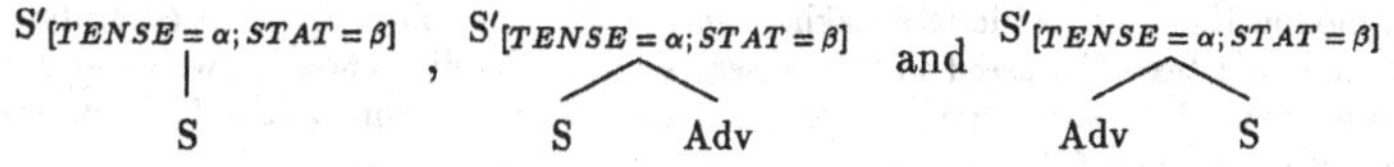

$S'_{[TENSE=\alpha;\, STAT=\beta]}$ → S , $S'_{[TENSE=\alpha;\, STAT=\beta]}$ → S Adv and $S'_{[TENSE=\alpha;\, STAT=\beta]}$ → Adv S

As we have seen, there is a fair number of distinctions we have to draw; which particular rule is to be employed depends, apart from

(i) the presence or absence of a temporal adverb,

also on:

(ii) the value of *TENSE*,

(iii) the value of *STAT*,

(iv) whether or not the sentence is the first of the discourse or text to which it belongs.

Since each of these factors is responsible for its own part in the rules' output, the most perspicuous way of presenting the family of rules would be in the form of a four-dimensional chart. As that is not so easily done on a two-dimensional sheet of paper, we will have to be content with a presentation that divides the cases defined by one factor further into subcases defined by another.

We first give the rules for discourse-initial sentences without adverbs. For these the rules are comparatively easy to state, as the issue of choosing a reference point does not arise.[23]

[23]The system of rules we present in this section is not our final one. In Section 5.4 we will find reason for a modification that, strictly speaking, affects the processing of all tensed sentences. For the sentences and texts discussed in the present section, the differences between the DRS-constructions proposed here and those of Section 5.4 are, however, minimal. The final system of rules will be given in Section 5.4.

CR.S$'_{TA=\langle TENSE,STAT\rangle}$ (for discourse initial sentences)

Triggering configurations $\gamma \in$ Con$_K$:

(i) $[S'_{TA}\ [S_{TA}]]$ (ii) $[S'_{TA}\ \text{Adv}\ [S_{TA}]]$ (iii) $[S'_{TA}\ [S_{TA}]\ \text{Adv}]$

Introduce into U$_K$: a new time discourse referent **t**

If $\gamma \neq$ (i), then introduce into Con$_K$: **Adv(t)**

If *STAT* = –, then:

Introduce into U$_K$: new event discourse referent **e**

Introduce into Con$_K$: $e \subseteq t$

If *TENSE* = *past*, then:

Introduce into Con$_K$: $t < n$

If *TENSE* = *fut*, then:

Introduce into Con$_K$: $n < t$

Replace γ by* S(e) △

If *STAT* = +, then:

Introduce into U$_K$: new state discourse referent **s**

If *TENSE* = *past*, then:

Introduce into Con$_K$: $s \bigcirc t$, $t < n$

If *TENSE* = *pres*, then:

Introduce into Con$_K$: $t \subseteq s$, $t = n$

If *TENSE* = *fut*, then:

Introduce into Con$_K$: $s \bigcirc t$, $n < t$

Replace γ by[24] S(s) △

---

[24]This is not entirely correct. In the cases where *TENSE* = *past* or *TENSE* = *pres*, γ should not be replaced by S(e) △ or S(s) △, but rather by a structure S(e) $\triangle_1$ or S(s) $\triangle_1$, which we get by changing the

Two remarks are in order. First, the case ⟨*STAT* = −; *TENSE* = *pres*⟩ does not arise in our fragment. (This feature value combination would correspond to event-sentences in reportive speech; but we have decided to ignore reportive speech.) Second, the case with feature values ⟨*STAT* = +; *TENSE* = *pres*⟩ and where **Adv** is present is not very common. This should not be surprising, for the feature values guarantee that the described state is interpreted as overlapping **n** in any case, so that the adverb can perform its usual function of providing the location only redundantly: it can only *confirm* information that is available independently. In fact, when we find a temporal adverb in a present tense sentence, its role is typically that of emphasizing a contrast with what was or will be the case at some time other than **n**. For instance, we say things like **I am happy now. (But only last week I was utterly miserable.)** or **These days people just don't care any more.** (As these examples show, consistency demands that the time denoted by the adverb overlaps with the utterance time.)

We now turn to the case of sentences that are not discourse-initial. When such a sentence contains a temporal adverb, its interpretation presents no problems that differ significantly from what we encounter with discourse-initial sentences. The contextually determined reference point may still have a role to play with such sentences, but only in that the location of the described eventuality does not lie entirely before it. With non-initial sentences without temporal adverbs, however, the matter is more complicated. Here, as we saw, the relation between described eventuality and reference time will in general depend on the rhetorical relationship between the sentence under consideration and the one by which the reference time was previously introduced. As the identification of rhetorical relations is something that lies beyond the powers of our analysis, we are forced to simplify. We adopt the principle, already enunciated earlier in this section, that a new event is interpreted as following the reference time (as in cases of "narrative continuation"), whereas a new state includes it. Moreover, we adopt this principle not only for sequences of past tense sentences but also for sequences of sentences in the future tense.[25]

---

finite form of the verb into its infinitive (see p. (519)). Similarly, in the case where *TENSE*=*fut* Δ_1 is obtained from Δ by eliminating the auxiliary **will** and the Aux-node immediately above it (cf. (5.85) and (5.86)).

[25]For present tense sentences the role of reference point is moot. We saw that present tense sentences (or at any rate the kind of present tense sentences included in our formal treatment) always describe states which include the time of utterance. There is no way, it seems, in which a contextually determined reference point could alter this; nor, for that matter, is there anything in what we have said about reference points which bears on the issue what the reference point for a present tense sentence might be. If we want to insist for the sake of uniformity that non-initial sentences in the present tense require the choice of reference point just as non-initial past and future tense sentences do, we could identify the reference point for a present tense sentence with **n**. The principle that a state always includes the reference time then comes to what we knew already: that the state overlaps with **n**.

The second simplification we adopt concerns the choice of the reference point. Here too we adopt the procedure which yields the desired results in the examples we have so far considered, but which is liable to lead to inadequate representations for discourses that are structured differently from those we have looked at. We focus on the case where the sentence S for which a reference time must be chosen is in the past tense. We distinguish two cases

(a) The part of the discourse preceding S contains an earlier event-sentence in the past tense. For this case we stipulate that the reference point be the discourse referent representing the event described by the most recent past tense event-sentence before S.

(b) The antecedent part of the discourse contains no past tense event-sentence. In this case we let the reference point be the location time of the most recent past tense state-sentence. Otherwise we set the reference point equal to some new arbitrary time (represented by a new discourse referent).

The reference times for future tense sentences are chosen in the same way – just replace in the recipe for choosing the reference time for a past tense sentence 'past tense' everywhere by 'future tense'.

Now that we have made our various simplifying assumptions, stating the rules for non-initial sentences has become quite straightforward. In fact, each rule involves the same operations as its counterpart for discourse-initial sentences, except that two new additional conditions have to be added to Con_K. (They will be, if and only if the antecedent discourse satisfies either the condition (a) or the condition (b) on p. 545.) The extra conditions that are to be added are (i) $\mathbf{Rpt} := \mathbf{o}$ where $\mathbf{o}$ is determined as above, and (ii) $\mathbf{o} < \mathbf{e}$, in case $STAT = -$, or $\mathbf{o} \subseteq \mathbf{s}$, in case $STAT = +$.

Exercises

1. Construct DRSs for the following discourses.

   (a) Bill left the house at ten. It was raining. He returned and fetched an umbrella. He arrived at the bank at 10:45.

   (b) The phone rang. Alan was just squirting the shaving cream onto his face. Susan was having a shower. She rushed to the kitchen and picked up the receiver.

   (c) Bill left at 10 o'clock. The sun was shining. Bill walked to the bus stop. He was smiling.

(d) Bill loves Suzie. Last week he bought her cat. It scratched him. Next week he will buy her dog. It will bite him.

2. (a) Develop a construction rule for PPs like **after 10 minutes** and construct a DRS for the following discourse.

   (b) Susan's alarm clock rang at 7:30. She turned it off. Then, after 10 minutes, she got up, made her way to the kitchen, switched on the electric kettle and lit the burner underneath the milk pan. Next she went to the bathroom and had a shower.

3. Which Thursdays are possible denotations of **on Thursday** in the following texts?

   (a) Alan arrived on Monday. He obtained a visa on Thursday.

   (b) Alan arrived on Monday. He had obtained a visa on Thursday.

   (c) Alan arrived exactly two weeks ago. He had left on the preceding Monday. On Thursday he had received an alarming telegram.

   (d) Alan arrived exactly two weeks ago. On Thursday he bought a new car.

5.2.5 Negation

We encountered negation as early as in Chapter 1. The treatment of it we offered there was quite straightforward: negation triggers the introduction of a complex condition involving a subordinate DRS K′; this condition is verified if and only if there is no way of verifying K′. It might be thought that tense has got nothing to do with this and that the earlier treatment could be imported into the semantics of this chapter more or less as it is.

As it turns out, things are not as simple as that. Both syntactically and semantically negations of tensed sentences involve complications which could be ignored in our treatment of negation in Chapter 1 but which now demand careful attention. The syntactic complications have to do with word order, specifically with the positions which **not** can occupy in sentences with compound tenses (i.e. tenses involving auxiliary verbs). In finite English sentences, **not** always comes immediately after the verb (main or auxiliary) which carries the tense. Thus one must say **Bill will not have been practicing**, not **Bill not will have been practicing**, **Bill will have not been practicing** or **Bill will have been not practicing**. This kind of constraint on word order is awkward to capture in a phrase structure grammar of the sort introduced in Chapter 0. But from our semantic perspective this is not a matter of importance. The phrase structure rules which give what is required can be found in Section 5.7.

The principal semantic complication has to do with the way negation interacts with tenses. First, let us consider the negation of an event-sentence.

(5.87) Mary did not write a letter on Sunday.

This sentence asserts that on the relevant Sunday there was no event of the kind described by the non-negated sentence: the Sunday in question contained no event of the type "Mary write a letter". In other words, the implicit existential quantification over events which is part of our semantic analysis of the non-negated sentence **Mary wrote a letter** is within the scope of (5.87)'s negation. A DRS representing this reading should have some such form as (5.88).

(5.88)

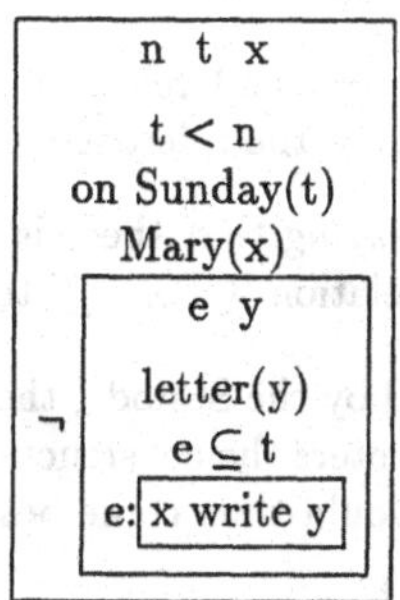

But what are the principles by which such a DRS could be derived? To see what principles might be involved consider the following two pairs of sentences.

(5.89) (1) (i) Mary looked at Bill. He smiled.
(ii) Mary looked at Bill. He was smiling.

(2) (i) Mary looked at Bill. He didn't smile.
(ii) Mary looked at Bill. He wasn't smiling.

(5.89.1.i) strangely suggests that Bill smiled after Mary started looking at him, perhaps as a reaction to her doing so. (5.89.1.ii), in contrast, implies that he was already smiling when she set eyes on him. The difference between (5.89.2.i) and (5.89.2.ii) is similar. (5.89.2.i) seems to say that Bill did not smile in reaction to Mary's looking at him, whereas (5.89.2.ii) has the interpretation that he was not in the process of smiling when she did. As this example indicates, the principles of relating the location time of a negated sentence to the context are the same as they are for the corresponding unnegated sentences. The difference between negated and unnegated sentences arises only for the further conditions in which the location time figures. In the cases we considered in the preceding sections this condition said that **t** stood in a certain relation ($\subseteq$ or $\bigcirc$) to the described event or state – or, to put it slightly differently, that there exists an event or state of a certain type that is thus related to **t**. The negated sentences deny the existence of such a state or event.

It is easy to see that this principle should yield the DRS (5.88), which has been our target for (5.87). Nevertheless, it raises two difficulties, one of a conceptual, the other of a more technical nature. The technical problem is this. As we set up the construction algorithm in Sections 5.2.2–5.2.4 a discourse referent for the described eventuality is introduced at the very start of sentence processing. For negated sentences this is clearly not the way to proceed. There the intuitively most natural procedure would seem to be this:

Step 1: Introduce a location time **t** and relate it to **n** (as well as to a suitably chosen reference point, in case the reference point is defined.)

Step 2: Introduce a condition saying that there is no event or state of a certain type which stands in the relation '$\subseteq$' or '$\bigcirc$' to **t**.

The first step should be triggered by the S′-node; the second step is to be triggered at the point where the negation enters the construction of the verb phrase complex. (Processing of the subject NP would thus come between the first and the second step.)

Not only does this seem to be a natural way of processing negated sentences; it also jibes with the construction algorithm for negation which we defined in Chapter 1. In fact, we can improve on the similarity by splitting step 2 into two steps, where the first introduces, just as the negation rule of Chapter 1, a negated DRS $\neg\boxed{\gamma}$, and the second reduces the condition γ by introducing the eventuality referent. But unfortunately, in adopting this strategy we introduce an inconsistency with the construction procedure we formulated, in Section 5.2.4, for non-negated sentences. For according to this procedure already the very first construction step introduces a state or event discourse referent **e** and then transforms the given syntactic structure into the claim that there is some **e** which satisfies a certain condition. The algorithm for negated sentences we just outlined introduces a comparable condition, to the effect that no such event or state exists, only at a later stage, when it reaches the (negated) VP-node.

Formally it would be quite possible to leave things as they are. But it would be awkward. So we will adapt the processing of non-negated sentences so that they are in line with what we have just come to see as the natural way of dealing with negations. In other words, the first construction step for a non-negated sentence such as

(5.32) Mary wrote the letter on Sunday.

will now involve only the introduction of a location time **t** and yield the result

(5.90)

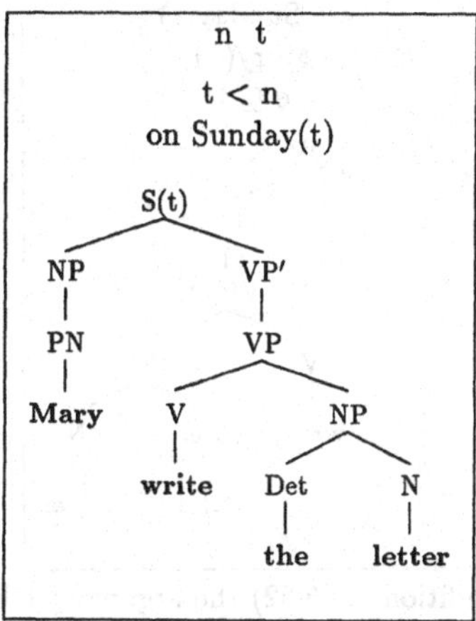

The next step deals with the subject **Mary** and yields

(5.91)

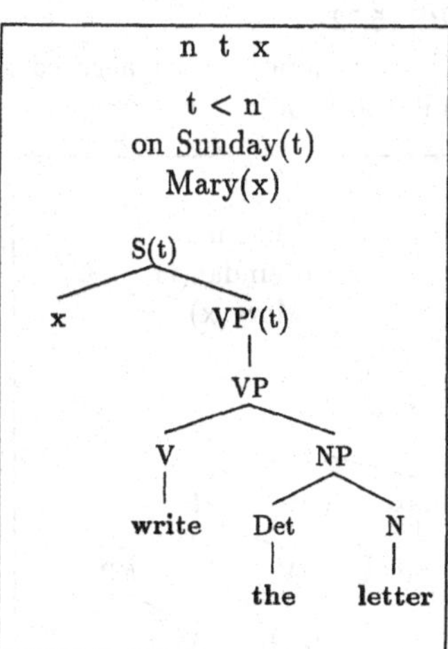

It is only the third step which introduces the event discourse referent **e**, with the result

(5.92)

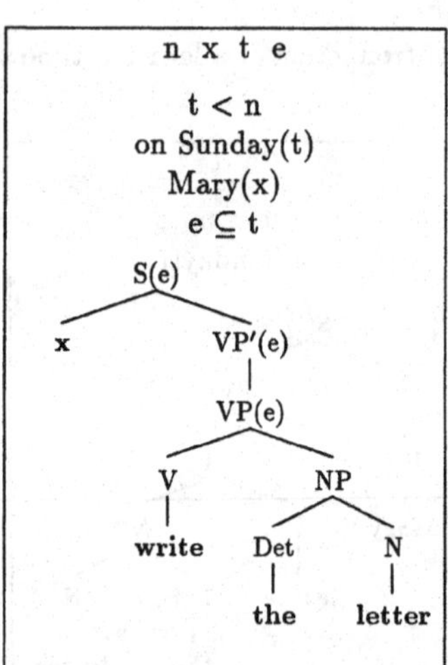

(Note that in the last condition of (5.92) the argument **t** has been replaced by **e**. This is meant to indicate that the condition no longer functions as a predication on **t** – **t**'s part is now accounted for by the separate condition **e** $\subseteq$ **t** – but as a predication of **e**.) The reduction of (5.92) proceeds as before and results, once again, in the completed DRS (5.72).

We now turn to the DRS-construction for the negated sentence (5.87). The first two steps yields a DRS similar to (5.90):

(5.93)

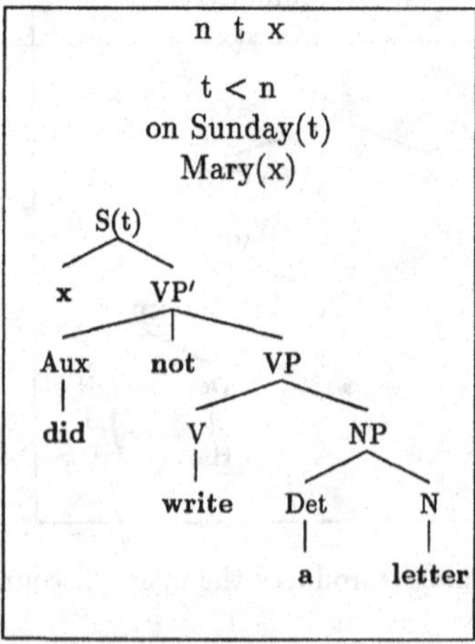

The next step converts (5.93) into (5.94), where the condition of the subordinate DRS is obtained from the last condition of (5.93) through processing of **did** and **not.** (5.94) gets then converted into (5.95) by the same construction rule that turns (5.91) into (5.92).

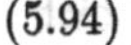
(5.94)

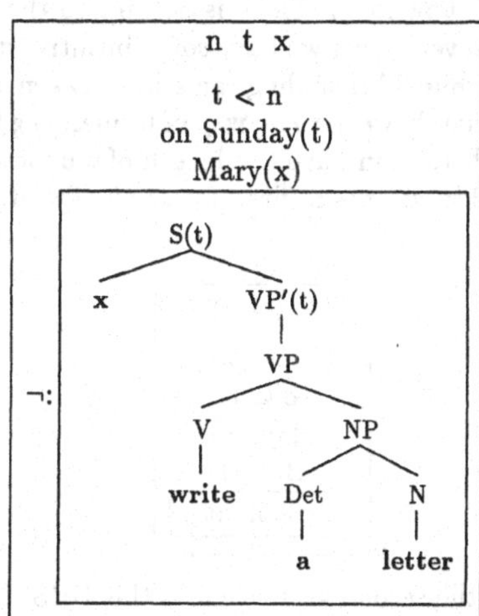

(5.95)

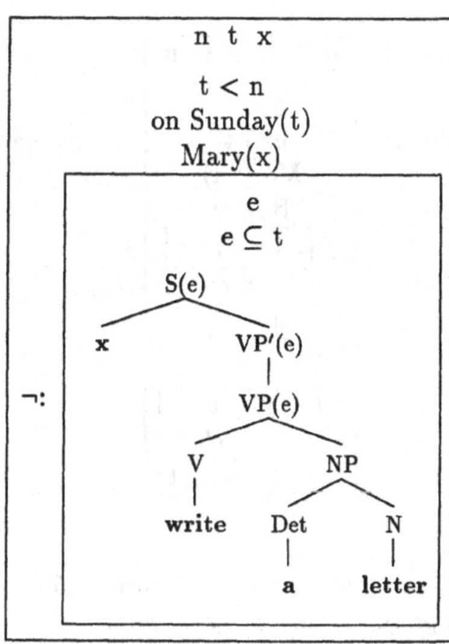

The other, conceptual, difficulty connected with negation does not arise in connection with negated sentences which, like (5.87), contain a temporal adverb. But we find it with negated sentences which lack such an adverb, such as the second sentence of (5.89.2). Intuitively (5.89.2.i) says something like "Mary's looking at Bill was not rewarded with a smile" – for some period t after Mary looked at Bill, he did not smile. But for how long? There is nothing in the sentence itself which tells us this explicitly. Nevertheless we have some intuitive understanding of how soon Bill would have to smile if his smiling can still be taken as "following" Mary's looking at him? Unfortunately we have no way of formalizing this kind of intuition. So we can do no better here than have the length of t undetermined. Proceeding in this spirit with (5.89.2.i) we obtain, first, for the first sentence

(5.96)

$$\boxed{\begin{array}{c} \mathrm{e\ t\ x\ y} \\ \\ \mathrm{t} < \mathrm{n} \\ \mathrm{e} \subseteq \mathrm{t} \\ \mathrm{Mary(x)} \\ \mathrm{Bill(y)} \\ \mathrm{e}: \boxed{\mathrm{x\ look\ at\ y}} \end{array}}$$

and then, incorporating the second sentence into this DRS

(5.97)

$$\boxed{\begin{array}{c} \mathrm{e\ t\ x\ y\ t'\ u} \\ \\ \mathrm{t} < \mathrm{n} \\ \mathrm{e} \subseteq \mathrm{t'} \\ \mathrm{Mary(x)} \\ \mathrm{Bill(y)} \\ \mathrm{e}: \boxed{\mathrm{x\ look\ at\ y}} \\ \mathrm{t'} < \mathrm{n} \\ \mathrm{u} = \mathrm{y} \\ \neg \boxed{\begin{array}{c} \mathrm{e'} \\ \\ \mathrm{e'} \subseteq \mathrm{t'} \\ \mathrm{e} < \mathrm{e'} \\ \mathrm{e'}: \boxed{\mathrm{u\ smile}} \end{array}} \end{array}}$$

Insofar as this admits t's of extremely short duration (5.97) does not reflect the truth conditions of the represented sentences correctly. For even when the smiling follows the looking quite quickly there may be a brief interval during which Bill isn't smiling yet. So (5.97) would be verifiable, whereas the discourse (5.89.2.i) would have to be judged as false. We have the determination of intuitively plausible constraints on the periods during which negated DRSs (such as the embedded DRS of (5.97)) are supposed to hold as a problem for further study.

Negations of stative verb phrases can be treated in much the same way as negations of non-stative verb phrases. Let's have a look at (5.98).

(5.98) Mary did not live in Stuttgart last year.

The only difference is that the negated sub-DRS now expresses the condition that the "location time" **t** is not overlapped by a state to the effect that Mary lives in Stuttgart.

(5.99)

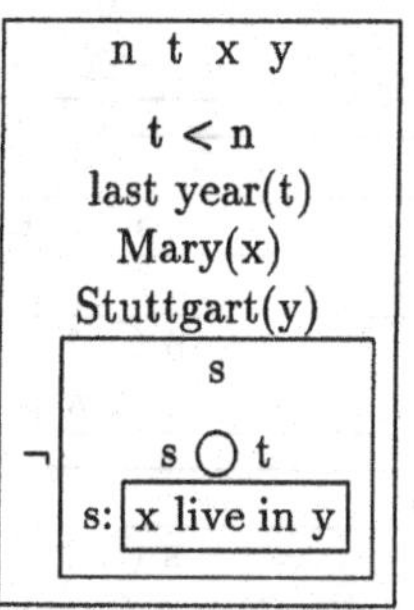

Of the first three processing rules needed to process negated sentences – which introduce location time, negation and eventuality discourse referent, respectively – we have explicitly stated only the last one, which deals with the VP′-nodes of non-negated sentences. The new S′-rule illustrated in (5.90) will have to be modified again (see Section 5.4). So too little would be gained by giving another preliminary formulation now. The rule for negation is rule CR.NEG on page 123.

CR.VP'$_{[TENSE=\alpha;STAT=\beta]}$

Triggering configuration $\gamma \in$ **Con$_K$:** VP'$_{[TENSE=\alpha;STAT=\beta]}$(t) | VP △

Choose Rpt: **Rpt := o**

If *STAT*= −, **then:**

Introduce into U$_K$: new event discourse referent e

If *TENSE*= *past*, **then:**

Introduce into Con$_K$: $o < e$, $e \subseteq t$

If *TENSE*= *fut*, **then:**

Introduce into Con$_K$: $o < e$, $e \subseteq t$

Replace γ **by** VP'(e) | VP △

If *STAT*= +, **then:**

Introduce into U$_K$: new state discourse referent s

If *TENSE*= *past*, **then:**

Introduce into Con$_K$: $s \bigcirc t$, $o \subseteq s$

If *TENSE*= *pres*, **then:**

Introduce into Con$_K$: $s \bigcirc t$, $o \bigcirc s$

If *TENSE*= *fut*, **then:**

Introduce into Con$_K$: $s \bigcirc t$, $o \bigcirc s$

Replace γ **by** VP'(s) | VP △

We conclude this subsection with the DRS-construction of a negated sentence in the present tense.

(5.100) Mary does not like Fred.

The construction principles just outlined yield for (5.100) the DRS (5.101).

(5.101)

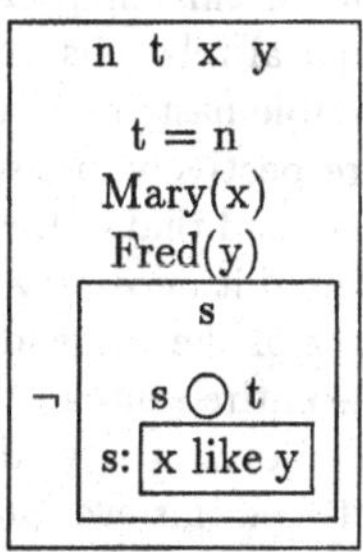

As it stands (5.101) assigns to (5.100) a representation saying that at the speech time **n** a state of a certain type does not obtain. This interpretation is compatible with what we said about negation in Chapter 1. That analysis, which does not involve reference to states at all, also admits of another elaboration, according to which there obtains at **n** the "negative" state of Mary not liking Fred. To get this second interpretation we would have to assume that negation has the effect of transforming a verb phrase (or sentence) with the feature $+STAT$ into another, negated, verb phrase (or sentence), again with the feature $+STAT$. It is tempting to see this assumption, that negations of stative sentences describe states characterized by negated predicates, as a special case of a more general thesis to the effect that negation always has the effect of transforming a verb phrase (or sentence) into a state description – that is, irrespective of whether the non-negated phrase has $STAT$-value + or −. But, the hypothesis would yield the wrong predications for examples like (5.89.2.i): if the sentence expressed a state, then our algorithm would predict for (5.89.2.i) the interpretation that in fact accrues to (5.89.2.ii).[26] It would still be possible to hold on to the assumption for the case where the underlying VP or sentence has $+STAT$; but nothing would be achieved this way, and so we won't.

The last considerations have moved us more closely than we had been so far to the subject of *aspect*. This is the topic of our next section.

[26]We owe this observation to Görel Sandstrom (personal communication).

Exercise

1. Construct DRSs for (5.89.1.i,ii) and (5.89.2.ii).

5.3 Aspect

5.3.1 Methodological Preliminaries

Throughout the preceding sections of this chapter we have been assuming that tenses express something like temporal relations. In Section 5.1, we discussed an analysis according to which the simple past, present and future tense express the relations of before, at and after, respectively, between the evaluation time of the "sentence" to which the tense applies and that of the tensed sentence resulting from its application. Subsequently we found it necessary to modify this proposal in several ways. First, the evaluation time of the embedded sentence was supplanted by the utterance time and that of the entire sentence (which contains the embedded sentence as a part) by the described eventuality. Second, we saw that tenses not only express temporal relations between this eventuality and the time of utterance, but that they often also imply a certain 'anaphoric' relationship between the eventuality and some time or event mentioned earlier. And third, we found that this second, anaphoric, relation will in general depend not only on the tense itself but also on whether the described eventuality is a state or an event. It is on this last complication, and on some others related to it, that we focus in this section.

Our first task in this section is to explain the distinction between tense and aspect. One problem with this task is that the terms "tense" and "aspect" have often been used without due concern for proper definition or consistency with earlier uses in the literature. Because of this lack of consistency, defining the notions in a way that does justice to all, or even most, of what has been said about them seems hopeless. So we have decided to set our concern for historical accuracy aside, and to use the terms 'tense' and 'aspect' in ways that are motivated primarily by the needs of our own theory. Nevertheless, the most salient characteristics common to earlier uses have, we think, been preserved.

For us *tense* and *aspect* are modes of classifying properties: certain properties fall within the province of tense, others within that of aspect. Some of these properties we have already encountered. For instance, among the properties that belong to the realm of tense there are those which determine how location time is related to the time of utterance: the property of having a location time lying before the utterance time, the property of having a location time coinciding with the time of utterance, and the property of having a location time which comes after the utterance time. In the last section, we represented these properties by means of the feature *TENSE*, with each property corresponding to one of the feature's three possible values. In fact, features are a convenient means of collecting properties into families; each value b of a given feature f determines one of the properties in the family, that property which is had by all and only those objects which f assigns the value b.

As we will be using the terms 'tense' and 'aspect' they will apply in the first instance to certain features – some features will be *tense features*, or *temporal features*, and others will be *aspect features*, or *aspectual features*. But since each feature determines a class of properties, the tense-aspect distinction can be directly transferred to those. Thus we will be in a position also to speak of temporal and aspectual *properties*.

Tense and aspect, then, are categories of properties. But properties of what? What sorts of things are the bearers of those properties? Here again the feature *TENSE* is to be our guide. As our use of it in the last section makes plain, *TENSE* is a function that is defined for certain types of expressions (viz. complete tensed sentences). This is what we will assume for temporal and aspectual properties generally: they are properties of natural language expressions, applicable in particular, though not exclusively, to finite tense sentences. As regards temporal properties, sentences will be the only expressions for which they are defined. (We will find reason in the next section to modify this slightly; but the change will be marginal.) The domain of aspectual properties, in contrast, will be larger. It will include not only full sentences, but also other syntactic categories, such as verbs and verb phrases.

With these formalities out of the way, we turn to questions of substance: Which properties of sentences, verb phrases etc. are the aspectual properties and which are the properties falling under tense? What is it that the aspectual properties have in common and that separates them from the temporal properties? And what is the importance of either kind of property for the processing of temporal discourse?

The present section is about aspect and will accordingly concentrate on aspectual properties. We have already said a fair amount in the preceding sections about temporal properties. A further group of temporal properties will be discussed in Section 5.4.

5.3.2 Aktionsarten

The aspectual properties to be discussed in this section presuppose one of the central assumptions of our treatment of temporal reference – the assumption that tensed sentences can be analysed as descriptions of eventualities. Thus far we have been talking about eventualities in a fairly undifferentiated way; we have merely distinguished between those eventualities that are events and those that are states. But if one looks more closely at the kinds of eventualities that are described by different verbs – or, more accurately, by different verb-argument combinations –

one realizes that many finer distinctions could be drawn. Only some of these finer distinctions are important for the semantics of English, and an even smaller set of distinctions are relevant to the analysis we want to develop in the present chapter.

The distinctions relevant here can all be drawn on the basis of a pair of quite simple structural schemata which seem to play a central role in our conceptualization of states and events. To explain the first schema, first consider a so-called *accomplishment verb*, such as **write**. The sentence

(5.102) Mary wrote the letter.

describes events which normally last through a certain interval of time – it takes some time to write a letter. This interval – the event's duration – comes to a natural conclusion when the letter is finished. Only when this conclusion is actually reached can the event be reported in the manner of (5.102); otherwise – i.e. when the letter is started but not completed – one would have to say some such thing as (5.103.i) or (5.103.ii).

(5.103) (i) Mary was writing the letter (but she did not finish it).

(ii) Mary started writing the letter (but she did not finish it).

The natural conclusion of the event, or *culmination point*, as it is often called, is followed by a period of which one can say: **Mary has written the letter.** And it is preceded by a period – that period covered by the event of writing which leads up to the culmination point, but does not include it – during which it is possible to say: **Mary is writing the letter.** (5.104) gives a schematic picture of the situation as we have described it.

(5.104)

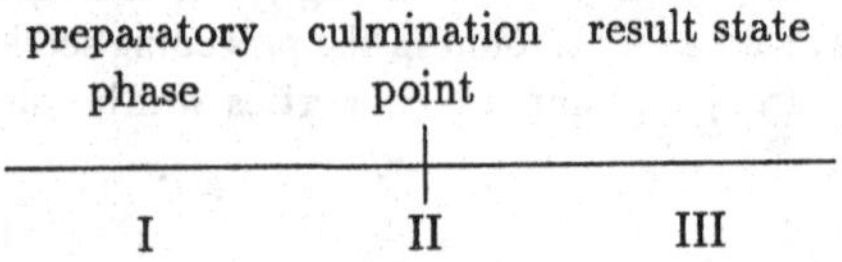

preparatory phase	culmination point	result state
I	II	III

The tense of a sentence (in the syntactic sense of the word) sometimes indicates which part or parts of this schema the sentence refers to. We already noted that a sentence in the simple past, such as (5.102), differs in this regard from the corresponding progressive sentence (5.103.i): (5.102) refers to the writing event as a whole (consisting of I and II in the diagram), (5.103.i) only to part I, and the present perfect sentence (5.105)

(5.105) Mary has written the letter.

refers to the state resulting from the event, i.e. to part III. These differences are for us paradigmatic differences of aspect: (5.102), (5.103.i) and (5.105) have distinct aspectual properties inasmuch as they refer to different parts of (5.104).

The aspectual properties that play a role in this chapter are all of this type. Each such property indicates which part or parts of schemata like (5.104) belong to the eventualities described by the expressions which have it.[27] As far as schema (5.104) is concerned, the only part-whole relations that are relevant are the three which we have already mentioned – the one where the part consists of I+II, where it consists of I and where it consists of III. These three possibilities define three mutually exclusive aspectual properties. As such they might be represented by a single three-valued aspectual feature. In this case, we will proceed in a slightly different way, however. Instead of one ternary feature we will employ two binary ones. The first of these is the feature *STAT*, which we introduced in Section 5.2.1. Since we need this feature in any case, we might as well make use of it in the present context, too. The second feature is *PERF*, with values *+PERF* and *−PERF*. The distinction between *+STAT* and *−STAT*, we have seen, corresponds to that between states and events: an expression has *+STAT* when it is used to describe a state, *−STAT* when it is used to describe an event. *PERF* will be used to distinguish between those expressions that refer to result states (these have *+PERF*) and those which refer to parts of the schema other than the result state part. Among the latter expressions, which we assign the value *−PERF*, are both simple past tense sentences like (5.102), which refer to I+II, and progressive sentences like (5.103.i) which refer only to part I. Result states are, as the term implies, always states. Therefore expressions with the feature *+PERF* will always have the feature *+STAT*.

(5.104) is only one of several schemata, corresponding to different types of verbs or verb phrases. As we said, (5.104) is the schema for accomplishment verbs. The term "accomplishment verb" stems from Vendler, whose aspectual verb classifica-

[27]Certain uses of the term "aspect" suggest that it should apply to a wider class of properties, including some which do not signify that the referential target is related to the schema as part to whole, but that the content of the expression is connected with the schema in some other way. For instance, the verbs **begin** and **stop** are often referred to as aspectual verbs. The idea behind this use of the term *aspectual* is that between sentences like

(5.106) (i) Mary began to write the letter.

(ii) Mary stopped writing the letter.

and the sentence (5.102) there exist semantic connections of the same general type as between, say, (5.102) and (5.103.i): in each case the meaning of the sentence can be explained by relating it to the schema (5.104). But in the case of (5.106.ii) the relation is not simply one of part and whole. Rather, the sentence *asserts* that the part leading up to the culmination point (part I) was broken off before the culmination point was reached. And (5.106.i) describes *initial phases* of writing events, i.e. initial segments of phase I of schema (5.104).

tion we adopt here.[28] Vendler distinguishes four verb types in toto: *accomplishment* verbs, *achievemement* verbs, *activity* verbs and *state* verbs. Among the achievement verbs are verbs like **win** and **die**. From an aspectual point of view, they are quite similar to the accomplishment verbs. In fact, the relevant aspectual schema associated with achievements is just the one given in (5.104). They differ from accomplishments on just one point. The events described by simple past tense sentences with achievement verbs such as

(5.107) (i) Mary won the marathon.

(ii) Mary died.

consist just of their culmination points; the phase leading up to the culmination point is not part of such an event. This becomes clear when we compare the relation between progressive and non-progressive tenses for achievement verbs with the corresponding relation for accomplishments. As we saw in the case of (5.103.i), the past progressive of an accomplishment verb refers to part of what is referred to by the corresponding simple past (to part I of (5.104) as opposed to I+II.) In contrast, past progressives of achievement verbs, as in

(5.108) (i) Mary was winning the marathon.

(ii) Mary was dying.

refer to episodes that are not included in those that are described by simple pasts of such verbs. For instance, if Mary died at 10:15 p.m. on January 29th, 1991, then she was, at that time, not dying. The sentence (5.108.ii) can have been true only with reference to times preceding this one, e.g. the seven hours (or twelve days or whatever time it "took her to die") leading up to the actual time of death.

In fact, the difference between accomplishment verbs and achievement verbs shows up particularly clearly when they are combined with "punctual" adverbs such as **at 10:15 p.m.** Thus

(5.109) Mary died at 10:15 p.m.

is fine; and if it is true, then

(5.110) Mary was dying at 10:15 p.m.

is not. For the times at which she was dying precede the time of her death. In contrast,

---

[28][Vendler 1967]

(5.111) Mary wrote the letter at 10:15 p.m.

is a peculiar sentence, as the events described by the verb phrase **write the letter** do not seem to be of the sort for which it makes sense to say that they occurred at some particular moment of time. Inasmuch as (5.111) is acceptable at all, we must take the phrase **at 10:15 p.m.** to refer, in the loose way in which we often use such phrases, to some fairly short interval located around the indivisible instant which the phrase **10:15 p.m.** denotes strictly speaking; and we must assume that the letter was short enough, and that Mary wrote fast enough, for the entire event to fit within this small temporal space. It is much more natural to say things like

(5.112) (i) Mary wrote the letter this morning.
(ii) Mary wrote the letter between 10:45 and 11:15 this morning.

And when these sentences are true the corresponding progressives

(5.113) (i) Mary was writing the letter this morning.
(ii) Mary was writing the letter between 10:45 and 11:15 this morning.

are true as well.

To sum up: With accomplishment verbs the episode referred to by the progressive is included in that referred to by the non-progressive tense; in the case of achievement verbs the first episode precedes the second.

Achievements and accomplishments are alike in that the events described by them have intrinsic culmination points – once this point has been reached, the event has necessarily come to its conclusion.[29] But not all verbs are like this. In fact, the verbs belonging to Vendler's two remaining verb classes, the stative verbs and the activity verbs, all lack culmination points. Typical examples of stative verbs are **know** and **trust**. The episodes described by simple past tense sentences with stative verbs do not have culmination points. Consider

(5.114) Mary trusted John.

[29]With achievement verbs the "culmination point" is all there is to the event, so the term "culmination point" is a little odd here; but it is nevertheless true that the event could not have extended beyond it.

(5.114) carries a certain presumption that the state it describes came to an end before the time of utterance. For if the state had not come to an end, and the speaker knew this, then it would have been more natural for him to say some such thing as (5.115.i) or (5.115.ii).

(5.115) (i) Mary has trusted John for some time now.
(ii) Mary has trusted John since ... .

However, termination is only an implicature here, which can be cancelled through the addition of another clause.

(5.116) Mary trusted John, and for all I know she still does.

In this regard stative sentences differ from, for instance, accomplishments.

(5.117) Mary wrote the letter this morning, and for all I know she is still writing it.

is simply incoherent. In contrast, (5.116) will be reasonable in a situation where the speaker knows, with regard to some past period t, that Mary trusted Fred, but has no knowledge whether she continued to trust him after that. This information entitles him to assert the first conjunct of (5.116); and it does not prevent him from adding the second conjunct. This shows that states of the type reported by the first conjunct do not have an intrinsic culmination point. For if they did, then assertion of this conjunct would have been justified only if the speaker had registered that this point had in fact been reached. But if he had registered that, he would have known that the state had come to an end and so the second conjunct would have been false. (5.117) is incoherent precisely because there the first conjunct *entails* that the culmination point of the described event was reached at some past time. So the speaker cannot at the same time convey the thought that he is unsure whether it was reached.

If there is no culmination point, then there is no intrinsic separation of two distinct periods. Consequently, the schema representing stative verbs is an extremely simple one. It consists of a single stretch, comparable to the part I (or III) of (5.104).

(5.118)

state

The difference between the schemata (5.104) and (5.118) correlates with a well-known contrast that sets stative verbs apart from achievement verbs and accomplishment verbs. Progressive forms are possible for the latter but not for the former – phrases such as **was knowing** or **was trusting** are awkward if not outright ungrammatical. The difference between (5.104) and (5.118) allows us to interpret this contrast as follows. As we indicated above, it is the semantic function of the progressive to select as the target of description that period which leads up to but does not include the culmination point. For this selection to be possible there *must be* a culmination point. So the progressive is well-defined only for those verbs whose schemata include a culmination point. So the progressive is fine for verbs which have (5.104) for their schema, but not for verbs which have (5.118).[30]

Activity verbs are in one way like statives, in another they are more like achievements and accomplishments. They are like statives in that the episodes they describe have no natural culmination points. Take the acitivity verb **walk**. A period of walking might have extended beyond its actual duration and still be a period of walking. But activity verbs are unlike statives in that they allow for the progressive. And not just that, the progressive is often required. For instance, the sentences

(5.119) (i) Mary walked.

(ii) Yesterday morning at 10 Mary walked.

are strange when used, as they are here, without antecedent context. In fact, (5.119.ii) is not good in *any* context that we can think of; the right form is

(5.120) Yesterday morning at 10 Mary was walking.

(5.119.i) is acceptable only in certain contexts. One such context is the following: you and I are discussing the ways in which Mary has been getting to work during the past week, when public transport was on strike. In the course of that discussion I say

(5.121) Most days Mary got a lift from Fred. But yesterday was different. Yesterday she walked.

What distinguishes the context set up by the first three sentences of (5.121) from a 'null' context, such as that which the recipient of (5.119.i) will assume by default, is that the former already contains a particular event **e**, that of Mary getting to work on the day preceding the utterance of (5.121). The last sentence can then be understood as providing a new description of this event **e** – of her getting to work on foot rather than by other means. In other words, an activity verb such as

[30]Cf. [Smith 1991].

walk is not able to introduce a new event into the discourse, but it can be used to *redescribe* the event once it has been introduced by independent means. With the independently introduced event comes, in particular, its termination point. It is this termination point which, we believe, activity verbs are unable to introduce on their own.

This does not mean that unless such a verb is in the progressive it can only be used to redescribe an event is already part of the context. A verb like *walk* can introduce a new event provided it is accompanied by a suitable complementary phrase. In fact, activity verbs allow for a variety of complements which have this effect. For instance, **walk** can be complemented as in (5.122.i) or in (5.122.ii).

(5.122) (i) Yesterday morning Mary walked to the beach.

(ii) Yesterday morning Mary walked for two hours.

In either case an end point is imposed, in (5.122.i) as the goal of the walk, in (5.122.ii) as the point of time two hours after the activity began. Both (5.122.i) and (5.122.ii) are fine without special contextual support.

These facts suggest the following assessment of activity verbs. Like the episodes described by stative verbs, those described by uncomplemented activity verbs lack a natural culmination point. But stative verbs and activity verbs differ from each other in that activity verbs are incomplete in a sense in which stative verbs are not: the simple non-progressive forms of activity verbs describe (or perhaps we should say, "try to describe") episodes that consist of a period leading up to some point which terminates the episode. But the activity verb is unable to provide such a bound by itself. So unless a bound is supplied by something other than the verb (by a constituent of the sentence or alternatively by the context in which the sentence appears) the verb won't describe what it is committed to, and thus defeats, as it were, its own purpose.

This analysis suggests in turn that the schema corresponding to activity verbs is like that for achievement and accomplishment verbs and not like that for the stative verbs. Thus accomplishment verbs, achievement verbs and activity verbs share the schema (5.104); they differ with regard to the part(s) of this schema that are available as denotations for sentences in the simple past. For accomplishment verbs and achievement verbs these are, we saw, parts I+II and part I, respectively. For activity verbs the denotations are, as they are for the accomplishment verbs, I+II. But since activity verbs do not provide part II themselves, this part has to be supplied externally. If it is not, then the non-progressive use of the verb is infelicitous.

The differences between accomplishments, achievements and activities, we have noted, reduce to the answers they provide to the following two questions: (i) do the episodes described by simple past clauses include part I? (They do in the case of activity verbs and accomplishment verbs; they do not in the case of achievement verbs) (ii) is part II given by the verb itself, or does it have to be supplied otherwise? (II is given by achievement verbs and accomplishment verbs; it is not given by activity verbs.)

We can represent these differences by augmenting (5.104) as below

(5.123)

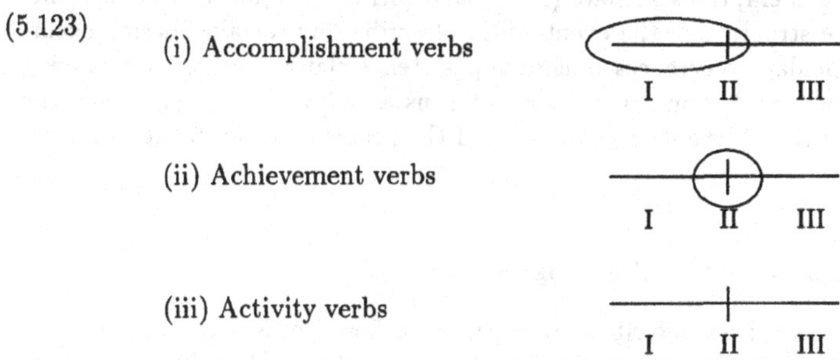

Here the circled parts are the ones described by certain non-progressive forms of the verb, in particular by its simple past. Note that the diagram for activity verbs has no circled part at all. This is to convey that such tense forms of activity verbs are not felicitous unless a "culmination point" is made available by something else.[31]

Aspectual verb classes such as the four distinguished by Vendler are often referred to as *Aktionsarten*.[32] According to the account we have just sketched, an Aktionsart is a certain set of aspectual properties, pertaining to (a) the basic aspectual schema for the class; (b) whether the verb itself makes available a culmination point; and (c) whether (in those cases where the schema includes a culmination point) the episodes described by simple clauses include a period leading up to the culmination point. (a), (b), and (c) might be thought of as three binary features, so long as we keep in mind that they are not independent: if the schema is that of the stative verbs, then the distinctions (b) and (c) do not arise; and where the

[31]The demarcation between activity verbs and accomplishment verbs is complicated by the problem which uses of the verb are to be counted as *simple*. We have been assuming that simple uses of a verb like **walk** are like those in (5.119) or (5.121), where the verb appears without a complement, like **to the beach**. In contrast, what we took to be the simple uses of the accomplishment verb **write** were those in which it is accompanied by an object phrase such as **a letter** or **the letter**. These ways of identifying the simple uses of **walk** and **write** accord with their usual classification as intransitive and transitive verbs; but note that a verb like **write** can be used transitively, as in **at 10 o'clock Mary was writing** and that intransitive **write** behaves very much like (uncomplemented) **walk**. Thus the division between accomplishment verbs and activity verbs depends in part on what we are prepared to count as the verb's arguments.

[32]The term *Aktionsart* was first introduced by the Junggrammatiker, a school of mostly German linguists which established itself during the final two decades of the 19th century. For an early use of the term see [Agrell 1908]. For a well known discussion see [Dowty 1979], p. 51ff.

schema is that of the non-stative verbs, only three of the four logically possible combinations of feature values for (b) and (c) are realized.[33]

5.3.3 Aspectual Operators and Aspectual Shift

As we explained them, the schemata (5.118) and (5.123.i–iii) not only show something about the structure of the eventualities described by certain "basic" occurrences (in particular occurrences in simple past tense clauses) of verbs belonging to the corresponding Aktionsart, they also tell us about what happens when the verb is put into the progressive. The effect of the progressive can be summarized as follows:

(5.124) **Semantic Effect of the Progressive:**

> The eventualities described by progressive forms of a verb **v** are of the type which is represented by that part of the schema corresponding to the Aktionsart of **v** which terminates in, but does not include, the culmination point.

When applied to the schemata in (5.123), (5.124) returns in each case the eventuality type defined by the portion marked as Part I (we will discuss in Section 5.3.4.2 what such an eventuality characterization really means). To schema (5.118), which has no culmination point, (5.124) cannot be applied at all, which accounts for the inability of stative verbs to take progressive forms.

The semantic effect of the perfect can be described in a similar way or, more accurately, it can when the verb is non-stative.

(5.125) **Semantic Effect of the Perfect:**

> The eventualities described by the perfect of a verb **v** are of the type which is represented by that part of the schema corresponding to the Aktionsart of **v** which starts at, but does not include the culmination point.

---

[33]It is not hard to see why the fourth case – that where the verb does not provide a culmination point and where the period "leading up to the culmination point" is not part of the episode described by a simple clause – cannot arise. A verb with these properties would, like an activity verb, need an externally supplied culmination point; but the external source can supply the culmination point only as the cut-off point for some episode supplied by the verb; and that is precisely what a verb with the presumed properties would fail to do.

Like (5.124), this principle is applicable to the schemata in (5.123) but not to (5.118). However, stative verbs admit the perfect just as readily as non-statives. So, (5.124) does not give an exhaustive account of the perfect; we need a complementary principle to characterize for the perfects of stative verbs and verb phrases.

As it turns out, we need not just one additional principle, but two. English perfects of stative verbs can be used in two quite different ways. To see this consider the sentence

(5.126) Mary has lived in Amsterdam for three years.

This sentence has two readings. It can mean that there was, somewhere in the past, a three year period during which Mary lived in Amsterdam. But it can also be taken to mean that Mary *is* living in Amsterdam now and that this state of affairs has already been going on for three years. The first reading – which seems to be the only one available when the perfect occurs by itself, as in

(5.127) Mary has lived in Amsterdam.

– closely resembles perfects of non-stative verbs: the state referred to is the one that comes about through termination of the episode described by the corresponding non-perfect verb form (i.e. the state of *having lived* in Amsterdam results through termination of the state of *living* in Amsterdam). This use of the perfect can be brought into line with what we have said about perfects of non-stative verbs, if we assume that the perfect of a non-stative verb can trigger a revision of its associated schema, in which the termination of the state is explicitly represented. Thus (5.118) is transformed into

(5.128)

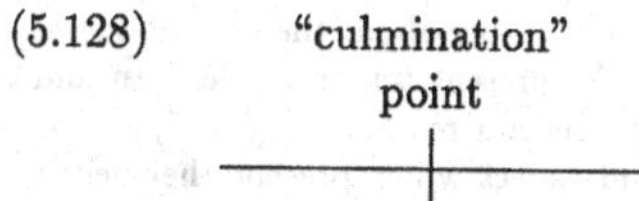

To this schema (5.125) can now be applied.[34]

The second reading of (5.126) cannot be quite so easily cast into the mould of (5.125). We should perhaps not be too much disturbed that this use of the perfect

[34]It may sound a little odd to talk about a "culmination point" in this context. For though a state can be brought to an end, this end is as a rule not an intrinsic part of what it is to be in the state (in the way in which completing a letter is an intrinsic part of the event of writing it). However, the event terminology is not important here. Substitute "termination point" for "culmination point" if that seems more appropriate!

proves to be the odd one out, for it appears to be something of an idiosyncrasy of English.[35] In German and French, for instance, languages into which most perfects – including (5.126) on its first reading – translate as perfects (**Marie a écrit la lettre, Mary hat den Brief geschrieben, Marie a habité ici pendant trois ans, Mary hat hier drei Jahre lang gewohnt**), one must use the simple present to capture the second reading of (5.126) (e.g. **Marie habite ici depuis trois ans, Mary wohnt hier seit drei Jahren**).

An account of why English uses the perfect to express this second reading must distinguish two separate questions: 1. Why *can* the English perfect be used to express this reading? and 2. Why does English *require* the use of the perfect for this purpose? We will set the second question aside.[36] The first, however, should get an answer.

But what kind of answer? Ideally one would hope for a basic account of the perfect that is compatible with all its uses, including the two readings of (5.126). Which reading or readings arise in particular contexts should then be explicable through the interaction of this account with additional features specific to those contexts. So what is it, we should ask, that all the above interpretations of the perfect have in common? Here is our hypothesis. We suggest that all readings fit the principle that the perfect VP describes a state r_s which results from the occurrence of a certain event. When the underlying VP is non-stative, this is an event described by the non-perfect VP itself; when the VP is stative, it is some event associated with a state s of the type described by this VP. So far, we have assumed that in this second case this event relates to the termination of s.[37] The puzzling second reading of (5.126) comes about when we take the event associated with s to be not its end but its beginning.[38]

[35]A similar use of the perfect is found in a few other languages. One finds it, for instance, in Swedish, but it is subject to somewhat different restrictions. (Görel Sandstrom, personal communication)

[36]Arguably this is not so much a question about the perfect, but rather about the present tense. What is it about the English simple present, as opposed to the present tenses of German and French, say, which prevents it from being used to express the second reading of (5.127)? This is one of many questions about the fine structure of tense and aspect which present themselves when the tense-and-aspect systems of different languages are compared. Most questions of this type go well beyond the scope of the present chapter.

[37]Our formulation suggested that the event consists of s together with its termination. However, one could just as well identify the event with the termination on its own; the resulting interpretation would come to the same.

[38]Identifying the beginning rather than the end of s as the event which produces the result state r_s described by the perfect VP has the consequence that r_s and s are concurrent. This is what sets this particular reading apart from the others. It may be responsible for the apparently marginal status that the option enjoys. (We saw that the perfects of French and German do not allow for this option at all. Moreover, in English it is limited to perfects that are accompanied by a **for**-phrase, or by one of a very restricted set of other phrase types (see Section 5.5.2)). We have no explanation of why the option is restricted in these particular ways.

The progressive and the perfect are often treated as *aspectual operators*, operators which transform the meaning of the underlying non-progressive or non-perfect verb, verb phrase or sentence into that of its progressive or perfect counterpart. The present proposal doesn't quite fit this picture, though it comes close. It doesn't quite fit because we have defined progressive and perfect as operating on the full schemata (5.118) and (5.123.i–iii) and not on those parts of them that are selected by what we have called the "simple" uses of the verbs or verb phrases in question. But this is a difference of no real importance. One always can, starting from the episodes described by those simple uses, first expand to the corresponding full schemata and then proceed in the manner we have described.

The progressive and the perfect are the only aspectual operators we discuss in this book. But natural language contains many others. For instance, most natural languages have aspectual verbs such as **start, continue, stop, finish.**[39] Semantically, such verbs can be regarded as operators which map the meaning of a verb phrase such as **write the letter** onto the meaning of the corresponding compound phrase (e.g., **stopped writing the letter**), in which the former occurs as an embedded gerund or infinitival, and in which it acts as argument to the aspectual verb. A verb like **stop** qualifies as aspectual by our criteria insofar as its effect can be described with reference to the schemata (5.118) and (5.123.i–iii) – in connection with non-stative verbs **stop** means that the episode leading up to but not including the culmination point in (5.123.i–iii) is terminated before the natural culmination point is reached; in connection with stative verbs it means simply that the state was terminated.[40]

There are many other natural language constructions that involve, in one way or another, aspectual change. But not all of these are naturally represented as aspectual operators. One example is the combination of prepositional phrases like **to the beach** and **for two hours** with an activity verb such as **walk.** As we saw in the last section, this combination produces verb phrases which allow for straightforward use in the simple past. In fact, the verb phrase **walk to the beach** behaves for all effects and purposes like accomplishment phrases such as **write a letter**, and so it should be considered an instance of the same Aktionsart. Much the same could be said about **walk for two hours.** A similar phenomenon, but one involving an aspect shift in the opposite direction, is the combination of accomplishment verbs with bare plurals as argument phrases. For instance, the verb phrases **wrote the letter, wrote a letter, wrote the letters, wrote several letters** all behave like accomplishments. But **wrote letters** does not. Thus **Mary**

---

[39]See footnote 27 on p. 559.

[40]**finish**, in contrast, means that the natural culmination point was reached – compare **Mary stopped writing the letter** and **Mary finished writing the letter**. Note also that **finish** is peculiar when combined with a stative verb – cf. **Mary finished trusting Bill**; **Mary finished being ill**, etc. – or with an activity verb – cf. **Mary finished running.**

wrote letters within two hours is odd, whereas it is perfectly natural to say **Mary wrote the letters within two hours**, etc.

These remarks only scratch the surface of a large complex of problems relating to aspect and aspectual change. We will not pursue this subject any further, except for what we will have to say in the next sections about the representation of perfects and progressives and some observations in Section 5.5 (see in particular 5.5.3). To conclude this general discussion of the topic, we note something that has emerged in the course of this discussion, but which we have not so far made explicit. The Aktionsarten are often presented as ways of classifying verbs; and it has been in this spirit that we introduced them in Section 5.3.2. In the present section, however, it has become plain that this classification ought to be applicable not only to single verbs, but also to larger syntactic units such as verb phrases and, arguably, even to full sentences. Once the application domain for aspectual distinctions has been thus enlarged, the central problem for the theory of aspect is to determine how the aspectual characteristics of complex phrases are determined by those of their parts.[41]

We are now ready to extend our construction algorithm to progressive and perfect tense forms.

5.3.4 DRS-Construction for Perfects and Progressives

We proceed in the following order: first, we consider sentences involving perfects of non-stative verbs. Next, we look at the progressive. The third and final part of the section will be concerned with perfects of stative verbs.

5.3.4.1 Perfects of Non-Stative Verbs

Consider

(5.129) Mary has met the president.

We assume for this sentence the following syntactic structure.[42]

---

[41] See in particular [Verkuyl 1972], to our knowledge the first essay in which the need for such an enlarged domain for the Aktionsarten is persuasively demonstrated and which at the same time engaged upon a serious programme for describing how the aspectual properties of complex expressions can be derived from the semantic properties of their syntactic constituents.

[42] We repeat our earlier warning: the distinction between VP and VP′ should *not* be understood in the sense of X-bar theory (e.g. [Chomsky 1970], [Jackendoff 1977]). (For a rationale behind our use of the category labels VP and VP′ see Section 5.7)

(5.130)

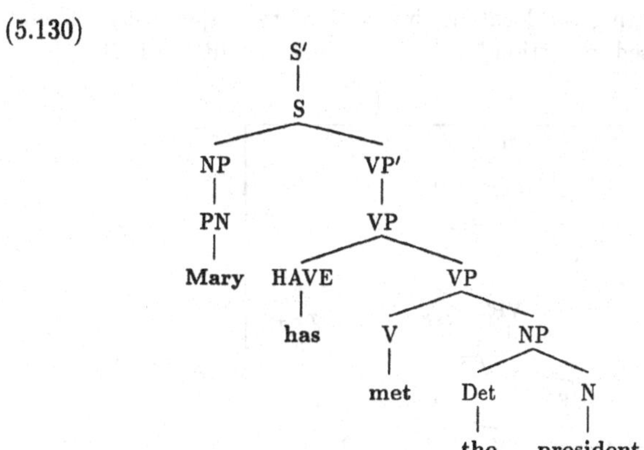

However, as in Section 5.2.1, mere configurational structure is not enough. We also need, at the right nodes, information about tense and aspect. Thus, if we are to proceed along the lines of Section 5.2.5, we must, at node VP′, have at our disposal the information encoded by *TENSE* and *STAT*. Moreover, we will need to know at some point in the course of our construction that the given sentence is in the perfect. The construction procedure for which we have opted requires this information at the higher of the two VP-nodes. We will also need to know that that VP results from "applying" the perfect to an underlying non-stative verb phrase. This information is attached to the lower VP. So the tree that is to serve as input to the construction algorithm will contain at least the feature information shown in (5.131).

(5.131)

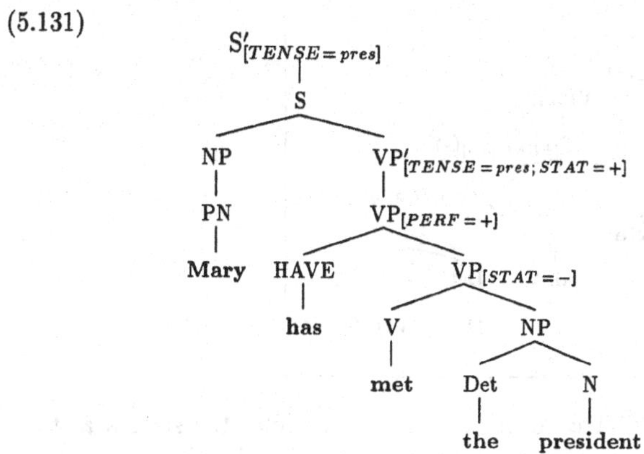

The first two construction steps to be performed on (5.131) introduce the discourse referents **t** and **x** representing the location time and Mary, respectively. These steps are like those discussed in Section 5.2.5. They yield the DRS (5.132).

(5.132)

n x t

Mary(x)

t = n

S(t)

x VP′$_{[TENSE = pres;\ STAT = +]}$

VP$_{[PERF = +]}$

HAVE VP$_{[STAT = -]}$

have V NP

met Det N

the president

The next step, triggered by the VP′-node, introduces a new state discourse referent **s**. This step too is familiar.

(5.133)

n s t x

t = n

t ⊆ s

Mary(x)

S(s)

x VP′(s)

VP$_{[PERF = +]}$(s)

HAVE VP$_{[STAT = -]}$

have V NP

met Det N

the president

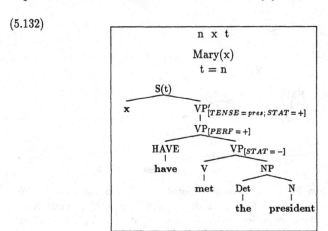

The third step is the one that concerns us here. It analyses the state **s** as the result of an occurrence of an event **e** of the kind described by the verb phrase corresponding to the lower VP. We only record the purely temporal dimension of the relation between **e** and **s**: **s** starts the very moment **e** ends; or, as it is sometimes put, **e** and **s** *abut*. We represent this relationship as $\mathbf{e} \supset\!\subset \mathbf{s}$. This step produces the structure

(5.134)

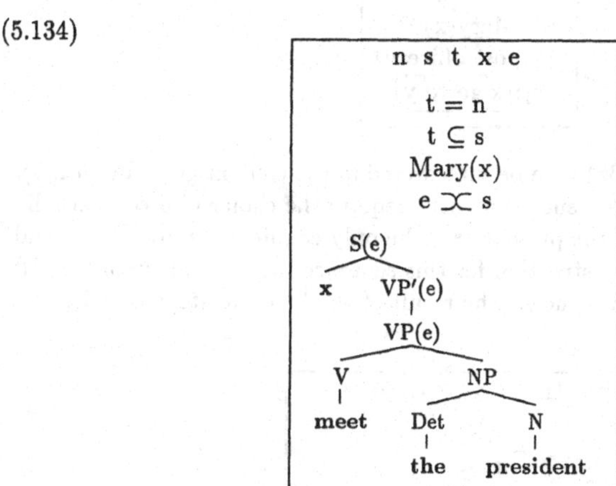

The one remaining step concerns the NP **the president**. Using the usual notation which ignores the internal structure of definite descriptions, and throwing away what syntactic structure remains, we obtain as final DRS (5.135).

(5.135)

n s t x e y
t = n t ⊆ s Mary(x) e ⊃⊂ s the president(y) e: [x meet y]

Our next example involves a past perfect.

(5.136) Mary went to the post office. She had written the letter.

The first sentence of (5.136) yields the DRS (5.137).

(5.137)

$$\boxed{\begin{array}{c} n\ t_1\ e_1\ x\ y \\ \\ e_1 \subseteq t_1 \\ t_1 < n \\ \text{Mary(x)} \\ \text{the post office(y)} \\ e_1{:}\ \boxed{\text{x go to y}} \end{array}}$$

The second sentence of (5.136) is to be interpreted in the context given by (5.137). As we argued in Section 5.2.2, such sentences require the choice of a contextually specified reference point. In the present case the only candidate is $\mathbf{e}_1$. The second step required by the DRS-construction for this sentence, which deals with the NP **she**, is of no particular interest now. The result of the first two steps is as in

(5.138)

$$\boxed{\begin{array}{c} n\ t_1\ e_1\ x\ y\ t_2\ s_2\ z \\ \\ e_1 \subseteq t_1 \\ t_1 < n \\ \text{Mary(x)} \\ \text{the post office(y)} \\ e_1{:}\ \boxed{\text{x go to y}} \\ \text{Rpt} := e_1 \\ s_2 \bigcirc t_2 \\ t_2 < n \\ e_1 \subseteq s_2 \\ z = x \end{array}}$$

S(s_2)
- z
- VP′(s_2)
  - VP$_{[PERF=+]}$(s_2)
    - HAVE — have
    - VP$_{[STAT=-]}$)
      - V — written
      - NP
        - Det — the
        - N — letter

The next step is analogous to the fourth step in the DRS-construction for (5.129). This and the remaining step produce the final DRS (5.139).

(5.139)

$n\ t_1\ e_1\ x\ y\ t_2\ s_2\ z\ e_2\ u$
$e_1 \subseteq t_1$
$t_1 < n$
Mary(x)
the post office(y)
e_1: $\boxed{\text{x go to y}}$
$s_2 \bigcirc t_2$
$t_2 < n$
$e_1 \subseteq s_2$
$z = x$
the letter(u)
$e_2 \supset\!\subset s_2$
e_2: $\boxed{\text{z write u}}$

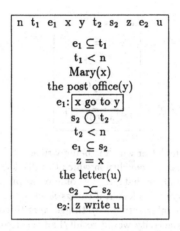

5.3.4.2 Progressives

In Section 5.1.3.2 we gave a provisional representation for a progressive sentence (the second sentence of (5.54)), in which we left the progressive VP **be wearing** untouched. As a consequence, the DRS reveals no information about the semantic relationship between this predicate and the one expressed by the non-progressive verb form **wear**. What we would like to offer at this point is a processing principle that reduces progressive VPs further and thereby makes this relationship explicit – much in the way we reduced perfect VPs in the last section. Unfortunately, we are not in a position to do this. In this respect progressives differ from perfects.

The difference which prevents us from improving significantly on our representation of (5.54) is this. The state described by a perfect can always be analysed as the result of an event that *actually* occurred; but the state described by a progressive verb phrase does not always lead to an event described by the corresponding non-progressive VP (See [Dowty 1979].). It would be wrong, for instance, to represent

(5.140) Mary is writing a letter.

by the DRS (5.141).

(5.141)

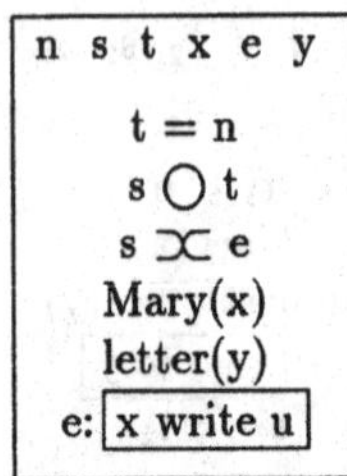

For (5.141) entails that the letter which is being written will be written, i.e. that it will be completed; and that is a conclusion which (5.140) does not support. All that (5.140) allows us to conclude is that what is going on at present is the sort of thing that *would* result in a completed letter, if things *were* to continue as planned. But what exactly does this counterfactual – *if* things were to continue/had continued as planned, *then* Mary's activity would result/had resulted in a finished letter – exactly mean; and, anyway, is such a counterfactual paraphrase of the progressive plausible also in other cases? These questions are still waiting for definite answers, in spite of the many attempts that have been made to deal with them.[43]

Since we have no answer to these questions, we cannot do much better here than we did in Section 5.2. Here as there we are forced to side-step the real issue. We do this by representing the predicates expressed by progressive VPs as the results of applying a certain operator **PROG** (the "progressive operator") to the predicates that are expressed by the corresponding non-progressive VPs. The semantic analysis of this operator we leave as a topic for further research.

With this proviso, the DRS for (5.140) will come to

(5.142)

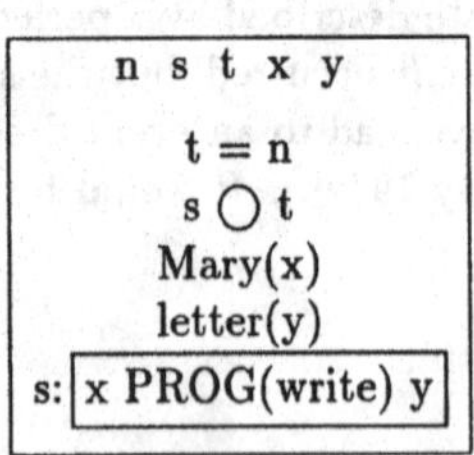

Here the condition **x PROG(write) y**, used to characterize the state **s**, simply says that **x** and **y** stand in the relation which we obtain when the operator **PROG** is applied to the relation **write**. But it doesn't say anything about how the two

[43]An insightful recent analysis of these problems can be found in [Landman 1992].

relations **write** and **PROG(write)** are connected.[44]

Now that we have decided to side-step the real semantic problem that progressives present, there is not much that needs to be said about the actual steps that are involved in constructing the DRS for a progressive sentence. But let us have a quick look at the one step that is new. We already gave an example of the syntactic structure we assume for progressive VPs in (5.58). Analogously, the syntactic tree for sentence (5.140) is assumed to have the form

(5.143)

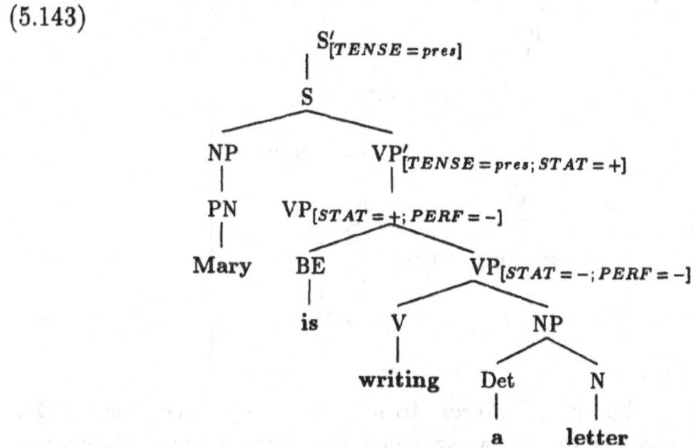

The first three processing steps convert this structure into (5.144).

[44]The progressives of verbs of creation, such as **write, build, bake** etc., pose a special problem. A sentence like (5.140) can be true in situations where the process is broken off, so that only a very small fragment of a letter is actually produced. Is it right in such a situation to analyse the sentence as expressing a relation between the subject **Mary** and some object **y** which is a letter? We think not. This is another difficulty that cannot be solved within the present framework. Its solution ought to be part of a general account of the semantic relationship between **PROG(v)** and **v**.

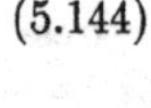

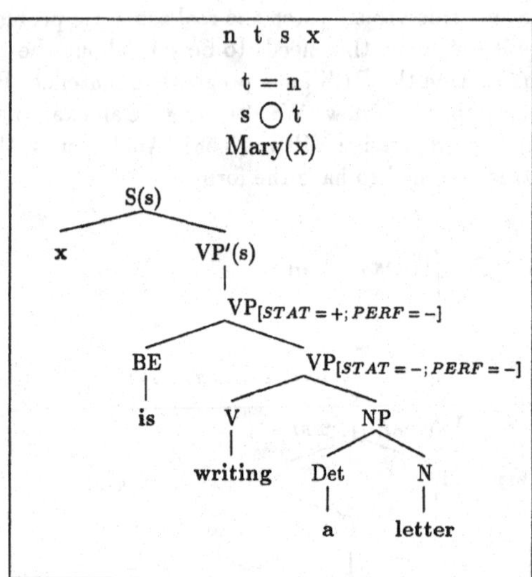

The next step – which is the one of interest to us here – introduces the PROG operator. However, and this is slightly at variance with what we said above, the structure of the tree in (5.144) makes clear that PROG is to be introduced as an operator acting on the *complex* phrase **write a letter**, and not exclusively on the verb **write**. The result may be represented as in (5.145).

(5.145)

n t s x

t = n
s ○ t
Mary(x)
s: [x PROG(write a letter)]

The final construction step should deal with the NP **a letter**. The possibility for which we will opt here is that according to which a discourse referent **y** representing this NP and the attendant condition **letter(y)** are introduced outside the scope of PROG, reanalysing PROG itself as operating on the verb only. The result of this is the DRS (5.142). As we noted already this way of analysing the progressive phrase is problematic, as part of a letter need not qualify as a letter (especially when it is a small, initial part). But, as we indicated an alternative analysis, in which the discourse referent introduced for **a letter** somehow remains within the scope of PROG raises problems which we cannot tackle with the tools available.

5.3.4.3 Perfects of Stative Verb Phrases

In Section 5.3.3 we observed that

(5.127) Mary has lived in Amsterdam.

has only one reading, whereas

(5.126) Mary has lived in Amsterdam for three years.

has two. We suggested that the VP of (5.127) should be interpreted as describing a state **s** resulting from the termination of another state **s′**, which latter state fits the description provided by the non-perfect VP. Thus the processing rule for the perfect in (5.127) has to be a little more complicated than the one used in Section 5.3.4.1, since it must also yield a representation of the event which terminates **s**. We show the effect of this rule by displaying the DRS immediately before its application and the one that directly results from it.[45]

(5.146)

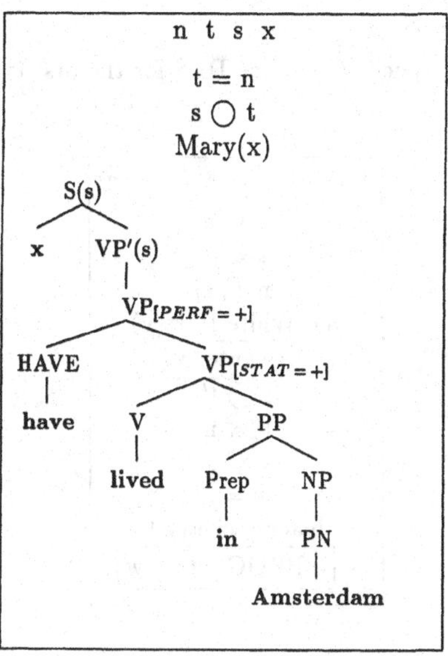

[45]The condition of (5.147) **e = end(s′)** is a new addition to our DRS-vocabulary. Its intended meaning should be clear, as should be that of the condition **e = beg(s′)**, to be found in DRS (5.158). For the formal semantics of **end** and **beg**, see Section 5.6.

(5.147)

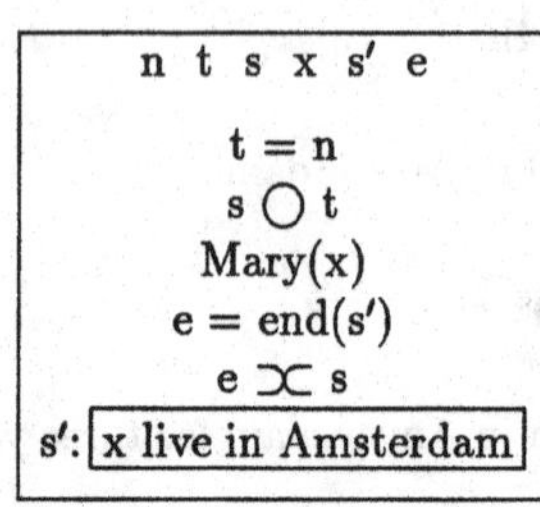

As a second example we consider a sentence, in which a perfect is applied to a progressive form. Suppose that we continue (5.54) after the second sentence as in (5.148).

(5.148) A man entered the White Hart. He was wearing a black jacket.
He had been running.

According to our latest specification, the DRS for the first two sentences[46] is

(5.149)

n e t x y s t′ u w

$e \subseteq t$
$t < n$
man(x)
the White Hart(y)
e: [x enter y]
s ○ t′
$t' < n$
$e \subseteq s$
$u = x$
black jacket(w)
s: [u PROG(wear) w]

The third sentence of (5.148) has the syntactic analysis given in (5.150)

[46] Compare (5.59′), p. 525.

(5.150)

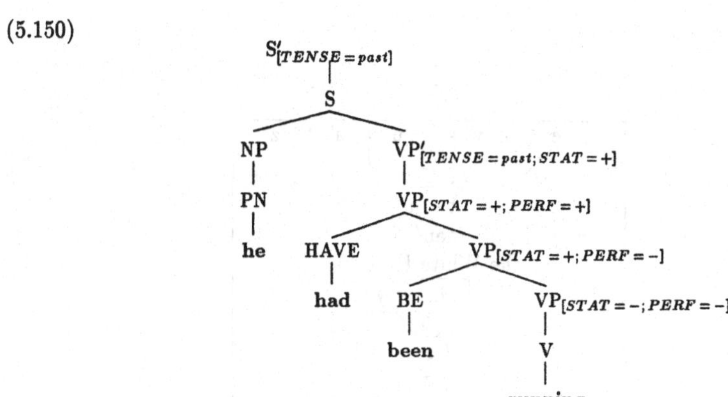

The first of the construction steps needed to integrate (5.150) into (5.149) introduces a new state **s'**, which it locates at a new location time **t''**, and chooses as reference time (just as was done for the second sentence) the last mentioned event **e**. After this step and standard processing of **he**, we get (5.151).

(5.151)

n e t x y s t′ u w s′ t″ z
$e \subseteq t$ $t < n$ man(x) the White Hart(y) e: [x enter y] $s \bigcirc t'$ $t' < n$ $e \subseteq s$ $u = x$ black jacket(w) s: [u PROG(wear) w] Rpt := e $s' \bigcirc t''$ $t'' < n$ $e \subseteq s'$ $z = x$
S(s′) [z VP′(s′) [$VP_{[STAT=+;\, PERF=+]}(s')$ [HAVE [have] $VP_{[STAT=+;\, PERF=-]}$ [BE [been] VP [V [running]]]]]]

The next step deals with the top VP-node, in the manner explained in Section 5.3.4, yielding

(5.152)

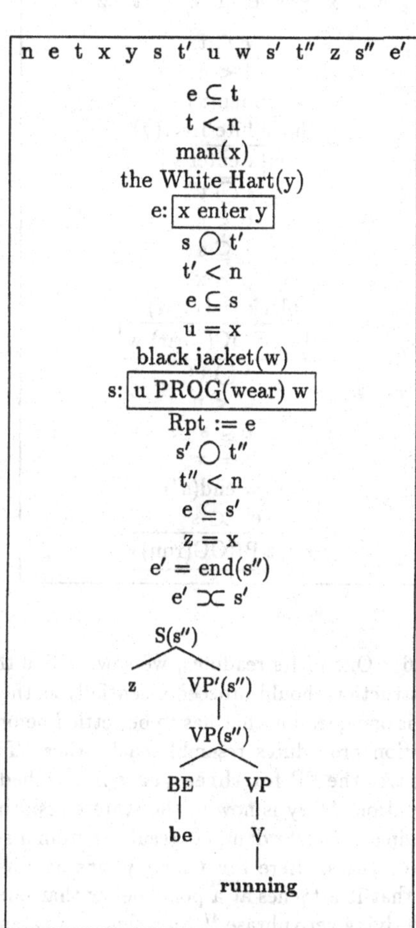

Now the rule for progressive VPs applies. It turns the structure under the higher VP of (5.150) into **PROG(run)**. So the final product is

(5.153)

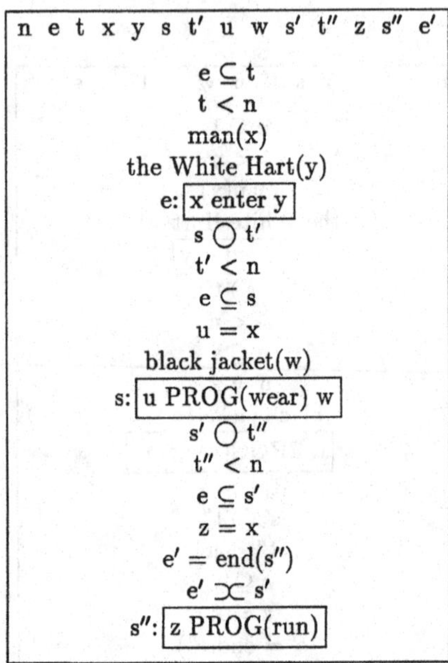

We now turn to (5.126). One of its readings, we saw, is like that of (5.127). For this reading DRS-construction should proceed essentially as the DRS-construction for (5.127). But there is one question that has to be settled before we can articulate how the two construction procedures resemble each other. This is the question where in the syntactic tree the PP **for three years** is attached. According to the reading under consideration, Mary is now in the state s resulting from a previous three year period of living in Amsterdam, i.e. resulting from a state s′ of her living in Amsterdam for three years. Here **for three years** acts as a qualification of s′. So we will assume that it attaches at a point below that one where the perfect combines with the underlying verb phrase.[47] Specifically, we assume that the phrase attaches at the same level as the PP **in Amsterdam**; in other words, we treat it as a further "argument" to the verb **live**:

[47]Attaching **for three years** in this particular place may be problematic for syntactic reasons. But given our earlier syntactic decisions it is the only option available to us; see Section 5.7.

(5.154)

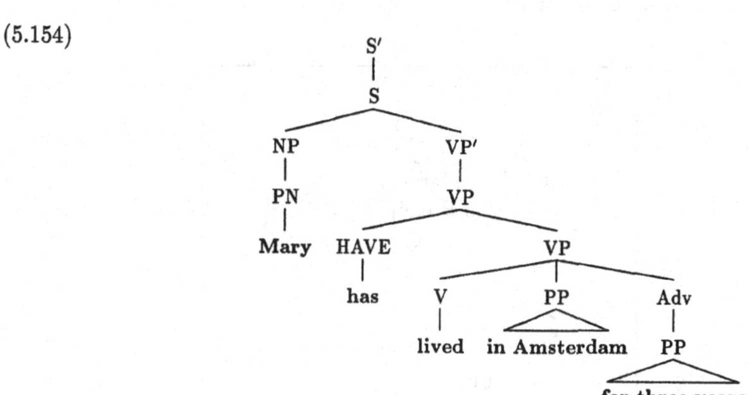

The semantic representation of (5.126) requires a semantic representation of **for three years**. We will have more to say about the semantics of **for**-phrases in Section 5.5.2. For now let it suffice that the phrase introduces a discourse referent **mt**, standing for an amount of time, which is characterized on the one hand as **three years** and on the other as the duration of the state s′; **dur** will be a function that maps intervals and eventualities onto the amounts of time they last. The DRS-construction for the reading of (5.126) which corresponds to that of (5.127) is now straightforward. The first construction step of interest here deals with the upper VP-node of (5.155)

(5.155)

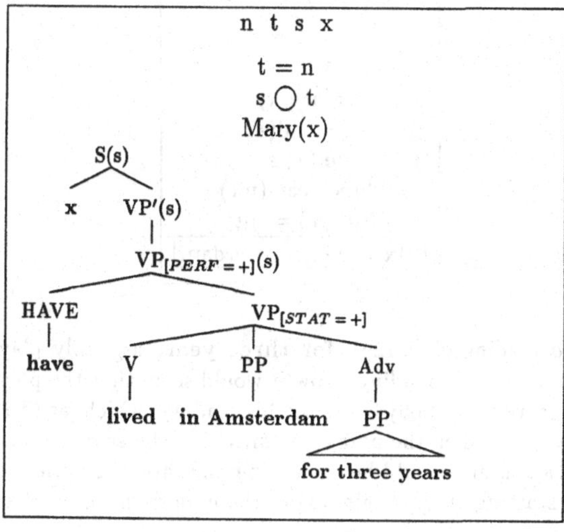

and yields the structure in (5.156).

(5.156)

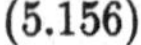

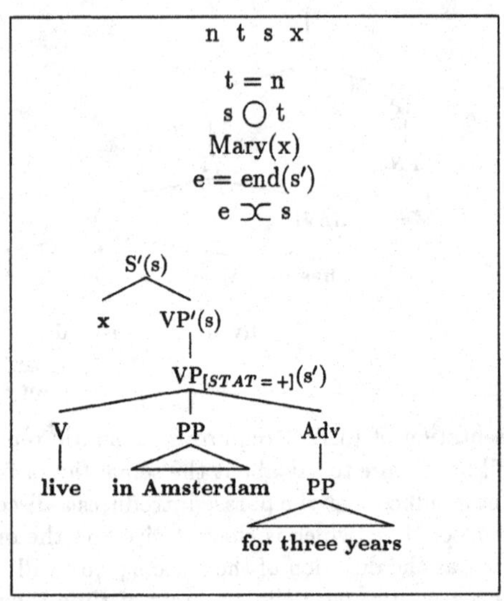

Next (5.156) will be reduced to

(5.157)

n t s x s′ e mt

t = n
s ○ t
Mary(x)
e = end(s′)
e ⊃⊂ s
three years(mt)
dur(s′) = mt
s′: x live in Amsterdam

In the second reading of (5.126), **for three years** arguably plays a different role than it does in the first reading. Now it would seem that the phrase combines directly with the perfect, thereby licensing this reading (which, as (5.127) shows, is in general not possible when the phrase is omitted). The semantics corresponding to this syntactic structure should be something like this: the perfect describes the result state **s** as starting at the beginning of the underlying state **s′** and as lasting for as long as three years, with the proviso that **s′** has not yet come to an end. As **s** and **s′** are concurrent in this case, it is hard to tell whether the **for**-phrase should be seen as characterizing **s** or **s′**. However, we know of no case where a **for**-phrase can be used as characterizing the result state described by a perfect.[48] So we assume that again, as in our analysis of the first reading of (5.126), **for three hours** acts as a characterization of **s′**.

This gives us all the factual information needed to state the construction rule that leads to the second interpretation of perfects with **for**-phrases. We will not go through the construction steps explicitly, but limit ourselves to the DRS which could be derived from (5.126) with the help of the construction rule given below.

(5.158)

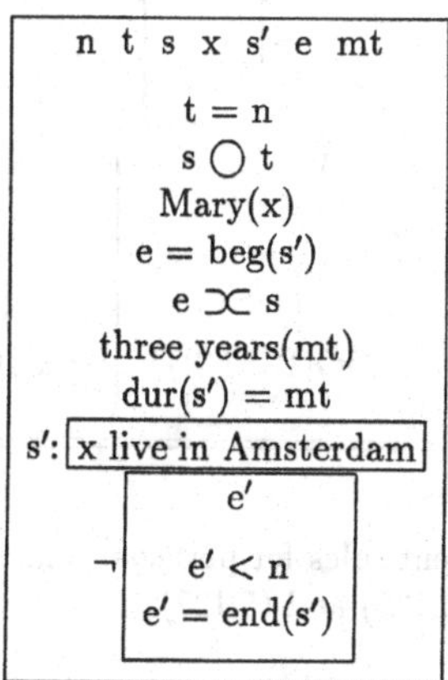

We end Section 5.3.4 with an explicit statement of the construction rules for perfects and progressives. We first give the rule for progressives. INF is an operator that maps β onto its infinitival form.

[48]For instance, it is impossible to interpret the sentence **Mary has eaten for half an hour** as meaning that she ate half an hour ago and has thus been for half an hour in the state of having eaten.

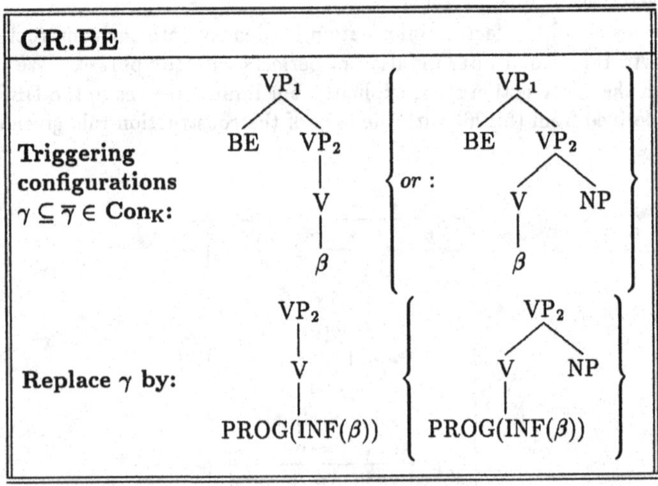

There are a number of different rules for perfects. The first two concern the standard cases, represented by (5.131) and (5.127).

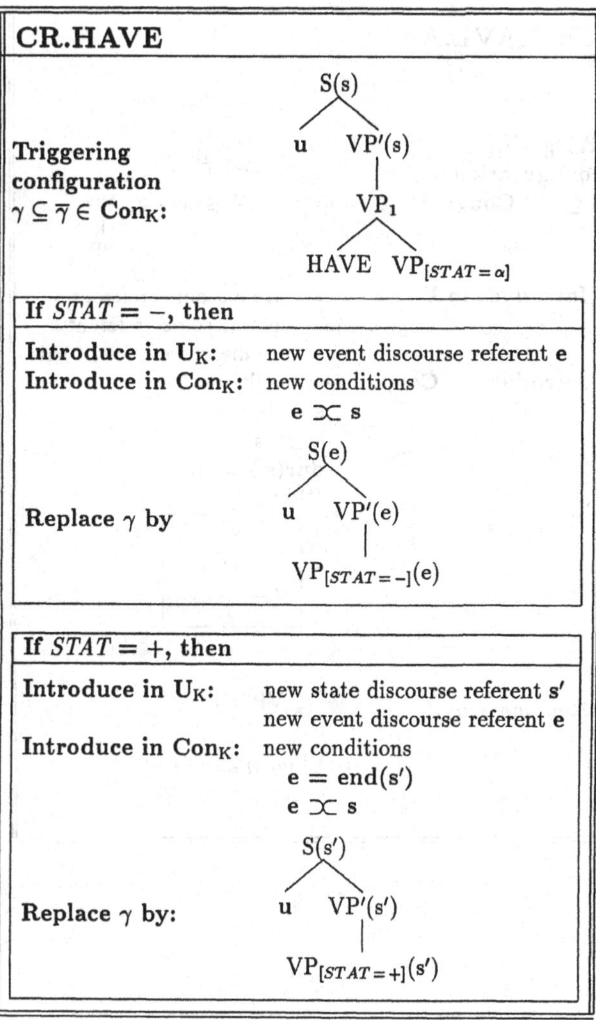

The next two rules deal with the two readings of (5.126).

CR.HAVE.Adv

Triggering configuration $\gamma \subseteq \overline{\gamma} \in Con_K$:

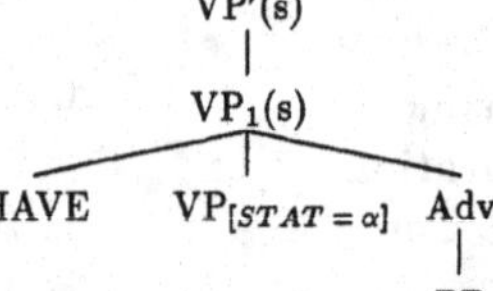

Introduce in U_K: new state discourse referent **s'**
new event discourse referent **e**
new time discourse referent **mt**

Introduce in Con_K: new conditions

$\mathbf{e = beg(s')}$

$\mathbf{e \supset\subset s}$

$\mathbf{dur(s') = mt}$

$\mathbf{PP(t)}$

$$\neg \boxed{\begin{array}{c} e' \\ \\ e' \leq n \\ e' = end(s') \end{array}}$$

Replace γ by:

$$\begin{array}{c} VP'(s') \\ | \\ VP_{[STAT=+]}(s') \end{array}$$

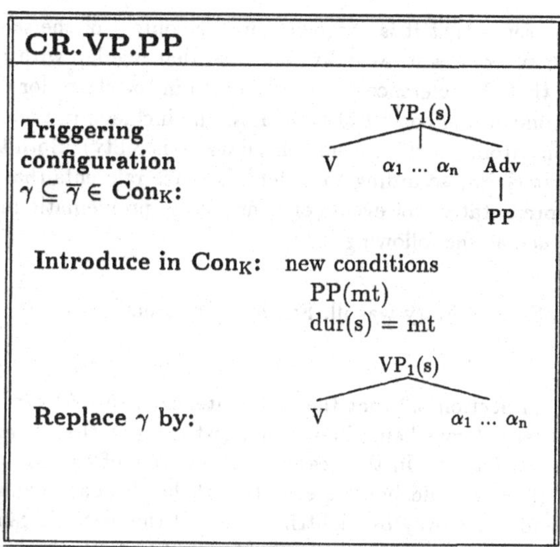

Exercises

1. Construct a DRS for the following discourse:

   My sister will send you a book which she bought yesterday. It is very funny. It is also quite obscene. I read it last night. She had not lent it to me. I had sneaked it from her bag. (From: Anonymous electronic mail)

2. Construct a DRS for the following discourse:

   (a) It was a tense moment. The phone was ringing, the baby was yelling, the kettle was screaming; at least the milk, which had boiled over and covered most of the stove, did not contribute to the noise. Susan was having a bath.

3. In Section 5.2.2 we made two claims about reference points for which we did not argue. The first was that the discourse referents that may be chosen as Rpts are either discourse referents for events or else discourse referents for times. The second point is that when the processed sentence has stative aspect, then the relationship between the discourse referents representing the described state and the Rpt is one of inclusion and not overlap (and thus differs from the relationship we assume to hold between a state and its location time). The second claim is motivated by an intuition which also finds expression in the term reference *point*. A reference point is a *reference*

point in the sense that it is conceived, in the context of the sentence whose interpretation requires it, as indivisible – so that overlap with a state **s** can only mean that the reference point is included in the state (for otherwise the reference point would consist of two parts, one included in the state and the other disjoint from it, which would entail its divisibility). Both this intuition and the first claim, according to which discourse referents that act as Rpts may be representatives of events or times, seem problematic in the light of examples such as the following

(5.159) On Sunday Mary was ill. She had a headache.

We argued in Section 5.2 that the first sentence of (5.159) can be true even in a case where Mary's being ill does not last through the entire Sunday but only covers part of it. In that case the same may of course be true of the headache: (5.159) could be true even though her headache and (therewith) her illnes had gone away by nighttime. But, if this is so, it cannot be right to take, when processing the second sentence of (5.159), the location time t of the first sentence as Rpt and then insist that the state of Mary having a headache includes this Rpt.

There are several possible answers to this predicament. The first is to weaken the relationship between Rpt and state to mere overlap. This would avoid the faulty analysis of (5.159) but it would have undesirable consequences elsewhere. In particular, it would lead to the wrong truth conditions for a discourse such as (5.136). (Check that this is so!) The second possibility is to weaken the first claim by allowing discourse referents for states to act as Rpts too – so that in the case of (5.159) the discourse referent representing the state described by the first sentence can be used as Rpt for the second sentence. The third possibility is to relinquish neither of the two claims, but to allow the choice of Rpts which are not introduced into the DRS by the construction algorithm as we have stated it, but which are associated in some systematic and transparent way with discourse referents that have been so introduced. In particular, the event which constitutes the onset of an already represented state, or the one which constitutes its termination would seem to be natural candidates.

Task:

(i) Construct a DRS for (5.159) according to each of the three alternatives mentioned.

(ii) Compare the three resulting DRSs as to intuitive plausibility.

(iii) Try to find other sentence sequences which could help us decide which of the three alternatives is to be preferred.

4. **Negations of Perfects:**
Construct DRSs for the sentences

(a) Mary has not written the letter.
(b) Mary did not write the letter today.

Show that (a) entails (b).

5. **Negation of Perfect and Progressive:**
Construct DRSs for the sentences

(a) Fred has not written a book.
(b) Fred has not been writing a book.

Show that (b) entails (a). Why is the converse implication not generally valid?

5.4 Temporal Perspective

In Section 5.2, we cited Reichenbach as the one who introduced the notion of reference point into the semantics of tense and aspect. This notion has proved to be of extraordinary importance, an importance which has been only partly revealed by what we have said about this notion so far. In fact, the examples that Reichenbach himself saw as central for his concept of reference point were not those we discussed in Section 5.2. Rather his point of departure were sentence sequences such as

(5.160) Fred arrived at 10. He had set off at 6.

in which a sentence in the past perfect is preceded by one in the simple past. The function of the past perfect in such passages, Reichenbach observed, is to situate the described state or event in the past of some point which is itself in the past of the time of utterance. In such cases Reichenbach speaks of the time intermediate between utterance time and described eventuality as "reference time".

According to this analysis the past perfect (as it occurs in passages like (5.160)) expresses a pair of temporal relations, one between reference time and utterance time and the other between reference time and described eventuality: reference time is before utterance time and described eventuality is before reference time.

Reichenbach extrapolated from this to an analysis which treats all tenses as expressing pairs of temporal relations. (His theory is sometimes referred to as the "two-dimensional theory of tense".)

We will follow Reichenbach in what we consider to be the spirit of his proposal, though not in its details. For some of the specific proposals he made do not seem to stand up to scrutiny. In fact, we believe that Reichenbach went astray when he wanted his notion of reference point to do too many things at once. In particular, he writes as if the reference time which is required for the interpretation of past perfects like the one in (5.160) is of a kind with the reference times we discussed in Section 5.2, where they were needed in the interpretation of sequences of sentences in the past progressive and simple past tense. That the two kinds of "reference time" should not be identified we can see clearly when we look at so-called *extended flashbacks.* Consider

(5.161) Fred arrived at 10. He had got up at 5; he had taken a long shower, had got dressed and had eaten a leisurely breakfast. He had left the house at 6:30.

All the past perfect clauses of (5.161) use the arrival time as their "reference time" in the sense of our analysis of (5.160). (It can only be the arrival time, as that is the only time between the described event and n that is represented in the context.) At the same time, however, the past perfect clauses of (5.161) form a narrative progression much like the sequences of simple past and past progressive sentences which we studied in Section 5.2.2 – sequences such as, e.g., (5.54). Both in (5.54) and in the flashback of (5.161) each clause provides a "reference time" for the clause following it – a time which the eventuality described by the second clause must follow or overlap.

Thus interpretation of the last four clauses of (5.161) involves both the perspectival analysis of the past perfect and the principle of narrative progression. On the one hand, each of those clauses requires a "reference time" in the sense of the narrative progression principle; in the present example this "reference time" changes from one clause to the next – it moves along with the narrative. On the other hand, all the past perfect clauses of (5.161) need the time of Fred's arrival as "reference time" in the sense explained in connection with (5.160). This "reference time" remains constant, and for each of the four clauses it is distinct from the "reference time" in the sense of narrative progression.

It should be clear from this discussion (i) that the analysis of certain sentences requires two reference points, and not just one; and (ii) that there are two distinct *notions* of reference time, which play entirely different roles. It is crucial that we keep these two notions apart. And so we must have different names for them. We propose to retain the term *reference point*, or *Rpt*, for the type of reference time which accounts for narrative progression. (Thus we remain consistent with the terminology we introduced in Section 5.2.) For reference times that arise in the two-dimensional analysis of the past perfect, we will use the term *temporal perspective point*, or *TPpt*. This term is meant to reflect our intuition that the intermediate time which Reichenbach recognized as essential to the interpretation of past perfects is the time *from which* the described eventuality is seen as past.

The role of the TPpt is easiest to recognize when the tense requires it to lie in the past. This is so in particular, we have just seen, for the past perfect. But there are more such tenses. A second one is the *past future*, as we find it in contexts like

(5.162) Mary got to the station at 9:45. Her train would arrive at 10:05.

Here the train's arrival is described as lying in the future of some other time – that of Mary's getting to the station – which is itself in the past of the utterance time. Here too, we maintain, the intermediate time identifies the point from which the described event is viewed – the point, in other words, which acts as TPpt. So the two relations corresponding to the past future are (i) TPpt before utterance time and (ii) described eventuality after TPpt.

There are also tenses which require that the TPpt be situated in the past and that the described eventuality overlaps it. These cases are not as easily identified as the instances of past perfect and past future we have just considered. But when we look more closely at the way in which tenses interact with temporal adverbs we find convincing evidence that tenses with this characteristic (i.e. tenses that are characterized by the relation pair ⟨*TPpt before the utterance time; described eventuality overlaps with TPpt*⟩) exist too. The evidence we have in mind involves the word **now**. A first attempt to say what **now** means might well be: **now** always refers to the utterance time of the sentence of which it is part (except when it occurs within direct quotation).[49] Little reflection is needed, however, to see that this is too restrictive. For **now** can also be used to refer to past times. An example is

(5.163) Mary had been unhappy in her new environment for more than a year. But now she felt at home.

Nevertheless, the contexts in which **now** can refer to a past time are severely restricted. For example, it seems to be almost impossible for **now** to refer to a past time if the clause in which it occurs describes an event rather than a state.[50]

[49] In fact, analyses of **now** based on this assumption can be found in the literature. See e.g. [Prior 1968] or [Kamp 1971].

[50] The constraint is particularly clear in a language such as French, where there are two past tenses, the Passé Simple and the Imparfait, the difference between which roughly corresponds to that between $-STAT$ and $+STAT$. The word **maintenant (now)** goes with Imparfait but not

Thus, (5.164) is awkward, and not nearly as good as (5.165),

(5.164) Bill had come home at seven. Now he wrote a letter.

(5.165) Bill had come home at seven. Now he was writing a letter.

even though the two passages are very similar in content. This restriction is reminiscent of what we noted earlier in relation to those uses of the present tense which we have included in our fragment: when so used, present tense sentences must, we saw, be descriptions of states, not events: the intuitive reason being that when one describes something as going on at the time of description, one must describe it as just that, viz. as something that *is* then going on. Apparently, this constraint is operative not only when what is going on at the time of speech is presented in the present tense, but also when one describes what is going on at some other time t from the perspective of that same time t. In other words, the restriction to eventuality descriptions with the feature $+STAT$ obtains whenever the eventuality overlaps the chosen TPpt. In (5.165), this TPpt lies in the past of the utterance time; with a sentence like

(5.166) Mary is writing a letter.

it is the utterance time itself.

With this last assertion we have committed ourselves to the next part of our version of the two-dimensional theory of tense: with some tenses – among them the present tense when used in the way we analysed in detail in Section 5.2 – the TPpt and the utterance time coincide. Thus, the present tense (when used that way) is characterized by the pair ⟨*TPpt coincides with utterance time; described eventuality overlaps with TPpt*⟩. This characterization differs from that of the past tense exemplified by the second sentence of (5.165), which corresponds to the pair ⟨*TPpt before utterance time; described eventuality overlaps with TPpt*⟩.

By our counts there are many tenses which locate the perspective point at the utterance time. One of these is the simple past when it is used in sentences which describe events. This claim is forced upon us if the TPpt is to explain why **now** can refer to a time before the utterance time only in those cases where it does. Evidently the explanation we proposed why **now** can figure in (5.165) would not be much good if it predicted this possibility also for a context like (5.164), where in fact it does not exist. So for simple past $-STAT$-sentences, where **now** appears to be impossible, the characterizing pair of relations should *not* be the one we proposed for the past tense of the second sentence in (5.162). To explain

with Passé Simple.

that **now** *cannot* occur in such sentences, their past tenses must not involve the relation *described eventuality overlaps TPpt.* The only plausible alternative is that such past tenses are characterized by the pair ⟨*TPpt coincides with utterance time; described eventuality precedes TPpt*⟩. Thus we are led to maintain that the English simple past must be seen as semantically ambiguous. Its interpretation can locate the TPpt either *at* the utterance time or *before* it.

Another tense that locates the TPpt at the utterance time is the simple future. Indeed, neither the simple future nor any other tense ever locates the TPpt in the future of the utterance time; this thesis is supported by the fact that **now** can never be used to refer to future times.[51] For the simple future we assume the relation ⟨*TPpt coincides with the utterance time, described eventuality after TPpt*⟩. This same analysis also applies to the future perfect, which, by our lights, is what the name implies: the result of combining the future tense with the aspectual operator *perf*.

We have seen that the simple past is ambiguous between two different relation pairs. When the past tense sentence has $STAT = -$, then its tense always corresponds to the pair ⟨*TPpt coincides with utterance time; described eventuality before TPpt*⟩. When $STAT = +$, we argued, the corresponding relations may be ⟨*TPpt before utterance time; described eventuality overlaps TPpt*⟩. In fact, there appear to be good reasons to allow for simple past $+STAT$ sentences also the alternative analysis which assigns them the same relation pair that is obligatory for past tense sentences with $-STAT$. For instance, of

(5.169) A man entered the White Hart. He was wearing a black jacket.
He sat down in the bar. Bill served him a pint of beer.

it would be odd to have to say that the perspective switches from the utterance time (for the first sentence) to the time of the man's entering the pub (for the second

[51]Perhaps this claim is too strong. It has been suggested to us (Görel Sandstrom, personal communication) that **now** can be used to refer to a future time in discourses which invite the interpretation that the perspective has been shifted towards the future, as in

(5.167) John will leave work at the usual hour and take the bus home. He will get there around 6:30. He will have had a hard day, so now he will want to relax with a cold beer.

We are inclined to agree that in this passage **now** does not seem out of place. And possibly the same may be said about the future tense counterpart of (5.163).

(5.168) Mary will have been unhappy in her new environment for more than a year. But now she will feel at home.

Nevertheless some of our informants report a considerable resistance towards such future tense discourses. So we have decided to admit for *TPpt* only the values $+PAST$ and $-PAST$. Those who share Sandstrom's intuitions may wish to adopt a third *TPpt*-value – indicating perspective shift towards the future, and adjust the two-dimensional analysis of tense accordingly.

sentence) and then back to the utterance time for the remaining two sentences; but this is what would be forced upon us if the progressive (and thus +*STAT*) sentence **He was wearing a black jacket** could only be analysed in the manner of (5.163).[52]

It will be convenient to extend our feature system so that it enables us to express distinctions like those between the two possible interpretations that are now available for simple past stative sentences. Since our revised theory of tense is two-dimensional, we need two temporal features rather than one, one feature to indicate the relation between TPpt and utterance time and one to indicate the relation between the location of the described eventuality and the TPpt.

The first, T(emporal) P(erspective), determines the relationship between TPpt and utterance time. It has two values, +*PAST* (meaning that TPpt lies before utterance time) and −*PAST* (meaning that TPpt and utterance time coincide). The second feature which determines the relation between the location time of the described eventuality and the TPpt, will be called *TENSE*. In fact, it is our old feature *TENSE*, except that we now interpret its values as determining the relation between location time and TPpt rather than between location time and utterance time.

By means of these two temporal features and the aspectual features *Stat* and *PERF* we can characterize the relevant interpretations of tensed clauses much as we have done up to now. For instance the two possible interpretations of simple past stative clauses can now be represented as ⟨−*PAST*, *past*, +*STAT*, −*PERF*⟩ and ⟨+*PAST*, *pres*, +*STAT*, −*PERF*⟩; the sole interpretation for simple past non-stative clauses is given by ⟨−*PAST*, *past*, −*STAT*, −*PERF*⟩

Another ambiguity arises with the past perfect. According to the analysis for which we have argued above, the past perfect involves the relations ⟨*TPpt before utterance time; location time before TPpt*⟩. But this is different from the account we offered in Section 5.3. There past perfects were interpreted in a manner directly suggested by their name, viz. as "past tense perfects" – past tenses of verb phrases which involve the aspectual operator *perf* (and thus carry the feature value +*PERF*). In contrast, we have been assuming in the present section that past perfects have the value −*PERF*; according to this account the auxiliary **have** does not represent the aspect operator *perf*, but is part of the verb's finite tense.

We maintain that the past perfect is ambiguous between these two possibilities: some past perfects should be analysed along the lines of 5.3, others along those of the present section. Past perfects occurring in typical flashbacks, like the examples we have discussed above, belong to the second category. A clear instance of the

[52]This argument is less than conclusive. In fact, we could formally get by with an analysis in which +*STAT* simple past sentences and sentences in the past progressive have only the one interpretation which locates the TPpt in the past. Nothing that is crucial here hangs on the decision to allow both interpretations.

first category is the second past perfect in

(5.170) Mary was content. The past two days had been strenuous.
But now she had sent off her proposal.

The second past perfect of (5.170) cannot be analysed in the manner of the present section. This follows from the presence of the adverb **now**. We have just seen that the presence of **now** in a clause implies that the clause describes a state holding at the TPpt. Thus a past perfect which appears in conjunction with **now** cannot be analysed, like the flashback examples of this section, as describing an eventuality which is located before the TPpt.

In fact, when we combine the considerations of 5.3 with those of the present section we find that past perfects are not just two-ways, but three-ways ambiguous. Besides the analysis exemplified above, which is characterized by the feature value combination ⟨ *+PAST*, *past*, *+/−STAT*, *−PERF*⟩, we get two possible analyses corresponding to the account of 5.3 – just as we get two different analyses for simple past stative sentences generally: when a past perfect is analysed as having *+PERF*, it is still possible to take its temporal features to be either ⟨*−PAST*, *past*⟩ or ⟨*+PAST*, *pres*⟩. The second of these two possibilities, characterized by the four values ⟨*+PAST*, *pres*, *+STAT*, *+PERF*⟩, is the only one possible when a past perfect is accompanied by **now**. In other cases, the choice between this analysis and the alternative ⟨*−PAST*, *past*, *+STAT*, *+PERF*⟩ may be difficult to make, just as it sometimes hard to make this choice for simple past stative sentences that are not perfects.

It might be argued that besides the three possible analyses for the past perfect that we have acknowledged there is a fourth one. This analysis would have the feature values ⟨ *+PAST*, *past*, *+Stat*, *+PERF*⟩ and thus impose the interpretation that the clause describes a result state, and that this result state is located at a time antecedent to some past TPpt. We are not aware of any convincing examples to show that the past perfect sometimes must be analysed in this way, so we shall not include this possibility among the options allowed by the theory.[53]

The many ambiguities which our theory predicts may seem to argue against it: how could a theory which implies alternative analyses for one and the same complex expression, between which it is not always possible to choose on rational grounds, be linguistically adequate? In fact, this objection has been raised more than once. We are in sympathy with it, but have no conclusive argument to counter it. Indeed, if a theory could be found which succeeded, without postulating apparently spurious ambiguities, to account for the same data as our own theory, we should be glad to

[53]In part, the problem is that any potential candidate for this analysis might in principle also be analysed as an "embedded" flashback, whose TPpt is itself a flashback event (or its location time), located in its turn before the TPpt of the "outer" flashback.

adopt it in its stead. But at present no such theory is known to us.

At the same time it should be pointed out that if a linguistic theory predicts ambiguities which do not reflect an immediate linguistic intuition, this should not automatically be seen as damning. Many theories, in syntax as well as in semantics, postulate such ambiguities, which arise out of general assumptions motivated by evidence that may be quite indirect. That speakers find it hard to "see" these ambiguities is by itself no conclusive ground for rejecting the theory. For, in fact, they often fail to perceive syntactic or semantic structure also in expressions which, on all accounts, are unambiguous.

In the light of the ambiguity that we have been led to attribute to the past perfect, one might be inclined to expect similar ambiguities for other forms involving the auxiliary **have**, such as the present perfect and the future perfect (as in **will have written**). For instance, does the present perfect, which we have thus far analysed as a present tense, not also permit interpretation as a kind of past tense, which locates the described eventuality in the past of a present TPpt just as the past perfect can be used to locate the eventuality before a past TPpt? Surprisingly, this interpretation does not appear to be available. This is, it seems, a special feature of English.[54] There are many languages (German and French among them) whose tense systems resemble that of English in many ways and in which the forms corresponding to the English present perfect can be interpreted as past tenses. But for English this is not so. (See Exercise 5) on p. 610)

With regard to the future perfect the possibility of an alternative intepretation is connected with the possibility, which we briefly discussed above, that the TPpt might lie in the future of the utterance time. For such an alternative interpretation would locate the described eventuality in the past of some future TPpt. Our earlier verdict was that there is insufficient evidence to support the existence of future TPpts. Indeed, this claim includes evidence from future perfect sentences as well as from sentences in the simple future. However, as we implied in footnote 51, we might be persuaded to admit future TPpts in the light of evidence we have overlooked. In that case the question whether the future perfect admits of more than one interpretation would have to be reconsidered. Much the same goes for the past tense analogue of the future perfect (the "past future perfect", as in **would have written**). Here too we get, on the assumptions to which we have now committed ourselves, just a single interpretation, according to which the sentence describes a result state, which lies in the future of a past TPpt.

We conclude this section with a table which gives for each of the English tenses we have so far considered the tuple or tuples of feature values which this form may represent.

---

[54]The same is true for Scandinavian languages.

present	$-PAST$	*pres*	$+STAT$	$-PERF$
future	$-PAST$	*fut*	$+/-STAT$	$-PERF$
simple past	$-PAST$	*past*	$+/-STAT$	$-PERF$
	$+PAST$	*pres*	$+STAT$	$-PERF$
past future	$+PAST$	*fut*	$+/-STAT$	$-PERF$
present perfect	$-PAST$	*pres*	$+STAT$	$+PERF$
future perfect	$-PAST$	*fut*	$+STAT$	$+PERF$
past perfect	$+PAST$	*past*	$+/-STAT$	$-PERF$
	$-PAST$	*past*	$+STAT$	$+PERF$
	$+PAST$	*pres*	$+STAT$	$+PERF$
past future perfect	$+PAST$	*fut*	$+STAT$	$+PERF$

5.4.1 Construction

In this section we revise the DRS-construction algorithm of Section 5.2 to account for the two-dimensional analysis of tense; at the same time we extend the algorithm to tense forms not so far considered.

To accord with our new, two-dimensional theory of tense the construction algorithm has to do a little more than it needed to do before. For now we must, as part of the processing of each tensed sentence, choose a suitable TPpt, and the location time will then have to be related, in accordance with the feature *TENSE*, to this TPpt. We have seen that when TP has the value $-PAST$, then the TPpt is always **n**. In this case everything happens essentially as before, for the relation which *TENSE* now imposes upon location time and TPpt is the same as the one previously imposed upon location time and n – which in this case just is the TPpt. When TP has the value $+PAST$, matters are a little more complicated. For, as we have seen from the examples in the preceding section, there is the additional problem of choosing the right element from the context DRS to serve as past TPpt. As with the choice of past Rpts this is a problem for which our theory does not offer a pat solution.

We begin with the DRS-construction of the first example of this section.

(5.171) Fred arrived at 10. He had got up at 5.

The first sentence of (5.171) has the syntactic representation (5.172).

(5.172)

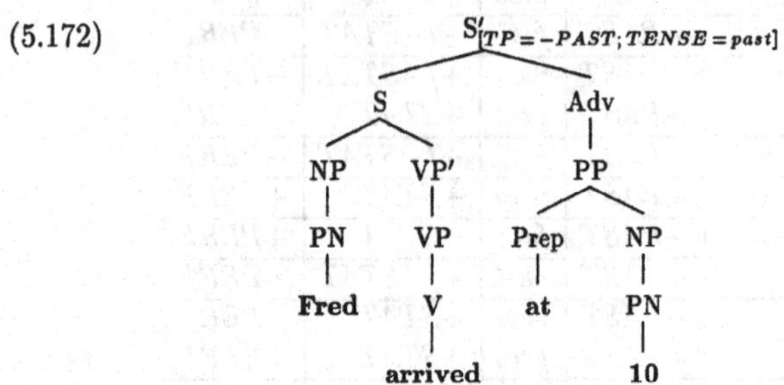

The only difference between this new structure and those we have been working with so far consists in the additional TP-feature.

The first step in the DRS-construction for (5.171) now involves choosing a TPpt. We mark this choice in the same way in which we have been representing the choice of Rpt, viz. in the form of a condition **TPpt** $:= \alpha$, where α is a discourse referent for an event or time which is already present in the DRS. In the present instance, of course, the choice is trivial, for the feature value $-PAST$ tells us that the TPpt should be identified with **n**.

The further operations involved in the first step are like those required by the first step in the construction procedure of Section 5.2. The only formal difference is that we now relate the location time $\mathbf{t_1}$ which the construction rule introduces to the chosen TPpt rather than directly to the utterance time. However, we implement this link with the TPpt by stipulating that the location time $\mathbf{t_1}$ stands in the relevant relation to the right-hand side α of the just introduced equation **TPpt** $:= \alpha$. So the result, the condition $\mathbf{t_1} < \mathbf{n}$, is in this case identical to what we would have obtained with the old rule.

(5.173)

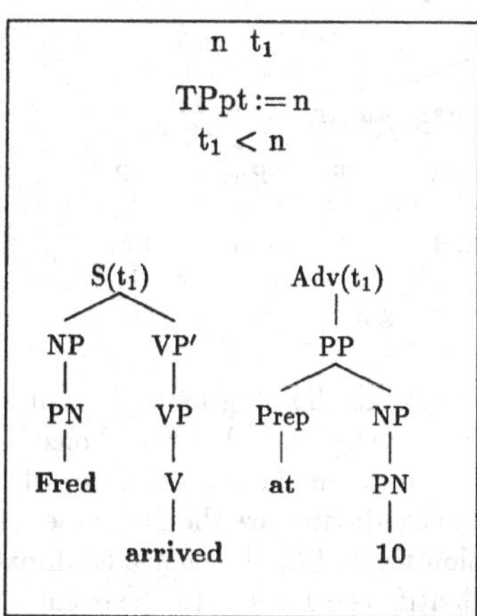

The remainder of the construction is identical with the earlier procedure. So what we end up with is the same DRS as before, except for the extra condition **TPpt := n**. However, conditions of the form **TPpt** $:= \alpha$ are, like conditions of the form **Rpt** $:= \alpha$, just bookkeeping devices needed in the course of interpreting a given sentence or clause; and like the Rpt-conditions they should be eliminated after the sentence or clause in question has been fully processed. So the final DRS is identical to the one generated by the rules of Section 5.2.

(5.174)

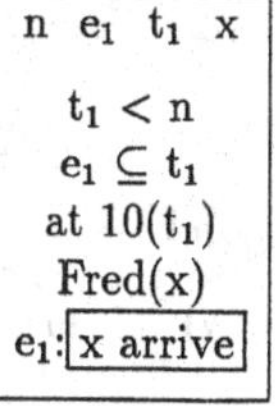

The second sentence of (5.171) is of more interest. Its syntactic structure is

(5.175)

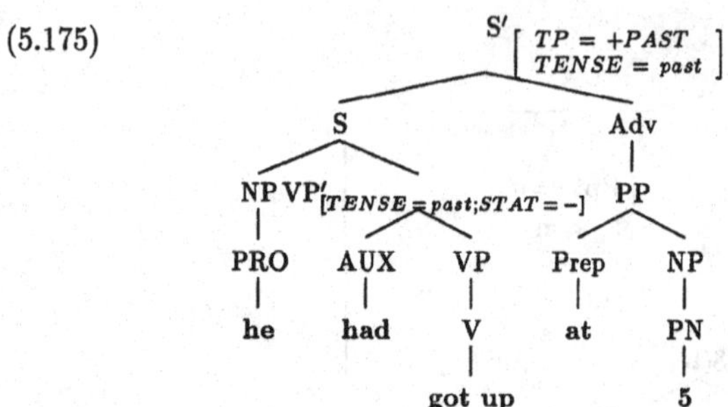

This time the first step involves choosing for the TPpt some discourse referent other than **n**. As with Rpts we stipulate that the choice is restricted to discourse referents for events and for times. In the present case, where our context is given by (5.174), the only possible candidates are the discourse referents $\mathbf{e_1}$ and $\mathbf{t_1}$. Since in this case $\mathbf{t_1}$ is the location time of $\mathbf{e_1}$ the choice is immaterial; as we did before in similar situations, we identify the TPpt with the event discourse referent $\mathbf{e_1}$. As with the first sentence of (5.171) the construction step will in addition introduce a location time $\mathbf{t_2}$. The effect of this first step is the following extension of (5.175):

(5.176)

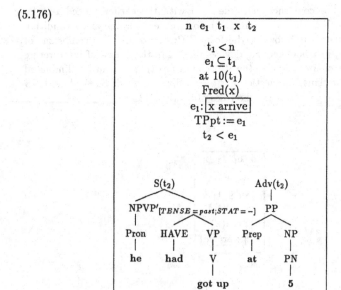

$\mathbf{n}\ \mathbf{e_1}\ \mathbf{t_1}\ \mathbf{x}\ \mathbf{t_2}$

$\mathbf{t_1} < \mathbf{n}$

$\mathbf{e_1} \subseteq \mathbf{t_1}$

at $10(\mathbf{t_1})$

Fred(**x**)

$\mathbf{e_1}$: | x arrive |

TPpt := $\mathbf{e_1}$

$\mathbf{t_2} < \mathbf{e_1}$

S($\mathbf{t_2}$) — Adv($\mathbf{t_2}$)

NPVP′[TENSE = past;STAT = −] — PP

Pron — HAVE — VP — Prep — NP

he — had — V — at — PN

got up — 5

The next step deals with the subject NP. Then the location time of the described event is placed in the past of the TPpt. In the present case there is no element in the DRS that could serve as Rpt (there are no elements α in (5.176) such that $\alpha < e_1$). So no Rpt is chosen. The result of these steps is

(5.177)

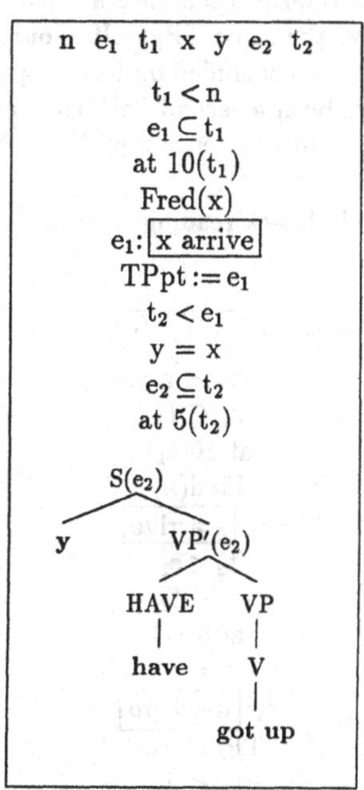

The remaining steps are left to the reader.

We consider one more example, in which an extended flashback requires the choice both of a past TPpt and of an Rpt for one and the same clause. The example will serve a double purpose, for it also contains a past future, and so permits us to show how that tense is processed.

(5.178) Fred arrived at 10. He had got up at 5. He had got dressed and had had a leisurely breakfast. He had left the house at 6 and he had been walking for sixteen hours. Now he was tired. Nevertheless he would continue his trip early the following morning.

The DRS for the first two sentences of (5.178) is virtually identical to that for (5.171) and we take its construction for granted. The third sentence is a conjunction of two tensed clauses. The conjunction reduction rule of Section 1.5 turns these into two separate sentences to be processed in sequence. We have a closer look only at the first of these, **he had got dressed.** The first step in the processing of this sentence requires the choice of a past TPpt. The content of (5.178) strongly suggests that the second and the third sentence are part of the same flashback, in other words that they involve the same TPpt. It should be noted, however, that this is a matter which cannot be concluded on formal grounds alone – in principle the third sentence could have been a second flashback, embedded within the first. In that case, the TPpt for the third sentence would have been the event introduced by the second sentence.

Opting for the extended flashback reading we obtain the DRS

(5.179)

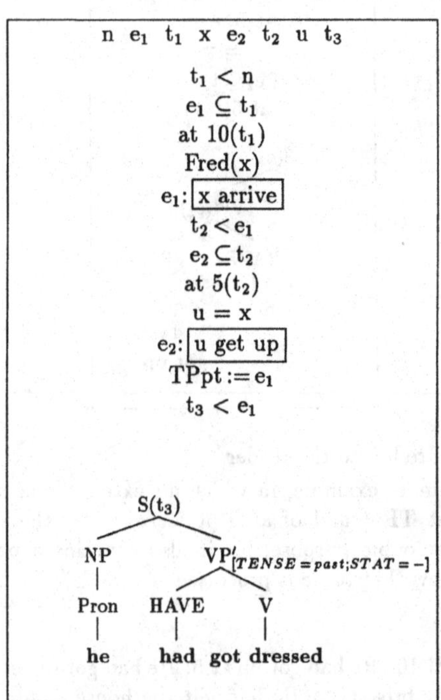

This time there is the possibility of choosing an Rpt from context, viz. the event discourse referent $\mathbf{e}_2$, and the next construction step should do so. The DRS (5.180)

shows the effects of this step together with those that are still needed to fully reduce the first conjunct of the third sentence, except for the final elimination of conditions of the form $\tau := \alpha$.

(5.180)

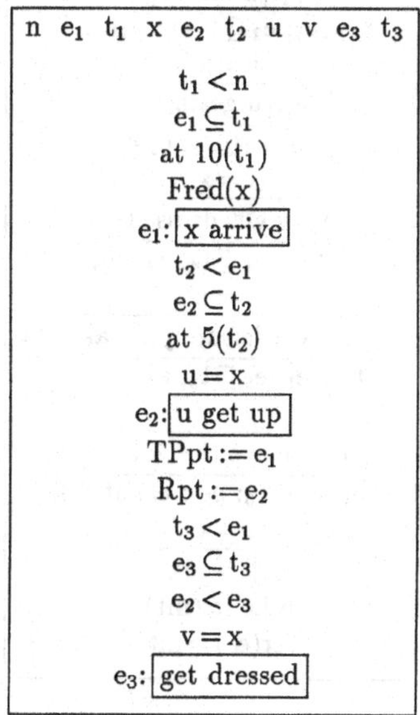

The intuitively correct interpretation of the second conjunct of the third sentence will employ once again $\mathbf{e_1}$ as TPpt and the last mentioned event $\mathbf{e_3}$ as Rpt. The fourth sentence is, like the third sentence, a conjunction, and can be reduced to its conjuncts in the same way. The first conjunct will use $\mathbf{e_1}$ as TPpt and the event $\mathbf{e_4}$ of Fred having his leisurely breakfast as Rpt; the second will have the same TPpt, whereas the Rpt shifts once more to the most recent event. We leave the task of going through the construction steps needed to deal with these three sentences to the reader and give the resulting DRS directly.[55]

[55]For reasons of space, some of the conditions of (5.181)–(5.183) are listed together on a single line, separated by semicolons. The conditions $\mathbf{s} \bigcirc \mathbf{t_6}$ and $\mathbf{t_6} = \mathbf{e_1}$ derive from the adverb **now**. We will explain the details of this representation in Section 5.5.

(5.181)

$$\begin{array}{|c|}
\hline
\text{n e}_1\ \text{t}_1\ \text{x e}_2\ \text{t}_2\ \text{u e}_3\ \text{t}_3\ \text{v} \\
\text{e}_4\ \text{t}_4\ \text{w e}_5\ \text{t}_5\ \text{y e}_6\ \text{t}_6\ \text{z mt} \\
\\
\text{t}_1 < \text{n};\ \text{e}_1 \subseteq \text{t}_1;\ \text{at } 10(\text{t}_1)\ ;\ \text{Fred(x)} \\
\text{e}_1\!: \boxed{\text{x arrive}} \\
\text{t}_2 < \text{e}_1;\ \text{e}_2 \subseteq \text{t}_2;\ \text{at } 5(\text{t}_2) \\
\text{u} = \text{x} \\
\text{e}_2\!: \boxed{\text{u get up}} \\
\text{t}_3 < \text{e}_1;\ \text{e}_3 \subseteq \text{t}_3;\ \text{e}_2 < \text{e}_3 \\
\text{v} = \text{x} \\
\text{e}_3\!: \boxed{\text{v get dressed}} \\
\text{t}_4 < \text{e}_1;\ \text{e}_4 \subseteq \text{t}_4;\ \text{e}_3 < \text{e}_4 \\
\text{w} = \text{x} \\
\text{e}_4\!: \boxed{\text{w have a leisurely breakfast}} \\
\text{t}_5 < \text{e}_1;\ \text{e}_5 \subseteq \text{t}_5;\ \text{e}_4 < \text{e}_5 \\
\text{y} = \text{x} \\
\text{e}_5\!: \boxed{\text{y leave the house}} \\
\text{t}_6 < \text{e}_1;\ \text{e}_6 \subseteq \text{t}_6;\ \text{e}_5 < \text{e}_6;\ \text{at } 6(\text{t}_6) \\
\text{z} = \text{x} \\
\text{e}_6\!: \boxed{\text{z walk}} \\
\text{16 hours(mt)} \\
\text{dur}(\text{e}_6) = \text{mt} \\
\hline
\end{array}$$

We now come to the processing of the fifth sentence. The **now** of that sentence requires its past tense to be analysed as involving the *TP*- and *TENSE*-values $\langle +PAST, pres \rangle$. Once more, therefore, we must choose a past TPpt; and once more the right choice seems to be the first event e_1, but again no strictly formal principle forces us to make this choice. The next step must introduce a state discourse referent, together with the condition that the corresponding location time coincides with the TPpt. Where, as here, the TPpt is an event (viz. $\mathbf{e_1}$) we express this condition as $\mathbf{t_7 = loc(e_1)}$ – **loc** assigning to an eventuality the interval of time it occupies. This step also has to confront the question what to do with the Rpt. The correct decision here should be the same as in the case of the present tense: since the described state overlaps with the perspective point, the choice of a reference point is irrelevant. Again we opt for the strictly formal solution of setting the Rpt equal to the TPpt. The fifth sentence requires one additional step, which interprets the pronoun. The result is the DRS (5.182), in which we have abbreviated the conditions of (5.181) as Γ.

(5.182)

$n\ e_1\ t_1\ x\ e_2\ t_2\ u\ e_3\ t_3\ v$ $e_4\ t_4\ w\ e_5\ t_5\ y\ e_6\ t_6\ z\ mt\ s\ t_7\ a$
Γ $t_7 = loc(e_1)\ ;\ s \bigcirc t_7$ $a = x$ s: [a be tired]

Now for the last sentence of (5.178). Once again we must choose a past TPpt and once again the intuitively correct choice is $\mathbf{e_1}$. The next step places the described event in the future of TPpt. A new complication arises in connection with the Rpt. (5.182) does contain a discourse referent, viz. **n**, which represents a time located after the TPpt $\mathbf{e_1}$ (the DRS contains the condition $e_1 < n$), and thus lies in a direction from the TPpt which accords with the value of *TENSE* (which in the present case is *fut*). Nevertheless our intuitions tell us that the described event has nothing whatsoever to do with **n** – that it acts in no sense whatever as "reference point" for this event. So Rpt should not be set equal to **n**; in fact it should remain undetermined. This seems to be a general rule applying to first sentences of both "flashbacks" and "flashforwards". (Here we have one of many rules concerning the identification of Rpt which are intimately connected with the rhetorical structure of discourse and which therefore lie beyond the reach of the theory developed in this book.) Eliminating the defining conditions for TPpt and Rpt in (5.182), and then performing the first two steps needed to interpret the last sentence we get (5.183).[56]

(5.183)

$n\ e_1\ t_1\ x\ e_2\ t_2\ u\ e_3\ t_3\ v$ $e_4\ t_4\ w\ e_5\ t_5\ y\ e_6\ t_6\ z\ mt\ s\ t_7\ a\ e_7\ t_8\ b$
Γ $t_7 = loc(e_1)\ ;\ s \bigcirc t_7;$ $a = x$ s: [a be tired] $e_1 < t_8\ ;\ e_7 \subseteq t_8$ early the following morning(t_8) $b = x$ e_7: [be continue his trip]

[56]The condition **early the following morning(t_8)** should be reduced further. This matter is addressed in Section 5.5. We have ignored the discourse particle **nevertheless**.

We are now in a position to state the construction rule that deal with the S′-node in its final form.

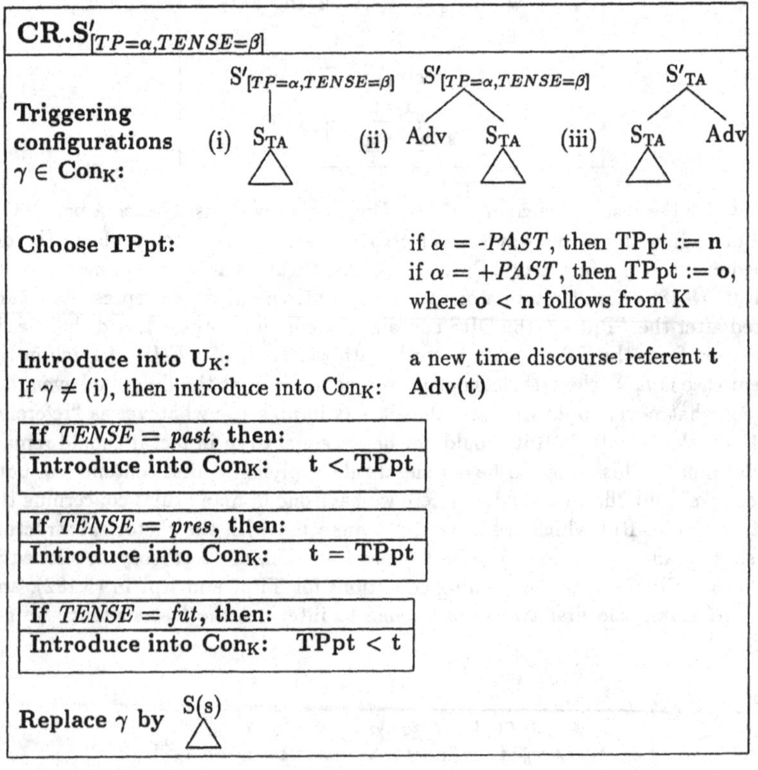

Exercises

1. (i) Construct a DRS for (5.165).

   (ii) Show that it is not possible to construct a DRS for (5.164),

   (iii) Construct a DRS for (5.162)

2. The theory of Section 5.4 allows for three different interpretations of the past perfect. Construct DRSs for (5.171) on each of the two interpretations not considered in the text.

3. Construct DRSs for (a) and (b):

(a) Fred left the house at 7 o'clock. He crossed the street and hailed a taxi. His train left at 7:15.

(b) Fred left the house at 7 o'clock. He crossed the street and hailed a taxi. His train would leave at 7:15.

Do these DRSs have the same truth conditions? If not, what is the difference?

4. Suppose we continue the first four sentences of (5.178) with

Now he had reached his goal.

Incorporate this sentence into the DRS (5.181)

5. (i) It was stated towards the end of Section 5.4 that the English present perfect only has the interpretation given by ⟨−*PAST*, *pres*, +*STAT*, +*PERF*⟩. In particular, it does not permit the interpretation given by ⟨−*PAST*, *past*, +/−*STAT*, −*PERF*⟩. Evidence for this lack of ambiguity is given by data such as the following:

   (a) Mary has written the letter today. (grammatical!)

   (b) * Mary has written the letter yesterday (ungrammatical!)

   (c) Mary has written the letter this morning. (o.k. if uttered in the morning, not when uttered in the evening or in the afternoon)

   Argue that these facts are compatible with the interpretation ⟨−*PAST*, *pres*, +*STAT*, +*PERF*⟩ but not with ⟨−*PAST*, *past*, +/−*STAT*, −*PERF*⟩.

   (ii) In German and French the counterparts of the ungrammatical sentences in (a) and (b) are grammatical, e.g.:

   (b) Marie a écrit la lettre hier. (grammatical!)

   (c) Maria hat gestern den Brief geschrieben.

   Argue that these sentences require an interpretation of the French and German present perfects (i.e. those forms which consist of present tense, Fr. **avoir**, Ger. **haben**) + past participle which is given by ⟨−*PAST*, *past*, +/−*STAT*, −*PERF*⟩.

5.5 Temporal Adverbials

In the preceding sections, we have come across quite a few sentences that contained temporal adverbs. But on the whole we didn't look at those adverbs in much detail. Mostly we needed them as explicit specifiers of location times, whose presence obviated the need to reconstruct the location time of the described eventuality from the antecedent context. Consistently with this purpose we largely ignored their interpretation. We simply recorded the semantic contribution made by the adverb in terms of a discourse referent t for the location time plus a condition in which the adverbial phrase as a whole was predicated of t. Only on one occasion did we discuss the meaning of an adverb in greater detail. This was the word **now**, which played a central part in our argument for the two-dimensional analysis of the simple past. Crucial to that argument was our assumption that **now** always refers to the Temporal Perspective Point (TPpt).

In the present section, we will study a variety of temporal adverbs in order to discover the principles according to which such adverbs refer. We will be especially interested in the context-sensitive aspects of their reference. It will emerge that context impinges on the reference of temporal adverbs in quite a number of different ways. In this regard temporal reference offers much more variety than e.g. nominal reference to persons or material things. **Now** is a case in point. The principle governing its reference – that **now** always refers to the time that acts as TPpt – displays context sensitivity of a sort that we do not find in the domain of physical things for the simple reason that there is no material analogue of temporal perspective.[57] The study of temporal locating adverbs thus reveals some important lessons about context sensitivity in general, and this is our principal reason for delving into the modes of adverbial reference as deeply as we will. We will be less concerned with the technical details of the construction algorithm, and often leave these details to be worked out by the motivated reader.

Besides the locating adverbs properly speaking, which will be discussed in Section 5.5.1, there are two further types of temporal adverbs which we will consider. The first category consists of the adverbs of quantification, or *frequency adverbs*, as they are also called – adverbs such as **always, often, rarely, mostly, never**. In a way these are locating adverbs, too. For the discourse referents they introduce act, like those introduced by the locating adverbs of Section 5.5.1, as specifiers of the temporal locations of described eventualities. But they differ from the adverbs of Section 5.5.1 in that their discourse referents do not act as representatives of particular times, but as bound variables. Frequency adverbs will be considered in Section 5.5.2.

The central members of the third category are prepositional phrases beginning with **in** or **for**, such as **in an hour** and **for an hour**. These phrases are not locating adverbs in any sense. Their function is not to locate the described eventuality along the temporal axis, but to determine its duration, its "temporal size". We will refer to these adverbs as *measure adverbs*. We will see, however, that there are also adverbs which simultaneously serve as location and as measure of the described

[57] Adverbials such as **now, on Sunday, last Sunday** behave in certain ways like *indexical* expressions. (See e.g. [Lewis 1970], [Kaplan 1979], [Zimmermann 1991].) However, in calling them all "indexical" one ignores the important differences between them.

eventuality. So it is not easy to draw a sharp dividing line between locating adverbs and measure adverbs. Measure adverbials will be the topic of Section 5.5.3.

In Section 5.5.4, we will have a brief look at a category of expressions that is strictly speaking a subset of the locating adverbs, but one that will be ignored in Section 5.5.1. These are temporal subordinate clauses, such as **when Mary opened the refrigerator, while Fred was clearing the rubble, before Kennedy was shot** or **until death do us part.** A subordinate temporal clause contributes to the meaning of the sentence in which it is embedded in much the same way as other locating adverbs. But where the adverb takes the form of a subordinate clause, interpretation of the sentence as a whole will require processing the temporal and aspectual features (*TP*, *TENSE*, etc.) twice over, once for the main clause and once for the subordinate clause. So we should be prepared for a certain interaction between these two sets of feature values. In view of such interactions, temporal subordinate clauses deserve separate consideration.

Relative clauses, which we first introduced in Chapter 1 but which have so far been ignored in the present chapter, raise similar questions. The section ends with a brief review of them.

5.5.1 Locating Adverbials

5.5.1.1 Calendar Names

Recall how temporal adverbials were processed in the earlier sections of this chapter: the construction rule dealing with the S′-node introduces a discourse referent for the location time; when a locating adverbial is present, it is turned into a condition on this location time. For instance, if we construct a DRS for the sentence

(5.184) Mary wrote the letter on April fifth, 1992.

after the recipe of Section 5.2 (compare the DRS-construction for (5.32)), we obtain (5.185).

(5.185)

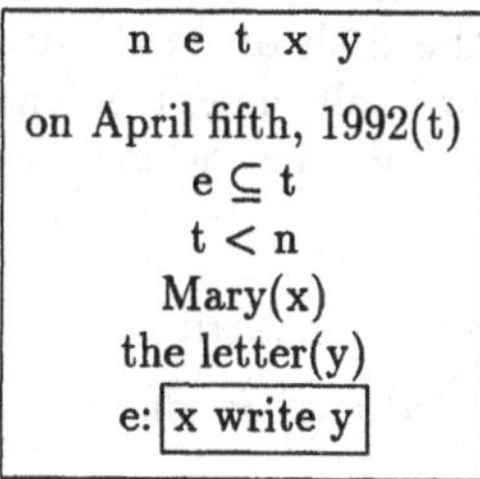

(5.185) contains the condition **on April fifth, 1992(t)**. Intuitively, this condition expresses that the time **t** is the fifth of April of the year 1992, a condition to which the preposition **on** and the NP **April fifth, 1992** each make their contribution. One of the tasks of the present section is to disentangle these separate contributions.

For the adverb under consideration, the matter is straightforward. The NP **April fifth, 1992** acts as a proper name, which rigidly designates one particular date. The preposition **on** relates this date to the location time of the described eventuality. We will assume that the relation it expresses is that of coincidence. The construction rule which reduces the condition **on April fifth, 1992(t)** splits it into two conditions, one of which, **April fifth, 1992(t′)**, specifies that the (newly introduced) discourse referent **t′** represents the day in question, while the other relates this discourse referent to the discourse referent **t** in the sense of **on**. When this rule is applied to (5.185), the effect is as in (5.186). (The relation **on** is conveniently represented as identity.)

(5.186)

n e t x y t′
April fifth, 1992(t′)
$t = t'$
$e \subseteq t$
$t < n$
Mary(x)
the letter(y)
e: [x write y]

5.5.1.2 'in April' and 'on Sunday'

In the context of our present inquiry adverbials like **on April fifth, 1992** are not of much interest. The NP **April fifth, 1992** is a fully explicit description of a particular time, and acts much like a proper name. Of more interest are what we might call "context-dependent calendar names" – NPs such as **April; the fifth of April; the fifth; 4 a.m. on the fifth of April; 4 a.m.; the first Sunday in April; Sunday**, and so on. For in all these, the denotation is dependent on the context in which they are used. Take, for instance, the NPs **April** and **Sunday**, as they occur in sentences such as

(5.187) (i) Mary moved to Paris in April.

(ii) Mary wrote the letter on Sunday.

Suppose (5.187.i) is asserted in a situation in which no context has yet been set up. In that case, **April** will be taken to refer to the most recent month of April. When the utterance is made in May or at some later time in the year, this will be the April of that same year; if the sentence is uttered in January, February or March, the referent will be the April of the immediately preceding year. The situation changes when the utterance context already represents certain past times. In that case **April** can refer to Aprils of other years. For instance, if

(5.188) Mary found that apartment in the Marais in February of 1978.
She moved to Paris in April.

is uttered some time in 1992, **April** is naturally taken to refer to the April following the mentioned February (that is, to April 1978). It needs little thought to see that **on Sunday** behaves in the same way.

These first observations permit us to draw two preliminary conclusions:

(i) context-dependent descriptions of calendar times, such as **April** and **Sunday**, apply to more than one portion of time. (If the world were to go on forever, they would be true of an infinite number.) In this respect, they are like descriptions such as **the kitchen** or **the post office**, which can be used to refer to many different kitchens or post offices.

(ii) which particular portion of time an NP such as **April** or **Sunday** selects when it occurs as part of an adverbial phrase **in April** or **on Sunday**, depends on the context. First, suppose that processing of the clause containing the adverb does not involve the choice of an Rpt, or alternatively that the Rpt is identified with the TPpt. In this case, the time designated by the NP is the one fitting its descriptive content and that is nearest to the TPpt in the direction indicated by the value of *TENSE*. Second, if an element other than the TPpt is chosen as Rpt and this element is distinct from the TPpt, then the denoted time may be *either* the one fitting the description that is nearest to the TPpt or else the one that is nearest to the Rpt, again in the direction that is compatible with the constraints imposed by *TENSE*.[58]

Besides the problem of articulating the general principles according to which tokens of adverbials such as **in April** and **on Sunday** determine their referents in context, there is the more modest one of deciding on a particular form for the DRS-conditions which articulate what the referents of such tokens are. The following DRS, for the sentence (5.32),

[58] We do not feel that we have done enough empirical spade work to be wholly confident about this conjecture. So we state it with reservations. We encourage the reader to try the hypothesis on more examples. If these show the hypothesis to be too restrictive (or to be defective in some other way) then the construction rule will have to be adjusted accordingly.

(5.32) Mary wrote the letter on Sunday.

illustrates how we propose to deal with this problem.

(5.189)

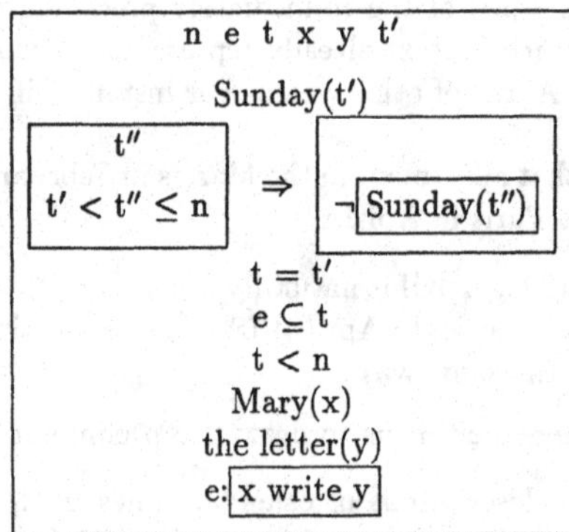

The condition **Sunday(t′)** expresses that t′ is some Sunday or other. The quantified condition says that no time that is entirely after **t′** but not later than **n** is part of another Sunday. Thus **t′** is the nearest Sunday to **n** in the direction of the past. These two conditions result when the condition **Sunday(t)** of (5.48) is subjected to further processing.

The prepositional phrases **in April** and **on Sunday** exhibit a number of properties that will also be important in connection with some other adverbs which we consider in this section. First, they cannot be used to refer to periods containing the utterance time. (5.188), for example, could hardly be used on a day in April as a way of saying that Mary moved to Paris earlier that same April. Similarly, if today is Sunday, and I know this, I cannot felicitously utter the sentence

(5.32) Mary wrote the letter on Sunday.

to mean that she wrote the letter earlier today. Nor can I say on Sunday afternoon

(5.190) Mary wrote the letter on Sunday morning.

to report that she wrote the letter that morning. In fact, the prohibition goes further. Not only would it be wrong to utter (5.32) in order to say that Mary wrote the letter that day; the sentence cannot be used either to say that she wrote the letter on the preceding Sunday; the same is true of (5.187). If the context in which it is uttered does not offer any past time to which the phrase **in April** can be related and the utterance falls within the month of April, then (5.187) is simply infelicitous, whether we take it as speaking about that same April or about the preceding one.

Our first, preliminary conclusions from these observations may be summarized as follows. (From now on we focus exclusively on **on Sunday**):

(iii) **on Sunday** cannot be used to refer to a day which contains the utterance time;

(iv) the day to which the phrase refers is the nearest Sunday to the utterance time in the direction indicated by the tense of the clause of which the phrase is part.

We saw that (5.32) and (5.190) are inappropriate when uttered on a Sunday. That observation, however, needs to be qualified. If we first introduce a past time or event which can then be exploited as Rpt in the interpretation of the next sentence, the use of either (5.32) or (5.190) is perfectly acceptable. Thus

(5.191) Monday three weeks ago Mary started to write her article.
She finished the article on Sunday.

can be felicitously uttered on a Sunday no less than on any other day of the week.[59] But there remains a difference between utterances of (5.191) that take place on a Sunday and utterances occurring on weekdays. When (5.191) is uttered on a Sunday, then **on Sunday** can only be interpreted as referring to the Sunday nearest to the Monday mentioned in the first sentence (or, more precisely in the present case: the Sunday nearest to this Monday in the right direction, that is the first Sunday after it). If the utterance falls on some other day of the week, then **on Sunday** is ambiguous between the interpretation just mentioned and that according to which it refers to the last Sunday before the time of utterance. The situation is different again when we change the **Monday** of (5.191) into **Sunday**, as in

(5.192) Sunday three weeks ago Mary started to write her article. She finished the article on Sunday.

(5.192) is unambiguous when used on a day which is not a Sunday; in this case it can only refer to the Sunday nearest to the day on which the utterance occurred. When (5.192) is uttered on a Sunday there is no felicitous interpretation for it.

The general underlying principle should now be clear. It is captured by the following conditions, which supplant (iii) and (iv):

[59]The same observations apply, *mutatis mutandis*, to (5.188).

(iii′) The interpretation of the adverb **on Sunday** requires the choice of an "origin of computation". This "origin of computation" is sometimes the utterance time, but it can also be some other contextually salient time.

(iv′) The day to which the phrase refers must be the nearest Sunday to the "origin of computation" in the "right direction".

(v′) A time cannot be used as "origin of computation" if it is itself part of a Sunday.

It seems to us that the second sentence of (iii′) can be strengthened to

(iii″) The "origin of computation" must be one of the following items

(a) the utterance time,
(b) the TPpt for the clause in which the adverb occurs,
(c) The Rpt chosen in the interpretation of the clause.

However, (iv″) is somewhat conjectural. It ought to be checked against more data than were available to us.

The interpretation procedure for **on Sunday** should take account of these conditions. In our framework this means that they ought to be reflected in the construction rule (or rules) needed to represent this adverbial phrase. We are already committed to a two-step interpretation procedure, in which the condition containing the prepositional phrase **on Sunday(t)** is decomposed into a condition $\mathbf{t = t'}$ which accounts for the contribution made by the preposition **on** and a condition **Sunday(t′)**, which expresses that the new discourse referent **t′** represents the day which the NP **Sunday** is taken to denote. It is the construction rule for reducing this last condition which should reflect the facts we have noted, and it is to this rule that we now turn our attention.

In formulating this rule, we are faced with a difficulty which we have not yet encountered. The use of a certain discourse referent $\mathbf{t_0}$ as "origin of computation" of the referent of **on Sunday** is subject, we argued, to the constraint that the time $\mathbf{t_0}$ may not itself be part of a Sunday. This constraint acts as a *presupposition* on the interpretation of the adverb: unless the constraint is satisfied, the phrase simply cannot be interpreted through computation from the time of speech. Thus it would be wrong to represent the constraint in the form of an additional condition in the DRS for the uttered sentence. For instance, it would not do to add

(5.193)

$$\neg \begin{array}{|c|} \hline \mathrm{n} \ \mathrm{t'''} \\ \hline \mathrm{n} \subseteq \mathrm{t'''} \\ \mathrm{Sunday(t''')} \\ \hline \end{array}$$

which states that the utterance time does not fall on a Sunday, to the DRS (5.189) for (5.32). For this would render utterances of (5.32) on Sundays false rather than infelicitous. And so we would be led to the conclusion that a negation of (5.32) like

(5.194) It is false that Mary wrote the letter on Sunday.

should be true, irrespective of what Mary did, simply because it was said on a Sunday. But of course this is absurd; when asserted on a Sunday, (5.194) is just as inappropriate as (5.32).

No, the construction rule should be such that when we apply it to an utterance of **on Sunday** on a Sunday, then the utterance time simply cannot be used as origin; and if no other time is available for this purpose, then the phrase, and with it the sentence of which it is part, cannot be interpreted at all. Presuppositional constraints, which block the application of a construction rule if certain conditions are not fulfilled, are no strangers to us. The rule for anaphoric pronouns, for instance, which we stated in Chapter 1, is constrained in just this way: it requires that the discourse referent for the pronoun be identified with some discourse referent already present in the context DRS (and occupies a position that is accessible from the position of the pronoun). If the context DRS does not contain any suitable discourse referents, then the pronoun is unprocessable and the sentence containing it fails to get an interpretation. But there is nevertheless an important difference between the constraint which governs the pronoun rule and the one which we need in connection with the rule for **on Sunday**. The former constraint only involved the form of the context DRS. In contrast, the one needed now has to do with how the represented utterance is located in the world; it involves not simply the form of the context DRS, but the way in which it is connected, via its discourse referent **n**, with reality. The recipient of an utterance of (5.32) will (in a context that makes no past times available as "origins of computation") register the utterance as odd when he is aware that it is Sunday – in other words, when the information that the utterance is being made on a Sunday is part of his context of interpretation. So, if the context DRS is to represent all the contextual information that is available to the interpreter, it will contain this information as well. This entails, however, that some parts of the context DRS make their way into it by means other than the processing of utterances or texts. For instance, there are many speech situations in which a large part of the relevant information will be due to visual perception.

The information on what day of the week a given utterance is or was made is essentially extralinguistic, too. If we nevertheless assume information of such extralinguistic provenance to be part of the context DRS, then we can state the constraint on the rule for **on Sunday** simply by requiring that the context DRS entails condition (5.193). We will pursue this use of DRSs – according to which they represent the information states of (human) interpreters of language – in Volume 2.

The next point that we must clarify before we can state the rule for **on Sunday** concerns the notions of "origin of computation" and of "right direction". We have mentioned the "origin of computation" several times already, always placing the term within scare quotes to make clear that it had not yet been properly introduced, but hoping that what we had in mind was sufficiently clear. As we said above, the general interpretation principle for the NP **Sunday** can be stated as: *the nearest Sunday, in the "right" direction, to* some given time t_0. Which Sunday this will be depends on the choice of t_0. The time t_0 is what we have been referring as the *origin of computation*. In other words, the referent of **Sunday** is the value which results when a certain function, given by the italicized description above, is applied to the origin of computation in question.

It turns out that the semantics of quite a number of temporal adverbials can be characterized with the help of such parameterized descriptions. In each of those cases we will speak of the parameter, as well as of the times which instantiate it in the interpretation of particular tokens of the adverb, as the adverb's origin of computation.

The meaning of "right direction" can now be described as follows. The interpretation of a tensed clause will typically involve a certain relation **R** between the described eventuality **e** and the time $\mathbf{t_0}$ which is used as origin of computation. This relation **R** determines the direction in which one should go from $\mathbf{t_0}$ to find the referent of the adverb. Formally we can define **R** as the relation such that the condition **e R** $\mathbf{t_0}$ is entailed by the DRS K under construction.

We now have all the bits and pieces we need to state the rule for **Sunday**. In our familiar format the rule looks as follows.

CR.Sunday

Triggering configuration $\gamma \subseteq \overline{\gamma} \in$ **Con$_K$:**

NP(t′)
|
PN
|
Sunday

Constraint: The clause from which this configuration derives has either *TENSE* = *past* or *TENSE* = *fut*.

Choose: Origin of Computation **t″** from the following items:

(a) **n**,
(b) the current TPpt, and
(c) the current Rpt.

Constraint: K entails the condition:

$$\neg \boxed{\begin{array}{c} t''' \\ \hline t'' \subseteq t''' \\ \text{Sunday}(t''') \end{array}}$$

Introduce into U$_K$: new time discourse referent **t**

Introduce into Con$_K$: **Sunday(t)**

(a) if K entails the condition **e < t″**, where **e** is the discourse referent for the described eventuality, add to Con$_K$ the conditions **t < t″** and

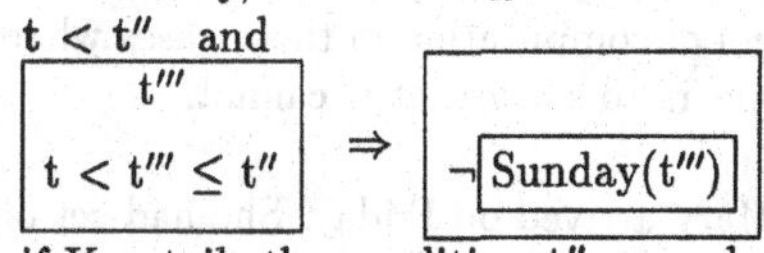

(b) if K entails the condition **t″ < e**, where **e** is the discourse referent for the described eventuality, add to Con$_K$ the conditions **t″ < t** and

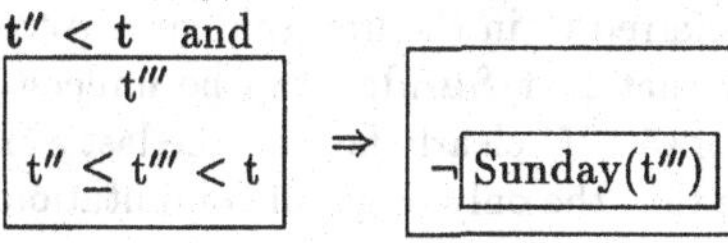

5.5.1.3 Alternatives to 'on Sunday'

It is interesting to compare the adverb **on Sunday** with some others that can sometimes serve as substitutes for it. The phrases we have in mind are: **last Sunday, next Sunday, on the previous/preceding Sunday, on the following Sunday**. First **last Sunday**. Observe that if we substitute this phrase for **on Sunday** in (5.32) or in (5.190).

(5.195) Mary wrote the letter last Sunday.

(5.196) Mary wrote the letter last Sunday morning.

we obtain statements with equivalent truth conditions. Or, more accurately, the statements we obtain this way are equivalent to the original ones so long as they are not uttered on a Sunday. For when the utterance falls on a Sunday, then each of the new statements is felicitous, while, as we saw, those with **on Sunday** are not. If **last Sunday** is uttered on a Sunday, its referent is just what it is when the utterance does not occur on a Sunday, viz. the most recent Sunday in the past.

We find a different effect when **last Sunday** is substituted for **on Sunday** in (5.191). When the utterance is not made on a Sunday, the new statement is unambiguous, the only possible referent for **Sunday** being the most recent Sunday before **n**. If the utterance is made on a Sunday, then the new statement differs from the old one. Again, **last Sunday** refers to the last Sunday before **n**, whereas **on Sunday** must in this case refer to the first Sunday after the Monday mentioned.

This gives us all but one of the empirical data needed to state the construction rule for **last Sunday**. The piece that is still missing is whether the TPpt can be used as origin of computation in those cases where it differs from **n**. The following example appears to show that it cannot.

(5.197) Mary arrived on Friday. She had set off last Sunday.

Suppose (5.197) is uttered on a Thursday. Then the last Sunday before **n** follows the Friday referred to in the first sentence. According to our intuitions this is the only Sunday that **last Sunday** can be understood to refer to here, even though the content of (5.197) clearly favours the last Sunday before the Friday mentioned. We conclude that the only origin of computation available for the interpretation of **last Sunday** is **n**.

These observations contain all that we need to know about the semantics of NPs of the form **last** α (**last Sunday, last April, last week, last night**, etc.).

We summarize the relevant conditions in analogy with our statement of the interpretation conditions for **on Sunday**.

(i) The time referred to by **last Sunday** is the nearest Sunday in the past of the "origin of computation".

(ii) The only origin of computation available for **last Sunday** is **n**.

(iii) **last Sunday** is not subject to the presuppositional constraint that **n** cannot be exploited as origin of computation when the utterance takes place on a Sunday.

A fully explicit statement of the rule also raises a question about syntax. On the surface, **last Sunday** appears to be an NP, not a PP. However, as a locating adverb it contributes to the semantic representation of the sentence in which it occurs not just the time to which it refers, but also the relation in which this time stands to the location of the described eventuality. In this regard, **last Sunday** is on a par with a PP like **on Sunday**, where the two contributions can be identified with the NP and the preposition, respectively. Indeed, from a semantic viewpoint **last Sunday** functions rather like a prepositional phrase, with an empty preposition whose semantic contribution is the same as that of **on** in **on Sunday**. This is what we assume the syntax of the adverb **last Sunday** to be. That is, we assume its syntactic tree to be of the form

(5.198)

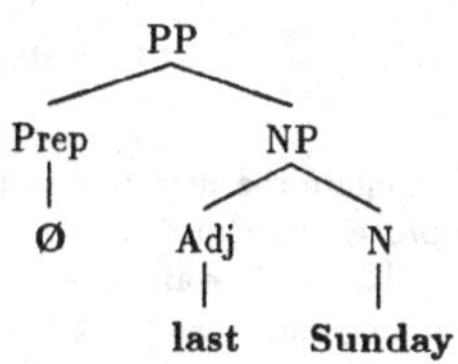

This syntactic analysis allows us to reduce conditions of the form **last Sunday(t)**, in which the top node of (5.198) is followed by the parameter **(t)**, in the same way as we did for **on Sunday(t)**. The construction rule directly applicable to conditions of this form reduces each such condition to two new conditions: **t** = **t′** (coming from the empty preposition **Ø**) and

(5.199)

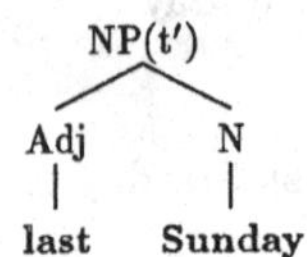

with **t′** a new discourse referent. The rule applying to (5.199) must then accomplish the equivalent of what the rule CR.**Sunday** accomplishes in the case of **on Sunday**. This rule, we implied above, ought to be factorized further into one dealing with the common noun **Sunday** and one dealing with the adjective **last**. We leave it as a task for the reader to determine how this is best accomplished.[60]

The phrase **on the preceding Sunday** differs from **on Sunday** in just the opposite direction from **last Sunday**. Substituting the phrase for **on Sunday** in (5.32) now produces a statement that differs from (5.32) both when the utterances are made on a Sunday and when they are made on some other day.

(5.200) Mary wrote the letter on the preceding Sunday.

In fact, without further context (5.200) is uninterpretable. And in contexts where it is interpretable, the prepositional phrase will pick out some Sunday other than the last one before the utterance time. We can see this more clearly when we substitute **on the preceding Sunday** for **on Sunday** in (5.191). The resulting discourse

(5.201) Monday three weeks ago Mary started to write her article.
She finished the article on the preceding Sunday.

[60]It is tempting to try and formulate the new rule in such a way that it becomes a special case of the general strategy for processing expressions of type N which consist of a superlative followed by a common noun. For that is after all what **last Sunday** amounts to from a purely syntactic point of view. Unfortunately there isn't much we can do along those lines here, since we are without a general treatment of comparatives and superlatives. As a superlative, **last** has the fairly unusual property that it involves a hidden parameter which can be made explicit by adding a Prepositional Phrase **before ...**, as in **last exit before the toll booth**. In the case of **last Sunday**, this parameter is precisely what we have been calling the origin of computation, which, we argued, must always be the utterance time **n**: treating **last Sunday** as the last Sunday before **n**.

In the absence of a general treatment of superlatives the best we can do is to formulate a set of construction rules for arbitrary NPs of the form **last** α, where α is either the name of a day of the week, the name of a month, or else is one of the words **week**, **month**, **year**, etc.

cannot be given a plausible interpretation. The phrase **on the preceding Sunday** must be interpreted as referring to the Sunday immediately preceding the Monday mentioned. But that interpretation is incompatible with the use of the tense (there should have been a past perfect instead) and even then it would have made no sense contentwise (one cannot finish a paper before starting it). Shuffling things around a bit, as in

(5.202) Wednesday three weeks ago Mary finished her paper. She had started it on the preceding Sunday.

we get a sentence pair that makes sense both qua grammar and qua content; and the sense it makes is unequivocally that the paper was started on the Sunday immediately before the Wednesday on which it was completed.

This shows that the origin of computation for **on the preceding Sunday** *cannot be* **n**. It can be an Rpt distinct from **n** and, as the next example shows, it can also be the TPpt, when that is different from **n**:

(5.203) Mary arrived on Friday. She had set off on the preceding Sunday.

These facts provide the empirical basis for the construction rule(s) for **on the preceding Sunday(t)**.[61]

The contrast between **last Sunday** and **on the preceding Sunday** is one of which we find many instances in natural languages: one of a pair of expressions is indexical in that its referent is related in a certain way to a deictically prominent element, whereas the other refers to items standing in that same relation to elements that differ from this deictically prominent element. We find a similar opposition between the first person pronoun **I** and the third person pronouns **he, she, it.** The former must always refer to the individual that stands to the utterance in the special relationship of being its author, while the third person pronouns are prohibited from referring to the authors of the utterances in which they figure.

5.5.1.4 'before' and 'after'

The three types of locating adverbs we have looked at in this section – **on Sunday, last Sunday, on the preceding Sunday** – are a small selection from a much larger family. Much more could be said, for instance, about words such as **yesterday, today,** and **tomorrow** (**today** behaves in many respects like **now**, but

[61]See Exercise 1 on p. 634.

not quite); about the words **then** and **next**; about **soon** and **recently**, and so on. An adequate discussion of the subject might well require a monograph on its own; certainly it could not be carried through in a subsection of a section of a chapter of a book. Thus the present section should be seen, not as offering an analysis of locating adverbs that aims to be in any way comprehensive, but rather as illustrating *some* of the problems with which a semantics of temporal adverbs must be able to deal. Our choice of the adverbs discussed above has been motivated by our belief that the problems they present are of particular interest in the context of discourse representation, and also that a careful analysis of these adverbs reveals some important morals about the phenomena of deixis and indexicality in general. In the remaining pages of this subsection, we briefly discuss temporal prepositional phrases which differ from the ones discussed so far primarily in how they relate the location time of the described eventuality to the times denoted by their NPs. The particular prepositions we consider are **after**, **before**, **since**, **until** and **from**.

We should say right away that prepositional phrases with **before** and **after** do not hold much interest for us as such. However, in Section 5.5.4, which deals with temporal subordinate clauses, we shall want to say something about clauses which have **before** and **after** for their conjunctions (subordinate clauses like **after Bill arrived** or **before Mary will hand in her paper**). These clauses have certain obvious properties in common with prepositional phrases such as **before 10** or **after the explosion**. Since we will need to articulate those properties somewhere, they are better discussed in the present section than in Section 5.5.4, where we will concentrate on the relations between the tenses of subordinate and main clause. Our reason for wanting to say something about **since** and **until** is another. Returning to these words is a kind of tribute to the past. We came to speak of **since** and **until** as early as in Section 5.1. At that point our perspective was one of formal logic rather than linguistics. With what types of English clauses **since** and **until** can form temporal adverbials, or how these adverbials interact in detail with the tenses of the main clauses – such questions were then beyond our purview. But they are the sorts of questions which have preoccupied us since. So it seems natural, now that we have had the experience of the intervening sections, to ask those questions also about our old acquaintances **since** and **until**.

But first **before** and **after**. Just as **at ten** or **in March**, adverbials like **before/after the explosion**, or **before/after the first of January, 1993** serve to characterize the location of the described eventuality. But the characterizations they provide are always partial characterizations only. For instance, **after the explosion** only says that the eventuality followed the explosion; it does not specify by how little or how much. What the phrase **after** α does is to divide the axis of time into two halves and to say of the described eventuality that it lies in the "upper half". **Before**-phrases do much the same, except that they locate the eventuality in the "lower half".[62]

According to this assessment of the meaning of **before**- and **after**-phrases, a sentence like

(5.205) Mary will move to Amsterdam after the first of January, 1993.

will get a representation of the form

(5.206)

n t t′ e x y
e ⊆ t
n < t
t′ < t
the first of January, 1993(t′)
Mary(x)
Amsterdam(y)
e: [x move to y]

However, in actual use **before**- and **after**-phrases often carry a certain implication about the distance between the described eventuality and the time or event mentioned by the adverbial. Thus in

(5.207) Bill arrived on Wednesday at five. He left after ten.

there is usually a strong implication that Bill's departure did not occur much after ten o'clock. For example, in most situations one would not want to assert (5.207) if Bill had left in the course of Thursday, let alone if he had left only the following week. Arguably this is a problem for pragmatics, and thus one that lies beyond the horizon of this book. That the matter is nevertheless of importance for semantics becomes visible in sentences involving adverbial quantification. For instance, if **after** e meant no more than "at some time or other following e", then the sentence

[62]There exists the possibility of using **before**-phrases in a kind of "virtual" sense which is not possible for prepositional phrases with **after**. In a case where the sentence

(5.204) George died before the completion of her novel.

is true, the completion of the novel presumably never took place. (We ignore the possibilities either that the book was finished by some other person or by George's ghost.) This use of **before** has given semanticists a good deal of trouble. (See in particular [Heinämäki 1973].) It is an issue which we will not pursue here.

(5.208) After a game of tennis Mary always smoked a cigarette.

would be true if Mary had smoked only once in her life, but at a time which happened to be later than all occasions on which she ever played tennis. This is clearly not what (5.208) says. (5.208) means something like "Mary always smoked shortly after playing tennis". But how short is short? Evidently that varies with the kinds of events the discourse is about and possibly with other aspects of the context as well.

While this additional constraint on the semantic import of **before**- and **after**-phrases is clearly important, it seems very difficult to give a reasonably precise treatment of it in a formal semantics of the kind we are pursuing. Not only is it hard to get an overview of the different factors which constrain the distance between desribed eventuality and the time or event denoted by the adverbial; there is also a problem of ineliminable vagueness. But vagueness is a subject in its own right and it is not one for this book.

5.5.1.5 'since' and 'until'

Since-phrases pose two interrelated problems. The first is: What times do **since**-phrases describe? The second: Why are the tense forms with which **since**-phrases can combine restricted in the way they are? As regards the second question, we note that English **since**-phrases are only compatible with perfect tenses. For instance, the sentences in (5.209) are all grammatical, whereas those in (5.210) are not:

(5.209) (i) Mary has lived in Amsterdam since 1975.
(ii) Mary had lived in Amsterdam since 1975.
(iii) Mary will have lived in Amsterdam since 1975.

(5.210) (i) *Mary lives in Amsterdam since 1975.
(ii) *Mary lived in Amsterdam since 1975.
(iii) *Mary will live in Amsterdam since 1975.

This is, like the special use of perfects with **for**-phrases which we discussed in Section 5.3, a feature of English that is not shared by languages such as German and French (for instance, the French and German translations of (5.209.i) are **Mary habite ici depuis 1975** and **Mary wohnt hier seit 1975**). So it seems reasonable to assume that **for**- and **since**-phrases trigger this same use of the English perfect. However, we have no better idea than we did in Section 5.3 why it should be precisely these adverbials that make this use of the perfect possible. It is a further question why perfects are obligatory in the presence of **since**-phrases. This question is also reminiscent of a similar problem we encountered in connection with **for**-adverbials: in order to say that Mary lives in Amsterdam and has lived there for the last three years, we *must*, if we are to express this proposition with the help of **for three years**, use the present perfect – in particular, it isn't possible to use the simple present tense sentence **Mary lives here for three years**.

The first problem – what does a phrase of the form **since** α denote? – must be seen in the context of what has just been said about the second. Consider (5.209.i): this sentence is true if and only if the state s′ of Mary living in Amsterdam holds at all times from (some time in) 1975 until (and including) the time of utterance. There is more than one way in which this relation between the time denoted by α and the temporal location of the state s′ could be articulated. One of them is as follows.

(5.211) The location of the state described by the sentence starts at the time denoted by α and continues up to some time that is to be recovered from the context.

But we do not think that this is quite right. Compare the sentences in (5.209) with those in (5.212), in which the **since**-phrase has been replaced by a phrase beginning with **from**.

(5.212) (i) Mary lived in Amsterdam from 1975.
(ii) From 1975 Mary lived in Amsterdam.
(iii) Mary lived in Amsterdam from 1975 onwards.
(iv) Mary lived in Amsterdam from 1975 until 1987.
(v) Mary lived in Amsterdam from 1975. Then, in 1987, she moved to Paris.
(vi) Mary has lived in Amsterdam from 1975 onwards.

As the sentences in (5.212) show, **from**-phrases can be combined with non-perfects – see (5.212.i–v) – as well as with perfects – see (5.212.vi). Moreover, there appear to be no general restrictions on the upper bound of the location time. According to what is said in (5.212.i–iii), the state described – that of Mary living in Amsterdam – could continue right up to the utterance time; but as (5.212.iv) and (5.212.v) show, they needn't. Thus **from**-phrases allow not only for greater variety of tense forms than **since**-phrases; they also can be used to describe a larger range of situations. In both respects, this greater flexibility is what the statement in (5.211) would lead one to expect. Thus, (5.211) (with **since** replaced by **from**) appears to be a correct description of the contribution of **from**-phrases rather than of **since**-phrases. A statement of the semantics of **since** α which could account for the syntactic and semantic restrictions that distinguish sentences with **since**-phrases from those with **from**-phrases ought to present the contributions that **since**-phrases make in a way which exploits the special features of those eventualities that are described by the type of perfect that we find in the presence of **since**-phrases – thus of that particular type of perfect which we identified in connection with **for**-phrases in Sections 5.3.3 and 5.3.4.3. According to the analysis we proposed in Section 5.3, such perfects describe states **s** which "result" from the onset of a state **s′** of the type characterized by the non-perfect verb phrase. It is this latter state, we argued, which is characterized by the accompanying **for**-phrase. We want to argue now that when the adverb is not a **for**-phrase but a **since**-phrase, that **since**-phrase also functions as a characterization of the underlying "non-perfect" state **s′**. This state, we already saw in Section 5.3.3, always continues up to and includes the location time **t** of the state **s** described by the perfect verb phrase. So **since** α in effect claims that the underlying state **s′** occupies the interval stretching from the denotation of α to **t**. And this is how we shall interpret the contribution it makes.

There is, however, one important difference between perfects with **for**- and those with **since**-phrases. The verb phrases that combine with **for**-phrases are invariably perfects of verb phrases that describe states or activities; the "result state" **s** is always brought about by the beginning of an underlying activity or state. The examples with **since**-phrases that we have so far considered shared this property.[63] But not all sentences with **since**-phrases are like this. In (5.214),

(5.214) (i) Since last summer Mary has moved to Paris.
(ii) Messiaen has died since the beginning of this month.
(iii) Since eight o'clock I have written ten letters.
(iv) Since the beginning of April Mary has written only one paper.

the underlying VPs – **write only one paper**, **write ten letters**, **die** – are accom-

[63] In fact, both the sentences with for-phrases and those with since-phrases we have so far looked at all had underlying stative verb phrases. But arguably activity VPs are also permitted in this environment. We are not absolutely certain of this. For while a sentence such as

(5.213) I have worked for three hours.

is surely grammatical, it is not entirely clear to us that it can have the reading according to which the period of working must extend up to the utterance time. These doubts notwithstanding, we will assume that both stative VPs and activities are possible in this construction.

plishments or achievements.[64] The existence of such sentences, and the meanings they have, evidently suggest the following:

(a) Since perfects with **since**-phrases allow for accomplishment and achievement verb phrases whereas the corresponding perfects with **for**-phrases do not, it may be presumed that the **for**-phrases are responsible for this restriction on the VPs they can combine with. Now, as we will argue in Section 5.5.3, it is a general property of **for**-phrases that they never combine with accomplishment or achievement verb phrases. This will entail the given restriction if we assume that the **for**-phrases of perfect sentences act as characterizations of the underlying eventualities. If, on the other hand, we were to assume that it is the eventuality described by the perfect VP which the **for**-phrase is used to characterize, then the restriction would remain unaccounted for since *this* eventuality will always be a result state, irrespective of whether the underlying VP is a stative or a non-stative one. (Note that this argument also supports the choice we made in Section 5.3.3 when we decided to treat the **for**-phrases of sentences in the perfect always as characterizations of the underlying state **s′** rather than of the result state **s**.)

(b) The result states described in (5.214) all require that the events of which they are the results took place after the times indicated by the **since**-phrases. For instance, the result state described in (5.214.i) holds in virtue of (i) the occurrence of a past event to the effect that Mary moved to Paris, and (ii) the fact that this event occurred *after* last summer – if Mary moved to Paris before that time, (5.214.i) is false. This is another piece of evidence suggesting that **since** α characterizes the location of the eventuality described by the non-perfect VP. The inclusion we have just observed – that this eventuality, Mary's move to Paris, lies within the period from last summer to the time of utterance – is consistent with what we said about the relation between location time and event in Section 5.2: if the underlying verb phrase is an accomplishment or achievement, then the eventuality is included in the location time. If the underlying verb phrase is stative, then, by the lights of Section 5.2, the relationship between eventuality and location time is rather the reverse (or at least it comes close to that). Indeed, this is what we find with the sentences in (5.209), where the underlying state must in each case have been going on for *at least as long as* the time given by the **since**-phrase.[65]

[64]How good achievements are in such sentences may be a matter of debate. (5.214.ii), for instance, seems to us a little awkward. But we believe the sentence are possible; we will assume that they are grammatical.

[65]There is a slight problem here with activity VPs. Sentences in which **since**-phrases go together with activity verbs require, like those with stative VPs, that the underlying eventuality includes the period characterized by the **since**-phrase, not that it be included in that period. In this respect, activity verbs behave like statives. We have no account of why activity verbs behave in this way.

We are now ready to state the semantic contributions made by **since**-phrases.[66]

(5.215) A phrase of the form **since** α serves to characterize the state **s** described by a clause in a perfect tense. **Since** α characterizes **s** indirectly, viz. by characterizing the location time **t′** for the eventuality described by the underlying non-perfect verb phrase. It describes this location time as beginning at the denotation of α and as ending with, and including the location time **t** for the state **s**. If the underlying verb phrase is stative, then **s** is the result of the onset of the state **s′** characterized by that VP; if the underlying VP is non-stative, then **s** results from the described event.

It is straightforward to convert (5.215) into a processing rule for sentences with **since**-phrases. We will spare ourselves this exercise and just present – in (5.216) and (5.217) below – the resulting DRSs for two such sentences, (5.209.iii) and (5.214.i).

(5.216)

n t s s′ e t′ t″ x y
$n < t$
$s \bigcirc t$
$e = beg(s')$
$e \supset\subset s$
$t' \subseteq s'$
1975(t″)
$t'' = beg(t')$
$t = end(t')$
Mary(x)
Amsterdam(y)
s′: [x live in y]

[66]There is one further problem with the analysis of since-phrases we have proposed. Contrary to what we have maintained up to this point, a since-phrase is not used to characterize the location time of the state s described by the sentence itself, but rather the location of some other, related, eventuality. As a matter of fact, this constitutes only a weak violation of the general principle governing location adverbs. For if the underlying VP is stative, then the two states run concurrently so that the since-phrase characterizes the location time of the result state. If the underlying VP is non-stative, however, there remains a problem. If the since-phrase is reinterpreted as characterizing the location time of the result state, then we would expect that this result state has lasted for at least as long as the since-phrase indicates. But as we have seen, normally this is not so. We do not know how this apparent contradiction is to be resolved.

(5.217)

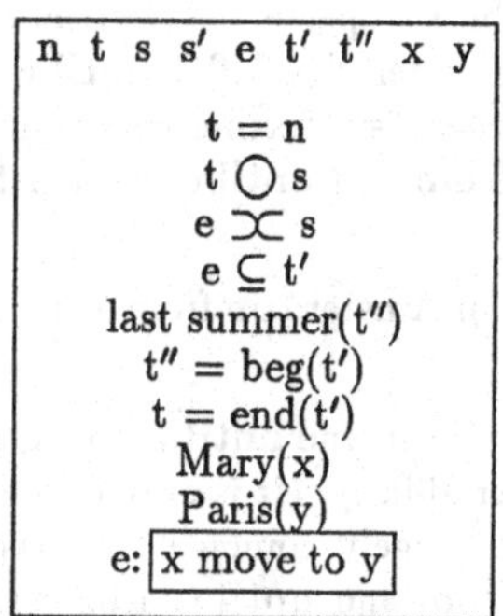

In Section 5.1, we discussed **since** in conjunction with **until** and we treated these two connectives as mirror images of each other. Their being each other's mirror images could seem plausible as long as we thought of past and future as mirror images of each other generally. However, in subsequent sections we found reason to reject this view. From a cognitive perspective, we argued, the future is fundamentally different from the past; so it should not be surprising that this difference manifests itself also in the ways in which language expresses propositions about past and future. In view of this general difference, we should also be prepared for certain differences between **since** and **until** that might have escaped our notice when our attention was focussed on logic rather than linguistics.

Indeed there are such differences. One is that **until** does not restrict the choice of tense in the way that **since** does. Thus, note that each of the following sentences is grammatical:

(5.218) (i) Mary lived in Amsterdam until 1987.

(ii) Mary had lived in Amsterdam until the beginning of 1975.

(iii) Mary will stay in Amsterdam until 1995.

(iv) Mary had remained in Amsterdam until the first of June 1975.

In fact, all non-perfect tenses are compatible with **until**-phrases – if any tense forms are excluded, then these are precisely the perfects. On the other hand, **until**-phrases are selective with regard to aspect: they only go with verb phrases which describe activities or states. For instance, a sentence like

(5.219) I will finish the paper until the first of June.

is ungrammatical. In both these respects – no restriction to the perfect, restriction with regard to aspect of the underlying VP – **until** resembles not so much **since** but, rather, **from**. In fact, there is a further connection between **from** and **until** which supports this claim: **from** and **until** can occur together, as in

(5.212.iv) Mary lived in Amsterdam from 1975 until 1987.

This possibility of combining **from**- and **until**-phrases into what appear to be single adverbials is evidence of their affinity. (It is only because the selection restrictions on **from**- and **until**-phrases largely coincide that the combined phrases are so readily available.) Indeed, **from** and **until** can be considered "mirror images" in the specific sense that they act, in the same types of sentential environments, as lower and upper bound to the location time of the described activity or state.

In a sentence like (5.212.iv), the location time is explicitly demarcated at both ends. Sentences which have a **from**-phrase but no **until**-phrase (such as those in (5.212.i,ii,iii)) or those with an **until**- but no **from**-phrase (as in (5.218)) provide explicit demarcations of one of the two ends only. The other end is then often implied contextually. For instance, if (5.218.iii) is said in a context in which no future times have yet been introduced, one will understand the described state to start at the utterance time; and in (5.212.v) the second sentence informs us that the state described by the first came to an end in 1987. But there are also cases where the context does not fix the missing end. (5.212.i), for example, can be felicitously used in contexts from which it is not possible to infer *until* what time Mary lived in Amsterdam.

What we have said about **from**- and **until**-phrases should suffice as guideline for the formulation of the pertinent construction rules and for applying those rules in the construction of DRSs for sentences like those in (5.212) and (5.218). We leave those rules and applications as an exercise.

Exercises

1. Formulate the construction for **the preceding Sunday** in the format of CR.Sunday (see p. 620). Check that this rule yields the intuitively correct interpretations for the sentences (5.200)–(5.203).

2. Similarly formulate construction rules for **last Sunday** and **next Sunday**. Check the rule for **last Sunday** against the examples (5.195)–(5.197). Use the rule for **next Sunday** and an equivalent rule for **next Friday** to construct a DRS for the following text:

Mary will phone her father next Sunday. She will visit him next Friday.

5.5.2 Adverbs of Temporal Quantification

Adverbs of temporal quantification stand to the locating adverbs we considered in the preceding section as quantifying NPs like **every student** or **many students** stand to definite noun phrases such as **Fred, the post office** or **Bill's children.** On the one hand, the two adverbial categories differ in that adverbs of quantification induce, like the quantifying NPs studied in earlier chapters, the tripartite quantificational structures we introduced in Chapter 4. Thus they make contributions to the meanings of the sentences in which they occur that are very different from the adverbs of the preceding section. On the other hand, quantifying adverbs have in common with those of the last section that they too characterize the location times of the described eventualities. In our terms: both types introduce discourse referents that play the *role* of location time. But while the discourse referent for a locating adverb in the sense of Section 5.5.1 represents a single time, those introduced by quantifying adverbs act as bound variables, ranging over sets of possible location times.

From a syntactic point of view, we find as much variety among the adverbs of temporal quantification as among locating adverbs: genuine adverbs (**always, often, mostly, rarely**), apparent noun phrases (**every morning, most Thursdays**) and prepositional phrases (**during every service, after many meals**). We begin by looking at an apparent NP, **every morning.** Consider the sentence

(5.220) In 1985 Mary went swimming every morning.

According to what we said in the last section, **in 1985** is a constraint on the location time of the eventuality which the sentence describes. In the present case, however, there isn't just one single described eventuality. Rather, the discourse referent **e** introduced by the tensed verb acts as a bound variable which takes values from a *range* of possible eventualities. Each of these eventualities must occur in the course of some morning or other – it is in this sense, we just said, that the quantifying adverb **every morning** functions as a locating adverb. At the same time, however, **in 1985** also functions as a locating adverb, but as one with a "global" function – the time it describes is to be understood as location time for *all* the eventualities in the range of the discourse referent **e**. In other words, it is the entire range of the quantifier **every morning** which is constrained by this second adverb. It is, we will assume, also the second adverb **in 1985**, which interacts with tense in the ways we have seen earlier. The general location time **t** is, one the one hand, constrained by the past tense to be situated before **n**, and, on the other hand, by the content of **in 1985**.

These observations should suffice as an informal guide to the kind of representation we want to propose for (5.220). We first present this representation and then consider the construction steps by which it is obtained.

(5.221)

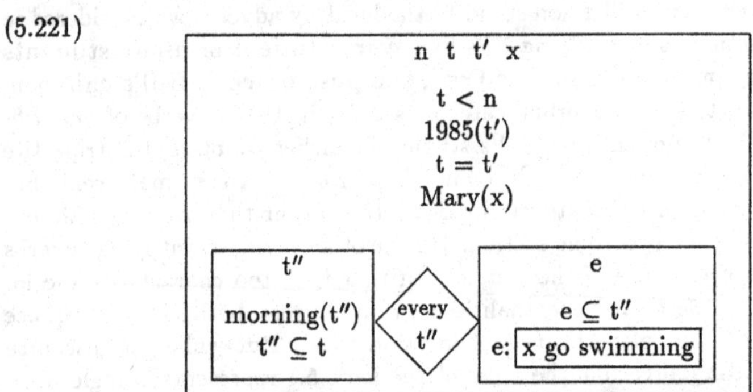

The construction (5.221) presupposes, as always, a syntactic input. With regard to the syntactic structure of quantificational sentences like (5.220), we adopt once again a pragmatic attitude. We assume, strictly for the sake of convenient processing, that the locating adverb and the frequency adverb form, jointly with the remainder of the sentence, a tripartite structure, as in (5.222).[67, 68]

(5.222)

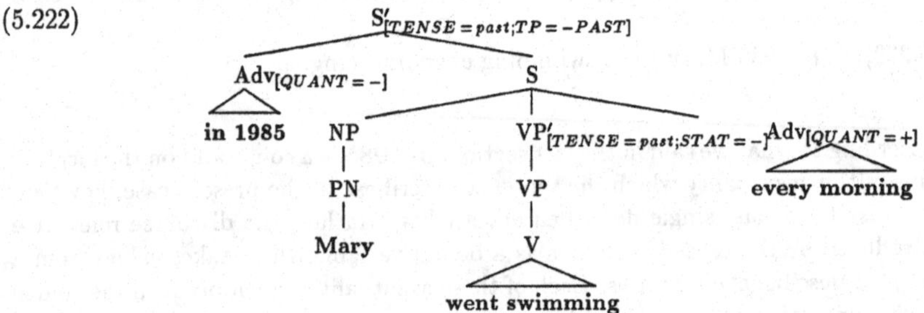

Given this syntactic structure, the construction of (5.221) should involve the following steps: the first concerns, as before, the choice of TPpt and the locating adverb

[67] The syntax presented in Section 5.7 does not include adverbs of quantification. So the sentences located in the present section are, like the phenomena discussed in Chapter 3, 'hors de concours'.

[68] For convenience we are treating **go swimming** as an unanalysable verb.

in 1985. In the present case, the TPpt must be **n**. The second step deals with the quantificational adverb **every morning**, setting up the quantifying condition given in (5.223)

(5.223)

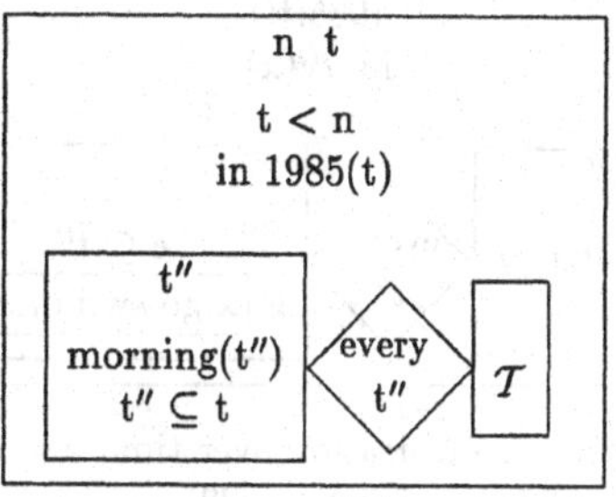

where $\mathcal{T}$ is

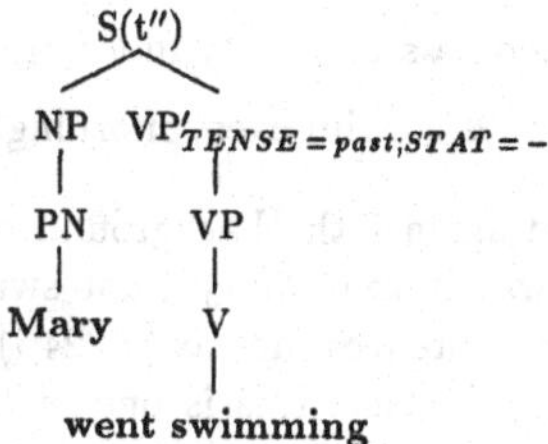

Still outstanding are the reductions of (i) the condition **in 1985(t)** and (ii) the condition $\mathcal{T}$. Reducing (i), following the processing strategy described in Section 5.5.1 and interpreting **in** as 'throughout', we obtain a new discourse referent **t′**, together with the conditions **t = t′** and **1985(t′)**. The reduction of (ii) proceeds as usual and yields

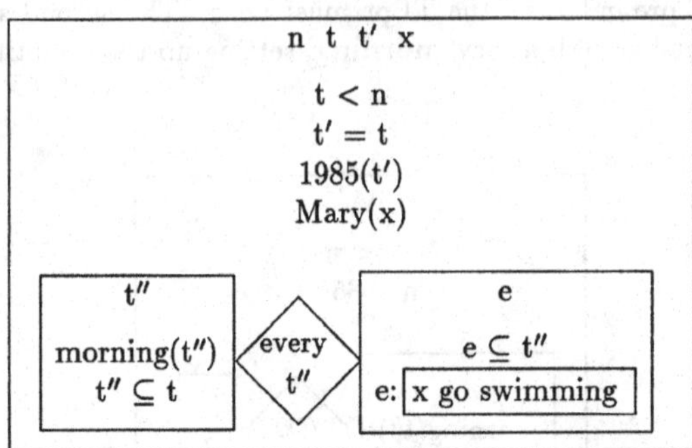

Most sentences that involve quantification over time involve complications which we were careful to avoid when choosing (5.220) as our first example. There are three kinds of problems which we will discuss. The first complication is illustrated by the sentences

(5.224) (i) Mary took a swim every morning.

(ii) Mary takes a swim every morning.

When (5.224.i) is used against the background of an empty context, it provokes the question: *When* was it that Mary went swimming every morning? In this regard, quantificational sentences such as (5.224.i) behave very much like sentences which describe states. (In fact, this is one of the reasons why quantificational sentences are sometimes classified as state-describing.) Such **when**-questions are either settled by a locating adverb, as in (5.220), or else they must be resolved contextually. When the question cannot be settled either way, the utterance strikes us as incomplete. Thus, reference time plays a similar role here as it did in earlier sections – except of course that the discourse referent which serves as reference time for a sentence like (5.224.i) must represent a period long enough to accommodate repeated instances of the described eventuality type.

(5.224.ii) presents a related problem. Again the period over which the described eventuality type – that of Mary taking a swim – is regularly instantiated must be long enough to accommodate repeated instances of such an event. And, just as with other sentences in the present tense, this period must include the time of utterance. As with past tense quantifications, the length of the period can be made explicit by an adverb such as **this week** or **this month** or **this summer**, or else the period may be contextually implied. But unlike (5.224.i), (5.224.ii) is quite acceptable in a context which does not specify the period. In this respect, (5.224.ii) is like other present tense sentences such as **Mary is sick** or **Mary is a graduate student**. Such sentences are often used to describe the status quo. For how long the status quo has lasted or for how long it will continue to hold in the future is left unspecified.

The second complication relates to adverbial quantifiers like **always**, as opposed to adverbs of quantification that have the overt form of noun phrases (such as **every morning** in (5.220)). Consider

(5.225) In 1975 Fred always had kippers for breakfast.

Clearly this sentence does not mean that at all times in 1975 Fred satisfied the predicate **have kippers for breakfast**, in the sense that each such time was a time at which he was having breakfast and was having kippers with his breakfast. Rather, the sentence would be understood to mean that at any time within the indicated period at which Fred was having breakfast, he was having kippers with it. It is fairly clear what a DRS with such truth conditions should look like. Here is one of several possible variants:

(5.226)

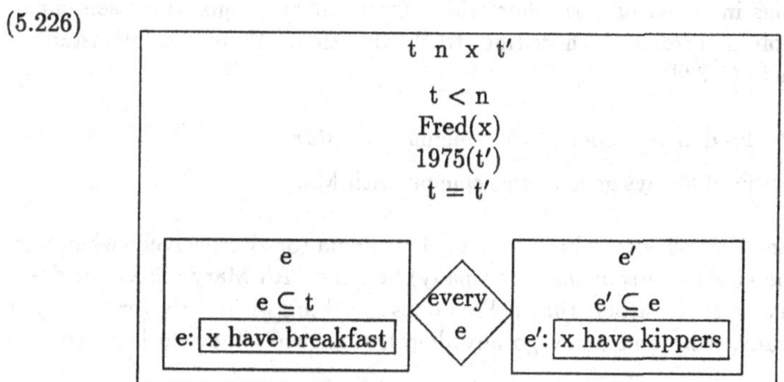

But how is such a representation to be derived from the syntactic representation of (5.225)? The crucial difficulty has to do with what goes into the left box of the duplex condition and what goes into the right one – or, to put it somewhat differently, how the material of the sentence is to be separated into that which goes into the left and that which goes into the right box. Thus far this never was an issue: the left-hand box was made up from the nominal of the quantifying NP and the right-hand box from the remainder of the processed sentence or DRS-condition. But no such simple strategy is available when the quantifier is an adverb.

This *separation problem* (as we will call it) which quantifying adverbs like **always** pose is closely related to an issue in semantics that we have not touched upon in this book, but which is of the greatest importance. This is the division of each sentence into its *topic* and its *focus*. Very roughly, the topic of a sentence constitutes that part of the information it contains which is presented as if it were already familiar to the recipient, whereas the focus constitutes the information that is presumed to be new to him. In spoken language, the distinction between topic and focus is often indicated by stress, with the stress falling within the focus part. Compare for instance

(5.227) (i) Fred sold his motorcycle to *Mary*.

(ii) Fred sold his *motorcycle* to Mary.

(5.227.i), with stress on **Mary**, would be natural in a situation where it is already known that Fred sold his motorcycle, but not to whom. In contrast, a natural context for (5.227.ii) is one where the recipient knows that Fred sold something to Mary but not what he sold her. The difference comes out particularly clearly when one considers (5.227.i/ii) as answers to wh-questions which query the respective issues: (5.227.i) is a felicitous answer to **Who did Fred sell his motorcycle to** but not to **What did Fred sell to Mary**. For (5.227.ii) it is the other way round. Such variations in stress pattern affect the interpretation of quantified sentences in that they often correlate with distinct truth conditions. Compare, for instance, the sentences in (5.228).

(5.228) (i) Fred always goes to the cinema with *Mary*.

(ii) Fred always goes to the *cinema* with Mary.

(5.228.i) means that whenever Fred goes to the cinema (or alternatively, whenever he goes to the cinema in someone's company) he goes with Mary. (5.228.ii) does not mean this. It says, rather, that if Fred does anything with Mary (or perhaps, more specifically, if he and Mary go anywhere), then what they do is go to the cinema.[69]

This may give some idea of the direction in which a solution of the separation problem might be sought. But it is very far from solving it. In fact, we have no very clear idea of how the problem is to be solved, though we see it as one of the

[69]Actually, the role of stress in quantificational sentences is more complex than this pair of examples indicates. For instance, if in (5.225) we put stress on **kippers**, the sentence will have the meaning represented in (5.226), which agrees with what we have just been saying. But when we put the stress instead on **breakfast**, then, contrary to what might have been expected from our comment on (5.228), the interpretation need not be that whenever Fred has kippers it is with his breakfast. With this stress pattern, the sentence could also be said in reply to the contention that Fred always had kippers with high tea. In that case it may be understood as a rectification of the previous utterance – that it is always when Fred *had breakfast* that he had kippers, and not always when he has high tea. For all the sentence conveys, in this context it is perfectly possible that Fred had kippers at times other than breakfast. (See in particular [Rooth 1985], [Rooth 1992].)

most urgent problems for natural language semantics.[70]

The separation problem is connected with another one, the problem of *contextual restriction.* This problem appears to be even more intractable. Consider the sentences

(5.229) (i) Mary always takes the Underground.
(ii) Fred always complains.

These sentences are like (5.225) in that they would not be taken to mean that at all times (of some substantial period surrounding the time of utterance) the subject satisfies the predicate – (5.229.i) doesn't require that Mary be engaged at all times in Underground travel; nor does (5.229.ii) entail that there is never a time when Fred shuts up. The interpretation which a recipient will attach to (5.229.i) is more likely to be something in the spirit of: 'Whenever Mary goes to work she travels by Underground – that is how she goes'. Similarly, (5.229.ii) might be taken to mean something in the vicinity of: 'Whenever Fred says anything at all, it will be to voice a complaint'. But these interpretations are only two of many that are possible, all with the same main clauses but with varying **whenever**-clauses. There is considerable scope for variation here, since the content of the **whenever**-clauses has to be guessed from the context and the context often provides no more than hints. As a consequence, sentences such as (5.229.i) and (5.229.ii) tend to be vague or ambivalent and are accordingly hard to refute. What, for instance, would establish that (5.229.ii) was false? Sure, if Fred never complains, then the sentence cannot be true. But provided Fred complains quite often, what must an occasion be like on which he does not complain if it is to count as one that actually refutes the sentence? As a rule, we would be hard pressed to give a precise answer to this question, just as hard pressed as we are to come up with a precise statement of the restricting **when**-clause in an explicit paraphrase of the sentence.

Often the separation problem and the problem of contextual restriction go hand in hand. In fact, (5.229.i) is a plausible case in point. The sentence is naturally read with stress on the word **Underground**, and is accordingly assigned an interpretation in which the content of the left-hand box is **Mary travels** and that of the right-hand box **Mary travels by Underground**. But in many contexts, the interpretation will be further restricted; e.g. the context may make clear that it is only Mary's trips to and from work that are at issue, or her movements within Central London, etc.

The third complication concerns adverbs such as **often, rarely, regularly.** These are like the determiners **many** and **few** in that they do not come with sharply defined truth conditions: How often is often; how rarely is rarely; how

[70]For the role of focus in the separation problem see in particular [Rooth 1985]. [Diesing 1990] discusses other, more syntactic constraints on separation.

regularly must events recur to justify the use of **regularly**? In connection with **many** and **few**, we noted that within our framework such problems are problems of DRS-evaluation, not of semantic representation, and we said we would not address them in this book.

(5.220) showed us one way in which frequency adverbials and locating adverbs can act together; the second adverb describes the period over which the first quantifies. But this is not the only way in which locating adverbs and quantifying adverbs interact. The locating adverb may also serve to specify the locations of the eventualities which correspond to (i.e. are the values of) the bound eventuality variable. This is the role, for instance, of **in the morning** in

(5.230) In 1985 Mary always went swimming in the morning.

In one reading, (5.230) has the same truth conditions as (5.220); and it should get a representation that is equivalent to (5.221). But the construction principles by which this representation is derived from (5.230) cannot be quite the same as those which derive (5.221) from (5.220). In particular, the construction of the DRS for (5.230) requires a principle which connects the adverb **in the morning** with the quantifying adverb **always**.

The connection is not entirely straightforward; in light of what we have said about the representation of quantification, it might have been expected that **in the morning** acts as a constraint on the variable bound by **always**, yielding a representation like

(5.231)

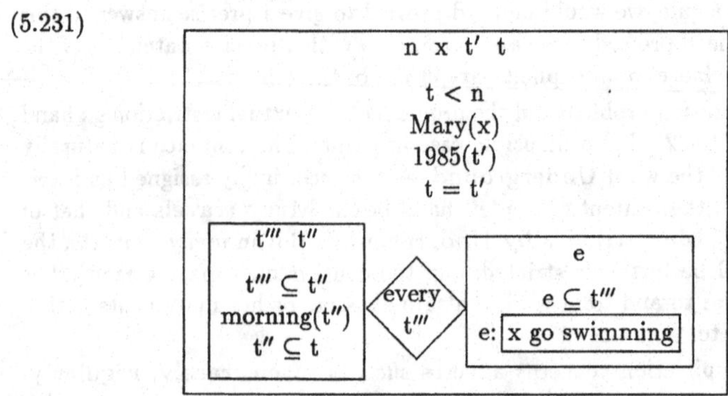

But (5.231) is far too strong. It requires that every time included in every morning in 1985 is a time at which Mary swims. This is much more than is claimed by (5.230), which only asserts that every morning includes some time at which Mary is

swimming, i.e. that Mary always took a morning swim. How could it be that (5.230) has this interpretation and not the one given by (5.231)? The reason appears to be that the locating adverb can act as a *constraint* on the location of the different eventualities which instantiate the eventuality discourse referent in the right-hand side box. In order that it can be interpreted as such a restriction, the location time represented by the discourse referent bound by the quantifier must be such that it *can* be so restricted. That is, the domain of quantification of **always** must consist of times from each of which the phrase **in the morning** can carve a proper part. The domain that naturally comes to mind in this connection is the set of *days* in 1985 – days are among the principal units in which the time of human experience is measured, and for each day there is a distinct proper subinterval determined by **in the morning**. Thus the adverb **in the morning** steers the interpreter towards one of the many possible contextual restrictions on the discourse referent bound by the quantifying adverb. The DRS which represents this interpretation has the following form

(5.232)

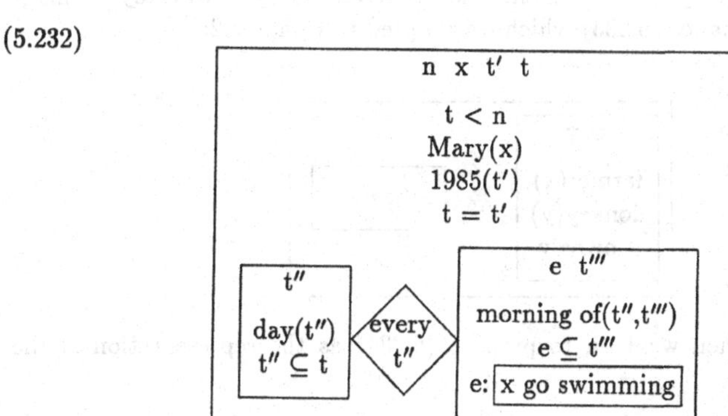

This still leaves us at a considerable distance from a precise statement of the construction rules which derive (5.232) from (5.230). However, as we are not presenting a formal algorithm for the processing of sentences with adverbs of quantification (not even for the less problematic cases such as (5.220)!) we are content to do no more than register the additional problems which a sentence like (5.230) would present to a formally precise theory in the spirit of our informal analysis.

We conclude the section with a discussion of two further issues. Again, the problems that we will mention are problems we will not be able to solve. If we mention them anyhow, it is once more because their importance extends well beyond the realm of the strictly temporal. In fact, they touch one of the central principles of Discourse Representation Theory as a whole. Not to mention these problems at all in this book would be a form of dissimulation.

Both issues were first discussed in a paper of David Lewis [Lewis 1975b] which antedates DRT by about seven years. One point Lewis observed is that while adverbs like **always, often, usually**, etc. often quantify over times, they do not always do this. In **A quadratic equation usually has two solutions**, for instance, **usually** apparently quantifies over quadratic equations, not times. (Another example is the second sentence of this paragraph, in which **often** and **always** are most naturally construed as quantifying over sentences with quantificational adverbs.) Lewis' second point is that adverbs of quantification appear to be polymorphic – they seem to have the capacity for binding several variables at once. Thus the sentence

(5.233) A farmer who owns a donkey usually beats it.

has, he suggests, a logical form in which the quantifier **usually** binds both the variable contributed by **a farmer** and that contributed by **a donkey**. This is precisely the analysis for (5.233) which we adopted in Chapter 2:

(5.234)

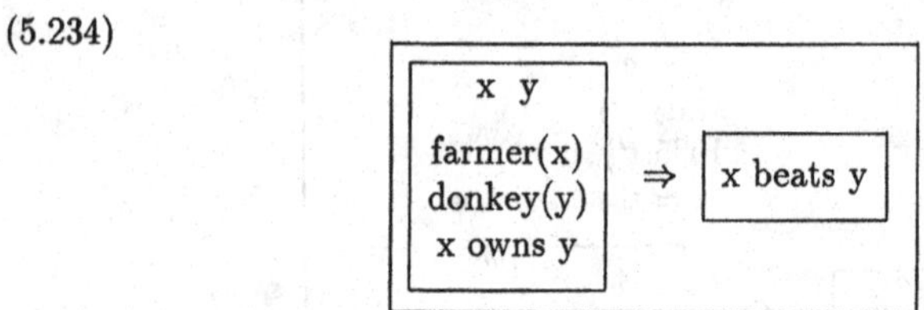

In Chapter 2 we then went on to propose (5.234) as the representation of the quantified sentence

(5.235) Every farmer who owns a donkey beats it.

as well as the conditional (5.237). This latter proposal was then revised in Chapter 4 in the light of the proportion problem. The representation we adopted instead involves a duplex condition, as in (5.236).

(5.236)

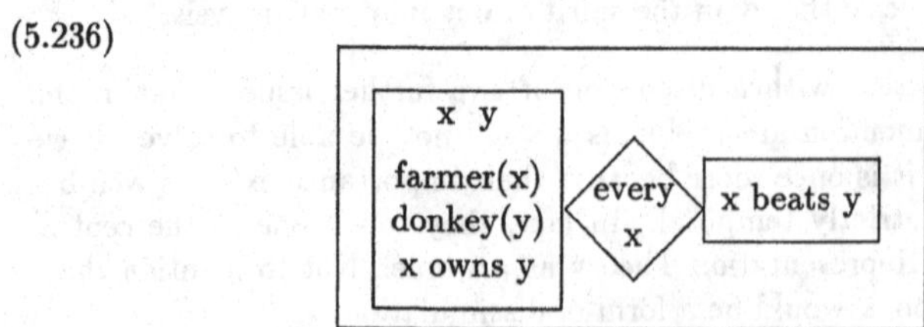

The crucial difference, recall, between $\Rightarrow$-conditions and duplex conditions is that the latter distinguish explicitly between discourse referents that are ***directly bound*** by the quantifier – these are the ones which occur in the central diamond – and those which are *indirectly bound* and which belong to the universe of the left-hand box but not in the centre. We decided, however, to retain representations of the type of (5.234) for conditional sentences such as

(5.237) If a farmer owns a donkey he beats it.

We were not in a position to motivate this decision at the time, for the proportion problem does not arise with conditionals of the kinds we studied in Chapter 2. But adverbial quantification alters this situation. In Section 5.5.4 we will argue that there is a close relationship between conditionals such as (5.237) and sentences involving adverbial quantification, like, say,

(5.238) Mostly a farmer who owns a donkey beats it.

(5.238) differs from

(5.239) Most farmers who own a donkey beat it.

in that it does not give rise to the proportion problem, or at least not in the same way. For instance, in a situation in which there is one farmer who owns fifty donkeys and beats them all and ten farmers with one donkey each to which they are very nice (5.238) can pass as true, whereas (5.239) cannot. It is tempting to connect this difference with the distinction between (5.234) and (5.236): adverbs like **mostly** are, as Lewis advocated, capable of binding several variables at once, while a quantifying noun phrase only binds the variable (discourse referent) it introduces itself. So (5.238) would get some such representation as

(5.240)

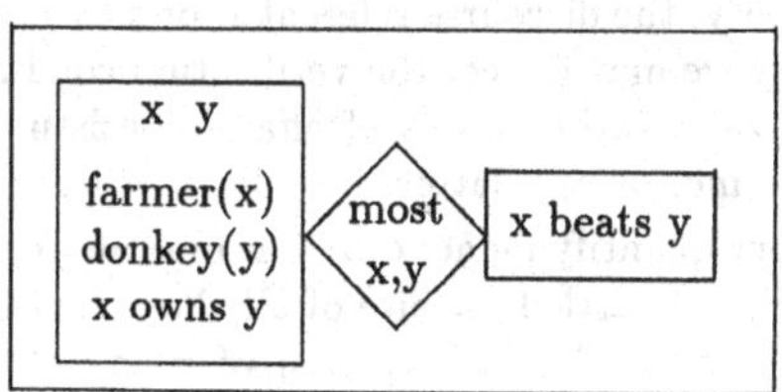

whereas the representation for (5.239) would remain as in (5.236) (with **most** replacing **every**). We should not forget, however, that neither representation is acceptable from the perspective of this chapter, since they both ignore all information relating to tense and aspect. Thus, (5.240) should be replaced by a representation of the sort indicated in (5.241)

(5.241)

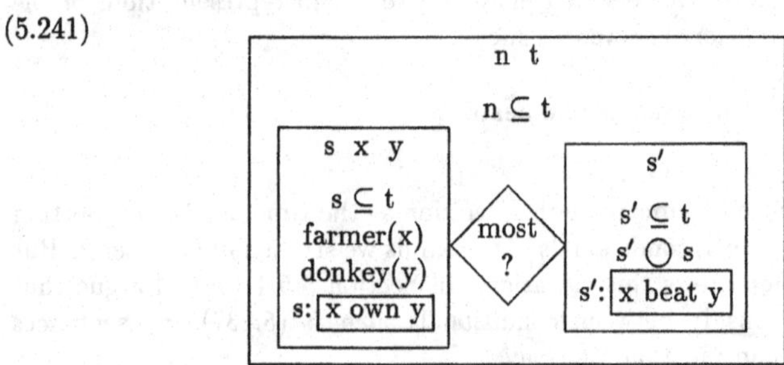

whereas (5.239) gets the representation

(5.242)

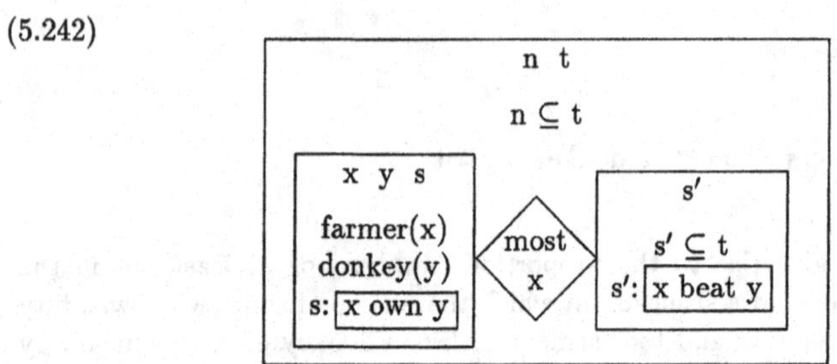

In (5.241), we have left open which discourse referent(s) is or are bound by the quantifier. Indeed, as far as the truth conditions of (5.240) are concerned (or, to be precise, the truth conditions of that reading of (5.238) on which it is true in the scenario of the one farmer with fifty donkeys and the ten farmers with one donkey each), it is immaterial whether we take the quantifier **most** to bind the discourse referents **x** and **y**, the discourse referent **s**, or **s** together with one or both of **x** and **y**. In each case we may expect the verification conditions of the complex condition to come out as counting states of affairs consisting of a farmer and a donkey such that the farmer owns a latter.

The question whether quantifying adverbs can bind more than one variable or discourse referent is still not settled, inspite of all the attention that the problem has received in recent years. For a discussion of many of the issues involved, see [Heim 1990].

5.5.3 Temporal Measure Adverbials

In the introduction to Section 5.5, we noted that there is a superficial similarity between the locating adverbials we went on to discuss in Section 5.5.1 and measure phrases like **in an hour** and **for an hour**, as we find them in

(5.243) (i) Mary wrote the letter in an hour.

(ii) Mary practiced the piano for an hour.

But as we also observed, the resemblance is mostly one of appearance. Semantically, locating adverbials and measure adverbials play quite different roles. Locating adverbials help to locate the described eventuality in time, measure adverbials like **for an hour** or **in an hour** specify the duration of the eventuality but do not locate it. Thus, the contribution of **for an hour** in (5.243.ii) is that the piano practicing went on for (at least) one hour; and the contribution of **in an hour** to (5.243.i) is that the writing of the letter took (at most) one hour.

A notable feature of measure phrases such as **in an hour** and **for an hour** is that they are sensitive to the aspect of the sentences with which they combine. Thus, the measure phrases of (5.243.i) and (5.243.ii) cannot be exchanged without leading to ungrammaticality. In general, **for**-phrases go with stative sentences and activity sentences, but not with achievement and accomplishment sentences; and with **in**-phrases it is the other way round. Thus, **in**-phrases go with those sentences which describe eventualities with an intrinsic culmination point and **for**-phrases with those that describe eventualities lacking such a point (see Section 5.3). The non-interchangeability of the two types of phrases invites the following informal assessment. **For**-phrases are used to say of something that could in principle go on indefinitely that it went on for such and such an amount of time; whether it went on for longer is left open. The function of **in**-phrases is to state an outer limit to the duration of an event that has, because of its intrinsic culmination point, a well-defined end. In both cases there is a tendency to take the duration mentioned by the **in**- or **for**-phrase as giving the exact duration of the described eventuality, rather than as some upper or lower bound for its duration. It is our impression, however, that where this stronger interpretation suggests itself, the implication is a pragmatic one.[71]

[71] Often when we hear someone *say* that Mary practiced the piano for an hour, we may nevertheless conclude that she practiced for an hour and no more. This inference is justified in most situations where the speaker knows for how long Mary practiced. Had she been practicing for more than an hour, the speaker would have known that, and so could have been expected to mention the total practicing time, rather than making the true but less informative statement (5.243.ii). The insight that there are many situations in which a statement, though true, would nevertheless be inappropriate, and that therefore from the assumption that the statement *was* appropriate further information can be deduced, is due to Grice. See in particular [Grice 1975].

It is indicative of the role which measure adverbs play that their noun phrase constituents typically denote quantities of time rather than particular parts of the time axis. The phrase **one hour**, for instance, applies equally to all intervals, past, present and future, that are an hour long, as well as to every eventuality whose duration is such an interval. So, inasmuch as **one hour** *denotes* anything at all, its denotation cannot be some particular interval, but rather a property of intervals, or something corresponding to such a property. There are two different ways in which we can think about amounts. The first sees them as numbers of measurement units – 12 ounces, 15 grams, 75 km, 20 miles, 250 metres, 55 cm, 20 years, 36 months, 5 weeks, 1 hour. In this perspective, amounts are real numbers assigned by two-place functions the first argument of which is a given quantity of stuff and the second argument a suitable unit of measurement. In particular, amounts of time would be numbers assigned by some function **dur** when applied to a given interval (or event or state) and a unit of time, such as **year**, **month**, **week**, **day**, **hour**, **minute**, etc. The other, more abstract, viewpoint is that amounts of stuff x are equivalence classes of portions of x, where two portions are equivalent iff they 'are-the-same-amount', i.e. if they yield the same numbers when measured in terms of the same unit.[72] Here it does not matter in which unit the measurements are expressed. For instance, if two periods last exactly the same number of weeks, they also last the same number of years or the same number of minutes. It is this second view point we will adopt. According to this view, amounts of time can be thought of as equivalence classes of intervals (and/or eventualities) under some suitable relation of "equal duration". (The analysis of this relation we take to be the task of chronometry and not of semantics.)

At the level of discourse representation, we need some more notation to represent the content of sentences such as (5.243.i,ii). In particular, we need to be able to refer to the function which maps intervals and eventualities on the amounts of time they last. We will denote this function as **dur**. We use the operator **dur** to form terms of the form **dur(t)**, **dur(e)**, **dur(s)**. These will occur only in DRS-conditions of the form $\mathbf{dur}(\alpha)\leq\beta$, $\mathbf{dur}(\alpha)=\beta$, $\mathbf{dur}(\alpha)\geq\beta$, where α is a discourse referent representing an event, a state or a time and β is a discourse referent repre-

---

Similar considerations apply, *mutatis mutandis*, to in-phrases.

[72]An *equivalence relation on* a set U is a binary relation R which is reflexive, symmetric and transitive on U. That is, for all **x**, **y**, **z** in U:

1. xRx
2. if xRy, then yRx
3. if xRy and yRz, then xRz

The *equivalence classes generated by* an equivalence relation R on U are all subsets V of U for which there exists a v in U such that V = {w ∈ U : vRw}. V is also called the *equivalence class (with respect to* R*) generated by* v, and is denoted by $[v]_R$.

senting an amount of time. Discourse referents for amounts of time will also occur in conditions specifying that the amount represented is the denotation of some noun phrase. Examples are **one hour(β)**, **three hours and 25 minutes(β)**, **several weeks(β)**, etc. We use **mt**, **mt′**, etc. as discourse referents for amounts of time.

With these notational conventions, (5.243.i) and (5.243.ii) can be represented as (5.244.i) and (5.244.ii).

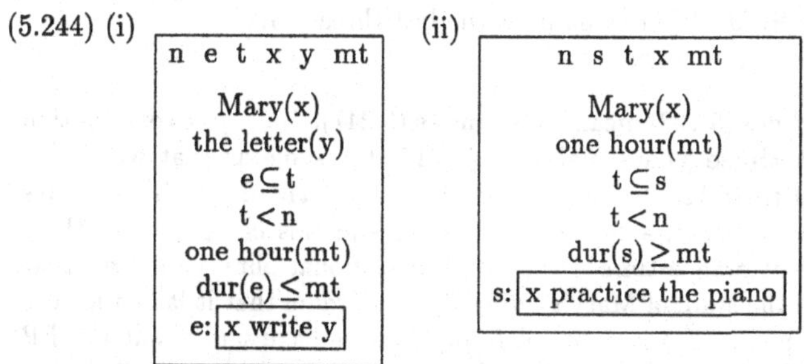

The construction rules producing these DRSs pose a problem similar to the one we encountered in our discussion of adverbs of quantification (see Section 5.5.2). In a sentence such as

(5.245) Yesterday Mary practiced the piano for an hour.

the construction algorithm will have to deal with (i) tense of the verb; (ii) the locating adverb **yesterday**; and (iii) the measure adverbial **for one hour**. It is easy enough to write a rule which performs, when triggered by the relevant combination of the features *TP*, *TENSE*, a locating adverb and a measure adverbial, all the necessary operations at once. But again, this is ad hoc in that it fails to exploit the systematic connections between sentences with and sentences without measure adverbials. The desirability of distributing the different construction operations over a number of distinct construction rules is revealed even more dramatically by sentences in which locating adverbs, adverbs of quantification and measure adverbials are all present together, as in

(5.246) Last year Mary always practiced the piano for an hour in the morning.

Once again we have this as a desideratum that an explicit algorithm should satisfy.

The distinction between measure adverbials and locating adverbials is not as clear-cut as the above discussion may have suggested. Compare, for instance, the by now familiar

(5.126) Mary has lived in Amsterdam for three years.

with

(5.247) Mary has lived in Amsterdam for the last three years.

In one of its two readings (5.126) means the same as (5.247). But is the contribution which **for the last three years** makes to (5.247) the same as that which **for three years** makes to (5.126)? This is not obvious for **the last three years** denotes, in the given context, a particular interval – in this case, the last three years preceding the utterance time – and the prepositional phrase **for the last three years** says of the state of Mary's living in Amsterdam that it lasted for the duration of *that* interval. This is different from what we have said about the PP **for three years.** That phrase, we said, asserts of the relevant state that it lasted for a certain amount of time, denoted by the measure phrase **three years.** It is only because other aspects of the sentence imply that this state has its end point at the utterance time that the total information conveyed by (5.126) ends up being the same as that carried by (5.247).

As we have just described, the contributions of **for three years** and **for the last three years** are clearly distinct for one involves reference to an amount of time and the other reference to some particular interval. But on reflection this might well be a distinction without a difference. Intuitively, the roles which the two **for**-phrases play in (5.126) and (5.247) seem very similar indeed. Both, it might be thought, have the function of determining the duration of the states they serve to characterize. That the phrase **the last three years** also specifies – supererogatorily, so to speak – the temporal location of those states does not alter this.

Once we think of **the last three years** as a measure phrase, a similar reassessement suggests itself for **since**-phrases for they too are found in the same syntactic environments, which fix the temporal location of the relevant eventuality by independent means. Ultimately it doesn't very much matter how we classify these adverbs – the semantics of the sentences containing them can be made to come out the right way – whichever way we think of them. But for that very reason their ambivalence appears to be unresolvable: they are locating phrases and measure phrases all in one; belonging to both categories at once, they defeat the possibility of a clear division between those categories.

5.5.4 Subordinate Clauses

Temporal adverbials often take the form of full subordinate clauses. Examples are found in the following sentences:

(5.248) (i) Mary left after Bill arrived.
(ii) Mary left before Bill arrived.
(iii) Mary left when Bill arrived.
(iv) Mary has been here since Bill left.
(v) Mary will be here until Bill arrives.

The subordinate clauses of (5.248.i,ii,iv,v) closely resemble prepositional phrases (such as **before/after/since/until 10 o'clock**). In fact, it is tempting to think of them as representing a special type of prepositional phrase, in which the clauses following the conjunctions **after**, ... act as noun phrases.[73] Whether this is really the correct syntactic analysis of such clauses is a problem for syntax which need not concern us here. But, syntactic questions aside, there is in any case a close semantic similarity between the phrases in (5.248) and prepositional phrases that begin with what is orthographically and phonetically the same word. For example, just as the PP **after the explosion** contributes to

(5.249) Mary left after the explosion.

the constraint that the described eventuality follows the mentioned explosion, so the clause **after Bill arrived** contributes to, for instance, (5.248.i) the constraint that Mary's departure followed Bill's arrival. This illustrates the function of such clauses in general: the eventuality of the subordinate clause is used to locate that of the main clause.

In our terms, this means that the discourse referents for the eventualities described by main clause and subordinate clause are connected by a condition which reflects the conjunction (or preposition) governing the clause, just as we proceeded with sentences containing prepositional phrases like **before ten** or **after the explosion**. We could leave matters at that, and in fact that is pretty much what we will do.

It is not at all obvious, however, that we have any right to be that cavalier, for temporal subordinate clauses raise questions which do not arise with other temporal adverbials. Each subordinate clause has a finite tense, which will have to

[73]This is also suggested by languages like German or French, in which such subordinate clauses consist of the "preposition" followed by a **that**-clause: **avant dix heures – avant que Bill arrive; nach zehn – nachdem Bill gekommen ist**.

be interpreted when the clause receives its semantic representation. But can we be sure that tenses in such subordinate clauses function in the same way as tenses in main clauses? And, secondly, couldn't there be some kind of interaction between the tense of the main clause and that of the subordinate clause – so that, e.g., certain combinations are excluded? As it turns out, both questions have positive answers. With regard to the first question, we note in particular that when a temporal subordinate clause refers to the future, the tense used is more often than not the present, and not the future, tense. Thus the sentences in (5.250)

(5.250) Fred will leave before/when/after Mary arrives.

are perfect; and they seem preferable to the alternatives in which tense of the subordinate clause is the simple future.

(5.251) Fred will leave before/when/after Mary will arrive.

We have no explanation why it is that English subordinate clauses allow for this use of the present tense, whereas main clauses do not (excepting the "time table use" of the present tense; but that is, we saw in Section 5.2.3, subject to severe restrictions).

The combinations of tenses in main and subordinate clause appear to be subject to special regulations also in other ways. The following two sentences, for instance, are deviant.

(5.252) (i) Bill will leave before Mary arrived.
(ii) Bill left before Mary will arrive.

But are these sentences unacceptable because they violate some (syntactic or semantic) rule of grammar? Note that (5.252.i) is semantically inconsistent in a particularly transparent way; the sentence says (i) that the main clause event is in the future; (ii) that the event of the subordinate clause is in the past; and (iii) that the first is before the second. Obviously that cannot be, and processing the temporal constituents of (5.252) will show this impossibility directly. (5.252.ii) is not inconsistent. But here the contribution of the subordinate clause is otiose: according to the tense of the main clause, the main clause event is in the past of **n**; so a fortiori it is in the past of any event that is itself in the future of **n**; and the tense of the subordinate clause tells us that its event is such an event. (5.252.i) and (5.252.ii) have in common that their locating adverbs fail to produce a genuine constraint on the set of times compatible with the interpretation of tense. This is a failure, however, which is not specific to temporal subordinate clauses and it produces similar effects of linguistic impropriety elsewhere. Consider, for instance, the sentences

(5.253) (i) The bridge will be completed in June of 1988.
(ii) The bridge was completed in June of 1998.

(5.253.i) seems odd (and not just false) when uttered at some time after June 1988. Likewise for (5.252.ii) when it is uttered at a time before June of 1998. Of course, the sentences in (5.253) differ from those in (5.252) in that their inappropriateness will be registered only by a recipient who is aware of the temporal relation between the utterance time and the date mentioned. Sentences like those in (5.252) bear their inconsistency on their sleeves, sentences like those in (5.253) do not. Nevertheless, the sense of impropriety which the sentences (5.252) provoke invariably and which is produced by utterances of the sentences in (5.253) only when the interpreter realizes they are uttered at the wrong time, has, we claim, the same cause. In each case, there is a violation of what we call the *non-triviality constraint.* This is the principle that the temporal adverb must impose a genuine restriction on the location time – that the set of times compatible with the restriction imposed by the adverb has a non-empty intersection with the set of times compatible with the tense of the sentence, but that this intersection be a proper subset of either of those sets. More precisely, the set of times compatible with the first constraint and the set of times compatible with the second should have an intersection that is non-empty, but smaller than either of them.

If this is the principle which rules out both the sentences in (5.252) and those utterances of the sentences in (5.253) which are perceived as taking place at the wrong times, then the apparent tense conflict we find in (5.252) is a secondary effect, deducible from this principle; since the principle seems to be needed anyway, there is no need to introduce a separate constraint on tense compatibility.

These brief discussions of the sentences in (5.250) and (5.252) do not add up to a systematic analysis of tenses in temporal subordinate clauses. But they may suffice to show that the treatment of their tenses cannot simply assimilate them to the tenses of main clauses. However, a detailed study of the differences and interactions between the tenses of main and subordinate clauses must wait for another occasion.

When all special conditions governing the use of tenses in subordinate clauses are set aside, the DRS-construction for sentences with such subordinate clauses becomes (not surprisingly) quite unproblematic. By way of example, let us see how to construct a DRS for (5.248.i). So as to be able to clearly discern what part is played by the tense of the subordinate clause, we first look at the DRS-construction for a sentence which is like (5.248.i) except that its locating adverbial is a prepositional phrase beginning with after, e.g.

(5.254) **Mary left after the 1st of January.**

According to what we proposed in Section 5.5.1.4, the DRS for (5.254) should look as follows

(5.255)

n t t′ e x
e ⊆ t t < n t′ < t the 1st of January(t′) Mary(x) e: [x leave]

The DRS for (5.248.i) differs from (5.255) in that the time t′ is now determined by the clause Bill arrived. Intuitively, t′ is the time of the event e′ described by this clause. We represent this relation between t′ and e′ by the condition loc(e′) = t′ (or "t′ is the temporal location of e′"). We display a number of stages in the DRS-construction for (5.248.i), concentrating on the immediate effects of the relevant steps which deal with the subordinate clause.

(Note that the transition from (5.256.i) to (5.256.ii) involves choosing a separate TPpt for the subordinate clause which in the present instance is n (since *TP* = −*PAST*). Care needs to be taken lest the TP points for main clause and subordinate clause become confused; but we forge the extra notation that this would require.)

(5.256) (i) (ii)

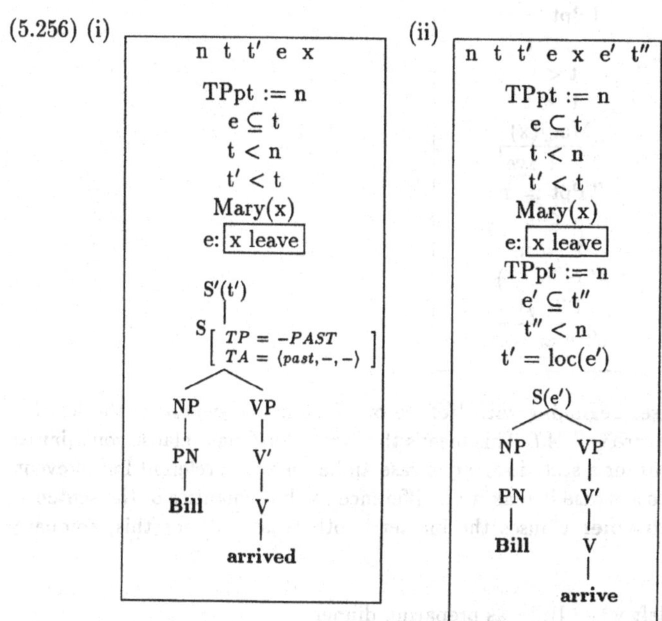

Neither (5.256.i) nor (5.256.ii) contains any conditions to determine Rpts. This might easily go unnoticed as we have been quite cavalier about Rpts in many earlier examples. But in the present case a comment is in order. Subordinate temporal clauses serve, as we said, to locate the eventuality described by the main clause. They are able to fulfill this function because they describe eventualities that can be identified or recognized by independent means – in this regard subordinate clauses are like definite rather than indefinite descriptions – and which consequently already have their determinate plan in the temporal order. So no Rpt is needed for their location. We will assume, therefore, that no Rpt needs to be chosen in the processing of a subordinate clause.

The main clauses of sentences involving subordinate clauses, on the other hand, require Rpts in the same way, and to the same extent as sentences with other types of locating adverbials. In the case of (5.248.i) this choice cannot be carried out as we are – as in so many earlier examples – processing the sentence as if it were a discourse-initial one. (See Section 5.2.3.)

(5.256) (iii)

n t t′ e x e′ t″ y
TPpt := n
$e \subseteq t$
$t < n$
$t' < t$
Mary(x)
e: [x leave]
TPpt := n
$e' \subseteq t''$
$t'' < n$
$t' = loc(e')$
Bill(y)
e′: [y arrive]

Subordinate clauses beginning with **before** or **after** may have either the feature $+STAT$ or the feature $-STAT$. This means that the subordinate clause contributes a discourse referent for a state in the one case and a discourse referent for an event in the other, but otherwise it makes no difference to the semantics of the sentence as a whole. With **when**-clauses the matter is otherwise. To see this, compare (5.248.iii) with

(5.257) Mary left when Bill was preparing dinner.

The natural interpretation of (5.248.iii) is that Mary left *upon* Bill's arrival. (5.257), in contrast, says that Mary left *while* Bill was preparing dinner. This difference is analogous to what we saw with sequences of main clauses. A sequence consisting of two past tense sentences without locating adverbials one of which has $+STAT$ while the other has $-STAT$ normally gets an interpretation according to which the event described by the $-STAT$ sentence is temporally included in the state described by the sentence with $+STAT$. But if both sentences have $-STAT$, then the temporal relation can be either precedence or overlap, depending on what rhetorical relation connects the sentences. In fact, the analogy goes further. In sentences where both the main clause and the subordinate clause have $-STAT$, the temporal relation between the described events may depend on the structural relation between main clause and **when**-clause as well as on world knowledge. For instance, in (5.248.iii), the event of Bill's arriving is naturally interpreted as the cause of Mary's leaving. Consequently, the main clause event is understood as following the event of the **when**-clause.

In contrast, in

(5.258) When they built the new bridge, they placed an enormous crane right in the middle of the river.

the main clause appears as an elaboration of the subordinate clause, and the event it describes is taken as temporally included in the **when**-clause event. But even where there is no apparent difference in rhetorical relations, our conclusion concerning the temporal relation between main and subordinate clause may vary according to what we know or assume about how things usually happen:

(5.259) (i) When they built the new bridge, a Finnish architect drew up the plans.
(ii) When they built the new bridge, the prime minister came for the official opening.

Both in (5.258) and in (5.259.i/ii) the relation between main and subordinate clause would seem to be elaboration. But in (5.259.i) we may be inclined to see the main clause event, i.e. the drawing up of the plans, as something preceding the building; and in (5.259.ii) the official opening may be seen as following it.[74]

5.5.4.1 'since' and 'until' as Subordinate Conjunctions

In 5.5.1.5, we returned to the words **since** and **until**, which made their first appearance in Section 5.1.2. In our second discussion of these words, we drew attention to their linguistic properties, properties from which the original discussion in Section 5.1 had abstracted away. In 5.5.1.5, however, we only considered "genuine" prepositional phrases, in which **since** and **until** were followed by such noun phrases

[74]The parallel between sentences with **when**-clauses on the one hand and pairs of main clauses on the other is not complete. Often it is not possible to rephrase a sentence with a **when**-clause as a sequence of two main clauses. (5.248.iii) is a case in point. Neither (i) nor (ii) of

(5.260) (i) Bill arrived. Mary left.
(ii) Mary left. Bill arrived.

are felicitous (except in special contexts). (5.260.i) can be improved by adding **then**.

(5.260) (iii) Bill arrived. Then Mary left.

(5.260.iii) is grammatical and it is a fairly close paraphrase of (5.248.i). Nothing we have said explains why (5.260.i) should be as awkward as it is and why adding **then** should improve it. There are other differences between **when**-clauses and main clauses; but none, it appears, can be explained with the apparatus at our disposal. The issues we touch upon here belong to a general theory of discourse structure, in which rhetorical relations must play an important role but which will also have to make use of many other concepts that play no part in the semantics developed in this book.

as **the explosion** or **last summer**. These uses are at variance with the **since** and **until** of Section 5.1, which, we recall, were propositional connectives, expressions that combine two sentences – the "main" and the "subordinate" clause – into one. We conclude the present section with a quick look at those other uses of **since** and **until**, in which they are followed not by NPs but by subordinate clauses. (In this way we come, as it were, full circle!) We will be brief. In particular, we will ignore the question what correlations there might be between the tense of a **since**- or **until**-clause and that of the main clause. We present three DRS-constructions, two for sentences with a **since**-clause and one for a sentence with an **until**-clause.

Here is our first sentence:

(5.261) Since she arrived, Mary has been busy.

The DRS-construction for (5.261) follows by and large the example of (5.217) in 5.5.1.5. The only difference arises in connection with the condition $\alpha(t')$, where α stands for the complement of **since** – in the sentence (5.214.(i)) represented by (5.217) in 5.5.1.5 this was the NP **last summer**, in the present case, it is the sentence **Mary arrived**. This means that now the entire sentence **Mary arrived** acts as characterization of some particular time; in this regard, the present example is like those we considered in the last section. But unlike in those examples the time characterized by the subordinate clause of (5.261) is not the location time of the main clause eventuality, i.e. of the result state expressed by the perfect verb phrase, but of the event which results in this state. In this second respect the **since**-phrase functions like that of (5.217). So, parallel to the DRS-construction for (5.217), we obtain, after processing the VP′-node the DRS:

(5.262)

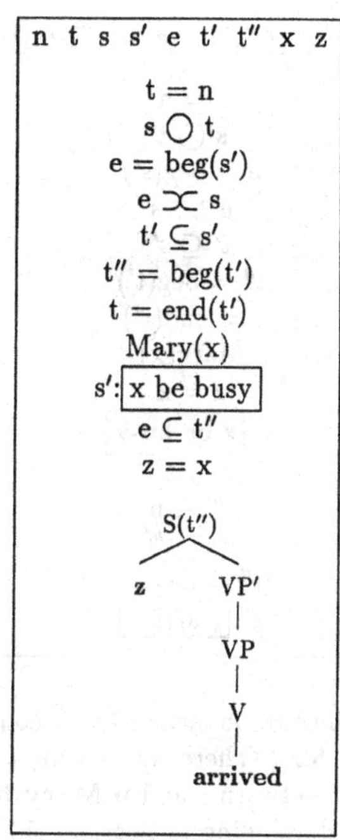

As we saw in the construction of (5.248.i), the reduction of a structure with a root node of the form $\mathbf{S}'(\tau)$ involves making τ into the location time of the eventuality the $\mathbf{S}'$-expression describes. Further reduction of the last condition of (5.262) produces the completed DRS

(5.263)

$$
\boxed{
\begin{array}{c}
\mathrm{n\ t\ s\ s'\ e\ t'\ t''\ x\ z\ e'\ t'''} \\
\hline
\mathrm{t = n} \\
\mathrm{s} \bigcirc \mathrm{t} \\
\mathrm{e = beg(s')} \\
\mathrm{e} \supset\!\subset \mathrm{s} \\
\mathrm{t'} \subseteq \mathrm{s'} \\
\mathrm{t'' = beg(t')} \\
\mathrm{t = end(t')} \\
\mathrm{Mary(x)} \\
\mathrm{z = x} \\
\mathrm{s'}: \boxed{\mathrm{x\ be\ busy}} \\
\mathrm{e} \subseteq \mathrm{t''} \\
\mathrm{t'''} < \mathrm{n} \\
\mathrm{e'} \subseteq \mathrm{t'''} \\
\mathrm{t'' = loc(e')} \\
\mathrm{e'}: \boxed{\mathrm{z\ arrive}}
\end{array}
}
$$

It is interesting to see how the two-quantifier truth condition which we presented for such sentences in Section 5.1 ("There was a time **t** before **n** such that **Mary arrive** held at **t** and for all **t′** between **t** and **n** **Mary be busy** held at **t′**") arises on the theory we have been developing in Sections 5.2–5.5. Inasmuch as (5.263) represents this truth condition, it is because (i) the event of Mary's arrival can be considered instantaneous, i.e. as occurring at one particular instant **t**; (ii) the state of being busy is one that is true of all instants in the interval between the time of Mary's arrival and the time of utterance. We have seen in what ways both of these assumptions are problematic. But even if we waive the difficulties they raise, there still remains one crucial difference between the truth condition given in Section 5.1 and what is implied by the analysis of the perfect which we proposed in Section 5.3: the truth condition of Section 5.1 excludes the utterance time, whereas our present analysis, which incorporates the account of Section 5.3, of the perfect includes them. How important this difference is from a logical point of view was noted already in [Lewis 1973], where it is shown that a **since**-like connective which includes the evaluation time among those at which the main clause is to be true has much less expressive power than the operator **S** defined in Section 5.1.

Moreover, the truth conditions of **since**- and **until**-sentences are quite different when the main clause has an accomplishment or achievement verb and not, as in (5.261), a stative or activity verb. This follows from what we said about such sentences in 5.5.1.5 (cf. the examples in (5.214)). The next example makes the point once more:

(5.264) Since she arrived, Mary has written a substantial paper on semantics.

The DRS for (5.264), given in (5.265) below, can be paraphrased as "There was a time **t** before **n** such that **Mary arrive** held at **t** and for some time **t′** between **t** and **n** **Mary write a substantial paper on semantics** held at **t′**". These truth conditions differ more radically from those of the S(ϕ,ψ)-formulas as defined in Section 5.1 than the truth conditions of e.g. (5.263). In fact, they can be expressed with the help of the simple past tense operator P and thus are representable in the much simpler tense logic TPL.

(5.265)

n t s e t′ t″ t‴ e′ x y z
$t = n$
$t \subseteq s$
$e \supset\!\subset s$
$e \subseteq t'$
$t'' = beg(t')$
$e \subseteq t'$
$t = end(t')$
Mary(x)
substantial paper(y)
$z = x$
e: [x write y]
$e' \subseteq t'''$
$t''' < n$
$t''' = loc(e')$
e′: [z arrive]

Our final example concerns **until**. For the sake of variation, we do not consider a single **until**-sentence but one that is part of a two-sentence text.

(5.266) Fred was very hungry. He had been waiting until Mary had arrived.

Note that the past perfect of the main clause of the second sentence of (5.266) is not (as it would have been had the adverbial been a **since**-phrase) the past of a perfect, but rather a "flashback past perfect" of the sort discussed in Section 5.4. The past perfect of the **until**-clause should get a similar – "flashback" – interpretation. We first present the DRS for the first sentence of (5.266), then the DRS resulting from processing the VP′-node of the main clause of the second sentence and finally the complete DRS for the two sentences together.

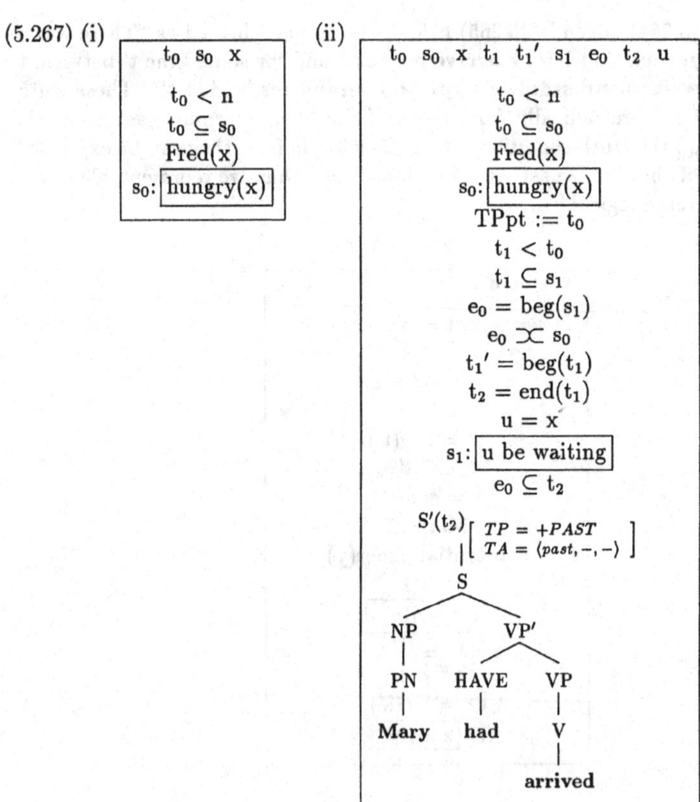

(iii)

t_0 s_0 x t_1 t_1' s_1 t_2 u y e_1 t_3 z
$s_0 < n$
$t_0 \subseteq s_0$
Fred(x)
s_0: \[hungry(x)\]
TPpt := t_0
$s_1 < t_0$
$t_1 \subseteq s_1$
$e_0 = beg(s_1)$
$e_0 \supset\!\subset s_0$
$t_1' = beg(t_1)$
$t_2 = end(t_1)$
u = x
z = x
s_1: \[PROG(wait)(z)\]
TPpt := t_0
$t_3 < t_0$
$e_1 \subseteq t_3$
Mary(y)
$t_2 = loc(e_1)$
e_1: \[y arrive\]

5.5.4.2 Relative Clauses

The fragment of English with which we dealt in Chapters 0, 1 and 2 included relative clauses. In the present chapter, relative clauses have so far been ignored. But of course, as they are tensed finite clauses, the matter of processing their tenses ought to be just as much of an issue as it is for main clauses; so it ought to be discussed. As it turns out, certain features which distinguish tenses in temporal subordinate clauses from those in main clauses also apply to the tenses of relative clauses. Thus, it seems that

(5.268) Next summer we will appoint someone who is working in industry.

can be understood as requiring that the person who will be appointed next summer will be working in industry then, not that she is working in industry now.

While this is a feature which temporal subordinate clauses and relative clauses have in common, the non-triviality constraint only affects temporal clauses – obviously it has no application to relative clauses since these do not primarily serve to the purpose of locating the eventuality of the main clause. Thus combinations of tenses which are excluded in the case of temporal clauses are fully legitimate with relative clauses. (5.269) is a case in point.

(5.269) Fred wrote a novel last year which will win a prize in 1995.

However, the very same circumstance – that it is not the prescribed task of relative clauses to provide a temporal location for the eventuality described in the main clause – makes for a complication which we do not find with temporal subordinate clauses. For while locating the main clause eventuality is not the raison d'être of relative clauses, they nevertheless *can* serve this purpose. But while they can, they do not need to, and often it is the main clause which helps to locate the eventuality of the relative clause rather than the other way round. The following sentences illustrate various possibilities.

(5.270) (i) In 1995 Fred wrote an autobiography which would be published after his death.
(ii) The story which Fred published in 1923 he had written before 1910.
(iii) The story that Fred wrote in 1909 was published three years later.
(iv) Fred published the novel which he wrote in 1910 only several years later.

In (5.270.i), the main clause provides the TPpt for the relative clause, while in (5.270.ii) it is the relative clause which provides the TPpt for the main clause. In (5.270.iii), the relative clause provides the Rpt for the main clause event, and in (5.270.iv), finally, the relative clause gets its Rpt from the main clause.

The temporal dependencies between main clause and relative clause constitute another topic that we must leave for further study. As with a number of other problems we have touched upon in the course of this chapter, the issue seems to depend closely on questions of discourse structure and thus points towards a theory of much greater complexity and sophistication than the one we have developed.

5.6 Model Theory

In the present section we deal with a matter that is long overdue. For most of Chapter 5 we have been discussing the form and construction of DRSs in which tensed discourse is represented. But so far we have said nothing about the model theory which is to assign those DRSs a definite meaning. In this respect the mode of presentation we have adopted in the present chapter follows that of Chapter 4 and differs from that of Chapter 1, where we introduced model theory as soon as it was at all possible. There is, however, an important difference between the model theoretic problems which we had to address in Chapter 4 and those which face us here. In Chapter 4 the adaptation of the earlier model theory of Chapters 1 and 2 was comparatively straightforward. In contrast, the model theory for the DRSs of the present chapter raises a substantial number of fundamental questions. Many of those were raised in earlier sections with a promise that they would be dealt with more properly in the present one. In view of those promises we must start with a warning. Those who expect from this section the solution of the metaphysical and logical problems touched upon in earlier parts of the chapter will be disappointed. It is true that the model theory we will present involves general decisions of considerable conceptual import. But for the most part these decisions were made on the strength of intuitions; proper philosophical justification is mostly lacking.

In Section 5.1, we presented the model theory for propositional tense logics. It was based on the comparatively simple idea that models for tense logic are temporally ordered sets of models of the sort considered in Chapters 1, 2 and 4. Later we argued that a model theory which characterizes satisfaction of a predicate at some non-instantaneous time **t** as satisfaction at every instant included in **t** is conceptually untenable. We also noted that an interval-based semantics is at risk of leading to truth value gaps, but that this problem is avoided when we pass from an interval-semantics to one based on events.

The crucial difference between an interval semantics and a semantics based on events is that in the latter events act as genuine arguments of predications. In our notation, this is made explicit in the DRS conditions which characterize events, such as (i) **e:** | **x write y** |. From an abstract point of view (i) says that a certain 3-place relation, expressed by **write**, obtains between **e**, **x** and **y**. (That **e** occupies a special position in (i) is from this perspective irrelevant.) A model reflecting this perspective will interpret verbs as having extensions in which an eventuality is always included. For instance, it will specify for the verb **write** a set of triples ⟨E,a,b⟩ where E is an event and a and b are individuals.

We saw in Section 5.2.5 that the threat of truth value gaps is thus averted. First, the extension of verbs such as **write** is now well-defined. For instance, a triple ⟨E,a,b⟩ either belongs to the extension of **write** or it doesn't. Second, our treatment of negation entails that of any pair of sentences such as, say,

(5.271) (i) Mary wrote the letter on Sunday.

(ii) Mary did not write the letter on Sunday.

precisely one will be true. For either there occurred an event E within the period denoted by **on Sunday**, such that E, **Mary** and **the letter** form a triple in the extension of **write**, in which case the first sentence is true; or else there occurred no such event and in that case the second one is true.

But there is a price to be paid. Our representations, and with them the models we will need, must admit besides such "ordinary" individuals as persons and letters, not only times, but also events. And as we have seen, events are problematic: their identity criteria are ill-defined; it is difficult to know under what conditions there exists, for two or more distinct events, a single new "sum" event which has those events for its parts; and it is not clear how events are related to other entities, such as, for instance, times.

As we said in Section 5.1, we have no conclusive answers to these questions, and presumably there are no clear, non-stipulative answers to be had. So what is to be done? There are two options that we can see. One is to adopt some exact but partly synthetic event concept. The other is to state the model theory so that it is compatible with a variety of distinct exact event concepts. A theory of this second kind offers two further options. It can either be taken as a genuine theory which accepts every model whose event structure instantiates one of the concepts compatible with the theory; or else it can be regarded as the skeleton of a theory, which may be turned into a theory properly speaking by adding some exact definition of an event concept whenever this is thought desirable.

We opt for the second of these three approaches – i.e. for a model theory which accepts a wide spectrum of possible models. One may worry that such an approach might be too permissive, in that it takes models on board which on closer inspection one should want to reject as improper. It is not so easy to assess, however, to what extent the presence of such improper models will distort the truth conditions which the theory assigns to the DRSs in which we are interested. Whether an improper model will do any real damage in this connection depends on the particular respect in which it is improper. Consider for instance a model which misrepresents (what might come to be seen as) the truth concerning event identity – e.g. a model which treats the event of Mary selling her motorcycle to Bill as distinct from that of Bill buying the motorcycle from Mary, although (we are assuming for the sake of argument) these really are one and the same event. To the DRSs of our fragment such a model will assign the same truth values as one which treats the event of Mary selling her motorcycle to Bill and that of Bill buying the motorcycle from Mary as one and the same. For in our DRSs event discourse referents only occur in conditions that are insensitive to this issue. (In the DRSs of the present chapter event discourse referents never figure as terms of equations of the form $\mathbf{e} = \mathbf{e}'$.) Thus in the context of our present investigation questions of event identity need not worry us.

Other kinds of impropriety, however, might affect truth conditons. Among them are misrepresentations of the relationship between events and times. Since this relationship does matter, we should be as clear about it as we can. We touched on the relation between times and events briefly in Section 5.1.3, promising to return to the issue in this section. We return to it now.

From a general ontological standpoint, the relation between events and times can take one of three forms; events might be definable in terms of times (together with other concepts, such as, say, property instantiation); times might be definable in terms of events; or there might be no definitional reduction either way. In Section 5.1 we rejected the first of these three possibilities. With regard to the second we mentioned the existence of a number of non-equivalent proposals; one of those, we said, would be discussed at some length in the present section.[75] To this we now proceed. We turn to the third possibility, in which there is no reduction either way, below, on page 671.

The reduction of times to events we are about to present defines temporal instants as maximal sets of pairwise overlapping events. The definition makes use of two temporal relations between events, the relation '$\bigcirc$' of temporal overlap and the relation '$<$' of temporal precedence. The basis for our definition is an event structure $\mathcal{E} = \langle \mathsf{E}, <, \bigcirc \rangle$, where E is a set of events and in which the relations '$\bigcirc$' and '$<$' satisfy the following postulates.

(P_1) $e_1 < e_2 \rightarrow \neg\, e_2 < e_1$

(P_2) $e_1 < e_2 \;\&\; e_2 < e_3 \rightarrow e_1 < e_3$

(P_3) $e \bigcirc e$

(P_4) $e_1 \bigcirc e_2 \rightarrow e_2 \bigcirc e_1$

(P_5) $e_1 < e_2 \rightarrow \neg\, e_2 \bigcirc e_1$

(P_6) $e_1 < e_2 \;\&\; e_2 \bigcirc e_3 \;\&\; e_3 < e_4 \rightarrow e_1 < e_4$

(P_7) $e_1 < e_2 \vee e_1 \bigcirc e_2 \vee e_2 < e_1$

We define an *instant* of $\mathcal{E}$ to be a maximal set of pairwise overlapping events. Consistently with this definition, we define the relation of 'going on at' (i.e. the relation which holds between an event e and an instant i iff e is going on at i) as membership of e in i. Finally, we define the relation '$<$' of precedence between instants as holding between i_1 and i_2 iff there are events which separate them, i.e. iff there is an event e_1 in i_1 and an event e_2 in i_2 such that e_1 completely precedes e_2.

[75] Detailed discussions of the various possible ways of defining times in terms of events can be found in particular in: [Whitrow 1961], [van Benthem 1983], [Eberle 1991].

Definition 5.6.1 Let $\mathcal{E}$ be an event structure. Then

(i) i is an *instant* of $\mathcal{E}$ if

(a) $\mathsf{i} \subseteq \mathsf{E}$;

(b) $\mathsf{e}_1, \mathsf{e}_2 \in \mathsf{i} \Rightarrow \mathsf{e}_1 \bigcirc \mathsf{e}_2$;

(c) if $\mathsf{H} \subseteq \mathsf{E}$, $\mathsf{i} \subseteq \mathsf{H}$ and for all $\mathsf{e}_1, \mathsf{e}_2 \in \mathsf{H}$, $\mathsf{e}_1 \bigcirc \mathsf{e}_2$, then $\mathsf{H} \subseteq \mathsf{i}$.

(ii) An event e *occurs at* an instant i iff $\mathsf{e} \in \mathsf{i}$.

(iii) For all instants $\mathsf{i}_1, \mathsf{i}_2$: $\mathsf{i}_1 <_{\mathsf{i}} \mathsf{i}_2$ iff there are $\mathsf{e}_1 \in \mathsf{i}_1$, $\mathsf{e}_2 \in \mathsf{i}_2$ such that $\mathsf{e}_1 < \mathsf{e}_2$.

It can be shown that '$<_{\mathsf{i}}$' is a linear order of the set of instants defined by (i). In this way each event structure $\mathcal{E}$ generates an instant structure $\mathcal{I}(\mathcal{E}) = \langle \mathsf{I}(\mathcal{E}), <_{\mathsf{i}}(\mathcal{E})\rangle$ where $\mathcal{I}(\mathcal{E})$ is the set of all instants in the sense of (i), and $<_{\mathsf{i}}(\mathcal{E})$ the precedence relation as defined in (iii).

We will assume that each model $\mathcal{M}$ includes an event structure $\mathcal{E}$ satisfying (P_1)–(P_7). The members of $\mathcal{I}(\mathcal{E})$ will then count as temporal instants of $\mathcal{M}$. However, the discourse referents that represent times will as a rule *not* represent instants of time but intervals. This presents no further problems, for intervals are readily defined from instants, viz. as the *convex* subsets of instants, i.e. as those instant sets X such that if $\mathsf{i}_1, \mathsf{i}_2 \in \mathsf{X}$ and $\mathsf{i}_1 <_{\mathsf{i}} \mathsf{i}_3 <_{\mathsf{i}} \mathsf{i}_2$, then $\mathsf{i}_3 \in \mathsf{X}$.

Given any instant structure $\mathcal{T} = \langle \mathsf{T}, <\rangle$, we let $\mathcal{I}nt(\mathcal{T})$ be the interval structure *derived from* $\mathcal{T}$, i.e. the structure $\langle \mathsf{Int}, <_{\mathsf{p}}, \bigcirc_{\mathsf{p}}\rangle$ where Int is the set of convex subsets of T and $<_{\mathsf{p}}$ and $\bigcirc_{\mathsf{p}}$ are defined as in Definition 5.6.2.

Definition 5.6.2 Let X, Y be intervals of an instant structure $\mathcal{T} = \langle \mathsf{T}, <\rangle$. Then

(i) $\mathsf{X} <_{\mathsf{p}} \mathsf{Y}$ iff for all $\mathsf{i}_1 \in \mathsf{X}$ and $\mathsf{i}_2 \in \mathsf{Y}$, $\mathsf{i}_1 < \mathsf{i}_2$.

(ii) $\mathsf{X} \bigcirc_{\mathsf{p}} \mathsf{Y}$ iff $\mathsf{X} \cap \mathsf{Y} \neq \{\}$.

(iii) $\mathsf{X} \subseteq_{\mathsf{p}} \mathsf{Y}$ iff for every instant $\mathsf{i} \in \mathsf{X}$, $\mathsf{i} \in \mathsf{Y}$[76]

Definitions 5.6.1 and 5.6.2 associate with each event structure $\mathcal{E}$ a corresponding interval structure $\mathcal{P}(\mathcal{E}) = \mathcal{I}nt(\mathcal{I}(\mathcal{E}))$. It is easily shown that $\mathcal{P}(\mathcal{E})$ satisfies, like $\mathcal{E}$, the postulates (P_1)–(P_7). $\mathcal{E}$ and $\mathcal{P}(\mathcal{E})$ are closely related. We can associate with each event e of $\mathcal{E}$ a corresponding interval $\mathsf{p}(\mathsf{e})$ by

[76]Precisely how many relations between intervals one wants to distinguish depends on the purpose to which one wants to put these relations. Much work in Artificial Intelligence is based on a set of 13 relations, which was brought into prominence through the work of Allen (see [Allen 1983]). The 13 relations can be graphically represented as follows (after [Vilain/Kautz 1986, p. 377]):

$$p(e) = \{i \in \mathcal{I}(\mathcal{E}) : e \text{ occurs at } i\}.$$

Then for any e_1, e_2 of $\mathcal{E}$.

(i) $e_1 < e_2$ iff $p(e_1) <_{\mathcal{P}(\mathcal{E})} p(e_2)$, and

(ii) $e_1 \bigcirc e_2$ iff $p(e_1) \bigcirc_{\mathcal{P}(\mathcal{E})} p(e_2)$.

Thus p is a homomorphism from $\mathcal{E}$ into $\mathcal{P}(\mathcal{E})$. In general, however, p is neither an isomorphism, nor is it onto $\mathcal{P}(\mathcal{E})$ for two events e_1 and e_2 may be simultaneous,

---

i_1: —— i_2: ⋯⋯

(1) (2) (3) (4) (5) (6) (7) (8) (9) (10) (11) (12) (13)

(The meaning of the diagrams should be clear: (1) stands for the relation which holds between i_1 and i_2 when i_1 lies entirely before i_2 and there is a gap between them; (2) for the relation of i_1 lying before i_2 while the end of i_1 touches the beginning of i_2, etc.)

The correspondence between these relations and the relations $<_p$, $\bigcirc_p$, $\subseteq_p$ is roughly as follows: $<_p$ corresponds to the disjunction of (1) and (2); $\bigcirc_p$ to the disjunction of (3) and (8) and $\subseteq_p$ to the disjunction of (4), (5), (6) and (7). (12) and (13) correspond to the converse of $<_p$. For details concerning this connection, see [Eberle 1991].

It is easily verified that these relations form an exhaustive and mutually exclusive set: any two intervals will stand in exactly one such relation. Moreover, they are the only relations definable from instants by purely *topological* means – i.e. by definitions which use no other relations between instants than identity and precedence – and which are insensitive to the distinction between closed and open intervals.

Allen's relations have been used mostly in the context of deduction ("theorem proving") from temporal information. In this context they are a natural choice. Our needs in this chapter are more modest and we can make do with a less finely differentiated collection of relations. But there is nothing sacro-sanct about our choice. Had we needed other relations than those we have introduced, we would not have hesitated to take them on board as well.

so that $p(e_1) = p(e_2)$, and yet not be identical; and not every interval need be the duration of some event. In particular, we should not expect there to be an event whose duration is all of time.

If the construction of times out of events we have outlined is to be applicable to the real world and imposes upon it a well-defined structure of instants and intervals, it must be based on a well-defined event structure $\mathcal{E}$. In the light of our complaints about the indeterminacy of the concept of an event, the assumption that the event structure of our world will have the required degree of definiteness may seem unwarranted. But things need not be as bad as they look.

First, one of the most serious problems for the theory of events, that of event identity – are the events of Fred selling the car to Mary and of Mary buying the car from Fred one or two? – is irrelevant to the outcome of the construction. For suppose we have two events here rather than one. Then these events will be exactly simultaneous, and thus precede, overlap or be preceded by exactly the same other events; so they will make precisely the same contribution to the construction of $\mathcal{I}(\mathcal{E})$ that would be made by the single event we would have if they were one.

Moreover, it may well be that the construction yields the same outcome whether it be applied to the structure of *all* events or to a certain substructure consisting, say, of all physical events of some closely circumscribed type, e.g. the class of all changes in the relative positions of physical particles, or of all changes in quantum states of local physical systems. Such restricted event structures may well be rich enough to account for as much temporal differentiation as can be found in our world at all. Including additional events in the basis for constructing instants from events will not alter the outcome, but produce an instant structure isomorphic to the one obtained from the restricted event structure. In this fashion the structure of time might turn out, somewhat paradoxically, to be more firmly determined than the event structure in which it is grounded.

But independence from the uncertainties that attach to our notion of event is not the only desideratum for the structure of time. Our modern conceptions of what the world is like are informed by, among other things, ideas about the nature of physical reality, and some of those involve quite definite assumptions about the nature of time. Prominent among these is the hypothesis that time has the structure of the real numbers (or alternatively that space-time has the structure of a 4-dimensional dense and continuous manifold). If our model theory is to conform to such conceptions concerning physical reality, then it should admit only models in which time fits those assumptions. To guarantee that it does one can proceed in one of two ways. One can either adopt the position that time should be construable from events (in the manner described above) and require of each model that its instant structure $\mathcal{I}(\mathcal{E})$ instantiates the conception of time that modern physics requires (e.g., the conception that time is isomorphic to the real number structure $\mathbb{R}$). This principle will then act as an indirect constraint on the underlying event structure $\mathcal{E}$: $\mathcal{E}$ must be such that the resulting instant structure $\mathcal{I}(\mathcal{E})$ is isomorphic to $\mathbb{R}$. Alternatively we can, dropping the requirement that times be definable from events, adopt time as a primitive category in its own right, stipulate that it has the structural properties of $\mathbb{R}$ and assume the connection between events and times to be related in some other way than by explicit definition.

It is this second alternative which we propose to adopt. With it we shift from the second of the three options mentioned on page 667, according to which time is definable, to the third, according to which both the event structure $\mathcal{E}$ and the instant structure $\mathcal{T}$ are irreducible primitives. However, in order to retain as much of the spririt of the second option as possible we assume that the "instant" structure $\mathcal{I}(\mathcal{E})$ is a substructure of $\mathcal{T}$. One way of expressing this assumption is as follows. We postulate that $\mathcal{E}$ and $\mathcal{T}$are related by a function LOC which assigns to each event e of $\mathcal{E}$ a closed interval of $\mathcal{T}$, which would be thought of as the smallest closed interval of $\mathcal{T}$ which temporally includes e, and which satisfies the following conditions:

(a) if $e < e'$, then LOC preserves $<$ in the sense that LOC(e) entirely precedes LOC(e′) in the order of T

(b) if $e \bigcirc e'$, then $\mathrm{LOC}(e) \cap \mathrm{LOC}(e') \neq \phi$

(c) for every $i \in \mathcal{I}(\mathcal{E})$ $\bigcap\{\mathrm{LOC}(e) \colon e \in i\} \neq \phi$.

Such a map LOC induces a homomorphic contraction $\mathcal{T}' = \langle T', < \rangle$ of $\mathcal{T}$, where T′ consists of all equivalence classes under the relation $\equiv$ defined by

$$t' \equiv t \quad \text{iff} \quad \forall e(t \in \mathrm{LOC}(e) \leftrightarrow t' \in \mathrm{LOC}(e)).$$

Moreover it is easily verified that for all $i \in \mathcal{I}(\mathcal{E})$, $t \in \bigcap\{\mathrm{LOC}(e) \colon e \in i\}$ and $t' \in \mathcal{T}$:

$$t \equiv t' \quad \text{iff} \quad t' \in \bigcap\{\mathrm{LOC}(e) \colon e \in i\}.$$

Thus the function which maps $i \in \mathcal{I}(\mathcal{E})$ onto $\bigcap\{\mathrm{LOC}(e) \colon e \in i\}$ is an isomorphism into $\mathcal{T}'$. In particular, in the kind of model which motivated our choice of the third option, i.e. in those models in which time is like the real numbers, condition (b) entails (c). So provided LOC is order preserving, it will guarantee the embeddability of $\mathcal{I}(\mathcal{E})$ in a homomorphic image of $\mathcal{T}$.

Our commitments so far are to models involving the following components:

(i) a time structure $\langle T, < \rangle$ that is linearly ordered and compact.

(ii) An event structure $\langle \mathcal{E}, <, \bigcirc \rangle$ satisfying the conditions (P_1)–(P_7) of p. 667;

(iii) a function LOC from $\mathcal{E}$ to closed intervals of $\mathcal{T}$ satisfying the conditions (b) and (c) above;

(iv) a set U of "ordinary individuals";

(v) a function Name which maps each name of the DRS-language onto a member of U;

(vi) a function Pred which assigns to each n-place event predicate P of the DRS-language a suitable extension for P in the model, i.e. a set of n+1-tuples $\langle e, a_1, ..., a_n \rangle$.

The next question we must consider concerns stative predicates and states. At the level of generality at which we have discussed events in this section there isn't much that distinguishes them from states. The very same questions we have been asking about events can be asked about states too, and the same answers seem possible a priori. Indeed, our discussion of events could be recast as a discussion about eventualities, about events and states together; and the option we have chosen could be taken as pertaining to eventualities as well. But that was not what we had in mind. When speaking of events we meant just them, excluding the states; which means that states should be given separate attention.

States and events, we noted in Section 5.1, stand to each other in a kind of dual relationship: on the one hand states can be seen as the pre- and post-conditions of events, and thus as providing their boundaries; on the other hand one might think of events as transitions between states of opposite types. The first image suggests an ontology in which the events are basic and the states definable from them; the second suggests a dependency in the opposite direction. To choose between these complementary perspectives is not easy; for each seems to have its paradigmatic instances, which make it look especially plausible. Thus there are events like turning red or becoming destitute or learning French which natural language presents, and which arguably we also conceive as transitions from one state to another (viz. from the absence of some quality to its presence); and there are certain states, such as being well-fed or having been knighted or being unopened, which are linguistically expressed and also seem to be conceived as the post- or pre-conditions of certain types of events. If the existence of these apparently clear examples of either kind may be taken at free value, then the family of primitive entities should include states as well as events. The two categories will be connected by certain general principles – such as that events produce the beginning and end of every bounded state, or that certain kinds of events always result in correlated result states, which begin as soon as the event is finished.

Opposed to this rather ecumenical conception of events and states are theories which accord events a primary status while they see states as epiphenomenal or unreal.[77] According to these views stative predicates are really predicates of (among other things) times, or alternatively predicates holding at times, much in the way of the interval semantics mentioned in Section 5.1. As they stand, models reflecting these views would not serve our present purpose, for they would fail to offer suitable embedding targets for discourse referents representing states. But it is quite possible to accommodate this deficiency by synthesizing "states" out of the pieces that such models will explicitly contain. For instance, one might construct states as triples of the form ⟨t,x,P⟩, where t is a period of time; x an individual and P a property, such that t is an interval at with x has P. Once states have been added by formal construction, there is little to choose between the ecumenical and the event-only-theory. Whether the states a model offers as correlates for the state discourse referents in the DRSs are "real" states or "pseudo-states" made up from periods, individuals and stative predicates matters little.

We have adopted the ecumenical view, according to which models contain states as well as events. In the light of the theory developed in this chapter this seems a natural choice. For the theory already commits us to equal status of states and events at the level of semantic representation. We must stress, however, that this is not a compelling reason. As we remarked earlier, a representational approach like the one we have pursued in this book holds the potential advantage of permitting a distinction between "real metaphysics" and "natural language-metaphysics" – between an ontology reflecting more or less directly the ways in which things are expressed in natural language and one which emerges when we dig below that surface and map out the world as it is suggested by science. From this perspective there is no reason why models in which states are first degree citizens would have to be preferred to models in which states do not constitute a basic ontological category. [78]

Our decision to include states among the basic entities of our models requires a reinterpretation of the "event structure" $\mathcal{E}$ which we listed on p.672 as one of a model's several components. We should now think of $\mathcal{E}$ as being more properly called an "eventuality structure", comprised of states as well as events in the strict

[77]See, for instance, [Galton 1984], [Löbner 1988].

[78]There is at least one further consideration that seems to point towards the thesis that states are as real as events. Both states and events appear as terms of causal relations. The breaking of the glass may be caused by dropping it; but also by its being left standing for several moments on the hot plate. And excessive drinking may cause a prolonged headache just as it may be the cause of falling down the stairs. Such examples seem to show that states can be related to events both as causes and as effects. We would hesitate to see this as a compelling reason for seeing states as being on an ontological par with events in all respects. For the nature of causation is a matter of dispute even to this day. So long as there is no consensus whether causal relations are real (rather than causal vocabulary being a loose and informal means of talking about the regularities captured by the laws of the natural sciences), no firm conclusions can be drawn about the nature of its apparent arguments.

sense of the word. In line with this reinterpretation we will refer to this structure henceforth as $\mathcal{EV}$ and to the set of its elements as EV. E will be the set of events properly speaking and S the set of states, EV being their union: $\mathsf{EV} = \mathsf{E} \cup \mathsf{S}$.

Having acknowledged states as primitives, we are faced with the question whether their presence affects the construction of times out of eventualities. Do we get a richer time structure when states are included in the base, or will their inclusion make no difference? Formally their inclusion could make a difference. Suppose for instance that all a model contains by way of events and states is a set consisting of three states s_1, s_2, s_3 and two events e_1 and e_2; that s_1 and s_3 are states to the effect that x has the property P, that s_2 is a state to the effect that x does not have P, that e_1 is the change from s_1 to s_2 and that e_2 is the change from s_2 to s_3. Thus graphically we can represent the eventuality structure of this model as $s_1 \supset\!\subset e_1 \supset\!\subset s_2 \supset\!\subset e_2 \supset\!\subset s_3$. Here each eventuality defines an instant on its own. So we get a set of five instants when we include the states in the base but only three when we don't. There are reasons, however, why the inclusion of states in the construction of $\mathcal{I}(\mathcal{E})$ might be expected not to make a difference, reasons which are roughly captured by the slogan "No time without change". Formally this intuition amounts to the assumption that for each state s and eventuality e such that $s \bigcirc e$, there is some event e' that is temporally included in s and overlaps e. If this principle is adopted, then the instant set generated by events and states together is isomorphic to that generated by the events alone. However, plausible as this principle seems to us, we have no independent arguments to support it and so we are reluctant to make it one of our general assumptions.

There is one more ontological category which our models must accommodate. This is the category of amounts of time. In Section 5.5.3 we proposed to identify amounts of time with equivalence classes of intervals of "equal duration". This means that our models need to have, as one of this components, the relevant equivalence relation '$\equiv$'.

However, not every equivalence relation between intervals qualifies as a relation of "equal duration". For instance if we have intervals $t_1 \subseteq t_2 \subseteq t_3$ and $t_1 \equiv t_3$, i.e. t_1 and t_3 are of equal duration, then t_2 should have that same length too, i.e. $t_1 \equiv t_2 \equiv t_3$. We might be tempted to think that this situation could arise only when t_1, t_2 and t_3 are identical – that from $t_1 \subseteq t_3$ and $t_1 \equiv t_3$ one could directly infer $t_1 = t_3$. However, we cannot assume this in general. It might be for instance that t_1 is an open and t_3 a closed interval, i.e. t_1 and t_3 differ only in that t_3 has a beginning and an end point which are missing from t_1. In such a case one may want to assign t_1 and t_3 the same duration. So we should allow for the possibility that $t_1 \subseteq t_3$, $t_1 \neq t_3$ but $t_1 \equiv t_3$; but then we should at the same time insist that $t_1 \subseteq t_2 \subseteq t_3 \equiv t_1$ always entails $t_1 \equiv t_2$.

In general we would want the relation '$\equiv$' to satisfy the following obvious constraint imposed by inclusion: if $t_1 \subseteq t_2$ then t_1 cannot be of longer duration than t_2. We make this principle explicit as follows. We define the following relation '$\leq$' on the equivalence classes generated by '$\equiv$'.

Definition 5.6.3

$[a] \leq [b]$ iff there are intervals c, d such that $a \equiv c \subseteq d \equiv b$.

We require that $\leq$ be a weak linear ordering, i.e. that $\leq$ satisfies the postulates

(MT_1) $[a] \leq [a]$

(MT_2) $[a] \leq [b]$ & $[b] \leq [a] \Rightarrow [a] = [b]$

(MT_3) $[a] \leq [b]$ & $[b] \leq [c] \Rightarrow [a] \leq [c]$

(MT_4) $[a] \leq [b] \vee [b] \leq [a]$

Evidently (MT_1)–(MT_4) imply that if b has a sub- and superinterval of equal duration, then b itself is also of that duration; if $a \subseteq b \subseteq b \subseteq c \equiv a$, then $b \equiv a$. On the other hand (MT_1)–(MT_4) are entailed by the conditions

(MT_5) for any intervals a, b either there is an interval f such that $a \equiv f \subseteq b$ or there is an interval g such that $b \equiv g \subseteq a$

(MT_6) if $a \subseteq b \equiv c \subseteq d \equiv a$ then $a \equiv b$

(MT_5) reflects the principle that for any two intervals a, b either b lasts at least as long as a, in which case there is a subinterval f of b which lasts exactly as long as a; or else a lasts at least as long as b, in which case there is a subinterval g of a which lasts exactly as long as b. (MT_6) is a slight generalization of the principle that when an interval b lies between two others that are of the same duration then it must itself be of such duration. Both (MT_5) and (MT_6) strike us as simple and reasonable; and they give us what we want. So we will assume that in each model $\mathcal{M}$ the relation $\equiv_{\mathcal{M}}$ satisfies these two postulates.

With '$\equiv$' and the function LOC we have the means to define the interpretation of the functor **dur**. Evidently the function which should interpret **dur** in M is the one which assigns each interval t the amount $[t]^{\equiv}$ and each eventuality e the amount $[LOC(e)]^{\equiv}$.

We have now discussed all the potentially problematic pieces from which our models are to be put together and so are ready to define models formally. Before we give this definition, however, we want to first assemble, also in the form of an explicit definition, the syntax of the DRS-language, introduced piecemeal in the course of this chapter, for which the models are to provide an interpretation.

Definition 5.6.4 I. Vocabulary

1. Discourse referents
   - (a) discourse referents for individuals: $x_1, x_2, \cdots$
   - (b) discourse referents for times: $t_1, t_2, \cdots$
   - (c) discourse referents for events: $e_1, e_2, \cdots$
   - (d) discourse referents for states: $s_1, s_2, \cdots$
   - (e) discourse referents for amounts of time: $mt_1, mt_2, \cdots$
2. Names : $PN_1, PN_2, \cdots$
3. Predicates
   - (a) 1-place predicates of individuals: $N_1, N_2, \cdots$
   - (b) n-place event predicates ${}^eP_1^n, {}^eP_2^n, \cdots$ (for $n \geq 0$)
   - (c) n-place stative predicates: ${}^sP_1^n, {}^sP_2^n, \cdots$ $PROG({}^eP_1^n), PROG({}^eP_2^n), \cdots$ (for $n \geq 0$)
   - (d) 2-place predicates of events, states and times: $<, \bigcirc, \supset\!\subset, \subseteq$
   - (e) 1-place predicates of times: $T_1, T_2, \cdots$
   - (f) 1-place predicates of amounts of time: $MT_1, MT_2, \cdots$
4. Functors
   - (a) 1-place functors on events and states: beg, end, loc
   - (b) 1-place functors on events, states and times: dur

II. Terms

1. any discourse referent is a *term*
2. if τ is a discourse referent for an event or state then beg(τ), end(τ) are terms for events and loc(τ) is a term for times
3. if τ is a term for events, states or times, then dur(τ) is a term for amounts of times

III. DRS-conditions

- (a) $PN_i(\tau)$ where PN_i is a name and τ a term for individuals
- (b) $N_i(\tau)$ where N_i is a predicate of individuals and τ a term for individuals
- (c) e_i: $\boxed{\Pi(\tau_1, ..., \tau_n)}$, where e_i is a discourse referent for events, Π an n-place event predicate and $\tau_1, ..., \tau_n$ terms for individuals
- (d) s_i: $\boxed{\Pi(\tau_1, ..., \tau_n)}$, where s_i is a discourse referent for states, Π an n-place state predicate and $\tau_1, ..., \tau_n$ terms for individuals
- (e) $\tau R \sigma$ where τ, σ are discourse referents for times, events, states and R is a 2-place predicate of events, states and times

(f) $\Pi(\tau)$ where Π is a 1-place predicate of times and τ is a term for times

(g) $\Pi(\tau)$ where Π is a 1-place predicate for amounts of time and τ is a term for amounts of time

(h) $\tau = \sigma$ where τ and σ are terms for the same type of entity

(i) $\neg$K, $K_1 \Rightarrow K_2$, $K_1 \langle \mathbf{Q}, x \rangle K_2$, where K, K_1, K_2 are DRSs, x is a discourse referent and **Q** a generalized quantifier.

IV. DRSs

A DRS is a pair ⟨U, Con⟩ consisting of a set U of discourse referents and a set Con of DRS-conditions

The concepts of *subordination*, *accessibility* and of a *proper* DRS are defined as in Chapter 1.

We now proceed to the definition of *model.*

Definition 5.6.5 A *model* M is a structure

$$\langle \mathcal{EV}, \mathcal{T}, \mathrm{LOC}, \equiv, \mathsf{Name}_{\mathsf{M}}, \mathsf{Pred}_{\mathsf{M}}, \mathsf{Fun}_{\mathsf{M}} \rangle$$

where

(i) $\mathcal{EV}$ is a quadruple ⟨EV, <, ○, E⟩ with ⟨EV, <, ○⟩ satisfying (P_1)–(P_7) (see page 667) and E ⊆ EV

(ii) $\mathcal{T}$ is a linear ordering ⟨T, <⟩

(iii) LOC is a function from EV to $\mathcal{Int}(\mathcal{T})$ which satisfies the conditions (a)-(c) on page 671.

(iv) '≡' is an equivalence relation on $\mathcal{Int}(\mathcal{T})$ which satisfies the postulates (MT_5) and (MT_6) of p. 675

(v) $\mathsf{Name}_{\mathsf{M}}$ maps the set of names onto elements of U

(vi) $\mathsf{Pred}_{\mathsf{M}}$ is a function, defined on the set of predicates, such that

(a) for each 1-place predicate N_i $\mathsf{Pred}_{\mathsf{M}}(N_i)$ is a subset of U

(b) for each n-place event predicate ${}^{e}P^{n}_{i}$ $\mathsf{Pred}_{\mathsf{M}}({}^{e}P^{n}_{i})$ is a set of tuples $\langle e, a_i, ..., a_n \rangle$ where $e \in E$ and $a_i \in U$

(c) for each n-place state predicate Π, $\mathsf{Pred}_{\mathsf{M}}(\Pi)$ is a set of tuples $\langle s, a_i, ..., a_n \rangle$ where $s \in EV - E$ and the $a_i \in U$

(d) when $\langle e, a_i, \ldots, a_n\rangle$ belongs to $Pred_M({}^eP_i^n)$ then there is a state $s \in EV\!-\!E$ such that $s \subseteq e$[79] and $\langle s, a_i, \ldots, a_n\rangle \in Pred_M(PROG({}^eP_i^n))$

(e) $Pred_M(<)$, $Pred_M(\bigcirc)$, $Pred_M(\supset\!\subset)$, $Pred_M(\subseteq)$ are the extensions of $<_{\mathcal{I}nt}(\mathcal{T})$, $\bigcirc_{\mathcal{I}nt}(\mathcal{T})$, $\supset\!\subset_{\mathcal{I}nt}(\mathcal{T})$ induced by LOC, respectively

(f) for each 1-place predicate T_i of times $Pred_M(T_i)$ is a subset of $\mathcal{I}nt(\mathcal{T})$

(g) for each 1-place predicate MT_i of amounts of time $Pred_M(MT_i)$ is a subset of the set of all equivalence classes under '$\equiv$'

(vii) (a) Fun_M is a function defined on the set of functors such that $Fun_M(beg)$ and $Fun_M(end)$ are functions from EV into E with the property that for each $ev \in EV$ $(Pred_M(beg))$ $((Pred_M(beg))(ev) = ev$ and $(Pred_M(end))$ $((Pred_M(end)(ev)) = ev$

(b) $Pred_M(loc) = LOC$

The definition of DRS-verification holds no surprises. First we define the *value* of a term τ in M under an embedding f, $[\tau]_{M,f}$.

(1) if τ is a discourse referent, then $[\tau]_{M,f} = f(\tau)$

(2) $[beg(\tau)]_{M,f} = Pred_M(beg)([\tau]_{M,f})$ and similarly for $end(\tau)$ and $dur(\tau)$

As before, we define, both for DRSs K and for DRS-conditions γ, what it is for K or γ to be verified by an embedding f in a model M. For f to verify K U_K must be included in DOM(f), and f must verify each of the conditions in

Con_K. Verification of complex conditions ($\neg K$, $K_1 \rightarrow K_2$, K_1 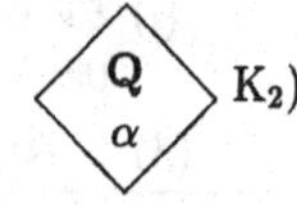 K_2) is defined as in Chapters 1, 2 and 4; verification of atomic conditions is given by the clauses (a)–(h) below:

(a) $[PN_i(\tau)]_{M,f} = 1$ iff $[\tau]_{M,f} = Name_M(PN_i)$

(b) $[N_i(\tau)]_{M,f} = 1$ iff $[\tau]_{M,f} \in Pred_M(N_i)$

(c,d) $[e_i{:}\boxed{\Pi(\tau_1, \ldots, \tau_n)}]_{M,f} = 1$ iff $\langle [e_i]_{M,f}, [\tau_i]_{M,f} \ldots [\tau_n]_{M,f}\rangle \in Pred_M(\Pi)$, similarly for $s_i{:}\boxed{\Pi(\tau_1, \ldots, \tau_n)}$

(e,f,g) $[\tau < \sigma] = 1$ iff $\langle [\tau]_{M,f}, [\sigma]_{M,f}\rangle \in Pred_M(<)$ and similarly for other predicates of events, states, times or amounts of time

(h) $[\tau = \sigma]_{M,f} = 1$ iff $[\tau_{M,f}] = [\sigma]_{M,f}$

[79] Here $ev_1 \subseteq ev_2$, for $ev_1, ev_2 \in EV$ is defined in terms of '$<$':
$ev_1 < ev_2$ iff $(\forall ev \in EV)$ $((ev_2 < ev \rightarrow ev_1 < ev)$ & $(ev < ev_2 \rightarrow ev < ev_1))$

Exercises

1. Show that the following conditions hold in $\mathcal{I}(\mathcal{E})$.

   (i) $(\forall t_1, t_2 \in T_\mathcal{E}) (t_1 <_\mathcal{E} t_2 \rightarrow t_2 \not<_\mathcal{E} t_1)$

   (ii) $(\forall t_1, t_2, t_3 \in T_\mathcal{E}) (t_1 <_\mathcal{E} t_3 \;\&\; t_2 <_\mathcal{E} t_3 \rightarrow t_1 <_\mathcal{E} t_3)$

   (iii) $(\forall t_1, t_2 \in T_\mathcal{E}) (t_1 \neq t_2 \rightarrow (t_1 < t_2 \vee t_2 < t_1))$

   (iv) $(\forall t_1, t_2, t_3 \in T_\mathcal{E}) (\exists e \in E) ((t_1 <_\mathcal{E} t_3 <_\mathcal{E} t_2$ $\;\&\; e \text{ occurs at } t_1 \;\&\; e \text{ occurs at } t_2) \rightarrow e \text{ occurs at } t_3)$

   (v) $(\forall e_1, e_2 \in E) (e_1 < e_2 \rightarrow (\exists t \in T_\mathcal{E}) (e_1 \text{ occurs at } t \;\&\; \neg e_2 \text{ occurs at } t))$

2. Suppose $\mathcal{E}$ satisfies the additional axiom

   $(\forall e_1, e_2 \in E) (e_1 < e_2 \rightarrow (\exists e_3, e_4 \in E) (e_3 \bigcirc e_4 \;\&\; (e_3 < e_2 \;\&\; e_1 < e_4)))$.

   Prove that the structure $\mathcal{T}_\mathcal{E}$ $(= \langle T_\mathcal{E}, <_p \rangle)$ is *dense*, that is

   $$(\forall t_1, t_2 \in T_\mathcal{E}) (t_1 <_p t_2 \rightarrow (\exists t_3 \in T_\mathcal{E}) (t_1 <_p t_3 \;\&\; t_3 <_p t_2))$$

3. Find a condition on $\mathcal{E}$ which is necessary and sufficient for the following property of $T_\mathcal{E}$.

   $$(\forall t \in T_\mathcal{E}) (\exists t' \in T_\mathcal{E})\, t <_p t'$$

5.7 Syntactic Rules

The English fragment studied in this chapter differs from the one defined in Chapter 0 primarily in regard of verb morphology. The fragment of Chapter 0 only contained verbs in the present tense. The only compound verb phrases that we had to deal with there were negated verb phrases such as **does not own** etc. In the present fragment compound verb phrases come in much greater variety; among them verified phrases like **will arrive, will not arrive, had been writing a letter, would not have been writing a letter**, and so forth. Our syntactic rules will have to make sure these and other grammatical compounds can be generated, while ungrammatical sequences – **will have not come, is having arrived, do not have written a letter, ...** – are excluded. As we remarked in Section 5.2, phrase structure rules of the kind we have been using in Chapter 0 are not particularly well-suited to this task. It is not hard to convince oneself that rules can be written which do the trick. But to get things right one either has to accept very large numbers of rules or else make use of a generous assortment of features. The final product is unappealing in either case. In particular, the set of rules which follows below is not one to be recommended for a beauty prize. In fact nothing much is lost, we feel, by those who choose to ignore these rules. This is why we have relegated them to this final section, which should be seen as a kind of appendix rather than as a genuine conclusion to the book.

Before we present the rules themselves a few explanatory remarks are in order. The most important general difference with the syntax of Chapter 0 is the distinction between the categories S and S′. As we described the difference in Section 5.2, S′ now represents the category of finite sentences, whereas S is the category of their corresponding "detensed", infinitival counterparts. In the syntactic structures we have displayed in the course of the present chapter, we have conveyed this difference by replacing the finite verb forms of syntactic structures whose roots are of category S′ by infinitival forms in the corresponding trees of category S. (Compare e.g. (5.47) and (5.48) of Section 5.2.). It must now be pointed out that structures of the latter kind, e.g. structures like the tree of (5.48), are not strictly speaking structures in the sense of the grammar we are about to present. (They may be seen as expressions belonging to the language of reducible DRSs, a language of which the language of the completed DRSs defined on p. 676 is a proper sub-language.) The grammar generates the verb complete with its finite morphology, i.e. each part of the verb complex is inserted into the syntactic tree in the form in which it appears in the sentence.

The construction algorithm we have developed in Sections 5.2–5.5 employs several temporal and aspectual features. By and large these same features also serve in the syntactic rules. But the overlap is not perfect. Our syntax makes use of the features *TP*, *TENSE*, *STAT* and *NEG*. But it does not use *PERF*. Instead it has a feature *AsA* (for "Aspectual Auxiliary") which, as we shall see directly, contains more information than *PERF*. The feature *AsA* is needed in the syntax in order to pass down to lower VP-nodes information about the introduction of certain auxiliary verbs. Suppose for instance that we expand a VP′-node to **do not** VP. Then this VP may be expanded neither to a perfect nor to a progressive verb form. This information must be encoded on the VP, so as to block the prohibited expansions later on. *AsA* serves to effect this encoding. Another, similar prohibition is that perfects cannot be reiterated. That is, once we have expanded a VP to say, **have not** VP, the VP may not be expanded to another combination of **have** + (**not** +) main verb. This prohibition must also be recoverable from the second VP, a need; *AsA* will serve this purpose as well.[80] The two cases mentioned show that

[80] A further prohibition of a similar sort is that progressive **be** cannot be followed either by a progressive VP or by a perfect. We do not need *AsA* to capture this prohibition, however, since progressives can be formed only from non-stative verbs, whereas both progressives and perfects are, according to our theory, statives themselves. So by insisting that only VPs with $STAT=+$

AsA ought to distinguish between three possibilities: (i) both the perfect auxiliary **have** and the progressive auxiliary **be** are excluded; (ii) **have** is excluded, but not **be**; (iii) neither **have** nor **be** are excluded. We capture these three possibilities by assigning *AsA* a space consisting of three values – **be, have** and **neither. Be** means that the VP so marked is to be expanded into a progressive phrase; **have** means that it is to be expanded into a perfect; and **neither** means it is to be expanded into a verb phrase that is neither a progressive nor a perfect. Thus the cases (i)–(iii) are represented by (i): **neither**; (ii): **be/neither**; (iii): a variable.

Although the feature *PERF* will not be directly represented in the syntactic structures which our grammar produces, its values can be read off those syntactic structures straightforwardly: *AsA* = *have* corresponds to *PERF*=+, and the other two values of *AsA* correspond to *PERF*= –.

In Chapter 0 a feature was always defined for all members of a syntactic category if it was for any of its members. In relation to the present fragment this requirement is not unnatural. For instance, we will want to have information about *TP* and *TENSE* associated with finite VPs; but for VPs that expand into gerunds or past participles these features are without significance. Even so we could have arranged matters in such a way that features always apply to syntactic categories wholesale; but this would have required some special provisions, which would have cluttered our grammar even more. Since nothing of substance would have been gained by these additional provisions, we have decided not to bother about them. Under the present more liberal management, the absence of a feature from the list of feature assignments that are attached to a given category symbol in a grammatical rule is to be understood as indicating that the feature is not defined for those members of the category which result through the kind of expansion which that particular rule describes.

While we have tried to formulate our rules so that they generate only those verb complexes that are grammatical, we have made no such effort in relation to temporal adverbs. Here our only ambition has been to generate a substantial variety of the adverbials discussed in Section 5.5. But the rules we give generate a great many "ungrammatical adverbs" besides. To block those productions would have required a further bevy of features. Anyone who has figured out how the rules we present manage to generate only grammatical compounds of verbs, will know enough to design a set of rules that will generate just the grammatical adverbs. But we expect that such a person will have seen enough also never to want to do anything of the sort.

We now proceed to list the syntactic rules. As in Chapter 0 they are divided into two groups, phrase structure rules properly speaking and lexical insertion rules.

---

may expand into perfects or progressives, and that the complement VP of progressive **be** must have the value *STAT*= –, we make sure that VPs with a progressive **be** or perfect **have** appearing under the scope of a progressive **be** will not be produced.

Quite a few of the rules are obtained by uniform transformations of corresponding rules from the grammar of Chapter 0. The rules that matter most from the point of the present chapter (and which make the system hard to understand!) are the VP′-rules (PS 4′) and (PS 5′) and the VP-rules (PS 6′), (PS 16′) and (PS 17′).

(PS 0.a) $S'\begin{bmatrix} Gap = \gamma \\ Fin = + \\ TP = \delta \\ TA = \langle\zeta,\eta,\theta\rangle \end{bmatrix} \rightarrow S\begin{bmatrix} Num = \alpha \\ Gap = \gamma \\ Fin = + \\ TP = \delta \\ TA = \langle\zeta,\eta,\theta\rangle \end{bmatrix}$

(PS 0.b) $S'\begin{bmatrix} Gap = \gamma \\ Fin = + \\ TP = \delta \\ TA = \langle\zeta,\eta,\theta\rangle \end{bmatrix} \rightarrow \text{Adv}\ S\begin{bmatrix} Num = \alpha \\ Gap = \gamma \\ Fin = + \\ TP = \delta \\ TA = \langle\zeta,\eta,\theta\rangle \end{bmatrix}$

(PS 0.c) $S'\begin{bmatrix} Gap = \gamma \\ Fin = + \\ TP = \delta \\ TA = \langle\zeta,\eta,\theta\rangle \end{bmatrix} \rightarrow S\begin{bmatrix} Num = \alpha \\ Gap = \gamma \\ Fin = + \\ TP = \delta \\ TA = \langle\zeta,\eta,\theta\rangle \end{bmatrix} \text{Adv}$

(PS 1′) $S\begin{bmatrix} Num = \alpha \\ Fin = + \\ TP = \delta \\ TA = \langle\zeta,\eta,\theta\rangle \end{bmatrix} \rightarrow NP\begin{bmatrix} Num = \alpha \\ Gen = \beta \\ Case = +Nom \end{bmatrix} VP'\begin{bmatrix} Num = \alpha \\ Fin = + \\ TP = \delta \\ TA = \langle\zeta,\eta,\theta\rangle \end{bmatrix}$

(PS 2′)–(PS 3′) : These are obtained from (PS 2)–(PS 3) of Chapter 0 in the same way that (PS 1′) is obtained from (PS 1).

(PS 4) is replaced by the following six rules.

(PS 4′.a)

$VP'\begin{bmatrix} Num = \alpha \\ Fin = + \\ Gap = \gamma \\ TP = \delta \\ TA = \langle fut,\zeta,-\rangle \end{bmatrix} \rightarrow AUX\begin{bmatrix} Num = \alpha \\ Fin = + \\ TP = \delta \\ TENSE = fut \end{bmatrix} VP\begin{bmatrix} Fin = - \\ Gap = \gamma \\ STAT = \zeta \\ AsA = \eta \end{bmatrix}$

(PS 4′.b)

$VP'\begin{bmatrix} Num = \alpha \\ Fin = + \\ Gap = \gamma \\ TP = \delta \\ TA = \langle fut,\zeta,+\rangle \end{bmatrix} \rightarrow AUX\begin{bmatrix} Num = \alpha \\ Fin = + \\ TP = \delta \\ TENSE = fut \end{bmatrix} \text{not}\ VP\begin{bmatrix} Fin = - \\ Gap = \gamma \\ STAT = \zeta \\ AsA = \eta \end{bmatrix}$

(PS 4′.c)

$$\mathrm{VP}'\begin{bmatrix} Num = \alpha \\ Fin = + \\ Gap = \gamma \\ TP = -PAST \\ TA = \langle past/pres, \zeta, + \rangle \end{bmatrix} \rightarrow \mathrm{AUX}\begin{bmatrix} Num = \alpha \\ Fin = + \\ TP = -PAST \\ TENSE = past/pres \end{bmatrix} \textbf{not} \;\; \mathrm{VP}\begin{bmatrix} Fin = - \\ Gap = \gamma \\ STAT = \zeta \\ AsA = neither \end{bmatrix}$$

(PS 4′.d)

$$\mathrm{VP}'\begin{bmatrix} Num = \alpha \\ Fin = + \\ Gap = \gamma \\ TP = +PAST \\ TA = \langle pres, \zeta, + \rangle \end{bmatrix} \rightarrow \mathrm{AUX}\begin{bmatrix} Num = \alpha \\ Fin = + \\ TP = +PAST \\ TENSE = pres \end{bmatrix} \textbf{not} \;\; \mathrm{VP}\begin{bmatrix} Fin = - \\ Gap = \gamma \\ STAT = \zeta \\ AsA = neither \end{bmatrix}$$

(PS 4′.e)

$$\mathrm{VP}'\begin{bmatrix} Num = \alpha \\ Fin = + \\ Gap = \gamma \\ TP = +PAST \\ TA = \langle past, \zeta, + \rangle \end{bmatrix} \rightarrow \mathrm{AUX}\begin{bmatrix} Num = \alpha \\ Fin = + \\ TP = +PAST \\ TENSE = past \end{bmatrix} \textbf{not} \;\; \mathrm{VP}\begin{bmatrix} Fin = part \\ Gap = \gamma \\ STAT = \zeta \\ AsA = be/neither \end{bmatrix}$$

(PS 4′.f)

$$\mathrm{VP}'\begin{bmatrix} Num = \alpha \\ Fin = + \\ Gap = \gamma \\ TP = +PAST \\ TA = \langle past, \zeta, - \rangle \end{bmatrix} \rightarrow \mathrm{AUX}\begin{bmatrix} Num = \alpha \\ Fin = + \\ TP = +PAST \\ TENSE = past \end{bmatrix} \textbf{not} \;\; \mathrm{VP}\begin{bmatrix} Fin = part \\ Gap = \gamma \\ STAT = \zeta \\ AsA = be/neither \end{bmatrix}$$

(PS 4′.a) and (PS 4′.b) cover the cases were AUX is expanded to **will** or **would.** Verb phrases beginning in this way may still be expanded into perfects as well as into progressives. So any AsA value is still admissible on the right-hand side. (PS 4′.c) replaces the old (PS 4), i.e. the **do**-supported negation which does not allow the VP to contain any form of **be** or **have**. Therefore the VP is marked with $AsA = neither$, whereas in the other two rules the value of AsA is not yet determined. And hence VPs with $AsA = neither$ must be expanded directly to an intransitive by (PS 7) or to a transitive verb and an NP by (PS 6).

If there is no AUX, we have

(PS 5′)

$$VP'\begin{bmatrix} Num = \alpha \\ Fin = + \\ Gap = \gamma \\ TP = \delta \\ TA = \langle past/pres, \varepsilon, - \rangle \end{bmatrix} \rightarrow VP\begin{bmatrix} Num = \alpha \\ Fin = + \\ Gap = \gamma \\ TP = \delta \\ TA = \langle past/pres, \varepsilon, - \rangle \\ AsA = \eta \end{bmatrix}$$

(PS 6′)

$$VP\begin{bmatrix} Num = \alpha \\ Fin = \beta \\ Gap = \gamma \\ TP = \delta \\ TA = \langle \varepsilon, \eta, - \rangle \\ AsA = neither \end{bmatrix} \rightarrow V\begin{bmatrix} Num = \alpha \\ Fin = \beta \\ Trans = + \\ TP = \delta \\ TA = \langle \varepsilon, \eta, - \rangle \end{bmatrix} NP\begin{bmatrix} Num = \zeta \\ Gen = \xi \\ Case = -Nom \\ Gap = \gamma \end{bmatrix}$$

(PS 7′) obtained from (PS 7) of Chapter 0 as (PS 6′) is obtained from (PS 6).

(PS 16′.a)

$$VP\begin{bmatrix} Num = \alpha \\ Fin = + \\ Gap = \gamma \\ TP = \delta \\ TA = \langle \varepsilon, +, + \rangle \\ AsA = be \end{bmatrix} \rightarrow BE\begin{bmatrix} Num = \alpha \\ Fin = + \\ TP = \delta \\ TENSE = \varepsilon \end{bmatrix} VP\begin{bmatrix} Fin = ing \\ Gap = \gamma \\ STAT = - \\ AsA = neither \end{bmatrix}$$

(PS 16′.b)

$$VP\begin{bmatrix} Num = \alpha \\ Fin = + \\ Gap = \gamma \\ TP = \delta \\ TA = \langle \varepsilon, +, + \rangle \\ AsA = be \end{bmatrix} \rightarrow BE\begin{bmatrix} Num = \alpha \\ Fin = + \\ TP = \delta \\ TENSE = \varepsilon \end{bmatrix} \textbf{not}\ VP\begin{bmatrix} Fin = ing \\ Gap = \gamma \\ STAT = - \\ AsA = neither \end{bmatrix}$$

(PS 16′.c)

$$VP\begin{bmatrix} Num = \alpha \\ Fin = -/part \\ Gap = \gamma \\ STAT = + \\ AsA = be \end{bmatrix} \rightarrow BE\begin{bmatrix} Num = \alpha \\ Fin = -/part \end{bmatrix} VP\begin{bmatrix} Fin = ing \\ Gap = \gamma \\ STAT = - \\ AsA = neither \end{bmatrix}$$

Have may be followed by a participial form of **be**. Thus we get

(PS 17′.a)

$$\mathrm{VP}\begin{bmatrix} Num = \alpha \\ Fin = + \\ Gap = \gamma \\ TP = \delta \\ TA = \langle \varepsilon, +, - \rangle \\ AsA = have \end{bmatrix} \rightarrow \mathrm{HAVE}\begin{bmatrix} Num = \alpha \\ TP = \delta \\ Fin = + \\ TENSE = \varepsilon \end{bmatrix} \ \mathrm{VP}\begin{bmatrix} Fin = part \\ Gap = \gamma \\ STAT = \eta \\ AsA = be/neither \end{bmatrix}$$

(PS 17′.b)

$$\mathrm{VP}\begin{bmatrix} Num = \alpha \\ Fin = + \\ Gap = \gamma \\ TP = \delta \\ TA = \langle \varepsilon, +, - \rangle \\ AsA = have \end{bmatrix} \rightarrow \mathrm{HAVE}\begin{bmatrix} Num = \alpha \\ TP = \delta \\ Fin = + \\ TENSE = \varepsilon \end{bmatrix} \ \textbf{not}\ \mathrm{VP}\begin{bmatrix} Fin = part \\ Gap = \gamma \\ STAT = \eta \\ AsA = be/neither \end{bmatrix}$$

(PS 17′.c)

$$\mathrm{VP}\begin{bmatrix} Num = \alpha \\ Fin = - \\ Gap = \gamma \\ AsA = have \end{bmatrix} \rightarrow \mathrm{HAVE}\begin{bmatrix} Num = \alpha \\ Fin = + \end{bmatrix} \ \mathrm{VP}\begin{bmatrix} Num = \alpha \\ Fin = part \\ Gap = \gamma \\ STAT = \eta \\ AsA = be/neither \end{bmatrix}$$

(PS 18′.a) Adv $\rightarrow$ Prep $\mathrm{NP}_{[\,Temp = +\,]}$

(PS 18′.b) Adv $\rightarrow$ Adverb

(PS 18′.c) Adv $\rightarrow$ Conj S′

We replace the lexical insertion rules (LI 15) and (LI 15) by

(LI 15′) $\mathrm{AUX}\begin{bmatrix} Num = sing \\ Fin = + \\ TP = -PAST \\ TENSE = pres \end{bmatrix} \rightarrow$ **does**

(LI 16′) $\mathrm{AUX}\begin{bmatrix} Num = plur \\ Fin = + \\ TP = -PAST \\ TENSE = pres \end{bmatrix} \rightarrow$ **do**

and add

(LI 30) $\mathrm{AUX}\begin{bmatrix} Num = \alpha \\ Fin = + \\ TP = -PAST \\ TENSE = past \end{bmatrix} \rightarrow$ **did**

$$\textbf{(LI 31)}\ \mathrm{AUX}\begin{bmatrix} Num=\alpha \\ Fin=+ \\ TP=+PAST \\ TENSE=pres \end{bmatrix} \rightarrow \textbf{did}$$

$$\textbf{(LI 32)}\ \mathrm{AUX}\begin{bmatrix} Num=\alpha \\ Fin=+ \\ TP=+PAST \\ TENSE=past \end{bmatrix} \rightarrow \textbf{had}$$

$$\textbf{(LI 33)}\ \mathrm{AUX}\begin{bmatrix} Num=\alpha \\ Fin=+ \\ TP=-PAST \\ TENSE=fut \end{bmatrix} \rightarrow \textbf{will}$$

$$\textbf{(LI 34)}\ \mathrm{AUX}\begin{bmatrix} Num=\alpha \\ Fin=+ \\ TP=+PAST \\ TENSE=fut \end{bmatrix} \rightarrow \textbf{would}$$

$$\textbf{(LI 35)}\ \mathrm{BE}\begin{bmatrix} Num=sing \\ Fin=+ \\ TP=-PAST \\ TENSE=pres \end{bmatrix} \rightarrow \textbf{is}$$

$$\textbf{(LI 36)}\ \mathrm{BE}\begin{bmatrix} Num=plur \\ Fin=+ \\ TP=-PAST \\ TENSE=pres \end{bmatrix} \rightarrow \textbf{are}$$

$$\textbf{(LI 37)}\ \mathrm{BE}\begin{bmatrix} Num=sing \\ Fin=+ \\ TP=-PAST \\ TENSE=past \end{bmatrix} \rightarrow \textbf{was}$$

$$\textbf{(LI 38)}\ \mathrm{BE}\begin{bmatrix} Num=plur \\ Fin=+ \\ TP=-PAST \\ TENSE=past \end{bmatrix} \rightarrow \textbf{were}$$

$$\textbf{(LI 39)}\ \mathrm{BE}\begin{bmatrix} Num=sing \\ Fin=+ \\ TP=+PAST \\ TENSE=pres \end{bmatrix} \rightarrow \textbf{was}$$

(LI 40) $\text{BE}_{\begin{bmatrix} Num = plur \\ Fin = + \\ TP = +PAST \\ TENSE = pres \end{bmatrix}} \rightarrow$ **were**

(LI 41) $\text{BE}_{[\, Fin = - \,]} \rightarrow$ **be**

(LI 42) $\text{BE}_{[\, Fin = part \,]} \rightarrow$ **been**

(LI 43) $\text{HAVE}_{[\, Fin = - \,]} \rightarrow$ **have**

(LI 44) $\text{HAVE}_{\begin{bmatrix} Num = sing \\ Fin = + \\ TP = -PAST \\ TENSE = pres \end{bmatrix}} \rightarrow$ **has**

(LI 45) $\text{HAVE}_{\begin{bmatrix} Num = plur \\ Fin = + \\ TP = -PAST \\ TENSE = pres \end{bmatrix}} \rightarrow$ **have**

(LI 46) $\text{HAVE}_{\begin{bmatrix} Num = \alpha \\ Fin = + \\ TP = -PAST \\ TENSE = past \end{bmatrix}} \rightarrow$ **had**

(LI 47) $\text{HAVE}_{\begin{bmatrix} Num = \alpha \\ Fin = + \\ TP = +PAST \\ TENSE = pres/past \end{bmatrix}} \rightarrow$ **had**

All the verbs in our original fragment were statives. Thus the rules (LI 19) and (LI 20) must be modified by adding to the left-hand side the feature specification *Stat* = +. In addition we will now supply ourselves with a stock of non-stative verbs. For a start we take

$\text{V}_{\begin{bmatrix} Trans = + \\ STAT = - \end{bmatrix}} \rightarrow$ **leave, reach, kiss, hit, scold, beat, ...**

$\text{V}_{\begin{bmatrix} Trans = - \\ STAT = - \end{bmatrix}} \rightarrow$ **leave, arrive, walk, sleep, come, shine, ...**

(LI 48) $\text{V}_{\begin{bmatrix} Num = \alpha \\ Fin = - \\ STAT = - \\ Trans = \beta \end{bmatrix}} \rightarrow \delta$, where $\delta \in \text{V}_{\begin{bmatrix} Trans = \beta \\ STAT = - \end{bmatrix}}$

Rules (LI 17) and (LI 18) are replaced by (LI 38) and (LI 39).

(LI 49) $\mathrm{V}\begin{bmatrix} Num = sing \\ Fin = + \\ STAT = \gamma \\ TP = -PAST \\ TENSE = pres \end{bmatrix} \rightarrow \langle \text{Pres, sing3}^{\text{rd}} \rangle(\delta)$, where $\delta \in \mathrm{V}\begin{bmatrix} Trans = \beta \\ STAT = \gamma \end{bmatrix}$

(LI 50) $\mathrm{V}\begin{bmatrix} Num = plur \\ Fin = + \\ STAT = \gamma \\ TP = -PAST \\ TENSE = pres \end{bmatrix} \rightarrow \langle \text{Pres, plur} \rangle(\delta)$, where $\delta \in \mathrm{V}\begin{bmatrix} Trans = \beta \\ STAT = \gamma \end{bmatrix}$

In addition we have

(LI 51) $\mathrm{V}\begin{bmatrix} Num = \alpha \\ Fin = + \\ STAT = \gamma \\ TP = -PAST \\ TENSE = pres \\ Trans = \beta \end{bmatrix} \rightarrow \text{Past}(\delta)$, where $\delta \in \mathrm{V}\begin{bmatrix} Trans = \beta \\ STAT = \gamma \end{bmatrix}$

(LI 52) $\mathrm{V}\begin{bmatrix} Fin = + \\ STAT = \gamma \\ TP = +PAST \\ TENSE = past \\ Trans = \beta \end{bmatrix} \rightarrow \text{Past}(\delta)$, where $\delta \in \mathrm{V}\begin{bmatrix} Trans = \beta \\ STAT = \gamma \end{bmatrix}$

(LI 53) $\mathrm{V}\begin{bmatrix} Fin = ing \\ STAT = \gamma \\ Trans = \beta \end{bmatrix} \rightarrow \text{Ger}(\delta)$, where $\delta \in \mathrm{V}\begin{bmatrix} Trans = \beta \\ STAT = \gamma \end{bmatrix}$

(LI 54) $\mathrm{V}\begin{bmatrix} Num = * \\ Fin = part \\ STAT = \gamma \\ Trans = \beta \end{bmatrix} \rightarrow \text{PPart}(\delta)$, where $\delta \in \mathrm{V}\begin{bmatrix} Trans = \beta \\ STAT = \gamma \end{bmatrix}$

(LI 55) Prep → **Ø, in, at, before, after, since, until**

(LI 56) Adverb → **now, yesterday**

(LI 57) $\mathrm{NP}_{[\,Temp = +\,]}$ → **Sunday, Monday, ..., January, February, ..., January 1st, January 2nd, ..., 1900, 1901, 1902, ..., 1 o'clock, 2 o'clock, ..., 10.30, 10.45, ...**

(LI 58) $NP_{[\,Temp = +\,]} \rightarrow$ Det $N_{[\,Temp = +\,]}$

(LI 59) $NP_{[\,Temp = +\,]} \rightarrow$ **day, week, month, year**

(LI 60) Conj $\rightarrow$ **before, after, since, until, from**

Bibliography

[Abusch 1988] Abusch, Dorit (1988), 'Sequence of Tense, Intensionality and Scope', *WCCFL* 7, Stanford University.

[Adams 1970] Adams, Ernest W. (1970), 'Subjunctive and Indicative Conditionals', *Inquiry* 6, pp. 39–94.

[Agrell 1908] Agrell, Sigurd (1908), *Aspektänderung und Aktionsartbildung beim polnischen Zeitworte.* (Acta Universitatis Lundensis / Lunds Universitets Årsskrift 4.1908, Nr. 2) Lund: Gleerup.

[Allen 1983] Allen, James F. (1983), 'Maintaining Knowledge about Temporal Intervals', *Communications of the ACM* 26, pp. 832–843.

[Aristotle, De Interpretatione] Aristotle, 'De Interpretatione', Ch. 9, in W.D. Ross (ed.), The Works of Aristotle, Oxford: Clarendon Press 1928.

[Asher/Wada 1988] Asher, Nicholas & Hajime Wada (1988), 'A Computational Account of Syntactic, Semantic and Discourse Principles for Anaphora Resolution', *Journal of Semantics* 6, pp. 309–344.

[Austin 1962] Austin, John Langshaw (1962), *How to do Things with Words*, Oxford: Clarendon Press.

[Bach 1981] Bach, Emmon (1981), 'On Time, Tense and Aspect: An Essay on English Metaphysics'. In: Peter Cole (ed.), *Radical Pragmatics*, New York: Academic Press, pp. 62–81.

[Barwise/Cooper 1981] Barwise, Jon & Robin Cooper (1981), 'Generalized Quantifiers and Natural Language', *Linguistics and Philosophy* 4, pp. 159–219.

[van Benthem 1983] van Benthem, Johan (1983), *The Logic of Time*, Dordrecht: Reidel.

[van Benthem & ter Meulen 1985] van Benthem, Johan & Alice ter Meulen (eds.) (1985), *Generalized Quantifiers in Natural Language*, (GRASS Series 4), Dordrecht: Foris.

[Bullwinkle 1977] Bullwinkle, Candace L. (1977), 'Levels of Complexity in Discourse for Anaphora Disambiguation and Speech Act Interpretation', *Proceedings of the Fifth International Joint Conference on Artificial Intelligence*, Cambridge, Mass.

[Chierchia 1991] Chierchia, Gennaro (1991), 'Anaphora and Dynamic Binding', *Linguistics and Philosophy* 15, No. 2, April 1992, pp. 111–183.

[Chomsky 1957] Chomsky, Noam (1957), *Syntactic Structures*, The Hague: Mouton.

[Chomsky 1970] Chomsky, Noam (1970), 'Remarks on Nominalization', In: I. Jacobs & P. Rosenbaum (eds.), *Readings in English Transformational Grammar*, Waltham, Mass.: Ginn & Co., pp. 184–221.

[Chomsky 1981] Chomsky, Noam (1981), *Lectures on Government and Binding*, (=Studies in Generative Grammar 9). Dordrecht: Foris.

[Church 1936] Church, Alonzo (1936), 'A note on the Entscheidungsproblem', *Journal of Symbolic Logic* 1, pp. 40f., 101f.

[Cocchiarella 1965] Cocchiarella, Nino B. (1965), *Tense and Modal Logic*, Thesis.

[Cole/Morgan 1975] Cole, Peter & Jerry L. Morgan (eds.) (1975), *Speech Acts* (= Syntax and Semantics 3), New York/San Francisco/London: Academic Press.

[Davidson 1967a] Davidson, Donald (1967a), 'The Logical Form of Action Sentences'. In: Nicholas Rescher (ed.), *The Logic of Decision and Action*, Pittsburgh: The University Press, pp. 81–95.

[Davidson 1967b] Davidson, Donald (1967b), 'Causal Relations (1967)', *Essays on Actions and Events*, Oxford: Clarendon Press 1980, pp. 149–162.

[Davidson 1967c] Davidson, Donald (1967c), 'Truth and Meaning', *Synthese* 17, pp. 304–323.

[Diesing 1990] Diesing, Molly (1990), *Syntactic Aspects of Semantic Partition*, PhD Thesis, University of Massachusetts, Amherst.

[Doron 1983] Doron, Edit (1983), *Verbless Predicates in Hebrew*, PhD Thesis, University of Texas at Austin.

[Dowty 1979] Dowty, David (1979), *Word Meaning and Montague Grammar*, Dordrecht: Reidel.

[Dowty et. al. 1981] Dowty, David R., Robert E. Wall & Stanley Peters (1981), *Introduction to Montague Semantics*, Dordrecht: Reidel.

[Eberle 1991] Eberle, Kurt (1991), *Ereignisse: Ihre Logik und Ontologie aus textsemantischer Sicht*, PhD Thesis, University of Stuttgart.

[Fodor 1975] Fodor, Jerry A. (1975), *The Language of Thought*, New York: Thomas Y. Cromwell. – Reprinted (1979). Cambridge, Mass.: Harvard University Press.

[Fodor 1983] Fodor, Jerry A. (1983), *Representations. Philosophical Essays on the Foundation of Cognitive Science*, Cambridge, Mass.: The MIT Press.

[Frege 1964] Frege, Gottlob (1964), *Begriffsschrift und andere Aufsätze*, Hildesheim: Olms.

[Frege 1967] Frege, Gottlob (1967), 'Über Sinn und Bedeutung', *Kleine Schriften*, Hildesheim: Olms, pp. 143–162.

[Frey 1989] Frey, Werner (1989), *Syntaktische Bedingungen für die Interpretation – über Bindung, implizite Argumente und Skopus –*, PhD Thesis, University of Stuttgart.

[Gärdenfors 1987] Gärdenfors, Peter (ed.) (1987), *Generalized Quantifiers. Linguistic and Logical Approaches*, (Studies in Linguistics and Philosophy 31), Dordrecht: Reidel.

[Galton 1984] Galton, Antony (1984), *The Logic of Aspect. An Axiomatic Approach*, Oxford: Clarendon Press.

[Gazdar 1979] Gazdar, Gerald (1979), *Pragmatics: Implicature, Pressupposition, and Logical Form*, New York: Academic Press.

[Gazdar et. al. 1985] Gazdar, Gerald, Ewan Klein, Geoffrey K. Pullum & Ivan Sag (1985), *Generalized Phrase Structure Grammar*, Oxford: Blackwell.

[Gödel 1931] Gödel, Kurt (1931), 'Über formal unentscheidbare Sätze der Principia Mathematica und verwandter Systeme I', *Monatshefte für Mathematik und Physik* 38, pp. 173–198; trsl. in: [van Heijenoort 1967], pp. 596–616.

[Grice 1975] Grice, H. Paul (1975), 'Logic and Conversation'. In: [Cole/Morgan 1975], pp. 41–58.

[Groenendijk/Stokhof 1990] Groenendijk, Jeroen & Stokhof, Martin (1990), 'Two Theories of Dynamic Semantics', in: Eijk, Jan van (ed.), *Logics in AI, European Workshop JELIA 1990'*, Berlin: Springer Verlag, pp. 55–64.

[Groenendijk/Stokhof 1991] Groenendijk, Jeroen & Stokhof, Martin (1991), 'Dynamic Predicate Logic', *Linguistics & Philosophy* 14, pp. 39–100.

[Grosz 1977] Grosz, Barbara Jean (1977), 'The Representation and Use of Focus in Dialog Understanding', PhD Thesis, Berkley California. In: Donald E. Walker (ed.) (1978), *Understanding Spoken Language*, New York: North-Holland.

[Grosz et.al. 1983] Grosz, Barbara Jean, Aravind K. Joshi & S. Weinstein (1983), 'Providing a Unified Account of Definite Noun Phrases in Discourse', *ACL Conference Proceedings.*

[Guenthner/Lehmann 1983] Guenthner, Franz & Hubert Lehmann (1983), 'Rules for Pronominalization', [Proceedings of the] *First Conference of the European Chapter of the Association for Computational Linguistics*, Pisa, pp. 144–151.

[van Heijenoort 1967] van Heijenoort, Jean (ed.) (1967), *From Frege to Gödel. A Source Book in Mathematical Logic, 1879–1931*, Cambridge, Mass.: Harvard University Press.

[Heim 1982] Heim, Irene (1982), *The Semantics of Definite and Indefinite Noun Phrases in English*, PhD Thesis, University of Massachusetts, Amherst. Distributed as *Arbeitspapier* 73, SFB 99, Konstanz. – Published (1988). New York: Garland.

[Heim 1990] Heim, Irene (1990), 'E-Type Pronouns and Donkey Anaphora', *Linguistics and Philosophy* 13, No. 2, April 1990, pp. 137–177.

[Heim, Lasnik & May 1991] Heim, Irene, Howard Lasnik & Robert May (1991), 'Reciprocity and Plurality'. In: *Linguistic Inquiry* 22, No. 1, pp 63–101.

[Heinämäki 1973] Heinämäki, Orwokki (1973), *The Semantics of English Temporal Connectives*, PhD Dissertation, University of Texas, Austin.

[Hirst 1981] Hirst, Graeme (1981), *Anaphora in Natural Language Understanding: A Survey*, Berlin: Springer.

[Hobbs 1985] Hobbs, Jerry R. (1985), 'On the Coherence and Structure of Discourse', *CSLI Report.*

[Hoeksema 1983] Hoeksema, Jack (1983), 'Plurality & Conjunction'. In: Alice ter Meulen (ed.), *Studies in Model-Theoretic Semantics*, Dordrecht: Foris, pp. 63–84.

[Jackendoff 1977] Jackendoff, Ray S. (1977), *X-Bar Syntax: A Study of Phrase Structure*, Cambridge, Mass: MIT Press.

[Kadmon 1987a] Kadmon, Nirit (1987a), *On Unique and Non-Unique Reference and Asymmetric Quantification*, PhD Thesis, University of Massachusetts at Amherst. Distributed by the GLSA.

[Kadmon 1987b] Kadmon, Nirit (1987b), 'Asymmetric Quantification'. In: Jeroen A. G. Groenendijk, Martin B. J. Stokhof & Frank Veltman (eds.), *Proceedings of the 6th Amsterdam Colloquium*, University of Amsterdam.

[Kadmon 1990] Kadmon, Nirit (1990), 'Uniqueness', *Linguistics and Philosophy* 13, No. 3, April 1990, pp. 273–324.

[Kamp 1971] Kamp, Hans (1971), 'Formal Properties of now'. In: *Theoria* 37, pp. 227–273.

[Kamp 1973] Kamp, Hans (1973), 'Free Choice Permission', *Proceedings of the Aristotelian Society.*

[Kamp 1979] Kamp, Hans (1979), 'Events, Instants and Temporal Reference'. In: Rainer Bäuerle, Urs Egli & Arnim von Stechow (eds.), *Semantics from Different Points of View*, Berlin: Springer.

[Kamp 1981] Kamp, Hans (1981), 'Evénements, représentations discursives et référence temporelle', *Language* 64, pp. 39–64.

[Kamp 1981b] Kamp, Hans (1981), 'A Theory of Truth and Semantic Representation', in: Jeroen A. G. Groenendijk, T. M. V. Janssen & Martin B. J. Stokhof (eds.), *Formal Methods in the Study of Language*, Mathematical Centre Tract 135, Amsterdam, pp. 277–322. – Reprinted in: Jeroen A. G. Groenendijk, T. M. V. Janssen & Martin B. J. Stokhof (eds.), *Truth, Representation and Information* (= GRASS Series No. 2), Dordrecht, pp. 277–322.

[Kamp 1990] Kamp, Hans (1990), 'Prolegomena to a Structural Theory of Belief and Other Attitudes'. In: C. Anthony Anderson & Joseph Owens, *Propositional Attitudes*, CSLI Lecture Notes 20, pp. 27–90.

[Kamp & Rohrer 1983] Kamp, Hans & Christian Rohrer (1983), *Temporal Reference in French*, Ms. University of Stuttgart.

[Kaplan 1979] Kaplan, David (1979), 'On the Logic of Demonstratives'. In: *Journal of Philosophical Logic* 8, 81–98.

[Keenan 1987] Keenan, Edward (1987), 'Unreducible n-ary Quantification in Natural Language'. In: [Gärdenfors 1987], pp. 109–150.

[Keenan 1987a] Keenan, Edward (1987), 'A Semantic Definition of "Indefinite NP"', in: Reuland, Eric J. & ter Meulen, Alice G.B. (eds.), *The Representation of (In)definiteness*, MIT Press, Cambridge, pp. 286–317.

[Kempson/Cormack 1981] Kempson, Ruth M. & Annabel Cormack (1981), 'Ambiguity and Quantification', *Linguistics & Philosophy* 4, pp. 259–309.

[Kneale/Kneale 1962] Kneale, William & Martha Kneale (1962), *The Development of Logic*, Oxford: Oxford University Press.

[Kripke 1972] Kripke, Saul (1972), 'Naming and Necessity'. In: Donald Davidson & Gilbert H. Harman (eds.), *Semantics of Natural Language*, Dordrecht: Reidel, pp. 253–355, 763–769.

[Kripke 1980] Kripke, Saul (1980), *Naming and Necessity*, Oxford: Basil Blackwell.

[Landman 1989] Landman, Fred (1989), 'Groups, Part I + II', *Linguistics and Philosophy* 12, pp. 559–606, 723–744.

[Landman 1991] Landman, Fred (1991), *Structures for Semantics*, Dordrecht: Kluwer.

[Landman 1992] Landman, Fred (1992), 'The Progressive.' *Natural Language Semantics*, Vol. I, Nr. 1, Dordrecht: Kluwer, pp. 1–32.

[Larson 1990] Larson, Richard K. (1990), 'Double Objects Revisited: Reply to Jackendoff.' *Linguistic Inquiry* 21, No. 4, pp. 589-632.

[Lasersohn 1988] Lasersohn, Peter (1988), *A Semantics for Groups and Events*, PhD Thesis, Ohio State University.

[Lasersohn 1990] Lasersohn, Peter (1990), 'Group Action and Spatio-Temporal Proximity', *Linguistics and Philosophy* 13, No. 2, April 1990, pp. 179–206.

[Lewis/Langford 1932] Lewis, Clarence I. & Cooper H. Langford (1932), *Symbolic Logic*, New York: Century (2nd ed. 1959).

[Lewis 1970] Lewis, David K. (1970), 'General Semantics'. In: *Synthese* 22, 18–67. – Reprinted in: Donald Davidson & Gilbert H. Harman (eds.) (1972), *Semantics of Natural Language*, Dordrecht, Reidel, pp. 169–218 .

[Lewis 1973] Lewis, David K. (1973), *Counterfactuals*, Oxford: Blackwell.

[Lewis 1975b] Lewis, David K. (1975), 'Adverbs of Quantification'. In: Edward Keenan (ed.), *Formal Semantics of Natural Languages*. Cambridge University Press.

[Lewis 1979] Lewis, David K. (1979), 'A Problem about Permission'. In: Esa Saarinen et al. (eds.), *Essays in Honour of Jaakko Hintikka*, Dordrecht: Reidel.

[Link 1983] Link, Godehard (1983), 'The Logical Analysis of Plurals and Mass Terms: A Lattice-Theoretical Approach'. In: Rainer Bäuerle, Christoph Schwarze & Arnim von Stechow (eds.), *Meaning, Use and Interpretation of Language*, Berlin/New York: de Gruyter, pp. 303–323.

[Link 1984] Link, Godehard (1984), 'Plural'. In: Dieter Wunderlich & Arnim von Stechow (eds.), *Semantik. Ein internationales Handbuch der zeitgenössischen Forschung*, Berlin: de Gruyter.

[Link 1991] Link, Godehard (1991), 'First Order Axioms for the Logic of Plurality'. In: J. Allgayer (ed.), *Processing Plurals and Quantification* (= CSLI Lecture Notes), Stanford

[Löbner 1988] Löbner, Sebastian (1988), 'Ansätze zu einer integralen semantischen Theorie von Tempus, Aspekt und Aktionsarten'. In: Veronika Ehrich & Heinz Vater (eds.), *Temporalsemantik. Beiträge zur Linguistik der Zeitreferenz.* Tübingen: Niemeyer.

[Lønning 1989] Lønning, Jan Tore (1989), *Some Aspects of the Logic of Plural Noun Phrases*, COSMOS-Report No. 11, Department of Mathematics, University of Oslo, Norway.

[Mann & Thompson 1986] Mann, William & Sandra Thompson (1986), 'Relational Propositions in Discourse'. In: *Discourse Processes* 9, pp. 57–90.

[Mann & Thompson 1987] Mann, William & Sandra Thompson (1987), *Rhetorical Structure Theory: A Theory of Text Organisation*, ISI Reprint Series.

[May 1985] May, Robert (1985), *Logical Form: Its Structure and Derivation.*, Cambridge/Mass.: MIT Press.

[de Mey 1981] de Mey, Sjaak (1981), 'Dependent Plural and the Analysis of Tense'. In: Victoria A. Burke & James Pustejowsky (eds.), *Proceedings of NELS* 11, Graduate Linguistics Student Association, University of Mass., Amherst.

[Milsark 1974] Milsark, G. (1974), *Existential Sentences in English*, Ph.D. Dissertation, MIT

[Montague 1974] Montague, Richard (1974), *Formal Philosophy. Selected Papers of Richard Montague*. Edited with an introduction by R.H. Thomason. New Haven/London: Yale University Press

[Mostowski 1968] Mostowski, Andrej (1968), 'On a Generalization of Quantifiers', *Fundamenta Mathematicae* 68, pp. 83–93.

[Ogihara 1989] Ogihara, Toshiyuki (1989), *Temporal Reference in English and Japanese*, PhD Thesis, University of Texas at Austin.

[Partee 1973a] Partee, Barbara (1973), 'Some Structural Analogies between Tenses and Pronouns in English', *Journal of Philosophy* 70, pp. 601–609.

[Partee 1973b] Partee, Barbara (1973), 'Some Transformational Extensions of Montague Grammar', *Journal of Philosophical Logic* 2, pp. 509–534.

[Partee 1984] Partee, Barbara (1984), 'Nominal and Temporal Anaphora', *Linguistics and Philosophy* 7, pp. 243–286.

[Partee 1984a] Partee, Barbara (1984), 'Compositionality', in: F.Landman, F.Veltman (eds.), *Varieties of Formal Semantics. Proceedings of the Fourth Amsterdam Colloquium* (= GRASS Series No. 3). Dordrecht: Foris, pp. 281–311.

[Partee 1988] Partee, Barbara (1988), 'Many Quantifiers'. In: *Proceedings of ESCOL*

[Pollock 1976] Pollock, John (1976), *Subjunctive Reasoning*, Dordrecht: Reidel.

[Prior 1967] Prior, Arthur (1967), *Past, Present and the Future*, Oxford: Clarendon Press.

[Prior 1968] Prior, Arthur (1968), 'Now', *Noûs*, Vol. 2, pp. 101–119.

[Quine 1953] Quine, Willard van Orman (1953), *From a Logical Point of View*, Harvard University Press.

[Reichenbach 1947] Reichenbach, Hans (1947), *Elements of Symbolic Logic*, London: Macmillan.

[Reichman 1985] Reichman, Rachel (1985), *Getting Computers to Talk like You and Me*, Harvard University Press.

[Reinhart 1983a] Reinhart, Tanja (1983a), *Anaphora and Semantic Interpretation*, London: Croom Helm.

[Reinhart 1983b] Reinhart, Tanja (1983b), 'Coreference and Bound Anaphora: A Restatement of the Anaphora Question', *Linguistics and Philosophy* 6, No. 1, pp. 47–88.

[Rescher 1967] Rescher, Nicholas (1967), 'Truth and Necessity in Temporal Perspective'. In: Richard M. Gale (ed.), *The Philosophy of Time*, Garden City (NY): Doubleday.

[Reyle 1986] Reyle, Uwe (1986), *Zeit und Aspekt bei der Verarbeitung natürlicher Sprachen*. PhD thesis, University of Stuttgart. 1986

[Riemsdijk/Williams 1986] van Riemsdijk, Henk & Edwin Williams (1986), *Introduction to the Theory of Grammar*, Cambridge, Mass.: The MIT Press.

[Roberts 1973] Roberts, Don D. (1973), *The Existential Graphs of Charles S. Peirce*, The Hague: Mouton.

[Roberts 1987a] Roberts, Craige (1987a), *Modal Subordination, Anaphora and Distributivity*, PhD Thesis, University of Massachusetts, Amherst.

[Roberts 1987b] Roberts, Craige (1987b), 'Plural Anaphors in Distributive Contexts', *Proceedings of WCCFL* VI, Stanford.

[Rohrer 1986] Rohrer, Christian (1986), 'Pour une sémantique du texte: La théorie des représentations discursive illustrée à l'aide du plusqueparfait et passé antérieur', *Linguistique générale et Linguistique Romane. Actes du XVIIe congrès international de linguistique et philologie romanes* 1.

[Rooth 1985] Rooth, Mats (1985), *Association with Focus*, PhD Thesis, University of Massachusetts, Amherst.

[Rooth 1992] Rooth, Mats (1992), 'A Theory of Focus Interpretation', *Natural Language Semantics*, Vol. I, Nr. 1, Dordrecht: Kluwer, pp. 75–117.

[Russell 1905] Russell, Bertrand (1905), 'On Denoting', *Mind* 14, pp. 479–493.

[Scha 1981] Scha, Remko (1981), 'Distributive, Collective and Cumulative Quantification'. In: Jeroen A. G. Groenendijk, T. M. V. Janssen & Martin B. J. Stokhof (eds.), *Formal Methods in the Study of Language*, Amsterdam: Mathematisch Centrum, pp. 483–512.

[Searle 1969] Searle, John R. (1969), *Speech Acts: An Essay in the Philosophy of Language*, Cambridge: Cambridge University Press.

[Sidner 1979] Sidner, Candace Lee (1979), *Towards a Computational Theory of Definite Anaphora Comprehension in English Discourse*, PhD Thesis, Mass. Institute of Technology.

[Smith 1991] Smith, Carlota S. (1991), *The Parameter of Aspect*, Dordrecht: Kluwer.

[Stalnaker 1968] Stalnaker, Robert (1968), 'A Theory of Conditionals'. In: Nicholas Rescher (ed.), *Studies in Logical Theory*, Oxford: Blackwell, pp. 98–112.

[Strawson 1950] Strawson, Peter F. (1950), 'On Referring', *Mind* 59, pp. 320–344. – Reprinted in: Antony G. N. Flew (ed.) (1956), *Essays in Conceptual Analysis*, London: Mac Millan, pp. 21–52.

[Thomason 1974] Thomason, Richmond H. (1974), Introduction to: *Formal Philosophy. Selected Papers by Richard Montague*, New Haven: Yale University Press, pp. 1–69.

[Thomason 1984] Thomason, Richmond H. (1984), 'Combinations of Tense and Modality'. In: Dov Gabbay & Franz Guenthner (eds.), *Handbook of Philosophical Logic*, Vol. II: Extensions of Classical Logic, pp. 135–165.

[Tarski 1933] Tarski, Alfred (1933), *The Concept of Truth in the Language of Deductive Sciences*, see [Tarski 1935/36].

[Tarski 1935/36] Tarski, Alfred (1935/36), 'Der Wahrheitsbegriff in den formalisierten Sprachen', trsl. in: [Tarski 1956], pp. 152–278.

[Tarski 1956] Tarski, Alfred (1956), *Logic, Semantics, Metamathematics, Papers from 1923 to 1938*, trsl. J. H. Woodger, Oxford: University Press.

[Veltman 1985] Veltman, Frank (1985), *Logics for Conditionals*, PhD Thesis, Department of Philosophy, University of Amsterdam.

[Vendler 1967] Vendler, Zeno (1967), *Linguistics and Philosophy*, Ithaca, N.Y.: Cornell University Press.

[Verkuyl 1972] Verkuyl, Henk (1972), *On the Compositional Nature of the Aspects*, PhD Thesis, University of Utrecht.

[Vilain/Kautz 1986] Vilain, Marc & Henry Kautz (1986), 'Constraint Propagation Algorithms for Temporal Reasoning', *Proceedings of the 5th Conference on Artificial Intelligence (AAAI-86)*, pp. 377–382.

[Vlach 1981] Vlach, Frank (1981), 'The Semantics of the Progressive', *Syntax and Semantics* 14, pp. 271–292.

[Webber 1978] Webber, Bonnie Lynn (1978), *A Formal Approach to Discourse Anaphora*, PhD Thesis, Harvard University. Published in the series: 'Outstanding Dissertations in Linguistics', New York: Garland 1979.

[Wiener 1914] Wiener, Norbert (1914), 'A Contribution to the Theory of Relative Position', *Proceedings of the Cambridge Philosophical Society* 7.

[Whitrow 1961] Whitrow, G.J. (1961), *The Natural Philosophy of Time*, London/Edinburgh: Thomas Nelson & Sons Ltd.

[Zanardo 1985] Zanardo, A. (1985), 'A Finite Axiomatization of the Set of Strongly Valid Ockhamist Formulas', *Journal of Philosophical Logic* 14, 1985, pp. 447–468.

[Zimmermann 1991] Zimmermann, Thomas Ede (1991), 'Kontextabhängigkeit'. In: Dieter Wunderlich & Arnim von Stechow (eds.), *Semantik. Ein internationales Handbuch der zeitgenössischen Forschung*, Berlin: de Gruyter, pp. 156–229.

Table of Construction Rules

Those marked with 'prel.' are preliminary versions.

Index of Symbols, Features and Feature Values

Index of Names

Index of Subjects

Studies in Linguistics and Philosophy

1. H. Hiż (ed.): *Questions.* 1978 ISBN 90-277-0813-4; Pb: 90-277-1035-X
2. W. S. Cooper: *Foundations of Logico-Linguistics.* A Unified Theory of Information, Language, and Logic. 1978 ISBN 90-277-0864-9; Pb: 90-277-0876-2
3. A. Margalit (ed.): *Meaning and Use.* 1979 ISBN 90-277-0888-6
4. F. Guenthner and S.J. Schmidt (eds.): *Formal Semantics and Pragmatics for Natural Languages.* 1979 ISBN 90-277-0778-2; Pb: 90-277-0930-0
5. E. Saarinen (ed.): *Game-Theoretical Semantics.* Essays on Semantics by Hintikka, Carlson, Peacocke, Rantala, and Saarinen. 1979 ISBN 90-277-0918-1
6. F.J. Pelletier (ed.): *Mass Terms: Some Philosophical Problems.* 1979 ISBN 90-277-0931-9
7. D. R. Dowty: *Word Meaning and Montague Grammar.* The Semantics of Verbs and Times in Generative Semantics and in Montague's PTQ. 1979 ISBN 90-277-1008-2; Pb: 90-277-1009-0
8. A. F. Freed: *The Semantics of English Aspectual Complementation.* 1979 ISBN 90-277-1010-4; Pb: 90-277-1011-2
9. J. McCloskey: *Transformational Syntax and Model Theoretic Semantics.* A Case Study in Modern Irish. 1979 ISBN 90-277-1025-2; Pb: 90-277-1026-0
10. J. R. Searle, F. Kiefer and M. Bierwisch (eds.): *Speech Act Theory and Pragmatics.* 1980 ISBN 90-277-1043-0; Pb: 90-277-1045-7
11. D. R. Dowty, R. E. Wall and S. Peters: *Introduction to Montague Semantics.* 1981; 5th printing 1987 ISBN 90-277-1141-0; Pb: 90-277-1142-9
12. F. Heny (ed.): *Ambiguities in Intensional Contexts.* 1981 ISBN 90-277-1167-4; Pb: 90-277-1168-2
13. W. Klein and W. Levelt (eds.): *Crossing the Boundaries in Linguistics.* Studies Presented to Manfred Bierwisch. 1981 ISBN 90-277-1259-X
14. Z. S. Harris: *Papers on Syntax.* Edited by H. Hiż. 1981 ISBN 90-277-1266-0; Pb: 90-277-1267-0
15. P. Jacobson and G. K. Pullum (eds.): *The Nature of Syntactic Representation.* 1982 ISBN 90-277-1289-1; Pb: 90-277-1290-5
16. S. Peters and E. Saarinen (eds.): *Processes, Beliefs, and Questions.* Essays on Formal Semantics of Natural Language and Natural Language Processing. 1982 ISBN 90-277-1314-6
17. L. Carlson: *Dialogue Games.* An Approach to Discourse Analysis. 1983; 2nd printing 1985 ISBN 90-277-1455-X; Pb: 90-277-1951-9
18. L. Vaina and J. Hintikka (eds.): *Cognitive Constraints on Communication.* Representation and Processes. 1984; 2nd printing 1985 ISBN 90-277-1456-8; Pb: 90-277-1949-7
19. F. Heny and B. Richards (eds.): *Linguistic Categories: Auxiliaries and Related Puzzles.* Volume I: Categories. 1983 ISBN 90-277-1478-9

Studies in Linguistics and Philosophy

20. F. Heny and B. Richards (eds.): *Linguistic Categories: Auxiliaries and Related Puzzles.* Volume II: The Scope, Order, and Distribution of English Auxiliary Verbs. 1983 ISBN 90-277-1479-7
21. R. Cooper: *Quantification and Syntactic Theory.* 1983 ISBN 90-277-1484-3
22. J. Hintikka (in collaboration with J. Kulas): *The Game of Language.* Studies in Game-Theoretical Semantics and Its Applications. 1983; 2nd printing 1985 ISBN 90-277-1687-0; Pb: 90-277-1950-0
23. E. L. Keenan and L. M. Faltz: *Boolean Semantics for Natural Language.* 1985 ISBN 90-277-1768-0; Pb: 90-277-1842-3
24. V. Raskin: *Semantic Mechanisms of Humor.* 1985 ISBN 90-277-1821-0; Pb: 90-277-1891-1
25. G. T. Stump: *The Semantic Variability of Absolute Constructions.* 1985 ISBN 90-277-1895-4; Pb: 90-277-1896-2
26. J. Hintikka and J. Kulas: *Anaphora and Definite Descriptions.* Two Applications of Game-Theoretical Semantics. 1985 ISBN 90-277-2055-X; Pb: 90-277-2056-8
27. E. Engdahl: *Constituent Questions.* The Syntax and Semantics of Questions with Special Reference to Swedish. 1986 ISBN 90-277-1954-3; Pb: 90-277-1955-1
28. M. J. Cresswell: *Adverbial Modification.* Interval Semantics and Its Rivals. 1985 ISBN 90-277-2059-2; Pb: 90-277-2060-6
29. J. van Benthem: *Essays in Logical Semantics* 1986 ISBN 90-277-2091-6; Pb: 90-277-2092-4
30. B. H. Partee, A. ter Meulen and R. E. Wall: *Mathematical Methods in Linguistics.* 1990; Corrected second printing of the first edition 1993 ISBN 90-277-2244-7; Pb: 90-277-2245-5
31. P. Gärdenfors (ed.): *Generalized Quantifiers.* Linguistic and Logical Approaches. 1987 ISBN 1-55608-017-4
32. R. T. Oehrle, E. Bach and D. Wheeler (eds.): *Categorial Grammars and Natural Language Structures.* 1988 ISBN 1-55608-030-1; Pb: 1-55608-031-X
33. W. J. Savitch, E. Bach, W. Marsh and G. Safran-Naveh (eds.): *The Formal Complexity of Natural Language.* 1987 ISBN 1-55608-046-8; Pb: 1-55608-047-6
34. J. E. Fenstad, P.-K. Halvorsen, T. Langholm and J. van Benthem: *Situations, Language and Logic.* 1987 ISBN 1-55608-048-4; Pb: 1-55608-049-2
35. U. Reyle and C. Rohrer (eds.): *Natural Language Parsing and Linguistic Theories.* 1988 ISBN 1-55608-055-7; Pb: 1-55608-056-5
36. M. J. Cresswell: *Semantical Essays.* Possible Worlds and Their Rivals. 1988 ISBN 1-55608-061-1
37. T. Nishigauchi: *Quantification in the Theory of Grammar.* 1990 ISBN 0-7923-0643-0; Pb: 0-7923-0644-9
38. G. Chierchia, B.H. Partee and R. Turner (eds.): *Properties, Types and Meaning.* Volume I: Foundational Issues. 1989 ISBN 1-55608-067-0; Pb: 1-55608-068-9

Studies in Linguistics and Philosophy

39. G. Chierchia, B.H. Partee and R. Turner (eds.): *Properties, Types and Meaning.* Volume II: Semantic Issues. 1989 ISBN 1-55608-069-7; Pb: 1-55608-070-0
Set ISBN (Vol. I + II) 1-55608-088-3; Pb: 1-55608-089-1
40. C.T.J. Huang and R. May (eds.): *Logical Structure and Linguistic Structure.* Cross-Linguistic Perspectives. 1991 ISBN 0-7923-0914-6; Pb: 0-7923-1636-3
41. M.J. Cresswell: *Entities and Indices.* 1990
ISBN 0-7923-0966-9; Pb: 0-7923-0967-7
42. H. Kamp and U. Reyle: *From Discourse to Logic.* Introduction to Modeltheoretic Semantics of Natural Language, Formal Logic and Discourse Representation Theory. 1993 ISBN 0-7923-2403-X; Student edition: 0-7923-1028-4
43. C.S. Smith: *The Parameter of Aspect.* 1991 ISBN 0-7923-1136-1
44. R.C. Berwick (ed.): *Principle-Based Parsing.* Computation and Psycholinguistics. 1991 ISBN 0-7923-1173-6; Pb: 0-7923-1637-1
45. F. Landman: *Structures for Semantics.* 1991
ISBN 0-7923-1239-2; Pb: 0-7923-1240-6
46. M. Siderits: *Indian Philosophy of Language.* 1991 ISBN 0-7923-1262-7
47. C. Jones: *Purpose Clauses.* 1991 ISBN 0-7923-1400-X
48. R.K. Larson, S. Iatridou, U. Lahiri and J. Higginbotham (eds.): *Control and Grammar.* 1992 ISBN 0-7923-1692-4
49. J. Pustejovsky (ed.): *Semantics and the Lexicon.* 1993 ISBN 0-7923-1963-X
50. N. Asher: *Reference to Abstract Objects in Discourse.* 1993 ISBN 0-7923-2242-8

Volumes 1–26 formerly published under the Series Title: Synthese Language Library.

Further information about our publications on *Linguistics* are available on request.
Kluwer Academic Publishers – Dordrecht / Boston / London